Hindu Architecture in India and Abroad

"What the learned world demand of us in India is to be quite certain of our data, to place the monumental record before them exactly as it now exists, and to interpret it faithfully and literally."

PREFACE

In this volume an endeavour has been made to give a brief survey of Hindu Architecture in India and Abroad. Materials are, however, not yet quite sufficient to attempt a full and complete history of the building activities of the Hindus in India itself. Architecture, in ancient India, was understood in a comprehensive sense, and included sculpture and a variety of other arts. In the preliminary section of the *Mānasāra* the ancient authorities themselves discussed the allied subjects. In the Introductory chapter of this volume a short account is given of what was understood as fine arts. Many of the fine arts are intimately connected with architecture. Thus a full history of Hindu architecture will be incomplete without a complete survey of all the allied arts. Besides, Hindu architecture was cultivated with success not only in its homeland and in its neighbouring countries, but also in far off colonies and apparently disconnected and distant countries. It has been now admitted by competent authorities that the Maya civilization of Central America spread from India, the motherland of the Maya clans, who, in the times of the great Epics, were known as *Dānavas* or opponents of Aryan invaders of India. Great explorers like Sir Aurel Stein have unearthed various Hindu monuments over an extensive area in Central Asia, which has been significantly designated as Serindia in order to keep its home connexion with India alive, especially in the matter of architecture, both Buddhist and Hindu. Numerous savants, especially French and Dutch scholars, have published particulars, with minute details, of Hindu and Buddhist monuments of colossal character in numerous island countries of the Indian Ocean and the inlands connected therewith. This extensive area, also, has been significantly designated as Insulindia for the same purpose of keeping fresh in the memory its home connexion with India. In the homeland itself the astonishing archaeological survey of General Sir A. Cunningham opened out an endless store of architectural materials of the Buddhist and later periods. The wonderful discoveries, at first of Mr. R. D. Banerji and, later, of Sir John Marshall and his colleagues, made especially at Mohenjo-daro and Harappa, have brought out an unexpected netherland, with its awe-inspiring cities and monuments which are stated to point to an Indian architecture of the pre-Vedic age, beyond 3000 B.C. These undreamed of discoveries have rendered quite stale the vigorous and learned controversy between Raja Rajendralal Mitra and James Fergusson regarding the architectural achievements of Vedic Indians, more specifically the question if the Indians of 2000 to 1000 B.C. knew the manufacture and use of burnt bricks. Convincing references are, however, available not only to burnt bricks and carved stones, but also to the storeyed mansions with a hundred doors and a thousand pillars which are described in the Vedic literature, and, subsequently, elaborated in the Buddhist scriptures and the Hindu Epics, *Purāṇas*, *Āgamas* and numerous other branches of Sanskrit literature. One of the fortunate results of this controversy has been, however, the publication of valuable books, especially of Fergusson's *History of Indian and Eastern Architecture*, containing life-like references to our architectural monuments of Buddhist and later periods. His noble example has been followed with greater zeal and clearer understanding by genuine friends of Indian culture like the late lamented E. B. Havell, Vincent A. Smith, and several others whose sacred memory deserves our respect, but who are too numerous to be quoted here. All these savants, however, had to restrict their researches to the trodden paths, which they enormously cleared, though they could explore no new avenue. Thus the period between 3000 B.C. and 500 B.C. remained practically unrepresented, so far as archaeological remains are concerned. This gap could only be filled by those vivid descriptions which can be gathered together from literature. The reality of non-technical literary and casual references has, however, been reasonably substantiated by the publication of the *Mānasāra* series. The treatises on *Śilpa-śāstra* were till very recently known only from casual references. The stores of manuscripts on the subject of architecture and other arts were practically closed for a long time. The publication of the *Mānasāra*, the leading and standard work on the subject, has made it possible to fill to a certain extent the gaps left vacant by the explorers, archaeologists, and historians.

This volume, purposely named, may justify its title, as it should supply a brief résumé of all sources of information generally indicated above. Parts of Chapters II, III, IV, V, VI, and VII were included in the writer's *Indian Architecture according to Mānasāra Śilpa-śāstra*, which was first published in 1927, but that edition was sold out in less than a year's time. The Government of the United Provinces accepted the proposal of bringing out a second edition, but preferred the scheme of the present volume, and consented to the change of the former title and the inclusion of illustrative drawings and photographs. The late lamented Mr. H. R. Harrop, the then Director of Public Instruction of the United Provinces Government, induced the writer to go much further and undertake the construction of a residential house in accordance with the rules and methods of the *Śilpa-śāstras*, with *such adaptations as would not violate the principles of Hindu architecture*, but, at the same time, would satisfy present-day requirements.

This volume opens with an account of the pre-Vedic architecture of 3000 B.C., which is based entirely on the Mohenjo-daro discoveries, and my grateful acknowledgment is due to Sir John Marshall and his co-workers. An endeavour has been then made to give a picture of the Vedic architecture such as could be drawn from copious literary references and inferred from the Mohenjo-daro finds of the preceding period, and corroborated by what happened in the succeeding classical period. The earlier part of this classical period, terminating roughly at the Christian era, depends also on literary references. But these literary references are different from and more substantial than those of the Vedic period. The accounts gathered from the Buddhist scriptures and the great Epics, the *Āgamas* and the *Purāṇas*, are, at many places, a technical description of the subjects. Moreover, from about the fifth century before Christ, architectural remains are available to supplement and to substantiate the vivid literary descriptions of the various types of monuments of purely Buddhist, Jain, and Brahmanical groups. This realistic background of Hindu architecture in its homeland is brought face to face with the pictures given in the avowedly architectural texts, which are unquestionably intended to serve as guide books to the practical builders and the professionals.

This brief survey of Hindu architecture in India itself may enable the reader to follow the natural course of its migration, not only to the border lands, but also into what is known as Serindia and Insulindia, and, to a certain extent, to China, Japan, and even Central America. The account of the Central Asian Hindu architecture is largely based on the Serindian explorations of Sir Aurel Stein, to whom the indebtedness of the writer is gratefully acknowledged. Insulindia comprises a much larger area, and contains in its wonderful island stores numerous colossal Hindu and Buddhist monuments which were necessarily erected because of their aesthetic and scientific merits, and because the builders and the rulers who colonized those islands went from India and were lovers of Indian arts. The accounts of such varied types and of such long duration had to be gathered from various sources, which have been specified in the footnotes for reference and for an expression of my gratitude. My grateful acknowledgment is, however, recorded here, also, to James Fergusson for the help received from his drawings and woodcuts in his *History of Indian and Eastern Architecture*, and to Dr. R. C. Mazumdar and other scholars who recently contributed to the Greater India series. While the influence of Hindu culture on Chinese and Japanese civilizations is generally known and acknowledged, it would be news to many that the Yucatan Peninsula, in the Mexican territory of Central America, contains some Hindu monuments. The Maya manuscript book records the migration to America of the clans whose chief, Maya, is stated in the great Indian Epic to have built a wonderful audience hall for the King Yudhishṭhira. The *British Museum Guide to the Maudsley Collection of Maya Sculptures* further confirms the building activities of Maya clans in America. But the credit is due to Dr. Gann and Professor Morley for the first discovery of the great city of Coba and the famous monolith of Aśokan type in the once populous site of the forests of Yucatan. The Mayas also erected magnificent temples and palaces, no doubt after Hindu originals, through the prototypes of Java. The conclusion of Professor Elliot Smith, of University College, London, which is gratefully reiterated here, is that 'the Maya civilization of Central America was directly derived from India.'

In Appendix I, an endeavour has been made to remove an erroneous notion that Hindu architecture was based on, or, at least, largely influenced by, the Persian architecture. The Persian had no temples, nor images, nor idols, while the glories of Hindu architecture are evinced nowhere more than in temples and sculptures. In Appendix II, a further endeavour has been made to remove a similar deceptive notion. Taking advantage of our present national awakening, certain time-servers and fortune-seekers have gone to the length of misleading even some big municipal corporations in matters of the so-called Indian style, which they enforced by legislation in certain quarters of their cities. This has also affected some truly patriotic builders, who have been persuaded to believe that their mission towards Hindu or Indian architecture will be fulfilled if they can discard everything European, especially English, and if they place a Gaṇeśa image or an elephant figure at the landing of their dwellings, a monkey on their school buildings, and a hawk symbol upon their hospitals. This leads to the more important question of ascertaining the future of Indian architecture.

Appendix III contains extracts from various shades of opinion which command respect and will help the solution of such a serious question. These observations are primarily on the *Mānasāra* archi tecture. 'Forms of ancient architecture' as supplied by the *Mānasāra* series, interested Dr. Rabindranath Tagore 'in a real human way.' Dr. Sir C. Y. Chintamani shared the view that 'our architectural policy of the past few hundred years, based on foreign imitation, has not proved successful, and that a trial may be given to our ancient methods and principles.' It is of particular interest to Professor Keith to see whether 'the true doctrines of the ancient Hindu authorities made available by the *Mānasāra* series can be turned to practical benefit for India and for its people,' and he looks forward to see 'a house built after the *Mānasāra* which may demonstrate that modern India has something to learn from the achievements of its past.' Mr. Hargreaves recommends to Indian architects 'to examine to what extent the principles laid down in the *Mānasāra* represent those of medieval Hindu architecture and art and to consider if they are suitable for modern practice.' Dr. Jha and Mr. Chatterjee are more than convinced about the practicability of the *Mānasāra* prin ciples of architecture. The former believes in 'the practical outcome of the experience of centuries, which is likely to be more adapted to the climatic conditions of the country than the ideas derived from experience in other climes and other countries, and which was likely to be extremely useful to the extensive town- and village-planning that was going to be undertaken in Bihar' after the disastrous earthquake, incidentally, but, for which, a wholesale trial of ancient methods is impracticable. Mr. Ramananda Chatterjee, after citing the examples of 'old Nepal temples which have withstood the earthquake shocks more than modern buildings,' appeals not so much to the Provincial Governments or the national leaders as to one's commonsense, to the effect that a trial must be given to the elaborate and practical handbook of *Mānasāra*, which 'embodies the age-long experience of many experts native to the soil and climate, and that to dismiss it without such trial is to insult ourselves as well as our ancestors.' [1]

Such exhortations naturally tempted the writer himself to make a trial, as no one else would be so anxious to see the actual result of his life-long researches. Thus at first a couple of tiny temples have been attempted with very great success. They are, however, erected in an out-of-the-way place, in his native village, Yajña-śāla, some five hundred miles east of Calcutta, in the Tippera District, East Bengal. One of these is a memorial Śiva temple on the cremation grounds of his parents. It faces south on the eastern bank of a tank, to the east of which, at a distance of some 400 yards, runs a nameless ancient river. This river rises from the mountains between Burma and India and falls into the Bay of Bengal, making a semi-circle of some two miles from north to south and a mile and a half towards the east from the temple. It is a very simple structure, 10 feet 6 inches long, 8 feet broad, and 12 feet high. It faces an eight feet high Nandi pillar and contains a phallus of Śiva, so carved by a sculptor in Benares as to symbolize the Ardha-Nārīśvara image. In a town it can be built at a cost of less than Rs.500.

The other is a Vaishṇava type of temple containing the images of the family deities, Lakshmī-Govinda and Rāja-Rājeśvara Nārāyaṇa. It is situated at some 400 yards to the west of the Śiva temple and is separated from the tank by a rectangular garden, 100 yards by 150 yards. It also faces the south, to which direction there are court-yard, garden, paddy-field, and the public road, east to west, to about 1,000 yards off the temple. The main shrine, a square of 16 feet a side, has a 7 feet 8 inches high and 10 feet 6 inches broad *śikhara* (spherical dome) of the *Mānasāra* pattern, rising above the roof 12 feet 4 inches from above the plinth and 16 feet above the ground. It has a colonnaded 6 feet wide verandah on all four sides, which may serve as the path for circumambulation on rainy days, the regular *pradakshiṇa* path being beyond the plinth. The pillars are of the *Mānasāra* type. This structure (Plates I*a*, I*b*) can be built in a town at a cost of less than Rs.4,500, with marble floor throughout.

These trial illustrations, being very much in an out-of-the-way place, are not likely to be scrutinized by many people. Besides, however religious-minded we are reputed to be, the success of the modern

[1] For further observations of a few more leaders of public thought, *see* Appendix III, pp. 422–449.

PLATES I (a) and I (b)

(TOP) RAJAJESVARA TEMPLE (EAST SIDE VIEW)

(BOTTOM) LAKSHMI-GOVINDA TEMPLE (WEST SIDE VIEW)

architecture must be judged by dwelling-houses and such other buildings as are more unavoidably connected with our earthly existence, with our worldly comfort and convenience, and with our town-life with its privileged amenities but having peculiar restrictions and requirements. Mr. Harrop, who, as the Director of Public Instruction, handled the publication of the *Mānasāra* for some fifteen years until he retired, was very much influenced by his own reading of the texts, as well as by the expert opinions, not only of scholars and leaders of public thought, but also of artists, engineers, and laymen,[1] to whose commonsense Mr. Ramananda Chatterjee so vigorously appealed. Thus, at his express suggestion and promise of some possible financial assistance from Government, who had already made a small profit, out of the sale-proceeds of the entire first edition, a bigger trial was undertaken in October, 1935.

The object has been to demonstrate a residential design from the *Mānasāra*. The Svastika plan of storeyed mansions described in Chapter XXXV has been selected. The structure has been built upon a site which answers the primary requirements demanded in the texts, regarding the natural slope for drainage purposes, the wind direction for ventilation, and the sun's course for a correct orientation of a dwelling-house in Allahabad. This Svastika Mansion is situated in a delta formed into a tableland by the three famous rivers, the Sarasvati, the Ganges, and the Yamuna, which no doubt once met below the Bharadvāj-Āśrama, some two hundred yards to the north of the site. The Sarasvati has now altogether disappeared, leaving behind its trace by a big dry drain which forms the southern boundary line of the site, but her roaring eloquence can be heard and her reality felt for an hour or two after a heavy shower of rain. The Ganges and the Yamuna have been diverted, the former to some three miles north and the latter about two miles south of the site, by dykes built by the Moghals. They now meet below the Fort of Akbar, at a distance of some two miles.

The site-plan (Plate II) will show the actual shape, size, and the surrounding views of the plot. The site commands a round frontage of six hundred and fifty-two feet, with a straight back of five hundred and eighty-seven feet, and has three road junctions on the circular part of the segment. At the east end of the segment Hamilton Road and Malaviya Road, coming from the south, and

[1] *See* Appendix III, pp. 422-449.

another new unnamed road coming from the north-east, merge into the provincial road locally known as Fort Road. About the middle point of the segment, and just facing the front entrance and the porch-pillar, another new road meets the Fort Road, coming straight from the dyke of the Ganges and running as if into the house, and thus may fittingly be named after the Svastika Mansion by the Municipal authorities. At this junction, also, ends the three-mile long Thornhill Road, the best street in Allahabad : it issues from the Cantonment area and passes through the Civil Lines, having the famous Alfred Park on the right and Muir College grounds and towers on the left at a distance of some two furlongs from the Svastika Mansion. At the west end of the segment this road is crossed below the Bharadvāj Park by Lowther Road, which at this junction, merging into the provincial road, connects the Ganges and the Yamuna. It runs from south to north and joins the East Indian Railway bridge on the Yamuna with the Curzon Bridge on the Ganges, and connects the city sides at two ends of the town. On the left of this important road stands the Government House Compound at a distance of some two furlongs, Bharadvāj-Āśrama at less than two hundred yards, and University grounds and main buildings at six furlongs; on the right lie the Swaraj and Anand Bhawans at some three hundred yards north, Prayag railway station at the distance of a mile, and the Chatham Lines fields and open country-side at one and a half miles. On the opposite side of Thornhill Road, between the central and western road junctions, is a triangular open ground, with a small tin-shed for public shelter, which terminates at another road-junction some fifty yards from the site, made of Lowther Road, provincial road, and Kamla Nehru Hospital-and-Annie Besant School Road.

The natural slope of the site is towards the south-east. Beneath the road-junction at this end of the segment the straight Sarasvati (drain) and the Fort Road drain meet at the road culvert and take away every drop of unwanted water and liquid refuse. The whole segment has been covered with boundary walls which demonstrate, in a modified form, the Buddhist railings of Sanchi and other places, really a variety of those referred to in the texts. The two main gates, specially made of wrought-iron to demonstrate an ancient design, are placed in a line with the eastern and western extremities of the main house. The central road-junction at the middle part of the segment, which supplies the axis to the house, faces a three-part

OSE-UP FRONT VIEW OF SVASTIKA MANSION, SHOWING THE OCTAGONAL TOWER,
GMENT-SHAPED PROCH, AND THE GRIHA-STAMBHA (MAIN PORCH PILLAR)

wicket-gate fitted with two closed and one open iron gates of special ancient design. The western main gate has a half wicket-door for servants and traders. About halfway between this gate and western end of the segment there is another twelve feet wide iron gate leading straight to the porch to the east, and to the garage, stable and outhouses to the south on the Sarasvati (drain).

The segment-shaped porch, a prototype of the site, coming out of the front portion of an eight-sided tower, is supported by a single main pillar (*gṛihastambha*) erected after the *Mānasāra* design, on the axis of the house. This tower, fifty feet high, supplies the grand stair hall to answer for the reception room (*rodana-gṛiha*) on the ground floor; the semi-circular gallery at the level of the porch-roof and first floor; and the segment-shaped tower hall at the roof-level of the first floor which serves the purpose of the family chapel internally, and, externally, an octagonal dome with two slightly rounded sides. The chapel has a colonnaded balcony in the straight front side, wherefrom the Ganges waters are visible when the river is full. At the back of it is a hexagonal boudoir, with one convex side, which serves as the shed over the grand staircase, and its doors at right and left open out to the roofs of the first floor rooms and of the slightly lowered back balconies. These roofs serve as terraces to the chapel and the boudoir. The boudoir has a corresponding hexagonal parlour on the ground floor. Both these rooms jointly form five sides of the octagonal tower, which has one flat side in front and two round sides on right and left. The tower has two wings on right and left, the single-pillared porch in the shape of the site in front, the hexagonal inner courtyard[1] at the back, the single-storeyed kitchen block and guest-rooms on the two back

[1] This irregular-sided courtyard is intended to represent the prescribed unsymmetric figure of the Spirit of the house (*Vāstu-purusha*) lying on its face. His five principal limbs are represented by the five set of staircases ascending from the ground to the high-plinthed verandahs, the head being on the landing, on the axis, from the parlour door; the right arm on the landing from the big verandah of the inner side of the dining- and the drawing- rooms; the left arm on the landing from the long verandah facing the library and the office rooms; the right leg on the landing from the verandah of the kitchen block; and the left leg on the landing from the verandah of the guest block.

The usual but unintelligible custom is still followed and the house-builders make on the actual building site a figure of the Spirit of the house with powdered chalk during the ceremonies of laying the foundations. That chalk-mark is, however, defaced in no time, while in the case of the Svastika Mansion the courtyard and its five landings, representing the Spirit of the house, may be expected to last as long as the house does.

sides of the inner courtyard. Thus the main structure with façades fulfils the plough-shaped *Svastika* plan,[1] and looks like an aeroplane (*vimāna*) from the distant front.

The eastern wing comprises, on the ground floor, the dining-hall, the drawing-room, and a large room partitioned into a shower-bath, flush latrine, wash-basin, and dressing-tables. The roadside of this wing is parallel to Fort Road, and the other outer side faces the east, having a covered verandah and an open platform which is connected with the main eastern gate. Below the raised platform is the terraced quadrangular lawn, having surrounding paved paths, and a well with high plinth and platform standing on the shortest side of the quadrangle. The drawing- and dining-rooms have a combined large back verandah terminating at two sides of the inner courtyard. From the end of this verandah, and covering two short sides of the courtyard, is erected from underground a pentagonal tower to the height of the first floor rooms. The lower part of this tower forms the underground summer-room, with two windows opening to the grassy courtyard, which, being covered by structures on all sides, is free from dust. Its top portion forms the strong-room, By one of its sides rises a flight of steps, forming a private staircase. By its two other sides proceed a corridor from the big verandah which separate the summer-room from the bathroom and the kitchen block. The same wing on the first floor comprises three bedrooms—one upon the dining-hall and two on the drawing-room—and a bathroom corresponding with the ground floor one with similar shower-bath, flush commode, wash-basin and dressing-table; a large balcony corresponding with the ground floor big back verandah; and two colonnaded front balconies, one overlooking the central road-junction and the other facing the lawn, the well and the road-junction at the east. The corridor from the large balcony runs between the bathroom and the strong-room to the terrace which forms the roofs of the kitchen block and guest rooms.

The western wing comprises, on the ground floor, the library, the office or business room, and a bathroom with all sanitary fittings and shower-bath, and runs parallel to Thornhill Road. This wing has a long inner verandah along the whole length of the library and the office room and terminating at the longest side of the courtyard. The first floor of this wing comprises another bedroom, the segregation or

[1] *Svastikaḥ lāṅgalākāraḥ*. Another characteristic is that it has three faces.

PLATE V

EASTERN WING OF SVASTIKA MANSION TOGETHER WITH THF TARRACED LAWN AND THE WELL.

PLATE VI (a)

... MANSION TOGETHER WITH THE OUTHOUSES AND ORCHARD GROUNDS

confinement room, and a bathroom covering the roof respectively of the library, the office, and the bathroom of the ground floor ; one outer balcony covering the bedroom and connecting the porch roof, and a long inner balcony corresponding with the ground floor verandah, which is connected with the terrace forming the roofs of the guest rooms and the kitchen block. The segregation room, which, like the chapel, was in ancient times an essential feature of a dwelling-house, big or small, has three ventilators or gable windows, five large windows and three doors, and will answer the requirements of a modern hospital.

All other rooms, also, are similarly furnished with sufficient number of ventilators, doors, and windows which are built after the directions of the texts. At Allahabad the wind blows from the north-east for four months and from the south-west for eight months. Thus all the living and public rooms of the present plan of the Svastika Mansion get a free passage of breeze throughout the year. The kitchen block being at the southern end of the courtyard, and being shaded by the two towers and the bathroom walls, its smoke cannot contaminate the air entering into the living or public rooms. All these rooms are daily flushed by the morning sun, but the glare of the evening sun is screened off by the situation of the two towers and four large balconies and verandahs, four bathrooms, and especially by the guest rooms and the kitchen blocks on the west and south of the courtyard. On the other hand, the bathrooms at the south-east corner of the ground floor and first floor get both the forenoon and the afternoon sun, and the two others at the north-west corner are thoroughly disinfected by the afternoon sun. The courtyard and the kitchen block also get the afternoon sun from midday till four in the afternoon. The two rooms in the guest block get the sun from nine till midday and from two to four in the afternoon.

The inner kitchen block on the south side of the courtyard comprises one non-vegetarian kitchen and one non-vegetarian Indian dining-room, and one vegetarian kitchen and a corresponding dining-room. Both the kitchens are furnished with smoke chimneys and have separate washing-rooms on their sides. There is also a shed at the eastern end which may be used for domestic animals or fowls. Rooms of the kitchen block are wire-netted in order to prevent the flies entering into them. All these rooms, as stated above, are daily disinfected by a flush of the sun's rays from midday till four in the afternoon. The guest block, comprising two rooms on the west side of the courtyard and a bathroom in continuation of the office room, with all the modern fittings, has a small verandah on the east and a large one on the west. It faces the outer courtyard, in continuation of which are laid the gardens. From this western verandah one can get a clear view of the Thornhill Road rising up and up, and of the Muir College tower and the dome of the Vijayanagaram Hall. The outer courtyard, protruding below the large verandah on the west of the guest rooms, has, on its left side, the store block, comprising five rooms. One of these rooms is intended to be used as a European type of kitchen, one for storing water and the other three are stores proper. In continuation of this block, but outside the outer courtyard wall, are built the outhouses, consisting of one stable and cow-shed, one garage, four servant quarters, and two latrines. The strip of land on the Sarasvati (drain) behind the kitchen block, store rooms and outhouses, contains the kitchen gardens ; and the grounds protruding from the outer courtyard beyond the outhouses form the orchard wherein a complementary pavilion may be built.

It should be noted that, owing to the extraordinary situation of the plot, which is, however, not always available in towns, the slope, the air-passage and wind direction, and the sun's course could be utilized exactly in the way demanded in the texts. This has further enabled the distribution of the rooms, blocks, courtyards, and gardens in accordance with the directions of the *Mānasāra* and other authorities. *These are really the matters of importance.* Once these facilities are available, it becomes easy to exercise one's free choice regarding the types of pillars, openings, screen-works, railings for verandahs and balconies, balustrades for staircases, and parapets for the roofs, all of which in the case of the Svastika Mansion bear, however, the hall-mark of ancient architecture with pleasing effect. The very few ornaments, which can be selected from anywhere, represent the simple patterns of ancient texts and are mostly in lines. They satisfy the aesthetic requirements and fulfil the tendency of modern times.

Much more ingenuity was, however, required in the technique of actual construction in accordance with the regulations, even in ancient times. For instance, the prescribed rock- or water-foundations, which no doubt provide a very long life to buildings, cannot always be made available in villages or towns where dwelling-houses have to be built. Thus, an adaptation has been made by the application of the modern device of a thick ferro-concrete slab resting on artificial sand-bed and a brick-soling at the bottom of the ten-feet deep pit. Similarly, the flat roofs have been made of reinforced stone

PLATE VI (b)

CLOSE-UP VIEW OF THE WESTERN WING

THE DEPTH OF THE FOUNDATION OF THE SVASTIKA MANSION

concrete slabs in place of the roofs of natural stone slabs, as prescribed in the texts. These slabs are supported by steel-girders that are converted by plaster to look like the prescribed wooden beams, which, in many places, would be uneconomical in these days. In the same way, stone concrete slabs have been used for the-sloping roofs which surround the whole of the main structure above the door and window levels in all the three storeys. These sloping roofs, incidentally, serve as rain-protectors and have given a very pleasing effect to the structure. In a like manner, stone concrete lintels just above the door-level run throughout the outer and inner walls, and will serve as earthquake bands, because the first-class brick walls are thus held fast between the roof slabs and the lintel slabs. They themselves have been mortared by well-ground lime and cinder, which has been found by experiment to be better than cement-sand mortar in dry climates with very scanty rainfall. Well-seasoned Burma teak of the B.B.T.C.L. brand has, however, been carved for the doors and the window frames, which latter have been panelled with diamond cut glasses of ancient design. Similarly, the floors have been laid upon a concrete bed, resting on sand and brick-soling, of precast mosaic tiles of various artistic colours and designs in order to economize the cost of coloured marble tiles, which have been used only in the reception hall.

These devices, it may be hoped, will serve the *real purpose of the ancient architecture*, namely, utility, stability, and beauty. These qualities have been preserved, also, in matters of modern fittings which are necessary to make the modern houses more comfortable. The United Provinces Electric Supply Company have made the electric installation with rubber-covered Indian cable (which is stated to have been manufactured specially to suit the tropical climate) resting on teakwood batten. Mr. C. G. L. Gamlen, the then Resident Engineer of the United Provinces Electric Supply Company, himself designed the artistic layout of the cables, and personally supervised the construction in order to make a demonstration. He holds the view that the installation should be lasting. With the same purpose of providing durability the G.E.C. fans have been used. Similarly, water pipes have been laid and rotary pumps fixed, although a well has been dug to the east of the lawn in accordance with the direction of the texts, with the remarkable result of a good supply of sweet water which is not available in the same quantity from wells of the neighbouring premises.

Individual tastes differ. Anything may be beautiful to its lover. But aesthetics have reached the status of a science and there are recognized standards by which beauty is to be judged. So far as architecture is concerned, proportion, uniformity, symmetry, and harmony are stated to be the chief elements of beauty. The business and originality of a builder, like those of an editor, lie in his ability in a wise compilation and in an aesthetic and economical adaptation from his authorities. The learned reviewer in *The Times*' Literary Supplement has quoted an instance from the *Mānasāra* that, 'if the staircase be less or greater the master would certainly be crippled,' and has himself emphasized that 'such might indeed happen from such a faulty construction.'[1] It is with a view to guarding against faulty constructions that one's choice is limited within the suggested alternatives in essential matters. In the non-essential particulars one is given an unrestricted liberty to introduce new elements, even the monkey symbol, if only the whole composition do not become incongruous and the principles of beauty be not violated.

The Svastika Mansion, it is hoped, will demonstrate all those principles. Its perimeters and dimensions of its rooms will illustrate several of the prescribed proportions, *śāntika* (peaceful), *paushṭika* (prosperous), *jayada* (progressive), *sarvakāmika* (fulfilling all desires), and *adbhuta* (wonderful).[2] Similarly the *Mānasāra* pillars, entablatures doors, windows, verandahs, balconies, platforms, courtyards, and boundary walls may demonstrate the harmony of the whole composition.

In the limited space of a Preface no further elaboration would be justified. This pen-picture may be elucidated by a reference to the line-drawings and photographs (Plates II–XI, XXVIII, XXXII). But only a personal inspection, with some previous knowledge of the ancient and modern authorities, will enable one to judge for himself as to what extent the Svastika Mansion demonstrates the ancient principles, wherein lies its adaptation, what is its supporting authority, and finally, what is the resultant success. An ordinary visitor may, however, testify to its actual comfort and convenience. The writer himself would treasure the censure of a distinguished engineer, Mr. T. A. Otto, much as did Ardhendu Śekhar Mustofi, the chief actor in Dīnabandhu Mitra's *Nīladarpaṇa*, who had the shoes of Pandit Iswara

[1] Page 443 of this volume.

[2] The height being, respectively, equal to, 1¼, 1½, 1¾, and twice the breadth, *see* the writer's *Encyclopaedia of Hindu Architecture*, under UTSEDHA, for further particulars.

PLATE VIII

AN INSIDE VIEW OF THE SVASTIKA MANSION FROM THE ROOF OF THE KITCHEN BLOCK AND GUEST BLOCK, SHOWING THE DEPTH OF THE OCTAGONAL TOWER AND PARTS OF THE TWO WINGS

PLATE IX (a)

AN INSIDE VIEW OF THE WESTERN WING SHOWING THE TYPES OF THE SCREEN WORK, PILLAR, PARAPET, AND RAILING

Chandra Vidyāsāgara thrown at him, when, owing to the very realistic performance on a Calcutta stage of the atrocities of the indigo-planters, the Pandit was so provoked that he forgot that it was a mere play. Mr. Otto, who worked as a Government builder for some thirty years and gained familiarity as an officer of the Department of Archaeology with the Hindu and Muslim monuments, remarked that the Svastika Mansion is but a 'schoolmaster's exercise-book meant to illustrate the rules and regulations of Hindu architecture in a pleasing manner,' while some learned colleagues are delighted to call it the complementary volume of the *Mānasāra.*

Time alone can prove the stability of the house, which quality emphatically distinguishes the old structures from the modern ones. Time will also show if anybody else will care to try the ancient methods and principles at a lesser strain and a greater economy.[1]

[1] In the construction of the Svastika Mansion, with its covered area of 11,361 (6495+4670+196) sq. ft., the total cost, including that of land, masonry retaining walls on both sides of some 800 feet long drain, and some 500 yards cement-concrete roads, is approaching a sum of six figures. It, however, does not represent a correct estimate on the house alone. That could be more accurately calculated on the basis of the following amount and quality of materials used, which would vary according to the size of similar houses, and in consideration of prices and rates which must necessarily vary in different places. (Smaller houses, retaining the *Mānasāra* style, can be built at much lesser cost, still less if cheaper materials are used) :

Bricks, 732,720 (first class 503,132, second class 181,339, third class 48,259).
Brick ballast, 9,651 c.ft.
Stone ballast, 3,488 c.ft.
Cement, 1,186 bags (about 60 tons).
White lime, 1,913 maunds 36 seers.
Kankar lime, 3,398 c.ft.
Sand, 9,754 c.ft.
Cinders, 24,133 c.ft.
Surki, 425 c.ft.
Iron—
  Joists, 127 maunds 36 seers.
  Rods, 279 maunds 20 seers.
  Miscellaneous, 68 maunds 35 seers.
  Railings, 38 maunds 28 seers.
  Gates, 33 maunds 35 seers.
  Wire net, 1,037 sq. ft.
Wood—
  Burma teak (B.B.T.C.L.), 4,016 sq. ft. for shutters, 117 c.ft. for frames.
  C. P. teak, 45 c. ft. for kitchen block.
Nepal sal, 296 c.ft. for kitchen block and outhouses.
Glass—diamond cut, 408 sq. ft. (for windows of main structure), and ordinary 286 sq.ft. (for windows of kitchen block, etc.).
Door fittings, polish, etc., Rs.663-9-6.
Precast mosaic tiles, 5,351 sq. ft.
Marble tiles, 212 sq. ft.
Marble chips, 549 lb.
Colours and paints, 924 lb.
Labour (including masons, carpenters, and labourers), Rs.9,902-1-9.
Cost of drawings, Rs.34.
Cost on estimator, Rs.544-2-6.
Architect's travelling allowance, Rs.43-11.
Miscellaneous things, Rs.590-9-9.
Water-pipes and bathroom fittings, Rs.1,063-12.
Electric installation and fittings and lightning conductors, Rs.1,985-2-6.

N.B.—Design in outline was supplied free by the architect, Mr. S. C. Mukerjee; the elaboration of the original plan, the supervision of construction, control of labour, purchase of materials, and keeping of accounts were carried out by the writer himself.

The expectations of scholars and other commentators have, however, not been fulfilled.[1] Neither the Bihar Government nor the Darbhanga Raj took their advice to experiment with the principles enunciated in our *Śāstras* when rebuilding the areas devastated by the earthquake of 1934. The expectation, too, that the engineering colleges might include the study of the *Mānasāra* series among their compulsory subjects remained unfulfilled; and it is a remarkable commentary on their interest in this important aspect of essential Indian culture that few copies of the first edition were purchased in India, the great bulk of them having been sold in Europe and America. The parent Governments themselves have not as yet made up their mind to give a lead to the private builders. The national importance of the *Mānasāra* and the value of the application of its principles to practical ends, as exemplified in the Svastika Mansion, still remain to be recognized. In other countries Governments and other bodies invite and grant awards of their own accord for improved housing schemes, competitive designs and economic plans to suit the needs of the people and to stand the weather and climate of their countries. With the present-day tendencies of all peoples to foster national culture Indian Governments might well, with sound reason, have adopted ere this the *Mānasāra* as a standard and revived the true Indian architecture by constructing public buildings according to the principles of an indigenous science which became almost lost and forgotten although it now shows the experience of generations and experiments of centuries. In these days of mob mentality people are helpless to think for themselves and to decide what to do until and unless they get a lead from the Government of the country, even in respect of food and clothes, not to speak of house and furniture. The introduction of a new style of architecture among the public will be facilitated if the Indian Governments, and the public bodies subordinate to them, take it as their own policy and have the courage to experiment on the lines of the *Mānasāra* in order to give a practical lead to the public. In this, as in other fields of endeavour, the natural hesitancy of individuals and non-Government institutions to try something new and untried can only be overcome by the example and the publicity provoked by builders constructing models of every-day utility, and publishing complete and detailed

[1] *See* Appendix III, pp. 422-449.

MĀNASĀRA TYPE OF PUŚPA-BANDHA AND SVASTI-BANDHA SCREEN WORKS

SCALE OF 1 ... 1 2 3 FEET

PLATE X

A VIEW OF THE PENTAGONAL TOWER RISING FROM ABOVE THE UNDERGROUND SUMMER ROOM

plans and costs thereof. But the demonstrations themselves need publicity for which again some signal recognition and special reward have been found necessary even in big international exhibitions in order to draw public attention. A more ready recognition and the consequent publicity to the *Mānasāra* and the principles exemplified in the Svastika Mansion might have been expedited if the series could have been completed during the regime of the great educationist Governor, Sir Harcourt Butler, who sanctioned the publication of the series by advancing money from public funds,[1] and if Mr. H. R. Harrop, the late lamented Director of Public Instruction of the local Government, who saw through the details of the publication and encouraged the construction, were in office till now. Nevertheless I acknowledge with respectful thanks the help received from the Government of the United Provinces and the Government of India during some thirty years I have been engaged in completing the *Mānasāra* series in seven big volumes involving as it did continuous and strenuous labour in addition to my professorial and other official duties.

During the closing months of his governorship of the United Provinces, Sir Maurice Garnier Hallett, G.C.I.E., K.C.S.I., I.C.S., who had appreciated our oriental scholarship in other provinces also, happened to inspect a volume of *Hindu Architecture* in an exhibition. Since then he took a personal interest in the architecture of *Mānasāra* and declared at a function: 'As Professor of Sanskrit and Head of the Oriental Departments of the Allahabad University since 1922, and as Dean of the Faculty of Arts for two successive terms, your work has been of a high order. Your monumental work, the *Mānasāra* series, which constitute a complete and illustrated survey and encyclopaedia of Indian Archaeology and Hindu Architecture, has been highly appreciated by eminent scholars all over the world. In recognition of your services in the promotion of Sanskrit scholarship and in the field of research, the title of "Mahāmahopādhyāya" has been conferred on you. I heartily congratulate you upon this well-merited distinction.' If his interest be supplemented by his successors in office it may

[1] At the suggestion of an Indian Adviser to the Governor, the local Government have decided that after the realization of the full sum of money advanced from the public funds for the cost of printing and publishing through the Oxford University Press, of the seven volumes, the further sale-proceeds, if there be any, will go to the successors of the writer.

be hoped that this series would ultimately attract the notice of the Indian public more effectively. The builders of this great country with its unrivalled achievements in science and arts may henceforth be induced to consult these volumes and to consider the advantages of adopting the architectural principles and methods of *Mānasāra*. On the eve of my own retirement this hope is a great consolation for me for my past 30 years' continuous labour on this task and I shall ever remain grateful to Sir Maurice for his congratulation. It remains for me to record my gratitude, in addition to Sir Harcourt Butler and Mr. Harrop, to Lieut.-Col. R. S. Weir, C.I.E., who succeeded as Director of Public Instruction, for his uniform sympathy and encouragement. To Lieut.-Col. D. W. Crighton, O.B.E., the then Superintendent, Printing and Stationery, and Mr. M. G. Shome, his successor, and his staff I owe much more than I can adequately express. Words fail me to give vent to my feeling of gratitude to Lieut.-Col. Crighton, not only for his faultless technical production, but also for his personal assistance in the matter of revision and linguistic amendments; in gathering together photographs and drawings from the Governments of Java, Sumatra, Siam, and French Indo-China, and from the Provincial Superintendents of the Department of Archaeology of the Government of India; and in preparing the correct plan, elevations, and illustrations of the Svastika Mansion.

I am in particular indebted to the Director General of Archaeology and his colleagues and staff and the Provincial Superintendents for the originals of Plates XIII, XIV*a*, XIV*b*, XV, XVI, XVII, XVIII, XIX*a*, XIX*b*, XIX*c*, XXIV, XXVII, XXIX, XXX, XXXI, XXXIII, XXXIV*a*, XXXIV*b*, XXXV, XXXVI, XXXVII, XXXVIII. I also take this opportunity to express my indebtedness to the Governments of Siam, Java, Sumatra, and French Indo-China for the supply of the photographic views of Plates XLIX, L, LI, LII, LIII, LIV, LV, LVI, LVII, LVIII.

To Mr. S. C. Mukerjee, B.A., G.D.ARC., A.I.I.A., the architect, more than a courtesy reference is necessary. He has supplied all the line-drawings, which needed a unique skill and personal interest in order to keep up the spirit and details of the texts. I am also indebted to him for working out the original plan of the Svastika Mansion. Mr. G. A. Sewell, the chief draughtsman of the Government Central Press, who got his training in Roorkee Engineering College, has cleverly redrawn the much-altered ground-plan and the present

PLATE XI(a)

ER VIEW SHOWING PARTS OF THE GALLERY, GRAND STAIRCASE, AND THE 26 FEET DEEP
TION HALL

PLATE XI (b)

AN INNER VIEW SHOWING PARTS OF THE GALLERY, GRAND STAIRCASE AND THE 26 FEET DEEP RECEPTION HALL

elevation of the house. Messrs. Zaidi Brothers, who, among all the local photographers consulted, had the courage and enthusiasm to take up the task, have supplied the photographic views which needed considerable skill. To both of them I record my thanks. For occasional technical assistance and guidance from time to time I am indebted to Mr. D. H. R. Rao, the University Engineer; Mr. Asutosh Gupta, the Assistant Engineer of the local Municipality; and Mr. T. A. Otto, a retired Chief Engineer of the Public Works Department, of considerable building experience and of very generous and scholarly temperament.

I am also grateful to late Sir Lalgopal Mukerji, a Judge of the Allahabad High Court, for his ready assistance and invaluable suggestions. For some special facilities in converting the site of the Svastika Mansion out of a strip of waste land into a beauty spot, I am grateful to the District and Municipal officers and the engineers of the combined Public Works and Public Health Departments. I am indebted to the then City Magistrate, Mr. A. D. Pandit, I.C.S., and the District Magistrate, Mr. G. W. M. Whittle, I.C.S., for enabling me to give a proper shape to the site and beautify the whole locality by straightening the drains, etc., and encroaching on a few yards of waste land whereupon nuisance was committed, for which, however, the then Indian Divisional Commissioner, imposed a fine of Rs.5 in order to put a check to such an endeavour. I shall ever remain grateful to Mr. W. G. P. Wall, once the Director of Public Instruction, Mr. A. D. Dixon, I.C.S., once the District Magistrate, and Mr. M. S. Singhal, Rai Bahadur, the then Divisional Commissioner, on whose combined recommendation the Governor of the United Provinces, Sir Maurice Garnier Hallett, was 'pleased to sanction, as a special case, the sale of Nazul plot no. 44, Thornhill Road' in my favour, which was originally held by me on lease for 30 years; the freehold right thus secured 'for ever' fulfils the requirements of a permanency of the costly demonstration of the Svastika Mansion built upon this plot.

To Dr. K. N. Katju, and Mr. R. N. Basu, the then Chairmen of Allahabad Municipal Board, to Rai Bahadur K. P. Mathur, the then Director, and Pandit S. G. Naravane, the Executive Engineer, of the Public Health Department, I owe the badly needed assistance and protection without which it is difficult for an ordinary builder to build a house at Allahabad.

Dr. Katju is a lover of arts and archaeology and appreciated my endeavour to demonstrate an ancient style of architecture. Mr. Basu, who has an inherited love for Sanskrit culture and Hindu civilization, read all about the *Mānasāra* architecture, developed a scholarly interest in the demonstration, and assisted me in the erection of the Svastika Mansion. To Rai Bahadur Braja Mohan Vyas, the then Executive Officer of the Municipal Board, I owe more than words can express. He is a brother scholar of Sanskrit and archaeology, and he evinced great enthusiasm in the construction of the Svastika Mansion, of which he laid the foundation. But for his own determination it would have been very difficult, if not impossible, for me to convert the plot of land out of recognition and to complete the construction. I shall ever remain indebted to these gentlemen. My acknowledgment is also due to the Superintendent of the Water-works, Mr. S. K. Mitra, for his generous assistance. I take this opportunity to record my gratitude to Mr. C. G. L. Gamlen, the then Resident Engineer of the United Provinces Electric Supply Company, to whose personal interest and skill I owe the artistic electric installation ; to Mr. V. M. Bhargava for tastefully fixing the lightning conductors and the aerial poles, and to Rai Amarnath Agarwal, Rai Ram Charan Agarwal, M.A., LL.B., and Lala Man Mohan Dass, *raises* and great builders, for their personal assistance and the occasional help of their well-organized machinery.

Last, but not least, I acknowledge my thanks to my colleague, Pandit Raghuvara Mitthulal, Shastri, M.A., M.O.L., for his assistance in settling some of the confusing passages of the Sanskrit text, and to our former research scholars, Mr. Bibhabasu Das, Shastri, M.A., M.O.L., for valuable assistance in making an elaborate index of this volume, and Mr. Madhav Saran Sharma, M.A., L.T., in arranging the drawings.

ALLAHABAD UNIVERSITY : P. K. ACHARYA.
April, 1944-46.

The Order of the Roman Characters and the Method of Transliteration adopted

a, ā ; i, ī ; u, ū ; ṛi, ṛī ; e, ai ; o, au ;

k, kh ; g, gh ; ṅ ; ch, chh ; j, jh ; ñ ;

ṭ, ṭh ; ḍ, ḍh ; ṇ ; t, th ; d, dh ; n ;

p, ph ; b, bh ; m ; y, r, l, v ;

ś, sh, s ; h ; ṁ ; ḥ.

CONTENTS

CONTENTS

LIST OF ILLUSTRATIONS

INTRODUCTION

FINE ARTS

ART IS SYNONYMOUS with *Silpa* and *Kalā*, or more precisely, with *Silpa-kalā* and is the subject-matter primarily of the *Silpa-śāstras*. The traditional list of sixty-four arts is, however, referred to in at least three other classes of our literature. The mythological group includes the *Śrīmad-bhāgavata*, the *Harivaṁśa* and the *Vishṇu-purāṇa*. The Buddhist-Jain group is represented by the *Lalita-vistara* and the *Uttarādhyāyana-sūtra*. And the erotic group consists of the *Kāma-sūtra* of Vātsyāyana and others. The mythological group makes mention of arts in connexion with the various kinds of knowledge acquired by Kṛishṇa and Balarāma. In the text of the *Śrīmad-bhāgavata*, however, only the number, not the specification of the arts, is given. It is stated that the sixty-four arts were learnt in so many, that is sixty-four, days.[1] But of its numerous commentators, some supply both the number and the specification, while others only the number.[2] The commentators Vīra-rāghavāchārya and Vijaya-dhvaja-tīrtha, who make mention only of the traditional number of arts as sixty-four, do not disclose the source of their information. Viśvanātha-chakravartin also does not specify the sixty-four arts, but he mentions the

[1] प्रोवाच वेदानखिलान् साङ्गोपनिषदो गुरुः ।
सरहस्यं धनुर्वेदं धर्मान् न्यायपरांस्तथा ॥
तथा चान्वीक्षिकीं विद्यां राजनीतिञ्च षड्विधाम् ।
सर्वं नरवरश्रेष्ठौ सर्वविद्याप्रवर्तकौ ॥
सकृन्निगदमात्रेण तौ संजगृहतुर्नृप ।
अहोरात्रैश्चतुषष्ट्या संयत्तौ तावतीः कलाः ॥

—(*Śrīmad-bhāgavata*, Part x, Chap. XLV, verses 33–35.)

[2] (*a*) अहोरात्राणां चतुःषष्ट्या चतुःषष्टिसंख्याकैर्दिवसैश्चतुःषष्टिविद्याः संजगृहतुः ।
—(Vīra-rāghavāchārya).

(*b*) चतुःषष्ट्या संङ्ख्यातैरहोरात्रै कालावयवैस्तावतीः तावत्सङ्ख्याः कलाः चतुःषष्टिकलाः जिद्या इत्यर्थः ।
—(Vijaya-dhvaja-tīrtha).

(*c*) तावतीश्चतुःषष्टिकलाः ताः शैवतन्त्रे द्रष्टव्याः ।
—(Viśvanātha-Chakravartin).

(*d*) तावतीश्चतुःषष्टिकलाः ताश्च शैवतन्त्रोक्ता लिख्यन्ते यथा गीतम् इत्यादि ।
—(Śrīdhara-svāmin.)

Saiva-tantra as his source. Srīdhara-svāmin and Vallabhāchārya also, who give a detailed account of the sixty-four arts, derive their information from the same source. The *Saiva-tantra*, however, it should be noted, is not the name of a book, but is a branch of mystic literature which can hardly be identified for the verification of the names and other details of the arts. Sukadeva, another commentator, who also specifies the sixty-four arts, quotes *in toto* from his authority named *Vidyāsaṅgraha-nibandha*, which, as its title indicates, is a mere compilation from some other sources. Lastly, Jīva-gosvāmin, who also describes the sixty-four arts in detail, appears to have derived his information from the *Vishṇu-purāṇa* and the *Harivaṁśa*, which is a supplement to the *Mahābhārata*. Thus, as quoted by Jīva-gosvāmin, the *Vishṇu-purāṇa*[1] and the *Harivaṁśa*[2] admit, indirectly though, a familiarity with the sixty-four arts, and state that the sixty-four (arts) were learnt in sixty-four days. The former, further, adds that it must be wonderful (*adbhuta*) to learn sixty-four arts in sixty-four days, while the latter explains this wonder by saying that Kṛishṇa and Balarāma had extraordinary memories (*śrutidhara*). The impracticability of learning sixty-four arts in no more than sixty-four days did not strike any of the commentators of the *Srīmad-bhāgavata*, presumably either because they were not at all familiar with the extensive knowledge demanded from and the wide field of study required for each of the sixty-four arts,

(*e*) अहोरात्रैश्चतुःषष्ट्या संयत्तौ तावतीः कलाः । संयत्तौ रामकृष्णौ चतुःषष्टिसङ्ख्या कैरहोरात्रैस्तावतीः चतुःषष्टिकलाः विद्याः संजगृहतुः । ताश्चोक्ता विद्यासंग्रहनिबन्धे ।

—(Śuka-deva).

(*f*) यावतीः कलाः संजगृहतुरिति चतुःषष्टिकलाः । संग्रहे एतावन्त्यहोरात्राणि अखिलवेदादिसंग्रहेणाप्यहोरात्राणि ज्ञेयानि । कलानां नामानि तैरेव लिखितानि, स्वरूपाणि तु लेख्यानि । तथा च श्रीविष्णुपुराणे हरिवंशे च ।

—(Jīva-gosvāmin).

(*g*) चतुःषष्टिसंख्यायुक्तैः अहोरात्रैः संयत्तौ तावतीः कलाः चतुःषष्टिकलाः संजगृहतुः । एकस्यां कलायां बहुप्रकाराः बह्वो ग्रन्थाः । शिक्षा च महतीं तथाप्येका कला एकस्मिन्नेव दिवसे शिक्षिता । ताः कलाः शैवतन्त्रोक्ता लिख्यन्ते गीतम् इत्यादि ।

—(Vallabhāchārya).

[1] सरहस्यं धनुर्वेदं ससंग्रहमधीयताम् ।
अहोरात्रैश्चतुःषष्ट्या तदद्भुतमभूद्द्विजे ॥

[2] तौ च श्रुतिधरौ वीरौ यथावत्प्रतिपद्यताम् ।
अहोरात्रैश्चतुःषष्ट्या सांगं वेदमधीयताम् ॥

or because they might have had no doubt about the superhuman ability of Kṛishṇa and Balarāma, which has been admitted on so many other occasions in the *Śrīmad-bhāgavata* itself. But though equally mythological in character, this point has struck both the *Vishṇu-purāṇa* and the *Harivaṁśa* wherein an explanatory note is purposely added. In the former it is stated that it was wonderful (*adbhuta*) for Kṛishṇa and Balarāma to learn sixty-four arts in sixty-four days, while in the latter they are stated to have been gifted with the power of remembering things by hearing only once (*śrutidhara*). The explanation of the *Harivaṁśa* is more expressly admitted in the *Śrimad-bhāgavata*, where it is stated that they retained everything by simply listening only once.[1]

But in spite of all these explanations one cannot help thinking that at the time of the *Śrimad-bhāgavata*, as well as in the different times of its commentaries, there was no practical knowledge of all the sixty-four arts; because, otherwise, the authors of these treatises could not have passed over the point so light-heartedly; further, in other literature such an indifference is not met with. In the times of the *Vishṇu-purāṇa* and the *Harivaṁśa*, however, the state of things seems to have been different. The arts were then living objects; they were then more real, more practical; at any rate people had more familiarity with them.

The heretic group refers to the arts in connexion with the schooling of Bodhi-sattva and of Mahāvīra. It is stated in the *Lalita-vistara*[2] that 'Whatever *Śāstras* are current in the regions, all figures and writings and calculations, all roots, all arts in their immensity current on earth were learnt by him in many millions of ages (*kalpas*).' In the *Uttarādhyayana-sūtra*[3] it is stated that 'He (Mahāvīra) studied the

[1] *See* above, p. 1, note 1; p. 2, notes 1 and 2.

[2] शस्त्राणि यानि प्रचरन्ति च देवलोके
संख्या लिपिश्च गणनापि च धातुतन्त्रम्।
ये शिल्पयोगपृथलौकिक अप्रमेया—
स्तेष्वेषु शिक्षितपुराबहुकल्प कोट्यः॥
—(Chap. X, 1, p. 142, ed. Rajendra Lal Mitra).

[3] बावत्तरी कलाओ य सिक्खई नीइकोविए।
जोव्वणेण य संपन्ने सुरूवे पियदंसणे॥
तस्म रूववइं भज्जंपियाज्जाणेइ रूविणि।
पासाए कीलए रम्मे देवी दोगुन्दओ जहा॥—(Chap. XXI, 6–7).

seventy-two arts, constantly applying himself to them, he was in the full bloom of youth, he had a fine figure and good looks. His father procured him a beautiful and beloved sweetheart, Rūpiṇi, with whom he amused himself in his pleasant palace, like a Dvikundaka god.' In the Buddhist and the Jain periods a far better knowledge of these arts are thus evinced. In the *Lalita-vistara* it is distinctly stated that 'all arts were current on the earth in their immensity (*aprameya*) and they were learnt in millions of years (*bahukalpa-koṭyaḥ*).'

That youth and beauty are essential conditions for the cultivation of arts has also been admitted in the *Lalita-vistara*. Therein it is stated that 'when the Prince had duly grown up, he was taken to the school under a hundred thousand auspicious arrangments. . . . Now Viśvāmitra, the school-master, feeling the beauty and glory of the Bodhi-sattva to be insufferable, fell prostrate on the ground.'[1]

In the *Uttarādhyayana-sūtra* the number of arts is limited to seventy-two, but they are not specified anywhere in the text. The context also demands a different reading for the expression *nī-i-kovi-e*,[2] as suggested in a similar context by the expression *bahu-kalpa-koṭyaḥ* (many millions of years) in the *Lalita-vistara*, in order to give a sense of the time or the close application of the mind required in learning the seventy-two arts. But what is really important is the fact that almost all the necessary circumstances under which the arts can be cultivated are more perfectly clear in this text. It is stated that 'the student of arts must be in the full bloom of his youth and must have a fine figure (*surūpa*) and good looks (*priyadarśaṇa*) himself; he must be united with a charming (*rūpavatī*) and beloved (*priyā*) wife, who should be the personified beauty (*rūpiṇi*) to keep him constantly amused and refreshed; and lastly, he must have a beautiful palace (*prāsāda*) to live in.' In other words, a student of arts should be surrounded with all beautiful things both internally and externally; he should live in an atmosphere of beauty and youth; all his sense organs must be in a state to appreciate and enjoy; the eyes to see pretty things, the ears to hear pleasant sounds, the nose to smell fragrance, the tongue to taste sweet things, the skin to touch delicately

[1] *Lalita-vistara*, Chap. X, Trans. (R. L. Mitra), p. 181.

[2] It has been very curiously translated as "an acquired knowledge of the world" (Jacobi, SBE, Vol. XIV, p. 108), which can hardly be the rendering of its Sanskrit equivalent *Nītikovida*.

soft objects, and, above all, the mind to think, to feel, and to will the beauties of arts.

Youth and beauty as an essential condition for the cultivation and development of arts reached a fuller recognition and a more elaborate treatment in the erotic group of literature. In the *Kāma-śāstra* youth and beauty is the main theme. Whatever is discussed therein is nothing but a reference to the natural inclinations of young hearts of cultured men and women in their æsthetic mood. *Kāma*, or sensual desires, can only arise in the mind of youth in an atmosphere of beauty. A seed cannot germinate in the desert, nor can an artistic idea grow up in the fossilised heart of an old person. This fact has been fully recognized in the mythological and the Buddhist-Jain groups of literature also, for, in spite of their spirit being avowedly religious, it was necessary to train Kṛishṇa and Balarāma on the one hand and Bodhisattva and Mahāvīra on the other in artistic and other matters, not in their advanced age but in their youth and in an atmosphere of beauty. This point can be abundantly developed by a reference to the extant arts of all countries, of all nations and of all sects. But before proceeding further with illustrations it would be convenient first briefly to examine the traditional list of arts. In the *Kāma-sūtra* of Vātsyāyana[1] the sixty-four arts are specified in connexion with the accomplishments to be acquired by men and women :

1. *Gīta*—Vocal music, including everything from composition to singing, in all scientific manner and comprising four or five main topics.[2]

[1] धर्मार्थाङ्गविद्याकालाननुपरोधयन् कामसूत्रं तदङ्गविद्याश्च पुरुषोऽधीयीत ॥
प्राग्यौवनात् स्त्री। प्रत्ता च पत्युरभिप्रायात्।
. . . गीतम्, बाद्यम्, नृत्यम्
. . . व्यायामिकानाञ्च विद्यानां ज्ञानम्,
इति चतुःषष्टिरङ्गविद्याः कामसूत्रस्यावयविन्यः ॥

[2] स्वरगं पदगं चैव तथा लयगमेव च।
चेतोऽवधानगञ्चैव गेयं ज्ञेयं चतुर्विधम् ॥ —(Yaśodhara on *Kāma-sūtra*).
तत्र गीतं गानशिक्षा गीतनिर्माणं स्वज़ातिरागभेदाः तालमात्रादिरचनाप्रकाराः सुधाक वाधकस्वरादिमेलनानां परिज्ञानञ्च। —(Jīva-gosvāmin on *Śrīmad-bhāgavata*).
गीतं गानशिक्षा गीतकारणं रागभेदाः तानमात्रादिरचनाप्रकाराः
साधकबाधकतानानां परिज्ञानञ्च एवमेकस्य गीतस्य।
—(Vallabhāchārya on *Śrīmad-bhāgavata*).

2. *Vādya*—Instrumental music, which also admits four or five varieties.[1]

3. *Nṛitya*—Dancing, which includes many more things than the ordinary connotations of the term.[2]

4. *Nāṭya*—Dramatic and scenic art, including acting. Vātsyāyana reads this much later in the list as *Nāṭakākhyāyikā-darśana*, which means both seeing dramatic representation and reading stories in prose and verse. This deals with the ten kinds of drama and numerous other details which are essentially artistic in matter, spirit and form.

5. *Ālekhya*—Painting, which includes six essential parts, namely, varieties of beauty, proportions, representation of sentimental grace, resemblance, colours, reliefs.[3]

6. *Viśeshaka-chchhedya*—Tattooing, specially referring to a kind of paint on the face which is stated to be liked very much by fashionable young ladies (*vilāsinī*).

7. *Taṇḍula-kusuma-bali-vikāra*—Obviously this refers to three separate things, namely, the artistic arrangements of rice-meal, flowers, and dishes. All the commentators[4] seem to have missed the point.

[1] धनञ्च विततं वाद्यं ततं सुषिरमेव च।
कांस्यपुष्करतन्त्रीभिर्वेणुना च यथाक्रमम्॥
—(Yaśodhara on *Kāma-sūtra*).

[2] करणान्यङ्गविद्याश्च विभावो भाव एव च।
अनुभावो रसाश्चेति संक्षेपान्न.त्यसंग्रहः॥
तद्विविधम् नाटचमनाटचञ्चेति। तथोक्तम्—
स्वर्गे वा मर्त्यलोके वा पाताले वा निवासिनाम्।
कृतानुकरणं नाटचमनाटचं नर्तकाश्रितम्॥
तन्त्रान्तरे तु नृत्यभेदज्ञापनार्थमेव पृथङ नाटचकलोक्तेति विज्ञेयम्।
—(Yaśodhara on *Kāma-sūtra*)

[3] रूपभेदाः प्रमाणानि भावलावण्ययोजनम्।
सादृश्यं वर्णिकाभङ्ग इति चित्रं षडङ्गकम्॥
—(Yaśodhara on *Kāma-sūtra*).

[4] तण्डुलानां कुसुमानां च पूजोपहाररूपाणां नानाप्रकाररचना।
—(Jīva-gosvāmin).
चणकाद्विदले हस्तिलेखनं तण्डुलानां कुसुमानाञ्च आरात्रिकारेण वलिविकाराः
पूजायां वा स्थापनप्रकाराः
—(Vallabhāchārya).
अखण्डिततण्डुलैर्नानावर्णैः सरस्वतीभवने कामदेवभवने वा मणिकुट्टिमेषु भक्तिविकाराः।
तथा कुसुमैर्नानावर्णैर्ग्रथितैः शिवलिङ्गादिपूजार्थं भक्तिविकाराः।—(Yaśodhara).

They have curiously divided the phrase thus : *Taṇḍula-bali-vikāra* and *Kusuma-vikāra*, and explain the former as referring to offerings to deities and the latter to making garlands also for worship. The context makes such interpretation untenable. These are essentially artistic matters and have nothing to do even with the worship of the god of love, as the commentator of the *Kāma-sūtra* thinks, as an alternative. Besides, worship of a deity is nowhere mentioned directly or indirectly in the list. The avowedly religious learnings are confined to the *Vedas*, *Upanishads*, *Dharma Śāstras*, etc., which are separately taught, as stated in the mythological group. Moreover, the foregoing and the following topics make such an interpretation quite unconnected. It is easily understandable that an accomplished young lady must cultivate these arts as arts and not as religion.

8. *Pushpāstāraṇa*—Making beds of flowers. It, of course, refers to gardening, which is separately mentioned later on.[1]

9. *Daśana-vasanāṅga-rāga*[2]—This also refers to three separate arts, namely, the staining of the teeth, dyeing of cloth, and colouring of the body by means of powder, etc.

10. *Maṇi-bhūmika-karman*–The art of setting jewels on the (marble) floor for use particularly in summer, as stated by Yaśodhara.[3]

11. *Śayana-rachanā*—The art of bed-making. According to Jīva-gosvāmin,[4] and probably Vallabhāchārya,[5] it refers to the making of bedsteads and couches, etc., which is an item of architecture mentioned as a separate art later on. According to Yaśodhara, this is necessary for digesting the food and for enjoyment.[6]

[1] Yaśodhara guesses an alternative sense also : viz., making garlands with flowers which is separately mentioned later on.

Vallabhāchārya passes it over, calling it as स्पष्टम् ।

Jīva-gosvāmin gives the real sense :

पुष्पादिभिः शयनरचनम् ।

[2] Curiously, Vallabhāhcārya detects a sexual sense here when he says :

शय्यादौ दशनवसनानां रागभेदाः अधरोष्ठयोः लक्षणपरिज्ञानं रसार्थमेषा परीक्षा ।

[3] According to Jīva-gosvāmin this should be done, as shown by the architect Maya in building a wonderful hall for the Pāṇḍavas (for details, *see infra*, p. 247 and the writer's *Indian Architecture*, 1st Ed., pp. 166, 167, note 4).

[4] पर्यङ्कादिनिर्माणम् ।

[5] शयनं शय्यास्थानम् तस्य निर्माणम् ।

[6] शयनीयस्य कालापेक्षया रक्तविरक्तमध्यस्थाभिप्रायादाहारपरिणतिवशाच्च रचनम् ।

This is fully elaborated in connexion with शयनोपचारिका (*vide infra*).

12. *Udaka-vādya*—Playing on an instrument known as *jala-taraṅga*,[1] or china-cups containing varying quantities of water to regulate the tune and produce harmonic notes like musical glasses, or an instrument (invented by Franklin) the sounds of which are produced from bell-shaped glasses placed on a frame-work that revolves on its centre, while the rims are touched by the moistened finger.

13. *Udaka-ghāta*—The art of making fountains, called *jala-stambha-vidyā* by Jīva-gosvāmin.[2]

14. *Chitra-yoga*—Pictorial arts, i.e. various kinds of painting.[3]

15. *Mālya-grathana-vikalpa*—The arts of making garlands.[4]

16. *Śékharāpīḍa-yojana*—The art of putting on ornaments (of flowers) on the hair and top of the head.[5]

17. *Nepathya-prayoga*—Scenic representations, the art consisting in putting on clothes and ornaments for the stage. This elaborates the art mentioned in the preceding item. According to Vallabhā-chārya this also includes the construction of the stage itself.

[1] According to Yaśodhara it is like the *muraja* or a drum. Vallabhāchārya does not think of it seriously when he says, ' as sounds are naturally produced on water ' :

यथा स्वत एवोदके नादाः स्पष्टीभवन्ति

Jīva-gosvāmin thinks that this music can be produced in a tank also :

सरोवरादिस्थापितभाण्डे उदकपरिपूरितपात्रे वा मधुरनानातानसमुत्थापनम्।

[2] Vallabhāchārya makes it a childish play with water :

यथा आहतमुदकमुपरि गच्छति अधो गच्छति विपरीतं वा गच्छति।

Yaśodhara also thinks it to be a play with water :

हस्तयन्त्रमुक्तैरुदकैस्ताडनम्,

and includes the preceding one also under a general heading of ' water-play.' In fact Śrīdhara-svāmin has included the two items (nos. 11, 12) under one heading.

[3] Practically all the commentators have found it difficult to explain this. Jīva-gosvāmin is vague when he interprets it as the means to see the various wonderful things :

नानाद्भुतदर्शने सम्यगुपायाः

Vallabhāchārya thinks it to be the garlanding of flowers (विचित्राः प्रकाराः). Yaśodhara, following him, sees sexuality everywhere and says that this supplements the act of कुचुमार, a separate item (*see* below):

नानाप्रकारदौर्भाग्यकेन्द्रियपलितीकरणादयः। ईर्ष्यया पराभि(? ति) सन्धानार्थाः। तानौपनिषदके वक्ष्यति। एते च कौचुमारयोगेषु नान्तर्भवन्तीति पृथगुक्ताः। कुचुमारेण तेषामनुक्तत्वात्।

[4] Jīva-gosvamin passes over these seven items as too easy to understand. Both Vallabhāchārya and Yaśodhara make it unnecessarily to mean the making of flowers-garlands for the head, which is mentioned in the next item.

[5] The skill consists here in artistically wearing and not making these ornaments.

18. *Karṇa-patra-bhaṅga*—Painting the cheeks before the ear with sandal and other pastes. Yaśodhara thinks it to be a part of scenic representation. No doubt it is a special kind of toileting.

19. *Gandha-yukti*—Perfumery, or the art of making perfumes.[1]

20. *Bhūshaṇa-yojana*—The art of putting on ornaments on the various parts of the body. Yaśodhara interprets it as the display of jewellery on the person for stage purposes and classifies under two heads, *Saṁyojya* and *Asaṁyojya*.[2]

21. *Aindra-jāla*—The art of jugglery; according to Vallabhāchārya it does not admit of a rational explanation and has twenty varieties which are, however, not specified.

22. *Kauchumāra-yoga*—The arts as taught by Kuchumāra, the author of the *Aupanishadādhikāra*. According to the commentators these refer to some unspecified tricks.[3] Kuchumāra need not necessarily mean the author of that name when no arts bearing his name are generally known. The term '*kucha*'[4] means the 'female breast'; hence it is just possible that the art may refer to the nursing or decoration of the female breast.[5]

23. *Hasta-lāghava*—Prestidigitation. The art is well known; this is extensively practised as an amusement in fashionable societies and considered to be an accomplishment for a young person.

24. *Vichitra-śāka-pūpa-bhakshya-vikāra-kriyā*—The cookery, or the art of cooking various kinds of vegetables, cakes, and (all other) eatables. The vegetables comprise ten different things, namely, root,

[1] Vallabhāchārya suggests an alternative interpretation also:
गन्धयुक्तिश्चन्दनादेः पुष्यवस्त्राद्याकारेण निर्माणं नानासुगन्धिनिर्माणं वा।

[2] तत्र संयोज्यस्य काण्ठिकेन्द्रच्छन्दादेर्मणिमुक्ताप्रवालादिभिर्योजनम्। असंयोज्यस्य कटककुण्डलादेर्विरचनं योजनम्। तदुभयं नेपथ्याङ्गम्। न तु शरीरे भूषणयोजनं तस्य नेपथ्यप्रयोगा इत्यनेन सिद्धत्वात्।

[3] स्वस्मिन्नाभारूपा व्यञ्जना।

—(Jīva-gosvāmin).

बहुरूपकाराः।

—(Vallabhāchārya).

सुभगंकरणाय उपायन्तरासिद्धसाधनार्थाः।

—(Yaśodhara).

[4] The reading '*kuchāmāra*' is not, however, available; but when the authors of the other reading (*kuchumāra*) are not clear about the sense, an emendation in the reading does not seem unjustified.

[5] It will be pointed out later on that some of these arts are meant for the females, some for males, and the rest for both males and females.

leaf, shoot (as of a bamboo), forepart, fruit, trunk, offshoot, skin, flower, and thorn.[1]

Cakes, including bread, are also of various kinds, but they are not specified. The eatables are divided into four classes, namely,

(*a*) *bhakshya* or *charvya*, things to be eaten by chewing,
(*b*) *bhojya* or *choshya*, things to be eaten by sucking,
(*c*) *lehya*, or things to be licked, and
(*d*) *peya*, or things to be drunk.

The *peyas* are divided into two classes, namely, cooked (with fire) and uncooked. The former is called *yūsha* and admits of two varieties known as soup and decoction. The latter also has two varieties called the *asandhānakṛita* and *sandhānakṛita*. The *saṁdhānakṛita* are those which are made by distilling, such as fermented or spirituous liquors, and are divided into *drāvita* and *adrāvita* : the former is made by mixing water, sugar, and tamarind, and is known as drink or spirituous liquor; and the latter is made of liquified herbs mixed with palmyra fruit and plantain flower (*mochā*),[2] and is called *rasa*, i.e. essence or juice.

25. *Pānaka-rasa-rāgāsava-yojana*—Preparation of beverages. According to both Yaśodhara and Vallabhāchārya *āsava* implies spirituous liquor and indicates intoxication of three kinds, namely, mild, ordinary, and high. The term *rāga* is stated to imply three things, namely, those to be licked, powders and liquids tasting salt, tamarind, pungent and slightly sweet.[3]

Yaśodhara thinks[4] this, and the preceding item, may be included under one heading, namely, cookery. But a number of most useful arts are referred to here which are even at the present time practised separately. It should be noted that the stages of development

[1] मूलपत्रकरीराग्रफलकाण्डप्ररूढकम् ।
त्वक् पुष्पं कण्टकञ्चेति शाकं दशविधं स्मृतम् ॥
—(Quoted from some unknown author by Yaśodhara.)

[2] Plantain grows out of this, which looks like the cauliflower or cabbage.

[3] रागो रागविधानज्ञैर्लेह्यश्चूर्णो द्रवः स्मृतः ।
लवणाम्लकटुस्वाद ईषन्मधुरसंयुतः ॥
—(Yaśodhara quotes from some unknown work.)

[4] एतच्चतुर्विधमास्वाद्यकलायां प्रपञ्चितम् शरीरस्थित्यर्थम् । योगविभागोऽग्निजानग्निजाकर्मदर्शनार्थः। तत्र पाकेन शाकादिक्रिया, विना पाकेन पानकादियोजनम्। अन्यथा ह्यस्वाद्यविधिरित्युक्तं स्वात्। तस्मात्कर्मभेदादास्वाद्यविधानज्ञोऽपि द्विविधः। तद्वशादेकापि कला द्विधा कृत्योक्ता।

and perfection in the art of making foods and beverages are the surest indication of the state of culture and civilization as well as of the economic condition of nations and communities.

26. *Sūchi-vāya-karman*—Tailoring and weaving. According to Yaśodhara tailoring is of three kinds, namely, *sīvana* or sewing of coat, etc., *ūtana* or darning of torn cloth, etc., and *virachana* or making of bed sheets, etc. Weaving implies manufacture of cloth or the whole textile industry, including making of yarn, which is separately mentioned later on (*see* no. 36).

27. *Sūtra-krīḍā*—The art of playing with thread and rope. According to Yaśodhara the play consists in showing by sleight of hand a piece of thread in perfect condition after tearing it to pieces or burning it to ashes, and would imply a kind of magic. According to Jīva-gosvāmin the play consists in moving dolls, etc., like living beings, with the help of a thread, and also walking on rope and unbinding oneself after having been bound up with a rope. This would imply acrobatism in addition to magic.

28. *Vīṇā-ḍamaruka-vādya*—Playing on lute and small drum.[1] These are included in the instrumental music, but they are specially mentioned, as Yośodhara says, first, because stringed instrumental music and lute music are very important, secondly, because they are difficult to learn especially at the commencement, and, lastly, because on these instruments the words (letters) played can be heard as distinctly pronounced.

29. *Prahelikā*—Solution of riddles, charades, etc.

30. *Pratimālā*—Modelling or making images, i.e. sculpturing. This interpretation is very definitely asserted by Jīva-gosvāmin and Vallabhāchārya.[2] But Yaśodhara interprets this in an entirely different way and says that it refers to a kind of versification beginning with a particular letter of a verse,[3] but that is separately mentioned under a different heading (*see* no. 56).

[1] *See* above, item no. 2.

[2] सर्ववस्तुप्रतिकृतिनिर्माणम् । —(Jīva-gosvāmin).
वस्तुनामनुकरणम् । —(Vallabhāchārya).

[3] यस्या अन्त्याक्षरिकेति प्रतीतिः। सा क्रीडार्था वादार्था च। यथोक्तम् (in some unknowr work):

प्रतिश्लोकं क्रमाद्यत्र सन्धायाक्षरमन्तिमम् ।
पठेतां श्लोकमन्योन्यं प्रतिमालेति सोच्यते ॥

Sculpture as an important art is well recognized and elaborately treated in a branch of literature like most of these arts.

31. *Durvāchaka-yoga*—Mimicry, i.e. the art of an imitative resemblance in one animal to another or to some inanimate object in sound or sense, as stated by Yaśodhara.[1]

32. *Pustaka-vāchana*—Elocution, i.e. the art of effective speaking, more especially of public speaking, regarding solely the utterance or delivery. This interpretation is supported by both Jīva-gosvāmin and Vallabhāchārya.[2] But Yaśodhara refers this to recitation in particular.[3]

33. *Nāṭakākhyāyikā-darśana*—Tableaux vivants, or what are called 'living pictures.' The art consists in exhibiting a motionless representation of a well-known character, painting, scene, etc., by one or more living persons in costume. That it is different from a dramatic performance is clear and needs no explanation.

34. *Kāvya-samasyā-pūraṇa*—Solution of verbal puzzles which are elaborately discussed in a class of literature known as *Alaṁkāra-śāstra.*

35. *Paṭṭikā(peṭikā)-vetra-vāna-vikalpa*—The art of making bows (? sofa, basket), sticks, canes, etc., with thread. According to Yaśodhara this art also includes the making of cane chairs, cane beds, etc.[4]

36. *Tarku-karaman*[5]—Making twist with a spindle or a distaff: this refers to the art of spinning. Weaving is separately mentioned (*see* no. 26).

[1] शब्दतोऽर्थतश्च। तस्य प्रयोगाः क्रीडार्था वादार्थाश्च।
Vallabhāchārya says that it refers to चतुरक्षरादिप्रकार ।
Jīva-gosvāmin adopts the ordinary sense:
यद्यद्वक्तुं न शक्यते तत्तद्वक्तुसुपायाः।

[2] अतिशीघ्रमविद्यमानानपि वर्णान् योजयित्वा तद्वाचनम्।

[3] भरतादिकाव्यानां पुस्तकस्थानां शृङ्गारादिरसापेक्षया गीततः स्वरेण वाचनम् । अनुरागजननार्थमात्मविनोदार्थं च।

[4] Vallabhāchārya reads it differently, *Patrikā-chitra-vachana-vikalpa*, and refers to ram-fighting, etc., which is however included under a separate heading (*see* no. 44).

[5] Both Śrīdhara-svāmin and Vallabhāchārya misread it as *Tarka-karman* (debating). In Vātsyāyana's *Kāma-sūtra* it is read as *Taksha-karmāṇi* (carpenter's works); and the commmentator Yaśodhara interprets it as कन्दुककर्माण्यपद्रव्यार्थानि (making of balls with inferior materials). But carpentry is expressly mentioned in the next item.

37. *Takshaṇa*—Carpentry, i.e. the art of wood-carving in making seats, beds, doors, etc.[1]

38. *Vāstu-vidyā*—Architecture, the different parts of which are assigned to *sthapati*, *sūtra-grāhin*, *vardhaki* and *takshaka*.[2] It refers to the art of building and includes everything built or constructed, from the palace to the bird's nest and from the image of a god to that of an insect.[3] Thus, in the first place, it 'denotes the construction of all kinds of buildings, religious, residential and military, and their auxiliary members and component mouldings. Secondly, it implies town-planning, laying out gardens, constructing market-places, making roads, bridges, gates, digging wells, tanks, trenches, drains, sewers, moats, erecting enclosure-walls, embankments, dams, railings, flights of steps for hills, ladder, etc. Thirdly, it denotes articles of house furniture, such as bedsteads, couches, tables, chairs, thrones, fans, wardrobes, clocks, baskets, conveyances, cages, nests, mills, etc. It also includes the making of garments and ornaments, etc. It discusses, as preliminary matters, selection of site, testing of soil,[4] planning, designing, finding out cardinal points for orientation of buildings, dialling, and astronomical and astrological calculations.'

Architecture also implies sculpture, like many of the other arts, and deals with the carving of phalli, idols of deities, statues of sages, images of animals, birds, fish and insects.

39. *Suvarṇa-rūpya-ratna-parīkshā*[5]—Testing of gold, silver and jewels.

40. *Dhātu-vāda*—Metallurgy, i.e., the art of setting, purifying, and mixing up of the metals such as earth(?), stone, and quick-silver.[6]

[1] Yaśodhara says that it refers to *vardhaki-karman*, but that is not correct because *takshaka* and *vardhaki* have got different works to do (*see* under the next heading *Vāstu-vidyā*).

[2] *See infra*, p. 98 and the writer's *Indian Architecture*, 1st Ed., p. 25, and *Dictionary of Hindu Architecture*, 1st Ed., pp. 709–712, 725–730.

[3] *See* the writer's *Dictionary of Hindu Architecture*, 1st Ed., Preface, p. viii, and *Indian Architecture*, 1st Ed., pp. 1, 2.

[4] This refers to practical geology. Mining is separately mentioned (*see* no. 41).

[5] The commentators have not included *suvarṇa* which is, however, found in a text of the *Kāma-sūtra*. It should be noted that the four items beginning with this fall under one category.

[6] स मृत्प्रस्तररत्नधातुनां पातनशोधनमेलनादिज्ञानहेतुरर्थः।

(Yaśodhara prefers the reading रत्न in place of रस.)

41. *Maṇi-rāga-jñāna* (*rāgaka-rañjana*)—Art of colouring precious stones.

42. *Ākara-jñāna*—Mining, or the art of ascertaining the existence of mines from external appearances.[1]

43. *Vṛkshāyurveda-yoga*—The art of gardening, which, according to Yaśodhara, includes planting, nursing, curing, and artistically arranging trees in private house gardens.[2] Vallabhāchārya refers it particularly to the fruit gardens.[3]

44. *Mesha-kukkuṭa-lāvaka-yudha-vidhi*—Ram-fighting, cock-fighting, quail-fighting. Such things are shown, according to Yaśodhara in the performance of a circus party.[4]

45. *Śuka-sārikā-pralāpana*—Teaching of parrots, etc., to speak. The art consists in a sort of singing and delivering (good) news through the birds.[5]

46. *Utsādana* (*-ne saṁvāhane cha kauśala*)—Massage or shampooing, i.e. rubbing the limbs with unguents, pomades, etc., both with hands and feet as Yaśodhara says.[6]

47. *Keśa-mārjana-kauśala*[7]—Coiffure or hair-dressing.

48. *Akshara-mushṭikā-kathana*—Guessing unseen letters and things held in a closed fist, as stated by Jīva-gosvāmin and Vallabhāchārya. But, according to Yaśodhara, the art consists in guessing things held in a closed fist, like the revealing of the hidden and suggested meanings in a poetic composition; it admits of two varieties, namely, *sābhāsa* (suggestive) and *nirābhāsa* (unsuggestive),

[1] Vātsyāyana does not include this. His commentator Yaśodhara says that this is found in some other texts.

[2] रोपणपुष्टिचिकित्सावैचित्र्याकृते गृहोद्यानार्थाः।

[3] वृक्षाणां जीवनप्रकाराः फलैर्निर्बीजकरणं वृक्षान्तरात्फलोत्पादनमित्यादि।

[4] सजीवद्यूतविधानमेतत्। तत्रोपस्थानादिभिश्चतुरङ्गैर्युद्धविधानं क्रीडार्थं वादार्थं च।

—(Yaśodhara).

[5] सुभाषितं पठन्ति सन्देशञ्च कथयन्ति।

—(Yaśodhara).

[6] मर्दनं द्विविधं पादाभ्यां हस्ताभ्याञ्च। तत्र पादाभ्यां यन्मर्दनं तदुत्सादनमुच्यते। शेषाङ्गेषु मर्दनं संवाहनम्।

For the purpose of the *Kāma-śāstra* such an erotic art has obviously a great use.

[7] केशग्रहणमत्रादरार्थम्। तत्र कौशलं पराराधनार्थम्।

—(Yaśodhara).

the object being twofold, namely, to guess hidden things and to make concise composition.[1]

49. *Mlechchhita-vikalpa*—Use of secret code language or modifying ordinary language so as to make it not ordinarily intelligible, as stated by Yaśodhara.[2]

50. *Deśa-bhāshā-vijñāna*—Knowledge of languages of different countries.[3]

51. *Pushpa-śakatikā-nirmita-jñāna*[4]—Making of flower carriages.

52. *Nimitta-jñāna*—The art of reading omens from the crowing of crows, etc., as stated by Vallabhāchārya.[5]

53. *Yantra-mātṛikā*—The art of making monograms, logographs, and diagrams. Yaśodhara attributes this to Viśva-karman and calls it *ghaṭanā-śastra* (science of accidents).[6]

[1] अक्षराणां सुष्टिरिव सुष्टिकागुप्तिरिति। सा साभासा निराभासा च । तत्र साभासा अक्षर मुद्रेति उच्यते। तया कथनं गूढ़वस्तुमन्त्रणार्थं ग्रन्थसंक्षेपार्थञ्च। निराभासा भूतसुद्रेत्यच्यते। तया कथनं गुह्यावस्तुमन्त्रणार्थम् ।

Yaśodhara illustrates this by quoting verses from the *Chandra-prabhā-vijaya-kāvya* of Ravigupta.

[2] यत्साधुशब्दोपनिबद्धमप्यक्षरव्यत्यासादस्पष्टार्थं तन्म्लेच्छितं गूढ़वस्तुमन्त्रणार्थम् । तस्य विकल्पा बहवः पूर्वाचार्योक्ताः। तद्यथा

कौटिलीयं यदि क्षान्तैः स्वरयोर्ह्रस्वदीर्घयोः।
विन्दुष्मणोर्विपर्यासाद्दुर्बोधमिति संज्ञितम् ॥

[3] अप्रकाश्यवस्तुज्ञापनार्थं तद्देशीयैर्व्यवहारार्थं च ।

—(Yaśodhara).

[4] Vātsyāyana divides this under two headings :

(1) *Pushpa-śākaṭikā* and (2) *nirmita-jñāna.* His commentator, Yaśodhara, simply says that

पुष्पाणि निमित्तीकृत्याहं प्रणीता।

Jīva-gosvāmin reads it as *Pushpa-śakaṭikā-nimitta-jñānam,* but fails to explain it

पुष्पशकटिकौपाधिकायां कस्याञ्चिद्विद्यायां निमित्तज्ञानम् ।

Śridhara-svāmin reads it as :

पुष्पशकटिकानिर्मितिज्ञानम् ।

[5] धर्मक्षमावर्गेऽन्तर्गतं शुभाशुभादेशफलम्। तत्र च प्रष्टुरभिज्ञानार्थम्। एवंरूपया स्त्रिया तव संप्रयोग इति कामोपहसितप्राया आदेशा इति। निमित्तज्ञानमिति सामान्येनोक्तम्।

[6] सजीवानां निर्जीवानां यन्त्राणां यानोदक (या नोदना) संग्रामार्थं (।) शास्त्रं विश्वकर्मप्रोक्तम्।

54. *Dhāraṇa-matṛikā*[1]—The art of composing enigmatic poetry. According to Yaśodhara it refers to a kind of science of remembering.[2]

55. *Sampāṭhya*—According to Yaśodhara it refers to a kind of reading which is practised for the sake of music and debate.[3]

56. *Mānasi kāvya-kriyā*—Extempore and mental composition of versified poetry. The art comprises the filling up of stanzas of which a portion is told, the versification of thoughts in someone else's mind, and composing verses beginning with certain given letters, etc.

57. *Abhidhāna-kośa*—Lexicography. The art consists in getting together all the synonyms of a term.

58. *Chhando-jñāna*—Knowledge of metres. The art consists in composing metrical verses. But according to Yaśodhara it refers to character-reading, especially of man by young ladies.[4]

59. *Kriyāvikalpa*—Derivation and conjugation of verbs in various ways. It refers to grammar and poetics, as Yaśodhara says.

60. *Chhalitaka-yoga*—Tricks. According to Yaśodhara the art consists in assuming by one the form of somebody else in order to deceive someone, as Śūrpaṇakhā and Kīchaka did.[5]

61. *Vastra-gopana*—Changing the appearance of fabrics, such as making cotton cloth appear like silk. But according to Yaśodhara the art consists rather in concealing by cloth the very existence of certain private parts of the body, putting on a torn piece of cloth in such a manner that it looks perfect, and wearing a long piece of cloth in skilful folding so that it appears small.[6]

1 Vallabhāchārya and Śrīdhara-svāmin read this along with the preceding one under the same heading.

2 श्रुतस्य ग्रन्थस्य धारणार्थं शास्त्रम्। यथोक्तम् --

यस्तु कोषस्तथा द्रव्यं लक्षणं केतुरेव च।

इत्येते धारणादेशाः पञ्चाङ्गरुचिरं वपुः ॥

3 सम्भूयक्रीड़ार्थं वादार्थञ्च। तत्रपूर्वधारितमेको ग्रन्थं पठति, द्वितीयस्तमेवाश्रुतपूर्वं तेन सह तथैव पठति।

4 पुरुषं दृष्ट्वैव तस्य छन्दोज्ञानम् अयमेवं वृत्तः इतिः कामिन्यादीनां मनोज्ञानं वा।

5 यद्रूपमन्यरूपेण संप्रकाश्य हि वञ्चनम्।

देवेतरप्रयोगाभ्यां ज्ञेयं तच्छलितं यथा ॥

दिव्यं शर्पणखा रूपमितरद्वायुनन्दनः।

छलितवानभिसृत्य श्रिया रामं च कीचकम् ॥ —(Quotations from some unnamed work.)

6 वस्त्रेणाप्रकाश्यदेशस्य संवरणं यथा तद्भूयमानमपि तस्मान्नापैति। त्रुटितस्यात्रुटितस्येव परिधानम् महतो वस्त्रस्य संवरणादिनाल्पीकरणम्।

62. *Dyūta-viśesha*—The art of various gamblings.

63. *Aksha-krīḍā*—Playing with dice, mentioned as a special game by Yaśodhara. Jīva-gosvāmin refers this to an unspecified game in which a distant object is drawn in.[1]

64. *Bāla-krīḍanaka*—The art of making dolls for children. According to a modern translator (Mitra) it refers to juvenile sports.

65. *Vainayikī-jñāna*—The art of etiquette, as Yaśodhara says.[2]

66. *Vijayikī-jñāna*—Art of warfare, including archery, etc. According to Yaśodhara, it admits of two varieties, divine and human.[3]

67. *Vyāyāmikī-jñāna*[4]—The art of physical exercises, including hunting and other sports, as stated by Yośodhara.[5]

From this list it is clear that under some headings more than one subject is discussed, that some subjects should better be discussed under one heading, and that the order is not logical. In fact, the number of arts as sixty-four is a fictitious one. Neither Vātsyāyana, nor all the commentators of the *Kāma-sūtra*, nor those of the *Śrīmad-bhāga-vata*, nor the author of the *Lalita-vistara* have been able to make up the number. Some of the commentators admit this.[6] In the *Uttarādhyana-sūtra* the number given, as pointed out above, is seventy-two, which are not, however, specified. Yaśodhara declares that the sixty-four are the basic arts, which may be subdivided into five hundred and eighteen.[7] These basic arts are classified under different groups in an unspecified text (of the *Kāma-sūtra*). Of these, twenty-four are stated to be the useful arts[8]; twenty refer to gambling, of

[1] As a matter of fact this and the former item should come under one heading.

[2] स्वपरविनयप्रयोजनाद् वैनयिक्यो आचारशास्त्राणि हस्त्यादिशिक्षा च।

[3] विजयप्रयोजना वैजयिक्यः। दैव्यो मानुष्यश्च। तत्र दैव्यो पराजितादयः। मानुष्यो याः सांग्रामिक्यः शस्त्रविद्याः।

[4] Both Śrīdhara-svāmin and Śuka-deva read it as *Vaitālikī*.

[5] व्यायामिक्यो मृगयाद्या :।

[6] केचित्त कलाः कल्पसंहितोक्ताः सुधियामेव प्रत्येकमेकाहोरात्रशिक्षणार्हाः क्षुद्रसिद्धिरूपाः परचित्तज्ञतादूरश्रवणदर्शनचिन्तारत्नाभृतविशेषनिर्माणाद्याः अन्या एवाहु :।—(Jīva-gosvāmin)·

पूर्वोक्ते वा अवान्तरभेदाः क्वचिद्ग्राह्याः।—(Vallabhāchārya).

[7] चतुःषष्टिर्मूलकलाः। आस्वेवान्तरनिविष्टानामन्तरकलानामष्टादशाधिकानि पञ्चशतान्युक्तानि।

[8] गीतम्, नृत्यम्, वाद्यम्, लिपिज्ञानम्, वचनं चोदारम्, चित्रविधिः, पुस्तककर्म, पत्रच्छेद्यम्, माल्यविधिः, आस्वाद्यविधानम्, रत्नपरीक्षा, सीव्यम्, रङ्गपरिज्ञानम्, उपस्करणक्रिया, मानविधिः, आजीवज्ञानम्, तिर्यग्योनिचिकित्सितम्, मायाकृतपाषण्डसमयज्ञानम्, क्रीड़ाकौशलम्, लोकज्ञानम्, वैचक्षण्यम्, संवाहनम शरीरसंस्कारः, विशेषकौशलञ्चेति।

which fifteen deal with theoretical things[1] and five with practical objects[2]; and sixteen are concerned with cohabitation[3] and four with subsidiary matters connected with cohabitation.[4] The last twenty are entirely private matters and are never meant for public discussion; they are too fine to be exhibited in a museum for fine arts, although indecent paintings of the sort are noticed in temples at Puri, Kanarak, Benares and elsewhere; they are stated to be practised in private.[5]

So far as the main list is concerned, it should be noticed, only the last twenty may be considered as exclusively feminine arts, the others from vocal music down to physical exercise being equally practised both by males and females. Even cookery, which includes the scientific preparation of all kinds of dishes and beverages, is a proper subject for the theoretical and practical study for man and woman alike. In fact, dietary is a section of the medical science. Another fact to which attention should be drawn is that barely one-fourth of the whole list can be called fine arts, which are meant only for mere culture or amusement, while others are really useful and productive arts both materially and culturally. This point is beautifully illustrated by Vātsyāyana in his *Kāma-sūtra* : ' Even an ordinary dancing girl possessing beauty and youth when trained in these arts rises to the status of a courtesan, is welcomed in respectable society, and is respected by kings and learned people. She becomes an object of notice and is desired by everybody. As regards princesses and daughters of high officials, they can keep captivated their husbands possessing a thousand other wives. And when they become widows

[1] द्यूताश्रया विंशतिः। तत्र निर्जीवाः पञ्चदश—आयुःप्राप्तिः, अक्षविधानम्, रूपसङ्ख्या, क्रियामागणम्, बीजग्रहणम्, नयज्ञानम्, करणादानम्, चित्राचित्रविधिः, गूढ़राशिः, तुल्याभिहारः, क्षिप्रग्रहणम्, अनुप्राप्तिलेखस्मृतिः, अग्निक्रमः, छलव्यामोहनम्, ग्रहदानञ्चेति।

[2] सजीवाः पञ्च—उपस्थानविधिः, युद्धम्, रुतम्, गीतम्, नृत्तम् चेति।

[3] शयनोपचारिकाः षोड़श–पुरुषस्य भावग्रहणम्, स्वरागप्रकाशनम्, प्रत्यङ्गदानम्, नखदन्तयोर्विचारः, नीवीस्रंसनम्, गुह्यस्य संस्पर्शनानुलोम्यम्, परमार्थकौशलम्, हर्षणम्, समानार्थता कृतार्थता अनुप्रोत्साहनम्, मृदुक्रोधप्रवर्तनम्, सम्यक्क्रोधनिवर्तनम्, क्रुद्धप्रसादनम्, सुप्त(शय्या)परित्यागः, चरमस्वापविधिः, गुप्तगूहनमिति।

[4] चतस्र उत्तरकलाः—साश्रुपातं रमणाय शापदानम्, स्वशपथक्रिया, प्रस्थितानुगमनम्, पुनः पुनः निरीक्षणञ्चेति।

[5] अभ्यासप्रयोज्यांश्च चातुःषष्टिकान् योगान् कन्या रहस्येकाकिन्यभ्यसेत्।

—(Vātsyāyana, Chap. III).

and deprived of their wealth they can honourably earn their livelihood even in another country. A man who is a skilful artist can command a hearing and proves a pleasant companion everywhere. Even being a stranger he can captivate the heart of young ladies in no time. Prosperity follows him in all places and at all times.'[1]

Lastly, none of these arts can be properly cultivated by a person, community, or nation who is not endowed with a sense of beauty and youth. In this matter age is no sure test of youth. The Great Buddha could renounce the world while yet a young man and in the midst of worldly prosperity because he had grown oldish in heart and had no interest for youth and beauty. Almost at the same age Chaitanya also renounced the world, but he was never deprived of a sense of beauty and youth, and the result has been the origin of *Saṅkīrtana*, a kind of very exciting mass music, as well as the establishment of *Nava-dvīpa*, and later *Vaishṇavism*, where many of the erotic arts developed under different garbs with a tinge of religion. On the other hand, poets like Rabindranath and others write highly erotic poems and love stories in their sixties and seventies, because, in spite of their age, they have kept alive an interest for beauty and youth in their heart. In fact, beauty and youth need not always be dependent upon a well-proportioned figure or any particular complexion or upon a particular age.

'Youth is not a time of life; it is a state of mind. It is not a matter of ripe cheeks, red lips and supple knees; it is a temper of the will, a quality of the imagination, a vigour of the emotions. It is the freshness

[1] अभिरभ्युच्छ्रिता वेश्या शीलरूपगुणान्विता।
लभते गणिकाशब्दं स्थानं च जनसंसदि॥
पूजिता सा सदा राज्ञा गुणवद्भिश्च संस्तुता।
प्रार्थनीयाऽभिगम्या च लक्ष्यभूता च जायते॥
योगज्ञा राजपुत्रो च महामात्रसुता तथा।
सहस्रान्तःपुरमपि स्ववशे कुरुते पतिम्॥
तथा पतिवियोगे च व्यसनं दारुणं गता।
देशान्तरेऽपि विद्याभिः सा सुखेनैव जीवति॥
नरः कलासु कुशलो वाचालश्चाटुकारकः।
असंस्तुतोऽपि नारीणां चित्तमाश्वेव विन्दति॥
कलानां ग्रहणादेव सौभाग्यमुपजायते।
देशकालौ त्वपेक्ष्यासां प्रयोगः सम्भवेन्न वा॥

—(*Kāma-sūtra*, Chap. III).

of the deep springs of life. Youth means a temperamental predominance of courage over timidity, of the appetite for adventure over the love of ease. This often exists in a man of fifty more than in a boy of twenty. Nobody grows old by merely living a number of years. People grow old only by deserting their ideals. Years wrinkle the skin; but to give up enthusiasm wrinkles the soul. Worry, doubt, self-distrust, fear and despair—these are the long long years that bow the heart and turn the greening spirit back to doubt. Whether sixty or sixteen, there is in every human being's heart the lure of wonder, the sweet amazement at the stars and at the starlike things and thoughts, in undaunted challenge of events, the unfailing, child-like appetite for what next, and the joy of the game of living. You are as young as your faith; as old as your doubt; as young as your self-confidence; as old as your fear; as young as your hope; as old as your despair.

'In the central place of your heart there is an evergreen tree, its name is Love. So long as it flourishes, you are young. When it dies, you are old. In the central place of your heart there is a wireless station, so long as it receives messages of beauty, hope, cheer, grandeur, courage and power from the earth, from men and from the infinite, so long are you young. When the wires are down, and all the central place of your heart is covered with snows of cynicism and the vice of pessimism, then you are grown old, even at twenty.'

Youth and beauty are an embodiment of what is called the sensual love. And love is the real life which is the source of all activities and of all arts. Life is, however, impossible without a body. Hence beauty and youth can be realized only with reference to an idol, an image, or a symbol.

Buddhism at its origin was a religion of renunciation. Buddha himself was not attracted to his young wife, newly-born baby boy, old parents, and an extensive kingdom and other royal prosperities. Buddhism itself required no idol to worship and needed no temple. Hence Buddhism has given rise, in architecture, for instance, to heaps of stone known as *stūpa*. These topes, the real representative structures, both of the Buddhists and the Jains, were of solid masonry for the preservation of relics and never intended to be artistic. No doubt they are found surrounded with beautiful stone railings and decorated with artistic gateways; but these were obviously incongruous with the original tumulus and must have been later additions. They formed no essential parts of the main structure, just like the other accessories, such as stone umbrellas, elaborately carved pillars, and abundant statuary, usually in the form of reliefs, representing scenes connected with their religions. They show the conversion of Buddhism and Jainism to idolatry and point to the period from whence the Buddhist and the Jain arts made their appearance.

Muhammadanism grew up in the Arabian desert. It is not a religion of renunciation, but it is non-idolatrous; hence there is no need for a temple; prayer could be said anywhere. Consequently the mosque does not represent any symbolic idea. It has been rightly stated that the Muhammadans 'designed like giants and their Hindu workmen finished like jewellers; but from the giant killed by Jack, right through the whole genus, giants have hitherto been noted for . . . immense strength.'[1] There is no room for any sculpture. Worship is congregational, but there is no need for music, which is considered to be a disturbance rather than an incentive to the worshippers in concentrating the mind upon one object. Priests are householders, but the God of daily worship is impersonal. Thus it is not a religion of love, rather one of obedience. The sensual love, however, embodies in itself beauty and youth without which no fine art can grow. Hence Muhammadanism could not give rise to many fine arts. It is, however, a fact that the Muslims have later on developed many arts, but that is due to their war-like spirit, their militarism, and not to their religion. The wonderful Taj Mahal is a secular monument of love for a beautiful wife. The great forts at Agra, Delhi, and other places were but military settlements. The famous Mughal paintings have no religious tinge about them. The *Quran* is composed in prose and is not a book of poetical hymns like the *Bible* or the *Vedas*. In fact, both Arabic and Persian poetry is predominantly secular.

Christianity, on the other hand, is a religion of love. Christ himself was born of extreme love of youth for beauty, and gave up his life under highly romantic circumstances. It is fundamentally a religion which cannot be practised in the absence of an idol, an image, or a symbol. Christ is idolized in every church, together with the cross, which was the deadly weapon upon which he was

[1] General A. Cunningham, *Archaelogical Survey Reports*, Vol. IV, pp. 56–57.

crucified. Idol-worship needs a temple. Hence the Christian form of worship is impracticable without the church or a chapel. Like Muhammadanism, it is also congregational, but, unlike the former, it is performed with music in an atmosphere of beauty ; the church is neatly arranged and the worshippers keep a fashionable dress for the Sunday or Church day. Its priests are householders ; they can eat all things, they can amuse themselves in all possible ways, even in hunting, gambling, drinking and dancing. In other words, it is full of life and vigour ; beauty and youth reign supreme in it. Thus the Christian churches of almost all ages and in all countries were lovingly conceived and beautifully executed. The Grecian gods and goddesses were vigorously carved and were always given a youthful and beautiful appearance. Young boys (and girls) in pretty uniform are required to sing psalms from the *Bible* in chorus. In painting, the romantic incidents connected with Christ played a great part. Greek, Latin, French, English, German, Russian, all literature of the followers of Christ is full of their mythological allusions. Poetry, lyric, drama, all are based mainly on the theme of beauty and youth. Vigorous and lively music is necessary everywhere in the church, for the funeral, in the battle-field, for a dinner-party, for the dancing hall, etc. Cookery or perfumery, jugglery or mimicry, weaving or tailoring, bull-fighting or hunting, in every art of the Christian world there is evinced a real life. The theme in all these arts is that of beauty and youth.

Hinduism combines in itself, at different stages of its development, the renunciation and respect for life of Buddhism, the stern discipline and brotherhood of Muhammadanism, and the love and life of Christianity. The inactive God beyond the conception of mind and word is impersonal, but the active God of worship is idolized to an extreme. In the early Vedic stage God is personified in natural phenomena ; then He is given a human body till at last He is conceived as having a thousand heads, a thousand eyes, a thousand arms, and so on.

Thus we see in the Paurāṇic age Brahmā is furnished with four heads, Siva and other deities with three eyes, the goddess Durgā or Sakti, i.e. the personified energy, with ten hands holding various attributes, and the goddess of learning with a musical instrument. In the *dhvānas*, or descriptions of various deities, all their characteristic features and qualifications are elaborately referred to. In these descriptions one feature, which is practically common to all the gods and goddesses, is that they are conceived at the height of their beauty. This is applicable not only to the goddess of love or wealth, but also to the goddess of fury or terror.

Temples had already been erected when God was fully idolized. But the priest who renounced the world, or went to the forest in his old age accompanied by his old wife alone, needed neither temple nor idol; he went on meditating on the impersonal God. The greater majority of priests, however, remain householders, enjoying life in all possible ways in an atmosphere of beauty and youth. Even in the early Vedic stage a worshipper had to be accompanied by, what is called in English, his *better half*. No religious observance would be complete unless one is accompanied by his wife. Rāma had to be accompanied by a golden image of Sītā for the performance of his horse-sacrifice in celebration of his suzerainty. And all possible phases and aspects of the conception of God were idolized. Thus Hinduism has given rise to an unparalleled pantheon and mythology. There is the god for creation, god for preservation, god for destruction. There is the god of death, there is the god of love, there is the god of war. There is a god for the fisherman, a god for the weaver, a god for the trader, a god for the hunter. All this statuary symbolizes the self-expression of youth in as beautiful a body as an artist can conceive. Sculpture being the handmaid of architecture such a variety of deities necessarily needed equally diversified types of temples, of which, though the ancient remains are not too numerous, there are convincing proofs in all branches of our literature, especially in the *Vāstu-śāstras*. Buildings have been distinguished as male, female, and neuter; as round, oval, rectangular, quadrangular, octagonal and of other shapes; as running to seventeen storeys; as having ninety-eight, forty-five, twenty, and ten types; as being high like the Himalayas; white like the swan, etc.[1] In the words of Fergusson, 'it will undoubtedly be conceded by those who are familiar with the subject that, for certain qualities, the Indian buildings are unrivalled; and that they display an exuberance of fancy, a lavishness of labour, and an elaboration of detail to be found nowhere else.' What remains to be added to this general

[1] *See infra*, pp. 186–196; the writer's *Dictionary of Hindu Architecture*, 1st Ed. pp. 830, 831, and the *Encyclopaedia of Hindu Architecture*, under *Prāsāda*.

characteristic is that Hindu architecture, much like sculpture, good, bad, or indifferent, was always inspired by a sensual love and executed in an atmosphere of beauty and youth.

The *Vedas*, which are the fundamental scriptures of Hinduism, have been recognized as first-class poetic productions, full of life, vigour and beauty. Thus the Hindu mind could not think but in poetry. Excepting the commentaries and explanatory notes as represented by the *Brāhmaṇas*, the *Sūtras*, and one or two other branches of literature, poetry has been the vehicle of expression everywhere else, including lexicons, law-books, political sciences, astronomy, mathematics, medicine, architecture, sculpture, painting, singing, dancing, even histories, not to speak of epic works, lyrics and dramas. Poetry can be woven only by the hand of youth in an atmosphere of beauty, whatsoever might be its nature, whatsoever might be its subject-matter and whatsoever might be its leading sentiment, either of love or laughter, pathetic or furious, heroic or terrible, expressing disgust or wonder, filial affection or spiritual resignation. Human love has always been a theme of Hindu poetry.

Poetry and music became almost identical at a very early stage; one of the scriptures is called a book of chants. Without music the Hindu life is impossible: it is necessary for wedding, for christening a child, for initiation, for amusement and for mourning, at birth and at death, for war and for peace. All music is but a beautiful expression of a heart full of youthful enthusiasm.

Although the arts like architecture, sculpture, poetry and music had their origin in the religion of the Christians and the Hindus in connexion with the form of worship, which is based on love, these arts, along with the others of the above list, became later entirely secular, and developed in various ways. In the *Kāma-sūtra* the arts have nothing to do with religion. Their object is neither salvation (*moksha*) nor ritualistic observances (*dharma*), but merely the gratification of material desires and sensual love. Cookery or perfumery, dancing or singing, painting or powdering, jugglery or physical exercise, gardening or weaving is undertaken to earn money or to enjoy oneself. This fact, as noticed above, has been repeatedly pointed out by the commentator Yaśodhara. In fact, material desires and sensual love can be nourished only by those who consider themselves ever young and immortal; in other words, no artistic matter can be cultivated by those who are in the grasp of death and decay.

Countries or nations deprived of a sense of beauty and youth for some reason or other could not give rise to many fine arts. While in the full bloom of her youth and beauty Africa, for instance, could think of erecting monumental pyramids and dream of devisiug means to preserve the perishable dead bodies in the form of mummies ; but since life and love have been taken out of her, there has been no artistic effort or expression in any way. The Grecian statuary no longer shows its former life and vigour, beauty and youth. The famous colossal buildings at Borobudur were built but once. The weavers of Bengal, who once manufactured the finest muslin in the world, could no longer be induced to produce even *khādi*.

So far as Hindu India of the past is concerned all the five hundred and eighteen arts, of which a mere mention is made, might not have been equally developed, but many of them, in the neighbourhood of a few hundred, did undoubtedly reach the status of a fully developed science and can each claim a *Śilpa-śāstra*. The revival of the *Śilpa-śāstras* would revive our art consciousness. The unearthing of our artistic treasures and unfolding of their worth and beauty may bring back life and love in us, and awaken that youthful artistic instinct which is our precious inheritance. Biggest fruits and best flowers can grow only in the healthiest young plants on a fertile soil.

In this volume an endeavour has been made 'to be quite certain of our data,' so far as Hindu architecture in India and Abroad is concerned, and 'to place the monumental records with a faithful interpretation before the learned world exactly as they now exist.'

PLATE XIII

GENERAL VIEW, NORTHEN SECTION, LOOKING SOUTH-EAST, MOHENJO-DARO

CHAPTER I

PRE-VEDIC ARCHITECTURE

Mohenjo-daro

The term 'Mohenjo-daro' is translated as the 'Mound of the Dead.' Why it is so called is not yet known. The place is locally known as 'the island.' It is 'a long, narrow strip of land between the main river (Indus) bed and the Western Nāra loop, its precise position being 27° 19′ N. by 68° 8′ E., some 7 miles by road from Dokri on the North-Western Railway, and 25 from Lārkāna town.' There are stated to have been several cities, one being superimposed upon the other. The remains of the uppermost city were hid by the mounds, averaging from 20 to 70 feet in height. 'The actual area covered by the mounds is now no more than about 240 acres.'[1] 'Originally, the site of Mohenjo-daro must have been much more extensive than it is today and have formed a more closely connected whole.'[2]

There is a main road, designated by the excavator as East Street, which runs across the site from east to west. There is another long street, but less important as the thoroughfare of the city, which crosses East Street at right angles and thus runs from north to south and is designated as First Street. 'From these two long streets, as well as from the short sections of others disclosed in other parts of the site, it is evident that the city was intersected by long streets or approximately straight thoroughfares mainly oriented north to south or east to west; and it is natural to suppose that one of these thoroughfares—perhaps the most important of them all—ran north to south through the broad depression which divides the *Stūpa* Mound from the rest of the site, in a line parallel to First Street and connecting at right angles with East Street.'[2] The main thoroughfares are all below the level of the buildings erected alongside of them.

The extent of ground covered by this city at successive periods is not definitely known, but it is clear that 'once it must have extended well beyond the existing limits.' Sir John Marshall, disagreeing with Mr. Mackay, asserts that the city must have been surrounded by walls. But it may be 'assumed that up to the time of its zenith

[1] *Mohenjo-daro and Indus Civilization*, Vol. I, p. 1. [2] *Ibid*, p. 8.

Mohenjo-daro went on steadily expanding, its centre would naturally continue to occupy the elevated ground formed by earlier settlements, while its outlying parts would overflow further and further on to the plain below.'[1]

Between the subsoil and the summits of the mounds remains of seven strata have been disclosed. The three last strata are distinguished from their predecessors 'by increasing signs of decadence in the size and construction of the buildings, and in some areas there is also a well defined break between the remains of the third and fourth strata from the top, as if the city had been reduced to ruin at that time and remained in that condition for an appreciable period before being rebuilt.' 'Of the seventh stratum only a very small extent has been uncovered, but the distinction of this and the sixth stratum is more than usually marked.' These seven strata have been divided into three major divisions or periods. The first of these comprising the first, second and third strata is called the 'Late Period'; the second comprising the fourth, fifth and sixth strata is called the 'Intermediate Period'; and the third represented for the present by the seventh stratum only is called the 'Early Period.'[2]

The layout of the whole city of any one of these periods or strata is thus missing from the account of Sir John Marshall and others. A provisional picture may, however, be imagined by joining up the various sections or areas as described by them. The city would thus look of irregular shape, the longer side in some cases being from north to south, and in others from east to west. The streets and lanes, however, are nearly straight. By the intersections of these the city is divided into different blocks. The central part appears to have been occupied by some public building or the Great Bath. Each block contained a number of buildings for the residence of the people of the same profession. The streets and lanes are all below the level of the buildings on their both sides. There appears to have been an extensive arrangement for drainage—a peculiarity which is strongly emphasized in the *Mānasāra* and other *Śilpa-śāstras*. The general city plan, excepting the irregularity, will also correspond to some extent to the plans elaborately described in the architecture of *Mānasāra*.

As in other ancient pre-historic sites, buildings at Mohenjo-daro have been discovered in different strata. The loftiest mound rising

[1] *Mohenjo-daro and Indus Civilization*, Vol. I, p. 9. [2] *Ibid*, p. 10.

some 72 feet above the surrounding country (and 227 feet above the mean sea-level) is crowned by the Buddhist tope and monastery. Below this earliest Buddhist pavement the lowest point so far reached goes down to a depth of 40 feet. Within this space seven different strata have been exposed, each stratum containing different kinds of structures built of kiln-burnt bricks.

The Buddhist monuments at the top of the uppermost stratum comprise an open quadrangle with a lofty tope in its middle and rows of monastic buildings enclosing it on the four sides. These monuments, including the tope, courtyard, and surrounding monastery, are stated to have been many times repaired or rebuilt 'on each occasion at a successively higher level. Thus the original pavement of the courtyard was 20 feet below the bottom of the *stūpa* drum, or 44 feet approximately above the level of the plain (and 199 feet above the mean sea-level). The next floor was 1 to 2 feet above it, and then followed a succession of at least three more floors, the last nearly 6 feet higher than the original one.'[1]

The general plans and details of these buildings follow those of the usual Buddhist monuments. But the *stūpa* is not situated in the centre of the quadrangle. The symmetry has been lost as the distance between the *stūpa* platform and the surrounding cells on the four sides is different, being 22½ feet on the north, 20 feet on the south, 12 and 14 feet on the west, and 34 feet on the east. The reason for this unusual want of symmetry is stated to be due to this building being erected first on this site and the courtyard and monastery being added later on the restricted space available on the summit of the mound.

'Measured from the first pavement to the base of the drum the height of the plinth is 20 feet. . . . The approach to it was in the middle of its eastern side, and was more than ordinarily elaborate. It consisted of a series of steps and landings which led upwards into a narrow vestibule. . . . On the opposite side of this vestibule was a short passage, from which two flights of steps ascended north and south to the top of the platform ; and closing the passage, at its western end was a small image-chapel, or a niche, which appears to have been 3¾ feet above the pavement of the passage. This image-niche (7 feet deep by 4½ feet wide) occupies a particularly

[1] *Mohenjo-daro and Indus Civilization*, Vol. I, p. 113.

prominent position, being directly opposite to, though slightly above, the approaching stairway. In it Mr. Banerji found some remains of a statue of Buddha, seated cross-legged, probably on a lotus throne. The core of the image, he says, was of brick covered with a coating of mud, which had originally been painted or gilt.'[1]

All that is left of the dome of the *stūpa* is the lower part of the circular drum of 33½ feet in diameter. This drum was probably hollow in the centre, wherein a relic casket of alabaster has been found. 'The fragments of plaster found on the western side of the plinth were coloured blue, yellow, red, and chocolate, and bore traces of figures and decorative designs, as well as fragmentary inscriptions in Brāhmi and Kharoshṭhi. Among the latter Mr. Banerji recognized the word *Samana* (Skt. *Śramaṇa*) in lettering of the Kushan epoch, but whether of the early or late part of it, is disputable.'[1]

Grouped about the main *stūpa* in the courtyard there were several smaller *stūpas*. There are series of cells and other apartments on all the four sides of the courtyard, all built like the *stūpa*, of kiln-burnt brick laid in mud and gypsum, as many of the pre-historic buildings were. Sir John Marshall assumes 'on the analogy of other monasteries of the Kushan period' that 'they (cells) possessed two storeys with a wooden verandah in front—facing inwards towards the courtyard—which would serve at once to shield them from the sun and provide access to the chambers on the upper floor. The roof would be carried on timbers and covered with mud, with a slight slope inwards towards the court.'[2]

'The entrance to the monastery was on the east side of the quadrangle directly opposite the steps leading up to the *stūpa*. Here there was a vestibule 25½ feet by 13½ feet. To the north of this vestibule there is a small chapel. On the floor of the chapel were two separate pavements of brick, corresponding to those in the large halls as well as in many of the cells.'[2] To the north of this chapel there is a long narrow chamber containing a staircase to the upper storey, where the monk quarters were situated. The large hall (44 feet by 26 feet), supposed to be a Hall of Assembly, a usual adjunct in the larger monasteries, is situated to the north-east corner beyond the staircase. The second large hall (41 feet by 22 feet), adjoining the entrance vestibule on the south, is entered from the courtyard by a doorway

[1] *Mohenjo-daro and Indus Civilization*, Vol. I, pp. 114–115. [2] *Ibid*, pp. 116–117.

PLATE XIV (a)

GENERAL VIEW OF FENESTARATED COURT IN BLOCK 5, MOHENJO-DARO

($5\frac{1}{3}$ feet wide), with two steps on the inner side. It might have been used as a common room or refectory.

'Thus on the east side of the monastery there were two large common rooms, an entrance vestibule, image shrine, and staircase leading to the upper storey. On the other three sides were the quarters of the monks. The majority of these comprised two apartments—an inner one for sleeping and an outer one for living purposes.'[1]

Of the seven strata, the first is represented by three walls, a square floor of brick, 'probably the floor of a bath room,'[2] near the south-east corner of the Buddhist courtyard. 'The second and the third strata contain portions of four buildings with a narrow lane between them and a number of more or less disconnected walls. One of these buildings is a well-built edifice of considerable size and is distinguished by the presence of a number of small paved bathrooms and particularly well-made drains, which suggests that it was mainly devoted to the bathing purposes and formed a part of the large hydropathic establishment to which the great bath and other structures on the west also belong. The fourth stratum contains a number of chambers at the north-west corner of the monastery, some fragments of walling a little to the north of them, a single wall running east to west on the east side of the *stūpa*, and two other walls. The fifth stratum is represented only by sections of two walls. One of these walls, from east to west, is situated at a depth of 13 to 17 feet below the Buddhist pavement. The other is a massive and finely built piece of walling, nearly 7 feet thick, pierced by an opening and provided on its southern face with an offset. It appears to have belonged to a building of importance. To the sixth stratum belong two small fragments of walling, one partly beneath the massive wall of the fifth stratum and the other near the north-west corner of the *stūpa*. The seventh stratum is represented only by a low wall and adjacent pavement in the deep trench outside the north-west corner of the monastery.'[3]

The buildings discovered at the different strata at Mohenjo-daro may be classified under the following heads: (1) dwelling-houses, (2) public baths of religious or secular character, (3) temples of some kind, and (4) raised platforms, possibly tombs.

'The houses varied much in size. The smallest, which may have been intended for menials' quarters, had no more than two rooms.

[1] *Mohenjo-daro and Indus Civilization*, Vol. I, p. 119. [2] *Ibid*, p. 125. [3] *Ibid*, p. 127.

The largest are on a scale that entitles them to be ranked almost as palaces or temples. One of the upper class houses has a frontage of 85 feet and a depth of 97 feet. Its surrounding walls are 4 to 5 feet in thickness and have a slight batter on the outside. Against its east and west sides other houses have been built. The front of the house was towards a quiet lane, and the entrance on this side measured nearly 10 feet across, afterwards narrowed to 76 inches by the insertion of an extra pier against the east jamb. Opposite the entrance is the porter's lodge, which is connected with an outside courtyard by a doorway almost as wide as the chamber itself, so that there might be no possibility of the occupant being hidden from view. To the right of the porter's lodge, a short passage led to the central courtyard of the house, which was open to the sky and provided light and air to the rooms grouped about it on both the ground and upper floors. The courtyard measures approximately 32 feet square, but the square is not a true one. Like other open courtyards it was paved with brick and provided with a covered drain. Of the rooms which encompass the courtyard, the one at the south-west corner contains a well and is entered up three steps from the passage near the vestibule. There is an apperture between it and the bathroom for conveying the well water direct into the bathroom. These bath- and the well-rooms are situated on the south side of the courtyard. Small rooms of irregular shape, numbering four, run along the east side of the courtyard. On the west side of the courtyard there is a curious chamber with a narrow exterior passage and having four niches in the inside walls. On the north of the courtyard there are three chambers which appear to be a northern projection of the house. The living- and the sleeping-rooms of the family were all on the upper floor, which was reached from the courtyard by way of the staircase. One of them and the passage-ways are raised up on a solid basement (in order to provide against the menace of floods, the idea being to have at least one fair-sized room where the family could find refuge if the rest of the house collapsed). The remainder of the upstairs rooms were disposed round about the central courtyard, following no doubt the same plan as the rooms below, but with a projecting balcony overhanging the courtyard from which the several rooms could be entered. The roof of this, as of most other buildings, was probably flat, and served as a terrace whereon the inmates of the house could sleep or take the evening air.[1] Another similar house[2] has a more elaborate plan. 'On its ground floor are four fair-sized courts, ten smaller rooms, three staircases, a porter's lodge, and a well-chamber. The front is towards First Street and here there are three entrances side by side, the principal one being in the middle. Besides these three front entrances, there is a small doorway alongside the well at the rear of the house, which seems to have been originally open, but was subsequently bricked up. Entering the house by the main door one finds oneself in a small vestibule, with the porter's lodge on the left and a second doorway directly opposite leading to the open court.[3] On the west side of it one of the three flights of steps ascends to the upper storey. On its south side is a broad brick pier, evidently intended for the support of the upper floor. On the north side of the court are three ornamental panels or recesses.'[4]

'To the left and right of this court are two other courts, one with its door communicating direct with First Street, the other with a small vestibule intervening between it and the street entrance. Of these two, the larger one, measuring about 25 feet in length, has a floor of brick-on-edge.'[4] Sir John Marshall surmises that it was perhaps 'roofed over its western half only, its eastern half being left open to the sky.'[4]

'The other apartments on this side of the house comprise the well-chamber at the far end and two other small rooms for menials. Crossing to the other side of the house, there are two smallish rooms, which for a time may have served as guest-chambers, but were subsequently bricked up and filled in solid as a precaution against floods. The tiny apartment next to them on the west was a latrine, from which a drain ran across the north side of the courtyard to a soak-pit in First Street, while in the wall of the latrine is the brick casing for a vertical pipe which descended from what was doubtless another latrine on the upper floor.'[5]

From the small size of this latrine pipe Marshall concludes that it was meant to convey fluid only, not solids, and 'this seems

[1] *Mohenjo-daro and Indus Civilization*, Vol. I, pp. 17, 18, 19, 20. [2] *Ibid*, Plate VI.

[3] 'A feature of the porter's lodge worth observing is the way in which the east wall has been built obliquely across it, so that the porter would be compelled to sit in full view of the entrance. The arrangement is at once clever and practical, and shows, like many other features, that the architect must have given a good deal of thought to the planning of this house.'

[4] *Mohenjo-daro and Indus Civilization*, Vol. I, p. 20. [5] *Ibid*, p. 21.

to be true of most of the house drains in Mohenjo-daro.' But he discovered other 'privies with seats (as to the character of which there can be no question) are directly connected with brick-drains of the usual type, which must therefore have been designed for sewage of any kind, solid or fluid.'[1]

'There is a small hall which is entered from the further side of the lobby. Its north and east walls are relieved by a series of ornamental recesses with single reveals. There appear to have been clerestory windows high up in the south wall. On this side there was a solid terrace, some 10 feet in height, abutting on to the hall, and windows with pierced lattice screens were contrived in the upper part of the wall. At the further end of this hall is the third and much narrower stairway leading to the upper floor, and alongside it another small room, above the doorway of which there was probably some sort of fanlight. All the remaining rooms on the ground floor are stated to have belonged to an older edifice, and were bricked up and filled in to form a solid terrace at the time when this house was built.'[2]

'In all except the smallest dwellings at Mohenjo-daro a certain portion of the ground floor,' asserts Sir John Marshall, 'invariably took the form of a terrace or plinth sufficiently high and strong to resist the floods which annually menaced the city.'[2] 'In this (second) of the larger houses the terrace thus constructed was some 25 by 30 feet, and quite large enough to support two or three fair-sized chambers.'

'To imagine that all the upper apartments were confined to such terraces and that the architects made the latter solid, because they knew no other way of adding a second storey, is entirely fallacious. The architects of Mohenjo-daro,' Marshall has no doubt, 'knew as well as anyone how to erect two- or perhaps three-storeyed houses according to the usual methods—houses, that is to say, in which the upper floors corresponded in plan with the lower.'[2]

'There is another group of buildings bounded on the east by First Street, and on the south by the First Lane. There are some five houses, four of which appear to be dwelling houses and the fifth one

[1] *Mohenjo-daro and Indus Civilization*, Vol. I, p. 24. Underground drains or sewers are frequently prescribed for larger houses in the *Mānasāra* and other *Śilpa-śāstras*; also writer's *Dictionary of Hindu Architecture*, 1st Ed., p. 209.

[2] *Ibid*, p. 21.

looks like a palace or a big temple. The first of these consists of only three rooms. The second one, immediately to the south of the first one, contains some seven rooms. The third house next door is a small structure consisting of only three rooms and they might have been a part of the second house. The fourth one was a larger building with a frontage of 62 feet. The fifth one was built in a block measuring 248 feet from north to south by some 145 feet from east to west. As many as 136 rooms have been uncovered in this block and divided tentatively into nine separate buildings. Besides the courts and rooms, numbered from 37 to 60 and 70 to 84, it probably embraced various other courts and rooms.' 'The spaciousness of its courts and general massiveness of construction,' asserts Mr. Sahni, 'suggest that this building could not have been an ordinary private house.'[1]

Sir John Marshall refers to a few more buildings of this type and comments, 'whether these spacious and elaborate edifices were private houses or not, has yet to be determined. Quite conceivably,' he asserts, 'some of them were temples.' In support of his assertion he refers to a foreign analogy. 'In Mesopotamia the temples of the gods were to all intents and purposes copies of the royal palaces—dwellings where a god could eat, drink, and make merry like any mortal prince, and even be wedded on occasions to his priestess.' But there is no need to go to Mesopotamia for such an analogy, because in India itself (of the later times) there are numerous instances of temples fully described in the *Silpa-sāstras* like the *Mānasāra*, which possess as many as seven courts and look like gorgeous palaces. 'The first, second, fifth, and sixth of these buildings,' continues Marshall, 'would have been specially appropriate for this purpose (as home for the gods), and it may be recalled,' he further asserts, 'that in one of them the excavators found a series of those peculiar ringstones which we have good reason for believing were objects of cult-worship.'[2]

This authoritative statement encourages Mr. Dayaram Sahni to say: 'It is gratifying to know that Sir John Marshall supports me in identifying them as phallic-emblems and the stone rings as their pedestals or *Yonis*.' He endeavours to strengthen this conclusion by adding that, 'This view is further corroborated by the evidence of similar objects discovered by Sir Aurel Stein in the course of his recent archaeological expeditions in Baluchistan.'[3] But Sir John Marshall

[1] *Mohenjo-daro and Indus Civilization*, Vol. I, pp. 188, 189, 190.
[2] *Ibid*, p. 22.
[3] *Ibid*, p. 191.

safeguards his position by noting under the phallic-emblem that 'the cones referred to are differentiated by me from the so-called gamesmen. The former I regard as baetylic and the latter as phallic.'[1] Mr. Sahni fully describes the ringstones, the cones and the gamesmen: 'There are eighteen large-sized stonerings with round tops and bottoms and differing in this respect from large undulating rings found at Harappa. The rings are 9 to 10 inches high and carefully smoothed, all perforated in the middle, the holes being 4½ to 9 inches in diameter and drilled in some cases from both sides. Some of them have shallow holes, neatly drilled on either side of the central perforation, while others have in the same positions long rectangular grooves, possibly for metal clamps. A few of them are also drilled with lines of small cup-marks. There are two round stone caps with rounded tops which resemble the tops of the so-called gamesmen, of varying sizes, found both at Harappa and Mohenjo-daro. Other objects of the same class are the cones of stone, terra-cotta, etc., but without the projecting ring at the top. One cone of this type, 11 inches high, unearthed at Harappa, bears similarity to the Śiva-Liṅga and it might have been fixed in a pedestal and worshipped in a tiny brick structure found close to it.'[1]

With regard to the existence of a temple, private or public, and of emblems for worship, Sir John Marshall appears to have been in a fix. He can neither deny the implications of his own finds nor can he get rid of some kind of prejudice. Thus in the following quotation he appears to deny the very thing which he seems to believe. 'All this, however, is sheer conjecture. Like the Minoans, the Indus people may have had no public shrines at all, or if they had them, the shrines may have been wholly unlike their ordinary residences. Among the buildings of Mohenjo-daro are several whose purpose we have not yet succeeded in discovering, and any one of these might have been a shrine as well as anything else.'[2] Then he refers to two buildings which bear all the essential features of a Hindu temple: 'There is the little building containing two chambers, one much larger than the other with a corridor at the side, and there is the larger structure, which comprises a large central chamber with a corridor on its western and southern sides, a well and two other small chambers at its southern end, and a group of somewhat larger

[1] *Mohenjo-daro and Indus Civilization,* Vol. I, p. 191, note. [2] *Ibid,* p. 22.

GENERAL VIEW FROM EAST AFTER EXCAVATIONS, HARAPPA

SEPULCHRES AT HARAPPA

Page 37

chambers at its northern, the original plan of which is obscured beneath later accretions. Little unfortunately is left of this interesting ruin except its foundations, but these are unusually massive, nearly 10 feet deep with a solid infilling of crude brick, and presuppose a correspondingly high superstructure, which might very well have taken the form of a corbelled *śikhara* over the central apartment.'[1]

One without a pre-conceived idea, but familiar with the common features of a Hindu temple, would feel no difficulty in identifying the above buildings as ordinary shrines, with a central room where a deity or an emblem is installed, with necessary side rooms and corridors, and, finally, surmounted with a *śikhara.*

Mr. R. D. Banerji, the explorer of Mohenjo-daro, ascribed these monuments, on the basis of hoards of square coins found therein, to the Maurya period, and inferred that 'the earliest floor was prior to the third century B. C. and the second prior to the second century B. C.' Sir John Marshall would bring down these monuments by several centuries, saying that, 'the *stūpa* may have been founded by one of the earlier Kushān kings, Kanishka or Huvishka, but in view of the conspicuous absence of any coins belonging to either of these kings in the monastery buildings, it is unlikely that the latter are older than the reign of Vasudeva I (A. D. 185–200).' He would also differ from Mr. Banerji regarding the period of their occupation. The latter put it from 300 B. C. to A. D. 200, while the former would 'vaguely' surmise and 'be on the safe side if, from start to finish, we place their history between A. D. 150 and 500.' Sir John Marshall, however, has no doubt about the seven strata below these Buddhist monuments 'all belonging to the Chalcolithic period,' and would assign the earliest and latest periods between '3250 B. C. to 2750 B. C.'[2]

HARAPPA

Harappa, on the old bed of the Ravi, is in the Montgomery District of the Punjab, south-west of Lahore, more than 400 miles north-west of Mohenjo-daro in the Larkāna District of Sindh. The area is a wide one, nearly 2½ miles in circumference, according to Cunningham, who visited it in 1833. The mounds, which rise conspicuously within this circuit, are of considerable elevation, the highest among them being 60 to 65 feet.

[1] *Mohenjo-daro and Indus Civilization*, Vol. I, p. 22.

[2] *Ibid*, p. 106.

'The site is manifestly of a great city covering a vast area and containing many strata of successive buildings.' By a careful comparison it has been found that the finds from Harappa and Mohenjo-daro belong to the same stage of culture and approximately to the same age, third to fourth millennium B. C. Peoples of both these places 'were living in well-built cities and were in possession of a relatively mature culture with a high standard of art and craftsmanship and a developed system of writing.'[1]

General Cunningham records the fact that 'the brick-remains within the mounds of Harappa had sufficed the contractors to ballast 100 miles of the Lahore-Multan railroad, and it was apparent that most of the actual walling had thus been long ago removed.'[2] Most of the mounds marking the site were thus completely honey-combed with the diggings of the modern brick-hunters. The three which seem to have suffered least have been excavated.

It has been determined that there are 'as many as seven successive layers of buildings, indicating a very prolonged occupation of the site'; no doubt there are other strata still unexposed below them. 'In the topmost stratum, which occurred at the depth of 13 feet from the summit of the mound, was revealed a round brick granary standing about 6 feet high. The next three strata were devoid of any structural remains (though the lowest of them was packed with a large number of undulating stone rings of the same character as those described by General Cunningham). In the fifth stratum from the top two brick structures were observed. One of these is a square room with thick walls and paved interior which was divided into two smaller chambers at a later date. A narrow covered drain in its south wall and two low masonry benches on the inside seem to point to its having been used as some sort of an image shrine.

In this connexion it is interesting to observe that, at this very spot, has been found the defaced terra-cotta of a statuette which might have been an object of worship.[3] The other structure found on this level is a confused mass of brick-remains in which a thick wall

[1] Sir John Marshall, *Archaeological Survey Report* for 1923–24, pp. 47, 48.

[2] *Ibid*, 1920–21, p. 50.

[3] Still Sir John Marshall finds it difficult to say whether idol worship existed in those early times. Rai Bahadur Daya Ram Sahni, on the other hand, has quoted Marshall's approval of the former's identification of phallus at Harappa (*Mohenjo-daro and Indus Civilization*, Vol. I, p. 191).

30 feet in length, resting partly on a solidly built platform, stands out prominently. A small square seal of white plaster in perfect preservation was sticking to this wall. The next lower stratum is represented by the somewhat better preserved structure which had been laid bare in this area and a number of tunnels left by the brick diggers. The seventh stratum will probably be found to be occupied by a building of considerable magnitude, though so far only a portion of its floor has been exposed. This floor consists of two courses of brick laid as stretchers and headers on a strong sub-stratum of pounded brick.'[1]

Portions of walls have also been found at several places. Most of these belong to dwelling houses. One of them has been followed up for a length of about 18 feet. There were also two other walls running parallel to it on the other side. 'This, however, turned out to be all that had survived of the buildings. That the structure was an important one is evidenced by several interesting objects which came to light in it.'[2] At another place have been discovered two thick walls running parallel to each other at a distance of about 2 feet. 'They are broken at both ends and contain no openings or doors. These walls came to light at the depth of 11 feet below the surface, but above them and intersecting them at right angles were two others that must be assigned to considerably later date. Two other trenches at this spot revealed a corner of a brick-building[3] in which two earthenware vessels containing human bones lay buried.'[4]

A well-preserved water reservoir, lined with brick and provided with a narrow covered channel, has been found at a depth of about 8 feet. 'By the side of the tank was standing a large earthen jar with its pointed bottom fixed in the ground. It was filled with earth in which were several smaller jars and terra-cotta figurines. The exact purpose of the reservoir has not yet been ascertained.'[5]

[1] *Archaeological Survey of India Report*, 1923–24, pp. 53–54.

[2] *Ibid*, p. 52.

[3] Bricks at Harappa are of uniform size, $11'' \times 5\frac{1}{2}'' \times 2\frac{1}{2}''$ to $3''$.

[4] *Archaeological Survey of India Report*, 1923–24, p. 53.

[5] A similar tank found at Mohenjo-daro was thought by Mr. R. D. Banerji to be a *charaṇāmṛita kuṇḍa* (a receptacle for the holy water used for the washing of the sacred image). But Sir John Marshall hesitates to accept this interpretation as he is doubtful about idol worship being in vogue at Harappa and Mohenjo-daro (*Ibid*, p. 52).

The other buildings brought to light are somewhat better preserved and include 'what appears to have been a temple with stout brick walls.' There is another large-sized structure consisting of a double series of parallel walls without connecting walls of any kind. The exact purpose and nature of this building are not known. 'Like the highest mound at Mohenjo-daro, the summit of certain mounds at Harappa would appear in later times to have been occupied by certain Buddhist structures of which only small fragments, with a few terra-cotta panels of the early Gupta period, have survived.'

'The inhabitants of Harappa appear also to have been in the habit of offering in their temples terra-cotta cones, with or without figures of animals, of which several specimens have been recovered. A large cone of dark stone, 11 inches high, resembling the Śiva-liṅga of modern times, must have been,' declares Rai Bahadur Dayaram Sahni, 'used for worship.'[1]

The ancient inhabitants of Harappa are stated to have cremated the dead, although there may have been some instances of burial. They are stated to have first burned the dead body on a funeral pyre and then to deposit a part of the cremated bones in earthen vessels or brick-structures resembling the *samādhi* of modern times. This is proved by the discovery of a well-preserved sepulchre constructed with the burnt brick of the usual size and lying east to west, with probably another structure of the same kind adjoining it on the south side, but placed at right angles to it. 'The former structure consists of a horizontal platform of a single course of bricks laid flat and protected on three sides by bricks standing upright on the narrow edge. The roof was composed of an inclined plane of a single course of bricks.' At the second stratum, also, there was a stout concrete floor, composed of nodules of hard overburnt brick, which was littered with burnt bones and ashes, indicating that the platform was probably used as the cremation floor. In the next stratum, also, another funeral structure has been uncovered in which a few cremated bones were found. 'The existence of two *samādhis* and the remains of cremations at several other spots appear to show that the whole of this area was at one time the crematorium of the ancient city. This view received some corroboration from the close proximity of

[1] *Archaeological Survey of India Report*, 1924–25, p. 74.

COARSE SANDSTONE LINGA AT HARAPPA

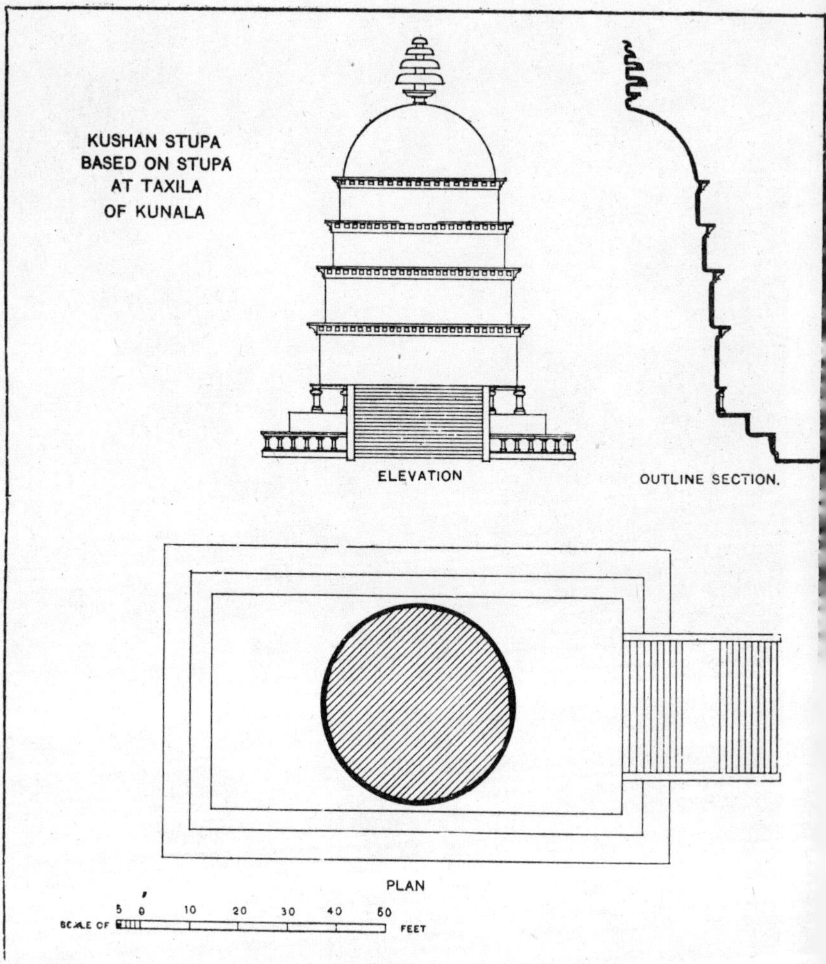

KUSHAN STUPA BASED ON KUNAL STUPA, TAXILA

the old bed of the river.'[1] In another place, underneath a platform, was a mass of cremated human bones, and about 16 feet from it, a large heap of ashes and charcoal with human bones 'which undoubtedly represents the remains of several funeral pyres.'[2] A double rectangular sepulchre has been found at the third stratum. It comprises two distinct compartments, one of which had an irregularly shaped relic-chamber, 1 foot 5 inches by 1 foot 4 inches by 1 foot 2 inches. The contents consisted of a number of cremated bones. Human bones were found scattered all over. One large collection of animal bones of dogs, sheep, oxen, and horses has been found buried. From this collection Rai Bahadur Daya Ram Sahni concludes that 'they might be the remnants of a big animal sacrifice.'[3]

A brick-built grave has also been uncovered.[4] A group of eleven burial jars has been found. Some of them contain fragmentary sculls and long bones, etc., of babies and adults of various ages.[5]

Of the other structures a series of fourteen walls, all running parallel to each other and of the same length, $51\frac{3}{4}$ feet, appear to represent an important construction. 'All of them terminated on the west on an open corridor, 24 feet wide, beyond which stretched a similar set of walls in precise correlation with those in the opposite series. These walls exhibit two distinct kinds, namely, a stouter kind and a thinner type. All these walls arise from a uniform level at the depth of 12 feet below the surface of the mound, and have finished ends towards the central aisle. The walls of the thicker type are arranged approximately at equal distances from each other, the interval between them being 17 to 18 feet in figures, and had it not been for the thin walls which intervene between them, it might have been thought that they enclosed a series of spacious rooms.'[6]

Two little circular structures paved in brick on a thick sub-stratum of hard burnt nodules of brick look like 'hearths or chimneys of some kind.'

Another little structure consists of a paved platform, surrounded by a single course of brick laid on edge, which might have been a bathing platform, as a large earthen jar was standing on one side of it.

[1] *Archaeological Survey of India Report*, 1924–25, p. 75. [2] *Ibid*, p. 77.
[3] *Ibid*, p. 79. [4] *Ibid*, p. 80. [5] *Ibid*, 1927–28, pp. 86, 87; 1928–29, pp. 76–77.
[6] *Ibid*, 1924–25, p. 76.

Fragments of solidly built structures have been discovered in several other places. A very big building of considerable dimensions has been found with an open courtyard between the two portions of the building with another open court at the back on the west side. 'One of the two rooms in the western portion measures 14 feet by 12 feet internally, while the other, which is separated from it by a passage or gallery, is incomplete. The former was provided with an entrance, 3 feet 10 inches wide on the east side, with a small rectangular drain and a masonry bench along one of the walls. Several strata of buildings came to light below this level, but they are too fragmentary. Two cells looking like kitchens or baths have been found. They are provided with drains and a gabled roof. Another solidly built house has been discovered. One complete room in this structure has internal dimensions of 15 feet by 5 feet 10 inches and is provided with one door on the south and presumably two on the north side.'[1]

A circular brick granary has also been found.[2]

In a structure composed of bricks three fragmentary terra-cotta panels have been found. 'One of the three panels represents a votary kneeling with the palm resting on the projected base of the sculpture. (The head of the figure is broken off and the feet are not indicated.) Another panel represents only the legs of a standing figure, while the third depicts a female figure rising from the ground after the fashion of the earth goddess in representations of the enlightenment of the Buddha.'[3]

'The inhabitants of Harappa appear also to have been in the habit of offering in their temples terra-cotta cones, with or without figures of animals, of which several specimen have been recovered.' Rai Bahadur Daya Ram Sahni is inclined to think that 'a large cone of dark stone, 11 inches high resembling the Śiva-liṅga of modern times, must have been used for worship.'[3]

Concerning the existence of the temples at Harappa, Sir John Marshall does not seem to have any doubt. Summarizing the account of Sahni, Marshall declares that 'the temples stand on elevated ground and are distinguished by the relative smallness of

[1] *Archaeological Survey of India Report*, 1924–25, p. 80. [2] *Ibid*, p. 78.

[3] *Ibid*, p. 78. In order to discover Buddhistic remains, the Rai Bahadur is anxious to identify the fragments of the three earthen jars with very narrow mouths with the Buddhist monk's bottles.

their chambers and the exceptional thickness of their walls—which suggest that they were several storeys in height. To a temple, also, doubtless belongs the spacious courtyard with chapels or other apartments on its four sides.' But he is doubtful 'whether the worship performed in these temples was iconic or aniconic. The only objects found in association with them and intended apparently for cult-worship are of two kinds, viz. "ring-stones" and "chessman." He, however, assures that 'the fact that no anthropomorphic images have yet been unearthed in these temples must not be interpreted as a proof that the worship of such images was unknown.' In proof of this he mentions that 'on a tablet of blue faience, which has just come to light, is depicted a figure seated crosslegged (like Buddha on a throne) with a kneeling worshipper to right and left and behind the worshipper a snake (*nāga*), while at the back is a legend in the pictographic script of the period. Now it is possible that this seated figure is nothing more than a royal personage, but the presence of the kneeling devotees, and particularly of the *nāgas*, certainly suggests that the central figure was intended to represent a deity rather than a king.'[1]

Further excavations[2] have brought to light numerous fragments of dwelling houses, including remains of pilasters and other members. There are also three circular structures but their purposes and other details are wanting.[3] The general account given above, however, represents fairly the kinds and conditions of structures at Harappa.

JHUKUN

With a view to tracing the Indus civilization, as disclosed by the finds made at Harappa and Mohenjo-daro, explorations have been conducted in the interior of Sind, which might have been once on or near the banks of the Indus, as well as further into Baluchistan. These Sind explorations have not yielded any substantial architectural or sculptural remains, although the so-called pre-historic pottery and implements have come out in abundance. The scanty remains, mostly of unidentified walls and of a few buildings, have, however,

[1] *Archaeological Survey of India Report*, 1924–25, p. 61.

[2] *Ibid*, 1926–27, pp. 97-103; 1927-28, pp. 85, 86-87; 1928-29, pp. 97, 103.

[3] *Ibid*, 1928-29, Plate XXX, (*a*).

been found not only along the old course of the Indus but also upon hills and around lakes.

The remains of buildings discovered at Jhukun, near Larkana (and about half way between Harappa and Mohenjo-daro), consist of 'over fifty rooms of varying dimensions' made of sundried bricks. 'The floor levels of these rooms show a variation of about 5 to 6 feet, resting at places on a foundation of debris and at others on a solid filling of sundried bricks on pure clay.' 'A masonry well was exposed on this mound at a level considerably lower than the floor of the rooms.'[1] This may indicate that the buildings whose purposes are unknown were dwelling houses.

The dates of these buildings are stated to have been indicated by the coins and the inscribed sealings discovered therein. 'A few of the coins are of the class represented by the thick round pieces issued by the Kushan King Vasudeva and his successors.'[2] This would, incidentally, show that those buildings were designed after the Hindu style, which is found applied in all Kushan structures.

Traces of three earlier strata, superimposed one upon another, have been uncovered. 'The surface layer has vertically a depth of about 12 feet. Of the dwellings of this period nothing but a paving of burnt bricks and a few traces of sundried brick walls had survived. At the middle stratum a number of walls of burnt bricks of Mohenjo-daro size were discovered. The bottom stratum also disclosed only a few walls of the same type.'[3]

Non-architectural remains, mostly of Buddhistic tablets depicting Buddha and Chaityas, have been found in southern Sind, in the delta country, at Tatta, Budhjo Takar, Mirpurkhas and other places.[4] Remains of walls and a drain have been uncovered also at Chanhu-daro.[5] Remains of walls of some late period have also been uncovered at Lohunjo-daro. But no traces of any complete structure have yet been found.[6]

The lake Manchhar is usually of 8 to 10 miles in length and breadth. It is situated at the foot of the Khirthar hills. Excavations at Masak, Lal Chhatto, Lohri, and Lakhiyo on the lake did not reveal any architectural objects except faint traces of some walls. But the

[1] *Memoirs of the Archaeological Survey of India*, no. 48, p. 6, Plate II, B, C, D.
[2] *Ibid*, p. 7. [3] *Ibid*, p. 9. [4] *Ibid*, pp. 19, 21.
[5] *Ibid*, pp. 36, 37, Plate IV, C. [6] *Ibid*, pp. 48–49, Plate V, C.

e Kohistan tract the excavation at Damb Barthi h
d scanty remains of ancient burial places, which in gener
emble similar structural remains at Nal in Baluchista
nsist of the outline walls of five chambers wherein huma
ve been found.[1] Pottery and such other remains have al
nd at Bandhni, Dhal, Maliri Landi, Pokhran Landi ar
.[2]

arizing the finds, Mr. Majumdar declares that the sites di
fall under two categories, namely, the places where the peop
inhabited and those where they carried on the flint-knappir
The walls of the buildings at the hill sites are stated
en made of stone at the base, up to a height of 2 to
stone blocks being rough hewn and often laid with mu
'The superstructure must have been built of mud an
rishable materials as reed and wood.' Though no defini
ion is available, yet it is stated that the roof of these hous
ave been made of reed and matting overlaid with mu
llings in and around lake Manchhar were of different type
ke sites have yielded neither stones nor bricks.' From th
jumdar concludes that 'here the people lived in pil
s, like the lake-dwellers of Europe, in the midst of the lak
to the edge of water.'[3]

BALUCHISTAN

a view to finding a connexion between the peoples of th
alley, whose cultural achievements have been disclosed b
overies made at Harappa and Mohenjo-daro, and of Baby
cavations have been carried out in Baluchistan, 'the countr
tween these two important river basins and where connec
between the two cultures' was expected to be recovered.
xcavations at Sampur Mound at Mastung, some 33 mile
Quetta, and at Sohr Damb at Nāl in Jhalawān in the Kalā
e 200 miles southward, do not appear to have yielded muc
ish that much-wished-for connexion.
the same view, further excavations have been carried ou
North-West Frontier from the Kuram river down throug

irs of the Archaeological Survey of India, pp. 115–116, Plate IX, C.
p. 120–131. [3] *Ibid*, pp. 147, 148.
argreaves, *Archaeological Survey of India Memoir*, no. 35, Preface, iii.

PLATE XIX (a)

BUDDHIST STUPA AT MIRPUR KHAS (VIEW FROM SOUTH-EAST)

PLATE XIX (b)

BUDDHIST STUPA AT MIRPUR KHAS (VIEW FROM NORTH-WEST)

PLATE XIX (c)

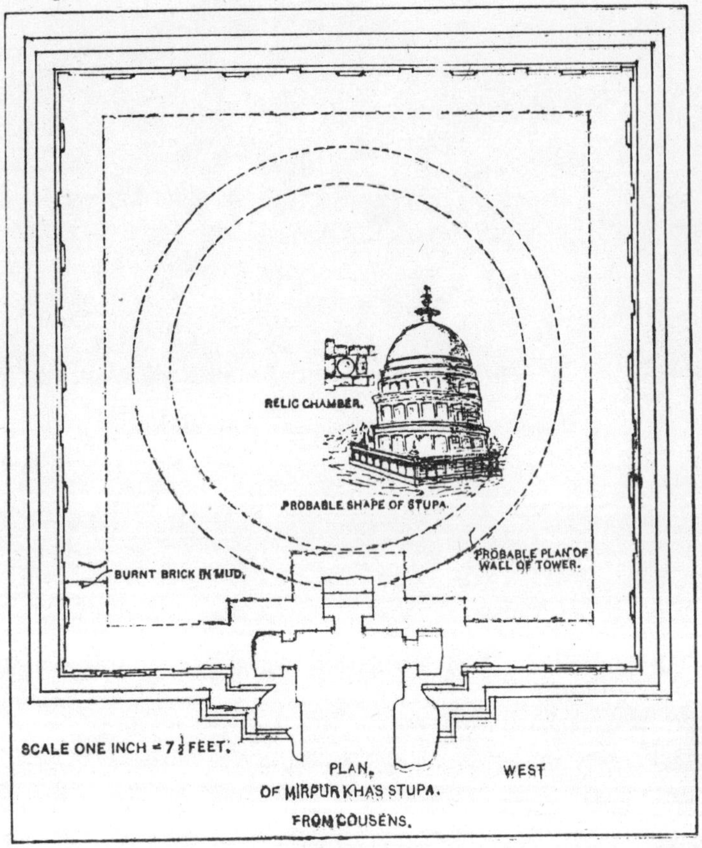

PLAN OF MIRPUR KHAS STUPA

Page 45

excavator declares that the 'explorations a
prove, for the first time, the existence of a la
during the later part of the Indus period.
the verge of the lake. Their ways of living c
different from those of the present dweller
boats with their families, or in huts constru
surface of water. These huts have a cur
lithic and Chalcolithic pile-dwellings of the
other European countries. Whether the
Manchhar used to have similar pile-houses
the data available. The pits and trenches e
and Mashak mounds have not revealed an
there any indication to show that the lake
these materials.'[1]

There are, however, abundant literary
Purāṇas, and *Silpa-śāstras* that special house
around the tanks and lakes during the early
the architectural details of these houses are
ever, exist at Puri, Bhuvaneśwara, Pushkar,
places. But these are more or less modern st

Johi, Sehwan, and Ko

Hill-dwellings have been traced at Johi,
At the Johi tract, the mounds, now known
covered the remains of an ancient fortress or f
races of many walls and a rampart. The wa
he basement of the various chambers and
he buildings were divided.[2] But these sc
lisclose the plan and other details.

The fort at Sehwan (Sindimana of Cun
o be of the time of Alexander the Great, i
Muslim origin. But the site itself might yet
buildings of early Hindu period upon wh
own has been built.[3] The remains of an a
learly found at Kohtras Buthi. But there a
tone-walls.[4]

[1] *Memoirs of the Archaeological Survey of India*, p. 65.
[2] *Ibid*, pp. 89–90, Plate VIII, B, C. [3] *Ibid*, p. 46

In t
uncover
may re
These c
bones h
been fo
Karcha
Sumn
covered
actually
industry
have b
feet, th
mortar.
such p
informa
might
The dw
'The l
Mr. M
dwellin
or close

With
Indus
the dis
lonia, e
lying b
ing lin
The
south o
State so
to estab
With
along t

[1] *Mem*
[2] *Ibid*,
[4] H. F

PLATE XIX (a)

BUDDHIST STUPA AT MIRPUR KHAS (VIEW FROM SOUTH-EAST)

PLATE XIX (b)

BUDDHIST STUPA AT MIRPUR KHAS (VIEW FROM NORTH-WEST)

PLATE XIX (c)

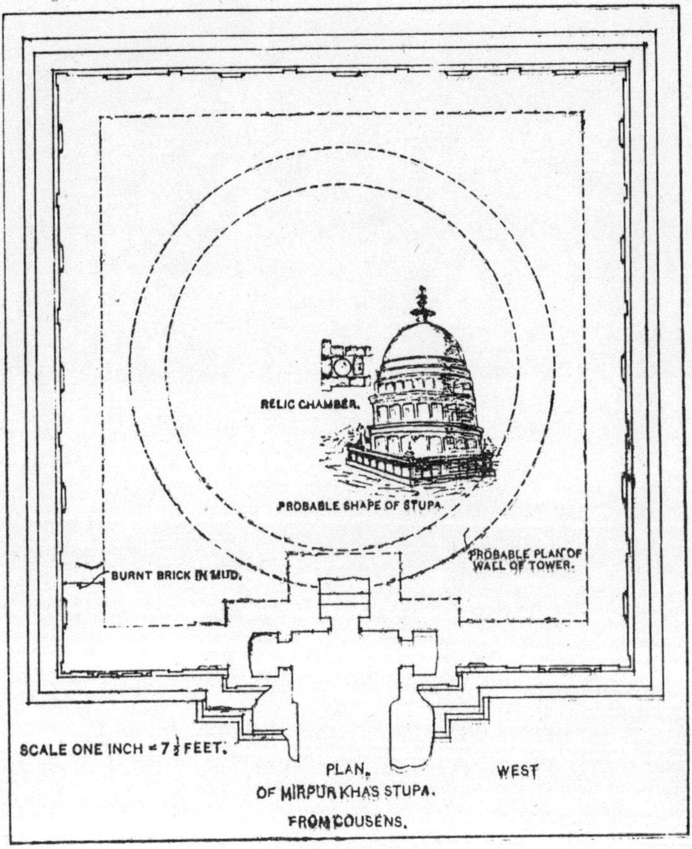

PLAN OF MIRPUR KHAS STUPA

excavator declares that the 'explorations around the Manchhar now prove, for the first time, the existence of a lake-dwelling people in Sind during the later part of the Indus period. Their settlements were on the verge of the lake. Their ways of living could not have been much different from those of the present dwellers, many of whom live in boats with their families, or in huts constructed on platforms on the surface of water. These huts have a curious likeness to the Neolithic and Chalcolithic pile-dwellings of the lakes of Switzerland and other European countries. Whether the ancient lake-dwellers of Manchhar used to have similar pile-houses it is difficult to say with the data available. The pits and trenches excavated on Lal Chhatto and Mashak mounds have not revealed any brick or stone, nor was there any indication to show that the lake-dwellings were made of these materials.'[1]

There are, however, abundant literary evidences in the *Epics*, *Purāṇas*, and *Silpa-śāstras* that special houses were built both on and around the tanks and lakes during the early Hindu period. Many of the architectural details of these houses are missing. Examples, however, exist at Puri, Bhuvaneśwara, Pushkar, Madura, and many other places. But these are more or less modern structures.

JOHI, SEHWAN, AND KOHISTAN

Hill-dwellings have been traced at Johi, Sehwan, and Kohistan. At the Johi tract, the mounds, now known as Ali Murad, have uncovered the remains of an ancient fortress or fortified palace. There are traces of many walls and a rampart. The walls are stated to represent the basement of the various chambers and apartments into which the buildings were divided.[2] But these scanty remains would not disclose the plan and other details.

The fort at Sehwan (Sindimana of Cunningham), once thought to be of the time of Alexander the Great, is now declared to be of Muslim origin. But the site itself might yet contain certain ancient buildings of early Hindu period upon which the present Muslim town has been built.[3] The remains of an ancient fortress have been clearly found at Kohtras Buthi. But there are only traces of two long stone-walls.[4]

[1] *Memoirs of the Archaeological Survey of India*, p. 65.

[2] *Ibid*, pp. 89–90, Plate VIII, B, C. [3] *Ibid*, p. 46. [4] *Ibid*, pp. 132–134.

In the Kohistan tract the excavation at Damb Barthi has uncovered scanty remains of ancient burial places, which in general may resemble similar structural remains at Nal in Baluchistan. These consist of the outline walls of five chambers wherein human bones have been found.[1] Pottery and such other remains have also been found at Bandhni, Dhal, Maliri Landi, Pokhran Landi and Karchat.[2]

Summarizing the finds, Mr. Majumdar declares that the sites discovered fall under two categories, namely, the places where the people actually inhabited and those where they carried on the flint-knapping industry. The walls of the buildings at the hill sites are stated to have been made of stone at the base, up to a height of 2 to 3 feet, the stone blocks being rough hewn and often laid with mud mortar. 'The superstructure must have been built of mud and such perishable materials as reed and wood.' Though no definite information is available, yet it is stated that the roof of these houses might have been made of reed and matting overlaid with mud. The dwellings in and around lake Manchhar were of different types. 'The lake sites have yielded neither stones nor bricks.' From this Mr. Majumdar concludes that 'here the people lived in pile-dwellings, like the lake-dwellers of Europe, in the midst of the lake or close to the edge of water.'[3]

BALUCHISTAN

With a view to finding a connexion between the peoples of the Indus Valley, whose cultural achievements have been disclosed by the discoveries made at Harappa and Mohenjo-daro, and of Babylonia, excavations have been carried out in Baluchistan, 'the country lying between these two important river basins and where connecting links between the two cultures' was expected to be recovered.[4]

The excavations at Sampur Mound at Mastung, some 33 miles south of Quetta, and at Sohr Damb at Nāl in Jhalawān in the Kalāt State some 200 miles southward, do not appear to have yielded much to establish that much-wished-for connexion.

With the same view, further excavations have been carried out along the North-West Frontier from the Kuram river down through

[1] *Memoirs of the Archaeological Survey of India*, pp. 115–116, Plate IX, C.
[2] *Ibid*, pp. 120–131. [3] *Ibid*, pp. 147, 148.
[4] H. Hargreaves, *Archaeological Survey of India Memoir*, no. 35, Preface, iii.

Waziristan and the northern district of Baluchistan, with no better results.[1]

Still further have been carried the excavations into the far-stretched portion of Gedrosia, comprising the territories of Khārān, Makrān, and Jhalawān, between the Arabian Sea in the south and the deserts adjoining Afghanistan in the north, but with the same fate.[2]

At Mastung, on the top of the mound, have been found only 'the interior wall of a small room. These walls were of kachcha (sundried) brick faced with mud plaster. No other rooms were traced elsewhere in this excavation.'[3] 'No stone or brick walls were found anywhere on this site, and the only kachcha walls recognized with certainty were those in the higher sections . . . and the room on the summit.'[4]

At Nāl, also, nothing more than the remains of the stone-walls of some structures, possibly rooms and courtyards, have been found. 'The word "room" is used for convenience for it is by no means certain that they are "rooms" in the ordinary sense of that word. The walls are at right angles and roughly oriented to the cardinal points. None are of any great height. In all probability the stone-walls were merely foundations. Any superstructures must have been of mud, brick or some light material which had entirely disappeared. No obvious entrances to the rooms can be traced. No traces of any roofing material or the charcoal of beams or rafters were discovered in this area. Most of the rooms had earth floors, but two rooms have pavements of small water-worn boulders and one had a particularly solid flooring consisting of three courses of stones carefully laid over a foundation of gravel.'[5]

Numerous burial places with human remains have been, however, uncovered in this area, but no architectural details are available.[6]

Waziristan

The antiquity of Waziristan is established by the mention of the river Kramu and Gomatī in the *Ṛig-Veda* (x, 75), which are identified with the present Kurram and Gumal in this region.[7] But the

[1] Sir Aurel Stein, *Archaeological Survey of India Memoir*, no. 37.
[2] *Ibid*, no. 43. [3] Hargreaves, *Memoir*, no. 35, p. 2.
[4] *Ibid*, p. 3. [5] *Ibid*, pp. 20–21. [6] *Ibid*, pp. 21–28.
[7] Stein, *Memoir*, no. 37, p. 2.

architectural structures discovered are nothing more than 'remains of rubble-built walls as well as single courses of large uncut stones at varying levels. They are likely to have served as wall foundations or floorings.'[1]

In Northern Baluchistan the remains at Zhob, Loralal and Pishin are also very scanty from the architectural point of view. 'The whole of this great mound (at Periano-ghuṇḍai in Zhob area) is composed of accumulations of clay and rough stones from decayed dwellings and permeated by layers containing ashes, bones, and decomposed refuse.'[2]

In the mound of Rāna-ghuṇḍai in Loralal District only 'the matrices left by charred beams, evidently of an old dwelling,' were traced. In places 'it was possible to make out large blocks of mud brick masonry.'[3]

At Tor-Dherai of the same district have been discovered the so-called 'written stones,' that is, Nagari characters and Svastika marks on the rocks. 'The line of a massive base of stone masonry' has also been traced.[4] A Buddhist relic deposit has also been found at an unrecognizable structure which was obviously a Buddhist *stūpa*, but no details are available.[5]

The antiquity of Pishin also is assured by its mention in Zoroastrian scriptures (*Vendi-dad*, i) among the principal territories of ancient Iran. But the architectural remains are practically missing. 'The central mass (at mound Spina-ghuṇḍai) shows almost everywhere nearly vertical walls of clay mixed with rubble, ashes, and potsherds.'[6]

At the Khārān area the only architectural remains consist of 'little roughly circular enclosures of stones only a few feet across. They recalled those funeral 'cairns' of similar appearance which at Moghal-ghuṇḍai in the Zhob Valley had proved to mark a burial ground of early historical times.' But here they contained only soft earth without any deposit of bones, ashes or objects.[7] Similar remains have also been traced at the Makrān coast.[8] No early or pre-Muslim remains of architecture have been discovered along the central valley of Jhalawān and Sarawān.[9]

[1] Stein, *Memoir*, no. 37, p. 6. [2] *Ibid*, p. 33. [3] *Ibid*, p. 52.
[4] *Ibid*, p. 65. [5] *Ibid*, p. 66. [6] *Ibid*, p. 82.
[7] Stein, *Memoir*, no. 43, pp. 34, 77, 86; also his *Northern Baluchistan Tour*, pp. 46 sqq.
[8] *Ibid*, p. 77 sqq. [9] *Ibid*, p. 170 sqq.

The discoveries made at Harappa and Mohenjo-daro have made it clear that the Indus peoples living in Sindh and the Punjab, and of the fourth and third millenia B. C., were in possession of a highly developed culture. 'At present our researches carry us back no further than the fourth millennium B. C., but even at Mohenjo-daro there are still earlier cities lying, one below the other . . . and also in other sites in Sindh and Baluchistan. One thing that stands clear and unmistakable both at Mohenjo-daro and Harappa, is that the civilization hitherto revealed at these two places is not an incipient civilization, but one already age-old and stereotyped on Indian soil, with many millenia of human endeavour behind it.'[1] Although 'India cannot be regarded as the cradle of human civilization, in fact no one country could be so regarded,' asserts Sir John Marshall, yet he would recognize India, along with Persia, Mesopotamia, and Egypt, 'as one of the most important areas where the civilizing processes of society were initiated and developed.'[1] But, so far as architecture is concerned, he has no doubt that 'there is nothing that we know of in pre-historic Egypt or Mesopotamia or anywhere else in Western Asia to compare with the well-built baths and commodious houses of the citizens of Mohenjo-daro. In those countries, much money and thought were lavished on the building of magnificent temples for the gods and on the palaces and tombs of kings, but the rest of the people seemingly had to content themselves with insignificant dwellings of mud. In the Indus Valley the picture is reversed, and the finest structures are those erected for the convenience of the citizens. Temples, palaces, and tombs there may of course have been.' He recognizes 'the evidence, in the Great Bath of Mohenjo-daro and in its roomy and serviceable houses with their ubiquitous wells and bathrooms and elaborate systems of drainage, that the ordinary towns-people enjoyed here a degree of comfort and luxury unexampled in other parts of the then civilized world.'[2]

He also recognizes another fact. Among the many revelations that Mohenjo-daro and Harappa have made, 'none, perhaps, is more remarkable than this discovery, that Śaivism has a history going back to the Chalcolithic age or perhaps even further still, and that it thus takes its place as the most ancient living faith in the world.'[2]

The other cultural achievements of the Indians of the Indus Valley

[1] Sir John Marshall, Preface (viii), Vol. I, *Mohenjo-daro and Indus Civilization.*
[2] *Ibid*, Preface v, vi.

have been correctly inferred from the Harappa and Mohenjo-daro finds. 'Their society is organized in cities; their wealth derived mainly from agriculture and trade, which appears to have extended far and wide in all directions. They cultivate wheat and barley as well as the date-palm. They have domesticated the humped zebu, buffalo and short-horned bull, besides the sheep, pig, dog, elephant, and camel; but the cat and probably the horse are unknown to them. For transport they have wheeled vehicles. . . . They are skilful metal workers, with a plentiful supply of gold, silver, and copper. Lead, too, and tin are in use, but the latter only as an alloy in the making of bronze. With spinning and weaving they are thoroughly conversant. Their weapons of war and of the charge are the bow and arrow, spear, axe, dagger, and mace. The sword they have not yet evolved; nor is there any evidence of defensive body armour. Among their other implements, hatchets, sickles, saws, chisels, and razors are made of both copper and bronze; knives and celts, sometimes of these metals, sometimes of chert or other hard stones. For the crushing of grain they have the muller and saddle-quern, but not the circular grindstone. Their domestic vessels are commonly of earthenware turned on the wheel and not infrequently painted with encaustic designs; more rarely they are of copper, bronze, or silver. The ornaments of the rich are made of the precious metals or of copper, sometimes overlaid with gold, of faience, ivory, cornelian, and other stones; for the poor, they are usually of shell or terra-cotta. Figurines and toys, . . . are of terra-cotta, and shell and faience are freely used . . . not only for personal ornaments but for inlay work and other purposes. With the invention of writing the Indus peoples are also familiar, and employ for this purpose a form of script which though peculiar to India, is evidently analogous to other contemporary scripts of Western Asia and the Nearer East.'[1]

The 'analogousness' of the Indus script to various other scripts of Asia, Europe and Africa has been suggested by scholars for the past fifteen years. It has not yet been deciphered. Nor is it known in which language the then Indians, of Sindh and the Punjab to be more particular, used to write and talk. Thus the antiquated theories of Bühler and others on the introduction of writing in India from the Phoenician source in 800 B. C. can now safely be discarded.

[1] Sir John Marshall, Preface, v vi, Vol. I, *Mohenjo-daro and Indus Civilization.*

The cultural achievements of the Indians revealed at Mohenjo-daro, Harappa, and other places in Sindh and Baluchistan can now be more confidently compared with those disclosed by the Vedas, not only with a view to revising the old notions that the Vedic Indians did not know the use of writing, but also with a view to understanding the casual references to the villages, towns, forts and cities with hundred enclosures or fortifications, stone houses, carved stones and brick edifices. For if the Indus peoples were the earlier residents, it will be curious to imagine that the later and highly cultured Vedic 'Aryans themselves were still in the village state and that their society was in other respects correspondingly primitive.'[1] Vedic Indians must have been aware of the art of building, illustrated in Mohenjo-daro. In that case one can hardly persuade oneself to believe that it was mere imagination when told that a Vedic sovereign 'sits down in his substantial and elegant hall built with a thousand pillars . . . residential palaces being vast, comprehensive and thousand-doored.'[2] Thus one can hardly share the obstinacy of the archaeologist when the latter expresses, in the absence of archaeological remains, his doubt about the Vedic forts being no more than 'simple earth-works, surrounded by palisades or rough stone-walls.'

The inhabitants of Harappa and Mohenjo-daro are surmised by Sir John Marshall to have been 'the pre-Aryan, probably Dravidian, people of India, known in the Vedas as the Dasyus or Asuras, whose culture was largly destroyed in the second or third millennium B. C. by the invading Aryans from the north.'[3]

In order 'to facilitate the co-ordination of the data of archaeology with literary evidences,' Rai Bahadur Ramaprasad Chanda has discussed some of the passages in the Vedic literature, comprising the *Saṁhitās, Brāhmaṇas and Sūtras*, 'the youngest in age among which is probably older than the third century B. C.'[4] He has endeavoured to show that the animosity between the invading Aryans and the original inhabitants of India, including those of the Indus Valley and farther south and the extreme east, was of such a nature that the former destroyed all the towns, cities (*pur*, *pura*) and forts (*durga*)

[1] *Indus Civilization*, Preface, p. v.

[2] *Ṛig-veda*. ii, 313 ; iv, 179.

[3] *Archaeological Survey of India*, *Report*, 1924-25, p. 63.

[4] *Archaeological Survey of India Memoir*, no. 31 (1926), pp. 12–14 ; no. 41 (1929), pp. 1–36.

of the latter, and that there was thus no possibility of any cultural influence between them.

'Two of the famous Ṛig-vedic kings, Divodāsa, the chief of the Bharatas, and Purukutsa, the chief of the Pūrus, are found engaged in war with the hostile owners of *puras* (cities). It is said (4, 30, 20) that Indra overthrew a hundred *puras* for his worshipper, Divodāsa. The greatest feat that Indra performed on behalf of Purukutsa, the chief of Pūrus, is thus described in a stanza (6, 20, 10) : 'May we, O Indra, regain new (wealth) through your favour; the Pūrus worship thee with this hymn and sacrifice. You destroyed the seven autumnal *puras* with thunder-weapon, slew Dāsas and gave wealth to Purukutsa.' 'If we can shake off our bias,' continues Mr. Chanda, 'relating to the absence of towns in the Ṛig-vedic period, we can recognize in these stanzas (5, 34, 7; 7, 25, 2; 1, 41, 3) references to both fort and town.' It is rightly declared that 'the recovery of the ruins of cities at Harappa and Mohenjo-daro leaves no room for doubt that the Ṛig-vedic Āryas were familiar with towns and cities of aliens.' He concludes that 'there existed, and the folk-memory remembered, that there once existed Ārya worshippers of Indra who waged wars against civilized aboriginal neighbours living in towns and fighting from within strongholds.'[1]

The Rai Bahadur has taken pains to quote passages from the later Vedic literature also, comprising the *Yajur-veda*, the *Brāhmaṇas*, together with *Āraṇyakas*, the *Śrauta* and *Gṛihya Sūtras*, and the subsidiary works, as Yāska's *Nirukta*, Saunaka's *Bṛihaddevatā*, and Pāṇini's grammar, to show that the Paṇis, the inhabitants of Ānarta, Aṅga, Surāshṭra, Deccan, Sind, also Gāndhāras, Sauvīras, Kāraskaras, Kaliṅgas, Vaṅgas, Puṇḍras, Keralas, Karkoṭas, Vīrakas, Bāhikas, Madras, Prasthalas, Vaśātis, Khaśas and others were treated by the Āryas as Nīchyas (low-born) or Apāchyas (ill-mannered ?). He has also endeavoured to show that, while the Āryas disposed of their dead by burning, these peoples adopted both cremation and burial.[2] But these data would hardly justify the inference that 'the Ārya conquerors were inferior in material culture,'[3] to the 'civilized aboriginal neighbours living in towns and fighting from within strongholds.'[4] Although Indra is called Purohā or Purandara (sacker of

[1] *Memoir*, no. 31, 1926, pp. 2, 3, 4.
[2] *Ibid*, pp. 6, 7, 8, 9–14.
[3] *Ibid*, p. 5.
[4] *Ibid*, p. 4.

cities), and the Aryan conquerors might have ' either destroyed the cities or allowed them to fall into ruin,'[1] there is, however, nothing to show that the former were inferior to the latter in the art of town planning and building fortified cities. In fact, the Rai Bahadur himself asks his readers to shake off the bias relating to the absence of towns in the Ṛig-vedic period. Thus, if there were towns like Mohenjo-daro, and if the Aryans themselves were living in extensive (*śatabhuji* or hundred winged) *pur* (town) made of copper or iron (*Ṛig-veda*, 7, 15, 4), it will be curious to think that the composers of Vedic hymns, the first effort of human beings to express thoughts in such language of grammar and metres, if not of some scripts also, were inferior to the ' cultured aboriginals ' in matter of house-building. If proper excavations could be made even the obstinate archaeologist might explore better types of cities of the Vedic Aryans, of which the literary description has been declared to be poetic exaggeration. In utter confusion the archaeologist assumes that ' the Ṛig-vedic Āryas reached the lower course of the Parushṇi long after the disappearance of the folk that built the ancient city of Harappa and when that city was already in ruins.'[2]

[1] *Memoir*, no. 31, 1926, p. 5. [2] *Ibid*, p. 2.

CHAPTER II

VEDIC ARCHITECTURE

Vedas

It is needless to say that the details of the art of building were systematically embodied for the first time in the avowedly architectural treatises. They are necessarily missing in non-architectural literature, especially that composed before the growth of the *Vāstu-śāstra.* But casual references to this art go as far back as the oldest existing literature of the world. That the people of that time had learnt the art of building, and used to reside in skilfully constructed houses and not in natural caves, is sufficiently clear, not only from the various synonyms for a house,[1] but also from the articles of furniture. 'The hymns of the *Atharva-veda*[2] give some information about the construction of a house, but the details are extremely obscure. . . . According to Zimmer,[3] four pillars (*upamit*) were set up on a good site, and against them beams were leant at an angle as props (*pratimit*). The upright pillars were connected by cross-beams (*parimit*) resting upon them. The roof was formed of ribs of bamboo cane (*vaṁśa*),[4] . . . The walls were filled up with grass in bundles (*palada*), and the whole structure was held together by ties of various sorts (*nahana, prāṇāha, samdaṁśa, parishvañjalya*).[5] It

[1] For *gṛiha, dhāma* or *dhāman, pastyā,* and *harmya* in the sense of the whole compound, *see*—

Ṛig-veda, III, 53, 6 ; IV, 49, 6 ; VIII, 10, 1.
Atharva-veda, VII, 83, 1 ; X, 6, 4.
Aitareya-Brāhmaṇa, VIII, 21.
Vedic Index, p. 229.

[2] III, 12 ; IX, 3. Bloomfield, *Hymns of the Atharva-veda,* 343, et seq. Weber *Indische Studien,* 17, 234, et seq. Whitney, *Translation of the Atharva-veda,* 525 et seq.

[3] *Altindisches Leben,* 153.

[4] 'It seems likely that, as the ribs were of bamboo and were probably fixed in the ridge, the roof was wagon-headed, like the huts of the Todas at the present day (*see* illustrations of rivers, *The Todas,* pp. 25, 27, 28, 51), and the rock-cut Chaityas or assembly halls of the Buddhists in Western India, in some of the earliest of which the wooden ribs of the arched roof are still preserved.' *See* Fergusson, *History of Indian Architecture,* II, 135, cf. 126.

[5] *A. V.,* IX, 3, 4, 5.

was composed of several rooms . . . and it could be securely shut up.'[1]

The above conclusion is no longer tenable, as will be shewn by what is quoted below.

The great variety of Vedic words[2] denoting a dwelling-house shows that the Vedic Indians were long settled with a tradition of house-building. Already in the early Vedic period houses were not simply unit family abodes, but were also individual private properties which could be acquired. Sometimes a ready-made house could be purchased for a considerable price (*A.-V.*, IX, 3, 15). A well-to-do person possessed several houses. Thus a rich householder is called *Pastyāvant* (*R.-V.*, I, 151, 2 ; IX, 97, 18). Some poet-singers are described as *purudama* (*A.-V.*, VII, 73, 1) and *āyatanas* are given as examples of prosperity (*Chhand. Upanishad*, VII, 24, 2).[3]

'The view of Zimmer and others after him (*Vedic Index*, I, 538 to 540), that Vedic India knew of nothing more solid and complex than the hamlet, like the early Germans and Slavs who had no castle-structures and town-life, is an extreme one ; for it is now being realized more and more as a basic fact that the Vedic Indians, like the Irānians, Hellenes, and Italians, were superimposed upon as earlier civilization. . . . Thus it becomes quite reasonable to find in *prithvī*, *ūrvī*, *śatabhuji*, *asmamayi*, or *āyasi purs*, or the massive, extensive, hundred-walled, stone-built, or iron-protected forts, the vivid descriptions of new and wonderful things the Vedic heroes actually saw ; and rather forced explanations discovering in them mysteries of myths and fancies of metaphor become unnecessary.'[4] The archaeological remains discovered at Harappa, Mohenjo-daro, and other places in Sind fully corroborate this view.

In addition to the noblemen's mansions (*harmya*, *śālā*) and king's palaces (*prāsāda*), comprising several storeys, casually referred to in *Vedas* and *Brāhmaṇas*, particulars of smaller houses may be inferred from the later Vedic literature like the *Atharva-veda*. Some early scholars, to whom the discoveries made in Mohenjo-daro, Harappa, and other places of pre-Vedic age were not available, have interpreted these details in a figurative sense which is no longer

[1] *R.-V.*, VII, 85, 6.

[2] e.g., *Stha*, *Viś*, *Pratishṭhā*, *Gaya*, *Dama*, *Dhāman*, *Śarma*.

[3] *Some Aspects of the Earliest Social History of India*, by S. C. Sarkar, p. 1.

[4] Sarkar, *ibid*, p. 19.

tenable. The *upamit*, *pratimit* and *parimit* really imply 'timber pillars and beams in various positions, vertical, horizontal and slanting.' The *vaṁśa*, or bamboos, were used mainly for the framework of roofing, the central horizontal bamboo supported on the main pillars (*sthhūṇa*) being prominent. The *akshu* was 'the wicker-work or split bamboo-lining over which was laid the thatch (*chhadis*) of hay, straw or long reedy grass (*palada* and *tṛiṇa*), fastened by net to keep the straw-bundles intact. The ridge on the top of the roofing (*vishuvant*) looked like parted hair. Fine clay for flooring and reed-work for walls completed the frame work of such a small house,' which is still in practice in most parts of East Bengal.

In keeping with the requirements of such a house for a family of Brahmanic custom in a village settlement, the accommodation provided was of modest character. There were 'several side-rooms with a central hall in bungalow pattern (*paksha*, *Kāth. Sam.*, XXX, 5; *Taitt. Brā.*, I, 2, 3, 1).' The *agni-śālā* (*lit.* hall of fire-altar), probably in the centre, served the purpose of both sacrifice and sitting-room. With it was connected the *havirdhāna* (sacrificial store-room) and *patnī-sadana* (women's apartments or bedrooms). 'A covered verandah ran all round the house. Altogether *bṛihach-chhandas* (well proportioned) house was covered by a many-winged roofing.'

'This type of dwelling-houses,' Sarkar correctly concludes, 'cannot have been the only one,' in the Vedic ages, and 'other varieties must have developed according to regional conditions.'[1]

The particulars of monumental stone structures erected over or near burnt or buried bodies are also available in the Vedic literature. The *Śatapatha Brāhmaṇa* (Chapter XIII) supplies the full details. The *śmaśāna* (funerary) structures are classified under three groups—*vāstu* (reliquary of bones), *gṛihān* (dwelling-house), and *prajñānam* (memorial pillars or stone-slabs). The etymological differences of these terms are fully borne out by the actual structures they represent. The *vāstu* type still survives in the name Kapila-Vāstu, which might have been originally built as the memorial *stūpa* of Kapila 'rather than the abode of Kapila as usually taken.' In this sense it would look like a solid stone or brick vault with stone enclosures and might have supplied the pattern of subterranean and rock-cut caves of

[1] *Some Aspects of the Earliest Social History of India*, by Sarkar (pp. 28 to 32) who compares this type with modern Bengal straw-houses with two, four, and eight slanting roofs (*chālās*).

later ages. 'The Roman catacombs and Egyptian cave-graves offer instructive parallels.'

The *gṛihān* means a dwelling-house with many chambers and implies that 'the funeral structure was either an actual house (mausoleum) with many rooms, erected over or beside the grave in memory of the deceased, and for the benefit of his soul dedicated to some religious order or philanthropic use.'[1] Its extensiveness is indicated by its other epithet, *harmya*, which has been frequently used in the early Vedic literature to imply a nobleman's residence and the king's palace.[2]

'Apart from the minor differences within the approved range as regards special forms for the several orders, the structural type that is regarded as unorthodox is described clearly as round and domes shaped (*parimaṇḍalā*, *Śat. Brā.*, XIII, 8, 1). That whereby the Easterners make the *śmaśāna* (funerary structure) separate from the earth is described by the usual Vedic word (*chamū*) for a large hemispherical bowl, which must here refer to something like a vault or dome of solid stone or bricks.[1] The structure is then 'enclosed by an indefinite number of enclosing stones'[3] (*Śat. Brā.*, XIII, 8, 2, 2) 'as in the case of fire-hearth.' The orthodox style is stated to be square or quadrilateral not separate from earth (*ibid*, XIII, 8, 1, 1; 8, 1, 2). Bricks one foot square are used in its construction (*ibid*, XIII, 8, 4, 11). A memorial mound like a fire-altar is prescribed for the builders of the same (*ibid*, XIII, 8, 1, 1).

'The former is the prototype of the Buddistic, Eastern and heretical *stūpa* architecture of the very next epoch, and through it of the Śaiva temple styles of subsequent ages (characterized by the round domes). The latter is a specially Brāhmanical style, associated with sacrificial altars and rectilineal figures, strikingly paralleled by the

[1] This is not a forced explanation dervied from the later Buddhist monuments (*vihāra*, *chaitya*). In the *Ṛig-veda* (VII, 89, 1) itself the grave is described as *mṛiṇmaya gṛiha*. It is more frequently mentioned in the *Atharva-veda*—'let these *gṛihasaḥ* be a refuge for him for ever' (*A.-V.*, XVIII, 3, 51 = *R.-V.*, X, 18, 12); 'make ye *gṛiha* for him according to his kindred' (*A.-V.*, XVIII, 4, 37), that is, the size and excellence depended on the number, position, and means of the kinsmen of the deceased (Sarkar, *ibid*, p. 44); 'as the five clans (*mānava*) implanted a *harmya* (edifice) for Yama, so I implant a *harmya* that there may be many of me' (*A.-V.*, XVIII, 4, 55).

[2] *See* the writer's *Encyclopaedia of Hindu Architecture* under *Harmya*, and compare *A.-V.*, XVIII, 4, 55, which refers to 'building a *harmya* for the dead.'

[3] Stones are used instead of the square bricks in the case of non-fireworshippers (*Śat. Brā.*, XIII, 8, 4, 11).

similar sacrificial and geometrical style of squares and bricks in ancient Babylonia, and represented recognizably in some later forms of Brāhmaṇical temple architecture' such as at Madura, Tanjore, and also in earlier monasteries or several storeys built pyramidically.[1]

Another remarkable feature of these funerary structures as described in the *Śatapatha Brāhmaṇa* is the regulation—'let there be *chitras* on the back of the *śmaśāna*.' The commentaries explain *chitras* as natural sceneries. In the case of the brick-built *tumuli*, these *chitras* would be paintings on suitable plaster, but in the case of the stone-built round *chamū* of the Easterners the most suitable *chitras* would be sculptured figures in relief. The nature of these *chitras* is indicated by the reason given: 'for *chitras* mean offspring.' Thus the figures painted or carved might have been of women and children, and possibly couples of men and women.

The third variety of the funerary monuments, the *prajñānam*, implies the monumental pillars (or slabs of stones). In the *Vedas* (*R.-V.*, X, 18, 3; *A.-V.*, XVIII, 3, 52) a pillar (*sthūṇa*) is stated to have been set up the grave, and a *loga* (clod, pole, also pillar) is erected after the earth is piled up from about the grave. On the *sthūṇa* (pillars) 'maintained by the Fathers, Yama makes seats for the departed' (*R.-V.*, X, 18, 3; *A.-V.*, XVIII, 3, 52). Seats on memorial pillars, like lion capitals of Mauryan age, may imply some sort of effigy or bust of the dead person. In the time of the *Śatapatha Brāhmaṇa* (XXX, 8, 4, 1; IV, 2, 5, 15; *Kat. Sr. Sut.*, XXI, 3, 31) 'a stone-pillar (*śaṅku*) was set up along with three timber ones at the four corners of the *śmaśāna* (grave or cemetery).'[2]

The symbolism of these *śmaśāna* structures might have been derived from the civic and sacrificial Vedic *drupadas* (posts)[3] to

[1] Sarkar further observes (*ibid*, pp. 40, 39, note 9) that 'from these indications, and from the recognition of round forms in the construction of altars and *śmaśāna* (funerary structures) in the later *saṁhitās* (*Taitt. Sam.*, V, 4, 11), it would appear that the antagonism to round and stone structures displayed by the *Śatapatha Brāhmaṇa* is a later development in the seventh century B.C., very likely due to the growing estrangement between the *prāchya* (eastern) and midland religions and philosophical doctrines in the Buddhistic reformation (arrangement of round and star-shaped bricks in a circle).'

[2] Sarkar further compares (*ibid*, p. 43) the account in the epic of the representation of the fertility goddess Jarā (or Jaṭā, the traditional village Spirit) on the palace walls of the King of Girivraja of a plump woman with children all around, and also the panels of female figures, amorous couples, etc., in the later *stūpa* and '*vihāra* architecture' and in Orissan temple sculptures.

[3] *R.-V.*, I, 24, 13; IV, 32, 23; VII, 86, 5; *A.-V.*, VI, 63, 3, 115, 2; XIX, 47, 9; *Vāj. Sam.* XX, 20.

which offenders and sacrificial victims were bound. 'The Buddhistic monolithic pillars erected beside the relic-*stūpas* and on the highways and public thoroughfares is probably the developed form of such memorial *śankus*. This is sufficient explanation of the Asokan pillars, and a theory of their Persepolitan origin is unnecessary.'[1]

The articles of furniture give more reality to architecture, especially regarding the residential buildings. Although conquest and religion were the chief characteristics of the Vedic Indians, fortified settlements, cities, forts and fortresses on the one hand, and fire-altars of various designs[2] in the absence of regular temples on the other, were not the only examples of Vedic architecture. The evidences gathered together above will amply justify the conclusion that civil architecture was probably the chief building activity of civilized conquerors like the Vedic Indians. Thus there are unquestionable references to noblemen's mansions (*harmya*) and king's palaces (*prāsāda*), which are corroborated by the Mohenjo-daro discoveries of earlier ages. But the matter of greater importance is the references to unpretentious dwelling-houses of priestly population in village settlements. These smaller houses, of which a pen picture has been drawn above and of which the main design is still followed in border lands like East Bengal villages, were furnished in a way which affords a real insight into the life of the remote past.

Thus the *Ṛig-veda* (VII, 55, 8) refers to 'married women occupying their commodious *talpas*, the new (and prospective) brides on the fashionable *vahyas*, other single women of the household on the broad *proshṭhas*, and a maiden on a *śayana*, which, as well as *paryaṅka*, are stated to be the ordinary bedsteads or couches. The *talpa* is the nuptial bed whereupon alone a legitimate son (*tālpya*) could be born (*Sat. Brā.*, XIII, 1, 6, 2). Its sanctity is further increased as it was reserved for the preceptor (cf. *Guru-talpa*, *Chhand. Upanishad*, V, 10, 9). *Vahya*, that which can be easily carried, is a lighter structure used specially in marriage ceremony of getting the bride and bridegroom lain on bed side by side (*A.-V.*, XIV, 2, 30), which ceremony may also be performed upon a humbler settee (*āsandi*). Upon it a weary bride mounts (*A.-V.*, IV, 20, 3), and women generally sleep' (*R.-V.*, VII, 55, 8 ; *A.-V.*, IV, 5, 3). Thus

[1] Sarkar, *ibid*, pp. 45, 46.

[2] *See* later p. 63, note 2.

it must be more than a mere litter or canopied sedan-chair. It must have been a regular bed spacious enough for two, 'bearing all forms' and of carved wood-work, furnished with a gold-embroidered coverlet (*rukma-prastaraṇa*). It formed a part of the principal dowry. The *proshṭhas* look like a 'combination of a settee and a coffer' and were also used as long benches and couches or beds, which were also sent as dowry along with the bride to her husband's home. They could also be fixed against the walls and furnished with turned legs. The term *proshṭha-pāda* as a proper name (arm-chaired or stretched-legged gentleman) may indicate it as an easy chair with provision for stretching the two legs. The *śayana*, or ordinary bedsteads, were also meant for 'a beloved woman or maiden' (*A.-V.*, III, 25, 1) who 'felt pain (*tuda*) of the silken coverlet' (because of the absence of a male companion). Pururavas and Urvaśī slept on such a soft couch (*Śat. Brā.*, XI, 5, 1, 2) and a Vedic student could also sleep on it (*A.-V.*, V, 29, 8).

The *āsandī* and *paryaṅka* 'originated with the ruling nobility, though in their ritualized and modified form (reed-covered and clay-daubed) these must have been subsequently used' in the ordinary priests' dwelling-houses. In the *Vājasaneyī Samhitā* of the *Yajur-veda* (XIX, 86; XX, 1) *āsandi* is regarded as the 'mother or womb of *Rājanyas*' (kings). In the same sense of a high seat it is referred to in the *Śatapatha Brāhmaṇa* also (V. 4, 4, 1). The *Aitareya Brāhmaṇa* refers (VIII, 5, 6) to its use at consecration and other ceremonies where it is 'mounted with the right knee first, then the left, approaching from behind and taking hold of it by both hands.' This king's *āsandi* was generally carried by two persons, while a god's *āsandi* called the 'throne of justice' was carried by four persons. While the height of the former reached the knee, that of the latter came up to the navel. Both were of great width and depth. The imperial *āsandi* for *samrāj* was shoulder-high, while the sacrificial one was a span-high, a cubit in width and depth. All were made of strong wood (*khadira* or *udumbara*), perforated (*vitṛiṇṇā*) and joined with straps, pleasant and soft seated, and covered with a tiger's or antelope's skin. 'The Brāhmaṇ's far-shining *āsandi* in an extensive hall of an invincible abode in a city was furnished with two fore-feet, two length-wise and two cross-pieces' (*Kaush. Upan.* I, 5; *Sāṅkh. Āraṇ.* III; *Jaim. Brā.*, *II*, 24).

The *paryaṅka* is 'a magnified *āsandi*, and like it associated with regal style and opulence, rather approaching a bedstead in later

Vedic times (*Kaush. Upan.*, I, 5; *Jaim. Brā.*, II, 24, *Sankh. Aran.*, iii), but yet used for sitting only; so also, later on, *āsandi* is taken to mean *paryaṅkikā*, or a smaller variety. But it developed to be of 'unmeasured splendour,' having same arrangement of feet and frame, and straps (*tantu*) stretched lengthwise and crosswise, with head-piece of the couch (*śīrshaṇya*), the supporting back (*upaśrī*), and cushion and pillow for the head (*uch-chhīrshaka*).'[1]

Various other smaller seats and smaller articles of furniture are referred to throughout the Vedic literature. [These will undoubtedly indicate a highly developed taste and culture.]

'The ritualistic types of furniture cannot, however, be taken as a faithful counterpart of the contemporary secular ones, for it is well known that sacrificial and ritual requisites almost always remain primitive and unchanged throughout long ages, and it is particularly true of India; so that the furniture of the priestly texts is almost that with which the Brāhmaṇic cult and civilization started. So great is the ritual conservatism in these respects that even where special circumstances required alteration in the sacrificial paraphernalia, the external items are transformed into Brāhmaṇical-looking accessories, by the employment of primitive materials sacred in ritual tradition.' Thus even today the *prastara*, a sacrificial seat, consists only of strewn grass (*darbha, R.-V.*, X, 14, 4; *A.-V.*, 2, 6; *Taitt. Sam.*, I, 7, 7, 4; *Vāj. Sam.*; II, 18; XVIII, 63; *Ait. Brā.*, I, 26; II, 3; *Śat. Brā.*, I, 3, 3, 5). Similarly *barhis* made of *bulbaja* grass strewn on the sacrificial ground and used as the seat for gods is a sort of litter. The *kūrcha* is a small square grass-mat (*Taitt. Sam.*, VII, 5, 8, 5; *Śat. Brā.*, XI, 5, 3, 4, 7; *Ait. Āraṇ.*, V, 1, 4; *Bṛihad. Upan.*, II, 11, 1). The golden *kūrcha* (*Śat. Brā.*, XIII, 4, 3, 1) is interpreted as a 'golden stool with feet, having a *kūrcha*-like pad over it,' or 'a wooden seat carved or painted so as to resemble a *kūrcha*.' The *bṛisī* (or *vṛishī*) is a cushion seat often spread over the grass *kūrcha*. The *kaśipu* (*A.-V.*, VI, 138, 5) implies a mat (or cushion) made from grass, but the chief priest (*hotṛi*) is stated to sit upon a golden *kaśipu*, which must be of stronger material than grass and of better craftsmanship. The *sadas*, wherefrom the term *sadasya* (councillor) is formed, must have been a 'raised seat and of a style specially associated with his office.' It is elsewhere (*Śat. Brā.*, XIV, 3, 1, 8) used as domestic

[1] For further details, *see* Sarkar, *ibid.*, pp. 52–56, and vide *Vedix Index* of Macdonell and Keith.

furniture and implies a seat in a dwelling-house. The *pīṭha* is a wooden low seat, square or rectangular. The *naḍvalā* (*Vāj. Sam.*, XXX, 16; *Taitt. Brā.*, III, 4, 12, 1) is also a mat or cushion made of reeds (*naḍa*). The *kaṭa* (*Taitt. Sam.*, V, 3, 12, 2) is a rattan mat made of split cane (*vaitasa*).

That these humbler articles of furniture, like their richer counterparts, were extensively in use is proved by the fact that there were professional (women) workers (*kārī*) who 'evidently turned out artistic seats and carpets, as is shewn in the early occurrence of *hiraṇya kaśipu* (*A.-V.*, V, 7, 10) in the sense of 'a gorgeous woman or courtesan with golden mantle' (*drāpi*).'

In the light of the above the following quotations need no longer be interpreted as imaginary or a mere poetic fancy.

Atri is stated to have been 'thrown into a machine room with a hundred doors, where he was roasted.'[1] Vasishṭha desired to have 'a three-storeyed dwelling' (*tri-dhātu-śaraṇam*).[2] Mention is made of a sovereign 'who, exercising no oppression, sits down in this substantial and elegant hall built with a thousand pillars,'[3] and of residential houses with such pillars and said to be 'vast, comprehensive, and thousand-doored.'[4] Mitra and Varuṇa are represented as occupying a great palace with a thousand pillars and a thousand gates.[5] Muir's comment that 'this is but an exaggerated description of a royal residence such as the poet had seen,'[6] is no longer tenable. If the Indians of an earlier age could built cities, towns, and villages with splendid buildings like those of Mohenjo-daro, there can be no reason to believe that they merely *exaggerated*, even in a poetic description, what they had actually seen and probably practised. But it is true that these Vedic gods did not occupy such palaces as referred to in the hymns, although such palaces might have existed at that time.

[1] *R.-V.*, I, 112, 7. Wilson's *R.-V.*, IV, 148. [2] *Ibid*, IV, 200.

[3] *Ibid*, II, 313. [4] *Ibid*, IV, 179.

[5] Compare *R.-V.*, II, 41, 5; V, 62, 6; VII, 88, 5; *A.-V.*, III, 12; IX, 3, which contains prayers for the stability of a house at the time of its construction.

[6] Muir, *Sanskṛit Text*, V, 455.

Compare R. L. Mitra, *Indo-Aryans*, I, 27: 'Pillars, spacious doors and windows, though frequently mentioned, are not decisive indications of the existence of masonry buildings, but bricks could not possibly have originated unless required for such structures, for it would be absurd to suppose that bricks were known, and made, and yet they were never used in the construction of houses.'

PLATE XX(a) (i)

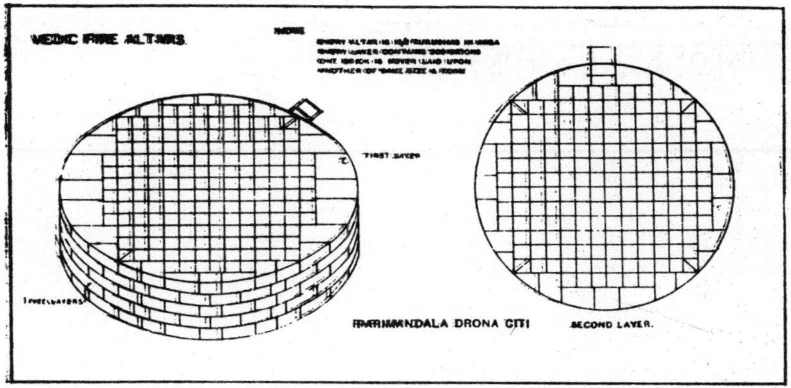

VEDIC FIRE ALTARS (PARIMANDALA-DRONA-CHIT)

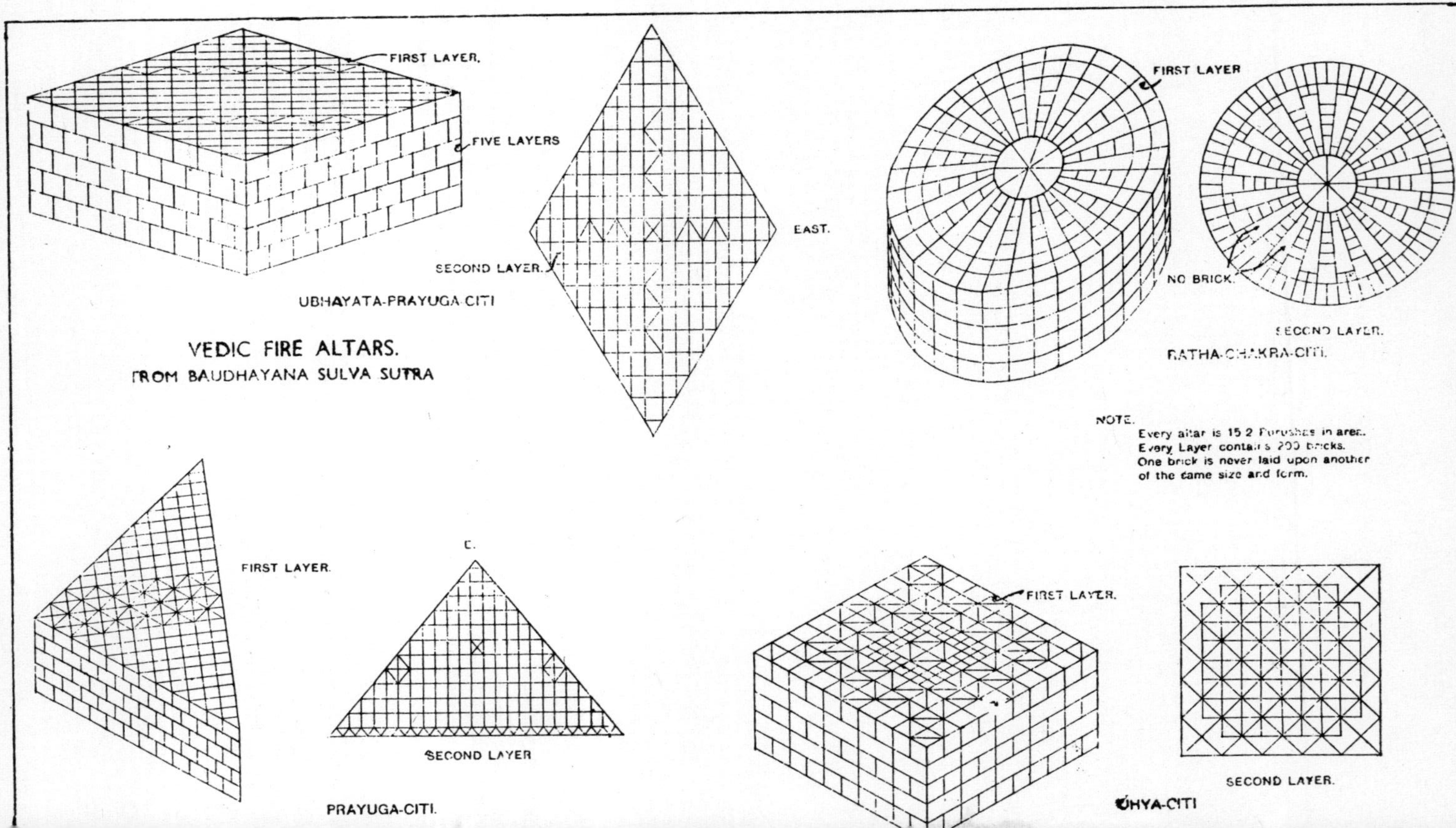
FIRST LAYER.
FIVE LAYERS
SECOND LAYER.
EAST.
UBHAYATA-PRAYUGA-CITI
VEDIC FIRE ALTARS.
FROM BAUDHAYANA SULVA SUTRA
FIRST LAYER
NO BRICK.
SECOND LAYER.
RATHA-CHAKRA-CITI.
NOTE.
Every altar is 15 2 Purushas in area.
Every Layer contains 200 bricks.
One brick is never laid upon another
of the same size and form.
FIRST LAYER.
SECOND LAYER
PRAYUGA-CITI.
FIRST LAYER.
SECOND LAYER.
ÚHYA-CITI

Brāhmaṇas and Sūtras

The *Sulva-sūtras*, which are but the supplementary portions of the *Kalpa-sūtras*, treating of the measurement and construction of the different *vedis* or altars, furnish us with some interesting structural details of the *agnis*, the large altars built of bricks. The construction of these altars, which were required for the great *Soma* sacrifice, seems to have been based on sound scientific principles and was probably the precursor of the temple which later became the chief feature of Hindu architecture.

These altars could be constructed in different shapes, the earliest enumeration of which is found in the *Taittiriya-Samhita*.[1] Following this enumeration,[2] Baudhāyana and Āpastamba furnish us with full particulars about the shape of all these different *chitis* (altars) and the bricks which were employed for their construction. Everyone of these altars was constructed of five layers of bricks, which together came up to the height of the knee ; in some cases ten or fifteen layers, and proportionate increase in the height of the altar, were prescribed. Every layer in its turn was to consist of two hundred bricks, so that the whole *agni* (altar) contained a thousand ; the first, third, and fifth layers were divided into two hundred parts in exactly the same manner ; a different division was adopted for the second and the fourth, so that one brick was never laid upon another of the same size and form.

[1] V, 4, 11.

[2] (i) *Chaturaśra-śyena-chit*—so called because it resembles the form of a falcon and the bricks out of which it is composed are all square-shaped.

(ii) *Kaṅka-chit*—in the form of a heron (cf. Burnell, Cat. 29, of a carrion kite) is the same as *śyena-chit* except the two additional feet.

(iii) *Alaja-chit*—is the same except the additional wings.

(iv) *Prauga-chit*—is an equilateral triangle ; and the

(v) *Ubhayataḥ-Praugachit*—is made up of two such triangles joined at their bases.

(vi) *Ratha-chakra-chit*—is in the form of a wheel, (*i*) a massive wheel without spokes, and (*ii*) a wheel with sixteen spokes.

(vii) *Droṇa-chit*—is like a vessel or tube, square or circular.

(viii) *Parichayya-chit*—has a circular outline and is equal to the *Rathachakra-chit*, differing in the arrangement of bricks which are to be placed in six concentric circles.

(ix) *Samūhya-chit*—is circular in shape and made of loose earth and bricks.

(x) *Kūrma-chit*—resembles a tortoise and is of a triangular or circular shape. Compare Thibaut, *J.A.S.B.*, 1875, part I.

'The first altar covered an area of 7½ *purushas*, which means 7½ squares, each side of which was equal to a *purusha*, i.e. the height of a man with uplifted arms. On each subsequent occasion the area was increased by one square *purusha*. Thus, at the second layer of the altar one square *purusha* was added to the 7½ constituting the first *chiti* (altar), and at the third layer two square *purushas* were added, and so on. But the shape of the whole and the relative proportion of each constituent part had to remain unchanged. The area of every *chiti* (altar), whatever its shape might be—falcon, wheel, tortoise, etc.—had to be equal to 7½ square *purushas*.'[1]

Frequent mention is made also of villages, towns and forts,[2] and cities with 'hundred enclosures or fortifications' are referred to.[3] On this Muir remarks that, 'although they are only alluded to as figurative expressions of the means of protection afforded by the gods, they no doubt suggest the idea of forts consisting apparently of a series of concentric walls, as actually existing in the country at that time.'[4]

From references like these, and in consideration of the prosperous condition of Indian architecture of the pre-Vedic age as disclosed by the discoveries made at Mohenjo-daro and other places, it may be safely concluded that the authors of the Vedic literature 'were not ignorant of stone forts, walled cities, stone houses, carved stones, and brick edifices.'

[1] Thus squares had to be found which would be equal to two or more given quares, or equal to the difference of two given squares; oblongs were turned into quares and squares into oblongs. Triangles were constructed equal to given squares or oblongs and so on. A circle had to be constructed, the area of which might equal as closely as possible that of a given square. *See* illustrations in *The Pandit*, new series, June, 1876, no. 1, Volumes I and IV; 1882, old series, June, 1874, no. 97. Volumes IX and X, May, 1876.

[2] *R.-V.*, I, 58, 8; 144, 1; II, 20, 8; IV, 27, 1; 30, 20; VIII, 3, 7; 15, 14; 89, 8; 95, 1.

[3] *Ibid.*, I, 166, 8; VII, 15, 14.

[4] Muir, *Sanskrit Text*, V. 451.

LIST OF BRICKS USED IN ŚYENA-CHIT ALTAR

(1) Indraṁbi; (2) Pṛthi; (3) Bhūrashi; (4) Sūrasi; (5) Jāsteya; (6) Birāṭ; (7) Samrājajyo; (8) Bṛihashpa; (9) Agneryā; (10) Devārāma; (11) Madhuśyāmādha; (12) Madhuścha; (13) Āshaḍhā; (14) Udamyaśrushmā; (15) Yāstejaḥ; (16) Machhande; (17) Pramāchhandaḥ; (18) Pratimā; (19) Aratrīvi; (20) Birāṭ-chhandasta; (21) Gāyatri-chhandastajā; (22) Trishṭup-chhandasta-chhid; (23) Jagatī-chhandanista; (24) Anushṭup; (25) Ushṇihā; (26) Paṁkti-ścharn; (27) Bṛihatī; (28) Māchhaṁ; (29) Pramāchhaṁ; (30) Pratimā; (31) Aratrīv; (32) Birāṭa-chhaṁ; (33) Gāyatrī-chhaṁ; (34) Trishṭupchhaṁ; (35) Jagati-chhaṁ; (36) Anushṭup; (37) Ushṇihā; (38) Paṁkti; (39) Bṛihatī; (40) Māchhanda; (41) Pramāchhandaḥ; (42) Pratimā; (43) Aratrī; (44) Biraṭa-chhaṁ; (45) Gāyatrīchhaṁ; (46) Trishtupachhaṁ; (47) Jagatī-chhaṁ; (48) Anushṭup; (49) Ushṇi; (50) Paṁkti-chhaṁ; (51) Bṛihatī; (52) Apāṁtve; (53) Apāṁ-tvodma; (54) Apāṁtvāta; (55) Apāṁtvā; (56) Apāṁtvāya; (57) Arṇave; (58) Samudre; (59) Salile; (60) Apaṁksa; (61) Apāṁsa; (62) Apāṁtvā; (63) Apāṁtvā; (64) Apāṁtvāyu; (65) Apāṁtvāyo; (66) Gāyatrī; (67) Apāṁtvā; (68) Trishtup; (69) Jagatī; (70) Anushṭup; (71) Paktiśchhaṁ; (72) Āravemvā; (73) Āyoshkṛi; (74) Āyoshpatva; (75) Vish; (76) Bṛihaspataye; (77) Adhmasaṁ; (78) Ṛitasadasi; (79) Salya-sadasi; (80) Tejaḥsadasi; (81) Vayaḥ-sadasi; (82) Yaśaḥ-sadasi; (83) Gṛiṇo; (84) Dhāmāsi; (85) Sanirasi); (86) Ritirasi; (87) Śakti; (88) Bhūtirasi; (89) Karmāsi; (90) Gudoshi; (91) Kshatraṁpā; (92) Kshatraṁpinva; (93) Kshatraṁjiṅva; (94) Kshatraṁyachha; (95) Kshatraṁdṛṅgaha; (96) Kshatramasi; (97) Viśveshutvā; (98) Viśveshutvā; (99) Viśveshutvādi; (100) Viśveshutvā; (101) Viśvāsutvā; (102) Viśvāsutvā; (103) Viśveshutvā; (104) Viśvāsutvā; (105) Viśvāsutvā; (106) Divisi; (107) Svarjiṁdasi; (108) Pūtanājid; (109) Bhūrijid; (110) Abhijid; (111) Viśvajid; (112) Sarvajid; (113) Satrājid; (114) Dhanajid; (115) Bhābhasi; (116) Vishpābhasi; (117) Prastrābhasi; (118) Sepatnaha; (119) Abhimati; (120) Arati; (121) Yātuhanaṁ; (122) Piśāchaha; (123) Rakshohaṇaṁ; (124) Śatruhanaṁ; (125) Udvadasi; (126) Ūditirasi; (127) Udatyasi; (128) Ātrumamā; (129) Ātrāmaṁtya; (130) Ākāntira; (131) Saṁkramamānā; (132) Saṁkrāmaṁ; (133) Saṁkrānti; (134) Sarmyāsi; (135) Svarasi; (136) Ishisī; (137) Urjisī; (138) Bhagesīda; (139) Draviṇesīda; (140) Sabhritesīda; (141) Pṛithivyāya; (142) Vishṇopṛishve; (143) Iḍāyāpaḥ; (144) Dhṛitavatisī; (145) Piṇvamave; (146) Samvatsare; (147) Parivatsare; (148) Idāvatsa; (149) Iduvatsare; (150) Idvatsare; (151) Vatsaresī; (152) Ekaṁsyāṁ; (153) Daśāsu; (154) Śateṁsī; (155) Sahasre; (156) Ayute; (157) Niyute; (158) Prayutesī; (159) Arbude; (160) Nyarbude; (161) Samudre; (162) Madhye; (163) Padme; (164) Antesī; (165) Parārdhasī; (166) Piṇvamānāsi; (167) Ṛitamasyṛita; (168) Satyamasi; (169) Sanirasi; (170) Saṅga-śṛitasi; (171) Sampada; (172) Āyusaḥ-prāṇaṅgasaṁ; (173) Prāṅadapānāṅgasaṁ; (174) Apānāduyānaṅgasam; (175) Vyānā-chakshuḥ; (176) Chakshushaḥśro; (177) Śrotātmanaḥ; (178) Manaso; (179) Vachaā; (180) Ātmanaḥ; (181) Pṛithivyā; (182) Antarvikshāddi; (183) Divaḥsudhaḥ; (184) Pṛithivī; (185) Antarikshaṁ; (186) Dyaurvaśā; (187) Rigvaśā; (188) Vidvaśā; (189) Trivṛite; (190) Paṁvadagaute; (191) Maptada; (192) Ekaviṅgagaute; (193) Tṛiṇavantejaḥ; (194) Manaso; (195) Tvāmasthe; (196) Lokaṁ; (197) Lokaṁpṛiṇā; (198) Lokaṁpṛiṇā; (199) Lokaṁpṛiṇā; (200) Lokaṁpṛiṇā.

CHAPTER III

CLASSICAL OR POST-VEDIC ARCHITECTURE

Buddhist Architecture

'In the Buddha's time and in that portion of Northern India where the Buddhist influence was most early felt—that is to say, in the districts including and adjoining those now called the United Provinces and Bihar, the arrangements of villages were practically similar. 'We nowhere hear of isolated houses. The houses were all together, in a group, separated only by narrow lanes. Immediately adjoining was the sacred grove of trees of the primeval forest. . . . Beyond this was the wide expanse of cultivated field, usually rice-field.' Villagers are described as 'uniting of their own accord to build mote hills and rest-houses and reservoirs, to mend the roads between their own and adjacent villages, and even to lay out parks.'[1]

The exact details of town-planning are not available. But 'we are told of lofty walls, ramparts with buttresses and watch-towers and great gates; the whole surrounded by a moat or even a double moat, one of water and one of mud. But we are nowhere told of the length of the fortifications or of the extent of the space they enclosed. It would seem that we have to think not so much of a large walled city as of a fort surrounded by a number of suburbs. . . . From the frequent mention of the windows of the great houses opening directly on to the streets or squares it would appear that it was not the custom to have them surrounded by any private grounds. There were, however, no doubt, enclosed spaces behind the fronts of the houses, which latter abutted on the streets.'[2]

[1] *Buddhist India*, Rhys Davids, pp. 42, 45, 49 : compare *Jātaka*, I, 199.

[2] *Ibid*, pp. 64-65.

Compare the hill fortress, Girivraja, four and a half miles in circumference, is said to have been built by Mahā-Govinda, the architect. Bimbisāra is stated to have built *Rājagriha*, king's house, which was three miles in circumference. 'The stone walls of Girivraja are the oldest extant stone buildings in India.' Mention is also made of Ayojjhā, Bārāṇasī, Kampilla, Kosāmbī, Mathurā, Mithilā, Sāgala, Sāketa, Sāvatthi, Ujjeni, Vesāli and other cities, of which, however, few architectural details are given (*Vimāna-Vatthu*, commentary, p. 82).

Compare *Diggha-Nikāya*, XIX, 36 :

दन्तपुरं कालिङ्गानमस्सकानाञ्च पोतनम् ।
माहिस्सती अवन्तीनम् सोवीरानञ्च रोरुकम् ॥
मिथिला च विदेहानम् चम्पा अङ्गेसु मापिता ।
वाराणसी च कासीनम् एते गोविन्द मापितेति ॥

See Rhys Davids, *ibid*, p. 38.

But detached references to individual buildings, as distinct from villages and towns, are found in abundance in the canonical texts, as well as the *Jātakas*. At places it appears as if Buddha were delivering discourses on architecture. As a matter of fact he enjoined upon his devotees the supervision of building construction as one of the duties of the order.[1] It is stated in one of the early texts that the Bhikkhus were told on a certain occasion by the Blessed One, after the delivery of a religious discourse, with respect to dwellings, thus : 'I allow you, O Bhikkhus, abodes of five kinds—*Vihāra*, *Arddhayoga*, *Prāsāda*, *Harmya*, and *Guhā*.'[2]

Buildings are thus divided into five classes. But the details of the distinguishing features are not methodically given in the texts obviously because these are not architectural treatises.[3]

[1] *Chullavagga*, VI, 17, 1 (Translation, pp. 212-216).

[2] *Vinaya text*, *Mahāvagga*, I, 30, 4, pp. 173-174 ; *Chullavagga*, VI, 1, 2, p. 158.

[3] The commentator Buddhaghosha has, however, submitted an explanatory note. *Vihāra* is the well-known Buddhist monastery. *Arddhayoga*, which literally means 'half-joining,' is stated by this commentator to imply *Suvarṇa-vanga-griha* or 'gold-coloured bungalow' as rendered by Oldenburg and Rhys Davids. P.T.S. *Encyclopaedia* does not accept this interpretation. Dr. B. C. Law (*Indian Culture*, April 1935, p. 717) would interpret it as *Garuḍa* (bird)-shaped house, but gives no authority. There appear, however, no such houses in Bengal, nor is this class of buildings mentioned in the *Silpa-śāstras*. It is clear, however, that these are meant to imply some sort of luxurious buildings of the then Bengal. Regarding *prāsāda*, Buddhaghosha simply says that it is a long *prāsāda*. Rhys Davids has made several conjectures—' a long-storeyed mansion, or the whole of an upper storey, or the storeyed buildings.' Sir M. M. Williams seems to explain this by 'the monks' hall for assembly and confession.' *Harmya* is stated to be a *prāsāda* with an upper chamber placed on the topmost storey. The references to the uses of *prāsāda* and *harmya* as found in the *Śilpa-śāstras*, general Sanskrit literature, and the archaeological records will be found in the writer's *Encyclopaedia* under those terms. *Guhā* literally means cave and would seem to refer to underground buildings. One of the *Jātakas* (*Ummagga*, p. 430) actually contains an elaborate description of an underground palace, and there are the rock-cut temples as in the famous Ajanta caves. According to Buddhaghosha these *guhā* buildings are of four kinds, namely, those built of bricks, stone, wood, or earth. Rhys Davids has rendered *śilāguhā* by hut made in a rock, and left out the translation of *paṁsu* (Sanskrit *pāṁśu*, meaning sand, dust, or crumbling soil) *guhā*. Buddhaghosha has thus explained the *pañcha-lenāni* under *Mahāvagga* 1, 30, 4 :

'अड्ढयोगो' ति सुवण्णवङ्गगेहम् । पासादो' ति दीघपासादो । हम्मियान् ति उपरि आकासतले पत्तिट्ठितकुटागारो पासादो येव । गुहा' ति इट्ठकगुहा सिलागुहा दारुगुहा पंसुगुहा ।

Compare also, Oldenburg and Rhys Davids, *Vinaya Texts*, Translation, *Mahāvagga*, p. 173, note, also *Chullavagga*, p. 158, note 2.

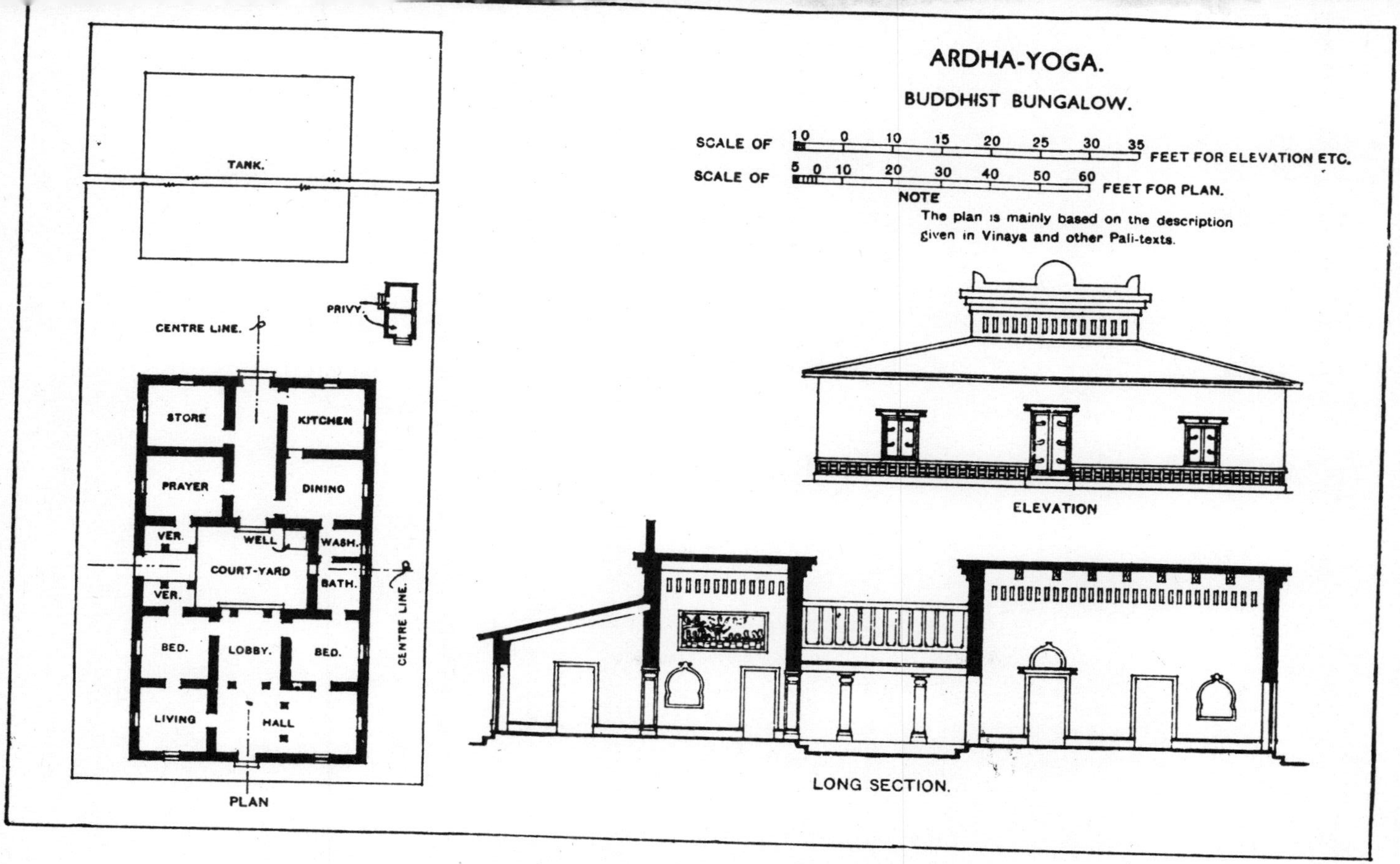

ARDHA-YOGA—TYPICAL ANCIENT BUNGALOW

Page 66

distinguished from one another, and till this is so, they must be considered, architecturally at least, as one.'[1]

The rails must be recognized as 'one of the most important features of Buddhist architecture. Generally they are found surrounding *topes*, but they are also represented as enclosing sacred trees, temples, pillars, and other objects. The Buddhist rails, however, in early ages at least, is never attached to the *tope*, and is used for so many other, and such various purposes.'[2]

The *chaitya* [3] is a more general term than *stūpa*, and may be applied to 'any building of the nature of a religious monument, but more correctly to the second division of *stūpas*, or those commemorative of acts, miracles, etc., or not funerary.[4] But it has further been restricted so as to correspond with the churches of the Christian religion; their plans, the position of the altar or relic casket, the aisles, and other peculiarities are the same in both, and their uses are identical in so far as the ritual forms of the one religion correspond to those of the other.'[5]

The *vihāra* with the Buddhists and Jains was a hall where the monks met and walked about; afterwards these halls came to be used as temples, and sometimes became the centres of monastic establishments. Like the *chaityas*, they resemble very closely the corresponding institutions among Christians. In the earlier ages they accompanied,

[1] *Dagaba* is a Singalese word applied to a *stūpa*, from the Sanskrit *dhātu*, 'relic,' 'element,' and *garbha* (in Pali *gabbho*), a 'womb,' 'receptacle' or 'shrine.' *Dhātugarbha* is thus the relic-receptacle or inner shrine, and is strictly applicable only to the dome of the *stūpa*, sometimes called the *aṇḍa* or egg. *Dhātus* were not merely relics in the literal sense, but memorials in an extended acceptation, and were classified as corporeal remains; objects belonging to the teacher, as his staff, bowl, robe, holy spots, etc.; and any memorial, text of a sacred book, cenotaph of a teacher, etc. *Stūpas* are known as *chaityas* in Nepal, and as *dagabas* in Ceylon.

The principal examples are at Bhilsa, Sarnath, Bodhagaya, Amaravati, Gandhara, Jalalabad and Manikyala.

[2] The principal examples are at Bharaut, Mathura, Sanchi, and Amaravati.

[3] The word *chaitya*, like *stūpa*, means primarily a heap or tumulus, but it also means a place of sacrifice or religious worship, an altar—from Sanskrit *chitā*, a heap, an assemblage, etc. Properly speaking, therefore, *chaitya* caves ought perhaps to be called 'halls containing a *chaitya*,' or '*chaitya* halls,' and this latter term is consequently used wherever any ambiguity is likely to arise from the use of the simple term *chaitya*.

[4] All structures of the nature of sanctuaries are *chaityas*, so that sacred trees statues, religious inscriptions and sacred places come also under this general name.

[5] Principal examples are at Sanchi, Ter Chezarla, Bhaja, Karle, Ajanta, Elura, etc.

Vihāras are the well-known monasteries or temples of the Buddhists, originally implying halls where the monks met. *Arddhayogas* seem to be a special kind of Bengal building, partly religious and partly residential. *Prāsādas* are wholly residential storeyed buildings; *Harmyas* are a larger and more pompous type of storeyed buildings. *Guhās* seem to be less dignified buildings, originally built underground for middle class people.

The various objects of Buddhist art, of which archaeological remains have been scrutinized by modern architects and historians of Fergusson's name and authority, are also classified into the five following groups, though, of course, it is at times impossible to separate them entirely from one another, and sometimes two or more of them must be taken together as parts of one monument.

The *stambhas*, or *lats*, are 'common to all the styles of Indian architecture. With the Buddhists they were employed to bear inscriptions on their shafts, with emblems or animals on their capitals. With the Jains they were generally *dīpadānas*, or lamp-bearing pillars, but sometimes supporting quadruple figures of a *Jina*. With the *Vaishṇavas* they generally bore statues of Garuḍa or Hanumān. With the *Śaivas* they bore the *Triśūla* symbol, or were *dīpadānas* and flag-staffs. But, whatever their destination they were always among the most original, and frequently the most elegant, productions of Indian art.'[1]

The *stūpas*, or *topes*, again, were 'primarily relic-shrines, but may be divided into two classes, according to their destination: first, *stūpas* proper, or monuments containing relics of Buddha or of some Buddhist saint[2]; secondly, the *stūpas*, or towers, erected to commemorate some event or mark, some sacred spot dear to the followers of the Buddha. If it were possible, these two ought to be kept separate, but no external signs have yet been discovered by which they can be

[1] The archaeological remains are scanty: Asoka pillar at Allahabad (Fergusson, Vol. II, no. 4, p. 57). Capital only at Sankisa (*ibid*, 58). Capital only at Tirhut (*ibid*, 58). Capital only at Karle, Bhaja, Bedsa (*ibid*, 60).

[2] The Jains in very early times had *stūpas* and worshipped at them. Even still the *Samosaranas* in some of their temples at Satrunjaya, Girnar, Abu, etc., are survivals of the earlier *stūpas*. They were also known as *Chaityas*—as *stūpas* are still called in Nepal and Tibet.—Bühler, *Legend of the Jaina Stūpa at Mathurā*, *Epigrahia Indica*, Vol. II, Plates at pp. 314-321; *Actes du Vienna Congres Int. Orient*, Vol. III, part ii, plate at p. 142, and *infra*, part iii, p. 130.

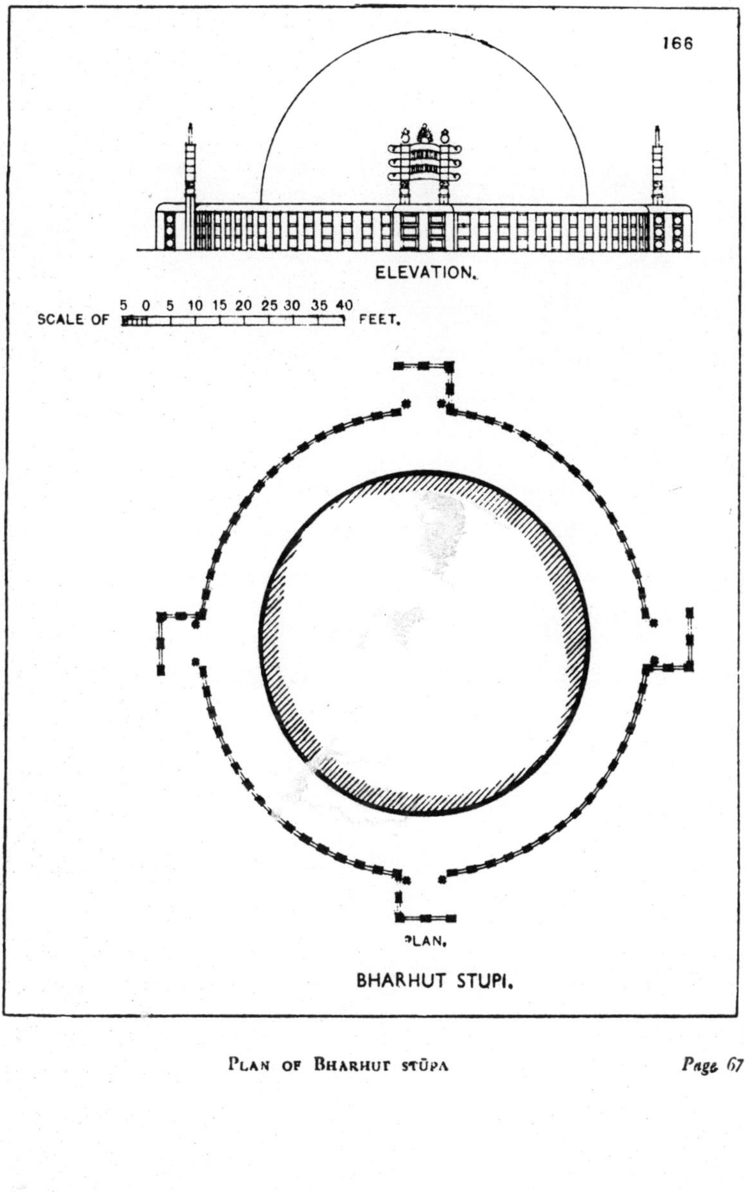

PLAN OF BHARHUT STŪPA

PLATE XXIII

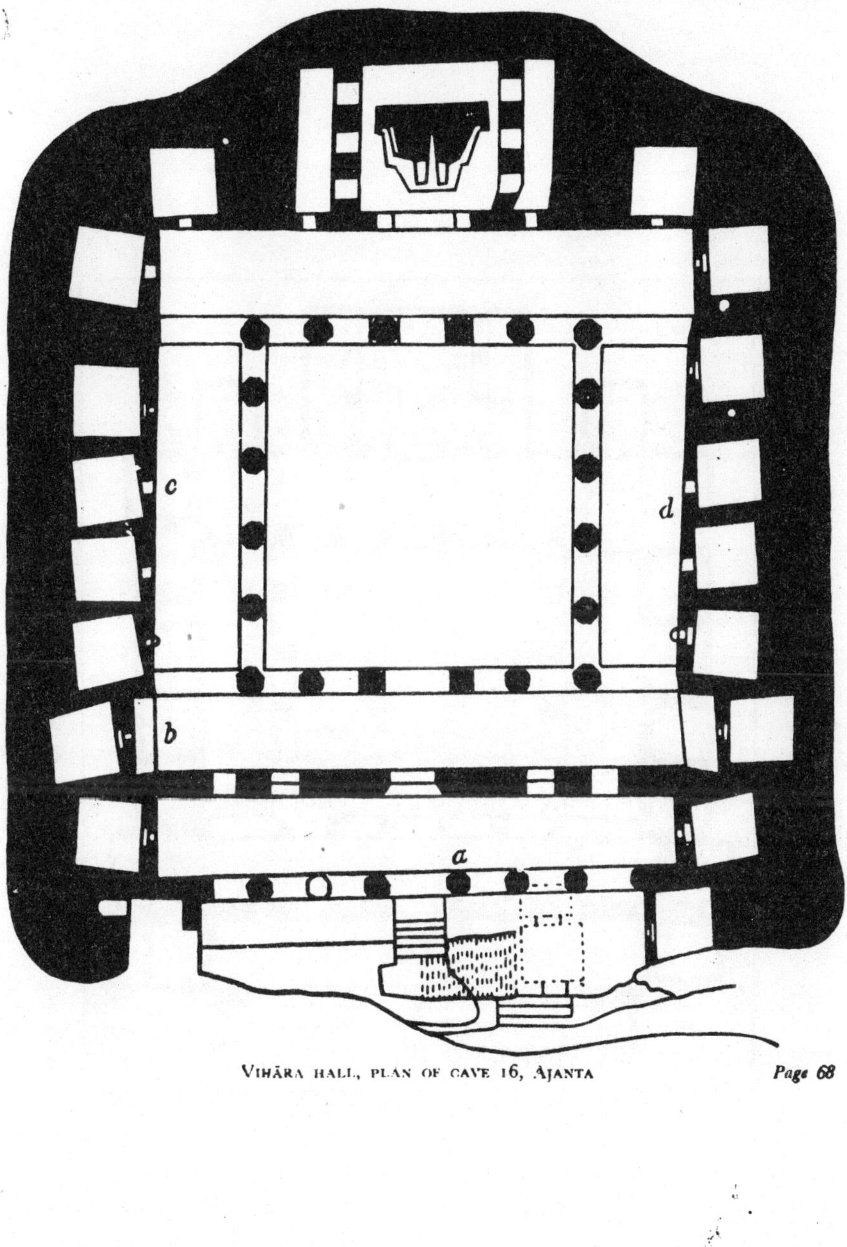

VIHĀRA HALL, PLAN OF CAVE 16, AJANTA

Page 68

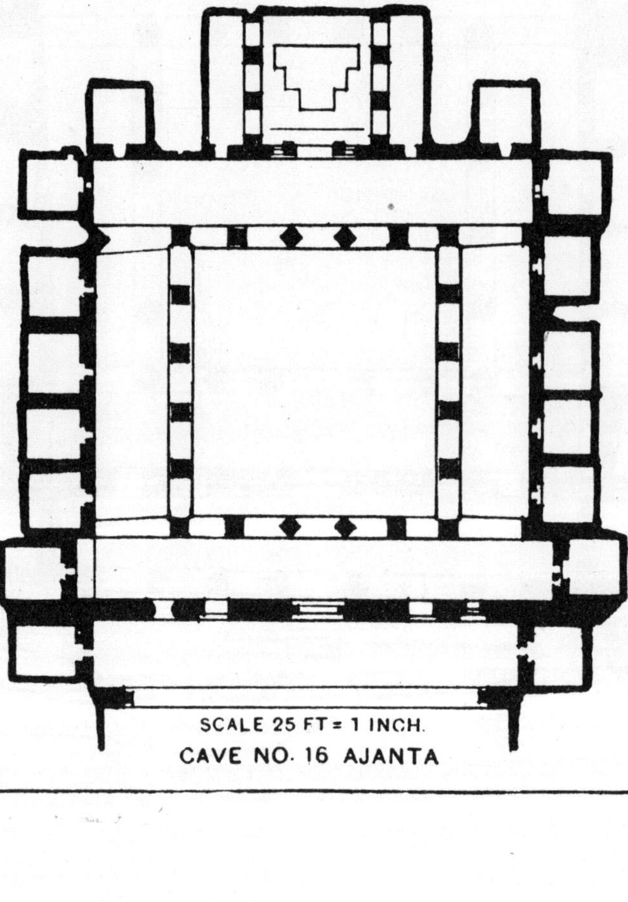

SCALE 25 FT = 1 INCH.

CAVE NO. 16 AJANTA

but were detached from, the *chaityas* or churches. In later times they were furnished with chapels in which the service could be performed independently of the *chaitya* halls which may or may not be found in their proximity.'[1]

The extensiveness of these buildings can be imagined not only from the colossal structures at Burobodur, Angkorvat, and other places, but also from the length of time devoted to getting a house completely built. Thus, it is stated that, 'with reference to the work of a small *vihāra*, it may be given in charge (to an overseer) as a *navakamma* (new work) for a period of five or six years, that on an *aḍḍhayoga* for a period of seven or eight years, that on a large *vihāra* or a *pāsāda* for ten or twelve years.'[2] That the long periods were not idled away will be clear from the following details of houses gathered from the *Vinaya texts*.[3]

'Even in the Buddha's time the size of these monuments had already reached very considerable dimensions. The solid dome erected by the Sākiyas over their share of the ashes from the Buddha's funeral pyre must have been about the same height as the dome of the St. Paul's measured from the roof.'[4]

The selection of building sites shows a highly developed good taste. The *ārāma* (rest-house), well fitted for quiet people, is stated to be built 'not too far from the town and not too near, convenient for going and for coming, easily accessible for all who wish to visit him, by day not too crowded, by night not exposed to too much noise and alarm. . .'[5] The whole compound is enclosed with ramparts (*prākāra*) of three kinds, namely, brick walls, stone walls, and wooden fences, which are again surrounded with bamboo fences, thorn fences, and ditches.[6]

[1]Fergusson, *Indian and Eastern Architecture* (1910), Vol. I, pp. 54–55.
The principal examples are at Mumallapura, Son-Bhandar, Nasik, Ajanta, Elura, Bagh, Dhamnon, Kuda, etc.

[2] *Chullavagga*, VI, 17, 1 (Translation, p. 214).

[3] *Ibid*, VI, 5, etc., and *Mahāvagga*.

[4] Rhys Davids, page 83–84. References to a large number of *topes* will be found in the writer's *Encyclopaedia* under *Stūpa*. Buddhaghosha's enumeration of the parts of a palace also shows the popularity of the subject of architecture in Buddhist literature. 'Ayam phasso nāma yathā pāsādam patvā thambho nāma, sesadabhasambhārānam balavapaccayo tulā saṁghāṭā bhitti pādakuṭagopānasipakkhapāsamukhavaṭṭyo thambhe baddhā thambhe patiṭṭhitā evam eva sahajātasampayuttadhamānam balavapaccayo hoti.' (*Atthasālini*, para. 286, p. 107, ed. Müller).

[5] *Chullavagga*, VI, 4, 8 (Translation, p. 187).

[6] *Ibid*, VI, 3, 7, 10 (Translation, pp. 176–177, 187).

Houses were built comprising 'dwelling-rooms and retiring-rooms, and store-rooms, and service halls, and halls with fire-places in them, and store-houses, and closets, and cloisters, and halls for exercise, and wells, and sheds for the wells, and bathrooms, and halls attached to the bathrooms, and ponds, and open-roofed sheds (*maṇḍapas*).'[1] These buildings are meant to be dwelling-houses; so it is stated that 'an *upāsaka* (devotee) has built for his own use a residence, a sleeping room, a stable, a tower, a one-peaked building, a shop, a *boutique*, a storeyed house, an attic, a cave, a cell, a store-room, a refectory, a fire-room, a kitchen, a privy, a place to walk in, a house to walk in, a well, a well-house, a *yantra-gṛiha* (which is supposed by Bühler to be 'a bathing place for hot sitting baths'), a *yantra-gṛiha* room, a lotus pond and a pavilion.'[2]

The inner chambers are divided into three classes, called *śivikā-garbha* or square halls, *nālikā-garbha* or rectangular halls, and *harmya-garbha* which appears to a be large dining-hall.[3] The verandahs (*alinda*) seem to have been a special characteristic of these buildings. The Blessed One (Buddha) says, 'I allow you, O Bhikkhus, covered terraces, inner verandahs, and over-hanging eaves.'[4] The storeyed buildings (*prāsāda*) are stated to be furnished with 'a verandah to it, supported on pillars' with capitals of elephant-head.[5]

[1] *Chullavagga*, VI, 4, 10 (Translation, p. 189).

[2] *Mahāvagga*, III, 5, 9 (Translation, p. 304), also III, 5, 6 (Translation, p. 303).

[3] About the last Buddhaghosha seems to be doubtful and says:

हम्मियग्भो ति कुटागारगब्भो मुदणुच्छादनगब्भो वा ;

But about the other two terms he is clear:

सिविकागब्भो ति चतुरस्सगब्भो ; नालिकागब्भो ति वित्थारतो द्विगुणतिगुणायामो दोघगब्भो (*Chullavagga*, VI, 3, 3). But Oldenberg and Rhys Davids seem to have been wholly misled when they translated these last two by 'palankeen shaped and quart measure shaped,' about the latter of which Indians of even today are quite unfamiliar.

[4] *Chullavagga*, VI, 3, 5 (Translation, p. 175), commented on by Buddhaghosha: आलिन्दो नाम पमुखं वुच्चति।

Compare *Abhidānappadikā*, verse 218:

पघनं नाम यं निखमन्ता च पविसन्ता च पादेहि हनन्ति, तस्स विहार द्वारे उभतो कुट्टं निहरित्वा कतपदेसस्स एतं अधिवचनम् पधानम् ति पि वुच्चति। पकुट्टनतिमज्झे गब्भस्स समन्ता परियागारो वुच्चति पकुटन् ति पाठो। ओसरको ति अनालिन्दके वंसं दत्वा ततो दण्डके ओसारेत्वा कतं छादनपमुखं।

[5] *Ibid*, VI, 14, 1 (Translation, p. 208): हत्थिनखकं supported on the frontal globes (*kumbha*) of elephants, says Buddhaghosha.

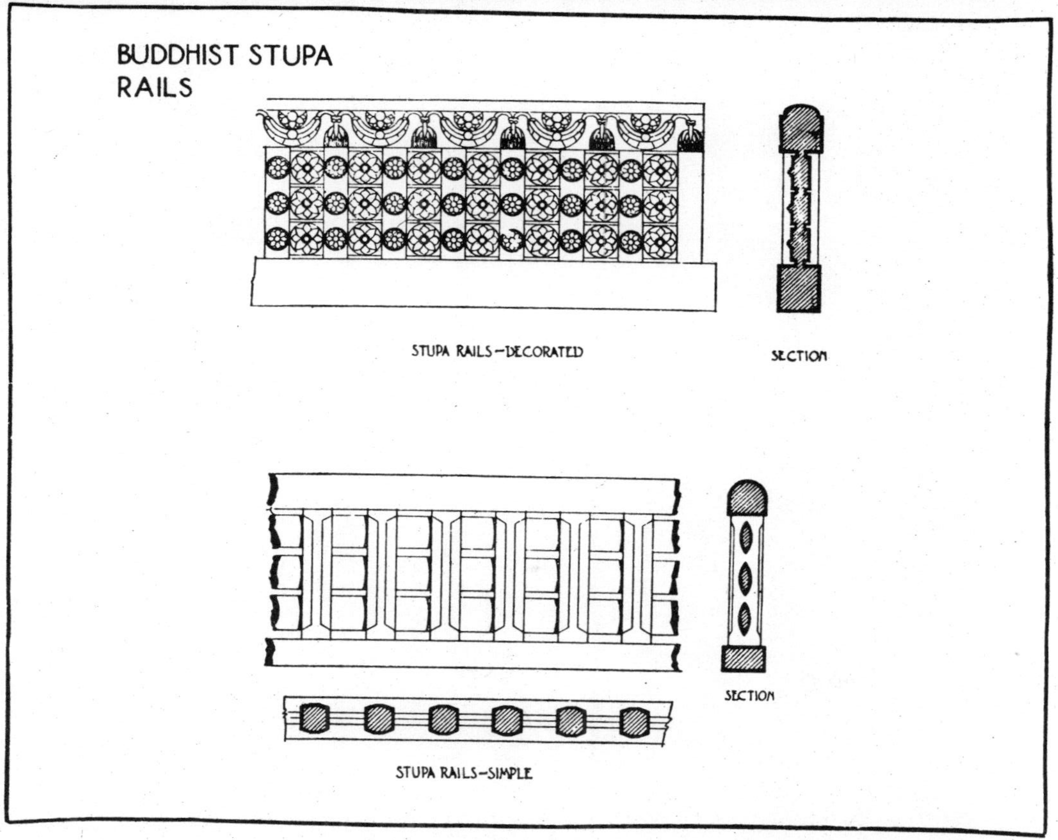

PLAN OF BUDDHIST RAILS

PRASADA OR ROYAL PALACE
FROM PALI TEXTS

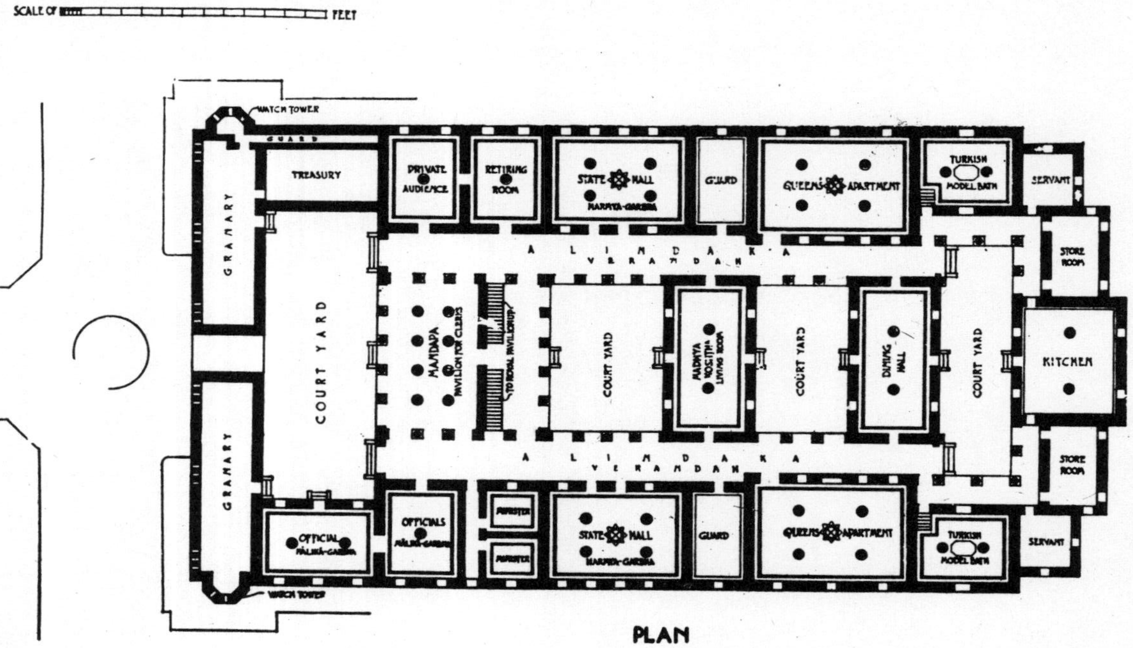

Details of gates, doors, and windows are also elaborate. Gateways are built with rooms and ornamental screen-work over them.[1] And gates are made of stakes interlaced with thorny brakes.[2]

Doors are furnished with 'door-posts and lintel, with hollows like a mortar for the door to revolve in, with projections to revolve in those hollows, with rings on the door for the bolt to work along in, with a block of wood fixed into the edge of the door-post, and containing a cavity for the bolt to go into (called the monkey's head), with a pin to secure the bolt by, with a connecting bolt, with a key-hole, with a hole for a string with which the door may be closed, and with a string for that purpose.'[3] The windows are stated to be of three kinds according as they are made with railings, lattices, and slips of wood.[4] The shutters are adjustable and can be closed or opened whenever required.[5] Five kinds of roofing are mentioned—brick-roofing, stone-roofing, cement-roofing, straw-roofing, and roofing of leaves.[6] The roof is first covered over with skins and plastered within and without; then follow whitewash, blocking, red-colouring, wreath-work and

[1] *Chullavagga*, VI, 4, 10 (Traslation, p. 189); 3, 10, तोरण of which excellent examples in stone have been found at the Sãñchi and Bharhut Topes (Translation, p. 178).

[2] *Ibid*, VI, 3, 10 (Translation, p. 178).

[3] *Ibid*, VI, 3, 8, also 2, 1 and 17, 1 (Translation, p. 177, 161, 213). Compare the distinction between कवाट (door proper) and द्वार (doorway or gateway) (Translation, p. 160, note 3). The keys are stated to be of three kinds, as they are made of bronze, hard wood, or horn (VI, 2, 1; Translation, p. 162).

[4] *Ibid*, VI, 2, 2, वेदिका बातपानं which according to Buddhaghosha means चेतिये वेदिकासदिसं, of which वेदिका has been explained by Rhys Davids in his note on *Mahā Sudassana Sutta*, 1, 60 (*see* R. D.'s *Buddhist Suttas*, p. 262). जालवातपा नाम जालकबदधं, of which जाल literally means 'net' but corresponds to lattice. R. D. advises to compare Anglo-Indian 'jalousic' (p. 162). सालक वातपानं नाम थम्भक वातपानं which 'possibly means with slips of wood arranged horizontally as in our Venetian blinds' (p. 163). In spite of all these, the learned Orientalists Rhys Davids and Oldenberg, would say that 'There were, of course, no windows in our modern sense, but only spaces left in the wall to admit light and air, and covered by lattices of three kinds" (note on *ibid*, VIII, 2, 2, Translation, p. 279).

[5] *Mahāvagga*, 1, 25, 18 (Translation, p. 160); *Chullavagga*, VIII, 2, 2 (Translation, p. 279).

[6] *Chullavagga*, VI, 3, 10 (Translation, p. 179). Compare also VI, 3, 8, 3, 3, etc.

creeper-work.[1] 'The floors were of earth, not of wood, and were restored from time to time by fresh clay or dry cowdung being laid down, and then covered with a whitewash in which sometimes black or red was mixed. From the parallel passage in *Mahāvagga* (I, 25, 15) and *Chullavagga* (VIII, 3, 1), it would seem that the red colouring was used rather for walls, and the black one for floors.'[2] It appears, however, that with a view to removing the dampness, gravel was spread over the floor.[3]

There were stairs of three kinds, namely, brick-stairs, stone-stairs, and wooden-stairs. And they were furnished with *ālaṁbana-bāhu* or balustrades.[4] A more detailed description of flights of stairs (*sopāna*) is given in the *Mahā-Sudasana Suttū* : 'Each of these had a *thambhā*, evidently posts or banisters; *sūchiyo*, apparently cross-bars let into these banisters; and *uṇhīsaṁ*, either a headline running along the top of the banisters, or a figure-head at the lower end of such a headline.'[5]

Thus it is clear that very minute details also are mentioned in this literature. The subject, therefore, seems to have been treated in a more than casual manner.

'The entrance to the great houses was through a large gateway. To the right and left of the passage-way were the treasury and grain stores. The gateway led into an inner courtyard round which were chambers on the ground floor. And above these chambers was a flat roof called the *upari-prāsāda tala*, the upper flat surface of the house, where the owner sat, usually under a pavilion, which answered the purpose at once of a drawing-room, an office, and a dining hall.'

'In the King's palace there was accommodation also for all the business of the State, and for the numerous retinue and the extensive *harem*. . . . The supplementary buildings included three institutions which are strange to us and of considerable historical interest.'

[1] *Chullavagga*, V, 11, 6 (Translation, p. 97); the rendering of the term *āgumpheti*, which also occurs in *Mahāvagga*, V, 11, by 'skins' seems doubtful and unsuitable. Buddhaghosa in his note at the latter place says अगुम्फियन्तीति भित्ति दण्डकादिसु वेठत्वा बन्धाति।

[2] Rhys Davids and Oldenberg, note on *Chullavagga*, VI, 20, 2 (Translation, p. 218).

[3] Compare *Chullavagga*, V, 14, 5.

[4] *Chullavagga*, V, 11, 6 (Translation, p. 96).

[5] *Maha-Sudasana Sutta*, 1, 59. *See* also R. Davids, *Buddhist Suttas*, p. 262, and compare *Chullavagga*, VI, 3, 3.

PLATE XXVI

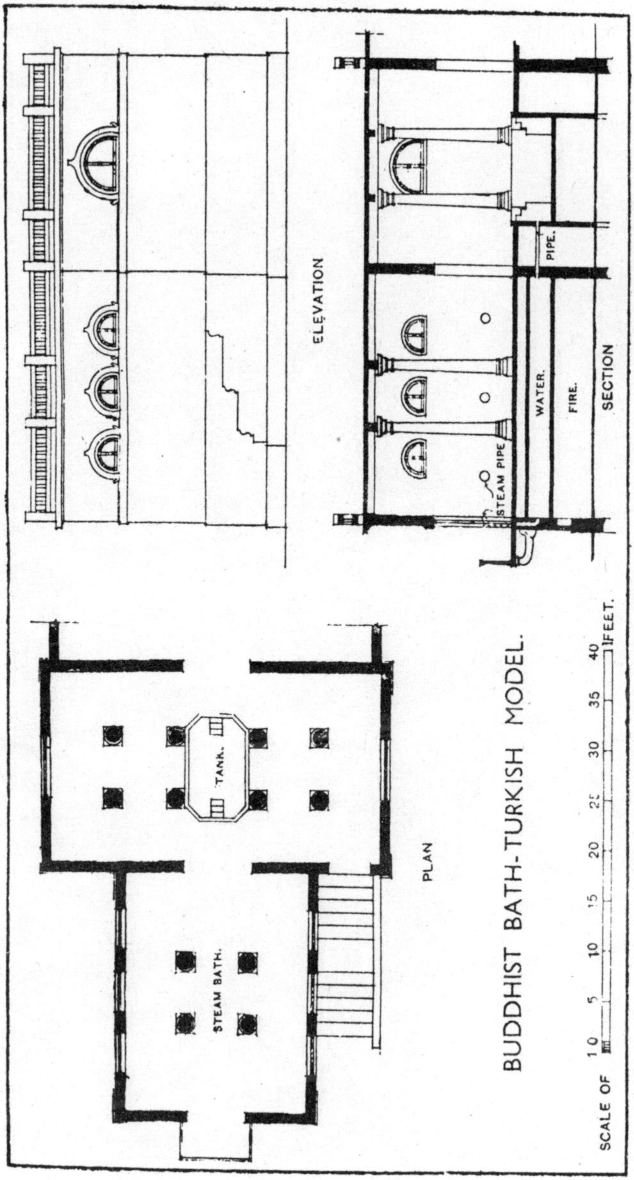

BUDDHIST BATH, GENERALLY KNOWN AS TURKISH BATH

'We are told several times of a building of seven storeys in height.'[1] Professor Rhys Davids seems to be of the opinion that these buildings must have some connexion with the seven-storeyed *ziggarats* of Chaldæa. 'But in India the use to which such seven-storeyed palaces were put was entirely private, and had nothing to do with any worship of the stars.' Still he would add that 'in this case also the Indians were borrowers of an idea.'

'Another sort of building historically interesting were the hot-air baths, described in full in *Vinaya texts*.[2] They were built on an elevated basement faced with brick or stone, with stone-stairs leading up to it, and a railing round the verandah. The roof and walls were of wood, covered first with skins, and then with plaster; the lower part only of the wall being faced with bricks. There was an ante-chamber, and a hot-room, and a pool to bathe in. Seats were arranged round a fire-place in the middle of the hot-room; and to induce perspiration hot water was poured over the bathers. . . .'

In the *Dīgha Nikāya*[3] there is a description of 'another sort of bath, an open-air bathing tank, with flights of steps leading to it, faced entirely with stone, and ornamented both with flowers and carvings.'

'The first step was probably merely to build the cairn more carefully than usual with stones and to cover the outside with fine chunam plaster to give a marble-like surface. The next step was to build the cairn of concentric layers of the huge bricks in use at the time, and to surround the whole with a wooden railing.'

The articles of furniture, which form an important part of the architectural subjects, are also elaborately described in the Buddhist literature. Benches were made long enough to accommodate three persons.[4] The bedstead (*pallaṅka*), or divan, was a separate piece or

[1] *Satta-bhumika-pāsāda*, *Jātaka*, 1, 227, 346; 5, 52, 426; 6, 577. R. Davids refers to a building 'still standing at Pulasti-pura in Ceylon and the thousand-stone pillars on which another was erected at Anurādhapura.' (*Buddhist India*, p. 70).

[2] III, 105–110, 297. 'After the bath there was shampooing, and then a plunge into the pool.' 'It is very curious to find,' observes Rhys Davids, 'at this very early date in the Ganges valley a sort of bathing so closely resembling our modern' so-called 'Turkish bath.' 'Did the Turks,' he asks, 'derive this custom from India?' (*Ibid*, p. 74.)

[3] *Buddhist Suttas*, translated by R. Davids (p. 262 foll.), who refers to 'several ancient baths still to be seen at Anuradhapura in a fair state of preservation in spite of the more than two thousand years that have elapsed since they were first constructed.' (*Ibid*, p. 76.) These baths may well be compared with those discovered at Mahenjo-daro.

[4] *Chullavagga*, VI, 13, 2 (Translation, p. 208).

furniture.[1] Large couches (*āsandi*), or chairs, seem to have been important articles of furniture.[2] Couches covered with canopies are also mentioned.[3] Mention is made of a large variety of chairs, namely, rectangular chair (*āsandako*), arm-chair, sofa (*sattaṅgo*), sofa with arms to it, state chair (*bhadda-pīṭham*), cushioned chair (*pīṭhikā*), chair raised on a pedestal (*etaka-padaka-pīṭham*), chair with many legs (*āmalaka-vaṇṭika-pīṭham*), leaning board (*phalakam*), cane-bottomed chair (*kochchham*) and straw-bottomed chair.[4] Mention is also made of the litter or sedan-chair.[5]

Valuable carpets, rugs, pillows, curtains, and such other luxurious decorations also are elaborately described. Thus mention is made of 'coverlets with long fleece, counterpanes of many colours, woollen coverlets white or marked with thick flowers, mattresses, cotton coverlets dyed with figures of animals, rugs with long hair on one or both sides, carpets inwrought with gold or with silk, large woollen carpets such as the nautch (dancing) girls dance upon, rich elephant housings, horse rugs or carriage rugs, panther or antelope skins, large cushions and crimson cushions.'[6] Pillows are of various kinds; they are stated to be of both 'the size of a man's head' and half 'the size of a man's body.' The Buddha allows the Bhikkhus 'to comb out the cotton, and make the cotton up into pillows if it be of any of these three kinds, cotton produced on trees, cotton produced on creepers, and cotton produced from *potaki* grass.'[7] The bolsters made for the use of high officials were of five kinds, as they were stuffed with wool, cotton cloth, bark, grass, or leaves. There were also coverlets

[1] *Chullavagga*, VI, 14, 1; VI, 8, 1, etc. (Translation, pp. 209, 197); *Mahāvagga*, V, 10, 3 (Translation, p. 27).

[2] *Ibid*, VI, 14, 1; VI, 8, 1, etc. (Translation, pp. 209, 197); *Mahāvagga*, V, 10, 3 (Translation, p. 27). Rhys Davids and Oldenberg under *āsandi*, twice by cushions and once by couches, and Childers by 'chairs' (*see* his Dictionary) It seems to imply Sanskrit *āsana*, which means 'a seat.'

[3] *Mahāvagga*, V, 10, 3 (Translation, p. 27).

[4] *Chullavagga*, VI, 2, 4 (Translation, p. 165). Renderings are mostly those made by Rhys Davids and Oldenberg depending on Buddhaghosha's note. Compare also *Chullavagga*, VI, 20, 2 and VIII, 1, 3. *Apassena-phalakam* as a 'board to lean up against' is also mentioned in *Mahāvagga*, 1, 25, 15, 16. For arm-chair and sofa there seems to be another expression, *apasayam*, *see* Buddhaghosha's note on *Chullavagga*, VI, 2, 4.

[5] *Mahāvagga*, V, 10, 2 (Translation, p. 27).

[6] *Ibid*, V, 10, 3 (Translation, p. 27).

[7] *Chullavagga*, VI, 2, 6 (Translation, p. 167); *see* also IV, 4, 4, and VIII, 1, 3.

for them.[1] The smaller articles like the floor cloth, mosquito curtain, handkerchief and spittoon did not escape the notice of the then house-decorators.'[2]

'It is almost impossible to over-rate the importance of architecture and its associated arts in elucidating and giving precision to our knowledge of Buddhist history and mythology, from the time when it became the religion of the State till it perished in so far as India was concerned.'

'In the rails at Bodhgaya and Bharaut, we have a complete picture of Buddhism as it existed during the great Maurya dynasty (320 to 180 B.C.). At Sanchi and western caves we have as complete a representation of the form it took from the second century before our (Christian) era to the third after it. At Amarāvati, and from the Gandhāra monasteries, we learn what modifications had been introduced between our era and the third century; and from the Ajanta and later caves we trace its history downwards through its period of decay till it faded away altogether.'

'During the first of this thousand years we have no contemporary records except those written in stone, and during the latter we have no books we can depend upon; but the architecture, with its sculptures and paintings, remain, and bear an indelible impress of the thoughts, the feelings, and the aspirations of those who executed them, and supply us with a vast amount of exact knowledge on the subject which is not attainable by any other means now known to us.'[3]

Jain Architecture

The Jainas are known as the Digāmbaras and Svetāmbaras. The former regard, at least theoretically, nudity 'as a sign of holiness, though they are now obliged to part from the outdoor practice of their theory.' The latter are supposed to be 'clad in white.' 'The Jaina religious theories and practices, in many respects, closely resemble those of the Buddhists.'[4] They have 'no veneration for relics like the Buddhists. The proper objects of their worship are the

[1] *Chullavagga*, VI, 2, 7 (Translation, p. 168).

[2] *Ibid*, VI, 20, 1 (Translation, p. 219); V, 14, 1 (Translation, p. 102); *Mahāvagga*, VIII, 18 (Translation, p. 227); for *cholaka*, or handkerchief, *see* also *Chullavagga*, VI, 19 and V, 9, 4.

[3] Fergusson, *Indian and Eastern Architecture*, Vol. I (1910), pp. 249–250.

[4] The Jainas acknowledge no supreme governor, believe in transmigration, regard all animal life as sacred, and revere the Jinas or *Tirthankaras*. They consist of ecclesistics—*Yatis* or *Sādhus*—and lay believers or *Śrāvakas*.

twenty-four Jinas or *Tīrthaṅkaras*, but, like the Buddhists, they allow the existence of Hindu gods, and have admitted into their sculptures at least such of them as are connected with the tales of their saints, among which are Indra or Śakra, Garuḍa, Sarasvatī, Lakshmī, Asuras, Nāgas, Rākshasas, Gandharvas, Apsaras, etc., forming a pantheon of their own, divided into four classes, namely, Bhavanādhipatis, Vyantaras, Jyotishkas, and Vaimānikas. In architecture both Buddhist and Jain structures are more closely connected with the Hindu ones. The Jain style was 'essentially Hindu,' declares Fergusson, 'and was doubtless largely common to all Hindu sects in Western India, but in its evolution it became modified by Jain taste and requirements.'[1] In fact the requirements alone have differentiated also the Buddhist architecture from the Hindu one. 'And, the Brāhmaṇas in turn, through the influence of the workmen, gradually accepted most of the stylistic improvements of their rivals. This seems to have been more especially the case in Gujrat and Rajputana, where the Jainas were very numerous and influential, and we might almost with equal propriety designate their style of architecture as a western Hindu style.'[1]

'The religion of the Buddhists and that of the Jains were so similar to one another, both in their origin and their development of doctrines, that their architecture must also at first have been nearly the same. A strong presumption that the architecture of the two sects was similar arises from the fact of their principal sculptures being so nearly identical that it is not always easy for the casual observer to distinguish what belongs to the one and what to the other; and it requires some experience to do this readily. The *Tirthankaras* are generally represented as seated in the same cross-legged attitude as Buddha, with the same curly hair, and the same solid contemplative expression of countenance. The Śvetambara Jains are also clothed much like the Buddhists.'[2] Thus, like those of the Buddhists, there are Jaina caves at Orissa, at Badami and Aihole, at Dharasinva, Ankai and Elura. There are again the Jain monolithic pillars at Elura and other places much like the Asoka pillars of the Buddhist style. But the Jain structural temples at Lakkundi, Palitana, Girnar, Mount Abu, Pareshnath, Ranpur, Gwalior, Khajuraho, Chitor and other places have more resemblance with the Hindu temples. In fact

[1] Fergusson, *Indian and Eastern Architecture*, II, 5.
[2] *Ibid*, pp. 6-7.

hardly any distinction is noticed between the Hindu temples and modern Jain temples at Sanogarh, Ahmedabad, Delhi and other places.

There is, however, a marked difference of the Jain architecture of the north and of the south. 'The first peculiarity that strikes one as distinguishing the Jain architecture of the south from that of the north, is the division of the southern temples into two classes. Bastis (*Basadi*, *Vasati*, monastery or temple) and Bettas (? *Vasahika*, buildings, including monastery and temple). The former are temples in the usual acceptance of the word, as understood in the north, and, as there, always containing an image of one of the twenty-four *Tīrthaṅkaras*, which is the object there worshipped. The latter are unknown in the north ; and are courtyards usually on a hill or rising ground, open to the sky and containing images, not of a *Tirthankara*, but of Gomata or Gomateśwara so called, though he is not known to the Jains in the north.' While the Jain Bastis at Sravana Belgola would look like an ordinary Hindu temple, the lamp-bearing pillar before it, as also at Guruvāyankeri, resembles the Buddhist free pillars. But the Jain temples at Undābidri and its pillars have similarities with the Buddhist pagodas and pillars of the far eastern colonies of the Hindus.[1]

Brāhmaṇical Architecture

The Buddhist and the Jain architecture, together with all other early Indian architecture, may be included under a general term which, for the want of a better designation, may be called Hindu architecture. Thus for the sake of clarity alone a new division, namely, the Brāhmaṇical architecture, has become necessary, because, otherwise the Buddhist and the Jain groups will be confusing, if not meaningless. Under the Brāhmaṇical group will be understood what are commonly known as Northern or Indo-Aryan architecture, and the Southern or Dravidian, Chalukyan and Pallava architecture. The former is illustrated by the extant Brāhmaṇical rock-cut temples at Elura, Badami, Elephanta, and other places, and structural temples at Pattadakal, Bhuvaneśvara, Kanarak, Puri, Cuttock, Jāspur, Benares, Vrindavan, Khajuraho, Udaipur, Amritsar, Pushkar and other places. The ancient village schemes and town plans have been superimposed by foreign invaders almost out of recognition. But historians

[1] *See* Chap. IX.

like Fergusson have endeavoured to illustrate northern Brāhmanical civil architecture by referring to certain cenotaphs, ghats (landings) reservoirs, dams, and modern palaces at Gwalior, Chitor, Amber and other places. But no dwelling-houses for ordinary people could be traced or reconstructed from archaeological remains.

The Dravidian architecture, also, is illustrated mostly by temples at Elura, Pattadakal, Dharwar, Mamallapuram, Conjeevaram, Tanjore, Tiruvalur, Srirangam, Chidambaram, Ramesvaram, Madura, Tinnevelly, Kumbakonam, Vellor, Perur and other places, as also by the civil architecture comprising palaces at Chandragiri, Madura and Tanjore, and Garden Pavilion at Vijayanagara. The illustrations of the Chalukyan architecture consist of the temples at Somanathpur, Belur, Halebid, and Dharwar, and memorial pillars at Worangul, Mysore and other places. The Pallava architecture is illustrated by the rock-cut temples excavated in the Districts of Trichinopoly, Chingleput, North Arcot, and South Arcot, and also by the ruins of the city of Mahendravādi, and of a great reservoir, the Mahendra tank, on the bank of which exists a Vishṇu temple. Thus the archaeological sources can supply only an imperfect and insufficient survey of Hindu architecture. In order to get an unbiased and more complete idea of our ancient architecture the literary sources are indispensable. Almost a perfect account, with full details of all varieties of architecture namely, religious and civil as well as military, is available from the literary sources, commencing with the epics and concluding with the numerous avowedly architectural treatises, one of which, the *Mānasāra*, attained the recognized position of a standard work and appears to have regulated the art and architecture of the whole country until it became subjugated by foreigners for mere political reasons.

The Epics

The Epics furnish copious description of cities, storeyed buildings, balconies, porticos, triumphal arches, enclosing walls, flights of stone masonry steps for tanks and a variety of other structures, all indicative of a flourishing architecture in the country.

The plan of the city of Ayodhyā is strikingly similar to the town-plan given in the *Mānasāra* and other architectural treatises.[1] 'The temples (*devāyatana*) in this city (Ayodhyā) were as resplendent as

[1] *See* writer's *Encyclopaedia* under *Nagara.*

the sky. Its assembly halls, gardens, and water-sheds or alms-houses (*prapā*) were most elegant; and everywhere were arranged extensive buildings crowded with men and women. . . . The houses were as mines of gems, and the abodes of the goddess of fortune. The steeples (*śikhara*) of the houses were as resplendent as the crests of mountains and bore hundreds of pavilions (*vimāna*) like the celestial palace of the chief among the Devas. The rooms were full of riches and corn, exquisitely gilt and decorated, and seemed as charming as pictures; and they were so arranged that men could pass from one room to another without perceiving any inequality (in the floor).'[1]

The *Mahābhārata* contains short but comprehensive accounts of the cities of Dvārakā (III, 15), Indraprastha (1, 207, 30ff.), a floating city (III, 173, 3), Mithilā (III, 207, 7), and others.

In the *Sabhā-parvan* there are interesting descriptions of some assembly halls. Maya built an assembly hall for the Pāṇḍavas (Chapter I). A description is given also of the assembly halls of Indra (Chapter VII), of Yama (Chapter VIII), of Varuṇa (Chapter IX), of Kubera (Chapter X), and of Brahman (Chapter XI).

These are poetic descriptions, but they must have been based on similar objects actually seen by the poets.

A large number of houses were needed for the accommodation of the kings invited to Indraprastha on the occasion of King Yudhishṭhira's royal feast, *Rājasūya*, and the poet describes the lodgings assigned to the guests: 'O king, these and many other princes of the middle country (India proper) came to the great ceremonial, *Rājasūya*, of the sons of Pāṇḍu. By order of the virtuous monarch to them were assigned dwellings replete with refreshments of every kind, and having by them charming lakes and ranges of ornamental plants. . . . Those houses were lofty as the peaks of the Kailāśa mountain, most charming in appearance, and provided with excellent furniture. They were surrounded on all sides by well-built high walls of a white colour. The windows were protected by golden lattices and decorated with a profusion of jewellery. The stairs were easy of ascent; the rooms were furnished with commodious seats, and clothing, and garlands; and the whole was redolent with the perfume of the finest agallochum. The houses were white as the goose, bright as the moon, and looked most picturesque even from a distance of four miles. They

[1] *Rāmāyaṇa*, I, 5, 10–15. Compare also the description of Laṅkākāṇḍa (VI), Sarga III.

were free from obstructions, provided with doors of uniform height, but of various quality, and inlaid with numerous metal ornaments, even as the peak of the Himālaya. The princes were refreshed by the very sight of those mansions.'[1]

'In the story of Nala, allusion is made to a lofty balcony from which men were seen from a great distance; and in the *Rāmāyaṇa*, Mantharā . . . looks out from an upper window of the palace to notice the rejoicings of the people in the street on the nomination of Rāma to the vice-kingship of Kośala.'[2]

'In the city (described in the Epics) special palaces existed for the king, the princes, the chief priests, ministers, and military officers. Besides these and humble dwellings (the larger houses being divided into various courts),[3] there were various assembly halls, courts of justice, and the booths of small traders, with goldsmith's shops, and the work-places of other artisans.'[4]

'The words *toraṇa*, arched gateway; *harmya*, masonry house; *devāyatana*, temple; *sabhā*, assembly hall; *prāsāda*, palace; *śikhara*, steeple; and *vimāna*, pavilion, in the above extract (from the *Rāmāyaṇa*) are noteworthy. None of them can consistently be applied to huts and thatched houses for which the poets invariably use different words. Prurient fancy may extol and exaggerate, but it never suffices to create names of material objects which the fanciful have never seen or heard of; a Ruskin may amuse himself and his readers by building an imaginary palace in the air,[5] but his ideas are always of the earth, earthly, taken from material objects with which he is familiar.'[6]

The Purāṇas

The *Purāṇas* generally deal with the subject of architecture in greater detail than the classes of literature referred to above. Casual references like those given above from the preceding classes of literature are frequently met with in all the nineteen great *Purāṇas*.[7] Some

[1] *Mahābhārata*, As. Soc. Edition, I, p. 354.
[2] R. L. Mitra, *Indo-Aryans*, I, p. 21.
[3] Compare the *Mānasāra*, under *Prākāra*, in the writer's *Encyclopaedia*.
Compare 'These courts have mosaic pavements of gold' (*R.*, VI, 37: 27, 58, *Mbh.* I, 185, 20; II, 33 and 34).
[4] Hopkins, *J. A. O. S.*, 13, under *City*.
[5] *The Queen of the Air*, by John Ruskin, 1869.
[6] Mitra, *Indo-Aryans*, pp. 22–23.
[7] वायु, स्कन्द (also called कुमार), मत्स्य, विष्णु, भागवत, पद्म, गरुड़, अग्नि, ब्रह्म, शिव, नारद, मार्कण्डय, वराह, वामन, लिङ्ग, कूर्म, ब्रह्माण्ड, ब्रह्मवैवर्त and भविष्य।

nine *Purāṇas* have, however, treated the subject more systematically, and have materially contributed to the later *Silpa-śāstras* themselves. The *Matsya-Purāṇa*, for instance, has eight comprehensive chapters dealing in great detail with architecture and sculpture.[1] In one of these chapters accounts are given of eighteen ancient architects.[2] One chapter is devoted to the column, which is the regulator of the whole composition of a building.[3] Columns are divided into five classes, as in the western system, and their component parts into eight mouldings exactly like those of the Græco-Roman orders.[4] Buildings are described in two chapters together with their architectural details, such as plans, measures, classifications, pavilions, halls, storeys, steeples, and cupolas.[5] Some of the building materials are also discussed in a separate chapter.[6] The remaining three chapters are devoted exclusively to sculpture.[7] One of these deals with a very technical subject, namely, the *tālamāna* or proportionate measures of an image[8]; and in the other two the images of the Phallus and its Pedestal are described.

The *Skanda*, which is another early *Purāṇa*, has devoted three chapters to the subject. One of these refers to the laying out of a large city.[9] In another, mention is made of the construction of a golden hall and three chariots in accordance with the descriptions supplied, and the names of the architects are added.[10] The details of the construction of a special pavilion for the wedding of a royal princess is described in another chapter wherein reference is made to the painting also.[11] Sculpture is associated with architecture; but painting is hardly mentioned in these works.

[1] Chapters 252, 255, 257, 258, 262, 263, 269 and 270.

[2] *See* p. 245.

[3] Chapter 255, स्तम्भमाननिर्णय ।

[4] For details, *see* pp. 228, 230.

[5] Chapters 269 (प्रासादलक्षण), and 270 (मण्डपलक्षण)

[6] Chapter 257, दार्वाहरण ।

[7] Chapters 258 (नवताललक्षण), 292 (पीठिकालक्षण), and 263 (लिङ्गलक्षण).

[8] For details, *see* p. 199.

[9] माहेश्वरखण्ड, Part II, Chapter 25—स्वयं विश्वकर्म द्वारा निर्मापितमहीनगरस्थापनवर्णनम् ।

[10] वैष्णवखण्ड, Part II, Chapter 25—निखिलसाहित्यसम्भारसंग्रहपत्रं श्रुत्वा इन्द्रद्युम्नाज्ञया पद्मनिधिना स्वर्णशालानिर्माणम् । नारदाज्ञया विश्वकर्मणा स्यन्दनत्रयनिर्माणम् । तस्य रथस्य नारद करेण स्थापनम् । तत्प्रसंगेन रथस्थापनप्रकारविधिवर्णनम् ।

[11] माहेश्वरखण्ड, Part I, Chapter 24—हिमालयन स्वसुताया विवाहार्थं गर्गाचार्यपुरोहितं पुरस्कृत्य विश्वकर्मद्वारा पूर्वमण्डपनिर्माणादिवर्णनम् । विवाहमण्डपे चातुर्येण सर्वदेवताप्रतिकृतिचित्रविन्यासं श्रुत्वा सर्वेषां देवानां शङ्काप्राप्तिः ।

The *Garuḍa-Purāṇa* makes some valuable additions to the contributions of this class of literature to architecture. One of the four chapters devoted to this subject deals systematically with all the three classes of buildings, namely, residential, military and religious, as well as with the laying out of pleasure gardens and pavilions therein. Thus, in this chapter residential buildings, forts and fortified towns, temples and monasteries are described along with garden-houses.[1] The following chapter treats exclusively of religious buildings.[2] The remaining two chapters are devoted to sculpture, one dealing with rules regarding the construction of an image and the other with the installation of images in temples.[3]

The *Agni*, among all the *Purāṇas*, has dilated on the subject at great length. There are sixteen chapters of which one deals with town-planning, two with residential buildings and the remaining thirteen with sculpture. The importance of its contributions to the *Silpa-śāstra* lies, however, specially in two things. First, it seems to have been aware of the *Mānasāra*, the standard work on architecture.[4] Secondly, its chapter on town-planning is a real addition to the *Purāṇas*' contributions to architecture.[5] Temples and residential buildings are described in two chapters.[6] The treatment of sculpture also is unique, and is the most exhaustive of all the accounts given in the *Purāṇas*. It deals with almost all classes of religious images, both of male and female deities, as well as of those not falling under either of these categories. Thus, of the thirteen chapters on sculpture, one is devoted to the description of the sun-god and his attendants,[7] one to the ten incarnations of Vishṇu,[8] two others also to Vishṇu under the name of Vāsudeva,[9] one to the guardian angel of the house,[10]

[1] Chapter 46—प्रासादारामदुर्गदेवालयमठादिवास्तुमानलक्षणनिरूपणम् ।

[2] Chapter 47—प्रासादलिङ्गमण्डपादिशुभवास्तुलक्षनिरूपणम् ।

[3] Chapters 45—शालग्राममूर्तिलक्षणम्, and 48—देवानां प्रतिष्ठाविधिः ।

[4] Compare तदूर्ध्वे च भवेद् बेदी सकण्ठा मानसारका । (Chapter 42, verse 16)
तृतीयो वेदिका त्वग्ने सकण्ठो मानसारकः । (Chapter 104, verse 11).
For details, *see* later p. 250.

[5] Chapter 106—नगरादिवस्तु

[6] Chapters 42—प्रासादलक्षणकथनम्, and 104—प्रासादलक्षणम् ।
For details, *see* later p. 189-190.

[7] Chapter 51—सूर्यादिप्रतिमालक्षणम् ।

[8] Chapter 49—मत्स्यादिदशावतारकथनम् ।

[9] Chapters 44—वासुदेवादिप्रतिमा, and 60 -वासुदेवादिप्रतिष्ठाविधिः ।

[10] Chapter 43—प्रासाददेवतास्थापनम् ।

one to the goddess of fortune,[1] two to the female deities in general,[2] four to the Phallus and its Pedestal,[3] and the remaining one to the stone gods, Sālagrāma and others.[4]

The *Nārada-Purāṇa* practically completes the *Purāṇas'* contributions to architecture. In a single chapter it describes the construction of pools, wells, and tanks, as well as temples.[5] The *Liṅga-Purāṇa* supplements the contributions by adding an account of the construction of sacrificial pits, together with a description of temples and the installation of deities therein.[6]

The *Vāyu*, which is one of the very early *Purāṇas*, maintains its unique position by dealing with the construction of various temples built upon mountain tops.[7] Examples of these temples are still found on several peaks of the Himālaya and the Vindhya ranges. For the *Brahmāṇḍa-Purāṇa* there was very little left to add. In a single chapter it describes the construction of temples and residential buildings.[8]

The *Bhavishya*, partly a late *Purāṇa*, has also nothing new to contribute. Three of its chapters are devoted to sculpture.[9] Architecture proper, comprising the description of temples, is treated in a single chapter.[10] The most striking feature of this *Purāṇa* is that the number, name, and other architectural details of the buildings described in it are identical with the twenty types found in the *Matsya-Purāṇa*, and the *Bṛihat-saṁhitā* of Varāhamihira.[11]

The *Brahma-vaivarta Purāṇa* has referred to the subject of architecture in some eleven chapters.[12] The cities of Dvārakā, Mathurā Vṛindāvana, and Golaka are described in five chapters.[13] The

[1] Chapter 62—लक्ष्मीप्रतिमाविधि: ।

[2] Chapters 50—देवीत्रतिमालक्षणम्, and 52—देवीप्रतिमालक्षणम् ।

[3] Chapters 53—लिङ्गलक्षणम्, 54—लिङ्गमानादिकथनम्, 45—पिण्डिकालक्षणम्, and 55—पिण्डिकालक्षणकथनम् ।

[4] Chapter 46—शालग्रामादिमूर्तिलक्षणम् ।

[5] Part I, Chapter 13—देवतायतनवापीकूपतडागादिनिर्माणम् ।

[6] Part II, Chapter 46—यागकुण्डविन्यासकथनपूर्वकं सर्वेषां देवानां स्थापनविधिनिरूपणम् ।

[7] Part I, Chapter 39—शैलस्थितविविधदेवालयकीर्तनम् ।

[8] Chapter 7—गृहादिनिर्माणम् ।

[9] The *Madhya-parvan*, Chapter 12—प्रतिदेवताप्रतिमालक्षणवर्णनम् ।
The *Brahma-parvan*, Chapters 131—मूर्तिस्थानम्, and 132—प्रतिमामानम् ।

[10] The *Brahma-parvan*, Chapter 130—प्रासादलक्षणवर्णनम् ।

[11] For details, *see* pp. 190–195, 244.

[12] *Śrī-Kṛishṇa-janma-khaṇḍa*, Chapters 2, 4, 5, 6, 10, 17, 72, 92, 103, 104 and 128.

[13] Chapters 103, 104 (vv. 6–22), 72 (vv. 2–14), 17 (vv. 14–27), 4 (vv. 73–169).

residential houses of Rādhā, Kubjā, and Nanda are referred to in three chapters.[1] The cars and the dancing court (*rāsa-maṇḍala*) are described in five chapters.[2]

The *Bṛihat-saṁhitā*, usually classed under the astronomical and astrological treatises, is but a semi-*Purāṇa*, dealing, as it does, with heterogeneous subjects like the *Purāṇas* themselves. Its authorship is attributed to Varāhamihira, who is supposed to be one of the nine traditional gems in the court of a mythical Vikramāditya,[3] and is thus stated to be a contemporary of Kālidāsa, a poet of unrivalled fame. In this treatise there are but five chapters devoted to both architecture and sculpture. But the subjects have been treated with a master hand. The chapters open with a definition of the science of architecture, and the author goes on to describe, briefly but succinctly and to the point, the suitable building sites, testing of soil, general plan, comparative measures of storeys and doors, and carvings thereon, and other important parts of a building. The preliminary subjects are described in the opening chapter.[4] Then follows the description of the buildings proper, under the same twenty types as in the *Matsya-* and the *Bhavishya-Purāṇas*, the names and details being identical.[5] The preparation of cement is discussed in a separate chapter.[6] One whole chapter is devoted to the construction of the necessary articles of house-furniture, such as bedsteads, couches, and seats.[7] Quite consistently with his sense of proportion Varāhamihira devotes only one chapter to sculpture, where, too, the details of images are described in a scientific manner which is missing in other ancient literature.[8] He is, however, accused of being 'in the habit of uncritically copying his authorities' and misappropriating their materials. But in his treatise seven architectural authorities are mentioned distinctly.[9]

[1] Chapters 5 (vv. 1–87), 92 (vv. 10–11, 41–60) and 72 (vv. 29–31).

[2] Chapters 2 (vv. 39–58), 6 (vv. 99–105), 10 (vv. 34–37), 128 (vv. 38–41) and 92 (vv. 26–53).

[3] For the names of the nine gems, *see* p. 241, note 1.

[4] Chapter 53—वास्तुविद्या ।

[5] Chapter 56—प्रासादलक्षणम् ।
For fuller details, *see* pp. 192, 193, 194.

[6] Chapter 57—वज्रलेपलक्षणम् ।

[7] Chapter 79—शय्यासनलक्षणम् ।

[8] Chapter 58—प्रतिमालक्षणम् ।

[9] गार्ग and मनु (LVI, 30-31), वसिष्ठ (LVIII, 8), भास्कर (LVIII, 52), विश्वकर्मन् (LI, 29), नग्नजित् (LVIII, 4, 15) and मय (LI, 29 ; LVII, 8).

The Āgamas

The term *Āgama* generally implies a traditional doctrine or precept, a sacred writing or scripture, and hence the *Vedas*. But there is a special class of work inculcating the mystical worship of Sivạ and Sakti like the *Tantras* : they belong to South India and are known as the *Āgamas*.[1] They are encyclopaedic works like the *Purāṇas*, whose ultimate object is also to discuss the worship of the Triad. The *Purāṇas*, however, deal with all the three deities forming the holy Trinity, although Vishṇu has received preference, and to his worship fourteen of the *Purāṇas* are devoted. The *Āgamas*, on the other hand, deal mostly with Siva. Obviously they are intended to represent the *Purāṇas* of South India. These *Āgamas* of *Dākshiṇātya* are in fact more extensive than the *Purāṇas* of *Āryāvarta*. There are as many as twenty-eight recognized *Āgamas*,[2] while the number of the great *Purāṇas* is not more than eighteen or nineteen.[3]

The *Āgamas*, like the *Purāṇas*, incidentally deal with architectural subjects ; their contributions to the *Silpa-śāstra* are, however, more extensive and valuable. Some of the *Āgamas* deal with very technical matters, which are not met with in the *Purāṇas*. Moreover, some *Āgamas* to all intents and purposes are but architectural treatises. The *Kāmikāgama*, for instance, devotes sixty chapters out of a total of seventy-five to architecture and sculpture, and its treatment of the subjects can hardly be surpassed by that of an avowedly architectural treatise. Just like a *Silpa-śāstra* it begins systematically with the preliminary matters, such as the testing and preparation of soil, selection of sites, scheme of measurement and the finding out of the cardinal points by means of gnomons for the orientation of buildings, and the site-plans. Buildings proper are described under twenty types, just as

[1] Compare the traditional definition of the *Āgama* :
आगतं पञ्चवक्त्रात्तु गतं च गिरिजानने ।
मतं च वासुदेवस्य तस्मादागममुच्यते ॥

[2] (1) कामिकागम, (2) सुप्रभेदागम, (3) योगजागम, (4) चिन्त्यागम, (5) करणागम, (6) अजितागम, (7) दीप्तागम, (8) सूक्ष्मागम, (9) सहस्रागम, (10) अंशुमानागम, (11) विजयागम, (12) निःश्वासागम, (13) स्वायंभुवागम, (14) असितागम, (15) विरागागम, (16) रौरवागम, (17) मुकुटागम, (18) विमलागम, (19) चन्द्रज्ञानागम, (20) बिम्बागम, (21) प्रोद्गीतागम, (22) ललितागम, (23) सिद्धागम, also called वैखानसागम, (24) सन्तानागम, (25) सर्वोक्तागम, (26) परमेश्वरागम, (27) किरणागम, (28) वातुलागम,
There are several other lists of these works. But this one appears to be the most authentic.

[3] *See* above, p. 80, note 7.

in the *Matsya-* and *Bhavishya-Purāṇas*, as well as in the *Bṛihat-saṁhitā*. But, unlike the *Purāṇas*, there is in the *Kāmikāgama* a discussion of architectural matters under some very highly technical classifications, such as the styles, *Nāgara*, *Drāviḍa*, and *Vesara*; shapes, masculine, feminine, and neuter; *Śuddha*, *Miśra*, and *Saṁkīrṇa*, depending respectively on a single material, mixture of two materials, and the amalgamation of many materials; *Saṁchita*, *Asaṁchita*, and *Apasaṁchita*, otherwise known as *Sthānaka*, *Āsana*, and *Śayana*, which, in case of temples, depend on the erect, sitting, and reclining postures of the image.[1] Another very technical matter referred to is *āyādi* formulas, so very important in selecting the right proportions.[2] For the close similarity of this *Āgama* with the *Śilpa-śāstras* it is, however, necessary to glance over the following *paṭalas* or chapters together with the corresponding chapters of the standard *Śilpa-śāstra*, the *Mānasāra*, which is referred to in more detail elsewhere in this volume[3]:

11. *Bhū-parikshā-vidhi*—examination of soil (*Mānasāra*, Chapter IV bearing the same title).
12. *Praveśa-bali-vidhi*—offerings (*M.*, VIII).
13. *Bhū-parigraha-vidhi*—selection of site (*M.*, V).
14. *Bhū-karshaṇa-vidhi*—ploughing the site (*M.*, V).
15. *Śaṅku-sthāpana-vidhi*—gnomons (*M.*, VI).
16. *Mānopakaraṇa-vidhi*—system of measurement (*M.*, II).
17. *Pada-vinyāsa*—site-plan (*M.*, VII).
18. *Sūtra-nirmāṇa*—making cord (*M.*, II).
19. *Vāstu-deva-bali*—offerings to the guardian angel of the house (*M.*, VIII), cf. 12.
20. *Grāmādi-lakshaṇa*—laying out villages and towns (*M.*, IX, X).
21. *Vistārāyāma-lakskaṇa*—dimensions (*M.*, XI).
22. *Āyādi-lakskaṇa*—a special kind of architectural and sculptural measurement used in selecting the right proportion (*M.*, LXIV).
24. *Daṅdikā-vidhi*—dealing with doors and gateways (*M.*, XXXVIII, XXXIX, XXXIII).
25. *Vīthi-dvārādi-māna*—roads and doors (*M.*, IX, X, XXXIX).

[1] For fuller information, consult the writer's *Encyclopaedia* under these terms, and also *see* pp. 187, 195.

[2] For details, *see* the writer's *Encyclopaedia* under *Shaḍvarga*, and also *see* p. 279, note 1.

[3] *See* Chapter IV, pp. 97–158.

26. *Grāmādi-devatā-sthāpana*—temples in villages and towns (*M.*, IX, X).
28. *Grāmādi-vinyāsa*—more details on villages and towns (*M.*, IX, X), cf. 20.
29. *Brahma-deva-padādi*—more details on site-plan (*M.*, VII), cf. 17.
30. *Grāmādi-aṅga-sthāna-nirmāṇa*—more details on villages and towns (*M.*, IX, X), cf. 20, 26, 28.
31. *Garbha-nyāsa*—foundations (*M.*, XII).
32. *Bāla-sthāpana-vidhi*—the installation of *Bāla*—not mentioned in *M.*
33. *Grāma-gṛiha-vinyāsa*—the arrangement of houses in villages and towns (*M.*, IX, X), cf. 20, 26, 28, 30.
34. *Vāstu-Sānti-vidhi*—not mentioned in *M.*
35. *Śālā-lakshaṇa-vidhi*—halls, etc. (*M.*, XXXV).
36. *Viśesha-lakshaṇa-vidhi*--not mentioned in *M.*
37. *Dvi-śālā-lakshaṇa-vidhi*—houses with two compartments, in many places in *M.*
38. *Chatuḥ-śālā-lakshaṇa-vidhi*—houses with four compartments, in many places in *M.*
40. *Vardhamāna-śālā-lakshaṇa*—more details on *Śālās* (*M.*, XXXV), cf. 35, 37, 38.
41. *Nandyāvarta-vidhi*—more details on *Śālās* (*M.*, XXXV), cf. 35, 37, 38, 40.
42. *Svastika-vidhi*—more details on *Śālās* (*M.*, XXXV), cf. 35, 37, 38, 40, 41.
43. *Paksha-śālā-vidhi*—more details on side-halls or ante-chambers (*M.*, XXXV), cf. 35, 37, 38, 40, 41, 42.
44. *Asti* (*Hasti*) *śālā-vidhi*—more details on *Śālās* (*M.*, XXXV), cf. 35, 37, 38, 40, 41, 42, 43.
45. *Mālikā-lakshaṇa-vidhi*—a special kind of buildings (cf. *M.*, XIX to XXX).
46. *Lāngala-mālikā-vidhi*—more details on *Mālikā* buildings, cf. 45.
47. *Maulika-mālikā-vidhi*—more details on *Mālikā* buildings. cf. 45, 46.
48. *Padma-mālikā-vidhi*—more details on *Mālikā* buildings, cf. 45, 46, 47.
49. *Nāgarādi-vidhi*—not separately treated in *M.*
50. *Bhūmi-lamba-vidhi*—dimensions of storeys (*M.*, XI)

51. *Ādyeshṭaka-vidhāna-vidhi*—laying the foundation stone, in many places in *M*.
52. *Upapīṭha-vidhi*—pedestals (*M*., XIII).
53. *Pāda-māna-vidhi*—pillars (*M*., XV).
54. *Prastara-vidhi*—entablatures (*M*., XVI).
55. *Prāsāda-bhushaṇa-vidhi*—the articles of house furniture (*M*., L).
56. *Kaṇṭha-lakshaṇa-vidhi*—the neck parts of buildings, in many places in *M*.
57. *Śikhara-lakshaṇa-vidhi*—the top parts of buildings, in many places in *M*.
58. *Stūpikā-lakshaṇa-vidhi*—steeples or domes of buildings, in many places in *M*.
59. *Nālādi-sthāpana-vidhi*—construction of water-ways and drains, in many places in *M*.
60. *Eka-bhumyādi-vidhi*—buildings of one and more storeys (*M*., XIX–XXX).
61. *Mūrdhni-sthāpana-vidhi*—construction of tops of buildings, in many places in *M*.
62. *Liṅga-lakshaṇa-vidhi*—the Phallus (*M*., LII).
63. *Aṅkurārpaṇa-vidhi*—literally sowing the seed, not separately treated in *M*.
64. *Liṅga-pratishṭhā-vidhi*—installation of the Phallus (*M*., LII).
65. *Pratimā-lakshaṇa-vidhi*—images (*M*., LXIV, etc.).
67. *Devatā-sthāpana-vidhi*—installation of images of deities (*M*., LI, LIV, LV, LVI, LXIV, etc.).
68. *Pratimā-pratishṭhā-vidhi*—more details on images, cf. 65, 67.
69. *Vimāna-sthāpana-vidhi*—buildings (*M*., XVIII).
70. *Maṇḍapa-sthāpana-vidhi*—pavilions (*M*., XXXIV).
71. *Prākāra-lakskaṇa-vidhi*—courts and enclosures (*M*., XXXI).
72. *Parivāra-sthāpana-vidhi*—temples of attendant deities (*M*., XXXII).
74. *Vṛishabha-sthāpana-vidhi*—the bull, the riding animal of Śiva (*M*., LXII).
75. *Gopura-sthāpana-vidhi*—the construction of gate-houses (*M*., XXXIII).

The *Karaṇāgama* also devotes much space to architecture and sculpture. There are thirty-seven chapters in this *Āgama*, which deal with those subjects exhaustively. It makes a distinct addition to the *Āgamas*' contributions to the *Śilpa-śāstras*. It contributes two valuable chapters dealing with the details of the nine and ten *tāla* measures.[1] This is also a highly technical matter concerning sculpture and entirely missing in the *Purāṇas*. This *Āgama* also has close similarities with the *Mānasāra*, which will appear, however imperfectly, from the following list of chapters :

Part I, chapters (*paṭalas*)—

3. *Vāstu-vinyāsa*—classification of building-sites (*Mānasāra, Vastu-prakaraṇa*, Chapter III).
4. *Ādyeshṭaka-vidhi*—laying the foundation stone, mentioned in many places in *M*.
5. *Adhishṭhāna-vidhi*—bases (*M*., XIV).
6. *Garbha-nyāsa-vidhi*—foundations (*M*., XII).
7. *Prāsāda-lakshaṇa-vidhi*—buildings (cf. *M*., XVIII, XIX—XXX).
8. *Prākāra-lakshaṇa-vidhi*—courts and enclosures (*M*., Chapter XXXI).
9. *Liṅga-lakshaṇa-vidhi*—the Phallus (*M*., LII).
10. *Mūrdhnishṭaka-lakshaṇa*—ornaments at the topmost parts of buildings—in many places in *M*.
11. *Pratimā-lakshaṇa*—images (*M*., LXIV, LI, LIV—LXII).
12. *Strī-māna-dasa-tāla-lakshaṇa*—intermediate type of *daśa* (ten) *tāla* measurement, used for the images of females (*M*., LXVI).
13. *Kaṇishṭha-daśa-tāla-lakshaṇa*—the smallest type of *daśa* (ten) *tāla* measurement (*M*., LIX).
14. *Nava-tālottama-lakshaṇa*—the largest type of *nava* (nine) *tāla* measurement (*M*., LIX).
16. *Bali-karma-vidhi*—offerings (*M*., VIII).
19. *Mṛit-saṃgrahaṇa-vidhi*—collection and preparation of soil (for images), not treated in a separate chapter in *M*.
20. *Aṅkurārpaṇa-vidhi*—literally sowing the seed, not treated in a separate chapter in *M*.
41. *Mahābhisheka-vidhi*—great coronation or anointing (cf. *M*., XLIX).
56. *Vāstu-homa-vidhi*—sacrificial offerings in connexion with the construction of a house (cf. 16).
59. *Liṅga-sthāpana-vidhi*—installation of the Phallus (*M*., LII), cf. 9.

[1] For detail, consult the writer's *Encyclopaedia* under *Tālamāna*, and *see* pp. 149, 153-154.

60. *Parivāra-sthāpana-vidhi*—the temples of the attendant deities (*M.*, XXXII).
61. *Bali-pīṭha-pratishṭhā-vidhi*—seat of sacrifice, not treated in a separate chapter in *M.*
62. *Ratna-liṅga-sthāpana-vidhi*—more details on the Phallus (cf. 9, 59).
66. *Parivāra-bali*—more details on the attendant deities (cf. 60).
88. *Bhakta-sthāpana-vidhi*—on the images of devotees (*M.*, LIX).
136. *Mṛit-saṁgrahaṇa*—more details on the collection and preparation of soil (cf. 19).

Part II, chapters (*paṭalas*)—

4. *Kīla-parīkshā*—the nail at the top, not separately treated in *M.*
5. *Gopura-vidhāna*—gate-houses (*M.*, XXXIII).
6. *Maṇḍapa-lakskaṇa*—pavilions (*M.*, XXXIV).
7. *Pīṭha-lakshaṇa*—pedestals (*M.*, XIII, LIII).
8. *Śakti-lakshaṇa*—female deities (*M.*, LIV).
9. *Grāma-śānti-vidhi*—villages (*M.*, IX, X).
11. *Mṛit-saṁgrahaṇa*—more details on soil (cf. Part I, 19, 136).
12. *Aṅkurārpaṇa*—more details on sowing the seed (cf. Part I, 20).
13. *Bimba-śuddhi*—purification of idols, not treated separately in a chapter in *M.*
14. *Kautuka-bandhana*—experimental yoking for the purpose of ploughing the building-site (*M.*, V).
15. *Nayanonmīlana*—chiselling the eyes (*M.*, LXX).
18. *Bimba-śuddhi*—purification of idols (cf. II, 13).
19. *Śayanāropaṇa*—bedsteads (*M.*, XLIV).
20. *Śiva-liṅga-sthāpana*—more details on the Phallus (cf. I, 9, 59).
98. *Maṭha-pratishṭhā*—monasteries, not separately treated in *M.*

The *Suprabhedāgama* has devoted not more than fifteen chapters to architecture and sculpture. Nor has it anything new to add to the *Āgamas*' contributions to the *Śilpa-śāstras*. But its unique nature consists in the fact that it has quite successfully summarized all important matter in a comparatively small space,[1] and in respect of brevity, explicitness, and precision it surpasses even the *Bṛihat-saṁhitā* of Varāhamihira.[2] This *Āgama* has apparently drawn upon a *Śilpa-śāstra*. Its similarities with the *Mānasāra*, discussed elsewhere in detail,[3] may be partly apparent from the following list of its chapters read

[1] *See* p. 196. [2] *See* pp. 194–195. [3] *See* pp. 187–189, 194–195.

together with the corresponding portions of the standard *Silpa-śāstra* mentioned above :

22. *Karaṇādhikāra-lakshaṇa*—on the constructive arts, dealing with, *ushṇisha* (head gear), *āsana* (seat, chair), *paryaṅka* (bedstead, couch), *siṁhāsana* (throne), *raṅga* (courtyard, theatre), and *stambha* (column), (*Mānasāra*, XLIX, XLIV, XLV, XLVII XV, etc.).
23. *Grāmādi-lakshaṇa-vidhi*—villages and towns (*M.*, IX, X).
26. *Taruṇālaya-vidhi*—a special kind of building, not separately mentioned in a chapter in *M.*
27. *Prāsāda-vāstu-vidhi*—buildings in general (*M.*, XVIII, XIX—XXX).
28. *Ādyeshṭaka-vidhi*—laying the foundation stone, mentioned in many places in *M.*
29. *Garbha-nyāsa-vidhi*—foundations (*M.*, XII).
30. *Aṅguli-lakshaṇa-vidhi*—the *aṅgula* (finger-breadth) measurement (cf. *M.*, II, LV).
31. *Prāsāda-lakshaṇa-vidhi*—more details on buildings (cf. 27).
32. *Mūrdhnishṭaka-vidhi*—an ornament on the topmost part of buildings in many places in *M.*
33. *Liṅga-lakshaṇa*—the Phallus (*M.*, LII).
34. *Sakala-lakshaṇa-vidhi*—images of Iśvara and other deities (*M.*, LI—LXIV).
35. *Aṅkurārpaṇa-vidhi*—sowing the seed, not treated in a separate chapter in *M.*
36. *Liṅga-pratishṭhā-vidhi*—installation of the Phallus (*M.*, LII); cf. 33.
37. *Sakala-pratishṭhā-vidhi*—installation of the images of Iśvara and other deities (cf. 34).
38. *Śakti-pratishṭhā-vidhi*—installation of the images of the female deities (*M.*, LIV).
39. *Parivāra-vidhi*—temples of attendant deities (*M.*, XXXII).
40. *Vṛishabha-sthāpana-vidhi*—the image of the Bull of Siva (*M.*, LXII).

The *Vaikhanasāgama* has two chapters on sculpture, one of which deals with the general description of images and the other with the ten-*tāla* measures.[1] The *Aṁśumad-bhedāgama*[2] has a single chapter

[1] पटल (Chapter) 22—प्रतिमालक्षण, and 43—उत्तमदशताल ।

[2] There is an architectural treatise bearing the title अंशुमद्भेद, the authorship of which is attributed to Kāśyapa. Consult the writer's *Encyclopaedia*, Appendix, and *see* pp. 162-165.

on the ten-*tāla* measures.[1] Instances like those given above can be culled from the remaining *Āgamas* also, but the multiplication of illustrations is not likely to furnish any new information. It is, however, clear that architecture was a favourite subject for the authors of the *Āgamas*.

Miscellaneous Treatises

The works on royal polity deal with architectural matters in a more than casual way. The Kauṭilīya *Artha-śastra*, for instance, devotes some seven chapters to the subject, containing a large number of structural details. There are interesting descriptions of forts, fortified cities, town-planning, and military and residential buildings.[2]

The *Sukra-nīti* deals with both architectural and sculptural objects. Rules and structural details are given together with interesting descriptions of forts and fortified towns, of temples and other kinds of buildings, and of various sorts of images.[3] In this treatise sculptural details are more numerous in some respects than even in the *Silpa-śāstras*. Repair of broken images, for instance, is an important matter in sculpture, which has been dealt with in detail in this treatise. Another important contribution made by the *Sukra-nīti* to the *Silpa-śāstras* is the

[1] पटल (Chapter) 28—उत्तमदशतालविधिः ।

[2] Chapter 22—जनपद निवेश । 23—भूमिच्छिद्रविधान । 24—दुर्गविधान । 25—दुर्गनिवेश । The last two deal with the laying out of fortified towns and forts. 65—वास्तुक, गृहवास्तुक (residential and military buildings). 66—वास्तुविक्रय, सीमाविवाद, मर्यादास्थापन, etc. For full details, *see* the writer's *Encyclopaedia* under *Durga*, *Nagara*, and *Grāma*.

[3] Chapter IV, Section 4 :

(1) देवमन्दिरनिर्माणव्यवस्था—the construction of temples and other kinds of buildings. For details of royal palaces, *see* the concluding portion of Chapter I.
(2) प्रतिमानिर्माणव्यवस्था—carving images in general.
(3) मूर्तीनां वाहननिर्माणव्यवस्था—the images of the riding animals of deities.
(4) गणपतिमूर्तिनिर्माणव्यवस्था—the image of Gaṇapati.
(5) शक्तिमूर्तिनिर्माणव्यवस्था—images of the female deities.
(6) बालमूर्तिनिर्माणव्यवस्था—images of Bāla (child Kṛishṇa).
(7) सप्ततालादिमूर्तिभेदस्य निर्माणव्यवस्था—the images measured in the seven (*sapta*) and other *tāla* measurements.
(8) पैशाचीमूर्तिनिर्माणव्यवस्था—the images of the demonesses.
(9) भग्नप्रतिमास्थापनव्यवस्था—the repair of the damaged images.
(10) उत्सवव्यापारव्यवस्था—Festival in connexion with installation of images.

Section 6—

(11) दुर्गनिर्माण—the construction of forts (and fortified towns).

For full details, *see* the writer's *Encyclopaedia* under *Tālamāna*.

description of the seven-*tala* measures which are generally applicable, both in India and the West, to well-proportioned human figures only.

Avowedly historical works are not numerous in Sanskrit. Of the two treatises, one is concerned with the reign of a single king, and the other with the events of a country, covering many reigns. In both these treatises architecture has been given its already well-recognized place.

The *Harsha-charita* is a history of Harshavardhana of Kanauj, during whose reign the famous Chinese traveller Hieun Tsang visited India. In this history it is stated that 'the palace had, besides the harem, always more than three courtyards; the outer one being for people and for state reception, the next inner one for chiefs or nobles, and the third one for intimate persons only. The palaces were stately buildings, though not of stone. The floors, however, are described as made of shining stones. The columns and walls were ornamented with gold and even precious stones. There was usually a several-storeyed building with inner gardens of flower-beds and large fruit trees.'[1] Mention is made also of detached buildings like the *maṇḍapas* or pavilions for the purposes of *sabhā* (council hall), *satra* (inn), *prapa* (water sheds), and *prāgvaṁśa* (an auxiliary shed to a sacrificial room).[2] The useful articles of house furniture, such as thrones (*siṁhāsana*), couches (*śayana*), and *āsandi*, meaning chairs, are also described.[3]

The *Raja-taraṅgiṇī* of Kalhana, dealing with the history of Kashmir, refers frequently to architectural objects like castles (*bāna-śālā*),[4] monumental buildings (*chaitya*),[5] and monasteries (*vihāras*).[6] But in these references very few structural details are to be met with. The references of Kalhana to temples and other buildings also generally lack constructive details.[7] But interesting structural details of some shrines merely referred to in Kalhana's work are elaborated

[1] *History of Medieval India*, Vaidya, p. 152. *See Harsha-charita*, p. 215–216, description of the palace of Prabhākara Vardhana of Thāneśvara.

[2] *Harsha-charita*, p. 176.

बहिरुपरचितविकटसभासत्रप्राग्वंशमण्डपैः प्रसूतागवे ग्रामैः ।

See also *ibid*, p. 137.

[3] *H. C.*, p. 103, *ibid*, 153.

[4] VIII, 1666.

[5] I, 103, 170; III, 380, 381; IV, 200, 204.

[6] I, 93, 94, 98, 103, 140–144, 146, 147, 169, 199, 200; III, 9, 11, 13, 14, 355, 380, 464, 476; IV, 79, 184, 188, 200, 210, 215, 216, 262, 507; VI, 171, 175, 303; VII, 696, 1336; VIII, 246, 248, 2402, 2410, 2417, 2431, 2433, 3343, 3352, 3353.

[7] Compare, e.g., the Śāradā temple (I, 37); Śāradā-sthāna (VIII, 2556, 2706), etc.

by Major C. R. Bates in the *Gazetteer of Kashmir*[1] and have been given in a note by Sir M. A. Stein.[2]

The astrological and astronomical treatises frequently refer to architectural topics, especially those bearing upon auspicious times. In a pamphlet of this class twenty-one things are stated to be observed in connexion with building a house.[3] A famous astronomical treatise, the *Gārga-saṁhitā*, deals with a large number of purely architectural subjects, such as the courts, compounds, compartments, rooms, dimensions, and location of doors.[4]

The more authoritative works like the *Sūrya-siddhānta*,[5] the *Siddhānta-Śiromaṇi*,[6] and the *Lilāvatī*[7] deal exhaustively with a very

[1] P. 339.

[2] 'The temple is approached from the lower slope of the hill . . . by an imposing stone staircase . . . which leads up in sixty-three steps to the main entrance of the quadrangular court enclosing the temple. It is about 10 feet wide and rises rather steeply between two flanking walls of massive construction, broken in six steps or flights. The entrance to the court is through a gateway, provided with the usual double porch of Kāśmīrian architecture.'

'The temple, which occupies the centre of the quadrangle, forms a square cella conforming in plan and elevation to the usual features of Kāśmīr architecture. It is raised on a basement 24 feet square and 5 feet 3 inches high. The walls of the cella proper recede about 2 feet from the edge of the basement. They are adorned on the north, east and south by trefoil arches and supporting pilasters both projecting in relievo. Below these arches are small trefoil-headed niches covered by double pediments.'

'The entrance to the interior of the cella is . . . approached by stairs 5½ feet wide with flanking side walls. There is an open portico in front of the door projecting about 4 feet beyond the pilasters on each side of the doorway. It is supported on the outside by two pillars . . . The interior of the cella forms a square of 12 feet 3 inches, and has no decoration of any kind.'

—(Kalhaṇa's *Rājataraṅgiṇī*, Vol. II, notes, p. 283 fol.).

[3] आयराशिश्च नक्षत्रं व्ययस्तारांशकस्तथा ।
ग्रहमैत्री राशिमैत्री नातिभेदगणेन्दवाः ॥
आधिपत्यं वारलग्ने तिथ्युत्पत्तिस्तथैव च ।
आधिपत्यं वर्गवैरं तथैव योनिवैरकम् ॥
ऋक्षवैरं स्थितिर्नाशो लक्षणान्यर्कविंशतिः ।
कथितानि मुनिश्रेष्ठैः शिल्पविधिर्गृहादिष ॥

—(*Laghu-Śilpa-jyotiḥ-sāra*, 3–5).

[4] The manuscript in the Trinity College, Cambridge, is in a mutilated condition. The contents of the first and second chapters, fols. 67–68, are almost illegible. The following are a little better :

(i) वास्तुविद्यायां चतुर्भागत्रिभागप्रतिभागविधिः (fol. 60a).
(ii) गार्गियायां वास्तुविद्यायां चतुःशालाद्वित्रिशालैकशालाविधिः (fol. 60a).
(iii) द्वारनिर्देशः (Chap. 3, fols. 57a and 68b).
द्वारप्रमाणविधिः (fol. 57b).
द्वारस्तम्भोच्छ्रायः (fol. 60b).
(iv) गृहप्रवेशः (fol. 68b).

[5] Chapter III, 1–4. [6] Chapter VII 36–49. [7] Part II, Chapter II, section vii.

technical matter bearing upon architecture, namely, the description of gnomons which were used for finding out cardinal points. The subject is architecturally very important, inasmuch as it refers to the orientation of buildings.[1]

The poetical works of Māgha, Kālidāsa, Bhavabhūti, and others refer occasionally to architectural matters. In the *Śiśupālavadha*, the sea-side city of Dvāraka, and the assembly halls and palaces of Yudhishṭhira and Kṛishṇa are described at length; the ornaments for the body and weapons, cars and chariots are also referred to.[2] In the *Vikramorvaśīya*, for instance, mention is made of a flight of stairs made like the waves of the Ganges; in the *Meghadūta* a market-place in Viśālā and the city of Alakā are elaborately described.[3] The *Uttara-Rāma-charita* refers to an architecturally important matte , namely, cement which is specially described in some *Śilpa-śāstras*.[4] In the same work Nala, the son of the heavenly architect Viśvakarman, is mentioned as an engineer who built the bridge joining India with Ceylon.[5]

Of this class of works, the *Mṛichchhakaṭika*, which deals with the ordinary affairs of wordly people, refers very frequently to architectural matters which are two numerous to be included here.[6] A very interesting description of the gateway and as many as eight courtyards into which the whole compound is divided is given in the fourth act.

[1] Compare the writer's *Encyclopaedia* under *Śaṅku*, and for full details, *see* pp. 100–101.

[2] III, 33–64, XIII, 51–63, II, 4–5, III, 2–11, 17–23, 27–28.

[3] गङ्गातरङ्गस्फटिकमणिसोपान, *see* also मणिहर्म्य (*Vikramorvaśīya*, Kale's ed. 1898, Act III, p. 73); *Meghadūta*, I, 33–34; II; 1–22.

[4] वज्रलेप, Act III, preceding verse 40.

[5] Act III, verse 45. Compare the *Rāmayaṇa* युद्धकाण्ड, Chapter 22, verses 41–42. In the *Mānasāra* also Nala is mentioned as an architect, *see Mānasāra*, Chapter II.

[6] Act I, गृहदेहली, threshold (verse 17); पक्षद्वारक, side entrance (38; also II, 83; V, 129; VI, 209, 211, etc.); चतु:शाला, courtyard (39); प्रासादबालाग्रकपोतपालिका dovecot on the top palace (52; VIII, 282, 283; IX, 347, 349, 350, 351).

Act II, श्रेष्ठिचत्वर, merchant quarters (88, 136); बहिर्द्वारशाला, outer hall (101, 117).

अभ्यन्तरचतु:शाला, inner court (107, 108, 109; VI, 204)

पक्वेष्टक, आमेष्टक, baked and unbaked brick (111).

Act V, प्राकार, fence (177); आरामप्रासादवेदिका, roof of the garden-house (177).

Act VI, प्रतोलीद्वार, main gate (216).

Act IX, व्यवहारमण्डप court of justice (289, 291).

अधिकरणमण्डप, court of justice (289, 302, 305, 307, 320, etc.).

दूर्वाचत्वर, grass lawn (291).

This description is full of further architectural details. This reference is specially important owing to the fact that in the *Mānasāra,* as well as the *Purāṇas* and the *Āgamas,* the compound, however big it may be, is divided into not more than five courts, the fourth of which is technically called *Prākāra* in the *Mānasāra.*

The construction of the play-house is referred to in the *Nāṭya-śātra* on dramaturgy, and several other texts on dancing, singing, and instrumental music. The *Nāṭya-śāstra* of Bharata describes in great detail the stage proper and the auditorium. The audience-house, as it is designated, admits of three varieties, namely, the circular or semi-circular, quadrangular, and triangular pavilions.[1] There is also given a similar account of the stage proper. On the two sides of it an entablature is raised over four pillars and green-rooms at the back and sides, and the platforms or theatre proper at the front are erected upon a higher level than the auditorium. Two of these three types of theatres have been referred to in the *Vishṇu-dharmottara.* The *Saṅgīta-makaranda*[2] of Nārada supplies an account of an unspecified type of the stage and the auditorium. The *Saṅgīta-Ratnākara* of Nihsanka-Śārṅgadeva[3] describes the auditorium alone.

Traces of an advanced state of architecture are found also in works like grammars and lexicons. Yāska in his *Nirukta* mentions several words which can be used for masonry houses only.[4] In the later lexicons, like the *Amarakosha,* lists of several architectural terms are met with.[5] Derivations of words like *bhāskara,* sculptor; *ishṭaka,* brick; *stambha,* pillar; *aṭṭālikā,* edifices, are found in Pāṇiṇi's grammar. They no doubt imply the existence of brick and stone buildings in those times.[6]

[1] Chapter II, 7, 8, 25.

[2] V. 2–9.

[3] VII, 1351–61.

[4] R. L. Mitra, *Indo-Aryans,* I, 25–26.

[5] *Amarakosha,* section on towns and houses (Chapter II, section ii, named *pura-varga,* verses 1–2; pages 116–126, ed. Sivadatta, Bombay, 1915).

[6] Mitra, *ibid,* I, 19.

CHAPTER IV

ŚILPA-ŚĀSTRAS

A Summary of the Mānasāra[1]

CHAPTER I

The Table of Contents (*Saṁgraha*)

The first verse is an invocation to Brahmā, the Creator of the Universe. In the second verse it is stated that the science of architecture (*Vāstu-śāstra*) had come down from Siva, Brahmā and Vishṇu, through Indra, Bṛihaspati, Nārada, and all other sages, to the seer (*ṛishi*) Mānasāra who systematized it.

After this genesis, titles of the chapters are given in order. The colophon of the last chapter, named *Nayanonmīlana*, in all the complete manuscripts gives the number of the chapter as 71. The manuscripts called I, the *codex archetypus* of my text, has made up the number 71 by repeating the chapter *Strīmāna-madhyama-daśatāla;* in one place it is numbered 66 and in the second 67. The only explanation of this number 71 for the last chapter is to suppose that the copyists of all complete and independent manuscripts were equally careless in numbering the chapters. This supposition is corroborated by the fact that the contents of the work do not show that any chapter is missing.

The last verse of the first chapter states the reason why the book is named *Mānasāra*, and explains the importance and authority of the work. It is called *Mānasāra* after a sage of that name. And as an authoritative work on art and complete in all respects, it has been accepted, it is stated, by the best among the leading artists.

CHAPTER II

The System of Measurement (*Mānopakaraṇa-vidhāna*)

The first part of this chapter gives a mythical genealogy of the artists. From the four faces of Brahmā, the Creator of the Universe, originated, in order, the heavenly architect Viśvakarman, Maya, Tvashṭar, and Manu. Their four sons are called respectively Sthapati,

[1] This summary has developed out of a Dissertation, which was accepted by the University of Leiden for the Ph. D. degree.

Sūtragrāhin, Vardhaki, and Takshaka. These four evidently represent the progenitors of the four classes of terrestrial artists.

The Sthapati is highest in rank ; he is the master-builder. The Sūtragrāhin is the *guru* of Vardhaki and Takshaka ; while the Vardhaki is instructor of the Takshaka.

The Sthapati must be well-versed in all sciences (*Sāstras*). He must know the *Vedas*. He must have the qualifications of a supreme director (*ācharya*).

The Sūtragrāhin also should know the *Vedas* and the *Śāstras*. He must be an expert draftsman (*rekhājña*).

The Vardhaki too should have a general knowledge of the *Vedas*. But the object of his special study is painting (*chitra-karman*).

The Takshaka must be an expert in his own work ; i.e. carpentry.

The second part of this chapter deals with the system of measurement :

The *paramāṇu* or atom is the smallest unit of measurement.

8 *paramāṇus*	=	1 *rathadhūli* (*lit.* car-dust).
8 *rathadhūlis*	=	1 *bālāgra* (*lit.* hair's end).
8 *bālāgras*	=	1 *likshā* (*lit.* a nit).
8 *likshās*	=	1 *yūkā* (*lit.* a louse).
8 *yūkās*	=	1 *yava* (*lit.* a barley corn).
8 *yavas*	=	1 *aṅgula* (*lit.* finger's breadth).

Three kinds of *aṅgulas* are distinguished, the largest of which is made of 8 *yavas*, the intermediate one of 7 *yavas*, and the smallest one of 6 *yavas*.

12 *aṅgulas*	=	1 *vitasti* (span).
2 *vitastis* or 24 *aṅgulas*	=	1 *kishku-hasta* (small cubit).
25 *aṅgulas*	=	1 *prājāpatya-hasta*.
26 „	=	1 *dhanurmushṭi-hasta*.
27 „	=	1 *dhanuragraha-hasta*.
4 *hastas*	=	1 *dhanus* (bow) or *daṇḍa* (rod).
8 *daṇḍas*	=	1 *rajju* (string).

Directions are given with regard to the use of the four different kinds of cubits (*hasta*) enumerated above. Conveyances (*yāna*) and couches (*śayana*) are said to measured in the cubit of 24 *aṅgulas*, *vimāna* in the cubit of 25 *aṅgulas*, buildings (*vāstu*) in general in the cubit of 26 *aṅgulas*, and villages, etc., in the cubit of 27 *aṅgulas*. The cubit of 24 *aṅgulas* may, however, also be used in measuring all these objects.

In the concluding portion of this chapter directions are given for the preparation of the yard-stick (*hasta*), the rod (*daṇḍa*), and the measuring-string (*rajju*). The former two objects should be made of the wood of certain trees, which are enumerated. In the same manner certain fibres are to be used as materials for the rope. The presiding deity of the yard-stick and the rod is Vishṇu, and that of the measuring-rope Vāsuki, the king of serpents.

CHAPTERS III, IV, V

The Classification of Vāstu (*Vāshtu-prakarana*) Examination of Soil (*Bhū-parīkshā*)—Selection of Site (*Bhūmi-saṁgraha*)

The first part of the third chapter defines *vāstu* (dwelling or habitation) and divides it into four classes. The place where men and gods reside is called *vāstu*. This includes the ground (*dharā*), the building (*harmya*), the conveyance (*yāna*), and the couch (*paryaṅka*). Of these, the ground is the principal one, for nothing can be built without the ground as a support. The building (*harmya*) includes *prāsāda*, *maṇḍapa*, *sabhā*, *śālā*, *prapā* and *raṅga*. The conveyance (*yāna*) includes *syandana*, *śibikā* and *ratha*. The couch (*paryaṅka*) includes *pañjara*, *mañchali*, *mañcha*, *kākāshṭa*, *phalakāsana* and *bāla-paryaṅka*.

The second part of the third chapter, as well as the fourth and fifth chapters, deal with the same subject, namely, the site on which a village, town, fort, palace, temple, or house, is to be built. The soil is examined with regard to its contour, colour, odour, features (*rūpa*), taste, and touch. The level of the ground, as well as the characteristic vegetation of the site, are also minutely examined.

If a plot of land is found to be satisfactory on all or most of these points, it should be selected for a village, town, fort, or house, as the case may be. But even after this selection it would be wise to test the ground in some other ways. A square hole of one cubit deep should be dug on the selected site and be filled with water. After twenty-four hours the chief architect should mark the condition of the water in the hole. If all the water be dried up by this time, the earth must be very bad. But if, on the other hand, there remains some water in the hole, the selected plot of land would be fit for any building purposes.

Another final test is this : a similar hole is dug on the plot and filled up with the earth taken out of it. If this earth fills up the hole exactly, the land is fair ; if this earth be not quite enough to fill up the hole the ground must be very bad, but if this earth overfills the hole, the soil must be very good for any building purposes. The import of both tests seems to be that in the former case porous soil is avoided, while in the latter case loose soil is said to be unfit for the construction of a building.

After this final selection the ground should be ploughed over. The concluding part of the fifth chapter gives a minute description of the oxen and the plough to be used in ploughing the selected site.

CHAPTER VI

THE GNOMON (*Śanku-sthāpaua-vidhāna*)

The object of this chapter is to lay down rules on the principles of dialling and for ascertaining the cardinal points by means of a gnomon.

The gnomon is made of the wood of certain trees. It may be 24, 18, or 12 *aṅgulas* in length, and the width at the base should bc respectively 6, 5, and 4 *aṅgulas*. It tapers from the bottom towards the top.

For the purpose of ascertaining the cardinal points, a gnomon of 12, 18, or 24 *aṅgulas* is erected from the centre of a watered place (*salila-sthala*) and a circle is described with the bottom of the gnomon as its centre and with a radius twice its length. Two points are marked where the shadow (of the gnomon) after and before noon meets the circumference of the circle. The line joining these two points is the east-west line. From each of these east and west points a circle is drawn with their distance as radius. The two intersecting points, which are called the head and tail of the fish (*timi*), are the north and the south points. The intermediate regions are found in the same way, through the fish formed between the points of the determined quarters.

As regards the principles of dialling, each of the twelve months is divided into three parts of ten days each and the increase and decrease of shadow (*avachchhāyā*)[1] are calculated for these several parts of the different months.

[1] Cf. *Vitruvius*, Book IX, Chap. VIII, '. . . the principles of dialling and the increase and decrease of the *days* in the different months' (translated by Gwilt).

Why the subject of the present chapter is important for architecture is evident from the rules regarding the orientation of buildings. Here it is said that a building should preferably face the east or the north-east, but that it should never be made to face the south-east, as this is considered inauspicious.

The chapter closes with a passing reference to the *khāta-śaṅku*, which appears to denote wooden stakes posted in different parts of the foundations made for constructing buildings thereon.

CHAPTER VII

The Site-plan (*Pada-vinyāsa*)

When a site is selected for constructing a village, town, or building thereon the ground is divided into different numbers of squares. Thirty-two kinds of such schemes are distinguished by as many different designations, according to the number of squares into which the whole area is partitioned out. The whole scheme has been arranged in such a manner that in each case the number of partitions represent the square of the serial number. The eighth plot, for instance, which is called *chaṇḍita*, comprises a division into sixty-four squares, while by the ninth plot, which bears the technical name of *paramaśāyika*, the ground is divided into eighty-one squares.

Each of these squares is assigned to its presiding deity. Some deities, however are lords of more than one square. The lord of the central square is always Brahmā. Charagī, Vidārikā, Pūtanā, and Rākshasī are the presiding deities of the four corners. A detailed description of all the squares of the eighth and the ninth plans is given in the text. Then the forty-four deities, who are enumerated in connexion with the *paramaśāyika* scheme, are described in the form of as many *dhyānas*. The portion is of some iconographical interest.

Finally, the presiding deity of the site (*vāstu-purusha*), who is described as hump-backed and of crooked shape, is said to occupy the habitated area (*vāstu*) in such a manner that his limbs cover the several squares or groups of squares, which, as set forth in the former part of the chapter, are assigned to and named after various deities. As he is supposed to lie down with his face turned downwards, his head being in the central square on the east side (assigned to Sūrya), his right and left hands must be in the partitions of Agni (S.E.) and Īśāna (N. E.) respectively, and his right and left feet on those of Nairṛita (S. W.)

and Vāyu (N. W.) respectively. The middle part of his body occupies the central portion of the plot, which, as we saw, is assigned to Brahmā.

CHAPTER VIII

The Offerings (*Balikarma-vidhāna*)

Different kinds of offerings (*bali*) are described for the various deitie enumerated in the preceding chapter, who are supposed to preside over the different partitions of the *paramaśāyika* or *maṇḍūka* (site, plan). These offerings consist of milk in its various forms, butter, rice and sesame, parched grain (*lāja*), honey and sweetmeat (*modaka*, offered to Sugrīva), incense and lamps, flowers and fruits. Blood is offered to Asura, dried meat to Mṛiga, dried fish to Roga (disease)- and sea-fish to Bhṛiṅgarāja. The four demonesses, namely, Rākshasīs Pūtanā, Vidārī, and Charagī, also receive their share, the first-mentioned evil spirit in the shape of meat of goats mixed with blood.

In the bringing of these offerings the master-builder (Sthapati) takes a leading part.

CHAPTER IX

The Village (*Grāmalakshaṇa-vidhāna*)

According to the *Mānasāra*, there is not much difference between a village, a town, and a fort. All are fortified places intended for the residence of people. A town is the extension of a village. A fort is in many cases nothing more than a fortified town, with this difference, that a fort is principally meant for purposes of defence, while a village or a town is mainly intended for habitation.

A detailed description of the plan of villages, towns, and forts, and the arrangement of the various buildings which they contain is given in the text.

Villages are divided according to their shapes into eight classes, called *daṇḍaka*, *sarvato-bhadra*, *nandyāvarta*, *padmaka*, *svastika*, *prastara*, *kārmuka*, and *chatur-mukha*.

Each village is surrounded by a wall made of brick or stone; beyond this wall there is a ditch broad and deep enough to cause serious obstruction in the event of an attack on the village. There are generally four main gates at the middle of the four sides, and as many at the

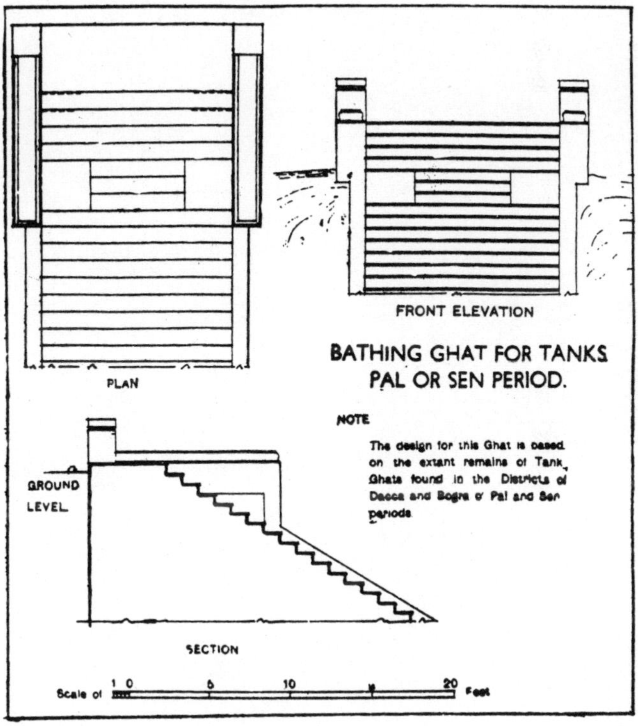

BATHING GHAT FOR TANKS

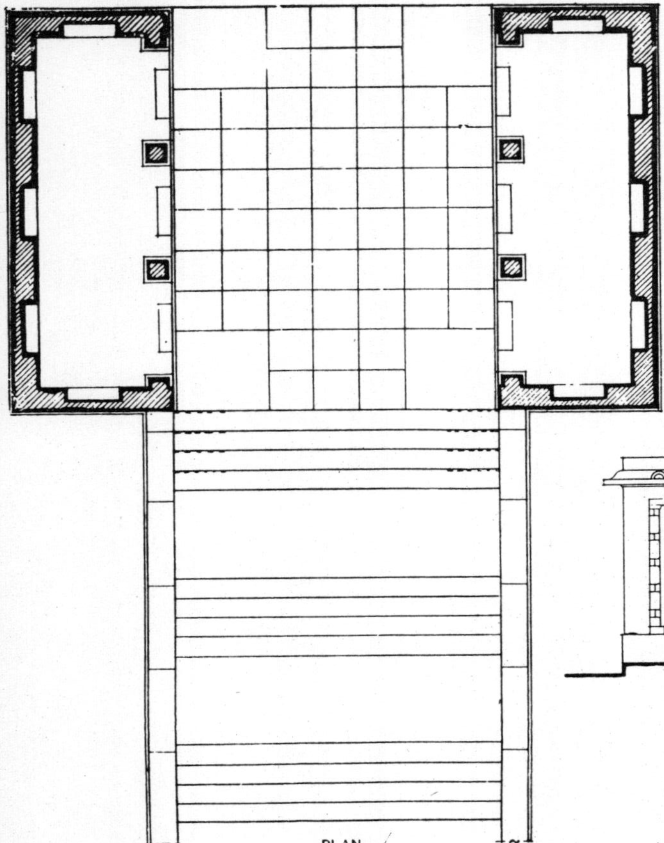

PLAN.

BATHING GHAT FOR RIVER
PAL OR SEN PERIOD

SCALE OF 1 0 5 10 15 20 FEET

SCALE OF 1 0 1 2 3 4 5 6 FEET FOR DETAIL

NOTE.

This design is based on the extant remains of old River Ghats found in Bengal.

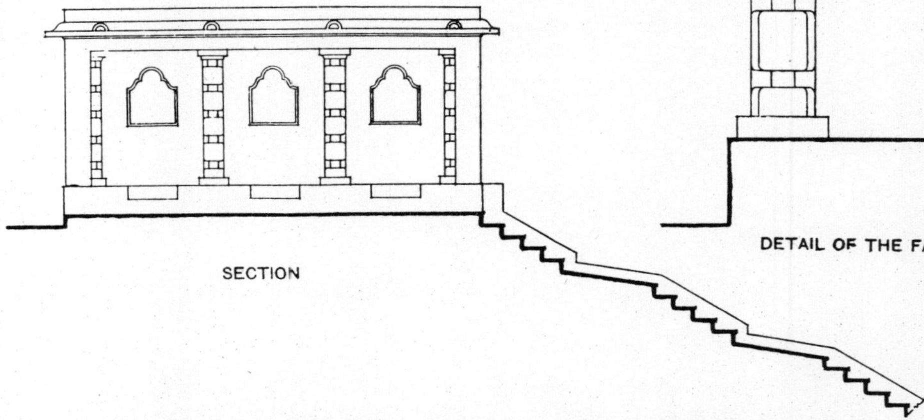

SECTION

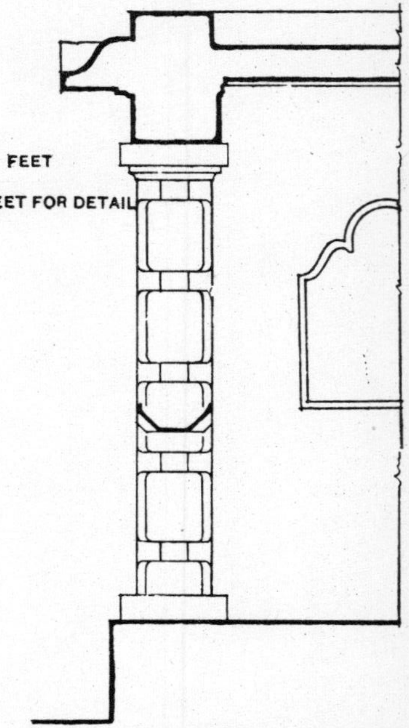

DETAIL OF THE FACADE

four corners. Inside the wall there is a large street running all round the village. Besides, there are two other large streets, each of which connects two opposite main gates. They intersect each other at the centre of the village, where a temple or a hall is generally built for the meeting of the villagers. The village is thus divided into four main blocks, each of which is again subdivided into many blocks by streets which are always straight and run from one end to the other of a main block. The two main streets crossing at the centre have houses and footpaths on one side of the street. The ground-floor of these houses on the main streets consists of shops. The street, which runs round the village, has also houses and footpaths only on one side. These houses are mainly public buildings, such as schools, libraries, guest-houses, etc. All other streets generally have residential buildings on both sides. The houses, high or low, are always uniform in make. Drains (*jaladvāra*, *lit.* water-passage) follow the slope of the ground. Tanks and ponds are dug in all the inhabited parts, and located where they can conveniently be reached by a large number of inhabitants. The temples of public worship, as well as the public commons, gardens, and parks are similarly located. People of the same caste or profession are generally housed in the same quarter.

The partition of the quarters among the various sects cannot be said to be quite impartial. The best quarters are generally reserved for the Brahmans and the architects. Such partiality to the artists is not met elsewhere in Sanskrit literature. The quarters of the Buddhists and the Jains are described in a few lines. The habitations of the Chaṇḍālas, as well as the places for cremation, are located outside the village wall, in the north-west in particular. The temples of fearful deities, such as Chāmuṇḍā, are also placed outside the wall.

CHAPTER X

Towns and Forts (*Nagara-vidhāna*)

As stated above, a town is a large village. According to the *Mānasāra*, it appears that the dimensions of the smallest town-unit are 100 × 200 *daṇḍas*; the largest town-unit is 7,200 × 14,400 *daṇḍas*. A town may be situated from east to west or from north to south according to the position it occupies. There should be one to twelve large streets in a town. It should be built near a river or a mountain, and should have facilities for trade and commerce with the foreigners (*dvīpāntara-vartin*). Like a village, it should have walls, ditches and gates, drains, parks, commons, shops, exchanges, temples, guest-houses, colleges, etc. For purposes of military defence, the towns are generally well fortified.

Towns are divided into eight classes: *rājadhānī-nagara*, *kevala-nagara*, *pura*, *nagarī*, *kheṭa*, *kharvaṭa*, *kubjaka*, and *pattana*. The distinction between them is slight, the general description given above being applicable to all. But it may be noted that the city called *pattana* is a big commercial port. It is situated on the banks of the sea or a river, and is always engaged in exchange and commerce with foreigners who deal specially in jewels, silk clothes, perfumes, etc., imported from other countries (*dvīpāntara*).

Forts are first divided into eight classes, called *śibira*, *vāhinī-mukha*, *sthānīya*, *droṇaka*, *saṁviddha* or *vardhaka*, *kolaka*, *nigama*, and *skandhāvāra*. There is a further division of these forts according to their position. They are known as mountain fort (*giri-durga*), forest fort (*vana-durga*), water fort (*jala-durga*), chariot fort (*ratha-durga*), divine fort (*deva-durga*), marsh fort (*paṅka-durga*), and mixed fort (*miśra-durga*).

The mountain fort is subdivided into three classes, according as it is built on the top of the mountain, in the valley, or on the mountain slope.

All these forts are surrounded with strong walls and ditches. The wall is made of brick, stone, and similar materials. It is at least 12 cubits in height and its thickness at the base is at least 6 cubits. It is provided with watch-towers.

CHAPTER XI

The Dimensions of Buildings of Various Storeys
(*Bhūmilamba-vidhāna*)

The name of this chapter is *Bhūmilamba*, which literally means the height of the storey. The *Kāmikāgama* (*paṭala* 50, verse 1) defines this name, *Bhūmilamba*, thus: '*Chatur aṁśādi-saṁsthānaṁ bhūmi-lambam iti smṛitam.*' The chapters on the subject, in both the works, *Mānasāra* and *Kāmikāgama*, deal with the measurement of length, breadth, and height of buildings of one to twelve storeys.

The various shapes of buildings are mentioned in the opening lines of the chapter. They may be square, rectangular, round, octagonal, or oval. Buildings of all kinds, such as the *vimāna* or temple, the *harmya* or palace, the *gopura* or gate-house, the *śālā* or storeyed mansion, the *maṇḍapa* or pavilion, and the *veśman* (residential houses generally) should have one of these five shapes.

Buildings are again divided into four classes—*jāti*, *chhanda*, *vikalpa* or *saṁkalpa*, and *ābhāsa*—which are frequently referred to in the subsequent chapters. These four classes seem to have different characteristics in different cases.

The proportion between height and width is expressed by five technical names, *śāntika*, *paushṭika*, *pārshṇika* (sometimes called *jayada*), *adbhuta*, and *sarvakāmika*. When the height of a building or idol is equal to its width, it is called *śāntika;* the *paushṭika* height is 1¼ times the width; the *pārshṇika* or *jayada* height is 1½ of the width; the *adbhuta* height is twice the width; and the *sarvakāmika* height is 1¾ of the width. This proportion of height and width is not, however, strictly followed all through. There is a slight variation in some cases. But the proportions given above are the most common. The measurement of length, breadth, and height is invariably divided into three types: large, intermediate, and small. The *śāntika* and the *paushṭika* heights are prescribed for the large type of measurement, the *pārshṇika* or *jayada* for the intermediate type, and the *adbhuta* and the *sarvakāmika* for the small type.

Five series of length and five series of breadth are prescribed here for each of the several classes of buildings of one to twelve storeys. But in some subsequent chapters as many as nine alternatives of length and breadth are prescribed for one and the same object.

The five series of breadth in the small type of one-storeyed buildings are 2, 4, 6, 8 and 10 units, and the five series of length are 3, 5, 7, 9 and 11 units. In the intermediate type the five series of breadth are 5, 7, 9, 11 and 13 units, and the five series of length 6, 8, 10 12 and 14 units. In the large type, the five series of breadth are 6, 8, 10, 12 and 14 units, and the five lengths are 7, 9, 11, 13 and 15 units.

All the classes of buildings of one to twelve storeys are in this way measured separately. The dimensions of the twelve-storeyed building in its three types are given briefly.[1] In the small type they are 35,

[1] The description of these dimensions is much clearer in the *Kāmikāgama* (*paṭala* 50). According to this work, the width of a twelve-storeyed building is 70 cubits and the height 100 cubits. It expressly states (*śloka* 33) that it is never desirable that buildings should be larger than 77 cubits in height and 70 cubits in width.

37, 39, 41, 43 units, in the intermediate type 36, 38, 40, 42, 44 units, and in the large type 37, 39, 41, 43, 45 units. These are the fifteen kinds of *vipula*, and the height should be as before.

These are the measurements in the *jāti* class of buildings. Three-fourths, half, and one-fourth of these are prescribed for the *chhanda*, the *vikalpa*, and the *ābhāsa* classes respectively.

The concluding part of this chapter prescribes the number of storeys allowed in edifices according to the social status of their occupants. In the first instance reference is made to the various classes of kings,[1] of whom the one highest in rank, namely, the *chakravartin* or universal monarch, is said to inhabit a palace of five to twelve storeys. The residence of the heir-apparent (*yuvarāja*), as well as those belonging to the chief feudatories (*sāmanta-pramukha*), should have one to three storeys.

CHAPTER XII

The Foundation (*Garbhavinyāsa-vidhāna*)

The foundation is classified under three heads, namely, for buildings, for villages, etc., and for tanks, etc. The last-named foundation is meant for a cistern, well or tank (*vāpī-kūpa-taṭāka*), etc.

The depth of the excavation (*garbha-bhājana*) in case of a village, a town, or a fort (*grāma, nagara, pura, pattana, kharvaṭa, koshṭha, kola*, etc.) is stated to be of five kinds, and varies in accordance with the size of the construction. Similarly, for a building or a well suitable depth of the excavation is prescribed.

The foundation of buildings is further divided into two classes as it may belong to temples or to human dwellings. Of temples, those of Vishṇu and Brahmā are dealt with, and the others are said to be like these.

For human dwellings there are four classes of foundations according to the caste of the occupier, Brahman, Kshatriya, Vaiśya, or Sūdra. In the laying of a foundation, ritualistic prescriptions play a prominent part, the actual process apparently being the same in all cases.

[1] Cf. below, Chapter XLI. In the present passage only six out of the nine classes are mentioned, the *maṇḍaleśa, paṭṭadhara* and *pārshṇika* having been omitted.

The depth of the excavation is equal to the height of the basement. The four corners and sides, built of brick or stone, are equal.

The depth of the excavation (*lit.* foundation-cave) should be as high as the basement of the building; the four sides (*lit.* corners or walls), made of brick or stone, should be equal; from its bottom should be removed water (if there comes out any), and all (kinds of) earth should be deposited therein. The floor of the excavation should be consolidated with seven kinds of earth, namely, from rivers and mountains, from ant-hills, crab-holes, sea-shores, from tops of trees (hills), and from near a cow-shed (*lit.* from the foreparts of cows' hoofs). Upon this (earth deposit) should be (further) deposited the root of the (white) lotus at the central part (of the excavation), to the east the root of the blue lotus, to the south the root of the water-lily, to the west *saugandhi* (grass), and to the north the *kākali* (gunja) plant. Upon this should be placed, in order, the following eight sorts of corn : *śāli* (corn) should be placed to the north-east and *vrīhi* (grains) to the east, *kodrava* (*Paspalum scorbiculatum*) to the south-east, *kaṅgu* (panic seed) to the south, *mudga* (*phaseolus mungo*) to the south-west, *māsha* (bean, *phaseolus raditus*) to the west, *kulattha* (*dolichos uniflorous*) to the north-west and *tila* (*sesamum indicum*) to the north. Upon this (finally depositing the other usual materials, e.g. concrete) the foundation should be raised up to the (upper) surface of the excavation.

As regard the measurement and the shape, it (the foundation) should be in conformity with buildings of one to twelve storeys. The twelve varieties of dimensions (of breadth and length) should begin respectively with three and four parts (*mātras*, i.e. *aṅgulas*) and end at twenty-five and twenty-six, the increment being by two. The depth of the excavation should be equal to its breadth and less by one-eighth or one-fifth, or similarly less by one-fourth. All these (measures) are stated to be (taken) in rods (of four cubits). The breadth of the excavation should be equal to the width of the (main) pillar of the building, or it may be made less by one-eighth, or be three-fourths of the breadth. The depth (of the excavation) should be made as aforesaid. The width of all the (four) walls should be one, two, or three parts out of the three parts into which the depth is divided. The depth of the excavation being divided into four parts one part is given to its base, two parts to its pillar and one part to the entablature. It (the excavation) should be shaped like a three-fold square pavilion at its entrance into the watery part (i.e. the bottom).

The concluding lines of this chapter deal with the measurement of bricks, with which buildings of one to twelve storeys are preferably built, and also with the ceremonies in connexion with the laying of the foundation-stone (*lit.* first brick, *prathameshṭaka*). The breadth of a brick may be from 7 to 29 or 30 *aṅgulas*. The length is greater than the breadth by $\frac{1}{4}$, $\frac{1}{2}$, $\frac{3}{4}$, or is twice the breadth. The thickness should be half of the breadth.

CHAPTER XIII

THE PEDESTAL (*Upapīṭha-vidhāna*)

The opening lines of the chapter describe the height of the pedestal as compared with the base. This height is said to be of nine kinds, which are worked out by nine proportions. Five of them are those expressed by the technical terms *śāntika*, *paushṭika*, *jayada*, *adbhuta* and *sarvakāmika* ($\frac{1}{3}$, $\frac{1}{4}$, $\frac{1}{5}$, $\frac{1}{6}$, and $\frac{1}{7}$). Rām Rāz, on the authority of a Tamil manuscript, says that the height of the pedestal is to be reckoned from one-quarter to six times of the height of the base.

The next topic of this chapter refers to the measurement of the projections (*nirgama*) of pedestals. The height of the pedestal is divided into 3, 4, 5, 6, 7, 8, 9, 10, 11, 12, 13, 14, or 15 equal parts; of these 1, 2, 3, 4, 5, 6, 7, or 8 are given to the projection. The nine kinds of projection are 1, $1\frac{1}{4}$, $1\frac{1}{2}$, $1\frac{3}{4}$, 2, $2\frac{1}{4}$, $2\frac{1}{2}$, $2\frac{3}{4}$, and 3 *hastas*. The projections may be 1, $1\frac{1}{2}$, 2, $2\frac{1}{2}$, 3, $3\frac{1}{2}$, 4, 5, 6, 7, 8, or 9 *daṇḍas*.

After this, the pedestals are divided into three classes known as *vedi-bhadra*, *prati-bhadra*, and *mañcha-bhadra*. Each of these is subdivided into four types. The measures of the mouldings of each of these twelve kinds of pedestals are given in detail.

The remaining portion of the chapter contains the names and measurement of the various mouldings which are to be employed in each of the twelve kinds of pedestal.

CHAPTER XIV

THE BASE (*Adhishṭhāna-vidhāna*)

The height of the bases is of twelve kinds, beginning at 30 *aṅgulas* and ending at 4 *hastas*, the increment being by 6 *aṅgulas*. These twelve heights are used respectively in twelve different storeys, one above the other. The heights of the bases are said to be 4 *hastas* in the houses of the Brahmans, 3 *hastas* in those of the Kshatriyas (kings), 2½ *hastas* in the houses of princes, 2 *hastas* in those of the Vaiśyas, and 1 *hasta* in the houses of the Śūdras.

Some sixty-four bases are described under nineteen different types called *pāda-bandha*, *uraga-bandha*, *pratikrama*, *kumuda-bandha*, *padma-kesara*, *pushpa-pushkala*, *śrī-bandha*, *mañcha-bandha*, *śreṇī-bandha*, *padma-bandha*, *kumbha-bandha* (or *kalaśa-bandha*), *vapra-bandha*, *vajra-bandha*, *śrī-bhoga*, *ratna-bandha*, *paṭṭa-bandha*, *kukshi-bandha*, *kampa-bandha*, and *śrīkānta*. Of each of the bases the mouldings and ornaments are described in detail.

CHAPTER XV

The Pillar (*Stambha-lakshaṇa-vidhāna*)

The opening lines divide the subject-matter into five heads, namely, the measurement of pillars, their shapes, their ornaments and mouldings, the collection of wood for the purpose of making pillars, which may, however, be made of stone, and the ceremonial and process of erecting pillars

The height of a pillar is measured from above the base to below the *uttara*, or above the pedestal from he *janman* to the *uttara*. The height of a pillar, in other words, is measured from the plinth up to the lowest member of the entablature, so as to include the capital. In an important passage in the *Kāśyapa*, quoted by Rām Rāz, it is stated that the measurement may also be taken from the cimbia of the shaft, exclusive of the base.

The height of a pillar is twice, one-and-a-half times, or one-and-a-quarter times that of its base, or the height of the pillar begins at 2½ *hastas* and ends at 8 *hastas*, the increment being by 6 *aṅgulas* or ¼ *hasta*. But according to *Kāśyapa*, the height of the pillar may be three times of the base; or six or eight times that of the pedestal. The width (diameter) of a pillar may be $\frac{1}{6}$, $\frac{1}{7}$, $\frac{1}{8}$, $\frac{1}{9}$ or $\frac{1}{10}$ of its height, or $\frac{1}{3}$, $\frac{1}{4}$ or $\frac{1}{6}$ of the height if it be a pilaster (*kuḍya-stambha*). The width of the pilaster, according to the *Mānasāra*, is 3, 4, 5, or 6 *mātras* (*aṅgulas*), and twice, thrice, or four times of these should be the width of the *kampa*. The height of a pillar being divided into 12, 11, 10, 9 or 8 parts, the one of these parts may be the breadth of the pillar, and at the top it is diminished by one-fourth.

The column admits of different shapes. A square pillar is called *brahma-kānta*. An octagonal one is called *vishṇu-kānta*. A sixteen-sided or circular one is known as *rudra-kānta*. A pentagonal one is called *śiva-kānta*, and the hexagonal one *skanda-kānta*. These shapes are stated to be uniform from bottom to top. But the base may be quadrangular.

With respect to dimensions and ornaments the five kinds of columns —*brahma-kānta*, *vishṇu-kānta*, *rudra-kānta*, *śiva-kānta*, and *skanda-kānta*— are called *chitra-karṇa*, *padma-kānta*, *chitra-skambha*, *pālikā-stambha*, and *kumbha-stambha*. A sixth one, *kostha-stambha*, in the latter division, is stated to be two-sided, and is the same as the *kuḍya-stambha* or pilaster.

It should be noticed that the former set of five names refers to the shapes of the shafts, whilst the latter set of five names is based on the shapes of the capitals; but in the detailed description both the capital and shaft are included.

Some special kinds of pillars are also described, such as *chitra-karṇa*, *padma-kānta*, *chitra-skambha*, *vīra-kaṇṭha*, *pālikā-stambha*, *kumbha-stambha* and *koshṭha-stambha*. Then follow the description and measurement of the mouldings of the pillars.

Columns, when in rows, must be in a straight line. 'The inter-columnation may be two, three, four or five diameters; it is measured in three ways, first, from the inner extremity of the base of one pillar to that of another; second, from the centre of the two pillars; and third from the outer extremities of the pillars including the two bases.' There seems to be no fixed inter-columnation. This has been left to the discretion of architects who are, however, required to be particularly careful with regard to beauty and utility.

Minor pillars should conform to the main pillar. A main pillar with one minor pillar (*upapāda*) is called *eka-kānta*, with two minor pillars *dvi-kānta*, and with three minor pillars *tri-kānta*. A main pillar with four minor pillars is called *brahma-kānta*, with five *śiva-kānta*, with six *skanda-kānta*, and with eight minor pillars it is called *vishṇu-kānta*.

There is a long description of the collection of wood for purposes of pillars. The details seem to indicate that at the time when the *Māna-sāra* was composed, wood was frequently used for making columns; stone pillars are also mentioned, but pillars made of brick alone are not particularly dealt with. It is, however, stated that stone, brick and wood were used for making different parts of a column. The square *ādhāra* or base of a stone pillar, it is stated, should be made of stone, and that of the wooden pillar of wood. But at the end of the next chapter, it is added that all the parts of a column should be made of stone (*śilā*), wood (*dāru*) or brick (*ishṭaka*). In the middle of the same chapter the use of these three materials is elaborately discussed. The pillars, etc., are called *śuddha* (pure) when made of one material, *miśra* (mixed) when made of two materials, and *saṁkīrṇa* (amalgamated) when made of all the three (or more) materials.

The concluding part of this chapter deals with ceremonies in connexion with erecting columns. They are essentially ritualistic. It is directed that the column should be posted (*veśayet*) at the side of a *maṇḍapa* or pavilion.

CHAPTER XVI

THE ENTABLATURE (*Prastara-vidhāna*)

The height of the entablature (*prastara*), as compared with that of the base (*adhishṭhāna*), is of six kinds. The height of the former may be equal to that of the latter, or less by $\frac{1}{4}$, or greater by $\frac{1}{4}$, $\frac{1}{2}$ or $\frac{3}{4}$; or it may be twice; or, in cubit (*hasta*) measurement these six kinds of height of the entablature begin at 7 cubits and end at $4\frac{1}{2}$ cubits, the decrement being by $\frac{1}{2}$ cubit. These six kinds of entablatures are respectively used in the houses of the gods, the Brahmans, the kings (or Kshatriyas), the crown-princes (*yuvarājas*), the Vaiśyas, and the Śūdras.

The height of the entablature is said to be $\frac{1}{4}$ or $\frac{3}{4}$ of, or equal to, that of the pillar (*pāda*), or greater by $\frac{1}{4}$, $\frac{1}{2}$ or $\frac{3}{4}$. Yet another set of six heights is described. The height of the pillar being divided into eight parts, seven, six, five, four, three or two parts may be assigned to that of the entablature.

The greater portion of the chapter is devoted to an enumeration of the various mouldings and the measurement of each of the eight different kinds of entablature.

In this chapter the roofing (*prachchhādana*) of buildings is described. It is stated that a brick-built building may be furnished with a wooden roof, and that the roofs of stone buildings should also be built of stone.

CHAPTER XVII

Wood Joinery (*Sandhikarma-vidhāna*)

The definition of the name (*sandhikarman*) of the chapter is given in the opening lines. The joining of pieces of wood for buildings is called *sandhi-karman.* Several kinds of wood-joining are described in detail. Pieces of wood are said to be joined in such a way as to make the *nandyāvarta*, *svastika*, *sarvato-bhadra* and such other shapes Some kinds of wood are strictly forbidden to be joined with some others. Fresh timber, it is stated, should under no circumstances be joined with seasoned wood.

It may be noted that wood was very largely used in constructing houses of various kinds; some parts of pillars too were made of wood, as has already been pointed out. Doors were mostly made of wood. The same was the case with couches, cars, chairs, etc.

CHAPTER XVIII

The General Description of Buildings (*Vimāna-vidhāna*)

The contents of the chapter are divided into the following headings: the classification of the *vimānas* of one to twelve storeys; the three styles of architecture; the characteristic features of the *stūpikā* or pinnacle, the *stūpī-kīla* or pinnacle staff, the *lupā* or loping roof, and the *mukhabhadra* or front portico; and the ceremonies of fixing the pinnacle staff.

The description begins with the making of the foundation; but this subject has already been dealt with in Chapter XII.

The classification of *vimānas* of one to twelve storeys is elaborately described here, their absolute dimensions having already been given in Chapter XI, called *Bhūmilamba-vidhāna.* Each of the twelve classes is subdivided into three types, according to their size—large, intermediate, and small. Whilst the width of the small type of one-storeyed building is 1, 2, 3, 4, 5, or 6 parts, it should be 5, 6, or 7 parts in the intermediate type, and 6, 7, or 8 parts in the large type. These 'parts' appear to be the partitions of the façade bordered by two pilasters (*pāda*).

The three styles of architecture are called *nāgara*, *drāviḍa*, and *vesara*, which are apparently geographical names. The distinguishing feature seems to be the general shape of the *śikhara* or spherical roof.

In the third place, the measurement and mouldings of the pinnacle (*stūpī* or *stūpikā*) are given in detail. The height of the *stūpī* is one cubit (*hasta*) in the houses of the Śūdras, two cubits in those of the Vaiśyas, two cubits and a half in the houses of the crown-princes (*yuvarāja*), three cubits in the houses of the kings (Kshatriyas), three cubits and a half in the houses of the Brahmans, and four cubits in the houses of the gods, that is, in temples.

Building materials are then discussed. Four kinds of materials are distinctly mentioned : stone, brick, wood, and iron (*lauha*).

Buildings are made of one, two, three, or all four of these materials, but preference is given to the use of one material alone. With regard to materials, buildings are divided into three classes, namely, *śuddha* (pure), made of one material alone, *miśra* (mixed) made of two materials, and *saṁkīrṇa* (amalgamated), made of three or more materials.

The term *stūpī-kīla* literally means the nail or pin of the *stūpī*. Its form is described clearly. It is quadrangular at the base, octagonal at the middle, circular at the top, and tapering gradually from bottom to top. The width at the top is one *aṅgula*.

Then two more architectural members are described, namely, the *lupā* and the *mukha-bhadra*. The former is explained by Rām Rāz[1] as 'a sloping and a projecting member of the entablature, representing a continued pent roof. It is made below the cupola (*śikhara*), and its ends are placed as if it were suspended from the architrave, and reaching the stalk of the lotus below.'

The *mukha-bhadra*, or front tabernacle or porch according to the same author,[2] indicates an ornamental niche, which occupies a central position in the façade of the building.

The chapter concludes with a description of the ceremonies in connexion with fixing the *stūpī-kīla*.

CHAPTER XIX

The One-storeyed Buildings (*Ekhabhūmi-vidhāna*)[3]

The chapter opens with various classifications of buildings. They are first divided into four classes called *jāti*, *chhanda*, *vikalpa*, and *ābhāsa*. Here they are considered with regard to their measurement.

[1] Rām Rāz, *Essay*, p. 52, footnote 2. [2] *Ibid*, p. 51, f.
[3] Cf. *ibid*, pp. 49–53, Plate XXI.

The *jāti* class is said to be measured in the *pūrva-hasta*, the first kind of cubit, i.e. the cubit of 24 *aṅgulas*. The *chhanda* is apparently measured in the cubit of 25 *aṅgulas*, the *vikalpa* in the cubit of 26 *aṅgulas* and the *ābhāsa* in the cubit of 27 *aṅgulas* (?).

A further classification is into *sthānaka*, *āsana* and *śayana*, which are also called, respectively, *saṁchita*, *asaṁchita*, and *apasaṁchita*. This classification also refers to measurement. In the *sthānaka* class the measurement of the height is considered, in the *āsana* the breadth is taken into consideration, and in the *śayana* the width is measured. It should be noted that these three classes, namely, *sthānaka*, *āsana*, and *śayana*, have a further signification with regard to the object of worship. In the *sthānaka* buildings the idol is in an erect posture, in the *āsana* buildings in a sitting posture, and in the *śayana* buildings in a recumbent posture.

A third classification refers to the shape. Buildings are classed as masculine (*purusha*) when they are equiangular or circular, and as feminine when they are rectangular. Male deities are installed in masculine temples, and female deities in feminine temples. It is added, however, that the images of the latter may be placed in masculine temples too.

After this introduction comes the description of one-storeyed buildings. The absolute measurement is referred to in the chapter called *Bhūmi-lamba* (dimensions of storeys). The comparative measurement and plan are described here at great length. The whole height of the building is divided into a certain number of equal parts which are distributed in a happy proportion amongst the different members, namely, the base, the pillar, the entablature, the neck, the dome, and the pinnacle. Similarly, the length of the entire temple is divided into a certain number of equal parts which are also distributed amongst various rooms and halls, namely, the *garbha-gṛiha* or shrine, the *antarāla* or anteroom, and the *maṇḍapa* or pavilion. These component parts of the building are described in detail in subsequent chapters, as also the gate-houses (*gopura*), courts (*prākāra*) and such other architectural members as doors, windows, arches, and so forth. In the present chapter a detailed account is given of the water-channel (*nāla*), which is meant to be an outlet for the water.

The eight kinds of one-storeyed buildings are known as *jayantika*, *bhoga*, *śrīviśāla*, *svasti-bandhana*, *śrīkara*, *hasti-pṛishṭha*, *skandhatāra*, and *keśara*.

The concluding portions of this chapter, as well as of the next eleven chapters, are devoted to an enumeration of the various deities with whose images the doors and walls of buildings should be decorated.

The Buddhist and Jain temples, dealt with in only two lines, are directed to be similarly built, with the difference that in these temples the images of the Buddhist and Jain gods should be installed instead of the images of the Brahmans.

CHAPTERS XX—XXX

Buildings of Two to Twelve Storeys

The contents of these eleven chapters of the *Mānasāra* may be conveniently summarized together. They deal respectively with two-storeyed (*dvi-tala*), three-storeyed (*tri-tala*), four-storeyed (*chatus-tala*), five-storeyed (*pañcha-tala*), six-storeyed (*shaṭ-tala*), seven-storeyed (*sapta-tala*), eight-storeyed (*ashṭa-tala*), nine-storeyed (*nava-tala*), ten-storeyed (*daśa-tala*), eleven-storeyed (*ekādaśa-tala*), and twelve-storeyed (*dvādaśa-tala*) buildings. In each of these chapters we find a classification of the peculiar kind of edifice under discussion followed by an account of certain details, in particular the location of the divine images with which the walls are decorated. Thus the buildings of two storeys are divided into eight classes which are called *śrīkara*, *vijaya*, *siddha*, *paushṭika*, *kāntaka*, *adbhuta* (also *prabhūtaka*), *svastika*, and *push-kala*. Those of three storeys are likewise divided into eight classes, called *śrikānta*, *āsana*, *sukhālaya*, *keśara*, *kamalāṅga*, *brahma-kānta*, *meru-kānta*, and *kailāśa*. The same eight-fold division is found in connexion with the four-storeyed buildings; here the names are *vishṇu-kānta*, *chatur-mukha*, *sadā-śiva*, *rudra-kānta*, *īśvara-kānta*, *mañcha-kānta*, *vedi-kānta*, and *indra-kānta*. The eight classes of the five-storeyed buildings are called *airāvata*, *bhūta-kānta*, *viśva-kānta*, *mūrti-kānta*, *yama-kānta*, *griha-kānta*, *yajña-kānta* and *brahma-kānta*. In the case of the buildings of six storeys there are no less than thirteen classes, the technical names of which are *padma-kānta*, *kāntāra*, *sundara*, *upakānta*, *kamala* or *kamalāksha*, *ratna-kānta*, *vipulāṅka*, *jyotish-kānta*, *saroruha*, *vipulākṛiti*, *svasti-kānta*, *nandyāvarta*, and *ikshu-kānta*. The seven-storeyed buildings are divided into eight kinds—*puṇḍarīka*, *śrīkānta*, *śrībhoga*, *dhāraṇa*, *pañjara*, *āśramā-gāra*, *harmya-kānta*, and *hima-kānta*. The eight classes of eight-storeyed buildings are called *bhū-kānta*, *bhūpa-kānta*, *svarga-kānta*, *mahākānta*, *jana-kānta*, *tapas-kānta*, *satya-kānta*, and *deva-kānta*. Those of nine storeys are divided into seven kinds—*saura-kānta*, *raurava*, *chaṇḍita*, *bhūshaṇa*, *vivṛita*, *supratikānta*, and *viśva-kānta*, of which the first four represent the small type of nine-storeyed buildings, the next two the intermediate type, and the last one the large type. The ten-storeyed buildings are divided into six classes, which are named *bhū-kānta*, *chandra-kānta*, *bhavana-kānta*, *antarīksha-kānta*, *megha-kānta*, and *abja-kānta*. Buildings of eleven storeys admit six varieties—*śambhu-kānta*, *īśa-kānta*, *chakra-kānta*, *yama-kānta*, *vajra-kānta* and *arka-kānta*. Finally, buildings of twelve storeys are divided into ten kinds—*pāñchāla*, *drāviḍa madhya-kānta*, *kāliṅga-kānta*, *virāṭa*, *kerala*, *vaṁśa-kānta*, *māgadha-kānta*, *janaka-kānta* and *sphūrjaka* (? *gurjara*). It deserves notice that in this instance the term by which the classes are designated are apparently geographical names.

In Chapter XXX we find, moreover, an elaborate account of staircases (*sopāna*).

CHAPTER XXXI

The Court (*Prākāra-vidhāna*)

The chapter begins with the announcement that five kinds of *prākāra* buildings will be described in connexion with *bali* (offerings), *parivāra* (attendant deities), *śobhā* (beauty), and *rakshaṇa* (defence). But the main object of the chapter is evidently to describe the various courts into which the whole compound is divided. The description of five such courts is given. The first or innermost court is called *antar-maṇḍala*. The second is known as *anta-hārā*, and the third as *madhya-hārā*. The fourth court is technically named *prākāra*. The fifth and last one is known as *mahāmaryādā* or the extreme boundary. As the title of the chapter indicates, the greater part of it describes only the fourth court. Here it may be briefly observed that this *prākāra* is also divided into the *jāti*, *chhanda*, *vikalpa*, *ābhāsa* and *kāmya* classes. Under each class a number of buildings (*śālā*) is exhaustively described. A further classification (*sankīrṇa*, etc.) is made with regard to the materials of which the *prākāra* buildings are made. These materials are the same as in other cases, namely, stone, brick, and timber.

The shrines of the attendant deities (*parivāra-vimāna*) and the gatehouses (*gopuras*) are very briefly described in conclusion, the next two chapters being entirely devoted to a special treatment of these two subjects.

SRI KASI-VISVANATHA TEMPLE, RAMESVARAM, TOGETHER WITH ITS COURTYARD, GOPURAM AND AUXILIARY BUILDINGS

Page 116

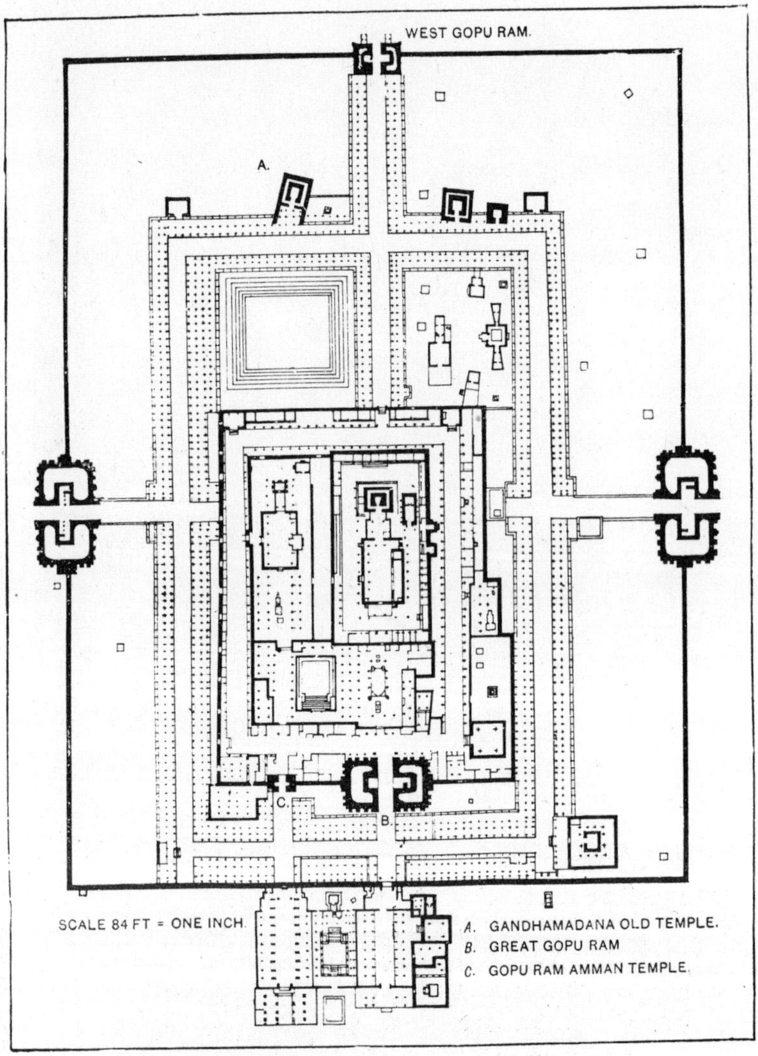

PLAN OF GANDHAMADANA OLD TEMPLE AND GREAT GOPURAM

CHAPTER XXXII

The Attendant Deities (*Parivāra-vidhāna*)

The temples of these deities are directed to be built round the *prākāra*. At the eight cardinal points of the innermost or the first court, the temples of a group of eight deities are built. Groups of sixteen and thirty-two deities are located in the second and the third courts respectively. Between the third and the fifth courts is said to be a special pavilion. After an elaborate description of the location of temples for each of the deities of the three groups, the attendant deities of Vishṇu are described in detail.

With regard to the family of Vishṇu, it may be pointed out that it also includes the same three groups of eight, sixteen, and thirty-two deities. The second group relating to Vishṇu includes Buddha too. The well-known ten incarnations of Vishṇu, except the *Matsya* (fish) and the *Kūrma* (tortoise), are included in the third group.

The temples of the Buddhists and Jains, it is expressly stated, should be constructed according to the rules of their own *Śāstras*.

It should be noticed that the description of the temples intended for so many deities does not contain any measurements, etc. The text is solely occupied with the location of these temples or deities in the compound. But a considerable portion of the chapter is devoted to the description of *maṇḍapas* (pavilions) for such purposes as bathing, sleeping, assemblies, performances of musicians and dancing girls, and stabling of cows and horses.

CHAPTER XXXIII

The Gate-house (*Gopura-vidhāna*)

Gate-houses (*gopura*) are built in front of each of the five courts into which the whole compound is divided. The *gopura* belonging to the first court (*antar-maṇḍala*) is technically called *dvāra-śobhā* or the beauty of the gate[1]; that belonging to the second court is known as *dvāra-śālā* or gate-house. The gate-house of the third court is called *dvāra-prāsāda* (gate-palace), and that of the fourth court (*prākāra*) has the name of *dvāra-harmya* (gate-edifice). The gate-house of the

[1] This term in *Prākrit* form (*duārasoha*) occurs in the *Mṛichchhakaṭika* (ed. Stenzler), pp. 72, 1, 13, in the description of Vasantasenā's palace (Act V), which is divided into seven courts.

fifth or outermost court (*mahāmaryādā*) is known as *mahāgopura* or the great gate-house.

Each of these five classes of gate-houses is subdivided again into three kinds—the small, the intermediate, and the large. Gate-houses are exhaustively described under these fifteen kinds. They are further divided into ten (? nine) classes with regard to the number of architectural members designated as *śikhara* (domes), *stūpikā* (pinnacle), *gala-kūṭa* (neck-peak), and *kshudra-nāsī* (vestibule). A *gopura* is thus technically called *śrībhoga* when its *śikhā* is like a *śālā*, and it has a circular surrounding *stūpikā*, and is furnished with a *gala-kūṭa*, four *kshudranāsīs*, and eight *mahānāsīs*. The remaining nine (eight) classes are called respectively *jaya*, *śrīviśāla*, *vishṇu-kānta*, *indra-kānta*, *brahma-kānta*, *skanda-kānta*, *śrīkara* and *saumya-kānta*. The name of one of these classes is evidently missing.

The fifteen kinds of gate-houses referred to above may have one to sixteen or seventeen storeys. But the details of those of one to five storeys only are given, others being left to the discretion of the artists and stated to be built in the same way as those described so minutely.

The measurements, both absolute and comparative, of length, breadth, and height of each storey belonging to each of the fifteen kinds of gate-houses are described at great length. The ornaments and mouldings of each storey are also given in detail. The *garbha gṛiha* (cella or sanctum), as well as all other rooms, together with their different parts, such as pillars, entablatures, walls, roofs, floors, doors, windows, etc., are exhaustively discussed.

The measurements, etc., of the gate-houses are discussed in comparison with those of the main buildings also. Then follows a lengthy description of their solid (*ghana*) and hollow (*aghana*) parts. The description of some interior members is also included in this section.

The chapter closes with an interesting description of windows, not only for gate-houses, but also for other kinds of buildings, both religious and residential. The general plan of windows seems to be this : a post or pillar is fixed in the middle to which are attached two perforated screens (*jālaka* and *pālikā*). These admit of various patterns, represented by the following names, by which they are classed with regard to their shapes, *nāga-bandha* (snake-pattern), *valli-bandha* (creeper pattern), *gavāksha* (cow's eye pattern), *kuñjarāksha* (elephant's eye pattern), *svastika* (cross pattern), *sarvato-bhadra* (ear pattern),

SHORE TEMPLE, MAHABALIPURAM

Page 118

PLATE XXXII

nandyāvarta (geometrical pattern) and *pushpa-bandha* (flower pattern). They are decorated with floral and foliated ornaments, as well as with decorative devices in imitation of jewels. The measurement of length, breadth, and thickness is entirely left to the discretion of the artist. But it is stated in conclusion that, according to some authorities, the width of the windows for gate-houses varies from 1½ to 5 cubits (*hasta*), the increment being by six *aṅgulas*. As stated elsewhere the height is regulated by five formulas, viz., 1¼, 1½, 1¾, 2, 2½ of the width.

CHAPTER XXXIV

THE PAVILION (*Maṇḍapa-vidhāna*)

The term *maṇḍapa* generally means a temple, pavilion, bower, shed or open hall. But the word has been used in three technical senses in this chapter. It is used to imply a single-storeyed house in the country, etc., or built on the sea-shore or the bank of a river, tank, or lake; secondly, it is used to imply all the detached buildings in a compound which is generally divided into five courts. But in the most general sense, it implies various sorts of rooms in a temple or residential building; for the greater part of this long chapter is devoted to a description of these rooms.

After an account of the architectural members indicated by the technical terms *bhitti* (foundation wall or floor), *alinda* (verandah), and *prapā* (shed), follows the lengthy description of *maṇḍapas*. Seven *maṇḍapas* are said to be built in front of the *prāsāda* or the main edifice. They are technically called *himaja*, *nishadaja*, *vindhyaja*, *mālyaja*, *pāriyātra*, *gandha-mādana* and *hema-kūṭa* respectively. One is said to be used for the purpose of a bath-room, another for a study or school (*adhyayana*), and so forth. Various parts of these buildings, such as walls, roofs, floors, verandas, court-yards, doors, windows, columns, etc., are described in detail. Besides these seven, various other classes of *maṇḍapas* are also described exhaustively. Their technical names, together with the main purposes for which they are built, may be given here.

The *meruja-maṇḍapa* is used as a library-room, the *vijaya* for marriage ceremonies, the *padmaka* as a temple kitchen, the *sicha* as an ordinary kitchen, the *padma* for collecting flowers, the *bhadra* for a water reservoir, store-house, etc., the *śiva* for unhusking corn, the *veda* for an assembly-hall, the *kula-dhāraṇa* for storing perfumes, the *sukhāṅga* for a guest-house, the *dārva* for an elephant's stable, and the *kauśika* for a horse stable, the *saukhyaka* and others built on the banks of the sea, river, lake, etc., are meant for purposes of pilgrimage, and the *jayāla* and others for summer residence. The plan, ornaments, etc., of each of these various classes are described in detail.

The chapter closes with a description of the forms of *maṇḍapas*. Those of temples and of the houses of the Brahmans should have the *jāti* shape. The *chhanda* shape is given to the *maṇḍapas* of the Kshatriyas, the *vikalpa* shape to those of the Vaiśyas, and the *ābhāsa* shape to those of the Śūdras. But according to some, these four classes are also said to be based on the form of the *bhadra* or front portico.

The *maṇḍapas* of two faces are called *daṇḍaka* and those of three faces *svastika ;* but the latter may also have the *lāṅgala* or plough shape. The *maṇḍapas* of four faces are known as *chatur-mukha,* those of five faces as *sarvato-bhadra,* and those of six faces as *maulika.*

A short description of *maṇḍapas* in villages or towns is given at the end. Their principal members are said to be the *lupā* (pent roof), *prastara* (entablature), *prachchhādana* (roof), *sabhā* (hall), *kūṭa* (pinnacle), etc. *Maṇḍapas* are also built on the roadside and elsewhere.

All classes of *maṇḍapas* mentioned above are described separately, according as they may belong to a temple or to the houses of the Brāhmaṇas, the Kshatriyas, the Vaiśyas, and the Śūdras respectively.

CHAPTER XXXV

The Storeyed Mansion (*Śālā-vidhāna*)

The Storeyed Mansions consist of rows of buildings varying from one to ten. The blocks of buildings varying in number of storeys up to twelve are artistically joined up. They are classified under six main groups called *daṇḍaka, svastika, maulika, chatur-mukha, sarvatobhadra,* and *vardhamāna.* Each of these is again subdivided into several types : the arrangement of the *daṇḍaka* mansion, for instance, is described under eight varieties. The *daṇḍaka* is an isolated mansion and consists of a single row of buildings and would look like a stick (*daṇḍaka*). The *svastika* mansion is plough-shaped and consists of two rows of buildings. The *maulika* mansion is shaped like a winnowing basket and consists of three rows of buildings. The *chatur-mukha* mansion is four-faced and consists of four rows of buildings. The *sarvatobhadra* mansion consists of seven rows of buildings, and the *vardhamāna* of ten rows. The huge buildings are naturally meant for kings, to the nine classes of whom they are assigned in accordance with the importance of the mansions and the rank of the king. But they are also stated to be used by the gods, the Brāhmaṇas, the Kshatriyas, the Vaiśyas, the Śūdras, the ascetics, the hermits, the priests, the Buddhists, the warriors fighting with the help of the horse, the elephant, and the chariot, the artists, and the courtesans. The lay-out, architectural members with dimensions, ornaments, and other details are fully described.

A special feature of the present chapter is the consideration of the times and season proper for the building of a *śālā*. Certain months and seasons are stated to be quite unsuitable for this purpose. Astrological and ritualistic considerations form another peculiarity of this chapter. Some classes of *śālās* are said to suit particular people born under the influences of certain planets and stars.

The chapter closes with an account of the rules of *shaḍ-varga* as applied to *śālās*, and with an enumeration of the various parts of a *śālā*.

CHAPTER XXXVI

The Situation and Dimensions of Dwelling Houses
(*Gṛiha-māna-sthāna-vinyāsa*)

The main object of the chapter is to describe the arrangement and situation of houses in the compound. The breadth of a house is said to be of five kinds, namely, from two or three *daṇḍas* to ten or eleven *daṇḍas*, the increment being by two *daṇḍas*. The length may be equal to twice the breadth. Houses are stated to be built in a village, town, port (*pattana*), grove, or hermitage, near a hill or mountain, or on the bank of a river, etc.

In Chapter XXXIV various sorts of *maṇḍapas* have been stated to be located in different parts of the five courts into which the whole compound of a temple is divided. In the present chapter, structures intended for various purposes are located in the different squares into which an inhabited area is divided, according to the *parama-śādhika* plan described in Chapter VII, called *Pada-vinyāsa*.

The *Brahma-sthāna*, or the central square, is stated to be unfit for a residential building. The temple of the family god is generally built in this part. Round this are constructed the dwelling-houses for the master of the family, his wife and children, and servants, sheds for cows, horses, poultry, etc., the kitchen and dining hall, etc., rooms for guests, for reading or study, for the daily sacrifices of the upper caste people, for amusements and music, for the dancing gīrls, and for all other domestic purposes. The arrangement of these different structures is, however, slightly different according to the caste and social position of the family. But the general plan of the dwelling-houses for a family is the same in all cases.

CHAPTER XXXVII

The First Entry into the House (*Gṛiha-praveśa-vidhāna*)

The ceremonies in connexion with the opening of and first entry into a house are described in detail. An auspicious day and moment, and the worship and sacrifice in this connexion, are still usually observed in India. The masters of the ceremonies are stated to be the *sthapati* and the *sthāpaka*. They lead the procession in circumambulating the village and the compound before the ceremonial entry into the house. The head of the family and his consort are usually the chief figures in these affairs. After completing the worship and sacrifice, a prayer is offered to the guardian angel of the house (*Gṛiha-Lakshmī*) to confer male offspring, wealth, and long life, on the master of the house.[1] After the solemn entrance into the house has been performed, the householder should feed the Brahmans, and present the architects and their followers with rich gifts.

CHAPTER XXXVIII

The Location of Doors (*Dvāra-sthāna*)

Doors and gates have already been described on various occasions. Two separate chapters are now devoted to the arrangement, location, measurement, and ornamentation of doors to be used in all kinds of buildings. Such a special description of windows has

[1] The *mantra* to be recited runs :
हे लक्ष्मीः गृहकर्तारं पुत्रपौत्रधनादिभिः ।
संपूर्णं कुरु चायुष्यं प्रार्थयामि नमस्तुते ।।

already been noted at the end of Chapter XXXIII on gate-houses (*gopura*).

It is stated in this chapter that four main doors are constructed on the four sides of all kinds of buildings of gods and men. In most cases four smaller doors are also made at the four corners. Many other smaller doors are prescribed in the intervening spaces. Drains (*jala-dvāra*) are made underneath the house.

The main doors are always furnished with a flight of steps. In many buildings the entrance-door is made, not at the middle of the frontage, but on either side of it. But in some houses they may be made in the middle of the front wall. In the case of kitchens, in particular, the main doors must be at the middle of the wall.

It is also stated expressly that where it is inconvenient to make so many smaller doors, as prescribed here, they should be replaced by windows.

The materials with which doors are constructed are mainly timber, but stone is used in some exceptional cases.

CHAPTER XXXIX

The Measurement of Doors (*dvāra-māna-vidhāna*)

The common rule is that the height of a door should be twice its breadth. But various alternative measurements are also given. The height of the larger doors may vary from 1½ cubits (*hasta*) to 7 cubits, the increment being by 6 *aṅgulas*. The height of the smaller doors varies from one cubit to three cubits, the increment being by 3 *aṅgulas*. In the former case, therefore, we have twenty-three, in the latter seventeen, varieties of dimensions.

These dimensions are prescribed for doors in the *jāti* class of buildings. But other measurements are given for doors in houses of the *chhanda*, *vikalpa* and *ābhāsa* classes. The alterative dimensions are modified by the application of the *shaḍ-varga* formulas.

The door-posts and other parts of the door are then described at great length. Doors are generally of double leaves, but those of single leaf are also mentioned.

Doors are profusely decorated with foliated and floral ornaments. The images of Gaṇeśa, Sarasvatī, and other deities should be carved over the entrance.

CHAPTER XL

THE ROYAL PALACE (*Rāja-griha-vidhāna*)

Palaces are divided into nine classes with regard to their size, according as they may belong to a king of any of the nine classes enumerated in the next chapter. Each class of palaces, whether of a *chakravartin*, *mahārāja*, *narendra*, *maṇḍaleśa*, etc., admits of nine sizes. For each one of the nine main classes it is further laid down that it should consist of a certain number of halls (*śālā*). Thus the palace of the *chakravartin*, universal monarch or emperor, should have from one to seven halls; that of the *adhirāja* (or *mahārāja*) from one to six halls; that of the *narendra* from one to five halls, and so forth.

Then the location of the various palace buildings is minutely described on the basis of the *Paramaśādhika* plan explained in Chapter VII called *Padavinyāsa*.

The *Brahma-pīṭha* is installed in the *Brahma-sthāna*, the square in the centre. The main palace of each of the nine classes of kings is then located in some of the remaining square —Indra, Varuna, Yama, Pushpadanta, etc. Among the other palace buildings enumerated we find mention of the residences of the queens, the princesses, and the private council-hall.

Other buildings, which are necessary adjuncts to the dwelling of an Indian king, are the coronation pavilion (*abhishekādi-maṇḍapa*), the arsenal (*āyudhālaya*), the store-house (*vastū-nikshepa-maṇḍapa*), the house for keeping ornaments (*bhūshaṇālaya*), the dining-hall (*bhojana-maṇḍapa*), the kitchen (*pāchanālaya*), the flower pavilion (*pushpa-maṇḍapa*), the baths (*majjanālaya*), the bed-chamber (*śayanālaya*), and several others. These all belong to the inner part (*antaḥ-śālā*) of the palace.

In the outer part (*bahiḥ-śālā*) are situated the residences of the crown prince (*yuvarāja*), of the family priest (*purohita*), of the ministers and others, likewise the hall of public audience (*āsthāna-maṇḍapa*), temples, etc.

Pleasure-gardens, flower gardens, groves, tanks, etc., are assigned their proper places. Stables for horses, elephants, and cow sheds, etc., are generally made near the main gate. Other animals, which are kept within the royal enclosure, are rams, cocks, deer, and antelopes, monkeys, tigers, and peacocks. Pavilions to witness ram-fights and cock-fights (*mesha-yuddhārtha-maṇḍapa*, *kukkuṭa yuddha-maṇḍapa*) are specially mentioned. The jail (*kārāgāra*) is located in a rather out-of-the-way place, such as the *bhṛiśa* or the *antariksha* part. At the end of the chapter it is stated that, for the rest, the arrangement is left to the choice of the king and to the discretion of the architects.

CHAPTERS XLI–XLII

Royal Courts and Characteristics of Kings
(*Rājāṅga-lakshaṇa, Bhūpāla-lakshaṇa*)

These two chapters deal with the royal courts, the classification of kings, the qualities which are required in a good ruler, and so forth.

Kings are divided, in descending progression of rank, into nine classes, namely, *chakravartin*, *mahārāja* (or *adhirāja*), *mahendra* (or *narendra*), *pārshṇika*, *paṭṭadhara*, *manḍleśa*, *paṭṭabhāj*, *prāhāraka*, and *astragrāhin*.

The opening and closing lines of Chapter XLI describe the general qualifications of all kings. They should know philosophy and religion and must be learned in all the *Śāstras*, and in the political, military, civil and moral laws. They should be haughty (*uddhata*), gracious (*lalita*), and generous (*udātta*) in their behaviour. They should have the direct knowledge of and control over the subordinate kings and ministers. They should themselves be great warriors and wise in all matters. The treasury should always be kept full and they should themselves be religious and of strict morals. They should be the protectors of their subjects. They should possess peace of mind, love of fame, good taste in matters of art, and fondness for music (*Gāndharva-śāstra*).

Then it is stated of each of the nine classes of kings what should be the number of his horses, elephants, soldiers, women, and queens. The *astragrāhin*, for instance, who is least in rank, is said to possess 500 horses, 500 elephants, an army of 50,000 soldiers, 500 female attendants, and one queen (*mahishī*). The *prāhāraka*, who follows next, has 600 horses, 600 elephants, 100,000 soldiers, 700 beautiful women, and two queens. The highest figures are reached in the case of the *chakravartin* or universal monarch.

Chapter XLII begins with the classification of kings mentioned above. The extent of their kingdoms and some special characteristics of each of the nine classes of kings are then described. The empire of the *chakravartin* reaches as far as the four oceans (*chatuḥ-sāgara*). He is the suzerain of all subordinate kings. He is strict in his judgment of right and wrong, but protects the people with kindness and mercy. He is famous and the most fortunate of all. The next king (*mahārāja* or *adhirāja*) is the lord of seven kingdoms. He has the six principal kingly qualities (*guṇa*), the six strengths (*bala*), and the three powers (*śakti*).[1] He is also versed in politics (*nīti*). He is born either in the solar or in the lunar race. The remaining seven classes of kings are similarly described.

A point of great historical interest in this passage is that royalty is no longer the monopoly of the Kshatriyas. A king may belong to any of the four castes—the Brahmans, the Kshatriyas, the Vaiśyas, and even the Śūdras. The *prāhāraka* is expressly stated to belong to any of the four castes.

The nine kinds of crowns, which pertain to these nine classes of kings, are then described. This subject, however, is more elaborately treated in Chapter XLIX (*Abhisheka-lakshaṇa*). Next comes the description of the nine kinds of thrones used by the nine classes of kings. Here other royal insignia, particularly the white umbrella (*dhavala-chhattra*), and the chowrie or fly-whisk made of the yak's tail (*chāmara*) are also mentioned. Thrones, it will be noticed, are fully dealt with in Chapter XLV (*Siṁhāsana-lakshaṇa-vidhāna*).

The next point of importance is the rate of royal revenue. The *chakravartin* takes only one-tenth of the produce as his share. The *mahārāja* takes one-sixth, the *narendra* one-fifth, the *pārshṇika* one-quarter, the *paṭṭadhara* one-third; the exact proportions of the other kings' shares are not given. No tax should be illegally imposed. Punishment and fines should be legal and moderate. The temples, as well as the Brahmans, the hermits and similar people should be supported by the state.

At the end of the chapter it is stated that this description of kings is made on the authority of the *Vedas*, the *Purāṇas*, and the *Śāstras*.

[1] The six qualities (*guṇa*) of a king are found in *Manu*, VII, 160:

सन्धिं च विग्रहं चैव यानमासनमेव च। द्वैधीभावं संश्रयं च षड्गुणं चिन्तयेत्सदा ॥

'Let him [the king] constantly think of the six measures of royal policy (*guṇa*), viz. alliance, war, marching, halting, dividing the army, and seeking protection (Bühler, *S. B. E.*, XXV, p. 241). But according to another source the six *guṇas* or qualities of a king are valour, energy, firmness, ability, liberality and majesty. The three royal powers (*śakti*) are found in the *Amarakosha* 2, 8, 1, 19—*śaktayas tisraḥ prabhāvotsāha mantrajāḥ*, 'the three powers come forth from majesty, energy, and good counsel.'

CHAPTER XLIII

Cars and Chariots (*Ratha-lakshaṇa-vidhāna*)

Cars and chariots are constructed for the ceremonial and ordinary use of gods, Brahmans and kings, as well as for war and other purposes. The wheels and other parts of cars, their shapes, their measurements, their ornamentations and mouldings are described in order.

The chapter begins with a minute description of the wheel, the most important part of the car. It is always circular, and is furnished with a strong tyre of similar shape. All its parts, together with their measurements, are described in detail—the *kukshi* (navel, *lit.* belly), *aksha* (axle), *śikhā* or *danta* (axle-band), *chhidra* (hole) and the *kīla* (axle-bolt, linch-pin), etc. Particular trees yielding timber for the wheel are enumerated. On a double support (called *ādhāra* and *upādhāra*), which rests on the axles, is raised a lofty structure which is provided with balconies (*bhadra*) and profusely decorated. It may have as many as nine storeys, the height of each upper storey being smaller than that of the one just preceding. The exact proportion is not given.

The forms of cars are next discussed. With regard to their shapes, cars are divided into seven classes—*nabhasvad-bhadraka*, *prabhañjana-bhadraka*, *nivāta-bhadraka*, *pavana-bhadraka*, *pṛishada-bhadraka*, *indraka-*(or *chandraka-*) *bhadraka*, and *anila-bhadraka*. The first of these is square, the second hexagonal, the third should have two *bhadras*, and the fourth three *bhadras*, the fifth and the sixth should have ten *bhadras*, and the last one should be furnished with twelve *bhadras*.

The description of the different shapes of cars is rather confusing. According to another classification given here, the square cars are called *nāgara*, the octagonal ones *drāviḍa*, the circular ones *vesara*, the hexagonal ones *āndhra*, and the oval ones *kāliṅga*.

These cars, in accordance with the different purposes referred to above, have various kinds of wheels and other members. Thus a fighting car has three wheels, the car for mock-fighting has four wheels, one for ordinary festivals (*nityotsava*) has five wheels, one for special festivals (*mahotsava*) may have six, seven, eight, nine or ten wheels. In the same manner the number of *vedis* (platforms) varies according to the special purpose for which a car is to be used.

Thus it is stated that the chariot of the universal monarch (*sārva-bhauma*) should have one to nine *vedikās*, that of the *mahārāja* one to seven *vedikās*, that of the *narendra* one to five *vedikās*, and so forth. The cars of Vishṇu and Śiva should consist of one to nine *vedikās*, those of Buddhist and Jain deities one to seven *vedikās*, and in the case of other gods the number should be four, or one to five.

These cars should be decorated with peacocks' feathers, chowries, arches (*toraṇa*), little bells, bright mirrors, fans and garlands. There should be also carved images of various deities, particularly on the upper part of the structure, while the basement is adorned with representations of lions, elephants, and crocodiles (*hari-kari-makara-rūpaiḥ*), with foliated ornamentation and with figures of dancers (*nāṭaka*), *bhūtas* and *yakshas*.

CHAPTER XLIV

Couches (*Śayana-vidhāna*)

Couches are meant for the use of deities, the twice-born, and members of other castes. They are said to be of two kinds, the small (*bāla-paryaṅka*) and the large (*paryaṅka*), the one being distinguished from the other by its size alone.

The measurement and various parts of the two kinds of couches are described separately. The width of the *bāla-paryaṅka* may vary from 11 to 25 *aṅgulas*, the increment being by 2 *aṅgulas*. This makes eight varieties. The *paryaṅka* proper admits of nine varieties, as they may be from 21 to 37 *aṅgulas* in width with increments of 2 *aṅgulas*.

It may be pointed out that they are generally furnished with four legs, and castors are attached to the legs so that they may easily be moved from one place to another. The legs of royal couches should be decorated with lions. The proportion of breadth to length shows that couches are generally rectangular in shape.

Special mention is made of swings suspended from four chains, which are said to be used by the gods, the Brahmans, the Kshatriyas, the Vaiśyas, etc.

The material of which couches and seats (*āsana*) are constructed is the wood of certain trees. For the legs special kinds of timber are recommended.

CHAPTER XLV

THRONES (*Siṁhāsana-lakshaṇa-vidhāna*)

The expression *siṁhāsana* implies a seat marked with a lion. This lion-seat or throne is made for the use of deities and kings. Royal thrones are divided into four classes. The *prathamāsana* is said to be fit for the first (*prathama*) coronation, the *maṅgala* throne for the coronation called *maṅgala*. The *vīra* throne for the *vīra* coronation, and the *vijaya* throne for the *vijaya* coronation. What is evidently meant is that these four thrones are employed for the four successive stages of the coronation of one and the same king.

As for the deities, the *nityārchana* throne, as the name indicates, is used for daily worship, the *nityotsava* throne for ordinary festivities, the *viśeshārchana* throne for special worship, and the *mahotsava* throne for great festivals.

Next comes a further division of thrones into ten kinds. An account of the general plan, as well as the measurements of the various parts of them, is given in detail. They are technically called *padmāsana*, *padma-keśara*, *padma-bhadra*, *śrībhadra*, *śrīviśāla*, *śrībandha*, *śrīmukha*, *bhadrāsana*, *padma-bandha* and *pāda-bandha*. Nine kinds of dimensions are given to each of the above-mentioned thrones. The right proportion in each case should be selected by the application of the rules of *shaḍ-varga*.

Of the ten kinds, the first, *padmāsana*, is used as the throne for Śiva or Vishṇu, the *padma-keśara* for the other gods and for the *chakravartin*, the *padma-bhadra* for the *adhirāja* (i.e. the *mahārāja*), the *śrībhadra* is suitable for the *adhirāja* and the *narendra*, the *śrīviśāla* for the *narendra* and the *pārshṇika*, the *śrībandha* for the *pārshṇika* and the *paṭṭadhara*, the *śrīmukha* for the *maṇḍaleśa*, the *bhadrāsana* for the *paṭṭabhāj*, the *padma-bandha* for the *prāhāraka*, and the *pāda-bandha* throne for the *astragrāhin*. It is expressly stated that lion-shaped legs should not be made for the throne of the last class of kings; but in the case of all other kings, the thrones are marked with lions and furnished with six legs. They are generally placed facing the east. The thrones of deities should face the four quarters.

At the end of the chapter the author says that the 'thrones of Vishṇu, Rudra, Jinaka, Indra, and all the other prominent gods, and also of the kings have thus been described.' It should be noticed that in the description itself no reference whatever is made to thrones of the Buddhist or Jain deities, as the term Jinaka would seem to imply.

CHAPTER XLVI

ARCHES (*Toraṇa-vidhāna*)

The *toraṇa*, or arch, is stated to be an ornament for the thrones (*āsana*) of gods and kings. It is supported on dwarf pillars (*aṅghri*), which rest on the pedestal (*pīṭha*) of the image. The arch admits of various shapes. It may be circular, triangular, crescent-shaped, bow-shaped, or of any other suitable form. Directions for making these arches, as well as the measurements of their constituent parts, are given in detail. With regard to their ornamentation, arches are divided into four kinds, technically called *patra-toraṇa* (foliated arch), *pushpa-toraṇa* (floral arch), *ratna-toraṇa* (jewelled arch), and *chitra-torana* (ornamental arch).

The various ornaments of arches are then described in detail. The top of the *toraṇa* should be decorated with figures of the heavenly musicians, Tumburu and Nārada, while *makaras* (crocodiles) are placed at the sides. The arch is supported by leogryphs (*vyāli*), which are placed on both sides of the pillars. For the rest the *patra-toraṇa*, as the name indicates, is mainly adorned with foliated ornaments, the *pushpa-toraṇa* with flowers, and the *ratna-toraṇa* with jewels. Among the other decorative devices mentioned we find the effigies of different classes of semi-divine beings, such as *yakshas*, *vidyādharas*, *kinnaras*, and *kinnarīs*. At the end of the chapter it is said that arches may also be made without any ornamentation (*chītra-hīna*).

CHAPTER XLVII

THE THEATRE (*Madhyaraṅga-vidhāna*)

In the first verse we meet with the expression *mukta-prapāṅga*, which appears to be used in the same sense as *madhya-raṅga*. It is provided with dwarf pillars or pilasters (*aṅghri-pāda*), and consists of various other members (*masūraka*, *vedi*, *mañcha*, *kuṭṭima*, *upapīṭha*, etc.), and is decorated with *uttaras*, *vājanas*, *mushṭi-bandhas* and *lupās*. It should be furnished with four *bhadras* (or with one *bhadra*) and with eight or sixteen *kshudra-nāsīs*. The upper portion is adorned with figures of leogryphs (*vyāli*) and crocodiles (*makara*). From the last but one verse of the chapter it is evident that there must be a close connexion between the *mukta-pārapṅga*, on the one hand, and the *siṁhāsana*, the *makara-toraṇa* and the *kalpa-vṛiksha*, on the other hand, the latter three subjects being discussed in the two immediately preceding and the following chapters.

From this verse it will be seen that the materials to be used for the *mukta-prapāṅga*, etc., are wood, stone, brick (terra-cotta ?) and various kinds of metal (*loha*, literally iron).

CHAPTER XLVIII

The Ornamental Trees (*Kalpa-vṛiksha-vidhāna*)

The name of the chapter is *Kalpa-vṛiksha*, which literally means a mythical tree granting all wishes or, in other words, an all-productive tree. But here it is undoubtedly a decorative device surmounting a seat (*āsana*) or throne. It is also mentioned in connexion with the *mukta-prapāṅga*, the *maṇḍapa*, and the *makara-toraṇa*.

The minute description and measurement of the various parts of the tree are given. Its trunk (*pāda*) is wound with a serpent, with expanded five-fold hood. The measurements of the snake, of its hood, and of its tail are described in detail. The number of branches as well as their size varies according to the special purpose of the throne, for the decoration of which the tree is meant. The tree is beautifully decorated with creepers, leaves, and flowers of various colours and forms. Jewels and garlands of pearls are inserted in suitable places. The figures of deities, *siddhas*, *vidyādharas*, monkeys, etc., are placed in the intervals between the branches.

Many other particulars regarding this ornamental tree are left to the discretion of the artist.

CHAPTER XLIX

Crowns and Coronation (*Abhisheka-lakshaṇa-vidhāna*)

The chapter is divided into two parts : the first part describes the crowns of gods and kings, and the second deals with the ceremonies of the coronation of kings.

The chapter opens very unusually with the description of the lavish presents to be made to the architects. These gifts consist, among other things, of girls, wealth, land, houses, and servants, both male and female.

After this introduction there follows an enumeration of the various headdresses used by gods and kings, namely, *jaṭā*, *mauli*, *kirīṭa*, *karaṇḍa*, *śirastraka, kuṇḍala* (*kuntala?*), *keśa-bandha, dhammilla, alaka, chūḍā, mukuṭa* and *paṭṭa* (turban).

Of these, the last-mentioned is subdivided into three kinds, called foliated, jewelled, and floral turbans (*patra-paṭṭa, ratana-paṭṭa,* and *pushpa-paṭṭa*).

The *jaṭā* (matted hair) and the *mukuṭa* (*lit.* diadem) are said to suit Brahmā and Śiva. The *kirīṭa* and *mukuṭa* are suited to Nārāyaṇa (i.e. Vishṇu). Other minor gods wear the *karaṇḍa* and *mukuṭa.* The love-goddess, Rati (Manonmanī), wears a *jaṭā, mauli, maṇḍala,* or *kuṇḍala.* Sarasvatī and Sāvitrī put on a *keśa-bandha* and a *kuṇḍala.* All the female deities may wear a *karaṇḍa* or *mukuṭa.*

Among the kings, the *chakravartin* (*sārvabhauma*) and the *adhirāja* wear the *kirīṭa.* The *narendra* puts on a *karaṇḍa,* and the *pārshṇika* a *śirastraka.* But the *chakravartin* and other kings may wear a *karaṇḍa* or *mukuṭa.* The *patra-paṭṭa* is suited to the *paṭṭa-dhara,* the *ratna-paṭṭa* to the *maṇḍaleśa,* the *pushpa-paṭṭa* to the *paṭṭabhāj,* and the *pushpa-mālya* (flower wreath) to the *prāhāraka* and the *astragrāha.*

The *kuṇḍala* (or *kuntala*) and *mukuṭa* are prescribed for the queen of a *chakravartin,* the *keśabandha* for the queens of an *adhirāja* and a *narendra,* the *dhammilla* and *kumuda-kuntala* for the queens of a *pārshṇika,* a *paṭṭadhara,* a *maṇḍaleśa* or a *paṭṭabhāj,* and the *alaka* and *chūḍā* for the queens of a *prāhāraka* and an *astragrāha.*

The height of a crown varies with the importance of the divine or royal bearers; it is set forth at considerable length. Next is described in detail the number of gold pieces and precious jewels in the crowns worn by the kings of various ranks and by their consorts. The forms of these crowns are then described.

The second part of the chapter deals with the royal coronation (*abhisheka*). In the coronation ceremonies of the *chakravartin* and other kings, four stages are prescribed, which are called *prathama* (here called *prāpta*), *maṅgala, vīra,* and *vijaya.* In this matter, too, the architects take a leading part. The *sthapati,* the *sthāpaka,* and the Brahman priest perform the *aṅkurārpaṇa* and all other ceremonies ending with the *adhivāsana.* Afterwards the king is anointed with various auspicious substances. This is the *abhisheka* proper. The king is then adorned with the royal robes, the sacred thread and various ornaments, and led to the coronation hall (*abhisheka-maṇḍapa*) which is furnished with the *madhra-raṅga,* the royal thrones, the wish-yielding tree (*kalpa-vṛiksha*), the ornamental arch (*torana*), and other emblems of empire.[1] The king and the queen take their places side by side on their thrones, the queen being on the left side of the king. The crown is held by the leading priests (*purohita-purogāḥ*) ; but it is actually placed on the king's head by the *sthapati* and the two *sthāpakas* at an auspicious moment during the pronouncement of *svasti* and other auspicious sounds. After this the king is garlanded, anointed, and besprinkled with various substances of good augury. Then the king mounts an elephant and circumambulates the city amidst acclamations of felicity. On the occasion of the entry into the palace, a curious ceremony takes place in order to determine the success awaiting the new king, as well as the future prosperity of the kingdom. Various auspicious and inauspicious things are arranged in a hall in the palace. The king is led there blind-folded and has to pick up anything he chooses. The thing thus picked up by the blind-folded king points to the prosperity of the people and victory of the king, or the opposite.

'If the rice-porridge or rice be touched [by him] there will be an increase of rice. If the heap of corn is touched by the [royal] hand there will be plenty of food (*subhiksha*). If gold and other precious metals be touched, it indicates that the subjects will prosper. If the sword or other weapons be touched, it bespeaks the king's prowess. It would be unfortunate for the whole kingdom, if any inauspicious things be touched by the king.'

The chapter closes with a recapitulation of the four forms of coronation, the directions as to the conduct of the ceremonial regal procession and a reference to the authorities (*Vedas* and *Purāṇas*) under which the coronation ceremonies are prescribed.

CHAPTER L

THE ORNAMENTS OF THF BODY AND ARTICLES OF FURNITURE (*Bhūshaṇa-lakshaṇa-vidhāna*)

In the first verse it is announced that the chapter is devoted to a description of the ornaments of gods and kings. In reality, only the first part of the chapter deals with ornaments proper, and the remaining

[1] Cf. Hultzsch, *South Indian Inscription*, Vol. I, p. 54, 11, 23-25, where in an Eastern Chalukya grant the *makaratoraṇa* is mentioned among the royal insignia. Professor Hultzsch quotes Sanderson's *Canarese Dictionary*, where the word is explained as 'an honorary wreath or string of flowers, etc., raised upon poles and carried in front of one, as an emblem of distinction.'

portion deal with certain miscellaneous articles of furniture, such as lamp-posts, fans, mirrors, swings, and so forth.

The first part is called 'ornaments of the body' (*aṅga-bhūshaṇa*), and the second, external ornaments (*bahir-bhūshaṇa*).

Ornaments proper are here divided into four classes, namely, *patra-kalpa*, *chitra-kalpa*, *ratna-kalpa*, and *miśrita*. All these are suited to the deities. The emperor or universal monarch (*chakravartin*, *sārvabhauma*) can put on all these ornaments excepting the *patra-kalpa*. The *adhirāja* and *narendra* can wear both the *ratna-kalpa* and the *miśrita*. The *miśra-kalpa* is prescribed for all other kings.

The *patra-kalpa* ornaments are so called, because they show foliated decoration. The *chitra-kalpa* kind consists of floral and foliated designs, precious stones, and images (*nāṭaka*). The *ratna-kalpa* variety is made of flowers and jewels. The *miśra-kalpa* decoration consists of leaves and jewels, and, in short, a mixture of all others. These four kinds, it should be observed, are specially made for the images of gods and kings only.

The following is a list of the personal ornaments mentioned in the course of the chapter :

Kirīṭa—a diadem, a crown.

Śiro-vibhūshaṇa—a head ornament.

Chūḍāmaṇi—a crest-jewel

Kuṇḍala—an ear-ring.

Tāṭaṅka (or *tāḍaṅka*)—a kind of ear ornament.

Makara-bhūshaṇa—an ear-pendant decorated with crocodile pattern (*makarāṅkita-kuṇḍala*).

Kaṅkaṇa—a bracelet.

Keyūra, *kaṭaka*—an armlet worn on the upper-arm.

Valaya—an armlet worn round the upper-arm (*bāhumūle*) or on the forearm (*prakoshṭha*).

Pūrīma—for the upper-arm.

Maṇi-bandha-kalāpa[1]—a jewelled ornament worn on the forearm.

Kiṅkinī-valaya—a bracelet (or anklet) fitted with little bells.

Aṅgulīyaka—a finger-ring.

Ratnāṅgulīyaka—a jewelled finger-ring.

Hāra[2] }
Ardha-hāra } —a string of pearls worn round the neck.

[1] Cf. *muktā-kalāpa* (*Kumāra-sambhava*, I, 43).

[2] According to *Bṛihat-saṁhitā*, LXXXII, 32, a chain of 108 strings is styled a *hāra* and a chain of 64 strings an *ardhahāra*. Kern's *Verspr. Geschr.*, Vol. II, p. 101.

Mālā—a garland or necklace hanging down from both shoulders.
Vana-mālā—a garland of wild flowers.
Nakshatra-mālā[1]—a necklace of 27 pearls.
Dāman—a garland or string worn round the shoulders.
Stana-sūtra / *Suvarṇa-sūtra*—a cord or chain worn round the breasts.
Pura-sūtra—a cord or chain worn round the chest.
Udara-bandha—a girdle worn round the waist.
Kaṭi-sūtra—a cord or chain round the loins.
Mekhalā—a girdle, a belt.
Suvarṇa-kañchuka—a golden cuirass (or bodice).
Nūpura—an anklet.
Valaya—a bracelet.
Pāda-jāla-bhūshaṇa—a net-like ornament worn on the feet.[2]

The following articles, which are reckoned to belong to the 'external' ornaments (*bahirbhūshaṇa*), are described in great detail : (1) the *dīpadaṇḍa* (lamp-post); (2) the *vyajana* (fan); (3) the *darpaṇa* (mirror); (4) the *mañjūshā* (basket, chest, box); (5) the *dolā* (swing or palanquin); (6) the *tulā* (balance) and (7) the *pañjara* (cage), *nīḍa* (nest) for domestic animals and birds.

The lamp-posts (*dīpa-daṇḍa*)[3] are of two kinds, the stationary, placed in front of the house, and the movable. The former are made of wood, iron, or stone, the latter of wood or iron. They may be square, octagonal, or circular in shape. The *vedikā* (platform) or the pedestal at the bottom of these is generally shaped like a lotus. Lamp-posts generally taper from the bottom upwards. Various other parts and also the mouldings of lamp-posts are described in detail. Their measurements are also given.

The fan-post (*vyajana-daṇḍa*), as well as the fan itself, is described in a like manner. These posts are made of timber or iron, but the fans appear to be made of leather.

[1] A *nakshatra-mālā* (*lit.* a star-cluster) consists of 27 pearls in accordance with the number of *nakshatras* or lunar mansions. Cf. *Bṛihat-saṁhitā*, LXXXII, 34.

[2] A few more terms of uncertain meaning are mentioned, namely : *viseshika* (=*tilaka ?*), *bālapaṭṭa*, *chulika*, *keśakuṭaka* and *mallika*.

[3] In literature we find the evidently synonymous expression *dīpavṛiksha* (*lit.* lamp-tree). *Mahabh.* XII, 7204 ; XIV, 1737. *Ram.* (ed. Gorresio), II, 5, 18 ; *Buddhacharita* (ed. Cowell), V, 44. Monumental lamp pillars of stone, now-a-days designated by the name of *dipdan*, are found especially in the South of India. Cf. Fergusson, *History of Indian and Eastern Architecture*, revised edition, Vol. I, pp. 347 sq., and II, 81.

Nine alternative measurements are prescribed for the mirror, namely, from 5 (or 6) *aṅgulas* up to 21 (or 22) *aṅgulas*. The mirror should be quite circular (*suvṛitta*), with the edge a little raised. The surface must be perfectly bright, the rim being decorated with linear ornaments (*rekhā*) and the reverse with the figures of Lakskmī and others. An account of the various parts is given in detail.

Three kinds of *mañjūshā* are described in detail. They are made of either timber or iron, and are square, rectangular, or circular in shape They generally consist of one, two or three compartments or chambers (*koshṭha*). The *parṇa-mañjūshā* looks like a box or trunk. The *taila* (oil) *mañjūshā* is apparently a receptacle for oil. It does not differ from the other, except in its greater height. The third kind is called *vastra-mañjūshā* and is easily identified with a wardrobe or linen-chest. Its breadth is said to vary from one to three cubits, the height and length being proportionate to the breadth.

The word *dolā* means both a swing and a palanquin; but as the description opens with the statement that the height of the post or pillar (*pāda*) varies from three to eight cubits, there can be little doubt that the passage refers to a swing. We may assume that the *phalaka*, which is repeatedly mentioned in this connexion, must be the swing-board. The swing is said to be used by both gods and men.

The balance[1] consists of the horizontal balancing rod or beam, the strings by which the scale pans are suspended, and the scale pans themselves. The two pans are made of iron, the rod of timber or iron, and the *jihvā* (*lit.* tongue) and the *toraṇa* (*lit.* arch) are always made of iron. The various parts of he balance are described minutely, together with their measurements.

A large portion of the chapter is devoted to a description of cages (*pañjara*). A number of birds and other animals are enumerated, and the size of the cage in which they are kept is given, the measurements

[1] From the description given in the text it may be conjectured that the royal balance in question was meant to be used by kings in performing the ceremony of having themselves weighed against gold and precious stones which were afterwards distributed among the Brahmans. This ceremony, known as *tulā-purusha-dāna*, was performed on certain special occasions, such as the coronation, or on the day of a solar or lunar eclipse, or on New Year's day. Cf. A. H. Longhurst, *The Tulā-purusha-dāna Monument at Hampi. Annual Report, Archaeological Survey of India for* 1912-13, pp. 142 sq., Plate LXXXIV.

admitting in each instance of nine different varieties. The following is a complete list :

	Size of cage	Increment
Mṛiga-nābhi-biḍāla (musk cat)	1—2 *hastas*	3 *aṅgulas.*
Suka (parrot)	9—23 *aṅgulas*[1]	2 ,,
Chātaka (rains-cuckoo or *cuculus melanoleucus*)	7—23 ,,	2 ,,
Chakora (partridge or *perdix rufa*)	7—23 ,,	2 ,,
Marāla (a crow-pheasant, a goose or duck)	7—23 ,,	2 ,,
Pārāvata (turtledove) ..	7—23 ,,	2 ,,
Nīlakaṇṭha (roller)	25—73 ,,	6 ,,
Kuñjarīya (ground-man) ..	5—21 ,,	2 ,,
Khañjarīṭa (wag-tail) ..	7—23 ,,	2 ,,
Kukkuṭa (cock)	15—31 ,,	2 ,,
Kulāla (*phasianus gallus*) ..	15—31 ,,	2 ,,
Nakula (mongoose, *viverra ichneumon*)	11—27 ,,	2 ,,
Tittiri (francolin partridge) ..	7—23 ,,	2 ,,
Godhā(*ra*) (alligator) ..	9—25 ,,	2 ,,
Vyāghra (tiger)	1½—3½ *hastas*	6 ,,

CHAPTER LI

THE TRIAD (*Trimūrti-lakshāṇa-vidhāna*)

The Indian Triad, to which the title of the chapter refers, consists of the three great gods, Brahmā, Vishṇu, and Siva. The chapter may be divided into two parts. The first part deals with the materials (*dravya*) of which the idols of all other deities, as well as of these three, are made. The second part describes the external features of the Triad.

The materials for making idols are nine, namely, gold, silver, copper (*tāmra*), stone, wood, *sudhā* (stucco, also mortar and plaster), *śarkarā* (*lit.* gravel or grit), *ābhāsa* (glass) and earth (terra-cotta). All the materials enumerated are well known except *ābhāsa*, of which a special description is given.

[1] Evidently there is a mistake here in the figures, which would yield only eight varieties of size. Another mistake seems to be in the size of cages, which in many cases is absurdly small.

Ābhāsa is subdivided into three kinds, called *chitra*, *ardha-chitra*, and *ābhāsa* proper. If it is perfectly transparent or visible (*sarvāṅga-dṛiśyamāna*, *lit.* which can be completely seen through), it is called *chitra;* if only half transparent or visible, it is known as *ardha-chitra* ; and in case it is partially (*lit.* one-fourth) transparent or visible, it is called *ābhāsa* proper.

The second part begins with an account of the different classes of images. An idol may be stationary (*sthāvara*) or movable (*jaṅgama*), erect, sitting, or recumbent. The movable images are used especially on the occasion of festivals. The three or four poses (*bhaṅga*), called *ābhaṅga*, *samabhaṅga*, and *tribhaṅga*, are discussed more fully at the end of Chapter LXVII.

The remaining portion of the chapter is devoted to a minute description of the images of Brahmā, Vishṇu, and Śiva, the three gods constituting the *Trimūrti*.

Brahmā should have four arms and four faces. He should wear a diadem and the matted hair of an ascetic (*jaṭā-mukuṭa-maṇḍita*). Two of his hands should be in the gift-bestowing (*varada*) and refuge-granting (*abhaya*) attitudes. The four attributes held in his hands are the water-pot (*kuṇḍika*), the rosary (*aksha-mālā*), and the large and small sacrificial ladles (*sruk-sruva*). The various ornaments, with which his body is to be adorned, are described in great detail. As to his clothes, he is said to wear a strip of bark (*chīra*) and an upper garment (*uttarīya*). His whole body should be of golden colour. Brahmā is accompanied by his two *śaktis* (female energies), the goddesses Sarasvatī and Sāvitrī standing to his right and left respectively.

Vishṇu is also four-armed (*chatur-bhuja*), but has one head. His headgear is the diadem called *kirīṭa*. He wears a yellow garment, while the colour of his body is dark blue (*śyāma*). His chest is adorned with the symbol called *śrīvatsa*. Two of his hands are in the gift-bestowing and refuge-granting attitudes. His attributes are the lotus flower, the mace (*gadā*), the discus (*chakra*), and the conch-shell called *pānchajanya*. Among the numerous ornaments which bedeck his limbs, special mention is made of the graceful garland of wild flowers (*vana-mālā*) which hangs down by both his legs. At the back of his head there is an ornamental nimbus (*siraś-chakra*, *lit.* a head-disc). Vishṇu is likewise attended by two goddesses (*Śakti*), apparently Lakshmī and Bhū-devī (the Earth-goddess).

Siva, the third member of the Triad, is four-armed and is, moreover, distinguished by a third eye, which is placed in the middle of his forehead. Like Brahmā, he wears the matted hair of the ascetic. The figure of Gaṅgā (the river personified), as well as the crescent, are inserted in his headdress, the latter on the left side. On the left side of his neck there is the mark of the deadly poison *kālakūṭa*. His dress consists of a tiger skin reaching down to the knees, and a waist-cloth. His complexion is said to be red.[1] Two of his hands are in the attitude of granting a boon (*vara*) and of conferring security (*abhaya*). In the remaining two hands he holds an antelope (*hariṇa*) and a tabor or hand-drum.[2] Śiva is accompanied by the goddess Pārvatī, who keeps standing or seated on his left side.

Images of the three members of the Triad are said to be measured in the largest type of the *daśa-tāla* measurement and those of their consorts in the middle type. The particulars of these two types of measurement are not discussed here, but reserved for an elaborate treatment in two separate chapters.

The pedestals are also dealt with in a separate chapter. Here it is very briefly stated that the pedestals of the Triad should be of the *padma-pīṭha* or the *mahā-pīṭha* kind, and be furnished with a *prapā* (canal), a *toraṇa* (ornamental arch), and *kalpa-vṛiksha* (ornamental tree).

The chapter closes with a statement that the particulars not mentioned here with regard to the making of these idols, should be supplied according to the rules of the *Śāstras*.

CHAPTER LII

The Phallus (*Liṅga-vidhāna*)[3]

Various classifications of phalli are given. They are classified first into six heads—*śaiva*, *pāśupata*, *kāla-mukha*, *mahâvrata*, *vāma*, and *bhairava*; secondly, into four—*samakarṇa*, *vardhamāna*, *śivāṅka*, and

[1] Elsewhere the complexion of Śiva is stated to be white.

[2] The name of the second attribute, which occurs also in the iconographic portion of Chapter VII, appears to be *ḍhakkā*. But this word usually indicates a large kettle-drum, whereas the tabor, which is one of Śiva's emblems, is called *ḍamaru*.

[3] The phallus worship is very popular in India : this is unmistakably proved by the fact that the number of *lingas* or phalli in India is estimated at thirty millions, of which the best known are Viśveśvara at Benares, Somanātha in Gujarāt, Mahākāla at Ujjayinī, etc.

svastika, fit to be worshipped by Brahmans, Kshatriyas, Vaiśyas, and Śūdras respectively; thirdly, into four, with regard to height—*jāti*, *chhanda*, *vikalpa*, and *ābhāsa;* fourthly, into three, with regard to width—*nāgara*, *drāviḍa*, and *vesara*; fifthly, into four—*daivika*, *mānusha*, *gāṇava*, and *ārsha*, the four together being called *svayaṁbhū*[1] or *udbhuta ;* sixthly, into two—*ātmārtha* (for one's own worship), and *parārtha*, (*lit.* for others, for public worship); again into two—*ekaliṅga* (single), and *bahu-liṅga* (phalli in a group); or into many—*vajra*, *suvarna*, etc., with regard to the material; and lastly into the *kshaṇika* (for temporary worship) class as constrasted with the permanent ones. All these kinds of phalli are described at great length. Various alternative measurements are prescribed for each of them. In some cases as many as thirty-six alternative heights are suggested. But in most cases their number is nine. The nine alternative heights of the phallus are determined in some cases by a comparison with different parts of the body of the worshipper (*yajamāna*). The height of the phallus may reach the worshipper's sex organ, navel, heart, breast, arm-joint (*bāhu-sīmānta*), chin, nose, eye, or be equal to his full length. Another comparative measurement is given with regard to the *garbha-gṛiha* (the cella of the temple in which the phallus is enshrined). Various absolute measurements also are given in some cases. These measurements vary according to the four classes, *jāti*, *chhanda*, *vikalpa*, and *ābhāsa*, mentioned above. In the *jāti* class the height may vary from 1 to 9 cubits (*hasta*), the increment being 1 *hasta*. The *chhanda* class admits of nine varieties, namely, from $\frac{3}{4}$ to $6\frac{3}{4}$ cubits, the increment in this case being $\frac{3}{4}$ *hasta*. In the third class (*vikalpa*) the hight varies from 1 to $4\frac{1}{2}$ *hastas* with increments of $\frac{1}{2}$ *hasta*, and in the fourth class (*ābhāsa*) from $\frac{1}{4}$ to $2\frac{1}{4}$ *hastas* with increments of $\frac{1}{4}$ *hasta*. Thus each of the four said classes admits of nine varieties of height. The breadth of the phallus is in like manner discussed at great length. The utility of so many alternative measurements is discussed in connexion with the application of the rules of *āyādi-shaḍvarga* described in detail at the end of the chapter.

The second part deals with the *pīṭha*, which is the stand upon which the phallus proper is placed. The *praṇāla* (*lit.* canal, drain) or

[1] The term *svayaṁbhū* (self-existent, self-created) indicates natural objects of worship. Such *svayaṁbhū-liṅgas* are even to this day worshipped at several *tīrthas* of Kāshmīr. Cf. *Kalhaṇa's Rājataraṅgiṇī*, a chronicle of the kings of Kāśmīr translated by M. A. Stein, Vol. I, p. 22 (note 1, 113).

yonidvāra, and all other parts of the *pīṭha* are described n detail, together with their measurements. The same subject is discussed in greater detail in the next chapter. The general appearance of a phallus is well known ; the *Mānasāra* does not deviate much from ıt. The *mūla* or the lower part, technically called *Brahma-bhāga* is square (*chatur-asra*, *lit.* four-cornered), whereas the middle part, called *Vishṇubhāga*, is octagonal (*ashṭāgrābha*), and the upper part, called *Śiva-bhāga*, is round. But these shapes of the three parts may be interchanged in some cases. The top is sometimes shaped like a bud (*kuḍmala*) or a leaf (*pattra*).[1]

The phallus proper and the *pīṭha* are generally made of the same material. But when they are made of very precious substances, such as jewels, gold, etc., the material of the two may differ. The *pīṭha* is mostly made of marbles of various colours such as white, red, yellow, black, etc. Precious stones are inserted in the different parts of the phallus.

The chapter closes with an account of the various fruits to be derived from phallus worship, and of the formulas of the *āyādi-shaḍvarga*.

CHAPTER LIII

THE ALTAR (*Pīṭha-lakshaṇa-vidhāna*)

It has been pointed out in the previous chapter that the *pīṭha*[2] forms the *yoni* or the lower part of the phallus. The *pīṭha* must match the phallus, of which it forms the lower member. There must, consequently, be as many kinds of *pīṭhas* as there are of the phalli. But the mouldings of the *pīṭha* are described under four classes, technically called, *bhadra-pīṭha*, *śrībhadra*, *śrīviśāla*, and *upapīṭha*. The principal parts of the *pīṭha* are the *nāla* (*lit.* canal), the *jala-dhārā* (*lit.* drain), the *ghṛita-vāri*, the *nimna*, and the *paṭṭikā*. These appear to have been intended to represent the various parts of which an ordinary *yoni* (female organ) is formed. The name of the principal mouldings are the following *prathama* or *janman*, *padma*, *kshepaṇa*, *kandhara*, *kampa*, *ūrdhva-padma*, *vājana*, *ghṛita-vāri*, and *vṛitta-kumbha*.

[1] A variant reading gives *chhattra* (an umbrella).

[2] The term '*pīṭha*' means a stool, seat, chair, throne, pedestal, an altar. The well-known fifty-one *pīṭha-sthānas* are the sacred spots where the parts of the body of Satī (Pārvatī), the consort of Śiva, fell after she had been cut to pieces by the discus of Vishṇu. As the *liṅga* or phallus symbolically represents Śiva, so the *pīṭha* does his consort Pārvatī.

A minute description and measurement of all these and other mouldings of *pīṭhas* of various kinds are given in detail. With regard to their shape, the *pīṭhas*, like the phalli (and, in fact, all other architectural and sculptural objects), are divided into three types, *nāgara*, *drāviḍa*, and *vesara*. The *pīṭhas* of the *nāgara* class are said to be square, those of the *drāviḍa* type are octagonal, and the *vesara* ones are round (*vṛitta*).

CHAPTER LIV

THE FEMALE DEITIES (*Śakti-lakshaṇa-vidhāna*)

The following female deities are specially described: Sarasvatī, the goddess of learning; Sāvitrī; Lakshmī, the goddess of wealth or fortune; Mahī, the Earth-goddess; Manonmanī, the goddess of love; Durgā; and the Seven Mothers (*Sapta-matṛi*) collectively so called. Of these, Lakshmī is distinguished into Mahā (great) Lakshmī, and Sāmānyā (ordinary) Lakshmī, the latter being installed in all the family chapels. The Seven Mothers consist of Vārāhī, Kaumārī, Chāmuṇḍī, Bhairavī, Māhendrī, Vaishṇavī, and Brahmāṇī. These seven goddesses are measured in the *nava-tāla* system, and all other female deities in the *daśa-tāla* system. The details of these measurements are discussed in two separate chapters, wherein the comparative measurements of the several parts of the various limbs of the body are given. It may be pointed out here that, according to the *daśa-tāla* system, the whole length of the body is ten times the face, while in the *nava-tāla*, it is nine times, and hence in the *ashṭa-tāla* it should be eight times the face, and so forth.

The characteristic attributes and poses, and the ornaments, decorations, etc., of each of these female deities are described in detail.

The goddess Sarasvatī is represented as seated on a lotus-seat. Her complexion is white like crystal. She is four-armed; in her two right hands she holds a *saṁdarśa*[1] and a rosary (*aksha-mālā*), and in her two left hands a book (*pustaka*) and a water-pot (*kuṇḍikā*). There exists, however, also a two-handed variety of the Sarasvatī image. Her ornaments, which are described in detail, include ear-pendants of the type called *grāha-kuṇḍala* (*makara-kuṇḍala*).

[1] Should we read it *ādarśa* (mirror)? The regular attribute of Sarasvatī, however, is the lute (*vīṇā*).

Sāvitrī, who is seated on a lotus-seat to the left of Brahmā, may be pink (white red, *śveta-rakta*) or dark blue (*śyāma*). She has two arms and two eyes, in other words she assumes a purely human shape. She holds a blue lotus flower (*utpala*) in her right hand, while her left hand is stretched out in the pose of granting a boon (*vara*). Sāvitrī, too, is adorned with various ornaments.

Lakshmī, the goddess of good fortune, looks benign (*prasanna-vadanā*) ; her complexion is pure gold. She has four arms. Her upper right hand is raised in the attitude of granting security (*abhaya*), and in her other right hand she holds either a red lotus flower (*padma*) or a rosary. The attributes held in her left hands are a tabor or hand-drum (*ḍiṇḍima*) and a blue or red lotus flower. As befits the goddess of luck, she is bedecked with gorgeous ornaments and jewels.

In contradistinction with the Great Lakshmī (Mahā-Lakshmī) thus described, the ordinary Lakshmī is said to have only two hands in each of which she holds a red lotus flower (*rakta-padma*). Her distinguishing feature is that she is placed between two elephants with uplifted trunks. A brief account is given about representations of Lakshmī as the spouse of Vishṇu.

The Earth-goddess (Mahī-śakti), who is placed on the other side of Vishṇu, is said to be two-armed and two-eyed. In her right hand she holds a blue lotus (*utpala*) ; with her left hand she indicates the granting of a gift. She has a dark blue (*śyāma*) complexion and wears *makara* ear-rings.

Durgā, also called Gaurī and Pārvatī, the consort of Śiva, is two-armed. She holds a blue lotus in her right hand and her left hand is in the pose of granting a gift (*vara*). She is distinguished by all the marks of female beauty and is profusely adorned with ornaments. She has a dark blue (*śyāma*) complexion and wears yellow garments. She is placed to the left of Śiva, or of his symbol, the *liṅga*.

Manonmanī(?), the goddess of love, is four-armed and three-eyed. Strange to say, her hair-dress is said to be the matted hair (*jaṭā*) of an ascetic. Two of her hands are in the attitude of assuming protection (*abhaya*) and of granting a boon (*vara*). In each of the two other hands she holds a lotus flower. Her complexion is pink (red white, *śveta-rakta*) or dark blue (*śyāma*). It appears that this *Śakti* also is reckoned as belonging to the retinue of Śiva, in whose temple she is worshipped.

Finally, the Seven Mothers are described. In general these *Saktis* have the same emblems and distinguishing features as their male counterparts. Brahmāṇī and Rudrāṇī, for instance, who are the *Śaktīs* of Brahmā and Rudra (or Śiva) respectively wear the matted hair of the ascetics. Brahmāṇī has four faces and four hands, in two of which she holds a rosary (*aksha-mālā*) and a water-pot (*kuṇḍikā*). Rudrāṇī has a white complexion, her attributes are the antelope (*hariṇa*) and the noose (*pāśa*). Vaishṇavī and Vārāhī, who are both *Śaktis* of Vishṇu, are distinguished by a dark blue (*śyāma*) complexion and hold the discus (*chakra*) and conch-shell (*śaṅkha*) which are the well-known emblems of Vishṇu. Vārāhī has a boar's head.

The chapter closes with a very brief reference to the plumb-lines which are more fully treated in a separate chapter.

CHAPTER LV

The Jain Images (*Jaina-lakshaṇa-vidhāna*)

The opening lines describe in detail the various kinds of measurements used in Indian sculpture.

The linear measurement is divided into six kinds, *māna*, *pramāṇa*, *parimāṇa*, *lamba-māna*, *unmāna*, and *upamāna*.

The measurement from the foot to the top of the head is called *māna*, which is in fact nothing but height. *Pramāṇa* is the measurement of breadth (*vistāra*); *parimāṇa* is the measurement of girth or circumference (*paritaḥ*); *lamba-māna* is the measurement along the plumb-line or the line drawn perpendicularly through the different parts of the body, the *māna* or the measurement of the height being determined by the surface of the body; *unmāna* is the measurement of thickness (*nimna*) or diameter; and *upamāna* is the measurement of interspace (*antara*), such as that between the two feet of an image; this measurement is evidently taken from one plumb-line to another.

The primary measurement (*ādi-māna*) refers to comparative measurement and is divided into nine kinds. The height of an image is determined firstly, by comparing it with the breadth (*tāra*) of the whole temple (*harmya*); secondly, with the height of the cella or sanctum (*garbha-gṛiha*); thirdly, with the height of the door (*dvāra-māna*); fourthly, with the measurement of the base (*adhishṭhāna*); fifthly, by expressing it in cubit (*hasta*); sixthly, in the *tāla* system;

seventhly, in *aṅgulas*; eighthly, by comparing it with the height of the worshipper; and ninthly, with the height of the riding-animal (*vāhana*) or with the height of the principal idol (*mūla-bera*).

Absolute measurement in cubits (*hasta*), etc. is given in the case of many architectural and sculptural objects.

The *aṅgula* (*lit.* finger) measurement has reference to both comparative and absolute measurements. Three kinds of *aṅgulas* are expressly distinguished, and a fourth *aṅgula* is added later.

(*a*) The *berāṅgula* is the measurement taken by the *aṅgula* or finger of the main idol.

(*b*) The *mānāṅgula* refers to the ordinary absolute measurement in *aṅgulas*, one *aṅgula* being equal to eight *yavas* (barley grains) or three-quarters of an English inch.

(*c*) The *mātrāṅgula* is the measurement determined by the length of the digit and the width of the middle finger in the right hand of the master (*kartṛi*).

(*d*) Another kind of *aṅgula* measurement is determined by dividing the whole length of the body of an image into a number of equal parts, each of which is called a *deha-labdhāṅgula* or simply *dehāṅgula*. In the last sense, *aṅgula* is used to mean simply a part. Thus both *aṅgula* and part (*aṁśa*, *mātrā*) are indiscriminately used throughout the work. If the length, etc., of a building or image is divided into a number of equal parts for some special purpose, each of them is called *aṅgula aṁśa*, or *mātrā* indiscriminately. This lack of discrimination has been very confusing in many places, rendering it extremely hard to distinguish an absolute measurement from a comparative one.

The height of the image is determined by comparing it with the height of the worshipper (*yajamāna*). It may be of nine kinds, according as it extends from the foot of the worshipper to his sex-organ, navel, heart, breast, arms, chin, tip of the nose, hair limit (on the forehead), or to his full height. The *tālamāna* admits of many varieties; the ten-*tāla* measurements vary from one *tāla* to ten *tāla*; each of these is again divided into three types, the *uttama* or the largest, the *madhyama* or the intermediate, and the *adhama* or the smallest. Thus an image is of the *daśa-tāla* measurement when its whole length, is equal to ten times the face. In the largest type of the *daśa-tāla* system, the whole length is divided into 124 equal parts, which are proportionately distributed over the different limbs of the body; in the intermediate type, the whole length is divided into 120 equal parts and in the smallest type, into 116 equal parts. In the *nava-tāla* system, the whole length would be nine times the face ; in the *ashṭa-tāla*, eight times ; and so forth. Several of these *tāla* measures are described in detail in the subsequent chapters.

The varieties of the alternative measurements in each case are simplified by the application of the rules of *āyādi-shaḍ-varga*.

The main object of the chapter, namely, the description of the Jain deities, is thus submerged in a lengthy discussion of the various measurements used both in architecture and sculpture.

Like all other idols, the images of Jain deities, too, may be stationary or movable ; they may be in the erect or in the sitting posture. They have a purely human shape, and wear neither robes nor ornaments. On the chest the *śrīvatsa* symbol is marked in gold. They are placed on a throne decorated with the *makara-toraṇa*, and the ornamental tree (*kalpa-vṛiksha*), and are attended by Nārada and other sages, by Yakshas, Vidyādharas, Siddhas, Nāgendras, and Lokapālas, etc. All these attendants, it should be observed, are also known as Hindu deities.

The twenty-four *Tīrthaṅkaras*, or Jain saints, are referred to but not specified.[1]

CHAPTER LVI

The Buddhist Images (*Bauddha-lakshaṇa-vidhāna*)

The account of these images, too, is very meagre. Evidently the author had in mind solely the effigies of Buddha, not of other Buddhist deities. This is clear from his description. These figures, he says, which may be either erect or in the sitting posture, are placed on a throne (*siṁhāsana*), and are distinguished by the *aśvattha* (holy fig) tree as well as by the *kalpa-vṛiksha* (mythic wonder-tree). The latter, as we have seen, is represented in connexion with other divine beings as well, but the *aśvattha* or *ficus religiosa* is characteristic of Buddha, as the Bodhi-tree, under which he attained enlightenment (*bodhi*), belongs to that species. Another peculiar mark of Buddha, which

[1] Cf. James Burgass, *Digambara Jaina Iconography*, *Indian Antiquary*, Vol. XXXII, pp. 459 sqq., for the full list of the Jain Saints ; *see* also the writer's *Encyclopaedia of Indian Architecture.*

PLATE XXXIV(a)

CARVINGS AT AMARAVATI STUPA

PLATE XXXIV(b)

has been duly noted by the author, is the *ushṇīsha* or protuberance of the skull (*ushṇīshojjvala-maulika*).[1] For the rest, the appearance of Buddha is purely human. He has a full face, a long nose, smiling eyes and elongated ears. His body is fleshy, his chest broad, his belly round, and his arms long. He wears a yellow garment (*pītāmbara-dhara*), and his complexion is white. Like other idols, the Buddha images are made of wood, stone, or iron (*loha*). They are measured according to the largest type of the *daśa-tāla* system.

CHAPTER LVII

Images of Sages (*Muni-lakshaṇa-vidhāna*)

The seven well-known patriarchs or sages (*ṛishi* or *muni*) are taken to illustrate the three varieties of the *tāla* measurement. They are Agastya, Kāśyapa, Bhṛigu, Vaśishṭha, Bhārgava, Viśvāmitra, and Bharadvāja.

Agastya is bright blue (*śyāma*) in colour; Kāśyapa, yellow (*pīta*); Bhṛigu, dark or black (*kṛishṇa*); Vaśishtha, red (*rakta*); Bhārgava, brownish (*piṅgala*); Viśvāmitra, red (*rakta*); and Bharadvāja, yellow (*haridra, lit.* turmeric-coloured). They are represented in a purely human shape, being two-armed and two-eyed; they wear yellow garments and the sacred thread (*yajña-sūtra*), and are distinguished by the matted hair of the ascetics (*jaṭājūṭa*). In their two hands they hold a staff (*daṇḍa*) and a book (*pustaka*). Of Agastya, who is mentioned first among the seven sages, it is stated particularly that he is corpulent (*bṛihatkukshi*) and hump-backed (*kubjākāra*).

Of these seven sages, Agastya is measued in the seven-*tāla*, Kāśyapa and Bhṛigu in the eight-*tāla*, and the rest in the nine-*tāla*. The details of these three *tāla* measurements are given subsequently.

In the *sapta*- or seven-*tāla* measurement, the whole length of the image is seven times the height of the face, which is generally twelve *aṅgulas* (9 inches) in the Indian system. This length is divided into $12 \times 7 = 84$ equal parts, of which the proportional distribution among the different limbs is explained at great length.

[1] The *urṇā*, or mark between the brows, which is another distinguishing feature of Buddha, is not noticed in the course of this description.

In the *ashṭa-* or eight-*tāla* system, the whole length is similarly divided into 96 equal parts, and in the nine-*tāla* into 108 equal parts.

CHAPTER LVIII

Images of Yakshas, Vidyādharas, etc. (*Yaksha-vidyādhara-vidhāna*)

The present chapter deals briefly with four classes of semi-divine beings, namely, *Yakshas*, *Vidyādharas*, *Gandharvas*, and *Kinnaras*. They are said to have two arms and two eyes, in other words, they assume a purely human appearance. They are adorned with the crown known by the name of *karaṇḍa*. The colour of the *Yakshas* is stated to be dark blue (*śyāma*) and yellow (*pīta*), that of the *Vidyādharas* dark red (*śyāma-rakta*) and yellow. The images, both of the *Yakshas* and the *Vidyādharas*, are measured according to the *nava-tāla* system. The *Yakshas* are distinguished from the *Rākshasas*, the latter being evil spirits, while the former are regarded as supernatural beings of a benevolent and inoffensive disposition. The *Yakshas* act as attendants (*anuchara*) and chowry-bearers of the gods. The *Vidyādharas* are a kind of fairies possessed of magical powers. Here, apparently, they are described as *Atlantes*. The *Gandharvas* are celestial choirs, and celebrated as musicians.

The description of the *Kinnaras* is contained in a *Mālinī* stanza at the end of the chapter : 'The legs are like those of an animal, the upper part of the body is like that of a man, the face is like that of Garuḍa (the bird of Vishṇu), and the arms are provided with wings. He is adorned with a diadem and a red lotus, has the beautiful hue of a flower, and holds a lute (*vīṇā*). These are the characteristic features of the *Kinnara*.[1]

CHAPTER LIX

Images of Devotees (*Bhakta-lakshaṇa-vidhāna*)

Devotees are divided into four classes according to the four stages of holiness and are called *sālokya*, *sāmīpya*, *sārūpya*, and *sāyujya*.[2]

[1] It may be noticed that the body of the *Kinnara* is a combination of the bodies of a man, an animal, and a bird.

[2] The *sālokyādi-chatushṭaya* is also mentioned in the *Bhāgavata-purāṇa*, IX, 4, 67. The literal meaning of the four terms in question is : dwelling in the same world (viz. as the deity), dwelling in the vicinity (of the deity), being in conformity with (the deity), and being united with (the deity).

VAJRASANA AT BODHGAYA

PLATE XXXV

INTERIOR VIEW OF RAMESVARAM TEMPLE

Sālokya is the result of devotion (*bhakti*), knowledge (*jñāna*), and renunciation (*vairāgya*). Knowledge combined with renunciation leads to *sāmīpya*. *Sārūpya* is produced in the worshipper by meditation alone, and *sāyujya* is attained by the true knowledge (of God).

The images of the *sālokya* class of worshippers are measured in the largest type of the *nava-tāla* system, in which the whole length is divided into 112 equal parts. Those of the *sāmīpya* class are measured in the smallest type of the *daśa-tāla* system, in which the whole length is divided into 116 equal parts. Those of the *sārūpya* class are measured in the intermediate type of the *daśa-tāla* system, in which the whole length is divided into 120 equal parts. And the figures of the *sāyujya* class are measured in the largest type of the *daśa-tāla* system, in which the whole length is divided into 124 equal parts.

The first two systems, namely, the largest type of the *nava-tāla* and the smallest type of the *daśa-tāla*, are minutely described in this chapter. The other two systems, that is, the intermediate and the largest types of the *daśa-tāla*, are treated subsequently in two separate chapters.

CHAPTER LX

Riding Animals of the Gods : the Goose

(*Vāhana-vidhāne Haṁsa-lakshaṇa*)

The chapter opens with the announcement that the *vāhanas* of the Triad (*Trimūrti*) will now be described. But only one of them, namely, the Goose (*haṁsa*), is described in this chapter, the other three, the Garuḍa, the Bull, and the Lion being described in the next three chapters. In these four chapters, the term *vāhana* is used to designate the various animals and birds used by the gods and goddesses for riding.

The goose is the *vāhana* of Brahmā. The limbs of the goose are said to be measured in the largest type of the *dvi-tāla* system. The details of this system are described minutely. The goose is white all over, with red legs and golden beak.

The chapter closes with the statement that rows of geese should be beautifully carved or painted in the temples of the gods and in the mansions of Brahmans and kings; they are figured on the entablature (*prastara*), on the upper part of the *uttara*, on the *kūṭa*, *nīḍa*, and *grīvā* (neck).

CHAPTER LXI

The Garuḍa (*Garuḍa-lakshaṇa-vidhāna*)[1]

The chapter opens with a lengthy discussion on the application of the rules of *āyādi-shaḍ-varga*, in order to reconcile various comparative measurements suggested for the Garuḍa and other riding animals of the gods.

Garuḍa is the *vāhana* of Vishṇu. His limbs are measured in the *nava-tāla* system, the details of which are given in a previous chapter. He is figured in an erect or sitting posture, and as meditating on Vishṇu with joined palms. The arrangement of his various limbs and their colour, etc., are described at great length. The Garuḍa is figured partly as a human creature and partly as a bird. He is provided with feathers, with wings painted in five colours, and with a beak (*tuṇḍa*); but, on the other hand, the description refers to his arms (*prakoshṭha*), his ears, and hair (*keśa*). He wears various ornaments (*sarvālaṅkāra-saṁyukta*), including a diadem of the kind called *karaṇḍa* (*lit.* a basket), and is gorgeously painted in a great variety of colours. He is described as being of a terrific appearance (*ugradṛiś*). His worship is stated to be conducive to the destruction of the enemy (*śatru-nāśa*).

CHAPTER LXII

The Bull (*Vṛishabha-lakshaṇa-vidhāna*)

The bull, Nandin,[2] is the animal of Śiva. Its image, which may be either recumbent or erect, is placed facing the Śiva temple on

[1] The Garuḍa is a mythical bird, the sovereign of the feathered tribes and the enemy of the serpent (*Nāga*) race. There is a tradition that Garuḍa is the son of Kāśyapa and Vinatā. Hence the metronymic Vainateya, by which he is often designated. The myth of the birth of Garuḍa is told in the *Mahābhārata*, *Ādi-parva*, Chapter XVI.

[2] The image of the bull Nandin is regularly found in front of temples dedicated to Śiva. A well-known example is the colossal recumbent bull, placed opposite to the famous *vimāna* of Tanjore. It is hewn out of one block of black granite and measures 16 feet in length and 13 feet in height. A remarkable bronze Nandin, which is found at Brāhmor (Chambā) in the Western Himālaya and which, on the evidence of an inscription, may be assigned to the seventh century A.D., is illustrated in the *Antiquities of Chamba State* (*Archaeological Survey of India*, New Imp. Series, Vol. XXXVI, Part I, Plate X).

pedestal (*pīṭha*), either inside the shrine, or in a pavilion (*maṇḍapa*) in front of the temple, or at the door. It is not measured in any *tāla* system. Various absolute and comparative measurements are prescribed. Its height, for instance, may be equal to the height of the idol (of Śiva), or up to its ears or arms, or the height may be from one cubit to nine cubits, or equal to three-fourths or one-half of the height of the door of the temple. The bull Nandin is made either solid or hollow, of iron (*lauhaja*), stone, wood, *ābhāsa* (glass), *ratna* (precious stone), *sudhā* (stucco), terra-cotta, and *śarkarā* (grit).

The description and measurements of the various limbs of the bull are given in great detail. From the description it would appear that the bull of Śiva is white in colour except the four legs, the hoofs, and the ears, which are red. He is covered with a tiger skin and wears not only garlands round the neck but even foot-rings or anklets (*nūpura*).

CHAPTER LXIII

The Lion (*Siṁha-lakshaṇa-vidhāna*)

The lion is the last of the four divine *vāhanas*, to which a chapter is d[illegible]

[illegible]ase of the bull, the image of the lion is not measured [illegible] *tāla* s[illegible]tem. The absolute measurements of the various parts of the lion, expressed in *aṅgulas*, are enumerated. The lion is made in an erect, sitting, or recumbent posture. His tail is generally equal to his height. His four legs are like those of the tiger. His colour is white, but his mane should be red. The shape of his nails and teeth is compared to that of the crescent (*bāla-chandra*, *ardha-chandra*).

CHAPTER LXIV

The Image (*Pratimā-vidhāna*)

This chapter, which is missing in all the manuscripts but one, opens with the announcement that herein will briefly be described

[1]At the beginning of the chapter (and again in the concluding verse) the lion is loosely indicated as 'the riding animal of the gods' (*devānāṁ vāhana*). It is, however, well known that the lion (or the tiger) is more particularly the animal of Pārvatī, the consort of Śiva. It is hardly necessary to point out that of the other deities, both male and female, each, as a rule, has his or her own *vāhana*, e.g. Kārttikeya, the peacock ; Gaṇeśa, the mouse ; Indra, the elephant ; Yama, the buffalo ; Sūrya, a chariot drawn by seven horses ; Varuṇa, a crocodile (*makara*) ; Kubera, a man (whence his epithet *nara-vāhana*), etc.

the measurements from head to foot of the sixteen attendant deities of the Vishṇu temple. It will be remembered that in Chapter XXXII on 'attendant deities' (*Parivāra-vidhāna*), groups of eight, ten, sixteen, and thirty-two deities have been mentioned, who are stated to occupy subsidiary shrines in the compound of a large Vishṇu temple.

But the contents of the chapter, in reality, do not expressly describe any of the groups of deities in question. The first part deals with the various kinds of comparative mea urements already discussed at the beginning of Chapter LV on the Jain deities. The second part elaborately describes the rules of the *āyādi-shaḍ-varga*, which have been repeatedly mentioned whenever a variety of measurements was suggested for any particular object.

The comparative measurement is distinguished into twelve kinds, according as it is compared with the phallus, the main Vishṇu image, the width of the sanctum (*garbha-griha*), the breadth of the main temple (*harmya, prāsāda*), the door, flagstaff (*vaṁsa*), basement, pillar; or is based on cubit (*hasta*) measurement, *tāla*-measurement, the measurement of the worshipper, and *aṅgula* measurement.

The *aṅgula* is further distinguished, as already pointed out, into three kinds; namely, *liṅgāṅgula* or *berāṅgula*; the *manāṅgula*, viz. *aṅgula* of eight *yavas* or three-quarters of an inch, and the *dehalabdha-aṅgula*, viz. one of the equal parts into which the whole length of an image is divided. The measurement obtained from a comparison with the height of the main idol or the worshipper is of nine kinds, as it may reach the full length (of the idol or the worshipper), his eyes, nostrils, chin, arms, breast, heart, navel, and sex organ.

Other measurements obtained from a comparison with the phallus, and various parts of the temple, such as the door, the pillar, etc., admit of many varieties and proportions.

CHAPTER LXV

THE LARGEST TYPE OF THE DAŚA-TĀLA MEASUREMENT

(*Uttama-daśa-tāla-vidhāna*)

In this system the whole length of an image is divided into 124 equal parts, which are proportionately distributed over the different parts of the body from head to foot. The measurement of breadth, etc., of the various limbs is not included in these 124 parts. The measurement of the hand, etc., is also excluded. All the numerous parts of the body are minutely described. Such minute measurement as that of the finger-digit, the interspace between two toes, etc., has not escaped the notice of the author of the *Mānasāra.*

CHAPTER LXVI

The Intermediate Type of the Daśa-tāla Measurement

(*Madhyama-daśa-tāla-vidhāna*)

The female deities of the higher order are generally measured in this system. The whole height of the image is divided into 120 equal parts, which are proportionately distributed over the various parts of the body from head to foot. The details are minutely described.

The face is taken as the standard of the *tāla* measurement, and is generally twelve *aṅgulas*, or about nine inches, in length. The face is stated to be of oval shape (*kukkuṭāṇḍa-samākāra, lit.* shaped like the egg of a hen). The eyebrow is shaped like the bow (*chāpākāra*), the eyes like a fish (*matsyākāra*), the nose like the sesame flower (*tilapushpākṛiti*), and the nostrils (*puṭa*) like a bean (*nishpāva-bīja*).

According to both Indian and European canons, a well proportioned male human figure is equal to eight times (*ashṭa-tāla*) the length of the face, and a female human figure is seven and a half times the length of the face. 'The other rules arrived at by the Indian artist do not appear to be divergent from those evolved by the European artist, and if in Indian sculpture the results are not good in some instances, it is the fault of the artist and not attributable to the guide book.'[1]

CHAPTER LXVII

The Plumb-lines (*Pralamba-lakshaṇa-vidhāna*)

The plumb-lines, as has already been pointed out, are lines drawn through the body of an image in order to find out accurately the perpendicular and the horizontal measurements of the different parts of the body.

This is done by means of an instrument called *pralamba-phalaka*, which is a square plank of four, three, two, or one *aṅgula* in thickness,

[1] T. A. Gopinath Rao, *Elements of Hindu Iconography ; see* p. 156, and the writer *Encyclopaedia* for further details under Tālamāna.

with the sides equal to three-fourths or one-half of the length of the image. Another plank of the same size is used as the stool on which the image is placed. The first mentioned plank (*pralamba-phalaka*) is fixed to the crown of the head of the image. The planks are kept parallel to each other. Holes are made in the upper plank, wherefrom are suspended strings at the other end of which are attached small balls of iron or stone. The number of holes and strings suspended from them, by which the plumb-lines are determined, varies from five to eleven, according to the different postures and poses of the image. The five principal plumb-lines consist of one drawn from the centre of the upper plank corresponding to the crown of the head, and four on the four sides of the body. Two other lines drawn adjoining the right and left sides of the face make the number seven. Another two lines drawn on the right and left sides of the back of the head make the number nine, and two lines drawn from the two armpits make the total of the lines eleven.

The line drawn from the crown of the head (*śikhā-maṇi*, *lit.* crest jewel) passes by the diadem and the headdress, the middle of the forehead, the eyebrows, the nose, the chin, the neck, the chest (*hṛidaya*), the navel, the sex organ, the thighs, between the knees, the ankles (*nalaka*), the heels, the soles of the feet, and the two big toes. This is evidently drawn along the surface of the body in a perfectly erect or straight posture of the image. The other plumb-lines, too, touch different parts of the body; but they are not particularly mentioned here.

Very minutely are described the comparative and the absolute measurements of the perpendicular distance between different parts of the body by a plumb-line, as well as the horizontal distance from one line to another. The distance, say, between the two big toes, is said to be eight *aṅgulas*. The variation of these measurements in different postures and poses is carefully considered.

The three postures of images, namely, erect or standing (*sthānaka*), sitting (*āsana*), and recumbent (*śayana*), are frequently mentioned in the *Mānasāra*.[1]

[1] Each of these three, of course, admits of a variety. The sitting posture (*āsana*) is in particular distinguished into various forms in Indian literature and sculpture, such as the *padmāsana*, *bhadrāsana*, *vajrāsana*, *vīrāsana*, *svastikāsana*, *yogāsana*, etc. In some books, even eighty-four postures are enumerated. These manners of sitting form part of the eight-fold observances of ascetics.

In the present chapter a special reference is made to the three *bhaṅgas* or poses which are distinguished in Indian sculpture. They are known as *sama-bhaṅga* or equipoise, *ābhaṅga* or a slight flexion, *ati-bhaṅga* or an excessive flexion, and *tri-bhaṅga* or of three flexions.[1]

CHAPTER LXVIII

The First Casting of the Image (*Madhūchchhishṭa-vidhāna*)

The chapter opens with an enumeration of the names of phalli and asceties (*muni*), as well as of architects,[2] but the subject proper is the casting of an image in wax (*madhūchchhishṭa*). The *sthapati* and the *sthāpaka* prepare the wax, but the manner of its preparation is not expressly described. All kinds of images, temporary or permanent, stationary or movable, are moulded in wax. The process appears to be this. Some part of the image is covered with a thin copper-leaf (*tāmra-patra*) and the wax is laid on two or three *aṅgulas* deep. Earth (*mṛittikā*) is spread above the part covered with wax. The idol is heated after it has been besmeared. If the master likes, the smearing may be done with melted iron too. One-half of the image, which is not covered with earth, is washed in water. The process is repeated several times. If any of the minor limbs be lost through this process, the image should be furnished with it again after having been heated. But if the head or the middle of the body (*madhyakāya*) be damaged, the whole image should be changed. If the master does not approve of the image, it should be recast. The whole process in its different stages has to be attended by many ritualistic ceremonies.

[1] The expression *tri-bhaṅga* (and *tri-bhaṅgin*) is applied to Kṛishṇa in his aspect of the divine cow-herd (Gopāla) playing the reed-pipe. Cf. *Een onbekend Indisch tooneelstuk* (*Gopālakeli-chandrikā*). *Tekst met inleiding door* W. Calland. (Verhand. Kon. Akad. v. Wetensch, te Amsterdam N. R. Dl. XVII, No. 3. Amsterdam 1917, p. 46, 1. 1 (*marakata-vibhaṅgojjvala-tri-bhaṅgāṅga-gopālena*) and p. 124, 132 (*tri-bhaṅgin*).

[2] The six kinds of phalli (*jyotir-liṅga*) enumerated here are : *śaiva, pāśupata, kāla-mukha, mahāvrata, vāma*(*na*) and *bhairava*. Cf. above, where the fifth class is called *vāma*. The names of the *munis* are Agastya, Kāśyapa, Bhṛigu, Gautama, Bhārgava, Gālava (?Gārga), etc., cf. above. The expert authorities on architecture are the following : Viśvakarman, Viśveśa, Viśvasāra, Prabodhaka, Vṛita, Maya, Tvashṭṛi, Manu, Nala, Mānavit, Mānakalpa, Mānasāra, Prashṭṛi, Mānabodha, Viśvabodha, Naya, Ādisāra, Viśāla, Viśvakāśyapa, Vāstubodha, Mahātantra, Vāstuvidyāpati, Pārāśarīyaka, Kālayūpa, Chaitya, Chitraka, Āvarya, Sādhakasāra-saṁhitā, Bhānu, Indra, Lokajña; and Saura.

In other texts the process of casting an image is much more clearly described :

'If images have to be cast in metal, the wax must first be melted and poured (out of the mould) and all defects removed with cloth.'[1]

'If the images be required to be made of earth, rods (of metal or wood) must be (inserted in them), if of metal, they must first be prepared well in wax.'[2]

'If an image is to be made of metal, it must first be made of wax, and then coated with earth; gold and other metals are purified and cast into (the mould) and a complete image is thus obtained by capable workmen.'[3]

'In regard to bronze images,' says Mr. Rao,[4] 'it is believed by some that India could not have known the *cire perdue* method of making metal images earlier than about the tenth century A.D., and that India must have therefore borrowed it from Europe. That the art of casting metals in wax moulds is much earlier in India can be shewn in more ways than one.' In support of his assertion, Mr. Rao cites the three above-mentioned quotations.

CHAPTER LXIX

The Defects of the Limbs (*aṅga-dūshaṇa-vidhāna*)

The chapter opens with the announcement that it will describe the evil consequences of a defective construction of buildings, which threaten the king, the kingdom, and the maker. It is laid down that no part of a building should be larger or smaller than what is prescribed. But nothing is further stated about the defects themselves. Nor are images separately mentioned. The penalties for defective construction are enumerated with regard to the different architectural members, such as doors, staircases, columns, walls, domes, spires, etc. Thus, it is stated that, if the altar (*vedikā*) be too small, the master will lose his eyesight; if the pinnacle (*stūpikā*) be too large or too small, the people will be afflicted with poverty; if the columns be too large or too small, the family of the master will be exterminated, and so forth.

[1] *Karaṇāgama*, II, V, 41.

[2] *Suprabhedāgama*, XXXIV, 21.

[3] *Vishṇu-saṁhitā, paṭala*, 14.

[4] *Ibid, Elements of Hindu Iconography.*

No such penalties, however, are mentioned for defects in sculptural objects.

CHAPTER LXX

The Chiselling of the Eye (*Nayanonmīlana-lakshaṇa-vidhāna*)

When the Indian sculptor has carved a divine image, the ceremony of chiselling (*lit.* opening) the eyes of the idol is the final function, by which it is, as it were, imparted with eyesight and rendered fit to be worshipped. The custom is quite ritualistic, although it is stated here that it should be carried out by the architect. The ceremonies consist in the worshipping of different deities, in performing the sacrifice with the holy fire, and in the *ratna-śuddhi* (*lit.* purifying the jewel), etc.

The setting of precious stones in the different parts of the phallus and in the images of the deities is also described in the present chapter.

This last chapter of the work closes with the statement that this science of architecture and sculpture was originally described by Brahmā, Indra, and all the other gods, and that the *Mānasāra* has been compiled on the basis of these authorities.

It will be noticed that of the seventy chapters of the *Mānasāra* the first eight are introductory, the next forty-two deal with architectural matters, and the last twenty are devoted to sculpture. In the introductory chapters full accounts are given of such preliminary matters as the table of contents, the system of measurement, the necessary training and qualifications of the different classes of architects, the selection of site, testing of soil, planning, designing, dialling, finding out cardinal points, and astronomical and astrological calculations. Next are given all the architectural details of various kinds of villages, towns, and forts; joinery, dimensions and foundations of buildings; pillars and their component parts, such as pedestals, bases, shafts, and entablatures; storeys varying from one to twelve in ordinary buildings and to seventeen in gate-houses; the artistic arrangement of mansions in as many as ten rows; compounds and courts of edifices, their gate-houses, their attached and detached buildings, their compartments, halls and chambers, their doors, windows and the openings; the steps and staircases for buildings, hills and rivers, etc.; their courtyards, quadrangles, and arches; royal courts, palaces, thrones, and crowns; cars, chariots, and other conveyances; articles of furniture, such as bedsteads, couches, tables, chairs, wardrobes, baskets, cages, mills, lamps; dresses and garments; and ornaments, such as various chains, armlets, anklets, head-gear and footwear. In the concluding portion are given the sculptural details of idols of deities of the Hindus, the Buddhists, and the Jains, statues of great personages, and images of animals and birds.

Thus it may be concluded that, as a standard work on architecture in the widest sense of the term, the *Mānasāra* is perfectly complete and methodical in all respects.

The Mayamata Silpa-śāstra

The next well-known *Silpa-śāstra* is the *Mayamata*, attributed to one Gannamāchārya.[1]

A detailed summary of this work is not necessary. The following list of thirty-six chapters, placed side by side with the similar chapters of the *Mānasāra*, will show that in respect of the titles of chapters, their sequence and contents, the *Mayamata* and the *Mānasāra* are identical[2]:

(1) *Saṁgrahādhyāya*—table of contents, *Mānasāra*, Chapter I.

(2) *Vāstu-prakāra*—classification of architectural subjects, *M.*,[3] IV, V.

(3) *Bhū-parīkshā*—testing of soil, *M.*, IV, V.

(4) *Bhū-parigraha*—selection of soil, *M.*, IV, V.

(5) *Mānopakaraṇa*—materials and system of measurement, *M.*, II.

(6) *Dik-parichchheda*—on finding out cardinal points, *M.*, VI.

(7) *Pāda-devatā-vinyāsa*—site plans, *M.*, VII.

(8) *Bali-karma-vidhāna*—offerings to gods, *M.*, VIII.

(9) *Grāma-vinyāsa*—villages, *M.*, IX.

(10) *Nagara-vidhāna*—town-planning, *M.*, X.

(11) *Bhū-lamba-vidhāna*—dimensions of storeys, *M.*, XI.

(12) *Garbha-nyāsa-vidhāna*—foundations, *M.*, XII.

(13) *Upapīṭha-vidhāna*—pedestals, *M.*, XIII.

(14) *Adhishṭhāna-vidhāna*—bases, *M.*, XIV.

(15) *Pāda-pramāṇa-dravya-saṁgraha*—columns, *M.*, XV.

(16) *Prastara-prakaraṇa*—entablatures, *M.*, XVI.

(17) *Sandhi-karma-vidhāna*—joinery, *M.*, XVII.

(18) *Sikhara-karaṇa-bhavana-samāpti-vidhāna*—making the finials and finishing the building, *M.*, XVIII.

(19) *Eka-bhūmi-vidhāna*—one-storeyed buildings, *M.*, XIX.

(20) *Dvi-bhūmi-vidhāna*—two-storeyed buildings, *M.*, XX.

[1] Oriental Manuscripts Library, Madras, Catalogue, Vol. XXII, no. 13038, also 13034–13039.

Cf. the colophon इति गन्नमाचार्यविरचितायां ते) मयमते शिल्पशास्त्रे ।

[2] The edition of the *Mayamata* by M. M. Gaṇapati Śāstri contains only the first thirty-four chapters. Besides, it does not seem to have made use of the manuscripts mentioned elsewhere. But there is reference to three other manuscripts in this edition.

[3] The *Mānasāra* has *Mānopakaraṇa* for Chapter II, which is placed in Chapter V of the *Mayamata*.

(21) *Tri-bhūmi-vidhāna*—three-storeyed buildings, *M.*, XXI.

(22) *Bahu-bhūmi-vidhāna*[1]—buildings of more than three storeys, *M.*, XXII—XXX.

(23) *Prākāra-parivāra*—courts, and temples therein of the attendant deities; in the *Mānasāra* these two subjects are treated in two chapters, XXXI, XXXII.

(24) *Gopura-vidhāna*—gate-houses, *M.*, XXXIII.

(25) *Maṇḍapa-vidhāna*—pavilions, *M.*, XXXIV.

(26) *Śālā-vidhāna*—storeyed mansions, *M.*, XXXV.

(27) *Gṛiha-mānādhikāra*[2]—(location and) measurement of houses, *M.*, XXXVI.

(28) *Gṛiha-praveśa*—first entry into a newly built house (opening or house-warming ceremony), *M.*, XXXVII.

(29) *Rāja-veśma-vidhāna*—royal palaces, *M.*, XL.

(30) *Dvāra-vidhāna*—doors; in the *Mānasāra* this subject is described in two chapters, XXXVIII, XXXIX.

(31) *Yānādhikāra*—conveyances, *M.*, II, XLIII.

(32) *Yāna-śayanādhikāra*—cars and chariots, couches and bedsteads, *M.*, XLIV, XLV.

Sculptural subjects are abridged in only four chapters:

(33) *Liṅga-lakshaṇa*—the phallus, *M.*, LII.

(34) *Pīṭha-lakshaṇa*—altars and pedestal of the phallus, *M.*, LIII.

(35) *Anukarma-vidhāna*—minor works on sculpture, *M.*, LI, LIV, LV, LXIII, LXV, LXX.

(36) *Pratimā-lakshaṇa*—images in general, *M.*, LXIV.

It should be noticed that in resp t of the titles of chapters, their sequence, except in one instance, contents, and method of treatment, the *Mayamata* runs exactly like the *Mānasāra*, step by step. It is hardly necessary to point out that in Chapter XXII of the former, the Chapters XXII—XXX of the latter are abridged, to the great relief of readers. So also Chapter XXX of the former is an abridgment of Chapters XXXVIII, XXXIX of the latter. Chapters XLI (royal courts) and XLII (characteristics of kings) of the *Mānasāra*, which have only an indirect use in an architectural treatise, have been prudently omitted in the *Mayamata*. Chapters XLV to L of the *Mānasāra* which deal respectively with thrones, arches, theatres,

[1] Cf. Śāstri, *ibid*, where *Chatur-bhūmyādi* is added at the beginning.

[2] Cf. Śāstri, *ibid*, where it is read *chatur-gṛiha-vidhāna*.

ornamental trees, crowns, ornaments, and articles of house furniture, are left out in the *Mayamata*, apparently as matters of detail.

Sculpture is said to be the hand-maid of architecture. This statement, in its restricted sense, is however appropriate only to religious architecture, that is, temple-building. But in a treatise which is concerned with all sorts of buildings—religious, residential, military —undue space and preference for sculpture have been economically avoided in the *Mayamata*. In this treatise, as has already been pointed out, sculpture dealing with the phalli, altars, images and minor matters, is described in four chapters, while in the *Mānasāra* nearly two-thirds of the whole book, comprising twenty chapters, is given to these subjects; and in the *Aṁśumad-bheda* of Kāśyapa, to be discussed presently, which is avowedly a sculptural treatise, nearly half the space, comprising Chapters XLVI to LXXXIV, is devoted to matters of sculptural detail.

It does not, therefore, seem unreasonable to suppose that in the compilation of the treatise named *Mayamata*, whether by Gannamāchārya, as stated in the colophon (of MS. no. 13038, Oriental Manuscripts Library, Madras, Catalogue, Volume XXII, page 8763) or by somebody else, the *Mānasāra* has been largely drawn upon.

In consideration of the fact that with the *Mayamata* (MS. no. 13037, fol. 213*a*), the *Mānasāra* (l*a*) has become mixed, I am further led to believe that the manuscript of the *Mayamata* in the Madras Oriental Library seems to be an abridgment of the *Mānasāra*.

The fact that one *Mayamata* is included in the list of thirty-two authorities mentioned in the *Mānasāra* itself does not present much difficulty in accepting this view. *Mayamata*, like *Manu* (or *Mānasāra*) is apparently a generic name, and the treatise catalogued under the title *Mayamata-vāstu-śāstra* need not necessarily be ascribed to the authority mentioned in the *Mānasāra*.

The Aṁśumad-bheda of Kāśyapa

This is another well-known treatise on architecture and about the next largest in size to the *Mānasāra*. There is also a striking similarity of the *Aṁśumad-bheda* with the *Mānasāra* as will be shown by the following list :

(1) *Karshaṇa*—ploughing of the selected site, *Mānasāra*, Chapter V.

(2) *Prāsāda-vāstu*—classification of buildings, *M.*, III.

(3) *Vāstu-homa*—sacrificial offerings to the presiding deity of the site, *M.*, VIII.

(4) *Prathameshṭaka-vidhi*—laying the foundations, *M.* XII (last portion).

(5) *Upapīṭha-vidhāna*—pedestals, *M.*, XIII.

(6) *Adhishṭhāna-vidhi*—bases, *M.*, XIV.

(7) *Nāla-lakshaṇa*—canals ; in the *Mānasāra* this subject is referred to in several places, e.g., Chapter XIX, L, LII, LXVI.

(8) *Stambha-lakshaṇa*—columns, *M.*, XV.

(9) *Phalakā-lakshaṇa*—planks, *M.*, LXVII.

(10) *Vedikā-lakshaṇa*—platforms, railings ; in the *Mānasāra* this is described in many places, Chapter IX, XV, XIX. XXII, etc.

(11) *Jālaka-lakshaṇa*—perforated windows, *M.*, XXXIII (concluding portion).

(12) *Toraṇa-lakshaṇa*—arches, *M.*, XLVI.

(13) *Vṛitta-sphuṭita-lakshaṇa*—in the *Mānasāra* this is not described in a separate chapter.

(14) *Stambha-toraṇa-vidhi*—arches upon columns, *M.*, XII.

(15) *Kumbha-tāla-lakshaṇa*—capitals of columns ; this also in the *Mānasāra* is referred to in many places, largely in Chapter XV.

(16) *Vṛitta-sphuṭita-lakshaṇa*—same as Chapter XIII.

(17) *Dvāra-lakshaṇa*—doors, *M.*, XXXVIII, XXXIX.

(18) *Kampa-dvāra-lakshaṇa*—a special door, *M.*, XXXVIII, XXXIX.

(19) *Prastara-lakshaṇa*—entablatures, *M.*, XVI.

(20) *Gala-vidhāna*—necks ; this is also referred to in many chapters in the *Mānasāra*, e.g., Chapter XVIII, XIX–XXX, etc.

(21) *Śikhara-lakshaṇa*—tops, finials ; in the *Mānasāra* this also is referred to in many places, e.g., Chapter XVIII, XIX, etc.

(22) *Nāsikā*—noses, wings ; in the *Mānasāra* this is described in several places, e.g., Chapter XVI, XVII, XIX, L, etc.

(23) *Mānopakaraṇa*—system of measurement, *M.*, II.
(24) *Māna-sūtrādi-lakshaṇa*—measuring strings, *M.*, II.
(25) *Nagarādi-vidhi*—towns, etc., *M.*, X.
(26) *Garbha-nyāsa-vidhi*—foundations, etc., *M.*, XII.
(27) *Eka-tala-vidhāna*—one-storeyed buildings, *M.*, XIX.
(28–30) *Dvi-chaturtha-tala-vidhāna*—two- to four-storeyed buildings, *M.*, XX–XXII.
(31) *Kūṭādi-lakshaṇa*—finials; in the *Mānasāra* referred to in many places, e.g., Chapter XV, XIX–XXX, LX, LXX, etc.
(32–39) *Pañcha-bhānu-bhūmi-vidhāna*—five- to twelve-storeyed buildings, *M.*, XXIII–XXX.
(40) *Trayodaśa-tala-vidhāna*—thirteen-storeyed buildings, and
(41) *Shoḍaśa-bhūmi-vidhāna*—sixteen-storeyed buildings, subjects of these two chapters (XL, XLI) are dealt with in *M.*, XXXIII.
(42) *Mūrdheshṭaka-vidhi*—the brick at the top; in the *Mānasāra* referred to in many places, e.g., XVIII, etc.
(43) *Prākāra-lakshaṇa*—courts, *M.*, XXXI.
(44) *Maṇṭa(-ḍa)pa-lakshaṇa*—pavilions, *M.*, XXXIV.
(45) *Gopura-lakshaṇa*—gate-houses, *M.*, XXXIII.

The remaining portion of this treatise, except the last two chapters on villages, deals with sculpture more elaborately than in the *Mānasāra*. It will be noticed that the purely architectural topics are more exhaustively described in the *Mānasāra.*

(46) *Sapta-mātrikā-lakshaṇa*—the seven mothers (female, images), *M.*, LXIV.
(47) *Vināyaka-lakshaṇa*—image of Vināyaka or Gaṇeśa; not specified in the *Mānasāra*, but see Chapters LVII, XLI.
(48) *Parivāra-vidhi*—images of attendant deities, *M.*, XXXII.
(49) *Liṅga-lakshaṇoddhāra*—unearthing the phallus, cf. *M.*, LII.
(50) *Uttama-daśa-tāla-purusha-māna*—the largest type of ten-*tāla* measure as applied to male deities, *M.*, LXV.
(51) *Madhyama-daśa-tāla-purusha-māna*—the intermediate type of the ten-*tāla* measure as applied to male deities, *M.*, LXVI, LXI.
(52) *Uttama-nava-tāla*—the largest type of the nine-*tāla* measure, *M.*, LVII, LXI.
(53) *Madhyama-nava-tāla*—intermediate type of the nine-*tāla* measure, *M.*, LVII, LXI.
(54) *Adhama-nava-tāla*—the smallest type of the nine-*tāla* measure, *M.*, LVII, LXI.

(55) *Ashṭa-tāla*—the eight-*tāla* measure, *M.*, LVII.

(56) *Sapta-tāla*—the seven-*tāla* measure, *M.*, LVII.

(57) *Pīṭha-lakshaṇoddhāra*—the altars and pedestal of the phallus, *M.*, LIII.

(58) *Sakala-sthāpana-vidhi*—the installation of the images of Iśvara and three other deities, *M.*, LI.

(59) *Sukhāsana*
(60) *Sukhāsana* } —posture of an image, *M.*, LXVII.

(61) *Chandra-śekhara-mūrti-lakshaṇa*—the image of Chandra-śekhara (Śiva), *M.*, LI.

(62) *Vṛishabha-vāhana-mūrti-lakshaṇa*—the image of the bull, the riding animal of Śiva, *M.*, LXII.

(63) *Nṛitta-mūrti-lakshaṇa*—the image of dancing (Śiva), *M.*, LI.

(64) *Gaṅgādhara-mūrti-lakshaṇa*—the image of the Ganges bearing Śiva, *M.*, LI.

(65) *Tripura-mūrti-lakshaṇa*—the image of Śiva in the pose of killing Tripura (demon), *M.*, LI.

(66) *Kalyāṇa-sundara-lakshaṇa*—the image of Kalyāṇa-sundara, *M.*, LI.

(67) *Ardha-nārīśvara-lakshaṇa*—the image of Śiva combined with his consort Pārvatī, *M.*, LI.

(68) *Gajaha-mūrti-lakshaṇa*—the image of Śiva as killer of demon Gaja, *M.*, XXIX, XXXII, XXXIX, XLIII, L.

(69) *Pāśupata-mūrti-lakshaṇa*—the image of Pāśupata (Śiva), *M.*, LI.

(70) *Kaṅkāla-mūrti-lakshaṇa*—the image of a skeleton, *M.*, not specified.

(71) *Haryardha-Hara-lakshaṇa*—the combined image of Vishṇu and Śiva, *M.*, LI.

(72) *Bhikshāṭana-mūrti-lakshaṇa*—the image of Śiva in the pose of a beggar, cf. *M.* LII.

(73) *Chaṇḍeśānugraha*, *M.*, not specified.

(74) *Dakshiṇā-mūrti-lakshaṇa*—the image of Śiva, *M.*, LII.

(75) *Kālaha-mūrti-lakshaṇa*—the image of Kālaha (Śiva), *M.*, LII.

(76) *Liṅgodbhava-lakshaṇa*—revelation of the phallus, *M.*, LII.

(77) *Vṛiksha-saṁgrahaṇa*—collection of wood, *M.*, XV.

(78) *Śūla-lakshaṇa*—the pike, *M.*, XVIII.

(79) *Śūla-pāṇi-lakshaṇa*—the image of Śūlapāni (Śiva), *M.*, LI.

(80) *Rajju-bandha-lakshaṇa*—binding of rope, *M.*, II, XLIV.

(81) *Mṛit-saṁskāra-lakshaṇa*—the process of casting images in earth, *M.*, LXVIII.

(82) *Kalka-saṁskāra-lakshaṇa*—preparation of mixtures.

(83) *Varṇa-saṁskāra-lakshaṇa*—preparation of colours.

(84) *Varṇa-lepana-medhya-lakshaṇa.*

The contents of Chapters LXXVIII–LXXXIV are referred to in several places in the *Mānasāra*.

(85) *Grāmādi-lakshaṇa*
(86) *Grāma-lakshaṇa* } —villages, *M.*, IX, X.

In this treatise, architecture proper is treated in the first forty-five and the last two chapters. These forty-seven chapters are similar in many respects to the first fifty chapters of the *Mānasāra*. The *Aṁśumad-bheda* deals much more elaborately with sculptural objects in thirty-nine chapters in place of some twenty chapters of the *Mānasāra*. But purely architectural topics are more exhaustively described in the *Mānasāra*, which seems in any case to have largely influenced the other work.

The Viśvakarma-Śilpa

The most popular treatise on architecture is naturally the one attributed to Viśvakarman, the heavenly architect. There seems to have been more than one title to this work : one is called the *Viśvakarma-Prakāśa* or *Viśvakarma-Vāstu-śāstra*, another is called the *Viśvakarmīya-śilpa*, apparently the same as the *Viśvakarmīya-śilpa-śāstra.*[1] The one designated as *Viśvakarma-Prakāśa* or *Viśvakarma-Vāstu-śāstra* deals with directions on the building of houses, the making of roads, tanks, etc. The treatise contains thirteen chapters in which the following topics are dealt with :

(1) *Maṅgalācharaṇa*—auspicious preliminaries (benediction).

(2) *Vāstu-purushotpatti-varṇanam*—the origin of the presiding deity of the house, *Mānasāra* VII, XXXV.

(3) *Bhūmi-lakshaṇa*—soil, *M.*, II, III.

(4) *Gṛiha-praveśa*—first entry into the house or house-warming, *M.*, XXXVII.

(5) *Khanana-vidhi*—digging (ploughing) the soil, *M.*, V.

(6) *Svapna-vidhi*—dreams.

(7) *Bhūmi-phalam*—fruit of the soil, *M.*, IV, V.

(8) *Gṛihārambhe samaya-vidhi*—auspicious time for beginning a building, *M.*, XXXV.

(9) *Dhvajādhyāya-phalāni*—flags.

(10) *Āya-vyayāṁśādīnāṁ phalāni*, *M.*, LII, XXXIX, IX, XXX, LXIV, LV.

(11) *Gṛiha-madhye devādīnāṁ sthāpana-nirṇaya*—installation of idols in temples, *M.*, in many places.

(12) *Dhurvādi-gṛiha-bheda*, *M.*, not specified.

(13) *Dvāra-mānāni*—measurements of doors, *M.*, XXXIX.

(14) *Stambha pramāṇāni*—columns, *M.*, XV.

(15) *Gṛihāṇāṁ śālā-nirṇaya*—halls of houses, *M.*, XXXV.

(16) *Gṛihārambha-kāla-nirṇaya*—almost the same as (8).

(17) *Gṛihārambhe lagna-kuṇḍalīstha-graha-phalāni*, *M.*, not specified.

(18) *Śayyā-mandira-bhavana-sumana-sudhārādi-gṛihāṇāṁlakshaṇāni* (*see* below the comparisons of the *Purāṇas* and *Āgamas*), referred to in many places in *M.*

[1] Egg. Catalogue, p. 1129. A treatise bearing the same title was published by the Veṅkaṭeśvara Press, Bombay, in Saṁvat 1952, Śaka, 1817, another at Benares in 1888. The same treatise is stated to have been translated into Bhāshā under the title *Pālārāma Vilāsa* by Mukula Śaktidhara Śarmā, at Lucknow, in 1896.

In the Oriental Manuscripts Library, Madras, there is a MS. bearing the title *Viśvakarmiya-Śilpa-Śāstram* (Catalogue, Vol. XXI, no. 13057).

(19) *Pādukā-upānaha-mañchādīnāṁ māna-lakshaṇa*—measurement of footwear, shoes, couches, etc., referred to in many places in *M*.

(20) *Śaṅku-śilā-nyāsa-nirṇaya*—finding out the cardinal points, etc., by means of a gnomon, *M*., VI.

(21) *Vāstu-deha-lakshaṇāni pūjanaṁ bali-dāna*—offerings, *M*., VIII.

(22) *Śilā-nyāsa*—referred to in many places in *M*.

(23) *Prāsāda-vidhāna*—palaces, *M*., XL.

(24) *Śilpa-vyāsa*, *M*., not specified.

(25) *Prāsāda-nirṇaya*, *M*., XIX–XXX.

(26) *Pīṭhikā-lakshaṇa*—pedestals (of the phallus), *M*., LIII, XIII.

(27) *Maṇḍapa*—pavilions, *M*., XXXIV.

(28) *Dvāra-lakshaṇa*—doors, *M*., XXXVIII, XXXIX.

(29) *Vāpī-kūpa-taḍāgodyāna-kriyā*—making of tanks, wells, pools, gardens, referred to in many places in *M*.

(30) *Dāru-chchhedana-vidhi*—cutting of wood, *M*., XV.

(31) *Gṛiha-praveśa-nirṇaya*—almost the same as (4), *M*., XXXVII.

(32) *Gṛiha-praveśa-kāla-śuddhi*, *M*., XXXVII.

(33) *Śayyāsana-dolikādīnāṁ lakshaṇa*—bedsteads, seats, palanquins hammocks, almost the same as (18).

(34) *Durga-nirṇaya*—forts and fortified cities, *M*., X.

(35) *Śalya-jñānaṁ, śalyoddhāra*—semi-astrological topics, referred to in many places in *M*.

(36) *Nāgara-saṁbandhi-rāja-gṛihādīnāṁ nirṇaya*—the palaces in cities, *M*., XL.

It should be noticed that most of these topics of this version of Viśvakarman refer to non-architectural and chiefly astrological matters. It is also worth noticing that this treatise leaves out sculptural topics altogether.

The *Viśvakarmīya-śilpa*,[1] apparently the same as is mentioned in Rājendralāla Mitra's notices of Sanskrit manuscripts, is a Nāgarī

[1] In Rājā Dr. Rājendralāla Mittra's *Notices of Sanskrit MSS.* (Vol. II, no. 73, p. 142).

Of the other version, *Viśvakarmīya Śilpa-śāstra*, the Madras MS. noted above, which was copied by Niṭla Sūrappa on Saturday, the 5th day of the bright fortnight of the Aśvija month in the year Jaya, contains a statement referring to Viśvakarma's debt to Brahmā, Indra, Maya, Bhārgava, Aṅgirasa, Dhruva, Gautama, Gārgeya, Manu, Vyāsa, and Bhṛigu. Agastya is also referred to. It is stated to have been founded on the revelation of Viśvakarman and traced back successively to Bṛihadratha, Parāśara, and Śambhu. In the *Mānasāra* the origin of the science is attributed to Śiva, Brahmā, and Vishṇu, and through Indra, Bṛihaspati, Nārada and others it was revealed to Mānasāra ; Viśvakarman, Maya, Tvashṭar, and Manu represent the heavenly architects, and Sthapati, Sūtragrāhin, Vardhaki and Takshaka form the guild of modern architects, but there are thirty-two other architectural authorities mentioned in the *Mānasāra*.

copy made in 1872 from an original written in the Hala-Kānādī character, the older codex being in the library of the Rāja of Tanjore. 'None of the MSS. examined by Mr. Burnell is perfect or even tolerably correct. This treatise is apparently a compilation, as it is written in the Tāntric style, having Śiva for its narrator.' The contents are classified under the following seventeen chapters :

(1) *Viśvakarmotpattiḥ karma-viśesha-bhedena vyavahṛitra-takshaka-varddha, kyādi-śabda-vyutpattiś cha*—origin of Viśvakarman, derivation of the words *takshaka*, *vardhaki*, etc., *M.*, II.

(2) *Satyādi-yuga-jāta-narochchatā-pramāṇaṁ, yajñīya-kāshṭhena prastareṇavā deva-pratimā-nirmāṇe mānādi*—height of man in different ages of the world, wood, and stone for the construction of images.

(3) *Takshakasya garbhādhānādi-saṁskāra-kathanaṁ, garbhotpatti-kathanādi cha*—sacraments for sculptors and carpenters.

(4) *Śiva-liṅgādi-pratishṭhārthaṁ sabhā-nirmāṇādi*—halls for the installation of Śiva's phallus and other gods, *M.*, LII.

(5) *Graha-pratimā-nirmāṇa-pramāṅaṁ, liṅga-pīṭha-nirmāṇa-pramāṇādi cha*—proportions of images of the planets and phalli.

(6) *Ratha-nirmāṇa-vidhi-kathanam*—cars and chariots, *M.*, XLIII.

(7) *Ratha-pratishṭhā-vidhiḥ*—consecration of cars, *M.*, XLIII.

(8) *Brāhmī-Māheśvaryādīnāṁ svarūpādi-varṇādi*—characteristics of Brāhmi, Māheśvarī, and other goddesses, *M.*, LIV.

(9) *Yajñopavīta-lakshaṇaṁ*—Brāhmaṇical sacred thread.

(10) *Suvarṇa-rajata-muñjādi-nirmita-yajñopavīta-kathanaṁ digbhedena devasthāpana-prakārādi, meru-dakshiṇa-sthita-hema-śilākathanādi cha*—sacred thread of gold, silver, muñja fibre, the cardinal points at which images of gods and goddesses are to be installed, qualities of (the stone-god called) Hema-śilā (*lit.* golden stone) to be found to the south of the Meru mountain.

(11) *Lakshmī-Brāhmī-Māheśvaryādi-devīndrādi-dikpāla-grahādi-mūrti-nirmāṇa-prakāra*—images of Lakshmī, Brāhmī, Māheśvarī and other goddesses, of Indra and other Dikpālas (quarter-masters), planets and other gods, *M.* LIV, etc.

(12, 13) *Mukuṭa-kirīṭa-jaṭā-mukuṭādi-nirmāṇa-prakārādi*—crowns, crests and headgear, *M.*, XLIX.

(14) *Sthāvarāsthāvara-siṁhāsana-nirmāṇa-prakārādi, punar viśesheṇa kirīṭa-lalāṭa-paṭṭikādi-nirmāṇa-prakāraḥ, Devatāyā mandirasya cha jīrṇoddhāra-prakāra*—movable and fixed thrones for images, crests, crowns, bands and other headgears, repairs of temples, *M.*, XLII, XLV.

(15) *Liṅga-mūrti-mandira-dvārādi-kathana*—proportions of doors of temples to phalli, *M.*, XXXVIII, XXXIX, LXIV.

(16) *Pratimā-mūrti-mandira-dvārādi-kathana*—proportions of doors of temples to (other) images, *M.*, XXXVIII, XXXIX.

(17) *Vighneśa-mūrti-mandirādi-nirmāṇādi-vidhi*—temples for the images of Vighneśa (Gaṇeśa) and other matters.

This portion of the treatise of Viśvakarman is chiefly sculptural. The treatment of the subject is in detail, although not so elaborate as in the *Aṁśumad-bheda* of Kāśyapa. I am inclined to think that the two versions form in fact the complete treatise attributed to Viśvakarman.

We have seen that Viśvakarman refers to the authority of Mayamata. If this Mayamata be the same person as the author of the *Mayamata* discussed above, and there seem reasons to think so, Viśvakarman might have been indebted to the *Mānasāra* through *Mayamata*, if not directly. Even the brief comparison of the two treatises given above may serve to indicate that there may have been such a relation of indebtedness between the *Viśvakarma-śilpa* and the *Mānasāra*.

The Āgastya

Āgastya is a name frequently cited, we have seen above, as an authority on architecture. Unfortunately, the manuscripts discovered are incomplete and devoted solely to sculpture. One of the manuscripts bearing the title *Āgastya-Sakalādhikāra* contains the following chapters :

(1) *Māna-saṁgraha*—system of measurement, *Mānasāra*, II, LV.

(2) *Uttama-daśa-tāla*—large type of the ten-*tāla* measure, *M.*, LXV.

(3) *Madhyama-daśa-tāla*—intermediate type of the ten-*tāla* measure, *M.*, LVI.

(4) *Adhama-daśa-tāla*—small type of the ten-*tāla* measure, *M.*, XLI.

(5) *Pratimā-lakshaṇa*—general rules on images, *M.*, LXIV.

(6) *Vṛishabha-vāhana-lakshaṇa*—bull, the riding animal of Śiva, *M.*, LXII.

(7) *Naṭeśvara-vidhi*—image of Naṭeśvara (dancing Śiva), *M.*, LI.

(8) *Shoḍaśa-pratimā-lakshaṇa*—sixteen images, *M.*, LXIV.

(9) *Dāru-saṁgraha*—collection of wood, cf. *M.*, XV.

(10) *Mṛit-saṁskāra*—preparing earth for images, mentioned in various places, cf. *M.*, LXVIII.

(11) *Varṇa-saṁskāra*—preparation of colours, mentioned in various places in *M.*

In a Madras manuscript the following topics are described[1] :

(1) *Māna-saṁgraha-viśesha*—specially on measures, *M.*, II, LV.

(2) *Uttama-daśa-tāla*—large type of the ten-*tāla*, *M.*, LXV.

(3) *Madhyama-daśa-tāla*—intermediate type of the ten-*tāla*, *M.*, LXVI.

(4) *Somaskanda-lakshaṇa*—image of Soma and Skanda, *M.*, not specified.

(5) *Chandra-śekhara-lakshaṇa*—image of Śiva, *M.*, LI, LII.

(6) *Vṛishabha-vāhana-lakshaṇa*—image of the bull, *M.*, LXII

Chapters 7 to 18 seem to be missing. It is not clear whether or not the following 7–14 (which numbers are not found in the compilation) are to be attributed to Agastya :

(7) *Tripurāntaka-lakshaṇa*—image of Śiva, cf. *M.*, LI, LII.

[1] In the Oriental Manuscripts Library, Madras, there are two fragmentary MSS. ascribed to Āgastya (Cat., Vol. XXII, nos. 13046, 13047). They deal with astrological matters bearing upon architecture. In the same library (Cat., Vol. XXII, no. 13058) there is a large manuscript of 429 pages, of 25 lines to a page, of paper 13½"× 8". Two large portions of this compilation are ascribed to Āgastya.

(8) *Kalyāṇa-sundara-lakshaṇa*—image of Kalyāṇa-Sundara.

(9) *Ardha-nārīśvara-lakshaṇa*—image of Śiva, *M.*, LI, LII.

(10) *Pāśupata-lakshaṇa*—image of Śiva, *M.*, LI, LII.

(11) *Bhikshāṭana-lakshaṇa*—image of Śiva as a beggar, *M.*, not specified.

(12) *Chaṇḍeśānugraha-lakshaṇa*—image of Śiva, *M.*, LI, LII.

(13) *Dakshiṇā-mūrti-lakshaṇa*—image of Śiva, *M.* LI, LII.

(14) *Kāla-dahana-lakshaṇa*—image of Śiva, *M.*, LI, LII.

(15–18) Apparently missing.

(19) *Pratimā-lakshaṇa*—images, *M.*, LXIV.

In another portion of the compilation the following chapters are numbered, as shewn in parallel column :

(20) (3) *Upapīṭha-vidhāna*—pedestal (for image), *M.*, XIII, LIII.

(21) (9) *Śūla-māna-vidhāna*—measurement of pikes for images, cf. *M.*, LXVII.

(22) (10) *Rajju-bandha-saṁskāra-vidhi*—making ropes, *M.*, II.

(23) (11) *Varṇa-saṁskāra*—preparation of colours mentioned in various places in *M.*

(24) (12) *Akshi-mokshaṇa*—chiselling of the eye, *M.*, LXX.

We have seen above that Āgastya is mentioned, together with Maya, as one of the authorities on which Viśvakarma's treatise is based. Āgastya was, therefore, presumably known to Viśvakarman. Owing to the incomplete nature of Āgastya's extant works the connexion of *Āgastya* with *Mayamata* and with the *Mānasāra* is not clear at present. It is true, however, that several chapters of *Āgastya* are strikingly similar to, if not taken from, the corresponding chapters of the *Mānasāra*.

The Sanat-Kumāra-Vāstu-Śāstra

Another authority frequently referred to is Sanat-kumāra. There are several fragmentary manuscripts of his treatise. But they are incomplete.[1] In one of the manuscripts the following subjects are dealt with[2] :

(1) *Griha-saṁsthāpana*—situation of houses, *M.*, XXXVI.

(2) *Nakshatra-graha-yoga-vidhi*—constellation of planets and stars (in determining the auspicious times) in connexion with the building of houses, *M.*, XXXV.

(3) *Graha-lagna-vidhi*—almost the same as (2).

(4) *Taru-tantra-vidhi*—on trees (wood, for building houses with), referred to in many places in *M.*

(5) *Bhū-parīkshā-vidhi*—examination of soil, *M.*, IV, V.

(6) *Nakshatra-tithi-vāra-śuddhi*—on auspicious time, *M.*, XXXV.

(7) *Nakshatra-lagna-phala-dvāra-bandha-śubha-sthāna-nirṇaya*—ascertaining auspicious time and place (in constructing doors), *M.*, IV, V, XXXV.

(8) *Gṛiha-preveśana*—first entry into the newly-built house, *M.*, XXXVII.

This treatise of Sanat-kumāra is stated to have been based on the works of Brahman, Śakra, Yama, Bhārgava, Āṅgirasa, Maya, Gautama, Gārgya, Manu, Vyāsa, Bhṛigu, Viśvakarman, and others.

The same list is differently given in another manuscript (no. 13064), where Śakra is replaced by Chandra, and Maya is omitted.

But in other manuscripts (nos. 13062, 13068) Śakra is not replaced by Chandra, although Maya is omitted.

As we have seen above, Viśvakarman acknowledges his debt to Maya. Sanat-kumāra mentions Viśvakarman as his authority; it is, therefore, not unlikely that of these lists the first one, which contains Maya, is correct. If the view that Maya is indebted to the *Mānasāra* be accepted on the grounds discussed above, it would be easy to infer that Sanat-kumāra may be also indebted, directly or indirectly, to the *Mānasāra*.

[1] Egg., III, 3151, 2680, Oppert, Vol. I, no. 8239, p. 580. In the Oriental Manuscripts Library, Madras, there are nine manuscripts (Cat., Vol. XXII, nos. 13060–13068).

[2] Madras manuscripts, no. 13060.

The Silpa-śāstra of Maṇḍana

The treatise of Maṇḍana, otherwise called Rāja-vallabha-Maṇḍana, Sūtradhāra-Maṇḍana, and also perhaps Bhūpati-vallabha, is unique in a sense. He seems to be a historical person. He is stated to have been 'in the employ of King Kumbhakarṇa of Medapāṭha, and the husband of Mirābai.' According to Tod, King Kumbha ruled over the country of Mewar from A.D. 1419 to 1469.[1] This treatise bears the titles *Silpa-śāstra*, *Vāstu-śāstra*, and also *Prāsāda-Maṇḍana-Vāstu-śāstra*.[2] It deals with the architectural disposition of houses, palaces and temples in the following fourteen chapters :

(1) *Miśraka-lakshaṇa*—classification, cf. *Mānasāra*, I, III.

(2) *Vāstu-lakshaṇa*—characteristics and classification of architectural objects, M. III.

(3) *Āyādi-lakshaṇa*—architectural formulæ of measurement, *M.*, LXVI.

(4) *Prākāra-yantra—vāpi-kūpa-taḍāga-lakshaṇa*—courts, tanks, wells, pools, machines, described in several places in *M.*

(5) *Rāja-gṛiha-niveśādi-lakshaṇa*—opening of the royal palaces, *M.*, XL, XXXVII.

The 28th verse of this chapter (V) mentions the *Matsya-Purāṇa* as an authority on the subject.

(6) *Eka-śālā-dvi-śālā-gṛiha-lakshaṇa*—houses with one and two halls or rows, described in many places in *M.*, cf. XXXV.

(7) *Dvi-śālā-tri-śālā-chatuḥ-śālā-gṛiha-lakshaṇa*—houses with two, three, and four sides, described in many places in *M.*, cf. XXXV.

(8) *Sayana-siṁhāsana-chhatra-gavāksha-sabhāshṭaka-vedikā-chatushṭaya-dīpa-lakshaṇa*—bedsteads or couches, thrones, umbrellas, windows, eight councils, four platforms, and lamps, an abridged collection of several subjects described in *M.*, XLIV, XLV, XXXIII, etc.

(9) *Rāja-gṛihādi-lakshaṇa*—royal palaces, *M.*, XL.

(10) (*Māpita*)-*Kshetrādbhuta-lakshaṇa*, building site, *M*, IV, V.

[1] Bhandarkar's Report, *ibid*, 1882–83, p. 37.

[2] Egg., 3142, 1291, 3147, 2253.

Apparently one of these manuscripts is published with some diagrams by Bhārati at Baroda, 1891.

Five other manuscripts are ascribed to Maṇḍana : (i) *Vāstu-Maṇḍana*, (ii) *Vāstu-Mañjarī*, (iii) *Vāstu-sāra*, (iv) *Rūpa-Maṇḍana*, and (v) *Āpa-tattva*.

(11) *Dina-śuddhi-gṛiha-niveśa-gṛiha-praveśa-vivāha-muhūrta - lakshaṇa*—auspicious times with regard to beginning the construction and entry into the house, and the wedding, cf. *M.*, XXXV, XXXVII.

(12) *Gochara-dina-rātri-māna-svarodaya-kūṭa-chakra-matṛikā - lakshaṇa*—astronomical calculations bearing upon architecture, cf. *M.*, XXXV.

(13) *Jyotisha-lakshaṇa*—astrological consideration, cf. *M.*, XXXV.

(14) *Śakuna-lakshaṇa*—auspicious signs, cf. *M.*, XV.

The manuscript bearing the title *Prāsāda-Maṇḍana-Vāstu-śāstra* by Sūtradhāra Maṇḍana (Egg., 3147, 2253) contains the following eight chapters, which, except the first one, are apparently in continuation of the fourteen chapters stated above.

(1) *Miśra-kalaśa*—the jug ornament, mentioned in many places in *M.*

(15) (2) *Āyatanādhikāra*—temples, buildings, cf. *M.*, XIX–XXX.

(16) (3) *Bhitti-pīṭha-maṇḍ[ap]a-vāra[dvāra]- garbha - gṛiha - udumbara-pramāṇa*—walls, pedestals, open courts, doors, shrines, etc., *M.*, XIII, XXXIV, XXXVIII, XXXIX, etc.

(17) (4) *Pramāṇa - dṛishṭi - pa(ā)da - sthāna - śikhara-kalaśa-lakshaṇa*—measures, sight (perspective), pillars, finials, towers, *M.*, II, XV, etc.

(18) (5) *Rājyādi-prāsādādhikāra*—royal kingdoms, palaces, etc., *M.*, XL, XLI, XLII, etc.

(19) (6) *Keśaryādi-prāsāda-jāti-lakshaṇa*, *pañcha-kshetra-pañcha-chatvāriṁśan-meru-lakshaṇādhyāya*—Keśari and other classes of buildings, forty-five types of buildings beginning with Meru; compare *M.*, XVIII, XIX–XXX, and see comparison of the *Mānasāra* with the *Purāṇas* and the *Āgamas* discussed below (p. 189–196).

(20) (7) *Maṇḍapā-bālāṇka-sambaraṇādhikāra*—open courts, etc. *M.*, XXXIV, etc.

(21) (8) *Jīrṇoddhāra-bhinna-dosha-sthāvara-pratishṭhā*, *Sūtradhāra-pūjā*, *Jina-pratishṭhā*, *vāstu-purusha-vinyāsa*—repairing and other defects, consecration of movable images, offerings to architects (carpenters), consecration of Jain images, description of the presiding deity of the house, *M.*, LXIX, II, VIII, LV, VII, etc.

As has already been suggested, these two parts of Maṇḍana's treatise in some respects seem to be two overlapping portions of one work. Other treatises ascribed to Maṇḍana are fragmentary and useless for any attempt to combine the several portions into a complete whole.

The important points relating to this historical treatise are well worth noticing. First its date is pretty certain, secondly it mentions the *Matsya-Purāṇa*, and lastly it contains a list of forty-five buildings, classified under five headings, bearing titles and giving details which correspond exactly to the lists and titles discovered in many important treatises.[1]

Another point to be noted is that many of its chapters contain matters which are, in fact, different topics and have been more logically described under different headings in the *Mānasāra* and other works. It is, therefore, likely that Maṇḍana's work is more or less a compilation from many sources.

[1] The *Agni-Purāṇa*, the *Garuḍa-Purāṇa*, also the *Matsya-Purāṇa*, the *Bhavishya-Purāṇa*, the *Bṛihat-saṁhitā* as well as the *Kāmikāgama*, the *Suprabhedāgama* and the *Mānasāra* (*see* pp. 189–196).

The Silparatna of Srīkumāra

This text comprises two parts, one of which is available and has been printed. It contains the following forty-six chapters, most of which are a literal abridgment of the *Mānasāra* in the same words, but without any recognition of its indebtedness. Only the last chapter appears to have been compiled from elsewhere :

(1) *Anukramaṇī*—table of contents, *Mānasāra*, Chapter I.

(2) *Mānasādhana*—system of measurement, *M.*, II.

(3) *Bhūmi-lakshaṇa*—examination of soil and selection of sites, *M.*, III, IV, V.

(4) *Sūdrapara-gṛiha-prakāra* (a wrong title for *sankusthāpana*), its contents are identical with Chapter VI of *Mānasāra* dealing with the gnomon.

(5) (8), (9) *Grāmādi-lakshaṇa*—villages and towns, *M.*, IX, X.

(6) *Pada-vinyāsa*—site plans, *M.*, VII.

(7) *Vāstu-pūjā*,—rites and ceremonies, *M.*, VIII.

(10) *Khāta-vidhi*, continuation of (3).

(11) *Dik-parichchheda*, continuation of (6).

(12) *Garbha-nyāsa*—foundation, *M.*, XII.

(13) *Vāstu-marma-vidhāna*, continuation of (7).

(14) *Dravya-vidhi*—on materials, compilations from various chapters of the *Mānasāra*.

(15) *Āyādi-lakshaṇa*—compilations from various chapters of the *Mānasāra*.

(16) *Prāsāda-lakshaṇa*—on palaces, *M.*, XL.

(17) *Pādādhishṭhāna-vidhāna*—on pillars, *M.*, XIV, XV.

(18) *Upapīṭhāvayava*—pedestals, *M.*, XIII.

(19) *Adhisṭhāna*—bases continuation of (17), *M.*, XIV.

(20) *Nāla*—channels, a compilation from *Mānasāra*.

(21) *Bhitti*—walls, a compilation from *Mānasāra*.

(22) *Dvāra*—doors, *M.*, XXXVIII, XXXIX.

(23) *Toraṇa*—arches, *M.*, XLVI.

(24) *Jālaka*—screened windows, compilation from *M.*

(25) *Kūṭa-koshṭhādi*—top rooms, compilation from *M.*

(26) *Pañjarāṇi*—cages, etc., compilation from *M.*

(27) *Vṛitta-sphaṭika*—an ornament from *M.*

(28) *Kumbha-latā*—an ornament from *M.*

(29) *Uttara*—an ornament from *M.*

(30) *Prastara*—entablature, *M.*, XVI.
(31) *Gala*—neck, a compilation from *M.*
(32) *Sikhara*—spherical roof, a compilation from *M.*
(33) *Lupā*—sloping roof, a compilation from *M.*
(34) *Mūrdheshṭakā*—topmost ornament, a compilation from *M*
(35) *Nāsikā*—vestibule, a compilation from *M.*
(36) *Stūpikā*—dome, a compilation from *M.*
(37) *Sāntikādi-niyama*—proportions of height, a compilation from *M.*, XXXIX.
(38) *Prāsāda-lakshaṇa*—palaces, a compilation from *M.*, LX.
(39) *Maṇḍapa*—pavilions, *M.*, XXXIV.
(40) *Prākāra*—courts, *M.*, XXXI.
(41) *Gopura*—gatehouses, *M.*, XXXIII.
(42) *Parivāra-vidhāna*—attendant deities, *M.*, XXXII.
(43) *Balipīṭha*—continuation of (42).
(44) *Dhvaja*—flags, a compilation from *M.*
(45) *Sandhi-karman*—joinery, *M.*, XVII.
(46) *Chitra-lakshaṇa*—paintings, a compilation.

Like many other such texts, the *Silparatna* shows a confused borrowing. The original sources have been distorted. The arrangement of chapters lacks in any method or reason. Śrīkumāra appears to have stolen unscrupulously, and, in order to conceal his indebtedness, has vainly endeavoured to displace the original order of the chapters, and to place the contents of one chapter under several headings.

The Samarāṅgana-Sūtradhāra of King Bhojadeva

This is also a huge compilation completed in eighty-three chapters, edited by Gaṇapati Śāstri, and printed in two parts from Baroda.

(1) *Mahāsamāgama*—deals with the arrival of the heavenly architect, Viśvakarman, to build villages, towns, and buildings, etc., *Mānasāra*, I.

(2) *Viśvakarmaṇaḥ putra-saṁvāda*—refers to the children of the heavenly architect, *M.*, II.

(3) *Praśna*—questions regarding houses, etc., cf. *M.*, III.

(4) *Mahadādi-sarga*—deals with the creation of things and the world.

(5) *Bhūparimiti*—deals with the division of the world into different countries and islands.

(6) *Sahadevādhikāra*—deals with the first human attempt to build houses with forest trees.

(7) *Varṇāśrama-vibhāga*—classification of human beings into castes and orders with a view to place them in various kinds of villages and towns.

(8) *Bhūparīkshā*—examination of soil, *M.*, Chapters IV, V.

(9) *Hasta-lakshaṇa*—scheme of measurement, *M.*, II.

(10) *Pura-niveśa*—moats, enclosures, etc., of villages and towns, *M.*, IX, X.

(11) *Vāstu-traya-vibhāga*—site-plans, *M.*, VII

(12) *Nāḍyādi-śirādi-vikalpa*—continuation of the site plans, *M.*, VII.

(13) *Marma-bheda*—continuation of site plans, *M.*, VII.

(14) *Purushāṅga-devatā-nighaṇṭvādi-nirṇaya*—spirit of the site, *M.*, III.

(15) *Rāja-niveśa*—forts and fortified towns for kings, *M.*, X.

(16) *Vana-praveśa*—to go to forests for wood and timber, *M.*, XV

(17) *Indra-dhvaja-nirūpaṇa*—instruments for cutting wood, etc., continuation of (16), *M.*, XV.

(18) *Nagarādi-saṁjñā*—towns, *M.*, X.

(19) *Chatuś-śālā-vidhāna*—houses with courtyard and buildings on four sides, compilation from several chapters of *Mānasāra* and other works.

(20) *Nimnochchādi-phala*—levels of the building site, *M.*, VII.

(21) (*Dvā-saptati*)-*triśāla-lakshaṇa*—certain-plan with buildings on three sides of the courtyard, *M.*, XXXV.

(22) *Dvi-śāla-gṛiha-lakshaṇa*—other plans with buildings on two sides of the courtyard, *M.*, XXXV.

(23) *Eka-śāla-lakshaṇa*—single-rowed houses, *M.*, XXXV.

(24) *Dvāra-pīṭha-bhitti-mānādi*—door, pedestal, wall, etc., *M.*, XXXVIII, XXXIX, XIII, etc.

(25) *Samasta-gṛihāṇām saṁkhyā-kathana*—Mansions of various kinds, *M.*, XXXV.

(26) *Āyādi-nirṇaya*—formulæ for verification of correct dimensions, compilation from various places in *M.*

(27) *Sabhāshṭaka*—eight kinds of halls, compilation from various places in *M.*

(28) *Gṛiha-dravya-pramāṇa*—mostly on doors, *M.*, XXXVIII, XXXIX.

(29) *Śayanāsana-lakshaṇa*—bedsteads and seats, etc., *M.*, XLIV, XLV.

(30) *Rāja-gṛiha*—royal palaces, *M.*, XL.

(31) *Yantra-vidhāna*—*lit.* architectural instruments (cf. engineering chapters of *Vitruvius*), compilation from various sources.

(32) *Gaja-śālā*—elephant stables, compilation from various places in *M.*

(33) *Aśva-śālā*—horse stables, compilation from various places in *M.*

(34) *Aprayojya-prayojya*—sculptures and paintings on palaces, continuation of (30), *M.*, XL.

(35) *Śilā-nyāsa-vidhi*—on foundation, *M.*, XII.

(36) *Bali-dāna-vidhi*—religious offerings, *M.*, VIII.

(37) *Kīlaka-sūtra-pāta*—nails, etc., compilation from various places in *M.*

(38) *Vāstu-saṁsthāna-māṭrikā*—distribution of houses in the plot, *M.*, XXXVI, XXXVII.

(39) *Dvāra-guṇa-dosha*—on doors, *M.*, XXXVIII, XXXIX.

(40) *Pīṭha-māna*—plinth, cf. *M.*, XIII.

(41) *Chaya-vidhi*—on plinth, continuation of (40), *M.*, XIII.

(42) *Śānti-karma-vidhi*—offerings, etc., *M.*, VIII.

(43) *Dvāra-bhaṅga-phala*—on orientation *M.*, VII.

(44) *Sthapati-lakshaṇa*—qualifications, etc., of the architects, *M.*, II.

(45) *Ashṭāṅga-lakshaṇa*—on site-plans, distribution of buildings, road-measures, etc., a confused compilation of several chapters in *M.*

(46) *Toraṇa-bhaṅgādi-śāntika*—on ritualistic matters, continuation of (42).

(47) *Vedi-lakshaṇa*—on platforms, pedestals, etc., in many places in *M.*

(48) *Gṛiha-dosha-nirūpaṇa*—on defective construction, cf. *M.*, LXIX.

(49) *Ruchakādi-prāsāda-lakshaṇa*—on palaces and *vimānas*, cf. *M.*, XVIII, XL.

(50) *Prāsāda-śubhāśubha-lakshaṇa*—continuation of (49).

(51) *Āyatana-niveśa*—dimensions of palaces, etc., continuation of (49).

(52) *Prāsāda-jāti*—classification of palaces, continuation of (49).

(53) *Jaghanya-vāstu-dvāra*—on doors, *M.*, XXXVIII, XXXIX.

(54) *Prāsāda-dvāra-māna*—on palace doors, continuation of (49).

(55) *Mervādi-shoḍaśa-prāsāda*—on palaces, continuation of (49).

(56) *Ruchakādi-chatuḥ-shashṭi-prāsāda*—on palaces, continuation of (49).

(57) *Mervādi-viṁśikā*—on palaces, continuation of (49) and (55).

(58) *Prāsāda-stavana*—on distribution of palaces to kings and gods, continuation of (49).

(59) *Vimānādi-chatuḥ-shashṭi-prāsāda*—on palaces, continuation of (49).

(60) *Śrī-kūṭādi-shaṭ-triṁśat-prāsāda*—on palaces, continuation of (49).

(61) *Pīṭha-pañchaka*—five varieties of plinth and pedestal, *M.*, XIII, LIII.

(62) *Drāviḍa-prāsāda-lakshaṇa*—Dravidian palaces of two to ten storeys, cf. *M.*, XX—XXVIII.

(63) *Mervādi-viṁśika-nāgara-prāsāda*—*Nāgara* palaces, *M.*, XIX–XXX.

(64) *Dig-bhadrādi-prāsāda*—on palaces, continuation of (49).

(65) *Bhūmija-prāsāda*—on local palaces, continuation of (49).

(66) *Maṇḍapa-lakshaṇa*—on pavilions, *M.*, XXXIV.

(67) *Sapta-viṁśati-maṇḍapa*—on pavilions, *M.*, XXXIV, continuation of (66).

(68) *Jagatyaṅga-samudayādhikāra*—on platform in palaces, continuation of (49).

(69) *Jagati-lakshaṇa*—continuation of (68).

(70) *Liṅga-pīṭha-pratimā-lakshaṇa*—on pedestal of the phallus and on altars and images, *M.*, LIII, LXIV.

(71) *Chitroddeśa*—on paintings, from several places in *M.*

(72) *Bhūmi-bandha*—on paintings, continuation of (71).

(73) *Lepya-karmādika*—on paintings and whitewashing, continuation of (71).

(74) *Aṇḍaka-pramāṇa*—on paintings, continuation of (71).

(75) *Mānotpatti*—on proportionate measures of images, same as *Tāla-māna* of *Mānasāra*, LXV, LXVI, LIV-LXIII.

(76) *Pratimā-lakshaṇa*—on images, *M.*, LXIV.

(77) *Devādi-rūpa-praharaṇa-saṁyoga*—on images, *M.*, LI, LIV, etc.

(78) *Dosha-guṇa-nirūpaṇa*—defects and merits in images, *M.*, LXIX.

(79) *Ṛijvāgatādi-sthāna-lakshaṇa*—on postures and attitudes of images, in many places in *M.*

(80) *Vaishṇavādi-sthānaka-lakshaṇa*—on erect and other postures, continuation of (79).

(81) *Pañcha-purusha-strī-lakshaṇa*—on images of birds, *M.*, LX, etc.

(82) *Rasa-dṛishṭi-lakshaṇa*—on expressions of images, continuation of (79).

(83) *Patākādi-chatuḥ-shashṭi-hasta-lakshaṇa*—on patterns and designs of paintings, in several places in *M.*

This outline of the contents of a modernized text will clearly show its compilation in a confused manner. There is no logical sequence or order in the arrangement of the chapters. The contents of the same chapter have been unnecessarily described in several chapters. The patron being a king, and the primary object being the royal palaces, some twenty-one chapters (XLIX-LXX) have been devoted to the same subject. Because the compilation was largely, if not wholly, based on the *Mānasāra*, however, some thirteen chapters at the end have been devoted to the subjects of sculpture and painting, as has been done in the *Mānasāra*, although the treatment is less methodical. The preliminary chapters dealing with the origin of the world and arrival of the heavenly architect are the only original, but entirely non-architectural, matters.

The Saṁgraha

This work is avowedly a compilation (*saṁgraha*). It bears the title *Śilpa-saṁgraha*, and, to our great relief, it expressly mentions the sources from which it has been compiled.[1] In fact, several of the architectural treatises compared above, and many more not mentioned here, are evidently compilations, although the authors have not acknowledged their debt, nor even mentioned the sources drawn upon. This point is convincingly illustrated in the following instance.

The following chapters in the order found in the manuscript are ascribed to

I.—*Mānasāra* :

Under 7, *Gomukha-lakshaṇa*—under this heading there is no separate chapter in the eleven manuscripts of the *Mānasāra* so far known to exist.

(13) *Upapīṭha-lakshaṇa*—pedestals (*M.* XIII).

Under 15, *Vṛishabha-lakshaṇa*—image of the bull, the riding animal of Śiva (*M.*, LXII).

II.—*Mayamata* :

Under 6, *Dik-parichchheda*—the cardinal points.

(23) *Maṇḍapa-vidhāna*—open sheds.

(9) *Grāma-vinyāsa*—villages.

(20) *Eka-bhūmi-ro(vi)dha(ā)na*—one-storeyed buildings.

Under 86, *Sthapati-lakshaṇa*—characteristics and qualifications of the architect.

(24) *Gopura-vidhāna*—gate houses.

(13) *Upapīṭha-vidhāna*—pedestals.

(1) *Adhishṭhāna-vidhāna*—bases.

(20) *Dvi-bhūmi-vidhāna*—two-storeyed buildings.

Under 20, *Tri-bhūmi-vidhāna*—three-storeyed buildings.

III.—*Kāśyapa* :

Under 7, *Prastara-lakshaṇa*—entablatures.

Under 7, *Adhisṭhāna-paṭala*—bases.

Under 7, *Nāla-pramāṇotsedhālaṅkaraṇa*—drains and canals.

Under 24, *Dakshinā-mūrti-paṭala*—an image of the god Śiva.

Under 22, *Nṛitta-lakshaṇa*—image of dancing Śiva.

[1] Oriental Manuscripts Library, Madras, Cat., Vol. XXII, no. 13058. It comprises 429 pages of 25 lines to a page of paper 13½″×8″.

IV.—*Viśvakarman* :

Under 6, *Gopura-lakshaṇa*—gate-houses.

Under 36, *Śayana-lakshaṇa*—bedsteads and couches.

(86) *Sthapati-lakshaṇa*—characteristics and qualifications of the architect.

(14) *Āyādi-sampad-artha-vidhāna*—the formula of Āya, etc.

V.—*Āgastya* :

Under 1, *Māna-samgraha-viśesha*—system of measurement.

Under 2, *Uttama-daśa-tāla*—the large type of the ten-*tāla* measure.

Under 3, *Madhyama-daśa-tāla*—the intermediate type of the ten-*tāla* measure.

Under 4, *Soma-skanda-lakshaṇa*—images of Soma and Skanda.

Under 5, *Chandra-śekhara-lakshaṇa*—image of Śiva.

Under 6, *Vṛisha-vāhana-lakshaṇa*—image of Śiva, riding on the bull.

It is not known for certain whether or not the following, under 6 and 19, are to be ascribed to Āgastya.

Under 6, *Tripurāntaka-lakshaṇa*—image of Śiva.

Under 6, *Kalyāṇa-Sundara-lakshaṇa*—image of Kalyāṇa-Sundara Śiva.

Under 6, *Ardha-nārīśvara-lakshaṇa*—image of Śiva.

Under 6, *Pāśupata-lakshaṇa*—image of Śiva.

Under 6, *Bhikshāṭana-lakshaṇa*—image of Śiva.

Under 6, *Chaṇḍeśānugraha-lakshaṇa*—image of Śiva.

Under 6, *Dakshiṇā-mūrti-lakshaṇa*—image of Śiva.

Under 6, *Kāla-dahana-lakshaṇa*—image of Śiva.

Under 19, *Pratimā-lakshaṇa*—images in general.

(3) *Upapīṭha-vidhāna*—pedestal.

(9) *Śūla-māna-vidhāna*—pikes.

(10) *Rajju-bandha-saṁskāra-vidhi*—preparation of ropes.

(11) *Varṇa-saṁskāra*—preparation of colours.

(12) *Akshi-mokshaṇa*—chiselling the eyes of an image.

VI.—*Bhṛigu* .

Under 7, *Ratha-nirmāṇa*—construction of chariots.

VII.—*Paulastya* :

Under 22, *Dakshiṇā-mūrti-nirmāṇa*—image of Śiva.

VIII.—*Nārada* :

Under 14, *Kṛishṇa-lakshaṇa*—image of Kṛishṇa.

IX.—*Nārāyaṇa* :

Under 20, *Rāma-Lakshaṇa*—image of Rāma.

X.—*Maushalya* :

Under 7, *Ratha-lakshaṇa*—chariots.

XI.—*Śesha-bhāshya* :

Under 36, (title missing).

Under 22, *Ekatāla-vidhāna*—one-storeyed buildings.

XII.—*Chitra-sāra* :

Under 14, (title missing).

(7) *Pratimāsāra* (?).

XIII.—*Sārasvata* :

Under 28, *Chaṇḍeśvara-vidhāna*—image of Chaṇḍeśvara.

(28) *Garuḍa-lakshaṇa-paṭala*—image of the Garuḍa bird ; *Rāma-Lakshmaṇa-paṭala*—the images of Rāma and Lakshmaṇa. (The term *paṭala*, usually used in the *Āgamas*, indicates that these chapters may have been borrowed from some *Āgamas*.)

Under 20, *Gopura-māna*—gate-houses.

(1) *Māna-saṁgrahādi*—the system of measurement.

XIV.—*Viśva-sāra* :

Under 20, *Aśva-māna-vidhi*—image of the horse.

Under 20, *Vīra-bhadra-lakshaṇa*—image of Vīrabhadra.

Under 20, *Skanda*—image of Skanda.

Under 20, *Tripuri*—image of Tripuri.

Under 20, *Pratimādi*—images, etc.

XV.—*Chitra-jñāna* :

Under 20, *Dhvaja-daṇḍa-paṭa-lakshaṇa*—flagstaff and banner.

Under 20, *Jīrṇoddhāra*—repairs.

XVI.—*Kapiñjala-saṁhitā* :

Under 20, *Garuḍa-lakshaṇa*—image of the Garuḍa bird.

XVII.—*Kaumudī* :

Under 29, *Pratimā-lakshaṇa*—images in general.

XVIII.—*Brahma-śilpa* :

Under 15, *Śayana-lakshaṇa*—bedsteads and couches.

XIX.—*Brahma-yāmala* :

Under 5, *Chāmuṇḍī-dhyāna*—characteristics of the goddess Chāmuṇḍī.

Under 20, *Daśāvatāra-lakshaṇa*—images of the ten incarnations of Vishṇu.

XX.—*Dīpta-tantra* :

Under 15, *Liṅga-lakshaṇa*—Phallus.

XXI.—*Dīpti-sāra* :

Under 8, *Gopura-lakshaṇa*—gate-houses.

Of these, it will be noticed, numbers I to V refer to treatises discussed above, VI to X refer to authors whose treatises are not mentioned here, and the rest refer to treatises and not to their authors. In fact, it is practically impossible to trace the authors of these latter treatises, as is the case with several others dealing with architecture and cognate arts.

The brief sketch of this compilation, as well as the other illustrative *Śilpa-śāstras* presented above, incidentally substantiate two theories. Most of the architectural treatises, whether or not ascribed to an author, historical or mythical, are but compilations. Some of these have actually acknowledged the sources drawn upon, while others have not. This practice of misappropriating somebody else's property is prominently shown in works like the *Purāṇas* and the *Āgamas* ; which in most cases are undeniably huge compilations gathered together from various sources dealing with heterogeneous subjects. The second theory is that the *Mānasāra*, though itself a compilation, because the author seems to have consulted some thirty-two authorities on architecture, appears to be the standard work on the subject, inasmuch as it is the most complete, scientific, and probably the oldest extant record. This last impression will be further strengthened by comparison of the *Mānasāra* with the architectural portions of the *Purāṇas*, the *Āgamas*, and the *Bṛihat-saṁhitā* in detail.

CHAPTER V

POSITION OF THE MĀNASĀRA IN LITERATURE

The Types of Buildings

With a view to ascertaining the position of the *Mānasāra* in relation to the non-architectural literature it will be necessary to discuss the points of similarity in detail. It is, however, practicable, in an article like this, to take into consideration only the architectural portions of works which deal with the subject specially. For the purpose of an elaborate treatment we propose to compare the *Mānasāra* with the *Agni-Purāṇa*, the *Garuḍa-Purāṇa*, the *Matsya-Purāṇa*, the *Bhavishya-Purāṇa*, the *Bṛihat-saṁhitā*, the *Kāmikāgama*, and the *Suprabhedāgama*.

It has been pointed out at the outset that architecture comprises a variety of subjects, but it cannot be denied that the fundamental business of the architect is with buildings, residential, religious, and military. It appears to be a fashion among many peoples of the past, as of the present, to designate individual buildings by proper names, with or without a meaning.[1] It seems to have been a custom among the ancient Hindu architects to describe buildings under some such names. In the eight treatises we have proposed to compare in detail, we find buildings bearing proper names classified and described in the following way:

1. In the *Mānasāra* the main buildings are described in some thirteen chapters.[2] Their common features from bottom to top are given under storeys, varying from one to twelve. They are also classified under styles—Nāgara, Vesara, and Drāviḍa—chiefly in accordance with the shape of the topmost part[3]; under sizes[4]—as Śuddha,

[1] Compare, for instance, Whitehall, Guildhall, Mansion House, Cosy Corner, Gordon Castle, Benmore, Barnes Castle, Svastika, Vijaya, Vipulāṅka, Indrakānta, Chatur-mukha, Pāñchāla, Drāviḍa Kamalā-Bhavana, Chitta-Viśrāma, etc.

[2] Chapters XVIII to XXX, *see* the summary of contents in the preceding section under XVIII.

[3] For details of these styles, *see* the writer's *Encyclopaedia*, under *Nāgara*.

[4] Large, intermediate, and small.

Miśra, and Saṁkīrṇa—in accordance with the materials of which they are built[1]; under Jāti, Chhanda, Vikalpa, and Ābhāsa in accordance with the various lengths of the cubit with which the buildings are measured[2]; under Sthānaka, Āsana, and Śayana, which are otherwise called Saṁchita, Asaṁchita, and Apasaṁchita respectively[3]; and under shapes, Puṁliṅga (masculine), Strīliṅga (feminine)[4] and Napuṁsaka (neuter).

The details of the ninety-eight types of buildings, described according to the number of storeys, are given below. The numerical figures on the left indicate the serial numbers, and those on the right refer to the lines or verses of the chapters.

I. The eight kinds of single-storeyed buildings with their characteristic features, Chapter XIX—

(1) Vaijayantika, with round spire (*śīrsha*), pinnacle (*śiraḥ*), and neck (*gīrvā*) (line 166); (2) Bhoga has *karṇa* or ears (187); (3) Śrīviśāla has the *bhadra* or front porch in it (168); (4) Svastibandha has octagonal finial (*śīrsha*) (168); (5) Śrīkara has quadrangular *śikhara* or steeple (170); (6) Hastipṛishṭha has oval steeple (171); (7) Skandatāra has hexagonal spire and neck (172); (8) Keśara has the front porches in the centre of the side-towers at the corners of the roof, and its nose, head. and neck are round or quadrangular (173–175).[5]

II. The eight kinds of two-storeyed buildings, Chapter XX (the general features are the same in all the eight kinds; the distinction lies in the different proportions given to the component parts from above the ground floor to the top)—

(9) Śrīkara (lines 94, 2–9); (10) Vijaya (94, 10–15); (11) Siddha (94, 16–18); (12) Paushṭika (94, 19–25); (13) Antika (94, 25–27); (14) Adbhuta (94, 28–33); (15) Svastika (95, 34–41); and

[1] (*a*) Śuddha, or pure, made of one material (brick, iron or wood); (*b*) Miśra, or mixed, made of two materials; (*c*) Saṁkīrṇa, or amalgamated, made of three or more materials. *M.*, XVIII, 139–142.

[2] *M.*, XIX, 2–5.

[3] Referring respectively to height, breadth, and length, *M.*, XIX 7–9, 10–11. The three latter sets also refer to the postures of the idols in case of temples, namely, erect, sitting, and recumbent.

[4] Equiangular and rectanguiar respectively. But in case of temples, the former contains the male deities, while the latter may contain both female and male deities, *M.*, XIX, 14–17. For the neuter class, *see* the *Kāmikāgama* below.

[5] For further details, *see* the writer's *Encyclopaedia*, under *Ekabhūmi*.

(16) Pushkala (94, 42–43). The projection, the general description, and the carvings on the doors, when these buildings are used as temples, are given (44–93, 96–116).[1]

III. The eight kinds of three-storeyed buildings, Chapter XXI (the general features and characteristic marks are similar to those of two-storeyed buildings)—

(17) Śrīkānta (lines 2–11); (18) Āsana (12–21); (19) Sukhālaya (22–30); (20) Kesara (31–32); (21) Kamalāṅga (33–38); (22) Brahmakānta (39–40); (23) Merukānta (41–49); and (24) Kailāśa (50–52).[1]

The general features, characteristic marks, and other details of the following kinds are similar to those of the two- and three-storeyed buildings—

IV. The eight kinds of four-storeyed buildings, Chapter XXII—

(25) Vishṇukānta (lines 3–12); (26) Chaturmukha (13–24); (27) Sadāśiva (25–33); (28) Rudrakānta (34–43); (29) Iśvarakānta (44–46); (30) Mañchakānta (47–57); (31) Vedikānta (58–59); and (32) Indrakānta (60–88).[2]

V. The nine kinds of five-storeyed buildings, Chapter XXIII—

(33) Airāvata (lines 3–12); (34) Bhūtakānta (13–15); (35) Viśvakānta (16–18); (36) Mūrtikānta (19–24); (37) Yamakānta (25–29); (38) Gṛihakānta (30–38); (39) Yajñakānta (33–40); (40) Brahmakānta; and (41–42) Mahākānta and Kalyāṇa.[2]

VI. The thirteen kinds of six-storeyed buildings, Chapter XXIV—

(41) Padmakānta (lines 3–12); (42) Kāntāra (13–14); (43) Sundara (15); (44) Upakānta (16); (45) Kamala-aksha (17–18); (46) Ratnakānta (19); (47) Vipulāṅka (20); (48) Jyoti(sh)kānta (50); (49) Saroruha (51–52); (50) Vipulākṛitika (53); (51) Svasti-kānta (53); (52) Nandyāvarta (54); and (53) Ikshukānta (55).[2]

VII. The eight kinds of seven-storeyed buildings, Chapter XXV—

(54) Puṇḍarīka (lines 3–23); (55) Śrīkānta (24); (56) Śrībhoga (25); (57) Dhāraṇa (26); (58) Pañjara (27); (59) Āśramāgāra (28); (60) Harmyakānta (29); and (61) Himakānta (30).[2]

[1] For further details, *see* the writer's *Encyclopaedia*, under *dvi-tala* and *tri-tala*.

[2] For further details, *see* the writer's *Encyclopaedia*, under *chatus-tala*, *pañcha-tala*, *shaṭ-tala*, *sapta-tala*, *ashṭa-tala*, *nava-tala*, *daśa-tala*, and *ekādaśa-tala*.

VIII. The eight kinds of eight-storeyed buildings, Chapter XXVI—

(62) Bhūkānta (lines 3–21); (63) Bhūpakānta (22–28); (64) Svargakānta (29–34); (65) Mahākānta (35–39); (66) Janakānta (40); (67) Tapa(s)kānta (41–42); (68) Satyakānta (43–45); and (69) Devakānta (46–47).[1]

IX. The seven kinds of nine-storeyed buildings, Chapter XXVII—

(70) Saurakānta (lines 5–9); (71) Raurava (10); (72) Chaṇḍita (11–12); (73) Bhūshaṇa (13–14); (74) Vivṛita (20–22); (75) Supratikānta (23–26); and (76) Viśvakānta (27–33).[1]

X. The six kinds of ten-storeyed buildings, Chapter XXVIII—

(77) Bhūkānta (lines 6–8); (78) Chandrakānta (6–8); (79) Bhavanakānta (9–13); (80) Antarikshakānta (14–15); (81) Meghakānta (16–17); and (82) Abjakānta (18).[1]

XI. The six kinds of eleven-storeyed buildings, Chapter XXIX—

(83) Śambhukānta (lines 3–7); (84) Īśakānta (8–9); (85) Chakrakānta (10–14); (86) Yamakānta (15–17); (87) Vajrakānta (18–24); and (88) Arkakānta (24–33).[1]

XII. The ten kinds of twelve-storeyed buildings, Chapter XXX—

(83) Pāñchāla (lines 8–10); (90) Drāviḍa (8–10); (91) Madhyakānta (11–14); (92) Kāliṅgakānta (14–16); (93) Varāṭa (Virāṭa?) (17–27); (94) Kerala (28–30); (95) Vaṁśakānta (31–32); (96) Māgadhakānta (33–34); (97) Jana(ka)kānta (33–36); and (98) Sphūrjaka (? Gurjaraka) (7, 37–84); description of the twelfth storey.[2]

2. *Agni-Purāṇa*, Chapter XLII, verses 1–9 (general plan), 10–25 (plan with reference to the idol), Chapter 104, vv. 1–11, 22–34 (further general plan), 11–21 (names, classes, shapes, and description of forty-five kinds of temples).

[1] For further details, *see* the writer's *Encyclopaedia* under *chatus-tala*, *pañcha-tala*, *shaṭ-tala*, *sapta-tala*, *ashṭa-tala*, *nava-tala*, *daśa-tala* and *ekadaśa-tala*.

[2] These ten kinds are named, it should be noticed, after the historic places, well marked in the ancient geography of India, which cover the whole length and breadth of the continent.

The topography of these places is described elsewhere (pp. 254–256). For the architectural details of these buildings, *see* the writer's *Encyclopaedia*, under these ten terms. The description of the twelfth storey is given under *dvādaśa-tala*.

Five divisions depending on five shapes (plans), each including nine kinds of temples (Chapter CIV, vv. 11–13)—

I. Vairāja—quadrangular (square)—includes (1) Meru, (2) Mandara, (3) Vimāna, (4) Bhadra, (5) Sarvatobhadra, (6) Charuka (in the Kāmikāgama, XXXV, 87, 91 : Ruchaka), (7) Nandika, (8) Nandi-varddhana, and (9) Śrīvatsa (Chapter CIV, vv. 14, 15).

II. Pushpaka—rectangular—includes (10) Ba(Va)labhi, (11) Gṛiharāja, (12) Sālāgṛiha or Sālāmandira, (13) Viśāla, (14) Sama, (15) Brahma-mandira, (16) Bhavana or Bhuvana, (17) Prabhava, and (18) Śivikāveśma (Chapter CIV, vv. 16, 17).

III. Kailāśa—round—includes (19) Ba(va)laya, (20) Dundubhi, (21) Padma, (22) Mahā-padmaka, (23) Varddhanī, (24), Ushṇi, (25) Śaṅkha, (26) Kalaśa, and (27) Svavṛiksha (Chapter CIV, vv. 17–18).

IV. Maṇika—oval (*vṛittāyata*)—includes (28) Gaja, (29) Vṛishabha, (30) Haṁsa, (31) Garutmat, (32) Ṛikshanāyaka, (33) Bhūshaṇa, (34) Bhūdhara, (35) Śrījaya, and (36) Pṛithivī-dhara (Chapter CIV, vv. 19–20).

V. Trivishṭapa—octagonal—includes (37) Vajra, (38) Chakra, (39) Svastika, (40) Vajra-svastika, (41) Chitra, (42) Svastika-khaḍga, (43) Gadā, (44) Śrīkaṇṭha, and (45) Vijaya (Chapter CIV, vv. 20–21).

3. *Garuḍa-Purāṇa* (Chapter XLVII) has exactly the same general plan (vv. 1–20, 32–47), five shapes, five classes (v. 21–23), and forty-five kinds of buildings (vv. 24–32), but the wording is not identical. The fourth class is read Mālikā (v. 21) in the general description, but the name ' Maṇika ' (v. 30) is given later on—

I. Vairāja—square (vv. 21–22)—includes the same nine kinds, but (7) Nandika is read as Nandana, and (6) Charuka is correctly read as Ruchaka (vv. 24–25).

II. Pushpaka—rectangular (vv. 22–23)—includes nine kinds where (10) Valabhī is correctly spelt, (13) Viśāla is read as Vimāna, which is apparently a mistake in the *Garuḍa-Purāṇa*, because (3) Vimāna is a kind of building included in the square (I) Vairāja class. But the reading of class (II) seems better in the *Garuḍa-Purāṇa*, which may be quoted—(10) Valabhī, (11) Gṛiharāja, (12) Sālāgṛiha, (13) Mandira, (14) Viśāla (text has Vimāna), (15) Brahmamandira, (16) Bhavana, (17) Uttambha, and (18) Śibikā-veśma (vv. 26–27).

III. Kailāśa—round (vv. 21—23)—has nine kinds, again perhaps with better readings—(19) Valaya, (20) Dundubhi, (21) Padma, (22) Mahāpadma, (23) Mukulī (in place of Varddhanī), (24) Ushṇīshi, (25) Śaṅkha, (26) Kalaśa, and (27) Guvā-vṛiksha (vv. 28–29).

IV. Maṇika—oval (vv. 30)—has nine kinds, of which (31), (32), and (33) are read as Garuḍa, Siṁha, and Bhūmukha respectively (vv. 29–30).

V. Trivishṭapa—octagonal (vv. 21, 23)—has nine kinds, readings again seem better here—(37) Vajra, (38) Chakra, (39) Mushṭika (preceded by Babhru, vv. 31), (40) Vakra, (41) Svastika, (42) Khaḍga, (43) Gadā, (44) Śrīvṛiksha, and (45) Vijaya (vv. 31–32).

4. The *Matsya-Purāṇa*, Chapter 269—

The description of the general plan (verses 1–7) is followed by that of the special plan (vv. 8–20).

The names (vv. 28–30), description of architectural details (vv. 31–46), measures (vv. 47–51), and division (vv. 53–54) of twenty types of buildings—

(1) Meru has 100 cupolas (*śṛiṅga*), 16 storeys (*bhūmika*), many variegated steeples (*śikhara*), and is 50 cubits broad (vv. 28, 31, 53); (2) Mandara has 12 storeys, many steeples and faces, and is 45 cubits broad (vv. 28, 37, 47, 53); (3) Kailāśa has nine storeys (many steeples and faces), and is 40 cubits broad (vv. 32, 47, 53); (4) Vimāna-chchhanda has eight storeys, many steeples and faces (*ānana*), and is 34 cubits broad (vv. 25, 32, 33, 47, 53); (5) Nandi-vardhana has seven storeys, and is 32 cubits broad (vv. 29, 33, 48, 53); (6) Nandana has seven storeys, and is furnished with *vishāṇa* or horns, and is 30 cubits broad (vv. 29, 33, 48, 53); (7) Sarvatobhadra has five storeys, 16 corners with various shapes, is furnished with art galleries (*chitraśālā*), and is 30 cubits broad (vv. 29, 34, 35, 48, 53); (8) Valabhī-chchhandaka has five storeys, many steeples and faces, and is 16 cubits broad (vv. 35, 50, 53); (9) Vṛisha should resemble the height and length of the bull, be round and without corners, should have five cupolas, two storeys, and should be 4 cubits broad at the central hall (vv. 30, 36, 44, 45, 53); (10) Siṁha resembles the lion and is 16 cubits broad, is adorned with the famous *chandra-śālā* (top rooms, gable windows), and by the width of the front neck six storeys high (vv. 29, 36, 40, 49, 53); (11) Gaja resembles the elephant, and is 16 cubits broad, and has many *chandraśālās* or top

rooms (vv. 36, 41, 49, 53) ; (12) Kumbha resembles the water-jar, has nine storeys, five cupolas (*aṇḍas*), and is 16 cubits broad (vv. 37, 49, 53) ; (13) Samudraka has 16 sides around, 2 *chandraśālās* (top rooms) at the two sides, two storeys (vv. 38, 53) ; (14) Padma has three storeys, 16 corners, a variegated steeple, and is 20 cubits broad (vv. 30, 39, 49, 53) ; (15) Garuḍa has the bird-design around, seven storeys, three top rooms, and is 8 cubits broad, and there should be 86 (?) compartments (*bhūmika, lit.* storeys, v. 42) all round the outside (vv. 41, 43, 51). There is a similar Garuḍa building with ten storeys, and a second Padmaka-building with two storeys more (? 12 storeys, v. 43) ; (16) Haṁsa, is 10 cubits broad (vv. 36, 51) ; (17) Vartula is 20 cubits broad (vv. 29 49, 53). No special description is given of the remaining : (18) Chaturaśra (four-cornered, vv. 28, 53) ; (19) Ashṭāśra (eight-cornered, v. 29, 53) ; (20) Shoḍaśāsra (sixteen-cornered, vv. 29, 53).[1]

Similar types of buildings are described almost in the same way in both the *Bhavishya-Purāṇa* and the *Bṛihat-saṁhitā.*

5. The *Bhavishya-Purāṇa,* Book I, Chapter CXXX, names (vv. 23–26), description of the architectural details and measures (vv. 27–35) of the twenty kinds of buildings (same as in the *Bṛihat-saṁhitā, see* below)—

(1) Meru, 39 cubits high and 32 cubits broad, has 12 storeys, various windows (*kuhara*), and four gateways (v. 27).

(2) Mandara, 30 cubits broad, and has ten storeys (v. 28).

(3) Kailāśa, 28 cubits broad, has steeples and eight storeys (v. 28).

The description of the following is clearer in the *Bṛihat-saṁhitā,* quoted below ; the names may be given here—

(4) Vimāna, with latticed windows (v. 29).

(5) Nandana (v. 29).

(6) Samudga (v. 30), Samudra (v. 24) as in the *Bṛihat-saṁhitā* (LVI, 28, 5).

(7) Padma (v. 30).

(8) Garuḍa (v. 31).

(9) Nandi-vardhana (v. 28, Naṁdī, v. 31).

(10) Kuñjara (v 32).

(11) Gṛiharāja (v. 32), *Bṛihat-saṁhitā* (LVI, 25) has Guharāja.

[1] Compare the three divisions of these buildings according to sizes.

(12) Vṛisha (v. 33).
(13) Haṁsa (v. 33).
(14) Ghaṭa (v. 33).
(15) Sarvatobhadra (v. 34).
(16) Siṁha (v. 35).
(17) Vṛitta (as in the *Bṛihat-saṁhitā*, LVI, 29, 49); but here (v. 33) it reads Vṛisha-like (12), which is apparently a mistake (*see* v. 30).

No special description is given of the remaining—

(18) Chatushkoṇa, four-cornered (v. 25), *Matsya-Purāṇa* (Chapter CCLXIX, vv. 28, 53) has Chaturasra; and *Bṛihat-saṁhitā* (VI, 28) has Chaturasra.

(19) Ashṭāsra, octangular (v. 25).

(20) Shoḍaśāsra, sixteen-cornered (v. 25).

Varāhamihira seems to have taken these from an earlier *Purāṇa* and improved them in the *Bṛihat-saṁhitā*.

6. The *Bṛihat-saṁhitā*, LVI, 1–19—

The religious merits acquired by building temples (vv. 1–2); suitable sites—in the garden, wood, banks of rivers (seas), tanks (vv. 3–8); ground (v. 9); general plan (v. 10); situation of doors (v. 10); comparative measures of length, breadth, and height (v. 11), of the adytum (*garbha*, v. 12), of the doors and their different parts (vv. 12–14); carvings on the door (v. 15); comparative measures of the idol, pedestal, and door (v. 16); the heights of storeys (v. 29–30).

This is followed by a classification (vv. 17–19) and an account of the architectural details (vv. 20–28) of the same twenty kinds of temples (*prāsāda*) as are given in the *Matsya-Purāṇa* and the *Bhavishya-Purāṇa*. The names of these buildings are given below, details being almost the same as in the *Purāṇas*—

(1) Meru (v. 20).
(2) Mandara (v. 21).
(3) Kailāśa (v. 21).
(4) Vimāna-(chchhanda) (vv. 17–22).
(5) Nandana (v. 22).
(6) Samudga (v. 23).
(7) Padma (v. 23).
(8) Garuḍa (v. 24).
(9) Nandivardhana (v. 24).
(10) Kuñjara (v. 25).

(11) Guharāja (v. 25).
(12) Vṛisha (v. 26).
(13) Haṁsa (v. 26).
(14) Ghaṭa (v. 26).
(15) Sarvatobhadra (v. 27).
(16) Siṁha (v. 28).
(17) Vṛitta (vv. 18–28).
(18) Chatush-koṇa (vv. 18–28).
(19) Ashṭāsra (v. : 18–28).
(20) Shoḍaśāsra (vv. 18–28).

7. The *Kāmikāgama*,[1] *Paṭala* LV—

The four classes—

Jāti (verse 128), Chhanda (v. 129), Vikalpa (v. 130), and Ābhāsa (v. 130).

Paṭala XLV—

Further classifications—

(1) Saṁchita, Apasaṁchita, and Upasaṁchita (v. 6).

(2) Nāgara (vv. 6, 12, 13), Drāviḍa (vv. 6, 14, 15), and Vesara (vv. 7, 16, 18).

(3) Jāti (vv. 7, 19), Chhanda (vv. 7–20), and Vikalpa (vv. 7–20).

(4) Śuddha (vv. 7, 21), Miśra (vv. 7, 22), and Saṁkīrṇa (vv. 7, 22).

(5) Puṁ-liṅga, or masculine, also called Saṁchita (vv. 8, 9), Strīliṅga, or feminine (vv. 9, 10), and Napuṁsaka, or neuter (vv. 11).

This class (5) does not refer (like the *Mānāsāra*) to the sexes of the deities. Here they appear more like residential buildings; their characteristic features are determined by architectural details. The distinguishing marks of the divisions in the other four classes (1 to 4) are similar to those of the *Mānasāra* noticed above.

In *Paṭala* XXXV, Śālās, in almost the sense of Prāsāda, are divided into five classes : Sarvatobhadra (vv. 87, 88), Vardhamāna (vv. 87, 88), Svastika (vv. 87, 89), Nandyāvarta (vv. 87, 90), and Charuka (vv. 87, 91).

Their technical names[2]—

(1) Sindhuka (XLV, vv. 23–28), (2) Saṁpūrṇa (vv. 29–30), (3) Merukūṭa (v. 31), (4) Kshema (vv. 32–34), (5) Śiva (vv. 35–38), (6)

[1] This *Paṭala* refers to the description of a single building and its component parts. So also does the *Paṭala* XLV (*see* under *Mālikā*), it is named *Mālikā-(lakshaṇa)* and does not mean anything but *Prāsāda* : cf. *Prāsāda-vyāsa-dirghochchā proktā prāsāda-mālikā* (11, 4).

[2] For further details, *see* the writer's *Encyclopaedia* under these terms and *Mālikā*.

Harmya (vv. 39–40), (7) Saumya (v. 40), (8) Viśāla (v. 41), (9) Sarvakalyāṇa (vv. 43–49), (10) Vijaya (v. 50), (11) Bhadra (v. 51), (12) Raṅgamukha (v. 52), (13) Alpa (vv. 53–54), (14) Koṇa (vv. 55–58), (15) Geya (vv. 58*a*–59), (16) Sāra (v. 60), (17) Pushkara (vv. 61, 63), (18) Adbhuta (v. 61*a*), (19) Saṁkīrṇa (62), and (20) Daṇḍa (v. 64).

8. The *Suprabhedāgama*, *Paṭala* XXXI (named Prāsāda)—

Three styles of temples—Nāgara, Drāviḍa, and Vesara (vv. 38–39).

Different kinds of temples—(1) Kailāśa, (2) Mandara, (3) Meru, (4) Himavat, (5) Nishadha (also called Nīlaparvata, Mahendra), (6) Nalīnaka, (7) Pralīnaka, (8) Nandyāvarta, (9) Śrīvarta (? Śrīpada), and (10) Parvata (vv. 40–52).

Maṇḍapas are first divided into four classes—

Deva-maṇḍapa, Snapana (bath)-maṇḍapa, Vṛisha (bull)-, Nandi-maṇḍapa, and Nṛitta (music)-maṇḍapa (vv. 96–97, 98–99) ; and further classified under epithets, Nandavṛitta, Śriyāvṛitta, Vīrāsana, Jayabhadra, Nandyāvarta, Maṇibhadra, and Viśāla (vv. 110–104).

The attention of readers is invited to the lists of the buildings described in the eight works under observation.

The list in the *Mānasāra* contains in 12 classes (storeys) 98 types of buildings; the *Agni-Purāṇa* has in five classes (or divisions) 45 types ; the *Garuḍa-Purāṇa* also has in the same five classes (or divisions) the same 45 types ; the *Matsya-Purāṇa* has in three divisions 20 types ; the *Bhavishya-Purāṇa* has left out the broader divisions but contains the twenty types ; the *Bṛihat-saṁhitā* in the very same way contains the twenty types ; the *Kāmikāgama* has in three divisions (of various kinds) twenty types ; and the *Suprabhedāgama* has left out all the minor divisions, but preserves the most important one, namely, the three styles (Nāgara, Vesara, Drāviḍa), which comprise ten types of buildings.

The various broader divisions, such as Śuddha, Saṁchita, Sthānaka, Jāti, Puṁliṅga, etc., we have seen in the *Mānasāra*, are repeated in the same terms and same sense as in the *Āgamas*. The most important division into the styles—the Nāgara, Vesara, and Drāviḍa—is also preserved intact in the latter works. These are purely architectural divisions, and they are not taken into consideration in the non-architectural treatises like the *Purāṇas* and the *Bṛihat-saṁhitā*. Even the broadest division into storeys, under which the *Mānasāra* describes the buildings in 12 or 13 chapters, has lost its prominence in the latter works.

Thus the *Mānasāra* has the largest number of the types, namely, 98. The *Agni-Purāṇa* and the *Garuḍa-Purāṇa* have 45 types each. The *Matsya-Purāṇa*, the *Bhavishya-Purāṇa*, the *Bṛihat-saṁhitā*, and the *Kāmikāgama* have twenty types each. The *Spurabhedāgama* has the smallest number of types, namely ten.

The technical names of these types of buildings are, as we have seen above, common in many cases. We have also seen that in some instances the architectural details are identical. The lists of the *Agni-Purāṇa* and the *Garuḍa-Purāṇa* on the one hand, and the *Matsya-Purāṇa* the *Bhavishya-Purāṇa*, and the *Bṛihat-saṁhitā* on the other, are strikingly similar. Of the works containing the lists of twenty types, the *Bṛihat-saṁhitā* has the best description. In respect of brevity, explicitness, and precision, the *Suprabhedāgama*, which contains the smallest number of types, surpasses all; and it happens that the smaller the types the better the description.

The common names of the types, the identity of their details, and the similarity in the description may not be accidental. The grades in the linguistic style and in the explicitness and precision of the description do not seem unconnected; while the variations in the number of types of buildings treated in these works also may not be meaningless. Before hazarding an opinion, it will be better to compare some of the other important points of similarity between the *Mānasāra* and the architectural portions of other works.

Amongst others, the three crucial features in architecture, at least so far as these ancient records are concerned, seem to be the measurement, the orders or columns, and the styles. Similarities in these respects are hardly accidental and may be ascribed to a common origin.

The Measurements

(*A*) The linear measurement is divided into six kinds[1] :

(1) *Māna*, (2) *Pramāṇa*, (3) *Parimāṇa*, (4) *Lamba-māna*, (5) *Unmāna*, and (6) *Upamāna* (*M*., LV, 3–9).

References to these measurements are met with, also, in non-architectural treatises, like the *Matsya-Purāṇa* (Chapter CCLVIII, verse 16) the *Suprobhedāgama* (*Paṭala* XXXIV, verse, 35), as well as in the *Bimbamāna* (British Museum, MSS. 658, 5292, verse 9).

(*B*) The primary measurement (*ādimāna*) refers to comparative measurements and is divided into nine kinds.

The height of an image is determined by comparing it with the

(1) breadth of the main temple,
(2) height of the adytum,
(3) length of the door,
(4) measurement of the basement,
(5) cubit,
(6) *tāla*,
(7) *aṅgula*,
(8) height of the worshipper, and
(9) height of the riding animal (*M*., LV, 10–15).

Each of the measurements is again divided into nine kinds (*M*., LV, 22)

Under (1), (2), (3), and (4), the proportions naturally vary on various occasions, but the general methods are similar in these treatises; compare for instances the *Suprabhedāgama* (XXXI, vv. –15).

The *aṅgula* (finger-breadth) and the *hasta* (cubit), (7) and (5), measures are in fact of the same class. The finger-breadth, equivalent to ¾ inch, is perhaps the earliest unit of measurement

[1] Measurement from the foot to the top of the head is called *Māna* (which is nothing but height) ;

Pramāṇa is the measurement of breadth;

Parimāṇa is the measurement of width or circumference (*paritaḥ*);

Lamba-māna is the measurement by the plumb-lines or the lines drawn perpendicularly through different parts of the body, the *māna* or the measurement of height being taken by the surface of the body ;

Unmāna is the measurement of thickness (*nimna*) or diameter ;

Upamāna is the measurement of interspace (*antara*), such as that between the two feet of an image.

Parimāṇa, unmāna, and *māna* are also mentioned in the *Śukra-nīti* (I, 310), but their meanings are not quite clear.

invented by human brain. Though not liable to being lost in the course of time, it has its own defects, namely, the finger of two persons is hardly of equal breadth and the finger of a person is liable to change owing to various natural causes. Apparently with a view to avoiding these defects, finger-breadth is ascertained by the measures of certain other objects, atom, car-dust, hair-end, nit, louse, and barley corn.[1] The largest size of finger-breadth is stated to be equal to 8 barley corns, the intermediate 7 barley corns, and the smallest 6 barley corns. Again, for the same purpose, this standard measure is divided into three kinds—*mānāṅgula*, *mātrāṅgula*, and *dehalabdhāṅgula*. Of these, *mānāṅgula*, which is equal to 8 barley corns, is meant to be the unit proper. *Mātrāṅgula* is the measure taken by the middle finger of the master who makes an image (or a building), *dehalabdhāṅgula* is the measure equal to one of the equal parts into which the whole height of a statute is divided for sculptural measurements.[2]

This *aṅgula* measure is practically the same in almost all the Indian works bearing upon measurement, for instance :

(1) *Mānasāra* (II, 40–45, 46–47, 48–52, 53–64, LXIV, 49–53, etc.).
(2) *Bṛihat-saṁhitā* (LVIII, 1-2).
(3) *Siddhānta-śiromaṇi*, ed. Bāpūdeva (p. 52).
(4) *Rāja-vallabha-Maṇḍana*, ed. Bhārati (Introduction).
(5) *Brahmāṇḍa-Purāṇa* (Part I, section 2, Chapter VII).
(6) *Matsya-Purāṇa* (Chapter CCLVIII, verses 17-18).
(7) *Vāstu-vidyā*, ed. Gaṇapati Śāstri (I, 3–5f).
(8) *Bimbamāna* (British Museum, MS. no. 558, 5292, verse 9f).
(9) *Suprabhedāgama* (XX, 1–9, 10–16, 20–26, etc.).
(10) *Kauṭilīya-Artha-śāstra*, ed. Shama Śastri (p. 106).

Compare also :

(11) *Manu-saṁhitā* (VIII, 271).
(12) *Rāmāyaṇa* (VI, 20, 22).
(13) *Śata-patha-Brāhmaṇa* (X, 2, 13, III, 5, 4, 5).
(14) *Aitareya-Brāhmaṇa* (VIII, 5).

[1] 8 atoms = 1 car-dust.
8 car-dusts = 1 hair-end.
8 hair-ends = 1 nit.
8 nits = 1 louse.
8 lice = 1 barley corn.
8 barley corns = 1 *aṅgula*.

[2] For further details, *see* the writer's *Encyclopaedia* under *Aṅgula*.

(15) *Chhāndogya-Upanishad* (V, 18, 1, etc).

(16) *Sulva-Sūtra of Baudhāyana* (*J. R. A. S.*, 1912, pp. 231–233, notes 1, 2).

The *tāla-māna* (under 6) is a sculptural measure. The length of face is taken as the unit of measurement.[1] But it seems more convenient to have the particular span, namely, the distance between the tips of the fully stretched thumb and middle finger, which is technically called *tāla*, as the unit.[2] It admits of many varieties : ten-*tāla* measures are mentioned in the *Mānasāra*,[3] while the *Bimbamāna* has reference to twelve kinds.[4] Each of these ten or twelve varieties is again divided into three types, namely, *uttama* or large, *madhyama* or intermediate, and *adhama* or small. Thus an image is of the ten-(*daśa*)*tāla* measure when its whole length is ten times the face. In the large type of the ten-*tāla* system, however, the whole length is divided into 124 equal parts, which are proportionately distributed over the different parts of the body ; in the intermediate type the whole length is divided into 120 equal parts ; and in the small type into 116 equal parts. In the nine-(*nava*)*tāla* system, the whole length would be nine times the face, in the eight-(*ashṭa*)-*tāla*, eight times, and so forth.

The principle of the *tāla* measure is fundamentally the same in all the works dealing with the subject, although certain differences in matters of details are noticed, compare for instance :

(1) *Mānasāra* (LX, 6–35; LVII, LIX, 14–64; 67–100; LXVI, 2–78; LXV, 2–179).

(2) *Bimbamāna* (verses 17–72, 91–138, and Appendix X).

(3) *Suprabhedāgama* (XXXIV, 30–34 ; XXX, 31–40).

(4) *Bṛihat-saṁhitā* (LVIII, 4).

(5) *Aṁśumadbheda* of Kāśyapa (fol. 251, Eg. 3148, 3012).

(6) *Bramhāṇḍa-Purāṇa* (Part I, *Anushaṁga-pāda*, VII, 97).

(7) *Matsya-Purāṇa* (Chapter CCLVIII, verse 19).

The details of the *tāla* measures from the following authorities are given by Mr. Rao[5] :

(8) *Śilpa-ratna*.

[1] *Matsya-Purāṇa*, Chap. CCLVIII, verse 19 :
Mukhamānena kartavyā sarvāvayava-kalpanā.

[2] *Aṁśumadbheda* of Kāśyapa, fol. 251. (MS. Egg., 3148, 3012).

[3] One to ten *tāla* (*M.*, LX, 6–35, etc.).

[4] One to twelve *tāla* (Appendix).

[5] *Elements of Hindu Iconography*, by T. A. Gopīnāth Rāo, Appendix B, pp. 9–28.

(9) *Aṁśumad-bhedāgama.*
(10) *Kā(?ki)raṇāgama.*
(11) *Vaikhānasāgama.*
(12) *Kāmikāgama.*

Another exclusively sculptural measure is that mentioned under (8), (9), namely, the height of an image as compared with the height of the worshipper (*yajamāna*), and the height of the riding animal (*vāhana*) as compared with the height of the main idol. Each of these admits of nine varieties. The height of an image may be equal to the full height of its worshipper, and may extend up to his hair-limit on the forehead (sometimes it is stated to be the eye-line), nose-tip, chin, arm-limit to the shoulder, breast, heart, navel, and sex organ. The height of the riding animal is in the same manner compared with the height of the main idol.[1]

Corresponding to the above-mentioned sculptural measures there are exclusively architectural measures also.

The architectural *gaṇya-māna*,[2] or the comparative heights of the component members of a structure, correspond to the sculptural *tāla-māna*, or the comparative heights of the component limbs of a statue.

The *ghana-mana*, or the measurement by the exterior, and the *aghana-mana*, or the measurement by the interior of a structure, are also exclusively architectural.[3]

In another architectural measure the height of a structure is compared with its breadth. It admits of five proportions, technically called, *Śāntika*, *Paushṭika*, *Jayada*, *Sarva-kāmika* or *Dhanada*, and *Adbhuta*, the height being respectively equal to breadth, 1¼, 1½, 1¾, and twice of the breadth.[4]

These latter items, highly technical and extremely minute in detail, are found in no other treatise under observation than the *Mānasāra*. Thus in respect of at least purely architectural and sculptural measurements the *Mānasāra*, of all these works, should occupy the first place.

[1] *Mānasāra*, LV, 30–33, etc.

[2] *See* the writer's *Encyclopaedia*; and compare the *Mānasāra*, XXVII, 36–40; XXIX, 35–38; XXXIII, 134–145, 216-217, 248; XLV, 86, 97–101; LIII, 29–34; XIII, 36–40, etc.

[3] *See* the writer's *Encyclopaedia, sub voce.*

[4] *See* the writer's *Encyclopaedia*, under *Utsedha.*

When a large number of absolute measures are prescribed for the one and the same object, the right proportion is selected by the test for the six formulas technically called, *āya*, *vyaya*, *ṛiksha*, *yoni*, *vāra*, and *tithi* or *aṁśa* (*see* details in the writer's *Encyclopaedia* under *Shaḍ-varga*).

The Five Orders

Like the five Græco-Roman orders, Doric, Ionic, Corinthian, Tuscan, and Composite, columns in ancient India also were divided into five main orders or classes. In the *Mānasāra*[1] they are called *Brahma-kānta*,[2] *Vishṇu-kānta*, *Rudra-kānta*, *Śiva-kānta*, and *Skanda-kānta*. These divisions are based on the general shapes of columns. With respect to dimensions and ornaments the five orders are called *Chitra-karṇa*, *Padma-kānta*, *Chitra-skambha*, *Pālikā-stambha*, and *Kumbhastambha*. A sixth variety in the latter division is pilaster and not pillar proper, and is called *Koshṭha-stambha* and *Kuḍya-stambha*.[3]

Among the *Purāṇas*, these details are very clear only in the *Matsya-Purāṇa*. In this *Purāṇa*,[4] as well as in the *Bṛihat-saṁhitā*,[5] the five orders are called *Ruchaka*, *Vajra*, *Dvi-vajra*, *Pralīnaka*, and *Vṛitta*.

Of the *Āgamas*,[6] the *Suprabhedāgama* contains the essential details. The names of the five orders according to this *Āgama*[7] are *Śrī-kara*, *Chandra-kānta*, *Saumukhya*, *Priya-darśana*, and *Subhaṅkarī*; the last one is stated to be the Indian composite order, being a compound of *Saumukhya* and *Priya-darśana*, just as the Græco-Roman composite order is a compound of Corinthian and Ionic.

Between the European and the Indian columns, however, there is obviously a striking point of difference. Of the Græco-Roman orders the five names have been left unchanged, while in India the names of the five orders have varied in various treatises referred to above. It is true, all the same, that the criteria of divisions are essentially the same in the *Mānasāra*, the *Āgamas*, the *Purāṇas*, and the *Bṛihat-saṁhitā*.[8] We have also seen above that the *Mānasāra* contains two sets of names of the five orders, one set referring, like the *Āgamas*, the *Purāṇas*, and the *Bṛihat-saṁhitā*, to the shapes of the columns, or more precisely the shafts, while the other refers mostly to the capitals. The works, other than the *Vāstu-śāstras*, as represented

[1] Chapter XV, 20–23, 31, 39, 40, 73, 204.
[2] Also mentioned in *Corpus Inscriptionum Indicarum*, Vol. III, p. 252, 253, *Epigraphia Indica*, XII, pp. 212, 216 verse 151.
[3] *Mānasāra*, XV, 84.
[4] *Matsya-Purāṇa*, Chap. CCLX, vv. 1–6.
[5] *Bṛihat-saṁhitā*, LIII, 27–30, also *J. R. A. S.* (N. S.), VI, p. 285, notes 1, 2.
[6] *See*, for instance, the *Kāmikāgama*, *Paṭala* XXXV, 24–26, 161, LV, 203, etc.
[7] *Suprabhedāgama*, *Paṭala* XXXI, 65–67.
[8] *See* references given above, and for further details consult the writer's *Encyclopaedia*, under *Stambha*.

by the *Mānasāra*, have not kept this distinction clear. What we can reasonably infer from this as regards the mutual relation of these treatises will be further elucidated by a consideration of the component parts of the column. The question of variation of the names of the five orders in the Indian works can perhaps be explained. While in Europe the origin of the names of the five orders is traced to historical geography,[1] in India the names were based on the shapes of columns. And as the Indians are comparatively religious and poetical, rather than historical in temperament and imagination, they chose mythological and poetical names according to the spirit of the times when these various works were composed. Thus in the *Mānasāra* we see the orders bearing the names of mythological deities, Brahmā, Vishṇu, Rudra, Śiva, and Skanda; as well as called *Chitra-karṇa* (variegated ears), *Padma-kānta* (graceful like lotus), *Chitra-skambha* (of variegated shaft), *Pālikā-stambha* (edged like a measuring pot), and *Kumbha-stambha* (of jug-shaped capital); while, in the *Āgama*, they bear highly poetical names: *Śrī-kara* (beautifying), *Chandra-kānta* (graceful like the moon), *Saumukhya* (of very charming face), *Priya-darśana* (sight-pleasing), *Śubhaṅkarī* (auspicious). In the *Purāṇas* and the *Bṛihat-saṁhitā* they are called *Ruchaka* (beautiful, pleasing), *Vajra* (club, hence lasting), *Dvi-vajra* (doubly lasting), *Pralīnaka* (firmly attached, hence a pilaster), and *Vṛitta* (round, hence solid and dignified).

With regard to the names and the functions of the component parts of the column, the variation is a little less marked; but these subservient parts, called mouldings and common to all orders, vary in number. Thus in the *Mānasāra*, which of almost all the treatises deals separately and exhaustively with the pedestal, the base, and the entablature, mention is made, in connexion with the pillar, of five mouldings,[2] apparently of the shaft, namely, *bodhikā*, *musṭi-bandha*, *phalakā*, *tāṭikā*, and *ghaṭa*. The *Suprabhedāgama* describes two sets of

[1] Doric is derived from the species of columns first seen in the cities of Doria (*Vitruvius*, IV, 1). That species of which the Ionians (inhabitants of Ionia) were the inventors has received the appellation of Ionic (*ibid*). Callimachus constructed columns after the model of the tomb in the country about Corinth, hence this species is called Corinthian (*ibid*). The other two orders, Tuscan and Composite, are of Italian or Roman origin. The Tuscan order has reference to the country of Tuscany, formerly called Etruria, in Italy (Gwilt, *Encyclopaedia of Architecture*, article 178).

[2] *Mānasāra*, XLVII, 16–18.

seven mouldings,[1] one set referring to the column of the main building and the other to that of the pavilion—*daṇḍa, maṇḍi, kaṇṭha, kumbha, phalakā, vīra-kaṇṭha,* and *potikā*; and *bodhikā, uttara, vājana, mūrdhikā tulā jayantī,* and *tala.* These increasing number of mouldings reached the significant number of eight in the *Matsya-Purāṇa,* the *Bṛihat-saṁhitā,* and the *Kiraṇa-tantra,* and bear the very same eight names,[2] to wit, *vahana, ghaṭa, padma, uttaroshṭha, bāhulya, bhāra* (or *hāra*), *tulā,* and *upatulā.*

The significance of the number eight referred to above lies in the fact that the component parts of the Græco-Roman orders also are eight in number,[3] and like the five orders themselves, their names are always the same ever since their introduction, though most of them have been given more than one name. They are called: (1) the ovolo, echinus, or quarter round; (2) the talon, ogée, or reversed cyma; (3) the cyma, cyma-recta, or cyma-tium; (4) the torus; (5) the scotia or trochilos; (6) the cavetto, mouth, or hollow; (7) the astragal; and (8) the fillet, listel, or annulet.

The *Mānasāra* refers to five mouldings; the *Suprabhedāgama* describes seven; and the *Matsya-Purāṇa,* the *Bṛihat-saṁhitā,* and *Kiraṇa-tantra* each makes mention of eight mouldings. But if the very large number of mouldings,[4] described in the *Mānasāra* in connexion with the pedestal, the base, and the entablature, be also taken into account, the *Mānasāra* will certainly exceed all other treatises under notice. Thus in the *Mānasāra* we can detect the following mouldings[5]: (1) *abja, ambuja, padma* or *saroruha* (cyma); (2) *antara,*

[1] *Suprabhedāgama, Paṭala* XXXI, 56–60, 107–108.

[2] *Matsya-Purāṇa,* Chap. CCLV, 1–6f, *Bṛihat-saṁhitā,* LIII, 29-30, *Kiraṇa-tantra, J. R. A. S.* (N. S.), VI, 285, notes 1, 2.

[3] *See* figures 867–874 and articles 2532, Gwilt, *Encyclopaedia of Architecture,* and *Glossary of Architectural Terms,* plate XXXIV.

[4] *See* the writer's *Encyclopaedia,* under *Upapīṭha, Adhishṭhāna* and *Prastara.*

[5] There are mouldings which bear a large number of names or synonyms, e.g.:

(i) *Kapota, prastara, mañcha, prachchhādana, gopāna, vitāna, balabhī,* and *matta-vāraṇa.*

(ii) *Prati-prastara, prati-vājana, anvanta, avasāna, vidhāna* and *vidhānaka.*

(iii) *Prati-rūpa, dalākāra, vijana, vājana, kshepaṇa, vetra, paṭṭa, uttara, paṭṭikā, kampa, trika, maṇḍa,* and *antarita.*

(iv) *Tulā-daṇḍa, jayantī* and *phalakā.*

(v) *Kapota, vakra-hasta, lupā, gopānaka* and *chandra.*

(vi) *Saṁgraha, mushṭi-bandha, maddala, uddhṛita-hasta, valabhī* and *dhāraṇa.*

(vii) *Nāṭaka, anta, mṛiṇālikā, vallikā, chitrāṅga* and *kulikāṅghrika.*

(viii) *Uttara, vājana, ādhāra, ādheya, śayana, uddhṛita, mūrdhaka, mahātauli* and *svavaṁśaka.*

antarita, *antarāla* or *antarika* (fillet); (3) *aṅghri*; (4) *aṁśu*; (5) *argala*; (6) *ādhāra*; (7) *āliṅga*; (8) *āsana*; (9) *bhadra*; (10) *bodhikā*; (11) *dala*; (12) *dhārā-(kumbha)*; (13) *gala*, *grīva*, *kaṇṭha* or *kandhara* (dado); (14) *ghaṭa*; (15) *gopāna-(ka)*; (16) *hāra* (bead); (17) *janman* (plinth); (18) *kapota*; (19) *kampa*, *kampana* (fillet); (20) *karṇa*; (21) *kumbha*; (22) *kumuda* (torus or astragal); (23) *kendra*; (24) *kshepaṇa*; (25) *mushṭi-bandha*; (26) *mūla*; (27) *mṛiṇāla* or *mṛiṇālikā*; (28) *nāṭaka*; (29) *nāsī*; (30) *nimna* (drip) (31) *paṭṭa* or *paṭṭikā* (fillet); (32) *prati* or *pratika*; (33) *prati-vakra*; (34) *prati-vājana*; (35) *prati-bandha*; (36) *pratima*; (37) *pāduka*; (38) *prastara*; (39) *phalakā*; (40) *ratna*, compounded with *kampa*, *paṭṭa*, and *vapra*; (41) *tāṭikā*; (42) *tuṅga*; *uttara* (fillet); (44) *upāna* (plinth); (45) *vapra* or *vapraka*; (46) *valabha* or *valabhī*; and (47) *vājana* (fillet).

There are a number of compound mouldings also, such as *kampa-karṇa*, *karṇa-padma*, *kshudra-kampa*, *kshudra-padma*, *kshepanāmbuja*, *mahāmbuja*, *padma-kampa*, *ratna-kampa*, *ratnapaṭṭa*, *ratna-vapra*, *vajra-paṭṭa*, etc.

Again, of all these treatises, only the *Mānasāra* and the *Āgamas* refer to certain highly technical and purely architectural matters. Thus in the *Mānasāra* we find the measurements and other details of 64 varieties of bases divided into nineteen classes,[1] called (1) *pāda-bandha*, (2) *uraga-bandha*, (3) *prati-krama*, (4) *kumuda-bandha*, (5) *padma-kesara*, (6) *pushpa-pushkala*, (7) *śrī-bandha*, (8) *mañcha-bandha*, (9) *śreṇī-bandha*, (10) *padma-bandha*, (11) *kumbha-bandha*, (12) *vapra-bandha*, (13) *vajra-bandha*, (14) *śrī-bhoga*, (15) *ratna-bandha*, (16) *paṭṭa-bandha*, (17) *kukshi-bandha*, (18) *kampa-bandha*, and (19) *śrī-kānta*.

In the *Suprabhedāgama* only four classes[2] of bases are mentioned, namely, *padma-bandha*, *chāru-bandha*, *pāda-bandha*, and *prati-krama*. The *Kāmikāgama* has only the general description of the base.[3]

In the *Mānasāra* sixteen types of pedestals are described in detail under three classes,[4] namely, *vedi-bhadra*, *prati-bhadra*, and *mañcha-bhadra*.

[1] *Mānasāra*, XIV, 11–387. *See* details in the writer's *Encyclopaedia*, under *Adhishṭhāna*.

[2] *Suprabhedāgama*, XXXI, 17 f.

[3] *Kāmikāgama*, XXXV, 22, 23, 114, 116, 122, LV, 202.

[4] *Mānasāra*, XIII, 37–127. *See* details in the writer's *Encyclopaedia*, under *Upapīṭha*.

Only scanty information of the pedestal is found in the *Kāmikāgama,*[1] the *Suprabhedāgama,*[2] and a Tāmil version of the *Mayamata.*[3]

As regards the entablature, various mouldings and their measurements are described under eight classes in the *Mānasāra.*[4] The *Kāmikāgama,*[5] the *Suprabhedāgama,*[6] and the *Vāstuvidyā*[7] have only briefly referred to the general description of the entablature.

The comparative measurements of the column proper and the pedestal, the base, and the entablature, are also given in more detail in the *Mānasāra* than in the *Āgamas* and some of the architectural treatises.[8]

Thus in respect of the names of columns, the number of their subservient parts called mouldings, and also the base, the pedestal and the entablature, as well as their comparative measurements, the *Mānasāra* will always occupy the first place among all the treatises under observation.

[1] *Paṭala* XXXV, 115, 122.
[2] *Paṭala* XXXI, 12.
[3] *Essay on the Architecture of the Hindus*, Rām Rāz, pp. 23, 26.
[4] Chapter XVI, 22–149. *See* details in the writer's *Encyclopaedia*, under *Prastara.*
[5] XXXV, 27–29, LIV, 1–4, 7-8, 9–46, 47.
[6] XXXI, 68–71, 72–74.
[7] Ed. Ganapati Śāstrī, IX, 23, 26.
[8] *See* details in the writer's *Encyclopaedia*, under *Stambha, Upapīṭha, Adhisṭhāna* and *Prastara.*

THE THREE STYLES

The style is also a technical and purely architectural subject. Thus it is not dealt with in the *Purāṇas*, not to speak of the epics or other poetical works where, as shown above, casual references to architecture and sculpture are met with. In some of the epigraphical documents and the *Bṛihat-saṁhitā* mention of the styles is occasionally made. The *Āgamas* contain a little more detail, while in the *Mānasāra* the subject is exhaustively treated.

The *Nāgara*, *Vesara*, and *Drāviḍa* are the three broad styles distinguished in the *Mānasāra*.[1] They are applied to both architecture[2] and sculpture.[3] With reference to the construction of cars or chariots a fourth style is mentioned.[4] This is called *Randhra*, which seems to be a corrupt form of *Andhra*. In an epigraphical record,[5] *Kaliṅga* is mentioned as a distinct style of architecture. But if the identification of *Vesara* with Telugu or *Tri-Kaliṅga* be accepted, the *Kāliṅga* and the *Āndhra* would be the two branches of the *Vesara* style. In the case of twelve-storeyed buildings, which are the most magnificent and imposing edifices as described, twelve special types, not necessarily the styles, of residential dwellings are also mentioned in the *Mānasāra*.[6] All these names are geographical, implying the twelve provinces into which the then India was divided architecturally, if not also politically. And these types are distinctly based on geographical divisions, in exactly the same way as the three styles, the *Nāgara*, *Vesara* and *Drāviḍa*, as also the two branches of the

[1] *Mānasāra*, XVIII, 92–104. The *Nāgara* style is distinguished by its quadrangular shape, the *Vesara* by its octagonal or hexagonal shape, and the *Drāviḍa* by its round shape. For details, *see* pp. 258–259 and the writer's *Encyclopaedia*, under *Nāgara*.

[2] *Mānasāra*, LIII, 53–54; XXI, 72–73; XXVI, 76; XLIII, 124–125, etc.

[3] *Mānasāra*, LII, 78, 100; LIII, 46–47, etc.

[4] *Mānasāra*, XLIII, 124–125.

[5] In the record itself, it is, however, stated that the *Nāgara*, *Vesara*, *Drāviḍa*, and *Kāliṅga* are four types, not styles, of buildings. (An inscription on the capital of a pillar in the Amriteśvara temple at Holal, Government of Madras G. O. no. 1260, August, 1915, Progress Report of the Assistant Superintendent for Epigraphy, Southern Circle, 1914–15, p. 90.)

[6] *Pāñchāla*, *Drāviḍa*, *Madhyakānta*, *Kāliṅga*, *Va(Vi)rāṭa*, *Kerala*, *Vaṁśaka*, *Māgadha*, *Janaka* and *Sphū(Gur)jaka* (*Mānasāra*, XXX, 5–7). We have seen in the previous section ninety-eight kinds of mansions are described in the *Mānasāra*. In the above-mentioned Holal inscription a reference is made to sixty-four kinds of mansions.

Vesara, the *Kāliṅga* and *Āndhra*, are based. The Græco-Roman orders, on which the European styles of architecture are mainly based, are also but geographical names.[1]

In the *Kāmikāgama*, as well as in the *Suprabhedāgama*, frequent references to the three broad styles, the *Nāgara*, *Vesara*, and *Drāviḍa*, are made.[2]

The distinguishing features of these styles are practically exactly the same in all the three works, namely, the *Mānasāra*, the *Kāmikāgama*, and the *Suprabhedāgama*.[3] The *Āndhra* and the *Kāliṅga* branches of the *Vesara* style are not mentioned in the *Āgamas*. But we have seen that the *Kāmikāgama*, like the *Matsya-Purāṇa*, the *Bhavishya-Purāṇa*, and the *Bṛihaṭ-saṁhitā*, describes twenty kinds of mansions, while the *Suprabhedāgama* has reference to ten kinds. These varieties of buildings, as also the sixty-four kinds mentioned in the Holal inscription, and the ninety-eight kinds described in the *Mānasāra*, do not, however, represent the styles which fall only under three broad divisions, namely, the *Nāgara*, *Vesara*, and *Drāviḍa*.

In the *Bṛihat-saṁhitā*,[4] clear mention is made only of the *Drāviḍa* style in regard to the measurement of the face, although the other styles may be said to have been implied. It is stated that according to one's own *aṅgula* (finger's breadth) the face (of an image) should be twelve *aṅgulas* (nine inches) broad and long ; but as stated by the architect Nagnajit the face should be twelve *aṅgulas* long and fourteen *aṅgulas* broad in the *Drāviḍa* style. Obviously, therefore, the former measurement refers to other existing styles or those which are not specified here.

In regard to the styles also, therefore, the *Mānasāra* must be undoubtedly given the first place amongst all these works which for the purpose of the present item of comparison comprise practically the *Āgamas*.

In the light of all these facts—merely to deal with the question in its aspects as they concern the *Mānasāra*—it seems to me impossible to resist the following conclusion. There appears to have been a relation of indebtedness between the *Mānasāra* and the other works, both architectural and non-architectural. Except in a few instances

[1] *See* p. 202 and footnote 7.
[2] *Kāmikāgama*, LXV, 6–7, 12–18, etc., *Suprabhedāgama*, XXXI, 37–39, etc.
[3] For details, *see* the writer's *Encyclopaedia*, under *Nāgara*.
[4] Chapter LVIII, 4.

noted above, it is, however, difficult to state definitely that the *Mānasāra* is the debtor or creditor to this or that work in respect of this or that matter. Most of the difficulties, it is needless to observe, hinge upon the chronology, which is the irritating point in the Sanskrit literature. If the chronology of the works discussed above were definitely known, it would have been easier to assume that the works earlier than the *Mānasāra* had been known to its author and those later than the *Mānasāra* had been influenced by it. Except in cases of support by archaeological records, epigraphical or non-epigraphical, the dates assigned to Sanskrit works are mostly but provisional. I have discussed elsewhere the available materials and the reasons which have induced me provisionally to place the *Mānasāra* somewhere in the fifth to seventh century of the Christian era. In view of the essential points of comparison and the accepted chronology of the works which have been critically studied by scholars, I should say that the *Bṛihat-saṁhitā*, and the later Āgamic and Paurāṇic works in respect of architectural and sculptural matters, as well as most of the avowedly architectural texts, are debtors to the *Mānasāra*; while it is a debtor itself in respect of the same matters to the Vedic and the early Epic works, as also to the early polytechnical treatises (like the *Kauṭīliya-Artha-śāstra* and the *Kāmandakīya*), and to the avowedly architectural works of the thirty-two authorities mentioned in the *Mānasāra*, which might have existed till its own time. Besides, it cannot but have been based on the actual observation and measurement of extant architectural and sculptural objects ; in this matter lies the special importance of the *Mānasāra*.

An objection may be raised here. It is possible that those works which are stated above to have been debtors to the *Mānasāra* might have been influenced directly by those which are asserted to have been the creditors to the *Mānasāra*. Such an objection, however, can be easily disposed of. The *Mānasāra*, in whichever period of history it is finally placed, has become a standard work on architecture and sculpture, because we have seen, firstly, it is the largest of its kind ; secondly, its treatment of the subjects is most exhaustive ; and, thirdly, in it the subject-matter has been scientifically classified and systematized. When there is a standard work existing, it is natural and highly probable that those who treat the subject rather casually or less exhaustively, should draw upon it instead of going to the original sources, except in some special instances. For the ordinary meanings or synonyms of a word we generally consult a standard dictionary, rather than attempt to trace the history, phonology, morphology, and semasiology of the word. An analogical instance may perhaps make the point clearer. Pāṇini's grammar makes mention of some nineteen pre-existing grammatical works, and it has been placed by later scholars somewhere in the fourth or third century before Christ. Like the works on rhetoric and prosody, grammars cannot be prepared without consulting the existing literature, because the sole business of these works is to generalize certain regulating features of literature. The methods of the pioneers of law books, as well as the grammar, the *Alaṅkāraśāstra*, and the *Silpa-śāstra*, must have been inductive. Pāṇini, as he acknowledges generously, has been indebted to his predecessors ; it is also clear from his work that he himself has consulted the preceding Vedic and post-Vedic literature. It is true that grammars have been prepared after Pāṇini also. But when Pāṇini's grammar reached the status of a standard work, his rules and regulations were naturally followed in the later literature. The later grammarians also must have been influenced by Pāṇini. In the field of grammar and literature Pāṇini's grammar is, therefore, the regulating and controlling standard work. In the same way, and more clearly and significantly, it seems to me, the *Mānasāra* occupies a unique position in literature, both architectural and non-architectural.

CHAPTER VI

THE MĀNASĀRA AND VITRUVIUS

As HAS ALREADY been pointed out in the Preface, the name *Mānasāra* is of ambiguous significance. It is, however, clear from the preceding chapters that the text bearing the title *Mānasāra* is a standard treatise on Indian architecture. It is divided into seventy chapters each bearing a distinct title. In 1834, in his *Essay on the Architecture of the Hindus*, Rām Rāz referred to the first few chapters of the *Mānasāra* from a single fragmentary manuscript to which he had access. Since then several manuscripts have been discovered ; but, owing to some serious difficulties stated in the Preface, nobody had made any attempt to deal with this huge text in any way for a period of 80 years till the present writer undertook in 1914 to edit it for the first time. This, the first edition, is based on all the eleven available manuscripts which are written in five different scripts in a language branded as 'barbarous Sanskrit.' Figures, sketches, or illustrations of any kind are absolutely wanting in all these manuscripts. The various scripts and the provenance of the manuscripts,[1] however, indicate that the *Mānasāra* was known and used in all provinces of ancient India.[2] Its extensive popularity has been further established by its unique position in literature, discussed in Chapter V.

Vitruvius is the name of a Roman architect. His treatise, on which, in a sense, all European architecture is based, seems to have been composed 25 years before the Christian era. 'The materials for a life of Vitruvius are only to be found in his own treatise. Among the ancient authors he is merely mentioned by Pliny as one of those writers from whom he compiled, and by Frontinus, in his treatise on Aqueducts, as the first who introduced the Quinarain measure.'

The title of Vitruvius's treatise is lost, if it originally had one. The *editio princeps*, printed at Rome in or about 1486, bears no title. The unique position of this treatise is, however, sufficiently clear from the fact that since its first appearance in the fifteenth century there have been, till 1807, forty-two editions of the work, practically in all the European languages. There are seventeen editions in Latin, eleven in Italian, two in Spanish, six in French,

[1] For details, *see Mānasāra* (text), Vol. III, Preface, pp. xi–xviii.
[2] *See* pp. 254–256, and notes.

four in German, and two in English.[1] It is divided into ten books, which, too, do not bear any titles. Each book contains a number of chapters varying from seven to twenty-two. The chapters also

[1] *See* Gwilt (XV—XXV) for fuller details of the following :
Latin editions—

1486—*Editio princeps*, printed at Rome by George Herolt begins, without title, *Sulpitius lectori salutem*. Polenus says, 'There are but few errors in this edition.'

1496—Printed at Florence. According to Fabricus the orthography of this edition is more correct than in the preceding one.

1497—The name of the editor does not appear. With a few slight variations this is little more than a reprint of the Florence edition. In this the chapters of the first book are differently divided from those of the two former editions.

1511—This is the first illustrated edition. It contains many wood-blocks and figures. Jocundus, the editor, altered the text of the two former editions in many places.

1513—The figures in this edition are the same as in the preceding, but considerably reduced and more imperfectly kept.

1522—This is a reprint of the preceding edition with the same blocks for the figures.

1523—This was probably edited by Will. Hayon of Lyons. This is a counterpart of the Giunta edition. Some of its figures are taken from the first Italian edition of 1521, which is noticed hereinafter.

1543—The text is nearly the same as that of Jocundus. The figures of the wood-blocks are partly borrowed from the Giunta edition and partly from the Italian edition of 1521.

1550—The text is the same as that of 1543 edition. But it contains notes of Philander which were first published at Rome in 1544.

1552—'Philander himself superintended this edition, chiefly following the Giunta text, which he collated with several MSS. The wood-blocks are better than in any preceding edition.'

1567—Darbaro in this seems to have mostly followed Philander's edition of 1552.

1586—Harwood says that 'the editor of this edition was Jo. Tornaesious, junior, and that it is more correct, though less elegant, than that produced by the father in 1552.'

1649—With commentary of Meibomius on those chapters relating to musical notation. This was the best edition of the author produced at that time. 'De Laet professes to follow the text of Philander's edition but neither was this accurately done, nor were the notes of Philander, nor the Lexicon of Baldus, given entire, as the title would import.'

1758—By Marchese Berardo Galiani at Naples, with an Italian version noticed under the Italian editions. Harwood says that this is 'a fair and valuable edition.'

1800—The text of this edition is of little value, nor its plates well executed. It has notes appended, but it contains the glossary in five languages.

1807—It contains notes.

1807—In the same year another edition was published. The second and third volumes are devoted to commentaries on the text. It contains, however, no plates. 'This is the best edition of the author which has appeared.'

Italian editions—

1521—This is one of the earliest and rarest versions of Vitruvius. It was translated, with the assistance of Benedict Jovius, by Caesar Caesarianus, who was one of the architects of the Cathedral of Milan. One of the plates contains a plan and two sections of this Cathedral.

have not any proper titles. The treatise deals with both civil and military architecture. The rules respecting military engines, 'now incomprehensible, but doubtless in his time sufficiently clear,' are laid down in the last book. The treatment of civil architecture includes both temples and residential buildings. 'That he should have met with opposition from his brethren is quite consonant with later experience, for the rabble of ignorant builders, and artisans, and draughtsmen are of the same class as those that flourished subsequently to Vitruvius.' From this remark of Gwilt it appears that Vitruvius was induced to 'write his treatise with a view to assisting the uneducated professional architects' who, like those of India, depended solely on the knowledge handed down to them from their equally uneducated forefathers.

1524—This is a repetition of the preceding edition, but without the notes of Caesar Caesarianus.
1535—This is copied from the preceding edition, but the index is not quite so copious.
1536—A translation of the first five books. Perugia.
1556—With Barbaro's commentary.
1567—With Barbaro's commentary.
1584—Similar to the preceding edition.
1629—Very similar to the preceding edition.
1641—Little differing from the preceding.
1758—In Napoli, accompanied with the Latin text.
1790—Another edition by Galiani, similar to the preceding, but without the Latin text.

Spanish editions—
1602—Without plates.
1787—Large folio, with plates.

French editions—
1547—First version in French, Jan Martin, Paris.
1572—A reprint of the preceding, Cavellat, Paris.
1618—Printed from the two preceding editions by Jean de Tournes at Geneva.
1673—Translated by Perrault. Figures are numerous and well executed.
1684—With plates, best of Perrault's editions.
1816—With plates, Bruxelles.

German editions—
1548—With plates on wood-blocks cut by Erard Schaen.
1575—A repetition of the preceding, Basil.
1614—Another repetition with a little different title.
1796—With a life of Vitruvius in the first volume. This edition contains many illustrations of the author.

English editions—
1771—Translated from the original Latin by Newton, London.
1791—Second volume with many plates. It exhibits defective knowledge of Latin, but the notes are good.
Latterly a portion was translated by Wilkins.
After Joseph Gwilt's translation there have been several others in English.

'Certain points of similarity between the *Mānasāra* and the treatise of Vitruvius are so striking that they raise a presumption that the two works are in some way connected with each other.' This thesis[1] is proposed to be illustrated in this chapter.

Practically seven-tenths of both the works is avowedly architectural.

Out of the seventy chapters of the *Mānasāra* the first fifty deal with architecture proper, and out of the ten books of Vitruvius the first seven deal with the same subjects.

The remaining twenty chapters of the former are devoted to sculpture, and the remaining three books of the latter deal mostly with war instruments, machines, and engines. Of the similar seven-tenths in both the works, the names of many chapters, and the contents, too, in most instances, are the same.

The *Mānasāra* opens, following the usual custom, with a prayer to the Creator Brahmā and touches upon the origin and development of the science of architecture, from Śiva, Brahmā, and Vishṇu, through Indra, Bṛihaspati, and Nārada, to the class of Ṛishis called *Mānasāra*, and concludes the introduction with a list of the chapters.

Vitruvius, too, opens with a prayer to his patron, Caesar, and acknowledging his obligations to Caesar's father and sister, concludes with a proposal to give an account of the magnificent edifices Caesar had built, and to develop all the principles of the art.

The next chapter (II) in the *Mānasāra* deals with two distinct subjects, the system of measurement (*mānopakaraṇa*), and the requisite qualifications of an architect (*śilpi-lakshaṇa*).

The corresponding chapter is marked 'I' instead of 'II' by Vitruvius, because the preceding chapter goes without any numbering, as it is called Introduction. This, the present chapter, deals exactly like the corresponding chapter in the *Mānasāra* with two distinct subjects under the heads, 'what architecture is,' and 'of the education of an architect.' The former of these two subjects has again been treated in the following chapter, namely III, of the *Mānasāra*, and is noticed below. The striking similarity in the training demanded of the architect by the two authorities may be noticed here.

According to Vitruvius 'an architect should be ingenious, and apt

[1] Submitted as such to Leiden University by the present writer.

in the acquisition of knowledge. He should be a good writer, a skilful draughtsman, versed in geometry and optics, expert at figures, acquainted with history, informed on the principles of natural and moral philosophy, somewhat of a musician, not ignorant of the sciences, both of law and physic, nor of the motions, laws and relations to each other, of the heavenly bodies.' The absolute necessity for these qualifications has been very satisfactorily elaborated by Vitruvius.

In the *Mānasāra* artists are first divided into four classes. Together they form the guild of architects, each an expert in his own department, but possessing a general knowledge of the science of architecture as a whole. They consist of the chief architect (*sthapati*), the draughtsman or the designer (*sūtra-grāhin*), the painter (*vardhaki*), and the joiner (*sūtra-dhāra*).

According to the *Mānasāra* the chief architect is expected to be well versed in all the sciences. He must possess a knowledge of all the *Vedas* and all the *Śāstras*. He must be proficient in law, mathematics, history, geography, painting, draughtsmanship, mechanics, and deep 'in the ocean of the science of architecture.' He must be very learned, meritorious, patient, and dexterous, a champion, of large experience, of industrious habits, and of noble descent, full of resource, and capable of application to all kinds of work. He must possess a wide outlook, bold temperament, and self-control. He must be above committing errors. He must have a good name and be faithful to his employers (*lit.* friends). He must be endowed with all the qualifications of a supreme managing director. He must not be deformed or have any disease or disability; he must also be free from the seven vices, namely, hunting, gambling, daydreaming, blackmailing, addiction to women, etc.

A similar set of qualifications is also demanded of each of the other three artists, but the *sūtra-grāhin* is expected to possess an expert knowledge of draughtsmanship, the *vardhaki* of painting, and the *sūtradhāra* of carpentry.

The utility or the possibility of so many attainments in a single person has not been expressly discussed in the *Mānasāra*. But Vitruvius has submitted an interesting explanation.

It is familiar to everybody that for success in any profession in life one must be clever, industrious, honest and generous. It is also easily understood that an architect, who has got to do both manual and brain work, must not be deformed, and must be free from any disease or disability.

According to Vitruvius he is required to be a good writer also, because an architect is to commit to writing his observations and experience, in order to assist his memory. Drawing is employed in representing the forms of his designs. Geometry, which forms a part of mathematics, affords much aid to the arhitect; to it he owes the use of the right line and circle, the level and the square, whereby his delineations of buildings on plane surfaces are greatly facilitated. Arithmetic estimates the cost and aids in the measurement of the works; this, assisted by the laws of geometry, determines those abstruse questions wherein the different proportions of some parts to others are involved. The science of optics enables him to introduce with judgment the requisite quantity of light according to the aspect. Unless acquainted with history, he will be unable to account for the use of many ornaments which he may have occasion to introduce. For history (the expression *purāṇa* is used in Indian literature), which implies ' ancient ' or mythological legends that are as a rule depicted in the buildings of a nation. There are, however, other uses of history for an architect.

'Moral philosophy,' says Vitruvius, 'will teach the architect to be above meanness in his dealings and to avoid arrogance, and will make him just, compliant, and faithful to his employer; and what is of the highest importance, it will prevent avarice gaining an ascendancy over him; for he should not be occupied with the thoughts of filling his coffers, nor with the desire of grasping everything in the shape of gain, but by the gravity of his manners and a good character, should be careful to preserve his dignity.' These precepts of moral philosophy are prescribed by our Indian authorities almost in the same terms. We have seen above that the architect is required to be of noble descent, pious, and compassionate. He must not be malicious or spiteful. He must be content and free from greed. He must be truthful and possess self-control. He must be above the seven vices. He must be faithful to his employer. He must not have excessive desire for gain. He must be of good behaviour and generous enough to forgive his rivals.

'The doctrine of physic is necessary to him in the solution of various problems, as for instance, in the conduct of water, whose natural force, in its meandering and expansion over flat countries, is often such as to require restraints, which none know to apply but those who are acquainted with the laws of nature.' This matter, too, has been more exhaustively discussed in various chapters of the *Mānasāra*.

'Music assists him in the use of harmonic and mathematical proportion.' In these matters, the *Mānasāra* is rather too elaborate; in most individual cases nine proportions have been suggested, and the selection of the right proportion and harmony has been made dependent on the application of the six formulas, which are treated in a very technical manner, based on mathematics. According to Vitruvius, music is, moreover, absolutely necessary in adjusting the force of the ballistae, catapultae, and scorpions, in whose frames are holes for the passage of the homotona, which are strained by gut-ropes attached to windlasses worked by hand-spikes. Unless these ropes are equally extended, which only a nice ear can discover by their sound when struck, the bent arms of the engine do not give an equal impetus when disengaged, and the strings, therefore, not being in equal states of tension, prevent the direct flight of the weapon. A knowledge of music is specially useful to the architect in building theatres, lecture rooms, and such other halls where the spread of sound is taken into particular considertion. Both Vitruvius and the *Mānasāra* are equally enthusiastic in speaking about it. The former further says that the architect 'would, moreover, be at a loss in constructing hydraulic and other engines if ignorant of music.' 'Skill in physic enables him to ascertain the salubrity of different tracts of country, and to determine the variation of climates, for the air and water of different situations, being matters of highest importance, no building will be healthy without attention to those points.' A very elaborate account of the selection of sites and the examination of soil is given in the *Mānasāra* and other architectural treatises.[1] The salubrity of the tracts is minutely ascertained with reference to the site where a village, town, fort, palace, temple, or dwelling-house is to be built. The soil is examined with regard to its contour, colour, odour, features, tastes, and touch. The level of the ground, as well as the characteristic vegetation of the site, as pointed out above, are also minutely examined.

[1] *Bṛihat-saṁhitā, Gārga, Viśvak, Kāśyapa, Vāstu-ratnāvali, Vasishṭha-saṁhitā, Vāstu-pradipa, Nārada, Gṛiha-kārikā, Bhṛigu, Śilpa-dīpaka, Bhavishya-Purāṇa. See* quotations from these works under *Bhū-parikshā* in the writer's *Encyclopaedia.*

'Law should be an object of his study, especially those parts of it which relate to party-walls, to the free course and discharge of the eaves' waters, to the regulation of cesspools and sewage, and to window lights. The laws of sewage require his particular attention, so that he may prevent his employers from being involved in law suits when the building is finished. Contracts, also, for the execution of the works, should be drawn up with care and precision, because, when without legal flaws, neither party will be able to take advantage of the other.'

Law, as explained by Vitruvius, is not mentioned in so many words in the list of accomplishments given in the *Vāstu-śāstras* quoted above. But most elaborate instructions are given in the *Arthaśāstra* and other treatises on party-walls, the sewage system, and on windows and other openings [1]

'Astronomy instructs him in the points of the heavens, the laws of the celestial bodies, the equinoxes, solstices, and courses of the stars; all of which should be well understood in the construction and proportions of clocks.' In the *Vāstu-śāstras* dialling is an important subject; but astronomy, which is always mixed up with astrology, has been drawn upon particularly with regard to the auspicious moment invariably observed in almost all matters.

Vitruvius has added an explanatory note on the expression 'all sciences' of which the architect is required to have sufficient knowledge. This explanation will indeed throw a clear light upon a similar expression, *sarva-śāstra*, used by the Indian authorities. But for the following note of Vitruvius, we might have taken the term *sarva-śāstra* as an exaggeration which is very often found in Sanskrit literature to imply nothing more than a general knowledge.

'Perhaps, to the uninformed mind,' begins Vitruvius, 'it may appear unaccountable that a man should be able to retain in his memory such a variety of learning; but the close alliance with each other of the different branches of science will explain the difficulty. For as a body is composed of various concordant members, so does the whole circle of learning consist in one harmonious system.'

'On this account, Pythius, the architect of the noble temple of Minerva at Priene, says, in his commentaries, that an architect should have that perfect knowledge of each art and science which is not even acquired by the professors of any one in particular.' This seemed

[1] *See* the writer's ***Encyclopaedia***, under *Jaladvāra* and *Vātāyana*.

rather too much to Vitruvius, so he asks 'how can it be expected that an architect should equal Aristarchus as a grammarian, yet should he not [*sic*] be ignorant of grammar. In music, though it be evident he need not equal Aristoxenus, yet he should know something of it. Though he need not exceed, as Appeles in painting, nor as Myron or Polycletus in sculpture, yet he should have attained some proficiency in these arts.'

'Thus, also, in the other sciences,' concludes Vitruvius, 'it is not important that pre-eminence in each be gained, but he must not, however, be ignorant of the general principles of each. For in such a variety of matters it cannot be supposed that the same person can arrive at excellence in each, since to be aware of their several niceties and bearings, cannot fall within his power. . . . Wherefore Pythius seems to have been in error, forgetting that art consists in practice and theory. Theory is common to, and may be known by, all, but the result of practice occurs to the artist in his own art only. The physician and musician are each obliged to have some regard to the beating of the pulse, and the motion of the feet, but who would apply to the latter to heal a wound or cure a malady? So, without the aid of the former, the musician affects the ears of his audience by modulations upon his instrument. The astronomer and musician delight in similar proportions, for the positions of the stars, which are quartile and trine, answer to a fourth and fifth in harmony. . . . Throughout the whole range of art there are many incidents common to all. Practice alone can lead to excellence in any one. That architect, therefore, is sufficiently educated whose general knowledge enables him to give his opinion on any branch when required to do so. Those unto whom nature has been so bountiful that they are at once geometricians, astronomers, musicians, and skilled in many other arts go beyond what is required of the architect.'

Further observations are perhaps unnecessary with a view to reiterating the striking similarities between the *Mānasāra* and Vitruvius on this point. This series of similarities between the injunctions of the two standard works on such an important matter as the training of the architect, the very soul of architecture, seem to have been due to something more than mere coincidence.

The next chapter (III) in the *Mānasāra*, called *Vāstu-prakaraṇa*, defines *vāstu* or habitation and divides it into four classes—ground, building, conveyance, and couch (*dharā*, *harmya*, *yāna*, and *paryaṅka*).

Chapter IV, called *Bhū-parīkshā* or examination of soil, deals with the site where a village, town, fort, palace, temple, or dwelling is to be built, and examines the soil thereof with regard to contour, colour, odour, features, taste, touch; the elevation of the ground; and the luxuriance of certain plants, trees, and grasses.

Chapter V, called *Bhūmi-saṁgraha* or selection of site, deals further with the soil before it is finally selected for a building site.

The next chapter (VI) considers the orientation of buildings, and recommends that a building should preferably face the east or north-east, and never the south-east. Reasons have not been discussed fully, beyond stating that this is auspicious or that is inauspicious. Incidentally, the principles, mechanics, and details of dialling have been exhaustively discussed.

The following chapter (VII) discusses the design or division of the site selected for a village, town, or house, into a number of plots. Thirty-two schemes are distinguished, each of which is divided into squares of various numbers.

Following the usual custom, this introductory section concludes with a chapter (VIII) on offerings to various deities. In this matter, too, the chief architect takes a leading part.

The corresponding chapter (II) of Vitruvius is called, 'Of those things on which architecture depends.' It deals with the fitness (*ordinatio*) and arrangement (*dispositio*), also proportion, uniformity, consistency, and economy, and is divisible into three heads, ichnography, orthography, and scenography, which considered together constitute design.

The next chapter (III) is called 'Of the different branches (building, dialling, and mechanics) of architecture,' and the chapter following (IV) is named 'Of the choice of healthy situation,' which deals with the climatic conditions and elevations of the building site, as well as with its aspects or orientation. Unlike in the *Mānasāra*, the consideration of fog, rain, heat, and cold, which are peculiarities of the European countries, has been given prominence here. The explanations of aspects recommended are satisfactory. 'A city on the sea-side,' it is stated, 'exposed to the south or west will be insalubrious, for in summer mornings a city thus placed would be hot, at noon it would be scorched. A city, also, with a western aspect would even at sunrise be warm, at noon hot, and in the evening of a burning temperature. Hence the constitution of the inhabitants of such places, from such continual and excessive changes of the air, would be much vitiated.' After citing opinions of physicians andot hers, and supporting by illustrations, it is further stated, 'When, therefore, a city is built in a marshy situation near the sea coast, with a northern, north-eastern or eastern aspect, on a marsh whose level is higher than the shore of the sea, the site is not altogether improper; for by means of sewers the waters may be discharged into the sea; and at those times, when violently agitated by storms, the sea swells and runs up the sewers, it mixes with the water of the marsh and prevents the generation of marshy insects; it also soon destroys such as are passing from the higher level, by the saltness of its water to which they are unaccustomed.' The frequent mention of the seaside, it is needless to point out, is due to the situation of the prominent Italian cities on the sea shore, and of Rome in particular, which was the object of special study to Vitruvius.

Vitruvius has also elaborately treated the subject of dialling in as many as four chapters (Book IX, Chapters I, II, VIII, IX).

In this matter of dialling, as in many others, Vitruvius, of course, differs in certain details from the *Mānasāra*. For instance, regarding the principles of dialling, each of the twelve months is, in the *Mānasāra* (VII), divided into three parts of ten days each, and the increase and decrease of shadow are calculated in these several parts of the different months. Vitruvius (Book IX, Chapter VIII), on the other hand, discusses 'the principles of dialling and the increase and decrease of the *days*,' not the *shadow* thereof, in the different months.

In both these works, therefore, this introductory section comprises exactly eight chapters, which bear similar titles and deal with the same subjects practically in the same way.

Town-planning is the next topic treated in both the works, and it covers exactly two chapters both in Vitruvius (Book I, Chapters VI and VII), as well as in the *Mānasāra* (Chapters IX and X).

The *Mānasāra* describes the subject under two heads, *Grāma-lakshaṇa* and *Nagara-vidhāna*, and three categories, village, town, and fort. Villages are divided into eight classes, called *daṇḍaka*, *sarvatobhadra*, *nandyāvarta*, *padmaka*, *svastika*, *prastara*, *kārmuka*, and *chaturmukha*; each of these, as the names indicate, represents a particular design and lay-out. Towns are also divided into eight classes: *rājadhānī*, *nagara*, *pura*, *nagarī*, *kheṭa*, *kharvaṭa*, *kubjaka*, and *pattana*. These refer more to the situation and distribution of buildings than to their shapes or designs.

Forts are first divided into eight classes: *śibira*, *vāhinīmukha*, *sthānīva*, *droṇaka*, *saṁviddha* or *vardhaka*, *kolaka*, *nigama*, and *skandāvāra*. According to their situation, they are further classified into mountain fort (*giri-durga*), forest fort (*vana-durga*), water fort (*jala-durga*), chariot fort (*ratha-durga*), gods' fort (*deva-durga*), clay fort (*paṅka-durga*), and mixed fort (*miśra-durga*). The mountain fort is subdivided into three classes, according as it is built on the top of the mountain, in the valley, or on the mountain slope.

According to the *Mānasāra* there is, however, not much difference between a village, a town, and a fort. The town is the extension of a village. And the fort is in many cases nothing more than a fortified town. There seems to be only this difference that a fort is chiefly meant for purposes of defence, while a village or town is mainly intended for habitation and commerce. But the village scheme seems, all the same, to have originated from the plan of the military camp.

Each village is surrounded by a wall made of brick or stone. It is supported by ramparts. Beyond this wall there is a ditch, broad and deep enough to cause serious obstruction in the event of an attack on the village. There are generally four main gates at the middle of the four sides, and as many at the four corners. Inside the wall there is a large street running all round the village. Besides, there are two other large streets, each of which connects two opposite main gates. They intersect at the centre of the village, where a public temple or hall is generally built in which the villagers may meet. The village is thus divided into four main blocks ; each of these is again subdivided into many blocks by streets, which are always straight and run from one end to the other of the main block. The two main streets crossing at the centre have houses only on one side, facing the street. The ground floor of these houses on the main streets consists of shops. The street which runs round the village, also, has houses only on one side. These houses are mainly public buildings, such as schools, colleges, libraries, guest-houses, and liquor saloons. All other streets generally have residential buildings on both sides. The houses, high or low, are always uniform in make. The drains and sewers are made towards the slope of the village. Tanks and ponds are dug in all the inhabited parts and located in such quarters as can conveniently be reached by a large number of inhabitants. The temples of public worship, as well as the public commons, gardens, and parks, are similarly located. People of the same caste or profession are generally housed in the same quarter. The habitation of the dead-body burners (*chaṇḍālas*), as well as the places for cremation, are located outside the village wall, to the north-west in particular. The temples of fearful deities, such as Chāmuṇḍā, are also located outside the wall.

A town may be situated from east to west or from north to south according to the position it occupies. There should be one to twelve large streets in a town. It should be built near a river or a mountain, and should have facilities for trade and commerce with foreigners. It should be furnished with walls, moats, ditches, gates, drains, parks, commons, shops, exchanges, temples, guest-houses, colleges, etc. The king and his court usually reside in a town, and traders and forum are essential elements in its population.

Forts are also surrounded with strong walls and large and deep ditches. The wall is made of brick, stone, and similar lasting materials. It is at least eighteen feet in height and its thickness at the base is at least nine feet. The wall is provided with watch-towers.

Fortified cities are specially honoured with the residences of the king, the princes, priests, ministers, and military officers. There are also humbler dwellings, as well as courts of justice, arsenals, traders' booths, shops, work-houses for artisans, various assembly halls, dancing halls, liqour saloons, and gambling halls.

According to Vitruvius (Book I, Chapter V) :

'When we are satisfied with the spot fixed on for the site of the city, as well as in respect of the goodness of the air, as of the abundant supply of provisions for the support of the population, the communications by good roads, and river or sea navigation for the transport of merchandize,[1] we shoud take into consideration the method of constructing the walls and the towers of the city. From the exterior face of the wall, towers must be projected from which an approaching enemy may be annoyed by weapons; from the ambrasures of those towns, right and left, an easy approach to the wall must be provided against; indeed they should be surrounded by uneven ground, and the roads leading to the gates should be winding and turned to the left from the gates. By this arrangement the right side of the attacking troops, which are not covered by their shields, will be open to the weapons of the beseiged.'

'The thickness of the walls should be sufficient for two armed men

[1] Cf. Chāṇakya's saying : 'Residential houses should not be built in such places where there are no rich men, no learned men, no kings, no rivers, and no physicians.'

to pass each other with ease. The walls ought to be tied, from front to rear, with many pieces of charred olive wood; by which means the two faces, thus connected, will endure for ages. . . .'

'The distance between each tower should exceed an arrow's flight. The walls will be intercepted by the lower parts of the towers where they occur, leaving an interval equal to the width of the tower, which space the tower will consequently occupy. The towers should be made either round or polygonal. A square tower is a bad form on account of its being easily fractured at the quoins by the battering ram; whereas the circular tower has this advantage, that, when battered, the pieces of masonry whereof it is composed being cuneiform, cannot be driven in towards their centre without displacing the whole mass. Nothing tends more to the security of walls and towers than backing them with walls or terraces; it counteracts the effects of rams as well as of undermining. . . .'

'In the construction of ramparts, very wide and deep trenches are to be first excavated, the bottom of which must be still further dug out for receiving the foundation of the wall. This must be of sufficient thickness to resist the pressure of earth against it. Then, according to the space requisite for drawing up the cohorts in military order on the ramparts, another wall is to be built within the former, towards the city. The outer and inner walls are then to be connected by cross-walls, disposed on the plan after the manner of the teeth of a comb or a saw, so as to divide the pressure of the filling-in earth into many and less forces, and thus prevent the walls from being thrust out.' The materials are stated to be 'what are found on the spot, such as square stones, flint, rubble, stones, burnt or unburnt bricks' (Book I, Chapter V).

'The plan of the city should not be square, nor formed with acute angles, but polygonal, so that the motions of the enemy may be open to observation' (Book I, Chapter V).

'The lanes and streets (of which no details are given) of the city should be set out, the choice of sites for the convenience and use of the state remains to be decided on; for sacred edifices, for the forum, and for other public buildings. If the place adjoin the sea, the forum should be seated close to the harbour; if inland, it should be in the centre of the town. The temples of the gods, protectors of the city, as those of Jupiter, Juno, and Minerva, should be on some eminence which commands a view of the greater part of the city. The temple of Mercury should be either in the forum, or, as also the temple of Isis and Serapis, in the great public square; those of Apollo and Father Bacchus near the theatre. If there be neither amphitheatre nor gymnasium, the temple of Hercules should be near the circus. The temple of Mars should be out of the city, in the neighbouring country, that of Venus near to the gate. According to the revelations of the Hetrurian Haruspices, the temples of Venus, Vulcan, and Mars should be so placed that those of the first be not in the way of contaminating the matrons and youth with the influence of lust; that those of Vulcan be away from the city, which would consequently be freed from the danger of fire, the divinity presiding over that element being drawn away by the rites and sacrifices performing in his temple. The temple of Mars should be also out of the city, that no armed frays may disturb the peace of the citizens, and that this divinity may, moveover, be ready to preserve them from their enemies and the perils of war. The temple of Ceres shall be in a solitary spot out of the city, to which the public are not necessarily led but for the purpose of sacrificing to her. This spot is to be reverenced with religious awe and solemnity of demeanour by those whose affairs lead them to visit it' (Book I, Chapter VII).

It should be observed that in the *Mānasāra* eight distinctive plans of villages and some twenty-five varieties of commercial cities and military forts have been described with all details. In town-planning the Indian authority has recommended almost all the suitable designs, square, rectangular, and polygonal. But Vitruvius recommends only the polygonal. In the matter of the disposition of temples within the city wall and outside, the two authorities very strikingly correspond. In both the treatises the fear-inspiring deities are similarly located outside the city wall.

The following seven chapters (XI to XVII) in the *Mānasāra* serve the purpose of a preamble to the subsequent chapters dealing with buildings.[1]

The first of these (XI) is named *Bhūmi-lamba*, or height of storey, in the *Mānasāra*. It is defined in the *Kāmikāgama* as the dimensions of the four sides. The contents of the chapter in the *Mānasāra* describe in detail the measurement of length, breadth, and height of buildings of

[1] Of these seven preliminary chapters the twelfth, on foundations (*garbha-nyāsa*), should have been in the place of the eleventh, which treats of dimensions of buildings (*bhūmi-lamba*), as in Vitruvius's treatise.

one to twelve storeys, assigned to persons of different ranks. The five forms, namely, square, rectangular, round, octagonal, and oval, are prescribed for buildings of different classes, *jāti*, *chhanda*, *vikalpa*, and *ābhāsa*. These shapes are equally applicable to religious, military, and residential buildings. A palace of five to twelve storeys is stated to suit the emperor or the universal monarch, highest in rank among the nine classes of kings. Residences of one to three storeys are assigned to the heir-apparent and the chief feudatories, and so on.

The title of the corresponding chapter of Vitruvius (Book VI, Chapter III) is more significant. It is called, 'Forms of houses suited to different ranks of persons.' As in the *Mānasāra*, buildings are divided exactly into five classes, though the criteria of classification are different. It is stated (Book III, Chapter II) that 'there are five species of temples, whose names are Pycnostylos, that is, thick set with columns ; Systylos, in which the columns are not so close ; Diastylos, where they are still wider apart ; Aræostylos, when placed more distant from each other . . . ; Eustylos, when the intercolumnation . . . is of the best proportion.' 'The conditions of temples are distinguished,' it is further stated (Book III, Chapter I), 'by their different forms. First, that known by the appellation, In Antis, then the Prostylos, Peripteros, Psuedodipteros, Dipteros, and Hypae-thros.' 'Circular temples are constructed of which some are Monopteral . . . others are called Peripteral' (Book IV, Chapter VIII).

As regards the distribution of buildings it is stated (Book IV, Chapter III) that 'temples of the Doric order are erected to Minerva, Mars, and Hercules, on account of whose valour their temple should be of masculine proportions and without delicate ornaments. The character of the Corinthian order seems more appropriate to Venus, Flora, Proserpine, and Nymphs of Fountains, because its slenderness elegance and richness, and its ornamental leaves surmounted by volutes, seem to bear an analogy to their dispositions. A medium between these two is chosen for temples to Juno, Diana, Bacchus, and other similar deities, which should be of the Ionic order, tempered between the severity of the Doric and the slenderness and delicacy of the Corinthian order' (Book I, Chapter II). As regards secular buildings, it is laid down that 'the houses of bankers and receivers of the revenue may be more commodious and elegant than those of persons of middling condition in life. For advocates and men of literature houses ought to be still handsomer and more spacious, to suit the reception of persons on consultations. But for nobles, who in bearing honours and discharging the duties of the magistracy must have much intercourse with the citizens, princely vestibules must be provided, lofty atria and spacious peristylia, groves, and extensive walks, finished in a magnificent style. . . . If, therefore, houses are erected thus adapted to the different classes of society . . . there will be nothing to reprehend, for they will be suitable to their destination.' 'I have thus described,' concludes Vitruvius, 'the proportions of town residences as I promised. I shall now proceed to those of houses in the country' (Book VI, Chapter VIII).

It is needless to point out that the subject-matter of this chapter is virtually the same in both the authorities. The small differences are due to the local conditions and requirements of the two different countries.

The next chapter (XII), called *Garbha-nyāsa* in the *Mānasāra,* deals with the foundations whereupon buildings, villages, and tanks are built. The foundation is excavated in the ground best suited for a structure to the depth of a man's height with uplifted arms. It is laid down that the bottom of the pit thus excavated must be rocky or watery, in other words, it must reach rock or water. It implies that the best soil for receiving foundation, when it is not erected on water, is rock, gravel, or closely pressed sandy earth.

The depth of the foundation-cave is equal to the height of the basement. The four corners and sides, built of brick or stone, are equal. This cave is filled with water and ten kinds of earth, thus the earth from an ant-hill, a crab-hole, etc., is placed at the bottom and closely pressed and hardened by means of wooden hammers shaped like the elephant's foot. Portions of certain plants are then deposited on the four sides, the root of the blue lotus to the east, the root of the white lotus to the south, and so on. Upon these are placed grains of ten kinds of cereals, such as *phaseolus mungo, phaseolus radiatus, dolichos uniflorus, seasamum indicum,* and so on. The vault is built thereon, the details of which need hardly be repeated here. Upon such 'strong foundations, the strength whereof varies according to the weights of the buildings above, various structures are constructed.'

'When we are satisfied,' says Vitruvius (Book I, Chapter V), 'with the spot fixed on for the site of the city . . . their foundations should be carried down to a solid bottom, if such can be found, and should be built thereon of such thickness as may be necessary for the proper support of that part of the wall which stands above the natural level of the ground. They should be of the soundest workmanship and materials, and of greater thickness than the walls above.' Importance of solid ground is emphasized and it is again stated (Book III, Chapter III), 'if solid ground can be come to, the foundations should go down to it and into it, according to the magnitude of the work, and the substraction be built up as solid as possible. Above the ground of the foundation, the wall should be one-half thicker than the column it is to receive, so that the lower parts which carry the greatest weight, may be stronger than the upper part. . . . Nor must the mouldings of the bases of the columns project beyond the solid. Thus, also, should be regulated the thickness of all walls above ground. The intervals between the foundations brought up under the columns, should be either rammed down hard, or arched, so as to prevent the foundation piers from swerving. If solid ground cannot be come to, and the ground be loose or marshy, the place must be excavated, cleared, and either elder, olive, or oak piles, previously charred, must be driven with a machine as close to each other as possible and the intervals between the piles filled with charcoal. The heaviest foundations may be laid on such a base.'

These details are also strikingly similar in both the authorities and this similarity seems to be due to something more than mere coincidence.

The next four chapters (XIII to XVI) in the *Mānasāra* deal with the column and its different parts, the pedestal, base, shaft, and entablature, and their various mouldings. Vitruvius also treats the subject in exactly four chapters (Book III, Chapter III, Book IV, Chapters I to III). But the titles of the chapters are a little different. They are named in the *Mānasāra*, *upapīṭha* or pedestal (XIII), *adhisṭhāna* or base (XIV), *stambha* or shaft (XV), and *prastara* or entablature (XVI). Vitruvius calls them, 'columns and their ornaments' (Book III, Chapter III), 'origin of the three sorts of columns and the Corinthian capital' (Book IV, Chapter I), 'ornaments of columns' (*ibid*, Chapter II), and 'Doric proportions' (*ibid*, Chapter III).

Vitruvius, in the Doric, Corinthian, and Tuscan orders, makes no mention of pedestals, and in the Ionic order he seems to consider them rather as a necessary part in the construction of a temple than as belonging to the order itself (Book V, Chapter VII). In the *Mānasāra* twelve kinds of pedestals are described with detailed measurements of the various mouldings of each pedestal. A comparison of these, with similar details of pedestals, quoted in full in the writer's *Encyclopaedia* from European authorities other than Vitruvius, makes it clear that the Indian pedestals surpass the Græco-Roman in variety, beauty of proportion, and the richness of ornaments.

As regards the base, also, there is in the *Mānasāra* a large variety of types, sixty-four in number, described in detail with their mouldings and ornaments. A comparison of the details gathered together in the writer's *Encyclopaedia* will show that the Indian bases and pedestals are made more systematically and afford a greater variety of proportions than those of the Græco-Roman orders. In European orders the forms and dimensions of both base and pedestal are fixed by invariable rules with respect to the orders in which they are employed, while in the Indian orders the choice is left to the option of the architects.

There are, however, more similarities between the Indian and the Græco-Roman entablatures, consisting of four parts, the capital, architrave, frieze, and cornice. But the massiveness of the Indian entablature offers a striking contrast to the lightness of the Grecian. This is shewn by a comparison of details given in the writer's *Encyclopaedia* of eight kinds of Indian and some five kinds of Græco-Roman entablatures.

But the point to be clear about is whether or not there is some fundamental resemblance between the Indian and the Græco-Roman column as a whole. This is a crucial point, because the column in a building is stated by authorities to be the regulator of the whole composition, and it is the one feature of the ancient architecture which 'illustrates its rise and progress as well as its perfection and weakness.'

Like the five Græco-Roman orders, called Doric, Ionic, Corinthian, Tuscan, and Composite, columns in ancient India were also divided into five classes or orders.

In the *Mānasāra* they are called *Brahma-kānta*, *Vishṇu-kānta*, *Rudra-kānta*, *Śiva-kānta*, and *Skanda-kānta*. These divisions are based on the general shapes. With respect to dimensions and ornaments, they are called *Chitra-karṇa*, *Padma-kānta*, *Chitra-skambha*, *Pālikā-stambha*, and *Kumbha-stambha.*

In the *Matsya-Purāṇa*, the *Bṛihat-saṁhitā*, and the *Kiraṇa-tantra* they are called *Ruchaka*, *Vajra*, *Dvi-vajra*, *Pralīnaka*, and *Vṛitta*. In the

Suprabhedāgama the names of the five orders are *Śrī-kara, Chandra-kānta, Saumuhkya, Priya-darśana,* and *Śubhaṅkarī.* This last one is expressly stated to be the Indian composite order, being a compound (*miśrita*) of *Saumukhya* and *Priya-darśana,* exactly like the Græco-Roman Composite order, which is a compound of Corinthian and Ionic.[1]

Between the European and the Indian columns that is a point of difference. In the Græco-Roman orders, the names of the five orders do not vary, while in India the names of the five orders have varied in the various treatises referred to above. It is true, all the same, that the criteria of divisions are essentially the same in all authorities. The variation of the names of the five orders can perhaps be explained. The names of the Græco-Roman orders, according to Vitruvius and other European authorities referred to in the *Encyclopaedia of Architecture* by Gwilt, are geographical.[2]

In India, on the other hand, the names of the orders were based on the shapes of the columns. And as the Indians are comparatively more religious and sentimental than critical in temperament and imagination, they chose mythological and poetical names according to the spirit of the times when these various works were composed. Thus in the *Mānasāra* we see the orders bearing the names of mythological deities, Brahmā, Vishṇu, Rudra, Śiva, and Skanda ; as well as the poetical names like *Chitra-karṇa* (variegated ear), *Chitra-skambha* (variegated capital), *Padma-kānta* (graceful like lotus), *Kumbha-stambha* (of jug-shaped capital), and *Pālika-stambha* (shaped like a measuring pot). In the *Āgama,* the names are more poetical : *Śrīkara* (beautifying), *Chandra-kānta* (graceful like the moon), *Saumukhya* (of a charming face), and *Śubhaṅkarī* (auspicious). In the *Purāṇa,* the *Bṛihat-saṁhitā,* and the *Kiraṇa-tantra,* the names combine beauty and utility : *Ruchaka* (pleasing), *Vṛitta* (round and dignified), *Vaira* (beautiful and solid like the club), *Dvi-vajra* (doubly so), and *Pralīnaka* (firmly attached).

With regard to the names and functions of the component parts of the column the variation is a little less marked. The number of these subservient parts, called mouldings and common to all orders, is very significant. Thus in the *Mānasāra,* which, of almost all the

[1] For references *see* above, pp. 201–202 and the footnotes, and the writer's *Encyclopaedia,* under *Stambha.*

[2] *See* p. 202, note 7. The contents of the four following paragraphs are discussed in more detail elsewhere (p. 201–206), and may be referred to.

treatises, deals separately and exhaustively with the pedestal, the base, the column or shaft, and the entablature, mention is made, in connexion with the pillar, of five mouldings apparently of the shaft. They are called *bodhikā*, *mushṭi-bandha*, *phalakā*, *tāṭikā*, and *ghaṭa*. But the total number of mouldings, when the base, pedestal, and entablature are also taken into consideration, is forty-seven. The *Suprabhedāgama* describes two sets of seven mouldings, one set referring to the column of the main building and the other to that of the pavilion. They are called respectively *daṇḍa*, *maṇḍi*, *kaṇṭha*, *kumbha*, *phalakā*, *vīra-kaṇṭha* and *potikā*; and *bodhikā*, *uttara*, *vājana*, *mūrdhikā*, *tulā*, *jayantī*, and *tala*.

This increasing number of mouldings has reached the significant number of eight in the *Matsya-Purāṇa*, the *Bṛihat-saṁhitā*, and the *Kiraṇa-tantra*, and bears the very same eight names—*vāhana*, *ghaṭa*, *padama*, *uttaroshṭha*, *bāhulya*, *hāra*, *tulā*, and *upa-tulā*.

The component mouldings of the Græco-Roman orders are also exactly eight in number, and, like the five orders themselves, their names have remained invariable ever since their introduction, though most of them have been given more than one name. They are called (1) the ovolo, echinus, or quarter round; (2) the talon, ogée, or reversed cyma; (3) the cyma, cyma-recta, or cymatium; (4) the torus; (5) the scotia or trochilos; (6) the cavetto, mouth, or hollow; (7) the astragal; and (8) the fillet, listel, or annulet.

Some of the eight mouldings of the Indian order can be identified, with a reasonable certainty, with the corresponding mouldings of the Græco-Roman order. *Padma*, for instance, implies lotus (petal), and cyma also suggests the same thing. *Uttaroshṭha*, literally the lower lip, and the cavetto, mouth, or hollow, are apparently the same. *Hāra*, meaning chain, seems to imply the same object as the torus, bead, or astragal. *Ghaṭa* means a pot, it may correspond to the ogée, talon, or reversed cyma. *Vāhana* is that which supports anything, and the abacus also serves the same purpose, so they may correspond to each other. *Tulā* and *upa-tulā*, otherwise called *vājana* and *uttara*, seem to correspond to the fillet, listel, or annulet.

The proportionate measurement of the columns is another important point of comparison. The details are discussed in the writer's *Encyclopaedia*. The first Indian order is six diameters high, the second seven diameters, the third eight diameters, the fourth nine diameters, and the fifth ten diameters high.

'Concerning the proportions of columns,' says Rām Rāz (page 38), 'the second sort of column in the Hindu arthitecture may be compared with the Tuscan, the third with the Doric, the fourth with the Ionic, and the fifth with the Corinthian or Composite pillar.' He further adds that 'there are other columns in the Indian architecture, not only one diameter lower than the Tuscan, but one to two diameters higher than the Composite.' The same is also the case with the European columns. 'The orders and their several characters and qualities,' says Gwilt (2538), 'do not merely appear in the fixed species of columns into which they have been subdivided, but are distributed throughout the edifices to which they are applied.'

'Both the Indian and Grecian columns are diminished gradually in their diameter from the base to the summit of the shaft, a practice which has never been observed in the Egyptian; on the contrary, a diametrically opposite rule has been observed in their shafts, which are made narrower at the bottom than at the top. The proportion in which the diminution at the top of the columns of the two former (Indian and Græco-Roman) is made seems to have been regulated by the same principle, though not by the same rule. The general rule adopted by the Hindu architects in this respect is that the thickness at the bottom, being divided into as many parts as there are diameters in the whole height of the column, one of these parts is invariably diminished at the top, but in the Grecian and Roman architecture the diameter of the upper part of the shaft, in a column of fifteen feet in height, is made one-sixth less than its thickness at the base, and in a column of fifty feet, the diminution is one-eighth. The higher the columns are, the less they diminish, because the apparent diminution of the diameter in columns of the same proportion is always greater according to their height, and this principle is supposed to have been discovered with greater scientific skill, and is adduced as one of the proofs of the highly refined taste of the Greeks; but we observe that precepts derived from the same principle have been taught and practised in India from time immemorial.'

The point at issue is not the actual identification. The striking similarities in the names of the mouldings, like *padma* or cyma, *hāra* or bead, or in the names of orders like the *Miśrita* or Composite, may sometimes be attributed to inexplicable coincidence. But in view of other striking similarities between Vitruvius and the *Mānasāra*, such as the classification of orders into exactly five, and the division of subservient parts, called mouldings, common to all the orders, into eight, and also the proportionate measurement varying equally from six to ten diameters and tapering almost in the same way, there would seem to have been something more substantial than mere coincidence. An influence, direct or indirect, of the one upon the other, seems highly probable. I venture to think, further, that there might have been a relation of indebtedness between the two authorities.

The concluding chapter (XVII) of this section in the *Mānasāra* deals with joinery. No separate treatment has been accorded by Vitruvius to this subject.

The next chapter (XVIII) in the *Mānasāra* is a summary of details concerning buildings of various storeys and kinds described in Chapters XIX to XXX. The following chapters (XXXI to XXXVI) deal with attached buildings of various descriptions and requirements. Chapter XXXVII refers to the first entry into a newly-built house. Doors are separately described in two chapters (XXXVIII and XXXIX), so also the royal palaces and courts are described in Chapters XL to XLII. Cars and chariots, couches and thrones, are treated in the next three chapters (XLIII to XLV). Arches are separately described in Chapter XLVI, so also the theatre (*madhya-raṅga*) is treated in Chapter XLVII. And this architectural portion of the *Mānasāra* ends with the description of ornamental trees (Chapter XLVIII), crowns (Chapter XLIX), and ornaments and articles of furniture (Chapter L).[1]

The sculptural portion of the work (Chapters LI to LXX) deals with the art of carving and measuring images. This portion practically comprises illustrations of the *tāla* measures. Vitruvius, as we shall show presently, has not treated the subject separately; he has mixed it up with the architectural description.

With regard to these subjects the comparison between the *Mānasāra* and Vitruvius need not be lengthy. Both these authorities in matters of detail must necessarily differ from each other, even if one were translated from the other, because the local conditions and national requirements are entirely different regarding not only residential buildings but also temples. On the broad lines of methods and principles, however, the comparison can be briefly continued in the expectation of fruitful results.

[1] For more details, *see* pp. 112-137.

Thus, in the *Mānasāra*, the whole compound of the house is divided into five courts (Chapter XXXI), each of which is furnished with a gate-house (Chapter XXXIII), and a large number of detached buildings are also built within each court (Chapters XXXII, XXXVI, XIX to XXX).

Vitruvius also divides the compound into exactly five courts, which are, however, not used simultaneously (Book VI, Chapters III to VII). 'There are,' says Vitruvius, 'five species of courts, which receive their names from their forms. The Tuscan, the Corinthian, the Tetrastylon (with four columns), the Displuviatum (open at the top), and the Testudinatum (roofed).' In the *Mānasāra* also, it should be noted, five technical names have been given to these five courts, *antar-maṇḍala* (innermost court), *anta-nīhāra* (the second court), *madhya-nīhāra* (the middle court), *prākāra* (the fourth court), after which the chapter has been named and which is stated to be first introduced in the *Mānasāra*, though as many as seven courts are described in the *Mṛichchhakaṭika*. The fifth one is called *mahā-maryādā*, or extreme boundary. Thus, in the *Mānasāra*, the courts receive their names from their situation, and not from their forms. Forms are discussed in the *Mānasāra* also. In fact the treatment of this subject, like all others, is by far the more exhaustive in the *Mānasāra*. Even the five gate-houses of the five courts have been treated at great length in a separate chapter (XXXIII) and given five technical names, *dvāra-śobhā* (beauty of the gate), belonging to the *antar-maṇḍala* or the first court, *dvāra-śālā* (gate-mansion, of the second court), *dvāra-prāsāda* (gate-palace, of the third court), *dvāra-harmya* (gate-edifice, of the fourth court), and *mahā-gopura* (great gate-house, of the fifth court).[1]

Within these courts, buildings of different requirements have been similarly distributed by the two authorities. For instance, in the *Mānasāra*, Chapter XXXVI is called *Gṛiha-māna-sthāna-vinyāsa*, literally meaning, 'location and measurement of house,' and Chapter XXXII is called *Parivāra-vidhāna*, meaning 'the buildings for the members of the family' (of gods). The corresponding chapters (Book VII, Chapters, I, II, IX) are named by Vitruvius, 'situation of buildings according to the nature of different places,' 'proportions of private buildings to suit the nature of the sites,' and 'proportions of houses in the country.' Detached buildings, situated both within the

[1] For further details, *see* p. 117–119.

compound and outside, have been described in the *Mānasāra* in two very long chapters (XXXIV and XXXV) called *Maṇḍapa* and *Sālā*. The term *maṇḍapa* is used to imply, first, a house or pavilion set up in a village or on the bank of a sea, river, tank, or lake; secondly, all the detached buildings within a compound, which is divided into five courts; lastly, it implies various sorts of rooms in a temple or residential building. *Śālā* also implies almost the same kinds of buildings, but they are more commodious and pompous mansions arranged in rows varying from one to ten, and their forms and twelve storeys are taken into special consideration. Chapter VI (Book I), called by Vitruvius, 'distribution and situation of buildings within the walls,' may be compared with *Maṇḍapa* and *Śālā* with respect to general principles and methods. But Vitruvius's treatment of the subject is comparatively brief. The brevity of his account of individual buildings also becomes obvious when the 'arrangement and parts of Grecian houses,' and 'interior of the cell and the arrangement of Pronaos,' described in two small chapters (Book VI, Chapter X, and Book IV, Chapter IV) are compared with the exhaustive description of similar subjects detailed in some thirteen chapters (XVIII to XXX) in the *Mānasāra*.

Doors are separately described by both the authorities. Vitruvius calls the chapter 'Proportions of the doors of temples' (Book IV, Chapter VI). In the *Mānasāra* the subject is treated under two chapters (XXXVIII and XXXIX) called *Dvāra-sthāna* (location of doors) and *Dvāra-māna* (measurement or proportions of doors). Both the authorities classify doors under three species. Vitruvius calls them Doric, Ionic, and Attic, and in the *Mānasāra* they are called *Chhanda*, *Vikalpa*, and *Ābhāsa*. Here is a striking point of similarity with respect to an important omission. In the *Mānasāra* the *Jāti* class always goes with the other three classes mentioned here. Vitruvius has also omitted Corinthian and Tuscan, which generally go with Doric and Ionic. In the *Mānasāra* the height of the door is stated to be, as a general rule, twice its breadth. 'Their width,' says Vitruvius, 'is found by dividing the height into two parts and a half, and taking one and a half for the width below.' Single-folded as well as double-folded doors are mentioned in the *Mānasāra*. Vitruvius has referred also to four-fold doors. Indian doors are decorated with foliated and floral ornaments, as well as with the images of deities. 'These doors,' says Vitruvius, 'are not to be inlaid (cerestrota), nor in two folds, but single-folded, and to open outwards.' According to Vitruvius, doors are generally constructed in the middle of the front wall. But according to the *Mānasāra* doors may also be constructed sometimes, not in the centre of the frontage, but on either side of the middle.

Windows are not separately described by Vitruvius. But in the *Mānasāra* a long account of them has been given at the end of Chapter XXXIII; similarly an account of staircases, omitted by Vitruvius, is found in the *Mānasāra* at the end of Chapter XXX. No separate mention has also been made by Vitruvius of arches, to which subject an entire chapter (XLVI) has been devoted in the *Mānasāra*. Vitruvius has left out the accounts, given in the *Mānasāra*, of cars and chariots (Chapter XLIII), couches (XLIV), thrones (XLV), crowns (XLIX), ornaments of the body and articles of house furniture (L), as well as the ornamental tree (XLVIII).

In the *Mānasāra*, on the other hand, a very brief reference is made to an object resembling a theatre, to which Vitruvius has devoted several chapters (Book V, Chapters III to IX). Vitruvius has not treated separately the royal palaces found in the *Mānasāra* (Chapters XL to XLII) nor does the *Mānasāra* contain any account of his special buildings, such as 'Forum and Basilica,' 'Treasury, Prison, and Curia,' 'Harbours and other buildings in water' (Book V, Chapters I, II and XII). Building materials, though frequently mentioned, are not described in the *Mānasāra* under separate chapters. Vitruvius has devoted some eight chapters (Book II, Chapters III to X) to the subject of building materials, namely, bricks (compare the *Mānasāra*, Chapter XII, last part), sand (*Mānasāra* XII), lime (*Mānasāra* LI), Pozzolona stone quarries (*Mānasāra* XV), timber (*Mānasāra* XV) and firs, called Supernas and Infernas, and the Appennines.

Vitruvius deals with painting and preparations of colours in the larger part of a book (VII) of fourteen chapters. This subject, as well as Vitruvius's books (VIII to X) on instruments, machines and engines, have no place in the *Mānasāra*. In place of these subjects, some twenty chapters (LI to LXX) of the *Mānasāra* have been devoted to sculptural matters, to which only the following brief and casual reference has been made by Vitruvius (Book III, Chapter I).

'In truth they (symmetry and proportion) are as necessary to the beauty of a building as to that of a well-formed human figure, which nature has so fashioned, that the face, from the chin to the top of the forehead, or to the roots of the hair, is a tenth part of the height of the whole body. From the chin to the crown of the head is an eighth part of the whole height, and from the nape of the neck to the crown of the head the same. From the upper part of the breast to the roots of the hair a sixth, to the crown of the head a fourth. A third part of the height of the face is equal to that from the chin to the under-side of the nostrils, and thence to the middle of the eyebrows the same, from the last to the roots of the hair, where the forehead ends, the remaining third part. The length of the foot is a sixth part of the height of the body. The forearm a fourth part. The width of the breast a fourth part. Similarly have the other members their due proportions by attention to which the ancient painters and sculptors obtained so much reputation. . . .'

'The navel is naturally placed in the centre of the human body, and if, in a man lying with his face upward and his hands and feet extended, from his navel as the centre, a circle be described, it will touch his fingers and toes. It is not alone by a circle that the human body is thus circumscribed, as may be seen by placing it within a square. For measuring from the feet to the crown of the head, and then across the arms fully extended, we find the latter measure equal to the former; so that the lines at right angles to each other, enclosing the figure, will form a square.'

'If nature, therefore, has made the human body so that the different members of it are measures of the whole, so the ancients have, with great propriety, determined that in all perfect works each part should be some aliquot part of the whole; and since they direct that this be observed in all works, it must be most strictly attended to in temples of the gods, wherein the faults as well as the beauties remain to the end of the time.'

This is all about the defects, to which in the *Mānasāra* practically a whole chapter (LXIX), one of the two concluding chapters of the work, is devoted. It is called *Aṅga-dūshaṇa* (*lit.*, defects of the limbs). In both the authorities the subject is discussed in connexion with sculptural objects, but curiously enough, defects and consequent penalties concerning images and idols have been entirely left out both by Vitruvius and the *Mānasāra*. Both the authorities have referred to the subject as concerning buildings only. This sort of similarity can hardly be due to mere coincidence.

'It is worthy of remark,' says Vitruvius, 'that the measures necessarily used in all buildings and other works are derived from the members of the human body, as the digit, the palm, the foot, the cubit, and that these form a perfect number, called by the Greeks *Téleios*.' Phonetically this sounds like what the Indians call *Tālas*, and there is a similarity in meaning also.[1] In the above quotation Vitruvius has briefly referred to only the eighth variety with which the male human figure is measured also by the Indian authorities. Details of the *tāla* measures given in the writer's *Encyclopaedia* need not be repeated here. It should also be noted that, in both the authorities, the face from the chin to the top of the forehead is taken as the standard of all the *tāla* measures, which number ten in the *Mānasāra*.[2]

The last point of comparison between Vitruvius and the *Mānasāra* is in respect of the linguistic style. We have already pointed out that *Śilpā-śastras*, or architectural treatises in India, were written in a very peculiar style. Sanskrit scholars like Dr. G. Bühler and Sir R. G. Bhandarkar have truly branded it as the 'most barbarous Sanskrit.' This remark really means that all possible sorts of violation of the rules of grammar and rhetoric have been committed in the language of the *Śilpa-śāstras*. Such a mixed dialect 'reads exactly like a piece from a stupid school-boy's exercise. It is also confirmed,' continues Dr. Bühler, 'by numerous analogies, such as the language of *janma-patras* (horoscopes) of the badly educated *Joshis* (astrologers) mentioned by Dr. Bhandarkar, the books of masons and carpenters, which have the rules for building houses in most barbarous Sanskrit, and many modern inscriptions composed by clerks.'[3] One of the theses presented by the writer before the Leiden University, and passed in his favour by that learned assembly after long discussion, was this :

'The ungrammatical style of Sanskrit revealed in the branch of literature of which the *Mānasāra* is a representative, is due to the want of literary proficiency on the part of the professional architects who seem to have been the authors of it.' With this the following apology, for ungrammatical style, of Vitruvius may very fruitfully be compared :

[1] *Teleios* is an adjective from *telo-s*, meaning *end*, and *tāla* is derived from *tala* and implies the distance between the *ends* of two fingers (*see* p. 199, and notes).

[2] *See* above, p. 199, and the writer's *Encyclopaedia*, under *Tālamāna*.

[3] *Ep. Ind.*, Vol. I, p. 37. For further details and illustrations from various sources, *see* the writer's *Indian Architecture* (1927), Appendix and pp. 211-214.

'I beseech you, O Cæsar,' says Vitruvius, 'and those who read this my work, to pardon and overlook grammatical errors; for I write neither as an accomplished philosopher, an eloquent rhetorician, nor an expert grammarian, but as an architect: in respect, however, of my art and its principles, I will lay down rules which may serve as an authority to those who build, as well as to those who are already somewhat acquainted with the science' (Book I, Chapter I).

I cannot help thinking that if the writers of the *Silpa-śāstras* generally, and the author of the *Mānasāra* in particular, were conscious of the nature of their style they would certainly have added to their treatises an apology like that of Vitruvius.

There is yet another curious similarity between Vitruvius and the *Mānasāra*. It is regarding the titles of both the works. Both are hidden in mystery. Vitruvius's work bears practically no title. It is called by his translators 'The architecture of Marcus Vitruvius Pollio.' It has been pointed out in the preface that the term 'Mānasāra' also admits of various interpretations. For a sage, Mānasāra is a very unfamiliar name. No such sage is mentioned in the various branches of Sanskrit literature except in this newly discovered *Vāstu-śāstra*. A king of Malwa, however, bore this name. As a derivative name, *Mānasāra*, meaning essence of measurement, and suitable for the title of a work like this, has some philological resemblance with *mensuration*. The derivative meaning of the term 'Vitruvius' is uncertain. The point, however, to which attention is invited, is the curious similarity between the treatise of Vitruvius and the *Mānasāra* in respect of the uncertain signification of their titles.

There is also an uncertainty lurking over the ages in which the architecture of Vitruvius and the *Mānasāra* were composed. 'It is *likely* that' the former 'was composed twenty-five years before the Christian era.' This conjecture is based mainly on Vitruvius's mention of his patron, Julius Cæsar. But there is no mention of anybody under whose patronage the *Mānasāra* might have been composed.

The similarities so briefly outlined will be more convincing to those who have carefully studied both Vitruvius and the *Mānasāra*.

Those who are, however, inclined to think like myself and refuse to attribute all these similarities to mere chance, will be anxious to find out the connecting link between the two authorities. The question was put before the Oriental Conference held in Calcutta in January,

1922, to point out the link, about the existence of which there seems no reasonable doubt. A learned discussion was then held on the paper, but no suggestion has yet been received on this point.

There is the expedition of Alexander the Great to explain the Grecian influence on the Gāndhāra sculpture. The 'Questions of Menander' may perhaps stand for the title *Milinda-pañha.* There is, again, the *Romaka-siddhānta* to indicate the influence of the Roman astronomy upon the Indian *Jyotisha-śāstra,* which had, however, already established itself as one of the six essential limbs of the Veda, the most ancient extant lore of human learning. Similarly, the art of building, which is intimately connected with all living beings, was developed at the early Vedic period, even earlier than that at Mahenjo-daro. But the *Silpa-śāstra,* which is but an analysis and commentary of the art, was necessarily evolved much later. There are reasons to think that the *Mānasāra* is not the first work in which the 'essence of measurement and the system of proportions' were codified in the form of *Śāstra,* though this may be the standard treatise.

Until the missing link is found, it is, however, possible to think that there was some work or works, or some floating traditions, which influenced both treatises. It will, therefore, serve no useful purpose in trying to further develop the nature of the various similarities between Vitruvius and the *Mānasāra.* I would not, therefore, hazard an opinion at present as to the precise nature of the connexion between these two treatises. There are arguments which might support a claim of priority on behalf of either work. I shall be content, for the present, if the learned world be convinced that there are undeniable similarities between the two standard works and that these affinities do not seem to be accidental.

CHAPTER VII

AGE OF THE MĀNASĀRA

IN TRYING TO establish, in the preceding chapter, a relation of influence between Vitruvius and the *Mānasāra*, one of my objects was to find out a landmark for the latter, as the date of the former is known approximately.

'From the fragments of inscriptions relative to the Vitruvia family found in the neighbourhood of Farmiae (the present Mola di Gaeta), is has been presumed, without a great stretch of probability, that it was in this territory Vitruvius was born. The age in which he lived was doubtless between the time of the death of Julius Cæsar and the battle of Actium, though some have assigned it to the reign of Titus. But his omission of the mention of a great number of magnificent buildings, erected after the time of Augustus, and his especial mention of the theatre of Pompey as the only one of stone, sufficiently prove that such a conjecture is not warranted by circumstances. The dedication, moreover, points to Augustus as the patron [of Vitruvius] and the incident of C. Julius, the son of Masanissa, who was born in the army of Julius Cæsar, having lodged with him, as related in the third chapter of his eighth book, seems clearly to indicate the time of his existence. It is likely that the following treatise (of Vitruvius) was composed when he was advanced in life, and that it was presented to his patron after he had assumed the title of Augustus, that is, twenty-five years before the Christian era, inasmuch as he speaks of a temple erected to Augustus, in his Basilica at Fano.'[1]

The other landmark may perhaps be supplied by the following thesis admitted by Leiden University. 'There seems to have been a relation of indebtedness between the *Mānasāra*, on the one hand, and on the other hand, the architectural portions of the *Agni-Purāṇa*, the *Garuḍa-Purāṇa*, the *Matsya-Purāṇa*, and the *Bhavishya-Purāṇa*, the *Kāmikāgama*, the *Suprabhedāgama*, and the *Bṛihat-saṁhitā*.' The reasons for and the arguments in favour of such a belief have been discussed in great detail elsewhere,[2] and need not be repeated here. For further scrutiny and more minute comparison, the *Bṛihat-saṁhitā*

[1] Professor Gwilt, Preface, xii.

[2] *See* pp. 186–209.

of Varāhamihira, one of the nine gems[1] at the court of a mythical Vikramāditya, is selected. Professor Kern has given a probable date, A. D. 550, to the *Bṛihat-saṁhitā.* The ages of the *Purāṇas* and the *Āgamas* mentioned in the thesis are more conjectural.

Although primarily not a treatise on architecture, the *Bṛihat-saṁhitā* has devoted five chapters[2] (LIII, LVI, LVII, LVIII and LXXIX) to this art. Three of these, called *Vāstu-vidyā* or the science of architecture, *Prāsāda-lakshaṇa* or the description of temples under twenty types, and *Śayyāsana-lakshaṇa* or the description of bedsteads and couches, deal with architecture proper, and the other two, called *Vajralepa* or the first casting of image, and *Pratimā-lakshaṇa* or the description of images, briefly refer to sculpture. The following similarities between the *Mānasāra* and *Bṛihat-saṁhitā* may be noticed :

	Mānasāra	*Bṛihat-saṁhitā*
Origin and development of the science of architecture ..	I, 1	LIII, 1.
Objects of architecture	III	LIII, 2–3 (details differ).
Testing of oil ..	IV–V	LIII, 95–97, 85–92, 115–117.
Site plan ..	VII	LIII, 42–69, 83–84.
Offerings to deities	VIII	LIII, 99–100.
Dimension of storeys	XI	LIII, 4–26, LVI, 29–30.
Columns ..	XV	LIII, 27–30, 112–113, 121–123.
Temple-buildings ..	XVIII	LVI, 3–8 (site), 9 (ground), 10–16 (general), 17–19 (twenty types).
One-storeyed buildings	XIX	LVI, 23, 26.
Five-storeyed buildings	XXIII	LVI, 27.

[1] धन्वन्तरिः क्षपणकोऽमरसिंहशङ्कुवेतालभट्टघटकर्परकालिदासाः।
ख्यातो वराहमिहिरो नृपतेः सभायां रत्नानि वै वररुचिर्नव विक्रमस्य॥
—(ज्योतिर्विदाभरण, Kern, B. S. 17).

The existence of these gems as contemporaries has been held to be untenable.

[2] This refers to Kern's edition published by Royal Asiatic Society, London. In some other editions, for instance, in that of Sudhākara Dvivedi, Benares, Vikrama era 1658, these chapters have got a different numbering. Our references to the *Bṛihat-saṁhitā* are mostly to Kern's edition.

	Mānasāra	*Bṛihat-saṁhitā*
Six-storeyed buildings	XXIV	LVI, 22.
Seven-storeyed buildings ..	XXV	LVI, 24.
Eight-storeyed buildings	XXVI	LVI, 21.
Ten-storeyed buildings	XXVIII	LVI, 20.
Halls and pavilions	XXXIII, XXXIV	LIII, 118.
Situation and measurements of houses ..	XXXVI	LIII, 70.
Ceremonial entry into a new y-built house ..	XXXVII	LIII, 125.
Situation and measurement of doors	XXXVIII, XXXIX	LIII, 26–27, 70–82 LVI, 10. 12–16.
Phalli	LII	LVIII, 53–55.
Images of female deities ..	LIV	LVIII, 56.
Images in general ..	LXIV	LVIII, 31–52, 57–58 (ends abruptly).
Largest type of ten-*tāla* measures ..	LXV	LVIII, 4–30.
First casting of images ..	LXVIII	LVIII, 1–8.

An elaborate discussion has already been introduced regarding the types of buildings[1] and the five orders.[2] Two other points of special and general importance may be elaborated here.

The site-plans are treated under twenty-four schemes in the *Mānasāra*. Of these, descriptions in detail are given of the eighth and the ninth schemes, which consist respectively of sixty-four and eighty-one squares. In the *Mānasāra* it is stated, by way of explanation, that these two plans were much in use. Varāhamihira also has described only these two plans. In the *Bṛihat-saṁhitā* there is not

[1] *See* pp. 187–197. [2] *See* pp. 201–206.

the slightest reference to the other twenty-two schemes. As is usual with him, Varāhamihira has changed the names or location of the squares here and there. Another striking point of similarity is that only the square plans are described in both the treatises, although in the *Mānasāra* five shapes or forms are given to the buildings. Varāhamihira also has referred to the round type of buildings. Corresponding to these shapes there should be the ground plans also. But these are unexpectedly missing in the *Mānasāra* and also in the *Bṛihat-saṁhitā*. The details of round or circular plans and also of triangular plans, both consisting of eighty-one squares, have been quoted from a mythical *Bharata-muni* by Bhaṭṭotpala, a commentator of the *Bṛihat-saṁhitā*. So, in matter of such a striking omission also, Varāhamihira seems to have faithfully followed the *Mānasāra*, Garga, or whatever else his sources might have been.

The other point proposed to be discussed here is that concerning the sources of the *Bṛihat-saṁhitā* in architectural matters. Varāhamihira says that the science of architecture has come down to him from Brahmā (Kamalabhū) through several generations of sages. He further admits that all matters relating to architecture are taken from Garga, and small portions of the architectural treatises of Manu and others have been put in from memory.[1]

The names of the sages passed over here may be gathered together from casual references. Mention is made of Vasishṭha, Maya, Viśvakarman, Bhāskara and Nagnajit.[2] The *Purāṇas* are not mentioned by Varāhamihira. But some of the *Purāṇas* are no doubt earlier than the *Bṛihat-saṁhitā*.[3]

[1] प्रासादलक्षणमिदं कथितं समासाद् ।
गर्गेण यद्विरचितं तदिहास्ति सर्वम् ॥
मन्वादिभिर्विरचितानि पृथूनि यानि ।
तत्संस्मृतिं प्रति मयात्र कृतोऽधिकारः ॥—(*Bṛihat-saṁhitā*, LVI, 30–31).

[2] चतुरङ्गुलं वशिष्ठः कथयति नेत्रान्तकर्णयोर्विवरम् ।—LVIII, 8.
मयकथितो योगोयं विज्ञेयो वज्रसङ्घातः ।—LVII, 8.
भूमिकाङ्गुलमानेन मयस्याष्टोत्तरं शतम् ।
सार्धहस्तत्रयं चैव कथितं विश्वकर्मणा ॥—LVII, 29.
सर्वप्रतिमास्वेवं शुभाशुभं भास्करोक्तसमम् ।—LVIII, 52.
आस्यं सकेशनिचयं षोडशदैर्ध्येण नग्नजित् ।—LVIII, 15.
नग्नजिता तु चतुर्दशदैर्घ्येण द्राविडं कथितम् ।—VIII, 4.

[3] *See* pp. 277–278.

It has been shown that with regard to the techincal names and other details of the twenty types under which temple-buildings are described, the *Matsya-Purāṇa* (Chapter CCLXIX, vv. 28–53), the *Bhavishya-Purāṇa* (Chapter CXXX, vv. 27–35), and the *Bṛihat-saṁhitā* (Chapter LVI, vv. 20–28) are identical.[1] The *Bhavishya-Purāṇa* (Chapter CXXX, vv. 15–26, 36 and 37, 27–35) can be read, letter for letter, in the *Bṛihat-saṁhitā* (LVI, 8–19, 30, 20–28). When verses 22, 36 and 37 of the former are compared with the identical verses 15, 29 and 30 of the latter, it seems as if Varāhamihira were the debtor.[2] It should be noted that the linguistic defects of the *Bhavishya-Purāṇa* are removed in the *Bṛihat-saṁhitā*.

Similar illustrations can be drawn from the *Matsya-Purāṇa* and the *Brihat-saṁhitā* also. For instance,[3] of the former, verses 2 (Chapter CCLV), 19 and 20 (chapter CCLXX) can be compared with the latter in respect of LIII, 28, and LVI, 12, 13. Varāhamihira's is apparently the improved version in the revised edition. On this ground one is tempted to place these *Purāṇas* before the *Bṛihat-saṁhitā*. But

[1] *See* pp. 190–195.

[2] शैलमङ्गल्यविहगः श्रीवृक्षः स्वस्तिकैर्घटैः ।
मानाष्टमेन भागेन प्रतिमा स्यात्सपिण्डिका ।। (22).
सहस्रत्रितयं चैव कथितं विश्वकर्मणा ।। (36).
प्राहुः स्थपतयश्चात्र मतमेकं विपश्चितः ।
कपोतपालिनीयुक्तमतो गच्छति तुल्यताम् ।। (37).
and शेषं मङ्गल्यविहगैः श्रीवृक्षैः स्वस्तिकैर्घटैः ।
मिथुनैः पत्रपल्लीभिः प्रमथैश्चोपशोभयेत् ।। (15).
सार्द्धं हस्तत्रयं चैव कथितं विश्वकर्मणा ।। (29).
प्राहुः स्थपतयश्चात्र मतमेकं विपश्चितः ।
कपोतपालिसंयुक्ता न्यूना गच्छन्ति तुल्यताम् ।। (30).

[3] रुचकश्चतुरःस्यात्त्वष्टास्त्रो वज्र ेच्यते । (255, 2).
and समचतुरस्त्रो रुचको वज्र ोऽष्टास्रिर्द्विवज्र को द्विगुणः ।—LIII, 28.
विस्तारार्धो भवेद्गर्भो भित्तयोऽन्याः समन्ततः ।
गर्भपादेन विस्तीर्णं द्वारं त्रिगुणायतम् ।। (270, 19).
and विस्तारार्धो भवेग्दर्भो भित्तयोऽन्याः समन्ततः ।
गर्भपादेन विस्तोर्णं द्वारं द्विगुणमुच्छ्रितम् ।।—LVI, 12.
again तथा द्विगुणविस्तीर्णमुखस्तद्वदुदम्बरः ।
विस्तारपादप्रतिमं बाहुल्यं शाखयोः स्मृतम् ।। (270, 20).
and उच्छ्रायात्पादविस्तीर्णा शाखा तद्वदुदम्बरः ।
विस्तारपादप्रतिमं बाहुल्यं शाखयोः स्मृतम् ।। —LVI. 13.

Varāhamihira himself has not admitted his debt to these authorities. In these circumstances priority might be claimed for him.

There is one other point which deserves special notice. In the *Matsya-Purāṇa* eighteen professors[1] of the science of architecture are mentioned, namely, Bhṛigu, Atri, Vasishṭha, Viśvakarman, Maya, Nārada, Nagnajit, Viśālāksha, Purandara, Brahman, Kumāra, Nandīśa (Śiva), Śaunaka, Garga, Vāsudeva, Aniruddha, Śukra, and Vṛihaspati. Of these eighteen professors, Garga, Maya, Viśvakarman, Vasishṭha and Nagnajit have also been mentioned in the *Bṛihat-saṁhitā*. Varāhamihira, the author of the *Bṛihat-saṁhitā*, has included Bhāskara and Manu, who are not met with in the *Matsya-Purāṇa*. The identity of these mythical sages is a vexatious matter in Sanskrit literature. One Bhāskara or Bhāskarāchārya was the author of the *Līlāvatī* and the *Siddhānta-śiromani*. Of Manu we shall presently speak more. But the *Matsya-Purāṇa* does not include these names in its lists, nor does it mention Varāhamihira.

In the *Mānasāra* there is a list of thirty-two authorities, namely, Viśvakarman, Viśveśa, Viśva-sāra, Prabodhaka, Vṛita, Maya, Tvashṭar, Manu, Nala, Māna-vid, Māna-kalpa, Māna-sāra, Māna-bodha, Prashṭar, Viśva-bodha, Naya, Ādisāra, Viśāla, Viśva-kāśyapa, Vāstu-bodha, Mahātantra, Vāstu-vidyāpati, Parāśarīyaka, Kāla-yupa,

[1] *Matsya-Purāṇa*, Chap. CCLV, 2–4.
Compare :

इति प्रोक्तं वास्तुशास्त्रं पूर्वं गर्गाय धीमते ।
गर्गात्पराशरः प्राप्तस्तम्मात्प्राप्तो बृहद्रथः ॥
बृहद्रथाद्विश्वकर्मा प्राप्तवान् वास्तुशास्त्रकम् ।
स एव विश्वकर्मा जगतो हितायाकथयत्पुनः ॥
वासुदेवादिषु पुनर्भूलोकं भक्तितोऽब्रवीत् ॥
—(*Viśva-karma-prakāśa*, Benares, 1888, XIII, 25 to 27).

प्रोक्तानि पंचरात्राणि सप्तरात्राणि वै मया ॥
व्यवस्तानि मुनिभिर्लोके पर्चाविशति संख्यया ।
हयशीर्षं तन्त्रमाद्यं तन्त्रं त्रैलोक्यमोहनम् ॥
वैभवं पौष्करं तन्त्रं प्रह्लादं गार्ग्यगालवम् ।
नारदीयं च संप्रश्नं शाण्डिल्यं वैश्वकं तथा ॥
सत्योक्तं शौनकं तन्त्रं वासिष्ठं ज्ञानसागरम् ।
स्वायंभुवं कापिलं च तार्क्ष्यं नारायणीयकम् ।
आत्रेयं नारसिंहाख्यमानन्दाख्यं तथारुणकम् ।
बौधायनं तथार्षं तु विश्वोक्तं तस्य सारतः ॥
—(*Agni-Purāṇa*, Chap. XXXIX, v. 1–5).

Chaitya, Chitraka, Avarya, Sādhakasāra-saṁhitā, Bhānu, Indra, Lokajña, and Saura. In the opening verse it is stated that the science of architecture has come down to the sage Mānasāra from Śiva, Brahmā, and Vishṇu, through Indra, Bṛihaspati, Nārada, and all other sages. In a mythical genealogy of the artists it is further stated that from the four faces of Brahmā originated the four heavenly architects, namely, Viśvakarman, Maya, Tvashṭar, and Manu. Their four sons, called respectively, Sthapati or the chief architect, Sūtra-grāhin or the designer, Vardhaki or the painter, and Takshaka or the carpenter, represent the guild of the modern architects.[1]

It should be noted that Viśvakarman, Maya, Manu, and Tvashṭar[2] are mentioned twice, once to represent the heavenly architects, and again as modern architects. In the same sense Indra is also mentioned twice.

Viśvakarman and Maya, to whom many extant architectural treatises are ascribed, are common in the *Mānasāra*, the *Matsya-Purāṇa*, and the *Bṛihat-saṁhitā*. The *Mānasāra* and the *Matsya-Purāṇa* have, therefore, in common five authorities, namely, Bṛihaspati, Indra (under the name Purandara in the *Purāṇa*), Viśālāksha (*alias* Viśāla in the *Mānasāra*), Viśvakarman, and Maya. The *Mānasāra* and the *Bṛihat-saṁhitā* have in common Viśvakarman, Maya, and Manu.

Viśvakarman, etymologically implying the Creator of the universe, is more or less a professional name for an architect. Manu is less so. This is a generic name. Mention is made of fourteen Manus,[3] namely, Svāyaṁbhuva, Svārochisha, Auttami, Tāmasa, Raivata, Chākshusha, Vaivasvata, Sāvarṇi, Daksha-sāvarṇi, Brahma-sāvarṇi, Dharma-savārṇi, Rudra-sāvarṇi, Rauchya-daiva-sāvarṇi, and Indra-sāvarṇi. Manu is a sort of second Creator, the Indian Adam, representative of man and father of human race. It seems clear, however, that there must have been an architect Manu also in the ordinary sense of the term, because with him several architectural works are associated. He is stated in the *Rāmāyaṇa*[4] to have built the ancient city of Ayodhyā, the capital of king Rāma.

[1] Chapters LXVIII, I, II, *see* pp. 155, note 3; 97, 98.

[2] Tvashṭar is mentioned in Padmagupta's *Navasāhasaṅka-charita*, as the sculptor of a crystal *śivaliṅga* (phallus).

[3] *Manusaṁhitā*, I, 63.

[4] अयोध्या नाम नगरी तत्रासील्लोकविश्रुता।
मनुना मानवेन्द्रेण या पुरी निर्मिता स्वयम्॥—(*Rāmāyaṇa*, *Ādikāṇḍa*, verse 6).

Maya is a more historical person. Several existing architectural treatises are ascribed to him.[1] He may not be as old as the *Zend-Āvesta*. Ahura-Mazda and Maya-Asura are perhaps not one and the same person. But he is mentioned in unmistakable terms as the architect of a wonderful council hall, of which it is stated there could not be any parallel in the world of the mortals, and whereon all heavenly ideas were depicted in bricks and stones. He declares himself as a great poet of architecture (*mahākavi*), a Ruskin, among the rivals of gods, and he is their Viśvakarman, who was the heavenly architect among the gods.[2] The town of Ratnavatī is stated to have been built by Maya, the prince of demons, in Padmagupta's *Nava-sāhasaṅka-charita*.

Like Manu, Maya is also a generic name. He is also known by some other personal names.[3] So the Maya of the *Mānasāra*, of the *Matsya-Purāṇa*, and of the *Bṛihat-saṁhitā* may not be one and the same person. It is just possible that there might have been a Maya who borrowed from, or based his treatises in any case, upon the *Mānasāra*.[4] In fact it is perfectly clear from the list of authorities quoted from the *Mānasāra* that there must have been at least one more Mānasāra, from whom or from which our *Mānasāra* has borrowed. It has also

[1] *See* the writer's *Encyclopaedia*, Appendix I, where a note on the latest discoveries of the Maya civilization in America is also given.

[2] अहं हि विश्वकर्मा वै दानवानां महाकविः।
सोऽहं वै त्वत्कृते किञ्चित्कर्तुमिच्छामि पाण्डवाः॥ (5)
ततो विचिन्त्य मनसा लोकनाथः प्रजापतिः।
चोदयामास तं कृष्णः सभा वै क्रियतामिति॥ (9)
यदि त्वं कर्तुकामोऽसि प्रियं शिल्पवतां वर।
धर्मराजस्य दैतेय यादृशीमिह मन्यसे॥ (10)
यां कृतां नानुकुर्वन्ति मानवाः प्रेक्ष्याधिष्ठिताः।
मनुष्यलोके सकले तादृशीं कुरु वै सभाम्॥ (11)
यत्र दिव्यानभिप्रायान् पश्येम हि कृतांस्त्वया।
आसुरान्मानुषांश्चैव सभां तां कुरु वै मय॥ (12)

—(*Mahābhārata*, *Sabhā-parvan*, Chap. I, 5, 9–12).

The famous commentator Nilakaṇṭha adds the following note:
विश्वं कर्मकृति साध्यं यस्य स विश्वकर्मा। महाकविः शिल्पपण्डितः। आसुरान् मानुषान् इत्युपलक्षणं देवगन्धर्वादीनामपि अभिप्रायान् लेपचित्रे लेख्यचित्रे च चतुर्दशभुवनान्तरस्थतत्तज्जातीय स्वाभाविकनानाविधलीलाप्रदर्शनेन मनोवृत्तीः पश्येम यद्दर्शनेन ब्रह्माण्डान्तर्वर्ति सर्वं वस्तुजातं दृष्टप्रायं भवतीत्यर्थः।

[3] *See* pp. 159–161.

[4] *See* p. 16.

been pointed out[1] that the term " Mānasāra " has been used to imply both a person and a treatise. The uncertain identities and the confusing chronology are indeed stumbling blocks in the field of Sanskrit researches.

In all items of comparison between the *Mānasāra* and the cognate works, we have seen[2] that the *Mānasāra* contains fuller lists. In the present instance also there are more than thirty-two authorities mentioned in the *Mānasāra*, while the *Matsya-Purāṇa* is content with a list of eighteen, and the *Bṛihat-saṁhitā* has specified only seven. But none of these three treatises has admitted the authority of either of the other two. From this it would appear as if they were quite ignorant of the existence of one another, being separated by an insuperable gap in time or space. Such a relationship is untenable, I should say improbable, between the *Matsya-Purāṇa*, the *Bhavishya-Purāṇa*, and the *Bṛihat-saṁhitā* in any case, unless, however, we choose to suppose that there might have been an unknown authority or some floating tradition by which these treatises have been influenced in the same way, even to the extent of chapter and verse, but without any knowledge of one another. I have failed to satisfy myself with such a hypothesis. For we have seen identical passages in these works.[3] All these three contain the same list of twenty types of buildings, bearing the same technical names and identical in other details.[4] Buildings are described under certain types in all the architectural works. Their technical names have no signification. Unless one list is copied from the other these names need not be identical. In fact such is the case with regard to the fuller list in the *Mānasāra*. Therein we have seen ninety-eight types of buildings described under more architectural divisions and with fuller achitectural details than in these non-architectural works.[5] Except in one or two solitary instances like *Kailāśa*, the names of these types of buildings are not identical. There are certain similarities. For instance, the *merukānta* of the *Mānasāra* is read simply as *meru* in the *Purāṇas* and the *Bṛihat-saṁhitā*. This is certainly an improved reading, first, because *meru* as the name of a mountain or as a geographical term is well known in Sanskrit

[1] *See* Preface, First edition (*Indian Architecture*, p. 3).
[2] *See* pp. 187–208.
[3] *See* pp. 245–247.
[4] *See* pp. 191–195.
[5] *See* pp. 187–189.

literature,[1] and secondly, *kānta*, in the expression *merukānta*, is meaningless. Similarly, the reading *vṛitta* of the *Purāṇas* and the *Bṛihat-saṁhitā* is an improved version, a good amended form of *vivṛita* of the *Mānasāra*. Almost similar is the case with regard to another architecturally very important object, namely, the column or order, for the columns are stated by the authorities to be the regulator of the whole composition. In this case also the *Mānasāra* contains a fuller list. It has two sets of five technical names for the orders, while the *Matsya-Purāṇa* and the *Bṛihat-saṁhitā* contain only one set of the five orders. The names of these orders in the *Mānasāra* are different from those in the *Purāṇa* and the *Saṁhitā*, but Varāhamihira has given the very same five names to the orders as the *Matsya-Purāṇa*, and they have also the very same eight names for the mouldings or the component parts of a column. The *Mānasāra*, as in all other cases, has a fuller list of mouldings also. It contains more than forty-seven mouldings for the pedestal, base, shaft, and entablature, the shaft being given five special mouldings. And as in the case of the types of buildings, there are some names of mouldings, for instance, *ghaṭa* and *hāra*, common in the *Mānasāra*, the *Matsya-Purāṇa*, and the *Bṛihat-saṁhitā*.

So in three important architectural matters, namely, the preceding authorities, the types of buildings, and the orders and their component parts, the *Mānasāra* has fuller lists than those in the *Matsya-Purāṇa* and the *Bṛihat-saṁhitā*, which are exactly identical in these matters. In these circumstances one is ordinarily likely to think that a later work only can make a thing more complete. But there is another essential point to consider, namely, that the *Mānasāra* is avowedly an architectural treatise, while the *Matsya-Purāṇa* and the *Bṛihat-saṁhitā* are not. Their treatment of architectural matters is but casual, and in fact they have entirely left out purely architectural description. It is clear beyond doubt that the *Purāṇa* and the *Saṁhitā* must have consulted an architectural treatise for their information and guidance in achitectural matters, just as they have, certainly, based their references, for instance, on medicine, to a standard medical treatise. If the Mānasāra had an opportunity of consulting Varāhamihira or the *Matsya-Purāṇa*, the reading like *vivṛita* for *vṛitta*, or

[1] For instance, *Naishadhacharita*, 16, *Bhartṛihari*, *Vairāgya-Śataka*, 150, etc. Compare the terms like *Sumeru*, *Uttarameru*, etc.

[2] *See* pp. 201–206.

merukānta for *meru*, could not have remained unamended in it. Besides, if the *Mānasāra* had been composed after the works like the *Matsya-Purāṇa* and the *Bṛihat-saṁhitā*, why should it not have added these two to its long list of authorities? It would be no argument to say that the author of the *Mānasāra* may not have consulted these authorities or may have been quite ignorant of their existence. For, though not primarily works on architecture, the *Matsya-Purāṇa* and the *Bṛihat-saṁhitā* have been well known to subsequent literature, and we shall presently show that the author of the *Mānasāra* had an extensive knowledge of things from a wide study and observation.

In these circumstances, though ready to re-adjust my views in the light of new facts, my present impression is that there must have been a direct influence between the *Matsya-Purāṇa*, the *Bṛihat-saṁhitā*, and the *Bhavishya-Purāṇa*; while the connexion between these treatises and the *Mānasāra* may have been indirect. The age of the *Mānasāra*, however, is indicated by other things also, and these will be discussed presently.

There are only a few treatises wherein the term "Mānasāra" is mentioned. The *Agni-Purāṇa*, as already pointed out,[1] has some passages of uncertain meanings wherein the term occurs. For instance, it is stated that above the *śuka-nāsa* (*lit.* parrot's nose) or gargoyles, that is, the water-spout in a building, there should be a *vedi* or platform furnished with a neck. And this should be as prescribed in the *Mānasāra* (*mānasāraka*), or the object of it is to make a passage for refuse (*malasāraka*).[2] This latter interpretation seems untenable, for the adjective is used in the neuter singular and ordinarily would not qualify a feminine singular noun. If the first rendering be acceptable, the expression would form a separate clause, *iti mānasārakam*, meaning this is in accordance with the rules of the *Mānasāra*.

There are reasons to think that a relation of direct influence exists between the *Agni-Purāṇa* and the *Garuḍa-Purāṇa*.[3] And, through the latter, the former may be connected with the *Matsya-Purāṇa*, the *Bhavishya-Purāṇa*, and the *Bṛihat-saṁhitā*.[4]

The *Sukra-nīti* is another important work, which, though not an architectural treatise, deals largely with subjects relating to

[1] *See* Preface, First edition. Compare also p. 245, note 1.

[2] तदूर्ध्वं तु भवेद्वेदी सकण्ठा मनसारकम् ? (मानसारकम् or मलसारकम्) ।
—(*Agni-Purāṇa*, XLII, 17).

[3] *See* pp. 189–191.

[4] *See* pp. 191–195, and the writer's *Encyclopaedia*, under *Prāsāda*.

architecture and sculpture.[1] It is a work on royal polity ascribed to an author, Śukrāchārya, whose age has not been clearly established. It appears to be anterior to the *Matsya-Purāṇa* for the reason that the latter has included *Śukra* as one of its eighteen authorities.[2] The question of the identity of Śukrāchārya with this *Śukra* must necessarily come in. But there is hardly a satisfactory answer to give.

In the *Śukra-nīti* we notice, also, a large number of passages common to it with another work called the *Kāmandakīya-nīti*. This has been assigned by Dr. R. L. Mitra to the fourth century of the Christian era on the ground of its dedication to Chandra Gupta, existence of Hindu temples, and the absence of any trace of Buddhism in the fifth century A. D. when the Chinese traveller Fa-hien visited Java,-where, in the island of Bali, the work was discovered.[3]

This *Kāmandakīya-nīti*, which has apparently borrowed from the *Artha-śāstra* of Vishṇu Gupta,[4] seems, in its turn, to have been freely drawn upon by the *Agni-Purāṇa*.[5] This *Purāṇa*, we have shown, may have borrowed from the *Mānasāra* also.[6]

This introduction of the *Śukra-nīti*, the *Kāmandakīya-nīti*, and the *Artha-śāstra*, together with the *Matsya-Purāṇa*, the *Agni-Purāṇa*, and the *Mānasāra*, may appear as an episode. But a time may come when the inter-relation of all these treatises will be more satisfactorily established.

The next external references to thè name of *Mānasāra* are met

[1] Chapter IV, Section 4 (1) देवमन्दिरादिनिर्माणव्यवस्था, (2) प्रतिमानिर्माणव्यवस्था etc. (*see* details in Appendix I, in the writer's *Encyclopaedia*)

[2] Page 164.

[3] यस्य प्रभावाद्भुवनं शाश्वते पथि तिष्ठति।

आजहार नृचन्द्राय चन्द्रगुप्ताय मेदिनीम् ॥—(*Kāmandakīya-nīti*, 1-5).

Here, it is argued, Chandra Gupta refers to the first or second Chandra Gupta of the Imperial Gupta dynasty, who are assigned respectively to A. D. 320–326 and A. D. 375–413.

[4] नीतिशास्त्रामृतं धीमानर्थशास्त्रमहोदधेः।

समुद्दध्रे नमस्तस्मै विष्णुगुप्ताय वेधसे ॥

—(*Kāmandakīya*, L. 6).

Dr. Jacob places the *Artha-śāstra* in the fourth century B. C. (Berlin Academy *Seitzungaberichte*, 1911, pages 954–973, 1912, pp. 832–849). Professor Keith tends to bring it down to the second or first century B. C. (*J. R. A. S.*, 1915).

[5] Dr. R. L. Mitra, *Kāmandakīya*, *Bibl. Ind.*, p. 4.

[6] *See* pp. 110–118.

with in a famous prose romance, the *Daśa-Kumāra-Charita*,[1] by a very eminent author, Daṇḍin, who 'probably dates from the sixth century A. D.' Therein Mānasāra is repeatedly mentioned in unmistakable terms as the king of Malava (modern Mālwa), with whom was engaged in war king Rājahaṁsa of Magadha or Pāṭalīputra, the modern Patna. The latter was the father of Rājavāhana, the chief of the ten princes or *Daśa-Kumāra*, after whom the work is named.

Here is a possibility of the *Mānasāra* being connected with the king of Mālwa bearing the name Mānasāra. There are several works in the Sanskrit literature which seem to have been named after their patron, for instance, the *Skanda-Purāṇa* is supposed by some scholars to have been associated with the name of Skanda-Gupta of the Imperial Gupta dynasty. The *Harsha-charita* has undoubtedly been named after king Harsha. But nothing more is known about king Mānasāra of Mālwa, nor is anything stated, directly or indirectly, about him in the *Mānasāra* itself. On the other hand, the internal references to the expression *Mānasāra*, which have been already introduced elsewhere,[2] prove that the term has been used in three different senses, namely, a treatise, an architect, and a class of sages or professors of architecture bearing the surname, like Manu or Maya, or the professional epithet, *Mānasāra*. In none of these senses, however, would the king of Mālwa fit in. If he were a real personage and had any connexion with this standard treatise on architecture, and preferred to remain incognito, the author of the *Mānasāra* would have added a fourth ambiguity referring to his anonymous patron. In the body of the *Mānasāra* there are several passages, which will be presently discussed, evincing on the part of its author not only a clear knowledge of man and things of the then Magadha and Mālwa, but also of all other chief cities and the broadest divisions of India of his time.

[1] Edited by Kale, Bombay, 1917; *see* page 4, repetition below is felt unavoidably necessary:

(i) Page 4, para. 2, line 3—मगधनायको मालवेश्वरं प्रत्यग्रसंग्रामघस्मरं समुत्कटमानसारं मानसारं प्रति . . . संग्रामाभिलाषेण रोषेण महताविष्टो निर्ययौ।

(ii) Page 8, para. 1, line 8—मालवनाथो जयलक्ष्मीसनाथो मगधराज्यं प्राज्यं समाक्रम्य पुष्पपुरमध्यतिष्ठत्।

(iii) Pages 12–13—राजहंसो मुनिमभाषत, भगवन्, मानसारः प्रबलेन दैवबलेन मां निर्जित्य मद्भोग्यं राज्यमनुभवति।

(iv) Pages 13–14—अवन्तिसुन्दरी नाम मानसारनन्दिनी . . . नगरोपान्तरम्योद्याने विहारोत्कण्ठया मनोभवमर्चयन्ती रेमे।

[2] *See* Preface, *Indian Architecture*, First edition.

The third external reference to (the architect) Mānasāra is found in two epigraphical records of uncertain reading. In these unpublished documents the epigraphist reads the expression, which is used in two inscriptions to imply the name of an architect, as *Mānasarpa* and not *Mānasāra*. In the light of information presented for the first time in our volumes, the epigraphist may perhaps be ready to revise his reading of the expression when the inscriptions are properly edited and finally published.[1]

In an architectural compilation, *Silpa-saṁgraha*, of apparently a very late date, we have shown already[2] that the *Mānasāra* is quoted in its true form. About the worth of considering this reference I am rather doubtful. Not that I am unwilling to bring down the *Mānasāra*, but because there are several facts which cannot fit in to a very late date like A. D. 1830, when a manuscript[3] of the *Mānasāra* was copied. The compiler could have easily consulted the *Mānasāra*. even if the latter were placed side by side with Vitruvius, or before Maya-Asura of the *Mahābhārata*, or Ahura-Mazda of the *Zend-Āvesta*.

Of the internal evidences from the *Mānasāra* the following points may be considered.

For the orientation of buildings it was necessary for the Indian architects to ascertain the right cardinal points. For this purpose the *Mānasāra*, in agreement with all complete works on architecture, including Vitruvius, makes use of a gnomon,[4] obviously because the mechanism of the compass was not known to the ancient architects. For similar purpose the astronomical treatises[5] also, like the *Sūrya-siddhānta* and the *Līlāvatī* and the *Siddhānta-śiromaṇi* of Bhāskarāchārya, use the gnomon. The calculation of the shadow is the main object in this matter, and the gnomon is used simply to ascertain the shadow. The sun's rays falling on an object like the gnomon causes the shadow. So at first the obstructed light, which gives rise to the

[1] Epigraphist's Report, Madras, 1901, nos. 207, 209. *See* page 4, note 2; 130, note 5; 176.

[2] *See* page 106.

[3] Called 'C' in the description of manuscripts attached to our edition of the *Mānasāra*. 'B' is dated 1677 of the Śālivāhana era (1823); 'D' is dated 1656 of the Śaka era (1734). The remaining eight copies—A, E, F, G, H, I, J, K, are not dated.

[4] For full description, *see* the writer's *Encyclopaedia*, under *Śaṅku*.

[5] *Sūrya-siddhānta*, III, 1–4, *Līlāvatī*, part 2, section 4, Chap. II; *Siddhānta-śiromaṇi*, last part, Chap. VII, 36–49. Cf. Vitruvius, Book I, Chap. VI; Book IX, Chaps. IV, VIII. The actual process of working the gnomon for ascertaining the cardinal points and dialling is described in full details from all these authorities in the writer's *Encyclopaedia*, under *Śaṅku*.

shadow, must naturally be taken from the sun. But the sun's light is uncertain and cannot be adjusted according to the requirements of scientific and advanced study. It is, therefore, not difficult to believe that the later astronomers easily found some artificial and adjustable light to replace the natural and unadjustable light from the sun. In the *Mānasāra* only the sun's light is made use of, while in the *Sūrya-siddhānta* and other astronomical works lamp-light was used in order to measure the shadow. These latter works also followed an improved method in ascertaining the level whereupon the gnomon was erected in order to calculate the movement of the shadow accurately. The methods followed in the *Mānasāra* are antiquated. It seems, therefore, that the *Sūrya-siddhānta* and other astronomical works must come after the *Mānasāra*.

The next internal evidence presented here for consideration is that concerning the knowledge evinced in the *Mānasāra* of the most prosperous countries throughout India. We have seen that ninety-eight types of buildings are described in the *Mānasāra* under twelve divisions, namely, of one to twelve storeys. Although sixteen-storeyed or even seventeen-storeyed gate-houses (*gopuras*) are mentioned, religious or residential buildings are not erected beyond twelve storeys.[1] The technical names of buildings of one to eleven storeys are more or less poetical. But the buildings of twelve storeys, largest and most gorgeous of all edifices, bear more significant names.

They are called *Māgadha*, *Janaka*, *Madhya-kānta*, *Vaṁśaka*, *Virāṭa*, *Pāñchāla*, *Sphū(Gū)rjaka*, *Kerala*, *Drāviḍa*, and *Kāliṅga*. These are the names of ten countries which cover the length and breadth of India. At one time or another they seem to have been very prosperous, possessing as they did distinctive types of the largest and most magnificent edifices.

Magadha[2] is the country of South Bihar, where the Pāli language was spoken. Janaka, or the country of some twenty-one generations of Janaka kings, otherwise called Videha, with capital city Mithilā, is North Bihar, which corresponds to the modern Tirhut and Purniyā divisions, between the Gaṇḍakī and Kośī rivers. Madhya-kānta

[1] *See* pp. 52, 47–51, 111–113.

[2] Magadha is also mentioned in the *Daśakumāra-charita*, अस्ति मगधेषु पुष्पपुरी नाम नगरी, which was conquered by king Mānasāra of Mālava (*see* Preface, *Indian Architecture*, 1st Ed., note). But Mālwais not honoured with a separate type of twelve-storeyed buildings, and it would appear strange and unusual if this king Mānasāra were the patron of the *Mānasāra*, the standard work on architecture.

stands for the Madhya-deśa, the middle country, or the tract situated between the Himālayas and the Vindhya range to the east of Vināśana and to the west of Prayāga or Allahabad.[1] Some authorities make it the Doab. Vaṁśaka is the country of the Vatsa kings, of which Kauśāmbī was the capital city. It apparently bordered on Madhya-deśā. Virāṭa[2] is the country in the vicinity of the modern Jaipur, wherefrom the Pāñchāla country begins. The present town of Bairat is one hundred and fifty miles south of Delhi. Pāñchāla is the Punjab, 'with a little territory in the more immediate neighbourhood of Hastināpura,' extending north and west from Delhi, from the foot of the Himalayas to the Chambal, Ahi-chhatra being the capital city of North Pāñchāla or Rohilkhand, and Kāmpilya of South Pāñchāla or the Gangetic Doab.[3] The reading of the name of the country mentioned next is uncertain. It may be read as Gūrjaka for Gurjara, as mentioned in the *Pañchatantra* and the *Rājataraṅgiṇī*, instead of Sphūrjaka,[4] and identified with the country of Gujarat. Kerala is the country of Malabar proper, on the western coast, extending farther down from Gujarat. Then comes Drāviḍa[5] or

[1] हिमवद्विन्ध्ययोर्मध्यं यत्प्राग्विनशनादपि ।
प्रत्यगेव प्रयागाच्च मध्यदेशः स कीर्तितः ॥ —(Manu, II, 21).

[2] It was at the court of the king of Virāṭa that the Pāṇḍava princes and Draupadī passed the thirteenth year of their exile incognito. The Virāṭa princess Uttarā was married to Arjuna'ss on Abhimanyu, who, at the age of sixteen only, gallantly challenged simultaneously seven most famous generals of the Kaurava army at the battle of Kurukshetra.

According to the *Mahābhārata*, king Virāṭa's capital was called Matsya, which Cunningham finds in the neighbourhood of Jaipur. Wilson says: 'Dinajpoor Rungpoor, and Cooch Behar.' Apparently there was more than one country of this name and one would appear in Northern India. Manu (II, 19) places Matsya in Brahmarshi-deśa.

[3] According to the *Mahābhārata* (Smith's History, p. 348), it would seem to have occupied the Lower Doab. Manu (II, 19) places it near Kanauj. Wilson will have it extending north and west from Delhi, from the foot of the Himālaya to the Chambal, and separated by the Ganges into Northern and Southern Pāñchāla. Cunningham considers North Pāñchāla to be Rohilkhand, with the capital city Ahi-chhatra represented by the ruins near Rāmnagar; and the South Pāñchāla to be the Gangetic Doab, with the capital city Kāmpilya between Budāun and Farrukhābad.

[4] This term seems to mean literally something belonging to the first union of lovers, characterized by joy in the beginning and some expectation of fear in the end. Of the ten names, it should be noted, this is the only one which, as the name of a country, can be doubted, if the amended reading be not acceptable.

[5] As applied to the classification of Brahmans (Pāncha-Drāviḍa, namely, Drāviḍa Karnāṭa, Gurjara, Mahārāshṭra, and Tailaṅga), it has a much wider application embracing Gujarat, Mahārāshṭra, and all the southern countries.

the country, where the Tamil language is spoken, extending from Madras to Cape Comorin. This tract is roughly bounded by the Vindhya range on the north, where Madhyadeśa ends; Kerala or Malabar coast on the west; and Kaliṅga or Coromandal coast on the east. Kāliṅga implies the twelve-storeyed buildings of Kaliṅga,[1] the country along the Coromandal coast, north of Madras, wherefrom the Drāviḍa country begins. It is clear, therefore, that India, comprising these ten provinces, extends from the Himalayas on the north to the Cape Comorin on the south, from Bihar, including perhaps North Bengal, on the east, to the Punjab and Gujarat on the west.

A number of questions may now arise. Did these ten provinces exist in a prosperous condition at any one time in the history of India? Did they ever possess gorgeous edifices of twelve storeys admitting of ten different types? How could the author of the *Mānasāra* come to know of them. Was the description of these buildings based on the details of the existing edifices, or was it meant to be an injunction to be followed in erecting edifices in these countries? Is there any reason to think that the *Mānasāra* is a technical treatise on architecture and not a work on polytechnics, like the *Bṛihat-saṁhitā*, dealing casually with architecture and sculpture, nor an encyclopaedic work like the *Purāṇas* of northern India and the *Āgamas* of southern India, which, too, have incorporated within them architectural and sculptural, as well as literary, religious, and scientific subjects?

That the *Mānasāra* is an avowedly architectural treatise meant for professional students of architecture and written by an architect there need be no doubt. This will be clear beyond doubt even to a casual reader of this volume, not to speak of those who care to look up the writer's *Encyclopaedia* and Text or Translation of the *Mānasāra*. To me it is, further, clear that the *Mānasāra* was largely based on details gathered together from the existing buildings and partly on details from the existing literature on the subject. It was, of course, meant to be a guide book, but it never aimed at being the sort of poem which is read for the beauty of its language or the general interest of its theme. It is very likely that the author of the *Mānasāra* was aware of the condition of buildings existing in the then India

[1] The *Calingae proximi mari* of Pliny.
जगन्नाथात्समारभ्य कृष्णातीरान्तगः प्रिये ।
कलिङ्गदेशः संप्रोक्तो वाममार्गपरायणः ॥ —(*Tantras*, *see* Apte's Dictionary).
उत्कलाद्दर्शितपथः कलिङ्गाभिमुखो ययौ । —(*Rāmāyaṇa*, IV, 38).

comprising the ten provinces mentioned above. There might not have existed simultaneously buildings of twelve storeys in all the ten provinces. What seems to be really meant is the distinctive types of magnificent buildings belonging to each of these provinces.[1] For the *Mānasāra* is not a history of buildings of any country, it is a guide book, and as such it must give illustrations and generalize its findings. It matters not, therefore, if these countries were not equally prosperous at any time. It is sufficient that these countries had flourished and that they were well known in the history of India, and also that everyone of these could at some time or other claim prosperity and magnificence. Of these, *Pāñchāla* and *Drāviḍa* are stated to be of the smallest types, next higher in size and importance are *Madhya-deśa*, *Kāliṅga*. *Virāṭa*, *Kerala*, and *Vaṁśaka*, the largest and most important are *Māgadha* and *Janaka*. *Sphūrjaka* is not specified (*Mānasāra*, XXX, 10–36).

The last question to answer is how the author of the *Mānasāra* came to know of these provinces or divisions of India. If these provinces were autonomous and independent of each other the knowledge of them must have been received through literature, should a tour all over India for a purpose like this be thought an improbability in days before the establishment of the British Government. If, on the other hand, the internal affairs of all these provinces were settled by a common and central authority, who alone could decide upon a policy for common good, and under whom alone guide books like the *Mānasāra* discussing general methods and principles of buildings for all provinces could flourish, there must have been an empire comprising all or most of these countries. The probability of the latter view is strengthened by the consideration of the styles of architecture, apart from the types of buildings discussed above. These styles are also designated by geographical names, which imply much broader divisions, namely, Northern, Southern, and Eastern. They are called *Nāgara*, *Drāviḍa*, and *Vesara*. In the case of some architectural objects *Vesara* admits of two other branches, namely, *Andhra* and *Kaliṅga*, the three together constituting *Tri-kaliṅga* or three *Kaliṅgas*.

[1] About the existence of these types there need not be much doubt, because, for instance, *Māgadha*, *Pāñchāla*, *Drāviḍa*, and others are used to imply types other than of buildings. For instance, *Māgadha* stands for a Prākṛit language? a tribe of people born of a Vaiśya mother and Kshatriya father; *Pāñchāla* stands for one of the four styles of composition; and *Drāviḍa* for a language, a class of Brahmans, etc. The point is sufficiently elaborated later on.

The *Nāgara* style is distinguished by its quadrangular shape, the *Drāviḍa* by its octagonal or hexagonal shape, and the *Vesara* by its round shape.[1]

'So far as is yet known, we cannot point to any buildings . . . of very early date, or before the sixth or seventh century, if indeed quite so early.'[2] This is the statement made by authorities like Fergusson, Burgess, Smith, and others. This may be referred to all parts and all styles of India. Cunningham has gathered together fragments of what he calls the Gupta style, of which, however, no single example in its entirety can be cited.

The Dravidian 'temples generally consist of a square base ornamented externally by thin tall pilasters, and containing the cell in which the image is kept. In front of this may be added a *manṭapam* or hall, or even two such, but they are not characteristic of the style. Over the shrine rises the *śikhara*, of pyramidal form, but

[1] वेदाश्रं नागरं प्रोक्तं वस्वश्रं द्राविडं भवेत् ।
सुवृत्तं वेसरं प्रोक्तमन्ध्रं स्यात्तु षडश्रकम् ॥ —(*Mānasāra*, XLIII, 124–25).

This is applied to cars and chariots. The rules referring to buildings proper are given in XVIII, 92–104 ; XXVI, 76 ; XXI, 72–73, etc. ; referring to sculpture proper, *see* for instance, LII, 78–100 ; LIII, 46–47 53–54, etc.

द्वारभेदमिदं प्रोक्तं जातिभेदं ततः श्रृणु ।
नागरं द्राविडं चैव वेसरं च त्रिधा मतम् ।
कण्ठादारभ्य वृत्तं यत्तद्वेसरमिति स्मृतम् ॥
ग्रीवामारभ्य चाष्टाश्रं विमानं द्राविडाख्यकम् ।
सर्वं वै चतुरश्रं यत्प्रासादं नागरंत्विदम् ॥—(*Suprabhedāgama*, XXXI, 37-39).

These also refer to buildings. For rules referring to sculpture, *see* the *Kāmikāgama*, LXV, 6–7, 12–18, and the *Bṛihat-saṁhitā*, LVIII, 4 (Kern's edition).

'An interesting record from Holal is the label cut out on the capita of a finely carved pillar in the Amṛiteśvara temple. It is called in the inscription a Sūkāra pillar. Speaking of the sculptor who made it, the record says that he, Bammaja, the pupil of Pādoja of Soge, was a Viśvakarman, i.e., the architect of the gods in this Kali age, the master of the sixty-four arts and sciences, the clever builder of the sixty-four varieties of mansions, and the architect who had invented [?discovered] the four types [styles] of buildings, viz., *Nāgara*, *Kāliṅga*, *Drāviḍa*, and *Veśara*.' (Progress report of the Assistant Archaeological Superintendent for Epigraphy, Southern Circle, 1914–15, p. 90.)

In another inscription (*Ep. Carnat.*, Vol. VII, Part I, Sorab Taluq, Inscription no. 275, Roman Text, p. 92, Translation, p. 46, note 1) these styles are called '*Drāviḍa*, *Bhūmijia*, and *Nāgara*,' of which *Bhūmija*, which literally means, 'grown up on the spot,' may refer to the *Veśara* style, with *Kāliṅga* and *Āndhra* as its two branches.

These and many other quotations will be found in the writer's *Encyclopaedia*, under *Nāgara*.

[2] *Imperial Gazetteer of India*, Vol. II, p. 171, para. 2.

PLATE XXXVII

CHANDAKESAVA TEMPLE OF BELUR, OF STAR-SHAPED PLAN

Page 258

PLATE XXXVIII

HOYSALESVARA TEMPLE, HALEBID

always divided into storeys and crowned by a small dome, either circular or polygonal in shape. Another special feature of these temples is the *gopurams* or great gateways, placed in front of them at the entrances to the surrounding courts, and often on all the four sides. In general design they are like the *vimānas* or shrines, but about twice as wide as deep, and very frequently far more important than the temples themselves. Another feature is the cornices of double curve; in other Indian styles the cornices are mostly straight and sloping downwards. As the contemporary northern styles are characterized by the prevalence of vertical lines, the Dravidian is marked by the prevalence of horizontal mouldings and shadows, and the towers and *gopurams* are storeyed. Then the more important temples are surrounded by courts enclosing great corridors or *prākāras*, and pillared halls.'

'The square rathas were evidently models of Buddhist *vihāras* and became the designs from which the temples proper or *vimānas* of Southern India were for long copied, and further, the oblong rathas, like Arjuna's temple, appeared to have given the first form to the great gateways or *gopurams*.'[1] Pierced stone windows are found at Ellora and other places.

Regarding the Chālukyan style, which covers the Hyderabad territory, the Central Provinces, Berar, the Marathi-speaking and a part of the Kanarese-speaking districts of the Bombay presidency, it is stated that 'the earliest temples within this area, however, are not very clearly marked off from the Dravidian and the more northern style—some of them have distinctly northern spires, and others are closely allied to the southern style.' For instance, 'the old temples of Pāpanāth at Pattadakal presents a curious combination of styles. The body of the temple is Dravidian, but the *Śikhara* is a curious approximation to the form of the early northern Hindu or Indo-Aryan order, while in details the temple shows a strong leaning to the Dravidian.' 'Still in Mysore, Dharwar, and Belgaum, as well as in Berār and Maharatha districts, sufficient remains still exist to illustrate the various development of the (Chālukyan) style.'[2]

'In the Chālukyan temples the corners are often made prominent by increments placed over them, or the whole plan is star-shaped,

[1] Burgess cites (*Imp. Gazetteer*, II, pp. 172, 171) as examples of temples at Madura, Rāmeśwaram, Tinnevelly, Śrirangam, Kanchipuram, Pattadakal (Virūpākhsha temple), Ellora (rock cut Kailāśa temple).

[2] Burgess, *ibid*, p. 175.

the projecting angles having equal adjacent faces lying in a circle as in the temple of Belur in Mysore (built about A. D. 1120).' There are other examples where ' the *Śikhara* did not preserve the southern storeyed form but was rather stepped, forming square pyramid with breaks corresponding to the angles in the wall, and with a broad band answering to the larger face in the middle of each exposed side of the shrine.' ' The pillars are markedly different from the earlier Dravidian forms, they are massive, richly carved, often circular and highly polished. Their capitals are usually spread out, while middle section of the shaft is richly carved with mouldings in the round. They are almost always in pairs of the same design.' The richly carved and richly ornamented pierced windows belong specially to this (Chālukyan) style as we see it at Ajanta and elsewhere, just like the pierced stone windows employed in Dravidian temples at Ellora and other places. ' The buildings are erected without mortar, and the joints were carefully fitted. The whole was covered with sculpture, often of geometric and floral patterns, intermixed with numerous mythological figures, and, in the later examples, the courses of the base were carved with the succession of animal patterns prescribed for them in the *Śilpa-śāstras.* This is very fully exemplified in the great temple of Hoysaleśvara at Halebid."[1]

These peculiarities of the Dravidian and the Chālukyan styles are taken from existing examples. Most of these details are also found under the *Drāviḍa* style of the *Mānasāra* which, however, does not refer to the Chālukyan style as a separate order.

The Northern or Indo-Aryan style of architecture covers the whole area once occupied by the Aryans, ' usually designated as Hindustan,' to the north of the Tāpti and Mahanadi rivers. ' What is known as the Jain style of architecture in Western India is a development or variety of this Indo-Aryan order, and was used by the Hindus and Jains alike all over Rājputanā, Mālwa and Gujarāt. It was employed in its most ornate form by the Jains in their famous marble temples on Mount Abu, and by both the Jains and Hindus at Nāgdā near Udaipur. At Girnār also and Śatrunjaya in Gujarāt, as well as Khajurāho in Bundelkhand, are clusters of temples of this order.'[2]

' Under this style are classified monuments of very various orders which may be separated into two or more distinct types.' The *Vesara* of the *Mānasāra* is apparently one of these orders.

[1] Burgess, *ibid*, pp. 176, 177. [2] *Ibid*, pp. 177, 179.

'The shrines and *maṇḍapas* are square, and only slightly modified by additions to the walls of parallel projections, which, in the earlier examples, were thin, the walls were raised on a moulded plinth (*pīṭha*) of some height, over which was a deep base (*adhishṭhāna*), the two together rising, roughly, to about half the height of the walls, over this is the paralleled face of the wall, usually of less proportionate height than in the Chālukyan style, and though devoted to figure sculptures in compartments, the tall thin pilasters of the southern style have disappeared, over this is the many-membered architrave, and cornice, above which rise the spire and roof. The spires follow the vertical lines of the wall, and present no trace of division into storeys, but vary in details with the age. In the earlier examples the summit was crowned by a large, fluted, circular block called *amala* (pure, shining) *śilā*, probably mistaken for *amalaka* (*Phyllanthus Emblica*). The finial over this is of the shape of a vase, known as the *Kalaśa* or *Karaka*.' 'One of the most striking features of the style is the richly carved domes over their *maṇḍapas* or porches. (Nothing can exceed the elaboration and delicacy of details in the sculptured vaults of the temples at Abu and Nāgdā.) These, with the diversified arrangement of variously placed and highly ornamented pillars supporting them, produce a most pleasing impression of symmetry and beauty.'[1]

'The earlier examples were apparently astylar, then—like the southern forms—with columns arranged in the *maṇḍapas* in groups of four, and later, especially in Western India, the larger domes on twelve pillars formed the central area of the halls. These *maṇḍapas* in early examples were roofed with long, sloping slabs, but, to provide for carved conical roofs inside, their outer forms represented courses of masonry, which were carved as in temples of Kanarak, Bhuvaneśvara (older), Ambaranāth, Baroli, Khajurāho, Abu and Chitor (mediaeval), Nāsik, Benares, Udaipur, Śatrunjaya, etc. (recent).'[2]

The peculiarities of the *Nāgara* style, except in one or two rather unessential points, would correspond to these details of 'Northern or Indo-Aryan style.' The *amala* or *amalaka-śilā* is not mentioned in the *Mānasāra* under this appellation, but the *mūrdhni-ishṭaka* (brick at the top) seems to serve the same purpose as the *amala-śilā*. The *kalaśa*, or dome, *śikhā*, and *śikhara*, are the distinguishing

[1] *Ibid*, pp. 178, 179.

[2] *Ibid*, pp. 180, 181.

features of the style found also in the *Mānasāra* in addition to the square shape.

'The temples at Bhuvaneśvara . . . differ very markedly from those in the west in being almost entirely astylar—pillars having been introduced in later additions. They have the early form of *śikhara*—nearly perpendicular below, but curving near the summit, and the crowning member has no resemblance to anything like the small domes on Chālukyan spires.'

Burgess, following the classification of Fergusson, has included the style found at Puri, Bhuvaneśvara, and Kanarak under the Indo-Aryan or Northern style. But he has admitted that it 'may be separated into a distinct order.' What is called the *Vesara* in the *Mānasāra* seems to be identical with this style. The main characteristic feature of this style is, according to the *Mānasāra*, its round shape, and this is clearly exhibited by temples and images in the Orissan countries.

The identification of *Nāgara* with Northern India needs, however, an explanation. It seems to have been never before used exclusively in that sense. Moreover, it is the name of an extensive division in Mysore, a part in Tanjore, and a number of ancient villages in the Deccan.[1] But it is found used more frequently as the names of villages, towns, and rivers in Bengal, Bihar, the United Provinces of Agra and Oudh, Rajputana, the Punjab, and Gujarat.[2] *Nāgara* is also the name of a portion of the *Skanda-Purāṇa*, of a sect of northern Brahmans, and of a script. The *Skanda-Purāṇa*, which to some scholars seems to have been named after Skanda-Gupta (A. D. 455–480), the seventh emperor of the early Gupta dynasty, contains a part called *Nāgara-khaṇḍa*. In this part of the *Skanda-Purāṇa* it is claimed that the Nāgara Brahmans are superior to all other Brahmans. It is held that they came over from the north and settled down in Gujarat at a place known as Nāgrānandana-pura. From these Nāgara Brahmans, it is said, came the use of the *Nāgarī* alphabet, which belongs exclusively to Northern India. Indeed, it is very famous as the name of a script, particularly of Northern India extending from Bihar on the east to the Punjab and Gujarat on the west,

[1] *See* the writer's *Encyclopaedia*, under *Nāgara*.

[2] *J. A. S. B.*, 1896, Vol. LXV, Part I, pp. 116–117. Basu's collection of references in this *Journal* and many other quotations will be found under *Nāgara* in the writer's *Encyclopaedia of Hindu Architecture*.

and from the foot of the Himalayas on the north to the Vindhya range on the south. This is the very tract which seems to have been covered by the *Nāgara* style about the time of the Mānasāra.

The southern and eastern tracts represented by the *Drāviḍa* and the *Vesara* styles can also be associated respectively with the Tāmil and the Telugu, including the Orissan scripts. As based on scripts and languages, these divisions, *Nāgara*, *Drāviḍa*, and *Vesara*, have existed apart from the architectural styles.

The expression *Nāgara* is certainly not coined in the *Mānasāra*. *Nagara* is a common name for the town, and *Nāgara* is an adjective therefrom and implies something connected with a city. Madurā of Southern India is apparently an identical name to Mathurā of Northern India. In the same way, the Nāgarakhaṇḍa of Mysore, the port Nāgore of Tanjore, and the village Nāgara of the Deccan can be accounted for. There are several things to prove conclusively that the Aryan influence and civilization were spread, from Aryāvarta or Northern India, all over the Dākshiṇātya or Southern India. It is true that the borrowed names sometimes became more prominent than those of which they are but imitations. New York of America, for instance, is much more prominent than old York of old England. Similarly the name *Nāgara*, though originated in and indicating Northern India, might have become more prominent in Southern India.

All these divisions are indicated by terms which were already in use as class names. The architecture of the country is divided into three broad styles and ten types, corresponding to the geographical divisions and the political entities. And there seems to have been a bond of union between these entities, however autonomous and independent they may have been in their mutual relation. In the total absence or rather non-existence of a unifying authority, the growth of a record of generalization, a guide book for the whole country, would be highly exceptional if not improbable. In other words, the presence of a standard work on architecture like the *Mānasāra* seems to pre-suppose an empire comprising countries having their own styles, methods, and principles, which are recorded and illustrated under so many divisions. Whether or not such books of generalization could have been written in those ancient days of India even without the patronage, active or passive, direct or indirect, of an imperial authority, it will be a useless, at any rate an unnecessary, discussion for our purpose. It is sufficient for me that the existence of such an empire may be taken to be conducive to the growth of such a treatise as the *Mānasāra.*

Existence of an empire at the time of compilation of the *Mānasāra* seems to be indicated also by the following facts.

In connexion with construction and disposition, according to ranks, of royal palaces, thrones, and crowns, royalty is divided into nine classes.[1] They are called, in descending order, *Chakravartin*, *Mahārāja* or *Adhirāja*, *Mahendra* or *Narendra*, *Pārshṇika*, *Paṭṭadhara*, *Maṇḍaleśa*, *Paṭṭabhāj*, *Prāhāraka*, and *Astragrāhin.* The number of storeys and halls in a palace, the divisions of the whole compound into different courts, the quarters for royal personages and officials, and other buildings which are necessary adjuncts of an Indian palace, are described The royal qualities, courts, army, and rate of revenue in accordance with the class to which a king belongs, are also incidentally mentioned. A consideration of these matters might have helped us in arriving at a time in the history of ancient India, if the historical materials and especially chronological data were available.

What, however, concerns us most here is to ascertain the relation existing between these nine classes of kings. They are mentioned by their common names, and not by proper and personal names.

An empire, in any case, has been expressly recognized in the *Mānasāra.* It is clearly declared that the *empire* of the *Chakravartin* or universal monarch reaches as far as the four oceans.[2] So it must include the whole of India, divided into three divisions, Northern, Southern, and Eastern, otherwise apparently known as Nāgara, Drāviḍa and Vesara. According to another classification we have seen, this empire seems to have comprised ten kingdoms. But here the empire is stated to have nine kinds of rulers.

The *Chakravartin* is the suzerain of all the subordinate kings who send up tributes and taxes to him.[3] The next king, called both *Mahārāja* and *Adhirāja*, is the lord of seven kingdoms.[4] *Mahendra* or *Narendra*

[1] *Mānasāra*, Chaps. XL, XLI, XI, *see* pp. 124–126, 104–106 of this volume.

[2] चतुःसागरपर्यन्तां महीं स्वीकृत्य बलवान्।
जित्वा द्वारस्य पुरतो घंटामावध्य संस्थितः। —(*M.*, XLII, 6–7).

[3] सर्वावनीन्द्रवन्द्योसौ चक्रवर्तीति कीर्तितः। —(*M.*, XLII, 10).
एवं क्षुद्राश्च भूपालाः स्वे स्वे जनपदे करान्।
स्वीकृत्य चक्रवर्त्यादिराजानां च कुर्वन्त्यपि॥—(*M.*, XLII, 75–76).

[4] *M.*, XLII, 11–13.

is the master of three kingdoms and more honourable than the *Pārshṇika*, *Paṭṭadhara*, *Maṇḍaleśa*, and *Paṭṭabhāj* classes of kings.[1] The *Pārshṇika* is responsible for the administration of one kingdom, and the *Paṭṭadhara* governs only half a kingdom.[2] The rest seem to be chiefs rather than kings, though they possess their own army and courts. The *Maṇḍaleśa* is stated to be content with a *maṇḍala* or province, while half a *maṇḍala* or province is left to the charge of the *Paṭṭabhāj*.[3] The *Prāhāraka* is the king of several *janapada* or divisions, and the *Astragrāhin* looks after several districts and is the ruler in a large city.[4]

About the *Adhirāja* it is stated that he must belong to the solar or the lunar race.[5] The kings of these races are Kshatriya by caste. Nothing is specified regarding the caste or castes of the other classes of kings. But the *Prāhāraka* is expressly stated to be born in a Brahman, Kshatriya, Vaiśya, or Śūdra family.[6] This state of things points to a time when the Śūdras were also recognized as kings.

There does not seem to be much doubt that the recognition of these divisions presupposes the existence of an empire, the extent and the boundaries of which are made clear by the geographical classification of the ten types of gorgeous buildings and the three styles of the architectural and sculptural objects. These various divisions seem to represent the different schools of one system, the different branches of one united civilization and culture. For such an empire it is not absolutely necessary to find out a political head who can keep together the apparently separate and exclusive entities under his direct military control.

When was there such an empire existing in India embracing the *Nāgara*, the *Drāviḍa*, and the *Vasara* portions all within itself? It is true, perhaps, that even in the time of Manu tracts of the country south of Vindhyas were known to the Aryans, and truer still that in the time of king Aśoka, who partially conquered a portion of what we are now describing as Vesara and Drāviḍa, there was a friendly intercourse subsisting between the north and the south. But the south was south still, and did not come to be considered as forming

[1] *M.*, XLII, 14–15.
[2] *M.*, XLII, 18, 21–22.
[3] *M.*, XLII, 23–28.
[4] *M.*, XLII, 29–35.
[5] *M.*, XLII, 12–13.
[6] ब्राह्मणक्षत्रियवैश्यशूद्राणामेककुलोद्भवः ।—(*M.*, XLII, 29).

along with the north part of one and the same whole. The idea of such an empire as would include the whole of India from the Himalayas to Cape Comorin, from Gujarat to Bengal, had not yet grown up. It was still to come, and arrived much later when all the different parts came to be united under one hand. This leads us to consider next the course of development of such an empire, the story of which as a matter of fact is the story of the gradual spread of the Aryan influence and power from Āryāvarta or Northern India southwards.

Dr. Bühler seems inclined to think that the Aryan conquest of South India took place 'a considerable time before the Vedic period came to an end, and it certainly was an accomplished fact long before the authentic history of India begins at the end of the fourth century B.C.'[1] According to Rhys Davids, till about the time of Buddha, Kaliṅga and part of the Deccan below the banks of the Godāvarī were outside the area of Hindu settlement.[2]

King Aśoka conquered Kaliṅga and annexed it to his empire. The same monarch in his edict (XIII) refers to the Cholas, Pāṇḍyas, and Keralaputras as his *pāchantas* or neighbours. It is evident from this edict of king Aśoka that the three South Indian powers—the Cholas, Pāṇḍyas and Keralaputras—were, till the third century B.C., quite independent of Magadha. But presumably the friendly relation which had existed between king Aśoka and those three powers opened for the first time the road of an exchange or amalgamation of two distinct civilizations, namely, the Aryan and the Dravidian. It is also not inconceivable that in or before the third century B.C., Andhra or Telugu country was in part Aryanized.

And, lastly, it is clear from the Allahabad pillar inscription of Samudragupta that this Indian Napoleon directed his campaigns against eleven kings of the south, nine named kings of Āryāvarta, besides many others not specified, the chiefs of the wild forest tribes, and the rulers of the frontier kingdoms and republics. He had also diplomatic relation with very remote foreign powers. 'Although it is at present impossible to identify every one of the countries, kings, and peoples enumerated in the inscription, enough is known to enable the

[1] *Āpastamba*, *S. B. E.*, II, pp. xxxvi and xxxvii.

[2] *Sutta-Nipāta*, 1011, *see* also *Aṅguttara Nikāya*, I, 213, IV, 252, 256, 260, Vinaya Texts, II, 146.

The account of Rāma's advance up to Ceylon as given in the *Rāmāyaṇa* reflects a travel rather than a conquest.

historian to form a clear idea of the extent of the dominions and the range of the alliances of the most brilliant of the Gupta emperors.'

He conquered South Kośala in the valley of the Mahānadi, subdued all the chiefs of the forest countries, which constitute the tributary states of Orissa, and the more backward parts of the Central Provinces, Pishṭapura, the ancient capital of Kaliṅga, the hill-forts of Mahendragiri and Kottur in Ganjam, the kingdom of Manṭaraja on the banks of the Kolleru lake, Vengi between the Kṛishṇā and the Godāvarī, Kāñchī to the south of Madras, Pālakka in the Nellore district, Devarāshṭra or the modern Mahratta country, and Erandapalla or Khāndesh. This would imply the whole of the Draviḍa country bounded by the Coromandal and the Malabar coasts. The only place left by Samudragupta for his son Chandragupta to conquer and to annex to the empire was Kathiawar in Gujarat.

'The dominions under the direct government of Samudragupta thus comprised all the countries of Northern India. It extended from the Hooghly on the east, to the Jamunā and Chambal on the west, and from the foot of the Himalayas on the north to the Narmadā on the south. Beyond these wide limits, the frontier kingdoms of Assam and the Gangetic delta, as well as those on the southern slope of the Himalayas, and the free tribes of Rajputana and Malwa, were attached to the empire by bonds of subordinate alliance, while almost all the kingdoms of the south had been overrun by the emperor's armies and compelled to acknowledge his irresistible might. The empire thus defined was by far the greatest that had been seen in India since the days of Aśoka. He maintained diplomatic relations with the Kushan kings of Gandhara and Kabul, and the greater sovereign of the same race, who ruled on the banks of the Oxus, as well as with Ceylon and other distant islands.'[1]

We now see that it was not until the time of the Imperial Gupta dynasty that the kind of empire implied in such a work as the *Mānasāra* came into existence. It is not our intention to say, indeed, that before or after this there had been nothing in the shape of an empire. It cannot certainly be gainsaid that there was a flourishing empire under king Aśoka. It cannot be denied either that there was an empire flourishing in the south independent of the Aryans, that of the Andhras, so far back as about the beginning of the Christian era. The Chālukyas also built up an empire after the fall of the early

[1] V. A. Smith, *History of India* (1908), pp. 271–72.

Guptas and remained powerful till about the middle of the eighth century, when the government of the country passed into the hands of the Rāshṭrakuṭas for more than two hundred years. Harshavardhana of Kanauj also built an empire which, however, did not include within itself the Dravidian countries. What appears clear to us is that not till the reign of Samudragupta (326–375) or until Chandragupta II (375–413) was there any one empire which comprised the whole land, including the Telugu- and the Tamil-speaking places. It is further clear from the Allahabad inscription of Samudragupta that some of his subordinated kings belonged to the Śūdra caste.

The next internal evidence to be considered is one regarding religion. This is illustrated in the *Mānasāra* by the indifferent treatment accorded to the Buddhists and the Jains, and also by the unusually dignified manner of addressing the Brahmans as the gods on earth (*bhū-sura*), and lastly by the predilection for Vaishṇavism.

Two separate chapters are, however, devoted to the description of the Jain and the Buddhist images.[1]

The description of the Jain deities, ostensibly the main object of a chapter, is submerged in a lengthy discussion of the various measurements used both in architecture and sculpture. The twenty-four *Tīrthaṅkaras* or Jain apostles are referred to, but not specified. The whole description of the Jain images is disposed of in a few lines at the fag end of the chapter. The Buddhist images are also described in a very small chapter of eighteen lines only. The account of these images too is very meagre. Evidently the author had in mind solely the effigies of Buddha, not of other Buddhist deities. This slight seems to have struck the author himself. So he adds in conclusion that the rest should be in accordance with the directions given in treatises specially dealing with these images.[2]

The Buddhists and the Jains have been mentioned, it is true, in connexion with all matters referring to people of different sects. But the indifferent treatment accorded to the followers of Buddhism and Jainism is clear beyond doubt. For instance, in connexion with the village scheme described in a chapter of five hundred and forty lines, only two lines are devoted to them. The slight is all the more prominent from the fact that rather unwelcome quarters are

[1] Chapters LV, LVI, *see* pp. 144–147 of this Volume.

[2] शेषं प्रागुक्तवत्कुर्यात्तत्तदागमवद्बुधः ।—(*M.*, LVI, 18, the last line).

reserved for the Buddhists and the Jains, and that the temples of their deities are built outside villages and towns.[1]

Similarly in connexion with buildings of different storeys they are treated with indifference, and nothing is specified about them.[2]

The same treatment is also apparent in connexion with the temples of attendant deities. The Buddhist and the Jain temples are passed over with the remark that they should be built according to the rules of their own *Sāstras.* It is true, however, that Buddha is recognized as one of the ten incarnations of Vishṇu, whose family consists of the three groups of eight, sixteen including Buddha, and thirty-two deities.

Again, in the chapter on pavilions (*maṇḍapa*), which consists of five hundred and seventy-six lines, only one is given to the Buddhists and the Jains.[3]

In connexion with the description of cars and chariots, it is stated in only one line that there should be one to seven platforms in the cars of the Buddhist and the Jain deities.[4] Thrones and seats for the Buddhists and the Jains are left undescribed with the remark that they are ' thus stated.'[5]

[1] बौद्धं वायुपदे चैव नैर्ऋत्ये तु जिनालयम् ।—(IX, 387).
दुर्गां गणपतिं चैव बौद्धं जैनं गतालयम् ।.
अन्येषां षण्मुखादीनां स्थापयेन्नगराद्बहिः ।।—(IX, 405–6).

[2] एवं तु चोक्तवत्कृत्वा बौद्धादिजिनकालयम् ।
तत्तद्विमानस्योर्ध्वेतु तत्तद्देवान्न्यसेत्क्रमात् ।।
—(XIX, 252–3, two lines out of 263 lines).
देवता दिशि चाष्टतो न्यसेद्विष्णोरीश्वरजिनादेरालये ।
—(XXI, 73–74, last two lines).
क्षुद्रमन्यमथ मुख्यं भौमके रुद्रविष्णुजिनकादिहर्म्यके ।—(XXII, 98–99).

[3] *See* the summary, Chap. XXXIV, pp. 119–129.
Compare the following :
नैर्ऋत्ये तु बौद्धं स्याज्जयन्ते पौत्रिकालयम् ।
बौद्धं च जिनकं चैव तत्तच्छास्त्रोक्तमार्गवत् ।
बौद्धस्यालये तज्जिनालयेऽपि क्षुद्रालये सर्वशः ।
शास्त्रस्यालयतोरणे कथितं तत्परिवारकं कुर्वीत ।।—(XXXII, 149, 157, 165–6).

[4] विष्णोस्त्र्यम्बकस्यापि चैकाद्ये (दि) नववेदिकाः ।
बौद्धादिजिनकान्तानां सप्तानां सप्तान्तं चैकादितः ।।
—(XLIII, 144–5).

[5] विष्णुरुद्राजनकेन्द्रमुख्यकानां सर्वदेवगणचक्रवर्तिनाम् ।
आसनानि कथितानि तानि वै चोत्सवानि कथितानि सूरिभिः ।।
—(XLV, 211–112, last two lines).

Lastly, in connexion with the general description of images, the Buddhists and the Jains are left unspecified with a similar remark as before.[1]

These are all the instances where the Buddhists and the Jains are at all mentioned. A significant point of omission also may be considered. Monasteries and such other architectural objects as are intimately associated with Buddhism and Jainism have not been referred to, while the minute details of Brahmanical Hindu temples have been rather elaborately described. From all this, two points seem to me to be clear. First, the Buddhists and the Jains, at the time of the *Mānasāra*, were not in a flourishing condition, secondly, they were not persecuted either. It was apparently a time of toleration for them.

The next point to be clear about, is, which religion had the preference? It was Vaishṇavism. The following references will, I hope, confirm this view.

In support of the indifferent treatment accorded to the Buddhists and the Jains, the passages quoted above contain references to Saivism and Vaishṇavism also. Vishnu and Iśvara, Vishṇu and Rudra, Vishṇu and Tryambaka, and Brahmā, Vishṇu, Rudra are mentioned alongside Buddha and Jina.[2] From this it must not be concluded, however, that Brahmā, Vishṇu, and Siva are treated in the same way as Buddha and Jina. In these passages it is directed how the latter should be treated, the former having been elaborately described. But in the treatment of Brahmā, Vishṇu, and Siva themselves a clear distinction and predilection have been shown. It is true that the opening verse is an invocation to Brahmā, not to Vishṇu or Siva, and that in the next verse the ultimate sources of the *Silpa-śāstras*, like many other *Sāstras*, have been ascribed to Siva, Brahmā, and Vishṇu.[3] These deities are described in the usual order of Brahmā, Vishṇu, and Siva in the chapter dealing with the images of the Hindu Triad.[4]

[1] ब्रह्माविष्णुरुद्राणां बुद्धस्य जिनकस्य च।
अन्येषां च प्रतिमानामेवं मानं तु संग्रहम्॥ —(XLXIV, 91–2)

[2] *See* p. 269, notes 2, 3, 4, 5.

[3] *Mānasāra*, I, 1, 2.

गङ्गाशिर, कमलभू, कमलेक्षण, this is the order; but in Sanskrit the order may be changed. Here, however, the terms form component parts of a *dvanda* compound where the order of terms has some significance.

[4] Chapter LI, *see* pp. 137–139.

In describing the riding-animals (*vāhana*) of the Triad, the same order has been followed, the goose, the *garuḍa* bird, and the bull being treated in turn.[1]

It is also true that the phallus of Śiva and his pedestal (*pīṭha*) have been elaborately treated in two separate chapters.[2] This, however, does not seem to have been due to the author's or his patron's predilection for Śaivism. For the phallus of Śiva is a very famous object of Hindu sculpture, and it would have been given the prominence all the same even if the artist had belonged to an entirely different sect, because without this his treatise would have been incomplete. Similarly the extollation of the phallus worship added in conclusion may be explained.[3]

Preference for Vaishṇavism seems clear also from the following points :

The whole compound of a large building is divided into five courts[4] around which the temples of attendant deities are built. Brahmā, Vishṇu, and Śiva may individually possess attendant deities. There are, therefore, no reasons why the attendant deities of any one of the Triad should be specially treated, unless the author were closely in touch with the temples of any one group of the attendant deities wherefrom his ideas and illustrations originated. In this connexion the groups of eight, sixteen, and thirty-two deities of the Vishṇu family alone arc illustrated. The ten incarnations of Vishṇu are also dealt with. But no mention is made of the attendant deities of Brahmā or Śiva.[5] This omission is significant, all the more because the *Mānasāra* is avowedly a treatise on architecture. If the work had been compiled in a place where Śaivism or Brahmā worship was favoured, the temples of their attendant deities could not but have been described in this connexion.

A similarly striking omission in connexion with the Śiva temples is also noticed in another important matter, namely, the foundations. Foundations of buildings are divided into two classes—according as they belong to temples and to human dwellings. Of the residential buildings there are four classes of foundations according to the four

[1] Chapters LX, LXI, LXII, *see* pp. 149–151.
[2] Chapters LII, LIII, *see* pp. 140–142.
[3] Chapter LII, *see* p. 141.
[4] Chapters XXXI, XXXIII, *see* pp. 116–117, 117–119.
[5] Chapter XXXII, *see* p. 117.

castes, Brahman, Kshattriya, Vaiśya and Śūdra.[1] Of temples, those of Vishṇu and Brahmā are illustrated. Śiva is not mentioned at all in this connexion beyond the author's usual method of passing on with the remark that the others should be similarly done. Very little is authoritatively known about the places in India where Brahmā worship was ever so much favoured as Vaishṇavism in Northern India, and Śaivism in Southern India. The author's predilection for Vaishṇavism seems to be indicated by this point likewise.

In the laying out of villages and towns also the Vishṇu temples have been given preference. It is stated that the Vishṇu temples may be built anywhere in the village under the innumerable epithets of Vishṇu, such as Śrīdhara in the east, Vāmana in the south, Vāsudeva, Ādi-Vishṇu or Janārdana in the west, Keśava or Nārāyaṇa in the north, Nṛisiṁha, Gopāla, Rāma and others at the four corners. No such details are given regarding the Śiva temples. It is simply stated that the Īśa (Rudra) temples may similarly be built in the quarters known as Rudra-jaya, Apa-vatsya, Jayanta, Parjanya and such other quarters, which are by no means prominent places in the village.[2]

[1] Chapter XII, *see* pp. 106–108.

[2] *Mānasāra*, IX, 255 f., and 383, for instance :

आर्यादिषु चतुर्दिक्षु ग्रामस्यापि चतुर्दिशि । (255)
एवं यथेष्टदिग्देशे विष्णुधिष्णं प्रकल्पयेत् ॥
अथवा बहिरङ्गे तु चेष्टदिग्विष्णोरालयम् ।
इन्द्रादिषु चतुर्दिक्षु विष्णुस्थानं तु राक्षसे ॥
पूर्वके श्रीधरं प्रोक्तं दक्षिणे वामनं तथा ।
पश्चिमे वासुदेवं वा चादिविष्णुं जनार्दनम् ॥
उत्तरे केशवं प्रोक्तं नारायणमथापि वा ।
अन्तः प्रागुत्तरदेशे विष्णुमूर्तिं यथेष्टकम् ॥
पितृदेवेशकोणे वा यथा नृसिंहालयं भवेत् ।
अग्निकोणे यथा रामं गोपालालयमेव च ॥
मित्रे च त्रितलं कुर्यात्स्थानकं चादिभूमिके ।
द्वितीये चासनं प्रोक्तं तृतीये शयनं भवेत् ॥
अथवा स्थानकं चोर्ध्वे शयनं मूलकस्थले ।
इष्टदिग्विष्णुहर्म्याणां द्वारं कुर्याद्विचक्षणः ॥
ग्रामस्याभिमुखं विष्णुं नरसिंहं पराङ्मुखम् ।

But in the case of Śiva it is simply stated :

ईशे वाथ जयन्ते वा पर्जन्यस्य पदेऽपि वा । (273)
एवमीशालयं कुर्याद्ग्रामस्य तु पराङ्मुखम् ॥

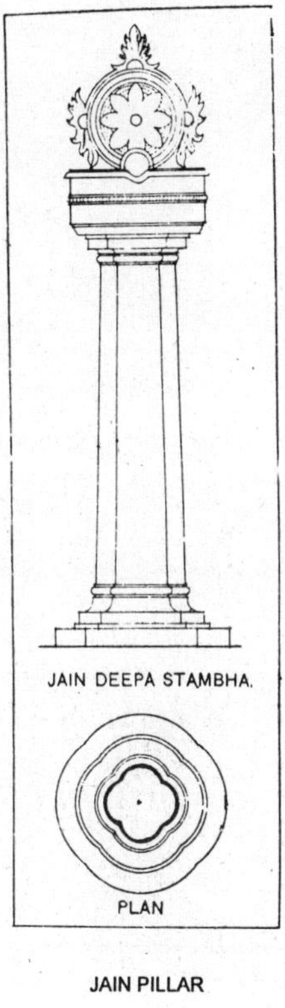

JAIN PILLAR

PLATE XL(a)

GUPTA DOOR

In the case of towns, the Vishṇu temples alone have been taken into consideration. In the capital cities, it is distinctly stated that the Vishṇu temples should be built at the main entrance.[1]

Similar illustrations from the body of the *Mānasāra* can be multiplied. But the point seems to be clear. Vaishṇavism appears to have been the leading religion of the place where the *Mānasāra* was compiled. The author himself may have had a personal preference for Śaivism or even for Brahmā-worship, but his patron or the influence under which the author was working apparently had a leaning towards Vaishṇavism in all its various phases and aspects, including even Buddha as one of the ten incarnations of Vishṇu. Buddhism and Jainism, though by no means favoured religions, were allowed to continue. The influence seems to be one of non-interference, a universal toleration, with special preference for Vaishṇavism.

In which period of the history of ancient India, then, could Buddhism and Jainism have got on alongside Brahmanical Hinduism? The state of things that is reflected in the generous treatment of the followers of different religions was possible only in the period from the fourth to the eighth or ninth centuries of the Christian era. For during the reign of Aśoka in the third century B.C., and some time after, Buddhism was in a very flourishing condition, while after the eighth or the ninth century both Jainism and Buddhism were declining.

During this period kings of three distinguished dynasties reigned in the country. The Gupta empire in its entirety dates from the

[1] *See* also 383, etc.

सर्व्वेषां नगरादीनां भेदं लक्षणमुच्यते।
नगरं राजधानीयं केवलं नगरं तथा॥
पुरं च नगरी चैव खेटं खर्वटमेव च।
कुब्जकं पत्तनं चैव शिबिरं वाहिनीमुखम्।
स्थानीयं द्रोणकं चैव संविद्धं कोलकं ततः।
निगमं स्कन्धवारं च दुर्गं चाष्टविधं भवेत्॥
नगरादीनि संग्रामं प्रोक्तदुर्गं च सत्तमम्।
राष्ट्रमध्ये नदीतीरे बहुपुण्यजनावृतम्॥
मध्ये राजयुतं चैव नगरे कृतमिष्यते।
तत्रागते नगर्यन्तं यदि विष्ण्वालयं भवेत्।
राजधानीति तन्नाम विद्वद्भिर्वक्ष्यते सदा।

—(*Mānasāra*, X, 37–47).

reign of Samudragupta (326–375), more accurately from the reign of Chandragupta II (375–413). The seventh and last emperor of the Gupta dynasty is Skandagupta. The imperial authority of the Guptas perished with Skandagupta (455–480), and the empire broke up, although the dynasty continued till about the middle of the seventh century or perhaps a little later. The Chālukyas came into power in the south at the beginning of the sixth century, after the fall of the Guptas, and remained powerful till about the middle of the eighth century, when the government of the Chālukya dominions passed into the hands of the Rāshṭrakuṭas for more than two hundred years. After their fall, the Chālukyas again came into power.[1] Harshavardhana (606–648) also built up an empire in Northern India about the time when the Chālukyas were powerful in Southern India. None of these empires, however, comprised the whole of India. Buddhism and Jainism could not have flourished alongside Brahmanical Hinduism under the Rāshṭrakuṭas. Some of the Rāshṭrakuṭa kings may have been in favour of Jainism, but none seems to have favoured Buddhism. 'Under them,' says Sir R. G. Bhandarkar, 'the worship of the Purāṇic gods rose to much greater importance than before. The days when kings and princes got temples and monasteries cut out of the solid rock for the use of the followers of Gautama Buddha had gone by, never to return.'[2]

'During the two centuries of the rule of the early Chālukya dynasty of Vātapi,' says Vincent Smith,[3] 'great changes in the religious state of the country were in progress. Buddhism, although, still influential, and supported by a large section of the population was slowly declining, and suffering gradual supersession by its rivals, Jainism and Brahmanical Hinduism. The sacrificial form of the Hindu religion received special attention and was made the subject of a multitude of formal treatises. The Purāṇic forms of Hinduism also grew in popularity, and everywhere elaborate temples dedicated to Vishṇu, Śiva, or other members of the Purāṇic pantheon, were erected. The orthodox Hindus borrowed from their Buddhist and

[1] The early Gupta kings, about 300–530, the later Guptas A. D. 535–720.
The Chālukyas of Bādāmi, A. D. 550–753.
The Rāshṭrakutas of Mānyakheṭa, A. D. 753–973.
The Chālukyas of Kalyāṇī, A. D. 973–1190.

[2] The *History of Dekkan*, p. 208.

[3] V. Smith, *ibid*, p. 386. *See* also Bhandarkar, *ibid*, p. 191.

Jain rivals the practice of excavating cave-temples.[1] Jainism was specially popular in the southern Marātha country.'

On the other hand, the history of the early Gupta dynasty has all the necessary features. The empire of the Guptas comprised all the countries and divisions indicated in the *Mānasāra*. Brahmanical Hinduism was the leading religion, but Buddhism and Jainism were tolerated. King Meghavarṇa of Ceylon was allowed to despatch a mission with valuable presents to king Samudragupta for permission to build a monastery near the sacred Bo-tree at Gaya. The reign of Chandragupta II, the son and successor of Samudragupta, is noted for the visit of the Chinese pilgrim Fa-hien, who, being a Buddhist pilgrim, necessarily saw everything through Buddhist spectacles. In his account, mention is made of a number of monasteries along his journey from the Indus to Mathura, in which neighbourhood he found twenty of these buildings. 'It is evident that, with a Brahmanical supreme government, Hinduism of the orthodox kind must have been far more prominent than his account would lead the reader to suppose.'[2] Fa-hien was never 'stripped by brigands, a misfortune which befell his successor Hiuen Tsang. Probably India has never been governed better. The government did not attempt to do too much but let the people alone, and was accordingly popular.' Though 'the sovereign was a Brahmanical Hindu, the tendency to the harassing kind of persecution, which a Buddhist or Jain government is apt to display, was kept in check, and liberty of conscience was assured.'

During the long and rather obscure reign of the next emperor, Kumāragupta (413–455), also Brahmanical Hinduism was the popular religion. This is clear from the fact that Kumāra, like his grandfather, celebrated the horse sacrifice, a ritual repugnant equally to Buddhism and Jainism. Both Skandagupta (455–480) and Narasiṁhagupta Bālāditya (485–535) 'continued to pay their devotions to the

[1] There is no reference in the *Mānasāra* either to cave-temples or rock-cut pillars. Nor have free pillars like those of Asoka been specially described in the *Mānasāra*. There is no reason to think that an author who gives particulars of all sorts of buildings found all over the country should have remained entirely ignorant of these wonderful architectural objects. Their omission seems to have been due to this: the *Mānasāra* is not an history of architecture. It is a guide book and was intended to help professional architects. Architectural objects like the cave-temples, rock-cut pillars, and free pillars had no more use for architects, presumably because they had become out of date at the time of the *Mānasāra*.

[2] V. Smith, *ibid*, pp. 292, 293.

Hindu gods, while exhibiting, like Harsha in the seventh century, a strong personal predilection for Buddhist doctrine.'[1]

'Whatever may have been the causes, the fact is abundantly established that the restoration of the Brahmanical religion to popular favour, and the associated revival of the Sanskrit language, first became noticeable in the second century, were fostered by the western Satraps during the third, and made a success by the Gupta emperors in the fourth century. These princes, although perfectly tolerant of both Buddhism and Jainism, and in two cases personally interested in the former, were themselves beyond question orthodox Hindus, guided by Brahman advisers, and skilled in Sanskrit. An early stage in the reaction against Buddhist condemnation of sacrifice had been marked by Pushyamitra's celebration of the horse-sacrifice towards the close of the second century. In the fourth, Samudragupta revived the same ancient rite with added splendour, and, in the fifth, his grandson repeated the solemnity. Without going further into detail the matter may be summed up in the remark that coins, inscriptions, and monuments agree in furnishing abundant evidence of the recrudescence during the Gupta period of Brahmanical Hinduism at the expense of Buddhism, and of the favour shown by the ruling power to classical Sanskrit at the expense of the more popular literary dialects, which had enjoyed the patronage of the Andhra kings.'[2]

It is, further, clear from coins, inscriptions, and monuments that Vaishṇavism was the predominating religion during the Gupta period. And this is the state of religious affairs evinced in the *Mānasāra*, namely, a Brahmanical Hinduism with preference for Vaishṇavism and tolerant of both Buddhism and Jainism.

[1] Paramārtha, Buddhist of the sixth century, who wrote the life of Vasubandhu states that 'Vikramāditya of Ajodhya, who at first was a liberal patron of the Sāṁkhya philosophy, which is considered to have a strong affinity to both Buddhist and Jain doctrines, was induced by the eloquence of the celebrated Vasubandhu of Peshāwar to turn a favourable ear to the teachings of Buddhism and to patronise its professors with equal liberality. The Queen and Prince Bālāditya, who afterwards, about A. D. 485, succeeded to the throne as Narasiṁhagupta, both became disciples of Vasubandhu, and Bālāditya, after his accession, continued his favours to the Buddhist sage. The coinage and official inscriptions of the Gupta kings are so distinctly Brahmanical that these statements might cause surprise.' But 'it is fully confirmed by Hiuen Tsang, who describes Bālāditya as a zealous Buddhist.'—V. Smith, *ibid*, p. 292; Takakusu, *J. R. A. S.*, 1905, p. 44: Watters, I, 288.

[2] Smith, *ibid*, p. 287.

The appearance of treatises like the *Mānasāra* during the period of the early Guptas seems to be indicated by other reasons also. Following the spread and consolidation of the Gupta empire under Samudragupta there came a time of peace and quiet, especially during the reign of Chandragupta II, favourable to the cultivation of art and literature, and an intercourse of ideas and thoughts between the different parts forming members of one empire. It was in this Gupta period that a general literary impulse was extended to every department. In this classical period of Indian history an all-sided improvement in arts, literature and science came to be achieved. It was, again, during this period that the *Sūtra* style of literature began to give place to the classic style. It has been shown elsewhere that the language of the *Śilpa-śāstras*, represented by the *Mānasāra*, seems to be the meeting place of the two.[1] Sanskrit was gradually raised to the position, which it long retained, as the sole literary language of Northern India.

'The literary revolution,' says Vincent Smith, 'necessarily was accompanied by corresponding changes in the art of architecture. The forms of buildings specially adapted for the purposes of Buddhist ritual dropped out of use, and remarkable developments in the design of the Hindu temple were elaborated, which ultimately culminated in the marvellously ornate styles of the mediaeval period, extending from the ninth to the end of the twelfth century.'[2]

The external evidences, mainly based on a comparison between the *Purāṇas* and the *Śilpa-śāstras*, also point to the same conclusions. The reasons have been elaborated for the belief that there is a relation of indebtedness between the *Mānasāra* on the one hand, and, on the other, the *Matsya-Purāṇa*, the *Bhavishya-Purāṇa*, the *Agni-Purāṇa*, and the *Bṛihat-saṁhitā*. 'To the same age probably (Gupta period)' says Vincent Smith, 'should be assigned the principal *Purāṇas* in their present form.'

Bāṇa, the author of the *Harsha-charita*, who wrote about A.D. 620, 'carries back the proof of the antiquity of the *Agni-Bhāgavata-*, *Mārkaṇḍeya-* and *Vāyu-Purāṇas* four centuries further back than Alberuni, who in 1030 gives the list of the eighteen *Purāṇas* as given in the *Vishṇu-Purāṇa*, having seen three of them himself.'

[1] *See* Appendix, and pp. 211–214 of the writer's *Indian Architecture* (1st Ed., 1927)

[2] Smith, *ibid*, p. 288, also refers to the seven characteristics of the Gupta style of architecture (*see* pp. 195–6 of this volume).

Cunningham, *Arch. Reports*, IX, 42, I, V, X, XI, XIV, XVI, XX and XXI.

The discovery of the Bengal manuscript written in Gupta hand has assigned the *Skanda-Purāṇa* to the middle of the seventh century on palaeographical grounds.[1] Many other early quotations from, or references to, the *Purāṇas* have been collected by Bühler, who points out that the account of the future kings in the *Vāyu-*, *Vishṇu-*, *Brahmāṇḍa-* and *Matsya-Purāṇas* seems to stop with the imperial Guptas and their contemporaries.[2]

'This last observation,' adds Vincent Smith, 'indicates that the date of the reduction of the four works named (including *Matsya-Purāṇa*, which seems to be intimately connected with the *Mānasāra*) cannot be very far removed from A.D. 500, the imperial Gupta dynasty having ended about A.D. 480. Bühler speaks of 'future kings,' because all the historical statements of the *Purāṇas* are given in the form of prophecy, in order to maintain the appearance of great antiquity in the books, which in their oldest forms were undoubtedly very ancient.'[3]

The *Mānasāra* seems, therefore, to point to the Gupta period in view of the accumulation of external and internal evidences, both political, religious, and social, namely, the date of the *Purāṇas*, the existence of an empire comprising the whole of India, the division of royalty into nine classes (including the Śūdras also), the popularity of the Brahmanical religion with predilection for the Vishṇu cult and non-interference and toleration of Buddhism and Jainism, a general impulse to arts and literature, the appearance of the peculiar Sanskrit of the *Śilpa-sāstras*, and characteristics of architecture and sculpture consisting mainly of the three styles and ten types of buildings.

At the time of the composition of the *Mānasāra* the memory of the first seven Gupta princes seems to have been fresh in the minds of the people. An expression *gupta-viṁśa* has been used in the

[1] *J. R. A. S.*, 1903, p. 193.

[2] *Ind. Ant.*, XXV, p. 323.

[3] *Ibid*, pp. 19, 20; compare also:

'The *Vāyu-Purāṇa* in its present shape seems to be referred to the fourth century A. D., by the well-known passage describing the extent of the Gupta dominions, which is applicable only to the reign of Chandra Gupta I in A. D. 320–326.'

The *Purāṇas* seem also to have been known to the author of the *Questions of Milinda* (*Milindapañha*), who composed a part of the work where the first references occur, almost certainly earlier than A. D. 300.

(*S. B. E.*, Vol. XXXV, pp. 6, 247.)

Mānasāra[1] to imply *sapta-viṁśa* or seven and twenty. *Gupta* in the sense of *seven* seems to have been coined in the *Mānasāra*. Perhaps it was due to the great fame and some patronage to the *Mānasāra* of the early Gupta princes, consisting principally of seven kings. For after the death of Skandagupta in A.D. 480, the seventh king of the dynasty, the empire broke up: the next princes, Puragupta, Prakāśāditya, and Narasiṁhagupta Bālāditya being but chiefs.

These conclusions are, however, in an apparent conflict with certain other matters. Cunningham has gathered together fragments of the Gupta buildings, wherefrom he draws the following peculiarities of what he calls the Gupta style.

'The chief characteristic features of the Gupta temples are:

(1) Flat roofs, without spires of any kind, as in the cave temples.

(2) Prolongation of the head of the door-way beyond the jambs, as in the Egyptian temples.

(3) Statues of the rivers, the Ganges and the Jumna, guarding the entrance door.

(4) Pillars, with massive square capitals ornamented with two lions, back to back, with a tree between them.

(5) Bosses on the capitals and friezes of a very peculiar form like the Buddhist Stupas or beehives, with projecting horns.

(6) Continuation of the architrave of the portico as a moulding all round the building.

(7) Deviation in plan from the cardinal points.'

None of these characteristics seems to be applicable in its entirety to the buildings described in the *Mānasāra*. Spires, or *śikhara* and *śikhā*, as well as the *kalaśa*, or domes, are the chief characteristic features of the buildings described in it. These seven characteristics would point to the antiquated period of structural architecture. And Cunningham himself admits the fact.

[1] तद्‌ऋक्षोऽष्टकवृद्धिः स्याद् गुप्तविंशक्षयो भवेत् ।
वारं ग्रहेण वृद्धिः स्यात्सप्तभिश्चक्षयो भवेत् ॥ —(*Mānasāra*, LXI, 32–33).

This refers to the following *shaḍvarga*, a set of six formulas, with which any particular measurement must conform before it can be accepted:

आय .. remainder of length × 8 ÷ 12
व्यय .. „ breadth × 9 ÷ 10
.. „ length × 8 ÷ 27
योनि .. „ breadth × 3 ÷ 8
वार .. „ circumference, thickness, or height × 9 ÷ 7
तिथि or .. „ C × 9 ÷ 30
अंश .. „ C × 4 ÷ 2

More details will be found in the writer's *Encyclopaedia*, under *Shaḍvarga*.

'The style is similar to that of the cave temples of Udayagiri, and of the structural temples at Eran.' 'The use of flat roofs would seem to show that these buildings must belong to the very earliest period of structural architecture. When the architect, whose work has hitherto been confined to the erection of porticoes in front of caves, was first called upon to build the temple itself as well as the porticoes, he naturally copies this only prototype, and thus produced in a structural form the exact facsimile of a rock-hewn cave.'[1]

This seems to explain away the main objection. What is designated as the *Gupta style* points really to buildings of much earlier periods. By the time the Gupta dynasty was consolidated, the methods and principles of architecture seemed to have considerably improved, the architect invented the use of domes and other ornaments over the 'flat roofs' copied in the earlier periods from the rock-hewn caves. In the Gupta period proper, as truly held by later scholars like Vincent Smith, 'remarkable developments in the design of the Hindu temples were elaborated which ultimately culminated in the marvellously ornate styles of the mediaeval period, extending from the ninth to the end of the twelfth century.' So the characteristics of the real Gupta buildings, notably those which existed under the Guptas and are discussed in the *Śilpa-śāstras*, would be different from those given by Cunningham. The buildings described in the *Mānasāra* would conform, we have seen, to the characteristics of the Indo-Aryan and Chālukya-Dravidian styles recorded from the existing examples by both Fergusson and Burgess. But none of these extant examples belonged to a period earlier than the sixth or seventh century A.D. These were, however, not the first of their class : buildings of this class must have existed long before the sixth or seventh century, because the extant examples themselves clearly show that they have passed through different stages in their development.

The next objection may be one concerning the *Gopuras*, *Prākāras*, and such other objects which have been exhaustively described in the *Mānasāra*. These are undeniably the peculiarities of southern architecure. This objection may be easily disposed of. There seem to be sufficient reasons to hold that the account of architecture in the *Mānasāra* has reference to buildings of all parts of India, comprising the northern, southern, and eastern styles. The southern style might

[1] Cunningham, *Archaeological Survey Report*, Vol. IX, p. 42. Some drawings are given in this volume as well as in I, V, X, XI, XIV, XVI, XX, etc.

be as elaborately described as the northern or eastern, even when the *Mānasāra* was compiled under the patronage of a northern emperor.

The mixture of styles or the preferential treatment of one style over the other may similarly be accounted for. The 'sporadic appearance of temples of a style removed from their proper area may be accounted for in various ways; great temples were constantly being visited by pilgrims on their way from one shrine to another, and the repute of any new fane was soon spread over all India, and thus, when a prince undertook to build a new temple, an architect (*sthapati*) of acknowledged ability might occasionally be sent for from the most distant province, and engaged to design the work which, of course, would be in his own style.'[1] In the very same way the author of the *Mānasāra* might have been sent for from Southern India to compose the standard work on Indian architecture.

The last point to be considered is the mention of Mānasāra in the *Daśa-kumāra-charita* as a king of Malwa. This king Mānasāra is the hero of a fiction. There are no doubt historical facts concealed in a fictitious work. But it is not easy to sift facts from fictions. Those who are, however, inclined to connect the *Mānasāra* with this king of Malwa would assign the treatise to the seventh century, because the author of the fiction, Daṇḍin, would be 'contemporary of Bhāravi,' who is mentioned in an inscription of A.D. 634,[2] and also of Harsha who reigned from A.D. 606 to 648.

Historical facts, as stated above, cannot generally be extricated adequately from the complexities of the fiction. Moreover, although some vague conclusion has been inferred from the circumstantial evidence about the period in which Daṇḍin, the undeniable author of the *Daśa-kumāra-charita*, lived, no such vague idea even is available about the period or periods in which the semi-historical incidents described in the *Dāsa-kumāra-charita* might have taken place. Besides, king Mānasāra of the *Daśa-kumāra-charita*, it may be incidentally pointed out, was not the hero or even one of the chief characters of the fiction. He is stated, as pointed out above, to be the king of Malwa and a contemporary of king Rājahaṁsa of Magadha, who was the father of Rājavāhana, the chief of the ten princes (*daśa-kumāra*). In the *Daśa-Kumāra-Charita* itself king Mānasāra is stated to have been engaged in a war with king Rājahaṁsa, that is all.

[1] Burgess, *ibid*, p. 178.

[2] Macdonell, *History of Sanskrit Literature*, pp. 329, 332.

There is in the fiction practically no direct or indirect reference made as to the nature of interest which king Mānasāra might have been in the habit of taking in literary or artistic matters. It must, however, be admitted that there were no real occasions for such a reference.[1] In this connexion another incident, too, may be advantageously taken into consideration: neither in the three styles mentioned in the treatise *Mānasāra* under three geographical names (*Nāgara*, *Vesara*, and *Drāvida*), nor in the ten types of buildings bearing, again, geographical names and provincial divisions (*Pāñchāla*, *Drāviḍa*, *Madhyakānta*, *Kāliṅga*, *Virāṭa*, *Kerala*, *Vaṁśaka*, *Māgadha*, *Janaka*, and *Sphurjaka*), is included Mālava, which was, presumably, the capital city and provincial kingdom of king Mānasāra of the *Daśa-kumāra-charita*. In the circumstances it would be really doubly unwarranted to take any decision about the possibility or otherwise of king Mānasāra's patronage or instrumentality in the production of the standard treatise on architecture which, as its title would seemingly indicate, might have been named after him. King Mānadeva of Nepal who ruled in the sixth century and was a great builder[2] would be a more historical patron of the *Mānasāra* if it could be associated with him.

In view of these facts we venture to expect that the reader may be inclined to consider more seriously the other evidences which are undoubtedly more authenticated and substantial, including those regarding the connexion of the *Mānasāra* with *Matsya-Purāṇa* (A.D. 450) on the one hand and the *Bṛihat-saṁhitā* (A. D. 550) on the other. On this assumption we shall perhaps be justified in placing the *Mānasāra* before the *Bṛihat-saṁhitā* and somewhere close to the *Matsya-Purāṇa*. In any event, we venture to hold that the evidences submitted above would warrant the extension of the period of the *Mānasāra* from A.D. 500 to 700, if not from the time of Vitruvius or earlier.[3]

[1] In his two recently discovered works, called the *Avanti-Sundarī-Kathā* in prose and the *Avanti-Sundarī-Kathāsāra* in verse, Daṇḍin, the author of the *Daśa-kamāra-charita*, is held to be 'well learned in architecture of royal and divine structures.' (*Proceedings of the Second Oriental Conference*, 1922, pp. 194, 196; *see* also p. 252, of this Volume.)

[2] *See* pp. 286–287.

[3] Until, however, the identity of the real author of the *Mānasāra* is established, and the missing link connecting the *Mānasāra* with Vitruvius is discovered and definitely ascertained, it would not be quite possible to be more precise about the date of the *Mānasāra*.

CHAPTER VIII

HINDU ARCHITECTURE IN INDIAN BORDER LANDS

TIBET

BOTH SAIVISM AND demon worship are practised along with Buddhism in Tibet. King Sron-bt[illegible]ram-po (A.D. 629 to 650) married two Buddhist princesses, on[illegible]om China and the other from Nepal, and thus Buddhism was introduced in Tibet. 'He is said to have built the monastery of Labrang, in the centre of Lhasa (A.D. 644), with perhaps the largest temple, as it is the most ancient in the country. His Chinese queen had brought with her a famous sandal-wood image of Sākyamuni and another of Ānanda, and for these was erected, about 650, the Ramoche temple, a little to the north-east of Labrang.'

Siva temples in Tibet are rare. But from the general history it can be assumed that they were of ordinary Hindu style with slight local variations. The Buddhist monuments in Tibet consist of numerous monasteries and the splendid tombs of the Grand Lamas.

The earliest Tibetan monastery is stated to be 'that of Sām-yas, about 35 miles south-east from Lhasa, near the Sang-po river. It was established by a famous teacher, Padma Sambhava, who went from Bihar with other Buddhist teachers about the middle of the eighth century. He is said to have modelled it after the great temple monastery of Odantapuri, near Nalanda, and it became the metropolis of the Red-cap order. The monastery, with its large temple and four separate colleges, is enclosed by a circular wall about a mile and a half in circuit, and contains a notable library and the State treasury. Another Indian Pandit, named Atisha, came from the Vikramasila monastery about 1038 A.D. and restored the Lamaism of his time, establishing what afterwards became the Yellow-cap or Gelupga order of Lamas, which became the State church when its chiefs, the Dalai Lamas, usurped the temporal power.'[1]

The most famous and magnificent of the Tibetan monasteries is, however, that of Potala, outside the city of Lhasa. Here the Dalai Lama resides. It is known as the Red Palace. Its centre is occupied by a great block, dominating the others, which contains the temples,

[1] Fergusson, *Indian and Eastern Architecture*, I, 293.

audience halls, and *chaityas* (tombs) of the Dalai Lamas. On its roof are the gilded pavilions of Chinese style that render it so conspicuous in the landscape. 'It was built by the first Dalai Lama between 1642 and 1650 on the ruins of the ancient fortress of Sron-btsang-gam-po, on a hill in the west of Lhasa, rising about 300 feet above the plain.'[1] The most of the remaining monasteries, even of later days, are, however, of Indian origin and style. One of these later monasteries is situated at Depung, three or four miles from Lhasa, and 'contains fully 7,000 inmates, mostly devoted to exorcism and magic. It was founded in 1414, and is said to be named or modelled after the early Indian monastery of Dhanyakataka or Amaravati.'[2] It is of the same plan as of other monasteries : 'within the enclosure is a large temple surrounded by four chapels, and a palace of Lhasa Lama.'

Sikim

Sikim is stated to have borrowed its architecture mostly from Tibet. But the doorway in the temple of Tashiding bears resemblance with the 'feature nearly universal in Bihar and early western caves.'[3] Another example is the temple at Pemiongchi 'the form of roof of which we are familiar with in the rock examples, and also as illustrating the extent to which the bracket capital of India may be carried under the influence of wooden architecture.'[4]

Thus while the Buddhist monuments of these regions are developed out of the northern Buddhist styles in India proper, the Brahmanical temples of the Śaiva and Vaishṇava faiths 'will become more intelligible when studied in connexion with the Dravidian and northern styles.'[5]

Nepal

There is a saying that in Nepal 'there are more temples than houses, and more idols than men.' In fact the number of the Buddhist, Śaiva, and Vaishṇava shrines in the three old capitals of Patan, Bhatgaon, and Kathmandu, which are within a short distance of one another, is estimated at 2,000. In Nepal no succession of styles can

[1] Fergusson, *ibid*, Plate vi, p. 292. [2] *Ibid*, p. 294.
[3] *Ibid*, wood-cut no. 163, p. 295. [4] *Ibid*, wood-cut no. 164, p. 297.
[5] *Ibid*, Vol. II, p. 297.

PLATE XLII (a)

WINDOW IN A NEPALESE TEMPLE

be, however, traced; 'no history in fact, for we hardly know when any of the three religions was introduced, but what we find is the Vaishṇava, Śaiva, and Buddhist religions existing side by side at the present day.'

'Like that of so many other countries of India, the mythic history of Nepal commences even before the Kaliyuga, and among its prehistoric visitors are mentioned Vipasyī and the other five Buddhas that preceded Śākyamuni, together with Mañjuśrī, Bodhisattva,' Śvayambhū, Śiva, as Paśupati, Vishṇu, and other gods of the Brahmanical pantheon. Tradition adds that king Asoka visited the valley and built five *chaityas*, one in the centre of Patan and the others at four cardinal points round it. The earliest inscriptions[1] belong to the later kings of the Lichchhavi dynasty 'whose ancestors seem to have come from Vaiśāli and established themselves in Nepal.' Some of them were Vaishṇavas and others Śaivas. Their inscriptions range from the fifth to the seventh century, when Aṁśuvarman founded a new dynasty.

'The Newars had entered the country from the north and were undoubtedly,' emphasizes Furgusson, 'of Tibetan origin,' their traditional connexion with the Nayyars of Malabar being stated to be a myth. These Newars were snake-worshippers, and 'the Buddhist missionaries who visited them accepted their legends and made them part of their system.' 'Hindu emigration into the valley must have begun early, and the kings of the long dynasty that ended about A.D. 600 all bear Hindu names, while their inscriptions indicate that they worshipped the Hindu gods. The Aṁśuvarman family or Thakuri dynasty were Vaiśyas and were succeeded by other Rajput families. In 1097 Nānyadeva, from Tirhut, invaded and subjugated the country, and again in 1324 Harisiṁha, of the same race, moved up from Simraun in the Tarai, and, overcoming the petty chiefs, assumed the government. His was a weak rule, the four chief towns, Bhatgaon, Banepa, Patan, and Kathmandu, each having their own princes till 1768, when a weak sovereign having called in the assistance of a neighbouring Gurkha raja, he seized the kingdom, and his successors still rule in Nepal.'

Owing to the prevalence, as in Tibet, of Tantric rites and sorcery, 'throughout in Nepal there is an exaggeration of all the most hideous

[1] Bhagwanlal Indraji, *Indian Antiquary*, IX, 411–428.

features of the religion.' The images of Durgā or Kālī are repulsive. Gods were propitiated with human sacrifices 'till warned in a dream to desist and substitute animals.'[1]

So far as the architecture of the Śaiva temples in Nepal is concerned, 'it seems to indicate that worship came into the valley from the north, rather than from the plains of Bengal. The architecture of the temples of Vishṇu, on the contrary, seems evidently to be an offshoot of the art of the plains.'[2] The shrine of Paśupati, three miles from Kathmandu, is a seventeenth century structure and comprises many temples and chapels. The little chapels along the side of the river are commemorative of the place where notable widows were burnt as *satis* along with the bodies of their dead husbands. The Bhavānī temple at Bhatgaon was built in 1703 by Bhupatīndra Malla to enshrine a secret Tantric goddess, which to this day is not allowed to be seen. It is five storeys in height and stands on a pyramid of five steps. The temples of Mahādeva and Kṛishṇa at Patan have the 'same characteristic form of roof, which is nearly universal in all buildings, civil or ecclesiastical, which have any pretension to architectural design. The temple dedicated to Kṛishṇa will be easily recognized by anyone familiar with the architecture of the plains from its *śikhara* or spire, with the curvilinear outline, and its clustering pavilions, not arranged quite like the ordinary types, but still so as to be unmistakably Bengali.'[3]

The Buddhist *chaityas* are regarded by authorities as the oldest monuments in Nepal. They are not called temples, since they contained no relics, but 'monuments intended to call forth pious thoughts.' In general appearance they are 'a hemispherical mound of earth, covered by a revetment of brick, surrounded by a plinth, also of brick, which serves as circular path. Four chapels are placed round the dome at the four points of the compass and joined to it, each containing the image of one of the four cardinal Buddhas—Amitābha on the west, Amogha-siddha on the north, Akshobhya on the east, and Ratnasambhava on the south (the centre being generally reserved for Vairochana). The temples of Svayambhū-nātha, a Buddhist monument, are perhaps the most elegant of all Nepal structures. It is beautifully

[1] *Account of the Kingdom of Nepal*, by B. Hamilton, pp. 35, 211.

[2] Fergusson, *Indian and Eastern Architecture*, p. 277, compare Paśupati temples (wood-cut no. 159), temples of Mahādeva and Kṛishṇa, Patan (photo no. 158), and Devī Bhavānī temple, Bhatgaon (photo no. 157).

[3] Fergusson, *ibid*, p. 283.

'extending through about five centuries (A.D. 600 to 1100), singularly uniform in their development and very local, being unlike any other style known in India.' This statement, however, does not mean that there is any structure in Kashmir whose origin cannot be traced to Hindu architecture or to the monuments of Brahmanical, Buddhist, or Jain faith. In fact Fergusson himself has admitted that 'in Kashmir we have a Buddhist period, developing by the eighth century into an original quasi-classical style that lasted till it, in its turn, was supplanted by that of the Muslim in the fifteenth century.'[1] Further, in describing the peculiarities of the Kashmir style, he takes the model of a small temple and says that 'such miniature temples are common in India and are copies of their larger prototypes'[2] Like this model instance, Kashmir temples are generally surmounted by roofs varying from two to four. 'All these roofs are relieved by dormer windows, of a pattern very similar to those found in mediaeval buildings in Europe, and the same steep, sloping lines are used also to cover doorways and porches, these being virtually a section of the main roof itself. The pillars which support the porticoes are by far the most striking peculiarity of this style, their shafts being so distinctly like those of the Grecian Doric, and unlike anything of the class found in other parts of India. Generally they are from three to four diameters in height, diminishing slightly towards the capital, and adorned with sixteen flutes, rather shallower than those of the Grecian order. Both the bases and capitals are, however, far more complicated than in the Grecian examples, though similar features are noticeable in Rome and Paestum.'[3] Another peculiarity is the trefoiled arch,[4] which is also noticed in Ajanta caves. Regarding this and other peculiarities Fergusson concludes by saying that, 'as in Kashmir and everywhere else in India, architectural decoration is made up of small model of large buildings applied as decorative features wherever required, it is by no means improbable that the trefoiled façade may have been adopted in Kashmir as currently as the simple horse-shoe form was throughout the Buddhist buildings of India proper.'[5]

The most typical and finest example is the temple of Martanda[6] situated about five miles east of Islamabad, the old capital of Kashmir.

[1] Fergusson, *ibid*, p. 274. [2] *Ibid*, p. 255, wood-cut no. 141.
[3] For example, *see ibid*, Vol. II, wood-cut no. 142, 143. [4] *Ibid*, wood-cut no. 144.
[5] *Ibid*, Vol. II, pp. 257, 258, 259. [6] *Ibid*, Vol. II, wood-cut no. 146, 147.

situated on a gentle eminence about half a mile from Kathmandu. Its history is not known. But the great Bodhnath *chaitya* is ascribed to king Mānadeva of the sixth century, as also to a Tibetan Lama, named Khasa, of later date. 'It is raised on three successive platforms or terraces, together about 45 feet high, on which stands the great dome, 90 feet in diameter, and rising another 45 feet, and over this is the pyramidal brick spire of about the same height.'[1] Another class of Buddhist *chaityas*, known as the *Koshṭhāgāra*, rise 'from a low, flat mound, one-tenth of its diameter in height, to a great height.' The curious thing about them is, 'among others there is a four-faced *Liṅga* of Śiva, with a corresponding emblem with four Buddhas, and altogether such a confusion of the two religions as is scarcely conceivable.'[2]

Kashmir

The earliest religious beliefs of Kashmir appear to have been the worship of Nāgas or serpent deities. The Nāga divinities were accepted by the Buddhists and worked into the mythology of the Māhayāna school. Until the sixth century this was probably the predominant religion of the country. Mihirkula, a white Hun who was a Śaiva, acquired the sovereignty about A.D. 530, and 'was a bitter prosecutor of the Buddhists, at the same time fostering the Brahmanical cult.'

When Hiuen Tsiang visited the country in the seventh century, Buddhism seems to have considerably revived. The kings of the Karkota and Utpala dynasties were tolerant and built Buddhist *vihāras* as well as Hindu temples. By the fourteenth century the Hindu rulers had become weak and effete, and a military adventurer from the south murdered Kota Rani, the widow of the last sovereign, A.D. 1339, and usurped the legal power as Sha Mir. As thus Muhammadanism rose in power, the old temples were either destroyed or were neglected and fell to ruin, as in northern India. There is thus no Buddhist *vihāra* in Kashmir and the few Hindu temples are in ruins.

The temples of Kashmir 'form a complete and homogeneous group,' as declared by Cunningham, Fergusson, and others,[3]

[1] Fergusson, *ibid*, pp. 278, wood-cut no. 155. [2] *Ibid*, p. 279, wood-cut no. 156.

[3] Cunningham, *Aryan Order of Architecture*, *J. A. S. B.*, Vol. XVII, Part II, pp. 241–327. Fergusson, *ibid*, Vol. II, pp. 251–252. Cole, *Illustrations of the Ancient Buildings in Kashmir, etc.* 1869.

PLATE XLIII

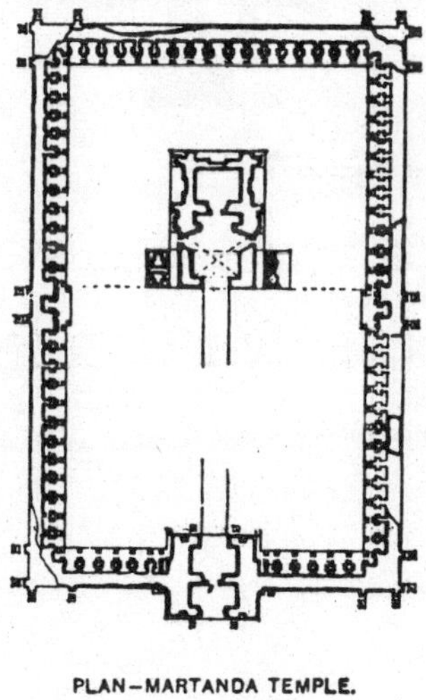

PLAN—MARTANDA TEMPLE.
SCALE 50 FT.=1 INCH.

MARTANDA TEMPLE

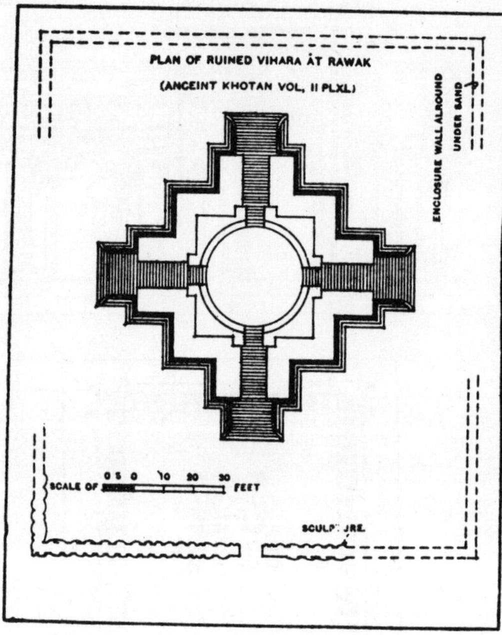

PLAN OF THE RUINED VIHĀRA AT RAWAK *Page* 289

It is called the architectural lion of Kashmir. It is, however, in a ruined condition and small in size, being 60 feet long by 60 feet wide and 60 feet high. The courtyard is more remarkable than the temple itself, its internal dimensions being 220 feet by 142 feet. On each face is a central cell, larger and higher than the colonnade in which it is placed. As stated in the *Rājataraṅgiṇī*, it was built by Lalitāditya-Muktāpīḍa who ruled about A.D. 725 to 760. Other important temples are those of Avantipur, half way between Srinagar and Islamabad, all erected by Avantivarman of the Utpala dynasty from A.D. 855 to 883. These are richer in detail than the Martanda temple. The temples at Pandrethan and at Payer are other remarkable examples, but without much difference.[1]

Kangra

The two famous temples in Kangra will complete the account of Hindu architecture in the Himalayan valleys. One of these is known as the temple of Vaidyanātha, situated in the village of Kiragrama some 25 miles from Kangra. It is clear from the inscriptions[2] that it was built by two merchants, Manyuka and Ahuka, under Lakshmana Chandra, brother-in-law of Jayachandra, king of Jalandhara or Trigarta, in about A.D. 1204. It is dedicated to Śiva and proved to be a Śiva temple by its porch, bull in front, and Gaṇeśa as its integral sculptures. But in the niche in the back there is the base portion of the image of Mahāvīra and a Jain inscription showing its consecration in A.D. 1240. 'This base must have been transferred to the Śiva temple after the destruction of the original Jain shrine,' says Fergusson, 'and probably owes its preservation, and that of a figure placed over it, to the ignorance of the priests of Vaidyanātha.'[3] In its composition it is an ordinary Śiva temple. It consists of a hall 20 feet square inside, with four round pillars supporting the roof, and a shrine for the Liṅga, 8 feet square, which is separated from the hall by a small ante-chamber. The roof and spire appear to have been rebuilt. The whole structure measures 51 feet by 31 feet and the walled enclosure is 120 feet long, 60 feet wide at the

[1] *See ibid*, pp. 268, 269, photo no. 152, 153.

[2] *Epigraphia Indica*, I, 97–118, II, 482, V, Appendix, p. 78. *Indian Antiquary*, XX, 154.

[3] The image of Pārśvanātha was found in the porch of a small Hindu temple at Kot Kangra (*Epigraphia Indica*, I, 120), Fergusson, *ibid*, II, p. 301.

east, and 75 feet wide at the west. Rooms for the priests and some small temples are situated within this area. But its chief interest lies in the shape of its pillars, particularly the capital. These pillars are styled the Hindu Corinthian order by Fergusson, who, however, says that the cylindrical shafts bear the Grecian proportions and that 'the bases are only slightly removed from classical design; the square plinth, the two toruses, the cavetto or hollow moulding between, are all classical (Grecian) but partially hidden by Hindu ornamentation of great elegance.'[1]

The other temple is known as that of Siddhanātha, situated at the west end of the town. It also consists of a four-pillared hall and a shrine, 33 feet by 20 feet, and with a *śikhara* of 35 feet height. It faces the east and has doorways on each side of the shrines leading into a circumambulatory passage.'[2]

CEYLON

The *Dipavaṁśa* and the *Mahāvaṁśa* are the chronicles of Ceylon. According to legends the kingdom of Ceylon was founded at the date of Buddha's *nirvāṇa*, 'which was placed in B.C. 543 and 236 years before the Council held in the eighteenth year of Aśoka.' About a century after the death of Buddha, in or about 370 B.C., his religion was introduced at Anurādhapur, the capital of Ceylon. But this capital city did not become sacred till 240 B.C., when it was considered one of the principal capitals of Buddhism, which position it continued to hold till the ninth century A.D. Thereafter, owing to the destructive invasions of the Malabars, an alternative capital was founded at Polonnaruwa, which in course of time became the sole capital till the thirteenth century. This later capital reached its greatest prosperity in the reign of Parākrama Bāhu I (1153–1186). After 1236, the seat of government was moved from place to place 'till the country fell into the hands of the Portuguese and Dutch, and finally succumbed to our (British) power.'[3]

[1] This type of capital is, however, found in the Śrī Yajña cave at Nāsik, in the courtyard of Viśvakarma at Elora, cave twenty-four in Ajanta, Hindu caves at Elora, at Eran of the Gupta period (about A. D. 400 to 600). Afterwards it became almost universal with the Jains till the advent of the Muhammadans. Compare Fergusson, *ibid*, pp. 298, 300, wood-cut no. 165, 166, 167.

[2] Cunningham, *Archaeological Reports*, Vol. V, Plate 44, which is stated to be incorrect by Fergusson, *ibid*, Vol. II, p. 301, footnote 2.

[3] Fergusson, *History of Indian and Eastern Architecture*, I, p. 228.

The Ceylonese monuments are situated in these two capital cities. Of all known countries Ceylon alone 'contains a complete series of Buddhist monuments extending from the time of Aśoka to the present day.' The two *dāgabas* of Anurādhpur are of the largest size known. The dome of the one, the Abhayagiri, is 'exactly hemispherical, and has a diameter of about 328 feet, being thus more than 1,000 feet in circumference, and with the base and spire must have made a total elevation of about 260 feet.'[1] It is ascribed to king Vattagamini Abhaya, who is stated to have built, in the first century B.C., a *vihāra* on the site of a Jain temple to commemorate the reconquest of his kingdom. Nothing is stated about the *dāgaba* or *chaitya* which must have been there. It was extended by Gajabāhu I in the second century A.D. 'The *stūpa* stands on a stone-paved platform 590 feet square, raised about 9½ feet above the ground level, and ascended on each side by a flight of steps 27 feet wide. The chapels or thrones for the Dhyāni-Buddhas (in this *stūpa*) are like those in Sanchi and Kalinga *stūpas*.'[2]

The second *stūpa* of Anurādhapur is the tope of Jetavanārāma. In form and dimensions it resembles the Abhayagiri. It was started by king Mahāsena in the fourth century A.D. and finished by his successor Meghavarna. In addition to these, there is a great number of *dāgabas* of various sorts scattered over the area once covered by the old city.

The Loha-Mahāpāya, or Great Brazen Monastery, has been fully described in the *Mahāvaṁśa*. 'It was erected by king Datta-gāmini in or about 100 B.C. Its plan is stated to have been received from heaven. It was 100 cubits or 250 feet square, and as high as it was broad. The height was divided into nine storeys, each containing 100 cells for priests, besides halls and other apartments. There were 1,600 pillars supporting the structure. They stand about 6 feet apart from centre to centre in a compact phalanx, 40 on each face, and covering a space of 250 to 260 feet each way. This monastery was originally of nine, and subsequently of five, storeys, each less in dimension than the one below it. The top one was surmounted, as at Māmallapuram, by a dome, but in this instance composed of

[1] The present total height is 232 feet (Smither, *Architectural Remains : Anurādhapur*, p. 47). Its traditional height, according to the *Mahāvaṁśa*, was 120 cubits of 2 feet $3\frac{6}{7}$ inch each.

[2] Fergusson, *ibid*, Vol. I, p. 230.

bronze—whence its name, and, 'gilt and ornamented as it no doubt was,' declares Fergusson, 'it must have been one of the most splendid buildings of the East.'

Besides these there are several other monuments, including *vihāras*, monasteries, halls for various purposes, rock-cut temples (like the one known as Isurmuniya), the sacred Bo-tree, stated to be a branch of the famous tree at Bodh-Gaya imported by Mahindra and Sanghamitta, the son and daughter of king Aśoka.

The ruins at Pulastipura and Kalingapura (now known as Topava or Polonnaruva) 'extend in a line nearly north and south for about a mile and a half from the palace to the Gal Vihāra and comprise two *dagabas*, besides a number of smaller edifices.' Most of these were erected during the reign of Parākrama Bāhu I (1153–1186). Most interesting of these is the Gal Vihāra. This is a rock-cut edifice, but is neither a residence nor a *chaitya* hall. 'On the left, on the face of the rock, is a figure of Buddha, seated in the usual cross-legged conventional attitude, 15 feet in height, and backed by a throne of exceeding richness.' Next to this is a cell with two pillars in front, on the back wall of which is another seated figure of Buddha. Beyond this is a figure of Ānanda, the cousin of Buddha, standing in the open, 23 feet high; still further to the right, another of Buddha, lying down in the attitude of his attaining *nirvāṇa*. This figure is 46 feet long.[1]

Close to the Gal Vihāra stands the Jetavana-vihāra temple, built of brick, 170 feet long by 70 feet wide and still about 70 feet high. 'It was divided into two halls, the inner or shrine being wider than the outer or eastern one, and containing an erect statue of Buddha, built of brick, 58 feet in height. The entrance is flanked by two polygonal turrets, on the bases of which were Dvārapālas or Yakshas in high relief, and the highly carved stone steps at the entrance were 20 feet long. On the north side of it is the Kiri Dagaba, about 70 feet in diameter and nearly 100 feet in height, with two smaller topes standing on raised platforms.' The whole space measuring 577 feet by 500 feet, once contained other monuments.

The Sāt Mahal Prāsāda[2] is a seven-storeyed temple. Its base is 28 feet 6 inches square, each storey diminishes in size and height, the uppermost being ruined, the total height is still 53 feet. Statues

[1] Fergusson, *ibid*, p. 244–245.

[2] Fig. 137. Fergusson, *ibid*, p. 246.

of stucco, in high relief, ornamented each storey. Fergusson suggests that the style of this tower was borrowed from Cambodia.

There is a unique circular building known as the Wata-Dā-ge.[1] 'It is a circular enclosure open to the sky, 58 feet 2 inches in diameter, and surrounded by a wall 14 feet high. Round the outer circumference of the wall is a narrow passage enclosed by a highly ornamental screen about 3 feet high, adorned with a range of 32 slender pillar shafts, 6 feet in height, with highly carved capitals. Below this is a richly carved stylobate, about 4 feet 6 inches high, standing on a circular platform 120 feet in diameter, about 20 feet broad and 4 feet 6 inches above the ground level. The principal entrance is from the north, but at other cardinal points also are flights of steps leading up to the enclosure. They all have highly carved thresholds or moonstones to start from. Their risers are each adorned with twelve figures of dwarfs, and their side-pieces, or jambs, are of exceptional richness, and each has a pair of *nāga*-headed *dvārapalas* at the sides of its steps.' Inside this were found the remains of a small brick-*dāgaba* and broken figures of Buddhas, and the broken shafts of pillars of two circles that had surrounded the *dāgaba.*

In this group there are, as stated by Fergusson, several buildings in the Dravidian style of architecture. One of these, 'miscalled the Dalada Māligāwa,' is really a Śaiva temple, erected probably by Nissanka Malla, about 1190.

'There are some interesting ancient bridges, formed on upright stone pillars, over which stone lintels are placed, and on these other stone beams, about 5½ feet in length from one lintel to another, to form the road.'

[1] Plate, *ibid*, p. 246–247.

CHAPTER IX

HINDU ARCHITECTURE IN SERINDIA OR CENTRAL ASIA

In addition to numerous literary references and travellers' accounts, archaelogical evidences, especially architectural and sculptural remains, have shown beyond doubt that Indian civilization marched further into Central Asia.

The area extends 'from the Hindukush valleys and the uppermost Oxus right across the whole length of the Tārim Basin to the province of Kan-su on the western marches of China proper.'[1] This region covers 'practically the whole of that vast drainageless belt between the Pāmirs in the west and the Pacific watershed in the east, which, for close on a thousand years, formed the special meeting-ground of Chinese civilization, introduced by trade and political penetration, and of Indian culture propagated by Buddhism.' This desert region contains 'relics of that ancient civilization which the joint influences of Buddhist India, China, and Hellenized Near East had fostered in the scattered oases of those remote Central Asian passage lands.'

Khotan

The Chinese records make it beyond doubt that Buddhism established in Eastern (Chinese) Turkestan, Khotan, Kasghar, oasis of Yarkand, and Karghalik, had been imported, directly or indirectly, from India. The migration of Indian culture in Central Asia was further corroborated by various archaeological evidences, including the discovery of the famous birch-bark codex by Colonel Bower from Kuchā the find of birch-bark leaves (containing a Buddhist text in early Prakrit language and in Kharoshthi script) by M. Dutreuil de Rhins at Khotan, and the Sanskrit texts (in Brahmi script) discover in the ruined shrines and monastic dwellings of Dandan-Uiliq Endere by Sir M. Aurel Stein, pointing to the study of Sansk. Buddhist literature in Khotan down to the end of the eighth century A.D The Central Asian explorations of Aurel Stein have supplied ample materials to identify in this region the Indian architectural and

[1] This region has been briefly designated by the French scholars as 'Serindia', depending on 'Learned popular etymology.' Sir Aurel Stein, Introduction, *Serindia*, Vol. I.

sculptural objects, including numerous articles of furniture. These are predominantly of Buddhistic style, but the purely Brahmanical names of deities and temples are not altogether missing. The village schemes and town-planning also appear to have been of Hindu origin in their general plan and other essential features. The differences may be easily accounted for by the climate, sandy desert, soil condition, and other local causes. That the territory of Khotan had been under Chinese supremacy for a long time during the Han and the Tang dynasties, and that the influence of Chinese civilization strongly asserted itself, are proved beyond doubt by the finds of Chinese records in wood and paper, Chinese graffiti, coins, articles of industrial art, etc. The finds of Tibetan MSS. and graffiti in the ruined fort and temple of Endere would also show the Tibetan influences. Despite these varied foreign influences at work, Eastern Turkestan, including Khotan, 'possessed during the pre-Muhammadan epoch a well-defined civilization of its own.' The religious predeliction and possibly the superiority of the Indian style may, however, have induced the migration of Hindu architecture in Central Indian colonies as in Indo-China and in Indonesian islands.

The remains consist of numerous mounds, *stūpas*, *vihāras*, sanctuaries, shrines, temples, palaces, pavilions, forts, and unrecognizable dwellings.

'The top of the mound (Kurghan-Tim) stands 70 feet above the ground level of the neighbouring fields, but it rises in reality to fully 85 feet above the lowest course of masonry at present traceable.' 'The whole mound consisted originally of sundried bricks of large size, laid in regular courses with thin layers of mud plaster to act as binding material.' 'The far advanced ruin of the whole structure makes it impossible to ascertain its original dimensions and constructive features. There can be no doubt as to the remains being those of a *stūpa*, built with a remarkably large dome, possibly of hemispherical shape. . . . The base was square and arranged in three storeys . . . its greatest length measuring about 160 feet from east to west, compared with about 130 feet from north to south.'[1]

The Mauri-Tim Stūpa bears similar features.[2] There are some common architectural similarities between these and the ruined *stūpas*

[1] *Ancient Khotan*, by Sir M. Aurel Stein, Vol. I, p. 74, photo no. 13, Plate (Vol. II) xxii.

[2] *Ibid*, Cf. *Mauri-Tim Stūpa* (pp. 81, 82, photo I, Vol. II).

of Takhtaband in Buner and of Bāhār near ancient Taxila,[1] in the Maṇikyala Stūpa, and in the numerous *stūpas* of the Kabul valley.[2] It is clear that there exists a close agreement in regard to the general architectural arrangement between all Turkestan *stūpas* and the corresponding structures in the Kabul valley and on the Indian north-west frontier. The development of *stūpa* architecture in India, as elucidated by M. Foucher,[3] will further show that the Turkestan *stūpas* conform closely to an Indian type.[4]

'The *stūpas* of Mauri-Tim, Topa-Tim, Niya, Endere, and Rawak all show the dome, which is the essential and unvarying feature of every *stūpa*, raised on a square base, and this is again arranged in three storeys. The relative proportion between these storeys varies considerably in the several structures, and so also do the shape of the dome and the relative height of the cylindrical portion or drum which intervenes between the top storey of the base and the copula proper. But the square shape of the base and its three-fold arrangement are constant features, and the former in any case is characteristic also of the great majority of *stūpas* in the border lands of India and Afghanistan. On the other hand the round base, which belongs to an earlier stage of *stūpa* construction, is represented in those territories only by a few examples, and seems completely absent in Eastern Turkestan.'[5]

'The king's new monastery,' comprising the splendid *stūpa* and temple of which Fa-hien has left a detailed description, were situated a little to the west of the Khotan capital. 'Seven or eight lea to the west of the city there is what is called the king's new monastery, the building of which took eighty years, and extended over three reigns. It may be 250 cubits in height, rich in elegant carving and inlaid work, covered above with gold and silver, and finished throughout with a combination of all the precious substances. Behind the tope there has been built a Hall of Buddha, of the utmost magnificence and beauty, the beams, pillars, venetianed doors and windows being all overlaid with leaf-gold. Besides these, the apartments for the

[1] Stein, *Report on Archaeological Tour with Buner Field Force*, p. 40, Plate viii, *Indian Antiquary*, 1900, p. 145.

[2] Cunningham, *Archaeological Survey Report*, Vol. V, Plate xxii.

[3] Foucher, *L'Art de Gandhara*, I, pp. 62–98.

[4] Stein, *Ancient Khotan*, p. 83, note 12.

[5] *Ibid*, p. 83.

monks are imposingly and elegantly decorated, beyond the power of words to express.'[1] 'From the great height mentioned,' concludes Sir Aurel Stein, 'it is clear that the structure was of wood, like the famous Vaiśravaṇa temple in the capital itself.'[1] Stein identifies this great shrine with the So-mo-je convent of Hiuen-Tsang and says that it 'must be located at the present village of Somiya, close to the west of Yot Kan.'[1]

Hieun-Tsang has left unusually full descriptions of various places of Buddhist worship outside the capital of Khotan. 'The nearest among these sanctuaries was the convent of So-mo-je, with a *stūpa* a hundred feet high in its centre a little over a mile to the west of the royal city.'[2] Hieun-Tsang ascribes its origin to a legend which really means that some architects were imported from India for its construction. The legend relates that: 'one time an Arhat coming from a distant foreign land had taken up his abode there in the middle of a wood. The miraculous light spread around by his spiritual power was noticed by the king as he stopped at night in a double-storeyed pavilion of his palace. Having been informed of its cause the king proceeded to the holy man and respectfully invited him into the palace. On the Śramaṇa refusing to leave the wood, the king full of reverence built a convent for him and a *stūpa*. When afterwards the king had procured a quantity of sacred relics and regretted not to have been able to insert them under the *stūpa*, the Arhat directed him to have the precious objects enclosed successively in receptacles of gold, silver, copper and stone. When this had been done and the relics had been transported by the king and his chief officers on an ornamented car to the convent, the Arhat raised the *stūpa* on the palm of his hand and held it while the king's workmen dug a place for the sacred deposit. Then, on the work being accomplished, the Arhat once more lowered the *stūpa* to its original position without any damage.[3]

[1] *Fa-hien's Travels*, Translation, Legge, pp. 19 sq.; Stein, *Ancient Khotan*, I pp. 194.

[2] Stein refers to *Memoirs*, II, pp. 235 sqq., *Si-yu-ki*, II, pp. 316 sq.: Remusat, *Ville de Khotan*, pp. 50 sqq., Watters, II, p. 297.

[3] This legend, and a somewhat similar one told by Hiuen-Tsang of a *stūpa* near Kapisa, (*Memoirs*, I, pp. 45 sq., *Si-yu-ki*, I, p. 60) have been discussed by M. Foucher, *L'Art de Gandhara*, I, p. 52, with reference to the light they throw on the purpose of *stūpa* construction.

Stein, *ibid*, p. 223.

The Tibetan form of the legend is slightly different. It is stated in the *Annals of Li-yul* that king Vijayavirya, the eighth successor of Vijaya-sambhava, under whom Buddhism was believed to have been first introduced, one day while looking out of *srog-mukhar* (life-fort) he perceived a light brilliant as gold and silver at the spot where now stands the Hgum-stir Chaitya. When the king learned that the Buddha had foretold that at that spot a *vihāra* would be built, he called to his presence the Buddhist Buddhadūta, and having made him his spiritual adviser, ordered him to direct the building of the Hgum-stir Vihāra.' Stein emphatically asserts that it refers to the same shrine and the Buddha-dūta corresponds to Hiuen-Tsang's Arhata.[1]

The buildings of the ancient Khotan capital are referred to in all Chinese records, and comprise magnificent temples, palaces and pavilions of which, however, the architectural details are not available. In a passage of the *Yini*, composed by Hui-lin in the eighth or ninth century,[2] reference is made to an important building. It shows that the famous temple of Vaiśravaṇa, which the legends related by Hiuen-Tsang and the *Annals of Li-yul* represent as the oldest shrine of the kingdom, stood in the city of Yu-tien, and that it was 'a tower built in wood seven storeys high. The god was supposed to reside on the summit. Hiuen-Tsang particularly extols the richness of the temple as it existed in his time.'[3]

This building is apparently of Indian origin as it bears the name of an Indian deity.

'As regards the royal palace,' says Sir Aurel Stein,[3] 'we learn from the account of the Chinese mission sent in 938 that it comprised a number of buildings all facing to the east, and among them a pavilion called that of the seven phœnixes.[4] An earlier notice, found in the *Liang Annals*, specially mentions the frescoes adorning the king's palace.[5] That the city was enclosed by walls we know from Hieun-Tsang. He adds that they were of no great height. . . . The ancient fortifications still existing at the sites of Endere,

[1] Stein, *Ancient Khotan*, I, p. 223.

[2] M. S. Levi, *Notes Chinoises L'Inde*, p. 39.

[3] Stein, *Ancient Khotan*, I, p. 202.

[4] Remusat, *Ville de Khotan*, p. 80, where the name of the palace is given as Chinise-tien.

[5] Remusat, *loc. cit.*, p. 16.

Karadong, Ak-sipil show that we may safely assume those walls to have consisted mainly of ramparts of stamped loess. At the gate of the city there used to take place the solemn reception by the king and the ladies of his court of the procession of great image cars of which Fa-hien has left us so vivid a description.'[1]

The Indian equivalent of the pavilion of seven phœnixes (*Nāga* and *Nāginī ?*) and of the Chinese name, Chin-ise-tien, of the palace are not quite clear. But the eastern orientation (façade), the fortified plan of the walled city with rampart around, and the procession of the great image cars are familiar objects of Hindu architecture described in great detail in the *Mānasāra* and other *Śilpa-śāstras*.

'In a convent known as the Ti-chia-po-fu-na Sanghārāma (*Dīrgha-bhavana*) and situated a little over 10 lea to the south-west of the capital, the pilgrim (Hiuen-Tsang) was shown the statue of a standing Buddha which was supposed to have miraculously come to this spot from Kuchā. A Khotan minister exiled to the latter state had secured his repatriation by assiduous worship of this image. . . . The minister then built for it this convent.' Stein identifies it with the Ziarat of 'Bowa-kambar,' which he found to consist of 'a large square cemetery enclosing the high mud-built tomb' of a saint. 'The level of the cemetery near its centre lies fully 12 feet below the surrounding fields. . . . A grove of fine old trees faces the eastern entrance.'[2]

By far the most imposing structure among the extant ruins of the Khotan region is the Rawak Stūpa and Vihāra. The greater part of the *stūpa* has gone, only its high base and enclosing quadrangle remaining. 'The *vihārā* court formed a great rectangle, measuring 163 feet inside on its south-western and north-eastern faces, and 141 feet on its shorter sides towards the north-west and south-east. It was enclosed by a wall about 3 feet 6 inches thick, solidly built of sun-dried bricks. At the south corner . . . this wall rose to a height of 11 feet, but was probably once still higher.[3] . . . The gate in the south-east face, 8½ feet to 10 feet wide, was the only entrance to the court.'

[1] Legge, *Travels of Fa-hien*, p. 19.

[2] Stein, *Ancient Khotan*, I, pp. 225–226.

[3] The bricks used in it, as well as in the *stūpa*, measured 20 by 14 inches with a thickness of 3½ to 4 inches, practically identical with the dimensions of the Ak-sipil bricks.

'The centre of the quadrangle is occupied by the imposing *stūpa* base which rises in three storeys to a height of 22½ feet above the floors of the court. . . . The lowest storey, 78 feet square and 7½ feet high, rests on a plinth of four steps showing aggregate elevation of 3 feet. The second storey is 45½ feet square, with a height of 9 feet. It is surmounted by a circular drum, 3 feet high and receding on the top, which serves as a plinth for another circular drum forming part of the *stūpa* dome.'[1] As the masonry of the dome is intact to a height of about 8½ feet, the exact elevation of the dome and the shape of the cupola cannot be determined. But the other indications will show that, like other monuments. it is also of the Indian style. This expectation is fulfilled by the other members of the *stūpa*.

'Considerable variation and originality was introduced into the ground-plan by a series of bold projections on each face of the base supporting well-proportioned flights of steps. Through these projections the ground-plan of the base has assumed the shape of a symmetrically developed cross, each of the four arms of which extends about 52 feet on the lowest level, as measured from the centre line of the *stūpa*. The broad flights of steps which occupied the centre of each of the four faces of the base, and, carried by the projecting portions, led up without a break from the level of the court to the very foot of the dome must have been an imposing architectural feature.'[1]

This obviously points to the Svastika plan of the *Mānasāra* architecture.

The extraordinary architectural features and imposing dimensions of Rewak monuments are quite in keeping with the rich series of relief sculptures decorating the walls of the enclosing *vihāra*. 'The main adornment of the walls, both towards the court and outside, consisted throughout of rows of relief statues in stucco over life-size. All the large reliefs represented Buddhas or Bodhisattvas; but from the varying poses, accessories, etc., still recognizable, a number of groups could be distinguished, arranged apparently with some regard to symmetrical disposition. Between the colossal statues at the frequent intervals were smaller representations of attendant divinities or saints. In numerous instances the walls were further decorated with elaborate plaques in stucco, forming haloes

[1] Stein, *Ancient Khotan*, pp. 483, 484, 485.

above the heads of figures, or, in some cases, where sufficient space had been allowed, even with complete aureoles in relief around them. . . . The whole of the relief work had been originally coloured, but the layers of paint had in most cases peeled off except where well-protected in drapery folds, etc. Thus the greatest portions of the stucco images presented themselves in the red ground colour of the clay in which they have been modelled.'[1]

'The total number of individual reliefs, most of them over life-size, amounted to ninety-one.' In the poses of these reliefs Sir Aurel Stein has identified the *Abhaya-pāṇi-mudrā* like in the Dandān-Uiliq and Kighillik reliefs, and the *Vara-mudrā* and *Bhūmisparśa-mudrā*, differing only by the pose of the hand with the palm turned towards or inwards. There are images of colossal, and small Buddhas and Bodhisattvas, both standing and seated with wave-lined draperies and characteristic nimbus, *vajras*, and other features. There are *dvārapālas* and female busts and heads of Yakshas and Yakshiṇis.[2] So far as the date of the Rawak remains is concerned, Sir Aurel Stein cautiously says that 'the fact of the Rawak sculptures approaching their Gandhara models much nearer than those of Dandān-Uiliq or Endere, and the total absence among them of any of those images with multiple limbs, etc., which characterize the later pantheon of Northern Mahāyāna Buddhism, may at once be accepted as a proof that they are older. But beyond this it would scarcely be safe to draw any further chronological conclusions from the evidence of the artistic remains themselves, seeing how scanty our data are for the chronology of the Graeco-Buddhist sculpture in Gandhara itself, and how little we know as yet of the historical development of its offshoot transplanted to Eastern Turkestan.'[3]

The ruins of Endere comprise the remains of a fort together with the remains of a *stūpa* and a temple. The fort is circular in shape, a variety described in the *Mānasāra Silpa-śāstra.* It is surrounded by a 30 feet wide rampart varying in height from 5 to 25 feet, with masonry parapet of 5 feet 6 inches height and 3 feet thickness at the entrance to the south. Behind the parapet ran a platform. The gate, 18 feet wide, was flanked on either side by a small square bastion or tower, projecting about 20 feet beyond the outer foot of the

[1] Stein, *Ancient Khotan*, p. 486.
[2] *See* photos nos. 61, 62, 63, 64, 65, 66, 67, 68; *ibid*, I, pp. 490–99.
[3] Stein, *ibid.*, I, p. 500.

circular rampart. To the west of the gate there is a guard-room.[1] Following the rules of the *Śilpa-śāstra*, the temple is situated just in the centre, which is technically known a the Brahmapīṭha. 'The cella of the temple formed a square of 18 feet 4 inches inside, enclosed by walls of timber and plaster having a thickness of 10 inches. The entrance lay to the east. The enclosing passage, the walls of which were of similar construction . . . was 5 feet wide, its plastered floor lay 3 feet higher than that of the cella.' 'It appears probable that, for purposes of lighting, the cella was provided with a raised roof in the centre.'[2] This would look like some form of Hindu *śikhara*. 'The four corners of the cella were occupied by plaster images, almost wholly detached and standing each on a basement to represent an open lotus with the petals pointing downwards. By the side of the statues in the north-east and south-east corners there were probably figures of *lokapālas* or guardians of regions.' 'The centre of the cella was occupied by a massive octagonal base or platform, 9½ feet long and 7½ feet broad. The base proper rose to a height of 2 feet 8 inches above the floor. On it four life-size relief statues in stucco must have stood, the lotus-shaped pedestals of three being still more or less intact.' 'On the north-east facet the fresco remains showed two rows of seated male figures, seven in each, apparently Buddhas or Bodhisattvas.'

The temple is surrounded by groups of small buildings to the north, east, south-west and north-west at a distance of some 50 feet. The purpose of all these buildings is not definitely established. Sir Aurel Stein surmizes one of these in the north to be a grain store. In the eastern group there is a half-open hall and a number of other rooms of various sizes and purposes. This is stated to be 'undoubtedly the main structure within the area enclosed by the ramparts, and judging from the size of its halls and rooms, and the general arrangement of its plan,' Sir Aurel Stein concludes that 'it had served as the residence of the officer and establishment, for the protection of whom the fort must be supposed to have been primarily intended.'[3] There appears to have been some dwelling-houses to the south-east also, which had distinctly an upper storey.

Sir Aurel Stein is doubtful if the whole structure could have been suggested by a Chinese Ya-men, because the disposition of the rooms,

[1] *See* Plate xxxvi, *Ancient Khotan*, by Stein, Vol. II.
[2] *Ibid.*, I, p. 424. [3] *Ibid.*, I, p. 432.

etc., is not compatible with Chinese architectural convention.[1] It would look more like an Indian fort with a public temple in the centre and with other features noted above.

The Endere *stūpa*, situated outside the fort towards the north-west, 'consisted of a square base, approximately oriented with its corners, and of a cylindrical dome rising above it. The base rose in three storeys according to the canonical arrangement previously explained, the lowest storey measuring 27 feet, with a height of 1½ feet. The next storey, receding 2 feet from the first and 6 feet high, formed the main portion of the base; above, the third, only 1½ feet high, also receded by 2 feet. The dome had a diameter of 16 feet, rising with its broken top to a height of 14 feet.'[2]

The date or rather the period of the antiquities in Eastern Turkestan has been fixed by Sir Aurel Stein with some definiteness. For this purpose he has taken into consideration not only the remains of ancient town-planning, buildings, sculptures, industrial arts, but also the languages and scripts (Kharoshṭhi, Indian Brāhmī, Central Asian Brāhmī, Tibetan, Chinese, and Hebrew) of the numerous manuscripts (and inscriptions) he has explored.

'The remains of the Rawak Vihāra . . . enable us better than any other ruins . . . to realize what the plan and decorative aspect must have been of large Buddhist shrines in ancient Khotan. The affinity which the Rawak reliefs show in style and most details of execution with the Graeco-Buddhist sculptures of Gandhara is far closer than that we have had occasion to observe in the plastic remains brought to light elsewhere. These considerations make it all the more important to determine the period, if only within approximate limits, to which the ruined *vihāra* belongs. The fact of the Rawak sculptures approaching their Gandhara models much nearer than those of Dandān-Uiliq or Endere, and the total absence among them of any of those images with multiple limbs, etc., which characterize the later pantheon of Northern Mahāyāna Buddhism, may at once be accepted as a proof that they are older. But beyond this it would scarcely be safe to draw any further chronological conclusion from the evidence of the artistic remains themselves, seeing how scanty our data are for the chronology of Graeco-Buddhist sculpture in Gandhara itself, and how little we know as yet of the historical development of its offshoot transplanted to Eastern Turkestan.'[3]

[1] *Ancient Khotan*, I, p. 432. [2] *Ibid.*, I, p. 437. [3] *Ibid.*, I, p. 500.

Although the Indian relics in Central Asia consist mostly of Buddhistic shrines, scanty remains of dwellings and forts are not altogether missing. In fact, in certain sites the existing dwelling-houses built according to old traditions are the only evidence of the past. 'Outside it (old Kafir house at Dawawish) looked at first sight like a large heap of stones. But closer inspection showed walls far more solid than usual in these parts, built of uncut but well-set slabs of stone. The most striking feature inside was a large central room or hall, showing elaborate carving on its massive pillars and along one wall decorative panelling in *deodar*. . . . The ornamentation chiefly consisted of a diaper of four-petalled flowers, closely resembling in style those . . . from the ancient wood-carvings of the Niya site and from Gandhara relievos. . . . The square pillars supported large corbels ending in elaborate volutes. . . . The opening in the centre of the roof (called *aiwān* or *kumāl* in Khowār), which alone admits light and air, showed the typical construction. It consists of successive overlapping courses of massive beams gradually reducing the square opening '[1]

The remains of another dwelling-house have been found within eleven yards of a shrine. 'It consisted of a room built with walls of sundried bricks, and a small room and verandah adjoining it on the north. Both were constructed with timbers and plaster walls. The room, about 17 by 12 feet, still retained its substantially built clay fireplace, and in the corner beside it a plastered sitting platform. The roof was probably made of rafters and reed bundles.'[2] At Niya site the remains of several other dwelling-houses have been discovered. In one of these 'the main room showed on three sides a sitting platform, 4 feet broad and 15 inches high, faced with sun-dried bricks 17 by 12 by 3 inches. There was found here a roughly carved round central pillar and a plain double-bracket, 8 feet long and 7½ inches wide, with ends curving upwards. . . . In another room there was a wooden pillar, 5 feet high and oval in section, with a longer axis of 9 inches and the sides showing sixteen facets. The top, both in front and on the back, was decorated in rough bold chip-carving with a design showing a vase from which issued two long curving stems ending in broad leaves and fruit pendants'[3].

[1] *Serindia*, I, pp. 35–36, Fig. 15, 16. [2] *Ibid.*, I, p. 199. [3] *Ibid.*, p. 239

A BUDDHIST STUPA OF CHIAO-TZU

A CLOSE-UP VIEW OF THE CAVES OF THE THOUSAND BUDDHAS

The idea of the central pillar (*griha-stambha*), around and by the standard of which the whole house used to be built, is a peculiarity of Hindu architecture, which has been specially referred to in the *Mānasāra* and other *Śilpa-śāstras*. The round (oval) pillar with sixteen facets is also a peculiarity of Hindu architecture. The wooden pillars[1] of Tang Fort, Endere site, are further examples of Hindu architecture.[2]

There is another larger house built partly in timber and plaster and partly with plastered rush walls. 'Room, i, to the north-east, served as an office and yielded sixteen well-preserved Kharoshṭhi tablets, mostly wedge-shaped or rectangular. The adjoining looks like a fireplace. Outside the large room, v, yet within the fenced enclosure of a court or garden, lay the remains of long twisted vine branches. The cattle-shed is on the north-east.'[3]

The remains of the old forts are scanty. No clear idea of the whole is available. 'They appeared to have been constructed of large uncut stones . . . and to have formed an oblong of over 40 yards in length and about 17 yards across.'[4] At the Wakhān region there are similar remains of 'three Kafir forts, which the natives believe to have been erected by the Guebers or fire-worshippers.'[5] They are known as Zamr-i-Ātish-parast, Zangibar, and Kala-i-Kāka, the latter on the right bank of the Oxus.[6]

The *stūpas* of Chitral region are like those of Khotan. 'There are the characteristic three bases successively receding . . . above them the high cylindrical drum; next, a projecting cornice surmounted by the proper *stūpa* dome, which is approximately hemispherical in shape. Above the dome, in conventional outlines and drawn with a rather primitive attempt at perspective, appear the orthodox succession of 'umbrellas,' apparently seven, the lowest resting on supports which seem to slant outwards from the top of the dome. Through the last three of the umbrellas is seen passing the central pillar which in reality carried the whole series of umbrellas, and which, according to an early tradition, symbolized the beggar's staff planted on the top of Buddha's own *stūpa* model.'[7]

[1] *Serindia*, Fig. 70, pp. 236–37. [2] *Ibid.*, pp. 237, 238.
[3] For plan and disposition of rooms, *see ibid.*, plate 16. [4] *Ibid.*, p. 36.
[5] Wood, *Source of the Oxus*, p. 218. [6] Stein, *Serindia*, I. p. 66.
[7] *Ibid*, I, pp. 37, *see* Fig. 5.

The shrines of Khādalik resemble the Hindu temples. One of these as reconstructed[1] would look like the Liṅga type of temples described in the *Śilpa-śāstras*. It 'formed a quadrangle of which the external measurements were 75 on the east and west, and 73 on the north and south. The middle of this quadrangle contained a cella, measuring on the inside a little over 28 feet. The centre of the cella was occupied by a badly decayed base or platform, 10½ by 9½ feet. It rose in its completely broken state to a height of about 2½ feet above the plastered floor. The space left between the outer walls and the cella, 21 feet on the north and south, and 20 on the other sides, seemed far too wide for the enclosing passage. . . . The remains revealed manifest remains of intermediate walls which seem to have divided this outer space into no less than three concentric passages.'[2] This shrine faces southwards.

The next shrine, which is Buddhist, 'consisted of a rectangular cella, measuring 25 by 24 feet inside and enclosed by a passage 8 feet wide on the north and 5 elsewhere, with a large hall adjoining the south passage. The walls are of sundried bricks and were strengthened by wooden posts.'[3] In the cella have been found some two dozens miniature *stūpa* models in clay, none higher than two inches.

'The structure immediately adjoining this shrine contained a single hall measuring some 47 by 42 feet. Its southern portion was occupied by a plastered platform, 15 feet wide, rising 10 inches above the floor. The foot of the platform showed a bold moulding 3 inches wide.'[3]

A few more shrines of the same type existed in this region. But the scanty remains do not give a clear idea of the whole. Their Indian origin is, however, assured by many indications, including the use of Kharoshṭhi script and an early Prakrit language for administrative purposes.[4]

The Mīrān site discloses two kinds of ancient monuments. 'The ruined fort of Mīrān, imposing as was the appearance, rises on the pebble-covered plain which extends, with a total width of 3 miles, from the belt of the vegetation watered by the present course of the Mīrān stream eastwards to an ancient river-bed. It is of irregular shape and construction. Its walls still rise to a considerable height.

[1] *See* Fig. 6, *Serindia*, I, pp. 4–5.
[2] *Ibid.*, I, p. 156.
[3] *Ibid.*, p. 157.
[4] *Ibid.*, p. 243.

The two first wall-faces measure about 240 feet each. The west and south faces are considerably shorter, being about 168 and 200 feet in length. Projecting oblong bastions of irregular shape and varying dimensions protected the corners. It is, however, of comparatively late origin and of Tibetan type a disclosed by the finds of abundant Tibetan records.'[1]

The other monuments of Mīrān are of Indian origin and comprise Buddhist shrines, including *stūpa* of the same pattern as in other sites, temple, remains of Buddhist sculptures, mural painting of a Buddhist legend in the cella, and Kharoshṭhi inscriptions.

The main structure 'presented itself as a solid mound built of sundried bricks, oblong in shape, but showing no readily recognizable surface features. Two storeys, however, could at once be distinguished, and of these the lower are measuring about 46 feet on its longer sides and a little over 36 feet on the shorter. Its height was about 9 feet above the original level of the ground. On the top of this solid platform or base there rose a second storey, also oblong in shape. Its ground-plan measured about 17½ by 15 feet. The corners of the whole structure were roughly orientated towards the cardinal points. . . . The niches had once contained stucco statues in relievo, probably a little under life-size.'[2] 'This clearly proves that the architectural design of this decoration, which places relievo images in niches divided by Indo-Persian pilasters, is one directly borrowed from Graeco-Buddhist art.'[3]

The colossal heads in soft stucco also showed the influence of Graeco-Buddhist sculpture 'in modelling and proportions.'[4] The outer wall is lined with a row of colossal stucco images of Buddhas seated with cross-folded legs and usual pose (meditation, *dhyānamudrā*) of the hands and drapery. 'The statues measured 7 feet to 7 feet 3 inches across the knees, which reached to a height of a little over a foot. The stucco bases occupied by the torsoes were 7 feet 6 inches long and 2 feet 4 inches wide, and rose to a height of 1 foot and 4 inches. The spaces dividing them were only 6 to 7 inches across in front, but widened towards the wall behind.'[5]

Further evidence of their Indian origin was supplied by the discovery of a palm-leaf *pothi* (book) written in Sanskrit language and Brāhmī characters of an early Gupta type.

[1] Stein, *Serindia*, p. 456. [2] *Ibid.*, p. 485. [3] *Ibid.*, p. 486.
[4] *See* Fig. 121, 122, *Serindia*, Vol. I, pp. 486–87. [5] *Ibid.*, p. 488.

'The shrine, square outside but circular within, had once been surmounted by a dome and enclosed a small *stūpa* in its centre. . . . The interior of the circular cella had been lit by windows passing through the centre of the side walls, which were approximately orientated to the south, east, and north. The width of the windows was 2 feet 3 inches, and their lowest portions reached down to a level of 2 feet 8 inches above the floor. The masonry enclosing the dome cella was 4 feet thick at the windows, increasing to fully 10 feet where it filled the square corners. It consisted of sundried bricks mixed with straw, measuring 16 by 10 inches, with a thickness of 5 inches. The dome must once have surmounted the square cella, which was enclosed by an outside passage.'[1]

'The peculiarity of this *stūpa* lies in the circular shape of the base instead of the usual square one. . . . It may be assumed that the choice of the round base, amply attested among the *stūpas* of India and the north-west border, was due to considerations of the space available within the small circular cella.'[2]

'On the lowest division of the base, 9 feet in diameter and 9 inches in height, there is placed a receding drum, 1 foot 6 inches high, terminated both below and above by a uniform series of mouldings. Then follows another plain division, 9 inches high and of the same diameter as the lowest, and above it a succession of small step-like mouldings, with a total height of less than 6 inches. From this rises the cylindrical member, about 2 feet 3 inches high which carries the dome, both being 6 feet 8 inches in diameter. The projecting frieze-like moulding, about 4 inches thick, which intervenes between drum and dome, is a feature seen with equal clearness in the *stūpa* carving of Pakhtardini, the wooden *stūpa* models of Niya and Lonlan, etc.'[3]

'Considering the influence of the *pradakshiṇa* custom it seems highly probable that the composition of the wall-paintings as a whole had its starting point on the left of the entrance to the cella and thus in the south-eastern segment.' There are various kinds of figures, representation of riding prince, saddle and horse-gear of mount, princess driving quadriga, white elephant in sylvan scene, prince leading elephant, figures of armed men, animals, etc.,

[1] Stein, *Serindia*, p. 493, Fig. 123, 128. [2] *Ibid.*, p. 494, Fig. 126, 129, 130, 131.
[3] *Ibid.*, 494. (This seems to be the very last outpost of Buddhist Central Asian monuments.)

representations of the story of *Vessantara-jātaka*, Prince Vessantara's exile, Indian ascetics with bushy hair and beards carrying the long staffs and small bowl for water (*kamaṇḍalu*), lastly, on a piece of frieze, is represented a low throne of the Indian *gadi* type, covered with drapery.[1] There are also figures like a girl playing on a mandoline, girl carrying decanter, bearded male head, bust of Indian prince, etc.[2]

Tun-huang Region

Sir Aurel Stein has frequently referred to this site.[3] 'To the south-east of its main oasis, at the foot of a barren dune-covered hill-chain, there lies the sacred site the 'Caves of the Thousand Buddhas.' Buddhist piety from about the fourth century A.D. onwards has here honey-combed the rock walls of a true thebais with hundreds of cave-shrines, still objects of worship.'[4] Their decoration with frescoes and stucco sculptures is very rich. In other respects also they would resemble the famous caves at Ajanta, Elora, and other places.

'Along the whole length of the scarp of the hill the precipitous portion of the rock-face shows an unbroken succession of grottoes (some 515 in number). Some high, some low, they are all closely serried laterally, and in most parts perched also one above the other. But the number of grottoes varies greatly in height. . . . At both the northern and southern ends the rock-face displays only a single line of cave-temples, while four or five successive tiers may be counted elsewhere. Only for short distances and between the two shrines containing colossal Buddha statues it is possible to recognize regular rows or storeys. The two last-mentioned temples stand in a separate category by themselves; for in order to secure adequate space for the giant clay images of seated Buddhas close on 90 feet high which they were meant to shelter, a number of halls were excavated one above the other. Each of these provides light and access for a portion of the colossus, which rises unbroken to the top through a continuous cavity at the back.'

'In front of most of the shrines there had been originally ante-chapels or porches of oblong shape carved out of the rock. Their

[1] *Serindia*, I, pp. 517, 518, 519, 520, 521, Fig. 127, 133, 134, 135, 136, 137, 138.
[2] *Ibid.*, I., pp. 525, 526, 527, Fig. 139, 140, 141, 143.
[3] *Ibid.*, I., Chap. XXIII, XXIV, XXV.
[4] *Ibid.*, I., Introduction, p. xii. *See The Portfolio of Thousand Buddhas*, by Stein, Plates i–xlviii.

back and side walls, as well as the ceilings, still retained paintings *in tempera*. . . . In most cases access to, and communication between, these upper shrines seems to have been assured by means of wooden galleries, now marked only by the wooden rafters which once served to support them, or more frequently still by the mere holes into which they were fixed. The rock-cut or wooden stairs, which were required for the same purpose, had crumbled away almost everywhere, and even rough ladders were to be found only before a few caves which had undergone manifestly recent restoration. . . . The interior arrangements and decoration of these upper shrines, mostly of modest size, did not differ in any essential way from those prevailing in the cave-temples carved into the foot of the cliff.'[1]

'The ground-plan and general structural arrangement of these caves showed a striking uniformity. Outside there came first a kind of oblong ante-chapel. . . . Where restoration had taken place recently, the front had been closed by a wooden construction with big doors and windows, and this feature is likely to have been present also in the original design. From this ante-chapel the cave-temple proper was approached through a high and rather wide passage, which alone admitted light and air to the interior excavation. This consisted everywhere of a single rectangular cella, usually almost square in shape and with sides up to 54 feet in length, hewn out of the solid rock and provided with a high conical roof. Within the cella, which is usually a little deeper than it is wide, the larger shrines had generally a big rectangular platform, elaborately decorated in plaster and facing the entrance.'[2]

'The centre was invariably occupied by a colossal stucco image of Buddha, by the side of which were grouped in a symmetrical fashion statues of smaller divinities, all of them often badly injured . . . usually a kind of screen and canopy combined had been left standing in the rock at the back of the principal image. Behind this, and between the platform and the cella walls, a passage was invariably left for the worshippers to perform the circumambulation (*pradakshiṇa*). In the smaller shrines similar groups of stucco images, with a seated Buddha in their centre, were ordinarily found placed in a kind of alcove or raised chapel. Only in a few instances a third type of internal arrangement was in vogue by which the centre of the cella

[1] Stein, *Serindia*, II, p. 793.

[2] *Ibid.*, p. 794.

A GENERAL VIEW OF THE VALLEY OF THE MYRIAD BUDDHAS

Page 310

FRESCO DECORATION IN THE INTERIOR OF A CAVE TEMPLE IN THE CAVES OF THE THOUSAND BUDDHAS

Page 311

was left unexcavated and the square block of rock used as a backing for statues.'[1]

The wall-paintings are all executed *in tempera*. ' It is in this modified, technically inaccurate, sense that the term ' fresco ' must be understood. The mural decoration in the passages and ante-chapels ordinarily represents rows of large Bodhisattvas moving in procession, or else seated in tiers. Diapers of small figures of Buddhas and Bodhisattvas . . . covered the walls in numbers of small cellas. Along with elaborate floral designs and tracery they had often been used also for the adornment of the ceiling in the large cellas. But it was on the walls of these last that the wonderful richness and variety of this pictorial art had found room to express itself fully. There the frescoes generally filled large panels, bordered by floral scrolls of striking beauty. They were arranged either singly or in a series. Painted dados, often representing figures of worshippers, in some cases monks or nuns, served to raise these panels to an appropriate height above the floor and the statue-bearing platform. Panels were almost invariably filled by elaborate compositions containing a large number of figures. Varied as the subjects were in details, two main classes could readily be distinguished among them. In one there appeared figures of Buddhas, surrounded by symmetrically grouped hosts of Bodhisattvas, saints, and other divine attendants, all shown in a carefully arranged architectural setting of pavilions, platforms, lotus tanks, etc. These panels were meant to represent scenes in Buddhist heavens. The other class of fresco panels displayed, in close juxtaposition and often bewildering variety, scenes which looked as if taken from mundane life, but often with sacred figures moving among them.' Sir Aurel Stein felt assured that 'these scenes in the mural paintings illustrated Buddhist Jātaka stories. [2]

There is another similar group of cave temples near Chiao-tzu, known as the ' valley of Myriad Buddhas.' This collection of cave temples ' could not compare in extent and importance with that of the Thousand Buddhas.'[3] ' What the site lacks in size seemed,'

[1] Stein, *Serindia*, II, p. 794.

[2] *Ibid.*, II, pp. 794–95. *See* Figs. 200, 214, 211, 212, 216, 217, 218, 219, 219–224, 228, 233–236, 230, 206, 209, 210, 220, 224, 231, 235, 217, 218, 221, 222, 233, 236, 202. For detailed descriptions, *see* pp. 847–91.

[3] *Ibid.*, Vol. III, p. 1109.

says Sir Aurel Stein, 'to be made up by the singular wildness of its setting.'

The temple grottoes of Wan-fo-hsia extend for a distance of over a quarter of a mile.[1] 'The condition of the sacred site harmonized very pleasantly with the picturesque seclusion and peace of this submontane thebais.' Numerous small shrines lay scattered along a raised terrace at the foot of the cliffs on the right bank of a river. None of the grottoes measured over 16 feet square and most of them 10 by 12 feet. In all essential points of architectural disposition and artistic decoration they 'show the closest resemblance to the average type of Chien-fo-tung shrines approximately assigned to the ninth-tenth century.'[2]

'The principal caves are found on the right bank ranged in two rows. The lower one opens on a terrace, about 20 feet above the river, the other extends on a level about 50 to 60 feet higher. The series of five main caves below starts on the south-east with one containing a colossal seated Buddha image, which rises up into the second storey. Next to it is a cave with a colossal figure of Buddha recumbent in *nirvāṇa*, fully 30 feet long. The five caves of the lower storey are supplied with verandahs in front and rendered very dark thereby.'

'The subjects of the larger panels appear to be chiefly assemblies of Buddhas and Bodhisattvas, set within a square frame of geometric design, and this again enclosed within a circle or oval of elaborate floral pattern. . . . The lower main caves, together with five or six small grottoes between them, containing new frescoes are the shrines which receive most attention from resident priests and pious visitors.'[3]

'The upper row of caves is approached by flights of stairs roughly cut into the rock, which start near some small grottoes serving as quarters for the priests. There is a line of 12 cave temples extending on a uniform level. All of them comprise a cella, square or nearly so, with sides varying from 20 to 32 feet; an ante-chapel, itself as broad as the cella, but only of moderate depth and separated from the cella by a shallow wide passage; a high porch or outer passage, in some cases 20 to 30 feet deep where it is intact, admitting light and air from the face of the cliff. The shrines originally communicated with each other by means of narrow plastered passages leading from one porch to the other through the facing part of the

[1] Stein, *Serindia* Vol. III, p. 1109. [2] *Ibid.*, Vol. III, p. 1109, Fig. 242, 243, 244.
[3] *Ibid.*, p. 1110.

rock wall. But where this had crumbled away or become unsafe, a rough tunnel connecting the ante-chapels had been driven through the rock. The uniformity with which this disposition is repeated in all shrines points to execution upon a definite plan and at no great distance of time, and with this the uniform style of their decoration seems in full accord.'[1]

'Throughout these cave-temples the walls bear paintings *in tempera*. . . . The walls of the porches ordinarily display on the one side rows of men dressed in dark-red robes with wide-brimmed black hats ; and, on the other, processions of ladies wearing rich wide-sleeved dresses and elaborate coiffure with flowers, bands, and pendants around bulb-shaped caps. These figures carrying offerings, which also recur on the side walls of the entrances to the cellas, are intended to represent donors and donatrices. The walls of the cellas and ante-chapels are decorated either with processions of large, richly robed Bodhisattvas moving under ornate canopies or with a variety of panels, showing familiar scenes from Buddhist Heavens, Buddhas enthroned among rows of Bodhisattvas, large representations of Mañjuśrī and Samanta-bhadra on their *vāhanas*, etc.'[2]

'The remaining shrines of the series are very small and dark. The side walls of cella of one of these (xix) are decorated with scenes from Buddhist Heavens and the back wall is occupied by a large representation of the 'wind-scene.' There are inscriptions in cursive Brāhmī, scribbled by the side of a donor figure.'[3]

These shrines of myriad Buddhas resemble in other respects also the Caves of the Thousand Buddhas. And both appear to have been largely influenced by, if not copied from, the cave-temples of India, particularly those of Ajanta and Ellora.

There are also other smaller remains of Buddhist *stūpas* and *vihāras* in several sites. There are Buddhist shrines, for instance, at Turfān, Yār-Khoto, mostly near the northern end of the town and in the open space beyond it. They consist of the central temple and part of the enclosing court of a large Buddhist *vihāra*, and the central group of *stūpas* at the northernmost Buddhist sanctuary.[4] At Kara-shahr there is a large group of shrines, including several massive temple ruins. There are also scattered numerous other structures mostly

[1] Stein, *Serindia*, III, pp. 1110–11.
[2] *Ibid.*, III, p. 1111, *see* Fig. 246, 247.
[3] *Ibid.*, III, p. 1113.
[4] *Ibid.*, III, pp. 1168–1169, Fig. 278, 279.

of modest size.[1] There are small cellas above the springs. There are also cave temples.[2] At Shorchuk, also, there have been discovered a ruined shrine, together with the ante-chapel and cella with relievo statues and circular image base, temple ruin, ruined *stūpa*, stucco reliefs, and stucco relievo sculptures.[3] There is here also a cave temple.[4] Buddhist shrines have also been found at Khora site.[5] Lastly at Mayaklik there are remains of Buddhist shrine, Buddha statue, Buddha image with painted base, and *tempera* painting.[6]

There appears to be no doubt about the fundamental influence of Hindu culture on the art and architecture of these Central Asian colonies. Sir Aurel Stein is equally emphatic on this point also. 'The most thorough proof of the dominating influence which Indian art exercised on the industries represented in this ancient settlement, was supplied by,' in addition to purely architectural and sculptural objects, 'the ornamental wood-carving of the chair.[7] . . . The height of the legs is 23 inches and the width of the chair 26 inches. . . . The great interest of this ancient piece of furniture lies in its ornamental carving, which shows the closest resemblance to decorative motives familiar from Gandhara reliefs. Referring for all details of the carving to the description given in the list, I may point out,' he continues, 'that the four-petalled flower of a shape closely approaching the large purple clematis, which forms its most frequent feature, is well known in Gandhara sculptures. We find it then,' he concludes by referring to their essential features, 'either complete and enclosed in squares forming ornamental bands, or else halved and placed within triangular spaces just as seen on the panels and legs of the chair.'[8] The zigzag arrangement of these halved flowers has also its exact parallel there. 'The eight-petalled lotus,' he emphatically asserts, 'is unmistakably Indian, while the central ornament of the front panel, with its conventionalized fruit (? pomegranate) and leaves, recalls decorative elements on certain Indo-Corinthian capitals.'[9]

[1] *Ibid.*, III, Fig. 281, 282, 284, 285, 287, pp. 1184–85.
[2] Stein, *Serindia*, Vol. III, p. 1184.
[3] *Ibid.*, Fig. 289, 290, 291, 292, 293, 294, pp. 1192–93.
[4] *Ibid.*, Fig. 298, p. 1199. [5] *Ibid.*, Fig. 300, p. 1224.
[6] *Ibid.*, Fig. 323, 324, 325, 326, 327, 328, pp. 1276–77, 1286–87.
[7] Preserved in the British Museum, London, Plate lxviii, *Ancient Khotan*, Vol. II
[8] Cf., Foucher, *L'Art de Gandhara*, I, Fig. 313 (sculptures from *Loriyan-Tengai Grūmwedat*, Burgess, *Buddhist Art*. Fig. 94).
[9] Stein, *Ancient Khotan*, I, p. 334.

SWĀT

The valleys drained by the Swāt river, together with the adjacent territory of Buner to the south-east, correspond to the ancient Uḍḍiyāna or Udyāna. The great fame attaching to this country in Buddhist tradition is amply attested by the records of the Chinese Buddhist pilgrims, as well as by manifold notices in literature of northern Buddhism.[1]

The ruins consist of the Buddhist *stūpa* of Top-dara,[2] small *vihāra* at Gumbatuna,[3] Bālo, Kandag Valley, Bir-kot,[4] ruined *stūpa* and monastery walls of Barrage, Tokar-Dar,[5] ruined mansions, dwellings and tower, monastic court, on ridge above Kotah,[6] ruined *stūpa* of Amluk-dara and of King Uttarasena, Shankardāra,[7] fortifications and ruined towers on Birkot Hill,[8] ruined *stūpa* of Shinasi near Batera,[9] Buddha's Foot-print near Tirāt.[10]

The architectural details of these ruins are similar to those described elsewhere and need no repetition here. The only points to be noted are that they are of Indian origin and that the local peculiarities are few.

[1] Sir Aurel Stein, *Memoirs of the Archaeological Survey of India*, no. 42, p. 1.
[2] *Ibid.*, Fig. 1, p. 6. [3] *Ibid.*, Fig. 5, p. 8. [4] *Ibid.*, Fig. 6, 7, p. 12.
[5] *Ibid.*, Fig. 8, 9, p. 14, Fig. 10, 11, .p 16. [6] *Ibid.*, Fig. 12, 13, 14, p. 18.
[7] *Ibid.*, Fig. 16, 17, p. 20. [8] *Ibid.*, Fig. 20, 22, pp. 24, 28.
[9] *Ibid.*, Fig. 34, p. 44. [10] *Ibid* Fig. 40, p. 54.

CHAPTER X

HINDU ARCHITECTURE IN INSULINDIA OR INDIAN ARCHIPELAGO

THE DERIVATION OF the term 'Insulindia' is not clear. Nor is there any general agreement about its geographical limits. Writers from time to time have used the term to imply various regions. Here it is used, for the sake of convenience, to indicate the mainland and islands to the east of the Indian continent, which, though now peopled by non-Indian races, professed Indian culture, both religious and secular, from time to time. The geographical boundaries and local names of the territories constituting the peninsular and insular regions have naturally changed with the change of governing authorities, and the monumental remains of the Hindu-Buddhist period have also suffered both from neglected indifference and deliberate destruction. Whatever traces, with inevitable modifications, of Hindu architecture have survived in some parts of the peninsula and the islands will show not only their Indian connexion, but also may supplement what have become extinct in India itself and what can only be recognized by a reference to the *Śilpa-śāstras* and literary sources of information.

The peninsula east of India is stated, on the basis of ancient inscriptions of an early date, to have included six regions, states or kingdoms: (1) Yavana-deśa, in the north-east, with its capital Chudhā-nagarī, now Luang Phrabang, on the Me-kong; (2) Champā-deśa, corresponding to Annam and extending to about 160 miles westwards of the Me-kong; (3) Śyāma-deśa, in the north-west, including Burma proper and the northern part of modern Siam east of the Salwin, of which Haripuṇyapura, now Lamphum on the Me-ping, was probably the capital; (4) Kambhoja-deśa included all Cambodia, Lower Cochin China, and Siam as far as Uttaradih; (5) Ramaṇya-deśa, on the west, comprised Pegu and Tenasserim; and (6) Malaya-deśa, the Malay Peninsula.[1]

[1] Fournereau, *Le Siam Ancient*, Part I, pp. 50 ff. quoted by Fergusson, *History of Indian and Eastern Architecture* (1910), Vol. II, pp. 373–374.

'The *Nagarakṛitāgama* and the *Pararaton* supply a list of the countries which belonged to the Majapahit kings, comprising all the islands between Java and New Guinea, including Borneo, Celebes, Buton, Buru, Ceram (Ambon), Banda, Banggai, Moluccas, Talaut, then the petty islets between Borneo and Malaya Peninsula, including Kedah, Kelang, Singapore, Penang, Kelantan, etc.'[1]

This list includes most of the islands, except Sumatra, Bali, and a few others, where remains of Indian architecture have been discovered.

Burma

Brahma-deśa, as the term would indicate, was situated in the Brahma-sthāna, or the centre of the then world. It is bounded on the west by India, on the north by China, on the east by Siam, and on the south by the Indian Ocean. In the historical period, Burma formed part of Siam and was inhabited by the same races of people. Burma was first of those countries which adopted the religion of Gautama Buddha at a very early period. It 'borrowed also many of the Indian forms of architecture,' probably from the Lower Bengal Provinces, which have become extinct in the land of their origin and present difficulty in explaining the differences.[2]

The architectural history of Burma is stated to begin with the foundation of Pagān in the middle of the ninth century. Its glory lasted for about four centuries until it was destroyed in 1284 by the Chinese or Tartar army of Kublai Khan.[3]

The ancient buildings in Burma are known by a curious expression, pagoda, coined by the early European visitors. The term 'Pagoda' (Payā in Burmese) 'seems to be applied by Europeans in Burma indifferently to two very different kinds of structure, namely, the bell-shaped *stūpas*, and the square temples.' The former was 'raised on a series of terraces or platforms and crowned with a conical finial. To these the term 'Tsedi,' or 'Zedi,' which corresponds with the Chaitya in Nepal, and Chedi of Siam, is sometimes given.' The latter was a type of 'temple which is square on plan with sometimes projecting porches or vestibules, and, n the thickness of the walls, narrow corridors, the walls of which are decorated with

[1] *India and Java*, I, p. 10.
[2] James Fergusson, *History of Indian and Eastern Architecture*, Vol. II, p. 339.
[3] Yule, *Marco Palo*, Vol. II, pp. 84 *et seq.*

frescoes or sculpture, with niches at intervals containing images of Buddha. Their roofs are pyramidal, consisting of a series of storeys of moderate height set back one behind the other and crowned with the curvilinear *śikhara* of the Indo-Aryan,' or northern style practised both by 'Jains and Hindus in the north of India, from the mouth of the Indus to the Bay of Bengal.'[1]

The earliest of the circular pagodas, or *chaityas*, is that at Bupayā, at Pagān, ascribed to the first years of the third century A.D. 'The centre portion, or bell, is of bulbous form, raised on a triple base and crowned with two features, the lower one a bold torus moulding, the upper one a conical finial, with cavetto sinkings between the bell and the torus, and between the latter and the finial.'[2]

The Banbangy pagoda of the seventh or eighth century, Ngakwe Nadaung of the tenth century, Shwe Dagon at Rangoon, Shwe-Hmaudan pagoda at Pegu, and several others are examples of this type.[3]

'The principal variations made in the design of the Zedi (*chaitya*) are those of the relative proportion of the bell to the east of the structure, the outline of the same and its superstructure, and the decoration employed. Thus in the Lokānanda Pagoda in Pagān, built by Anaurahtā in 1059, the bell is of immense size, being three-sevenths of the total height of the structure, including the triple base and finial.'[4]

'Some of the pagodas have in the centre of each face a flight of steps leading to the upper terraces, and on the level of the first platform an arch-way similar to the examples in Boro-Budur. In one or two cases also there are porches in front of each flight of steps, cruciform in plan, similar to those of the temples of Cambodia.'[5]

The history of the Shwe Dagon pagoda at Rangoon would explain the growth of most of the Burmese pagodas. 'Originally it is said to have been only 27 feet high and to have attained its present height

[1] Fergusson, *loc. cit.*, Vol. II, p. 341. [2] *Ibid.*, pp. 341–342.

[3] A crowd of smaller pagodas of all sizes, from 30 feet to 200 feet in height, surrounds the larger one. In fact there is scarcely a village in the country that does not possess one or two of these structures, and in all the more important towns they are numbered by hundreds. They are in fact innumerable (Fergusson, p. 348). For a description of the pagodas at Thaton and Prome, *see* Fergusson, pp. 357–359, 359–360.

[4] Fergusson, *loc. cit.*, Vol. II, p. 343. [5] *Ibid.*, p. 344.

and dimension by repeated casings many feet in thickness. About the middle of the fifteenth century the height of the pagoda was raised to 129 feet, terraces were built round the hill, and the top—a platform—was paved with flagstones. In 1768 it reached its present height of 321 feet, not including the new Hti, which was presented by king Mindon Min. The platform now measures 900 feet by 685 feet and rises about 165 feet above the base of the hill.'

It is stated 'to have been commenced about 2,300 years ago, or about the era of Buddha himself.' Its antiquity is further indicated by the belief that it contained in its Dhātu-Garbha (relic-chamber) not only eight hairs from the head of the last (Gautama) Buddha, but also relics of his three predecessors. 'After numerous miraculous indications, on this spot were discovered the staff of Kakusandha, believed to have lived some 3,000 years B.C., the water-dipper of Konāgamana, and the bathing garment of Kassapa, which, with the eight hairs above mentioned, are enshrined within this great pagoda.'[1]

The Mingun-payā is the other huge pagoda commenced by Bodauhpayā, who spent twenty-five years over it and died in 1819, leaving it incomplete. It represents the square form borrowed from early Indian Buddhism. 'It stands on a basement of five successive terraces, of little height, the lower terrace forming a square of 450 feet. From the upper terrace starts the vast cubical pile of the pagoda, 230 feet square in plan, and rises, in a solid mass, to the height of about 100 feet, with slightly sloping walls. Above this it contracts in successive terraces, three of which had been completed, raising the mass to a height of 165 feet at the time the work was abandoned.'[2] 'If completed, it would have risen to the height of 500 feet. It is even now a solid mass containing between 6,000,000 and 7,000,000 cubic feet of brick work. Had it been carried out, it would have been the tallest building in the world.'[3]

The Lemyet-hnā, built in the eighth and ninth centuries, is the earliest example of the square temples. 'It is about 24 feet square and is built in brick, with a solid pier 8 feet square in the centre, surrounded by a corridor 4 feet wide. On each face of the pier are

[1] *Asiatic Researches*, Vol. XIV, p. 270, referred to by Fergusson, *loc. cit.*, Vol. II, p. 347.

[2] *Mission to the Court of Ava*, p. 169.

[3] Fergusson, *loc. cit.*, Vol. II, p. 351.

bas-reliefs carved in stone which are lighted from four entrance doorways, one on each side of the temple.'[1]

'The two most interesting temples of this class are those at Nan Payā and Nagāyon, just south of Pagān. The first is considered to have been built by king Anaurahtā about 1050 and the second by Kyantsilthā in 1064.'

'It is, however, remarkable, considering the close connexion between India and Burma, so far as architectural style is concerned, to find the arch and vault employed systematically throughout the latter country in buildings many of which are said to have been built by Indian workmen, and further to note that those features appear only when they became an actual necessity, as in doorways requiring wide openings, or the covering cover of corridors and small internal chambers with a permanent incombustible material to carry these roofs. Those roofs were, as a rule, in the square temples, not flat terraces, but assumed an ogee section following the rise of the vault.'[2] This is shown in the temples of Ānanda, the Kyanktaùgyi, and Abhayadāna, south of Pagān.[3]

The Ānanda is the most remarkable of some 800 to 1,000 temples of Pagān ruins which 'extend about 8 miles in length along the river, with an average breadth of about 2 miles.' It is stated to have been built by Kyantsitthā (1057–1085). 'It is a square of nearly 200 feet on each side, with projecting porticos on each face, so that it measures 280 feet across each way. It is several storeys in height, the two lower ones are square with square turrets at each end, the three above have seated lions at each angle. The plan of these storeys, as also the base of the *śikhara*, follows that of the latter, being set back at the angles. The *śikhara* is crowned with the conical finial and Hti. The setting back of each storey, one behind the other, gives the whole a pyramidal form, which in this case rises to the height of 183 feet.'

'Internally the building is extremely solid, being intersected only by two narrow parallel corridors, but in rear of each projecting transept is a niche artificially lighted from above, in which stands a statue of Buddha more than 30 feet in height.'[4]

[1] Fergusson, *loc. cit.*, Vol. II, p. 352. [2] *Ibid.*, p. 353.
[3] *Ibid.*, Plate XLI, XXXVIII, XXXVI.
[4] *Ibid.*, pp. 360–361, Plate XLI.

This is the arrangement in the Chaumukh temple at Pālitānā and at Rānpur,[1] both Jain temples of the fifteenth and seventeenth centuries, while the Ānanda temple belongs to the eleventh century (A.D. 1066). This apparent anomaly is explained by the fact that the general basic principle was borrowed from India and the forms were unlike.

Of the other temples[2] at Pagān, the Mahābodhi was built by Nandaungmya Min in A.D. 1198 in imitation of the Bodh-Gaya temple.

There is, however, remarkable dissimilarity between the generality of temples at Pagān and their Indian originals. 'They are not *stūpas* in any sense of the term, nor are they *vihāras*.' The seven-storeyed *prāsāda* at Polonnaruva, however, appears to be exact original of Pagān temples, the resemblance being so striking.'[3]

There are two other classes of religious structures, known as the Thein and the Pitakat-Taik. The former is the ordination hall for priests, which would seem to correspond with the Bot of Siam, except that they are not as a rule found in the temple enclosure, as in the latter country. The Upali-Thein in Pagān, dating from the thirteenth century, is 'rectangular on plan and is divided into nave and side aisles by arcades and arches. The centre aisle or nave is loftier than the side aisles, and in section the structure is similar to that of a *Chaitya* temple (or of a Christian church, except that there are no clerestory windows). The summit of the roof is decorated with terra-cotta ridge tiles, and in the centre is an attenuated *dāgaba*. On the top of the nave and aisle walls is a cresting or pierced parapet similar to that which crowns the terrace walls of the pagodas. The interior is said to be decorated with fine and brilliant frescoes.'[4]

There are other examples also. The Pitakat-Taik is the sacred library at Pagān, which was built by Anaurahtā in 1057 to house the Buddhist scriptures that he brought away from Thaton. 'It was probably built by the masons whom he brought over from Thaton,[5]

[1] *See* Plate XXII, Fergusson, Vol. II, p. 47.

[2] The other famous temples at Pagān are Dhammayangyi (built by Narethu in A.D. 1160) and Thatpyinuyu (built by Alaungsithu, A.D. 1144).

[3] Compare *Sat Mahal Prasada* (Fergusson, Vol. I, p. 246) and *Pitakat-Taik*, Plate XL (Fergusson, Vol. II, 356–357).

[4] Fergusson, *loc. cit.*, Vol. II, p. 356.

[5] The ancient Suvarṇa-Bhūmi, Golden Chersonese of classical geographers, situated on the Sittang River, about 40 miles north of Martaban, destroyed in A.D. 1050 by Anaurahtā, King of Pegu (*Phoenix*, Vol. II, pp. 204 *et seq.*, *J. A. S. B.*, Vol. XLII, pp. 23 *et seq.*, Fergusson, *loc. cit.*, Vol. II, pp. 357–358).
But Sumatra is better known as Suvarṇa Bhūmi.

and was presumably a copy of the original library there. The plan of the structure is square, with, apparently, judging from the roof, four parallel corridors round the central chamber or hall.' The ground storey appears to be of moderate height. The roof consists of four storeys, set back one behind the other, with ogee roofs between, resting direct on the vaults of the corridors.[1]

The monasteries are another class of buildings of which the ideas were borrowed from India. But the Burmese 'monasteries are, in almost all instances, less magnificent than the pagodas to which they are attached, and are, with scarcely an exception, built of wood—a practice destructive of their architectural character, and also depriving them wholly of that monumental appearance of stability which is so essential to true architectural expression.'[2]

The residential buildings from those of the poorest to the palaces of the kings, were also constructed from time immemorial of the perishable material. 'The custom has now passed into a law, that no one shall have the power of erecting buildings of stone or brick, except it be the king himself, or unless the edifices be of a purely religious character.'[2]

Thus no idea of ancient Burmese civil architecture can correctly be formed.

Siam

The ancient Śyāma-deśa was the north-western one of the six states forming the peninsula east of India and south of China. It then included Burma proper and the northern part of modern Siam[3] east of the Salwin, of which Haripuṇya-pura, now Lamphum, on the Me-ping, was probably the capital. It was thus bounded on the west by India and the Indian Ocean, on the north by China, on the east by the Champā-deśa, and on the south by the Kambhoja-deśa, the sea (Śyāma-Sāgara) and the Malaya-deśa.

This ancient Siam is known from the epic tradition of the *Rāmāyaṇa* in connexion with the search for Sītā, stolen by Rāvaṇa; from the Buddhist tradition of Asoka and Kanishka having sent missionaries

[1] Fergusson, *loc. cit.*, Vol. II, pp. 356–357. *See* Plate XL, and compare with the library buildings mentioned in connexion with the Nalanda University.

[2] *Ibid.*, Vol. II p. 366.

[3] The modern Siam is of much limited area. It has Burma and the Indian Ocean on the west; the Shan States of Burma, China, and Laos on the north; Annam (Champa) and Cochin China on the east; and Cambodia, Gulf of Siam, and the Malay Peninsula on the south.

for propagation of Buddhism; from the inscriptions discovered in Champa and Cambodia; from the Siamese chronicles; from the annals of Ceylon, Malay Peninsula and Java; from the Chinese records and Japanese documents; and, lastly, from the accounts left by the Chinese and European travellers.[1]

The ancient Chinese empire claims to have extended in 585 B.C. up to the regions of the barbarians, including all the provinces south of the great Yang-tse-kiang.[2] Many and various tribes appear to have been included amongst these barbarians. 'Most of them were Tai people, the ancestors of the Siamese, Lao, and Shans of today.'[3] These Tai people were driven from their original home, Nanchao, and became 'the first inhabitants of Siam, long before the dawn of history.' 'Later on, Siam was inhabited by three races whose descendants may still be seen. In the south were two types, a curly-headed people of Negrito origin, and a wavy-haired Indonesian race,' represented by the naked and squalid Sewang and Sakai respectively, still wandering in the forests of the Malay Peninsula.[4] The northern Siam was inhabited by the Was or Lawas, distinguished as wild and tame, the former 'chiefly known through their habit of collecting human heads and decorating the approaches of their villages with rows of skulls,' and the latter inhabiting Shan States and Siam and professing Buddhism, known 'as peaceful cultivators or hunters in their mountain villages.' 'Many hundreds, perhaps thousands, of years before the Christian era, another race of men settled in Southern Siam, known as the Khmers, represented by the Cambodians, the Mohns or Talaings of Pegu, the K'amuks of French Laos, and the K'as and other smaller tribes in the Shan States.'[5]

'The Khmer civilization, the monumental remains of which have so astonished all investigators, was of purely Indian origin. It is not possible to say for certain when the first Indian settlers came to Siam or Cambodia, but there is no reason to suppose that any of their buildings, the remains of which are in existence, date from pre-Buddhist times.' But General Wood admits the fact that 'there were Indian settlers in pre-Buddhistic times. They must have

[1] Compare Phanindranath Bose, *The Indian Colony of Siam*, pp. 3–17.
[2] Demetrius Boulger, *History of China*.
[3] W. A. R. Wood, C.M.G., C.I.E., Consul-General, *A History of Siam* (1933), p. 31.
[4] Wood, *loc. cit.*, p. 40. [5] *Ibid.*, pp. 41, 42.

professed Brahmanism.' There is, however, reason to suppose that despite all the ancient stone inscriptions found in the region peopled by the Khmers being purely south Indian (Dravidian) both in lettering and language, 'the first great influx of Indians into this region dated from the time of king Asoka's invasion of Kalinga and that the settlers were natives of Kalinga' and 'formed colonies at various points along the coasts of the countries now known as Pegu, Siam, Cambodia, and Cochin-China.'[1] This view has been further substantiated by Fergusson when he says of Burma that it 'adopted the religion of Śākyamuni (Buddha) and borrowed also many of the Indian forms of architecture, but with differences we are now at a loss to account for. It may be that, as we know nothing practically of the architectural forms of the lower Bengal provinces before the beginning of the sixth century, these forms may have been taken to Prome and Pegu before that time'[2] and may have migrated also to Siam.

Support to this view is received also from the *Mahāvaṁśa*'s list of ten Buddhist missionaries sent forth to various parts of the world by king Asoka, including Suvarṇa-bhūmi (land of gold), variously identified with 'the region extending from Pegu right down through the Malay Peninsula,' with 'southern Siam,' and also with the island of Sumatra. Further, 'Prince Damrong and other competent authorities believe that the original *stūpa* over which the existing large pagoda of Nak'on Prat'om was built dates from the time of king Asoka.'[3] General Wood quotes Hiuen Tsang to the effect that king Śilāditya of Kanoj sent missionaries to foreign countries, who must have visited Siam also 'since images peculiar to that period have been discovered at Nak'on Prat'om, Nak'on Srit'am-marat, and in other parts of Siam.'[4]

According to a Tamil inscription[5] of the eighth or ninth century A.D. Indian merchants appear to have been in trade-relation with Siam in the early centuries of the Christian era, and they are stated to be the Tamil Vaishṇava soldiers who settled in Siam and built the temple of Vishṇu there.[6]

[1] Wood, *loc. cit.*, pp. 42, 43.
[2] James Fergusson, *History of Indian and Eastern Architecture* (1910), Vol. II. p. 339.
[3] Wood, *loc. cit.*, pp. 43–44.
[4] *Ibid.*, 45–46.
[5] E. Hultsch, *Note on a Tamil Inscription in Siam*, *J. R. A. S.* (1913), pp. 337–339.
[6] Bose, *loc. cit.*, p. 21.

The architectural remains of Indian origin are very scanty and poor in Siam, especially in comparison with those in the neighbouring countries of Champa and Cambodia. In fact the Hindu monuments consist of a few unimportant temples and images of Vishṇu, Lakshmī, Śiva, and others. Even the Buddhist monuments are rather unimportant architecturally, but numerous in number, and include monasteries, *stūpas*, *chaityas*, pagodas, and images of Buddha.

Temples at Sukhodaya, Phra, Pathom, Sajjanālaya, Ayuthia, Lophaburi, Sangkalok, and Bangkok have been referred to by travellers and historians. There are various structures built within the enclosures of temples. Their general classification and description may be gathered from an account of any one temple.

'The outer enclosure of a temple was always rectangular, and generally of greater length than width. The enclosure walls were as a rule about 3 feet thick, and from 12 to 14 feet high. The most important building in the *vāt* (enclosure) was the *bot* (the sacred temple) and usually the first built. The *bot* was rectangular in plan, and was divided into central and side aisles by columns in stone, carrying open timber roofs covered with glazed tiles in bright colours. The roofs over the side aisles were at a lower level than that of the central aisles, leaving space for a clerestory, which consisted of pierced terra-cotta slabs. Similar perforated screens were built in between the outer columns of the aisles. In important temples the *bot* had double aisles on each side.'

'The principal feature in the *bot*, admission to which was confined to the priests, was the great altar carrying a gilded statue of Buddha, which was always placed in the central aisles, in the last bay but one.'

Just like the ordinary shrine, the *bot* (of Vāt Jai at Sukhodaya) stood opposite the main entrance in the east and had a porch in front. 'In its rear was the principal *phra* (*stūpa*) of the temple, of which there were two types of design,[1] the *phra-prang* and the *phra-chedi*. The former is of a type peculiar to Siam, about half way up is the cell, with its entrance door on the eastern side, access to which was obtained by a steep flight of steps, and recessed niches on the three other sides.' Thus it differed in many essential respects from similar structures in India or Burma. 'The top, or upper part,

[1] Fergusson, *loc. cit.*, Plate XLVI.

has a domical shape, which we can easily fancy to be derived from the *stūpa*, but the upright part looks more like the *śikhara* of a Hindu temple than anything Buddhist.'

'The *phra-chedi* (of Vāt Jai at Sukhodaya) is based apparently on the *stūpas* of India, the cells containing the relics of Buddha, however, being placed underground, and reached in the larger examples by secret passages in the thickness of the walls. The enormous structures now existing of the Pathom *chedi* is the second enclosure or envelope of the original *chedi*, and rises to the height of 344 feet. It is surrounded by a triple gallery with numerous pavilions, the roofs of which were in the last rebuilding (of 1862) copied from those of Angkor Vāt in Cambodia.'[1]

The *vihāns* (*vihāras*) and *kamburiens* are similar in design to the *bot*, but smaller in size. Therein also people assembled to offer up prayers and listen to sermons.

There are two other types of buildings found only in the royal temples. They are known as *chuttamukk*, that is, *chaturmukha* (four-faced), and *mora-dob*, *mondob*, i.e. *maṇḍapa* or pavilion, both elaborately described in the *Mānasāra Śilpa-śāstra*. 'The former, cruciform (*svastika*) in plan, was originally built to shelter a statue of the four-faced Brahmā; this has been destroyed, and its place taken by four niches, placed back to back, each with a statue of Buddha facing the cardinal points.' The finest example is stated to have been found in the Vāt Maṇḍapa Si Nā at Sajjanalaya.

The *maṇḍapa* (or pavilion) is 'usually a rectangular building, containing a statue of Buddha. In the Vāt Si Jum at Sukhodaya, it measured 57 feet wide by 70 feet deep, and sheltered an immense statue of Buddha, nearly 50 feet high, which was constructed in brick, coated with stucco and gilded. The walls of the *maṇḍapa* were also built in brick, and they carried a lofty roof or tower of the same material; at a height of 32 feet from the ground the brick courses commenced to project one in front of the other. till they met at the top, thus forming in section an inverted pyramid.'[2]

Smaller pavilions were built 'to hold the Buddha-pāda, the mythical representation of the sacred feet of Buddha.'[3]

[1] Fergusson, *loc. cit.*, Vol. II, pp. 406, 407, 408.

[2] *Ibid*, Vol. II, p. 408.

[3] Locally known as Phrabat, wheel of the Law, the most famous example in Siam being 12 miles from Lophaburi.

The other types of buildings are the Belfry (Ho' Rakhang) and the sacred Library (Ho' Trai), the latter found only in the royal temples. The sacred tank in the enclosures was known as Sa, equivalent to the Cambodian Sra and the Indian Saras.

' The principal *phra* differs slightly in design (from those already described), the upper part being partly *chedi* and partly *prang*. It is raised on a platform and surrounded by eight smaller towers, consisting of a lower storey, with niche on each side containing a statue of Buddha, with a superstructure recalling the entrance doorways of Cambodia and Java, though the sculpture is very inferior. Above the architrave, carried by rectangular piers with moulded capitals, is a pediment enclosed with richly carved moulding, with dragons' heads on each side, and in the tympanum, which forms a niche, is a figure of Buddha in the *nirvāṇa* posture, with other figures. Above, there is a second storey with a repetition of the pediment and niche to a smaller scale, and there may have been a third storey, rising about 25 feet in height, the great *phra* in the centre being 80 to 90 feet high. Three towers of a similar kind, placed side by side, exist in the Vāt Sisavai, also at Sukhodaya where they take the place of the *phra*. Above a plain ground storey, with three angle projections, are other storeys, of which six still exist in the western tower on the right, and on each face is a niche with trefoil head and *nāga* terminations enclosing a statue, and, on the angle projections, antefixae carved with heads of *garudas* and other deities. The upper storeys are only slightly set back, one behind the other, so that they may be the prototypes of the *phra prang*.'[1]

' Of some of these structures many examples would be found in the same enclosure. Thus in the Vāt Jai at Sukhodaya, the most important temple illustrated by Fournereau, there was one great *phra-chedi* and its annexes, two *bots*, six *vihāns*, three *kamburiens*, one *maṇḍapa*, ten small pavilions, five *phra-prang*, and over a hundred *phra-chedi*, most of these being erected by private persons as funeral monuments and memorials—altogether nearly two hundred structures.'[2]

The design of the *phra-prang* is found in the crowning members of the (modern) pagodas of Bangkok. But their ' elaboration of

[1] Fergusson, *loc. cit.*, Vol. II, p. 409. Plate XLVII.

[2] *Ibid.*, Vol. II, pp. 408–409.

detail and exuberance of coloured ornament' is disapproved by Fergusson, and stated to have been 'here carried to an extent truly barbarous.' But they show 'the innate and irrepressible love of architecture they display.' Fergusson comments, however, in strong terms when he says, 'but it also shows how easily these higher aspirations degenerate into something very like vulgarity, when exercised by a people in so low a stage of civilization as the modern Siamese.'

'The same remarks apply to their civic buildings: palaces and porticos, and even dwelling-houses, are all as rich as carving and gilding and painting can make them; but, as in the pagodas, it is overdone and fails to please, because it verges on vulgarity.' Being in despair of the future even, Fergusson concludes that 'the new civilization is not indigenous, but an importation. The men of progress wear hats, the ladies French gowns, and they build palaces with Corinthian porticos and sash-windows.' He truly deplores the similar state of affairs in India when he says, 'it is the sort of civilization that is found in the bāzār in Calcutta, and it is not desirable, in an architectural point of view, at all events, if, indeed, it is so in any other respect.'[1]

The pagodas generally built on the banks of ruins are, however, 'like so many monastic towns in the middle of nice gardens with shrines dedicated to Lord Buddha. There are preaching halls and temporary accommodation for pilgrims and houses for monks.'[2]

The country of Siam appears to have been markedly connected with India from the time of king Asoka. The religions, tradition, culture, and population are of Indian extract. Some 98 per cent. of Siamese at present profess Buddhism. Before the time of Asoka, there are reasons to believe, Hinduism was prevalent there. The images of Vishṇu, Gaṇeśa, and other deities, and of Rāma, Sītā, as well as the incidents of the *Rāmāyaṇa* and the *Mahābhārata* are found depicted in temples and monasteries in Siam. The names of places like Ayodhya, Saurashtra, Maharastra, Vishṇu-loka, etc., as also of persons, are Indian in origin. The name of the country itself sounds like Indian.

Of architecture and sculpture there are numerous examples, as indicated above, to show that India contributed the leading principles.

[1] Fergusson, *loc. cit.*, Vol. II, pp. 412, 413.
[2] Bose, *loc. cit.*, p. 102.

PLATE L

A PAGAN PAGODA TOGETHER WITH A MONASTERY SHOWING THE HINDU SIKHARA. INSET: –HINDU SIKHARA IN A SIAMESE TEMPLE

Page 329

'The story of the *Rāmāyaṇa* is illustrated on the walls of the royal temple at Bangkok.' The stories of Jātakas were sculptured in Sukhodaya. Thus in religion, in literature, in art, in sculpture, in architecture Siam owes a lot to India. There are kings with Indian titles, ministers and officers bearing Indian names, and Indian customs and ceremonies practised in Siamese families.

The Brahmans are stated to have still maintained a leading position in the royal court of Siam. 'They preside over coronation and other important ceremonies, and occupy as honourable a position as the Buddhist monks in the royal court. They compose the names of the princes, towns, and temples in Sanskrit. They also act as *Hora*, or astrologers, and *Āchār* (i.e. Achārya, preceptor) of pagodas.'[1]

CHAMPA

Champa is the eastern portion of the Indo-Chinese peninsula in continuation of Burma, comprising Siam, Laos, Annam, Cambodia, and Cochin-China. It corresponds with Annam. It is bounded by the Sea of China on the east, and on the west there is a range of hills along the valley of Me-kong river, on the south is French Cochin-China, and on the north lie the parts of the sea, Laos, and Siam. It is about 160 miles from east to west up to the Me-kong.

The original inhabitants, who were conquered by the Indians, probably in the second century A.D., belonged to the Austronesian race.

The earliest mention of Champā-deśa is in that passage of the *Rāmāyaṇa* where it is stated that king Sugrīva sent out emissaries in search of Sītā, stolen by Rāvaṇa. The king Asoka's messengers also may have visited the country of Champa. According to the Arakanese traditions, the first king of Champa was the son of a king of Benares, who settled at Rāmāvatī, the present Rāmbyi or Ramri.[2] According to another tradition, the first Indian kings of Champa were known as the Kauṇḍiṇya of the lunar race.

Mainly on the basis of the Vo-chanh inscription in Sanskrit of the second or third century of the Christian era, it is clear that Champa

[1] Bose (*loc. cit.*, p. 109) refers, as his authority, to *Siam* in *E. R. E.*

[2] Phayre, *History of Burma*, p. 7, quoted by Dr. R. C. Majumdar, *Ancient Colonies in the Far East*, Vol. I, 'Champa,' 'Introduction,' p. xviii.

had already been under a 'Hindu or Hinduized dynasty.' Dr. R. C. Majumdar takes Śrī Māra as the first historical Hindu king of Champa In support of this, Majumdar refers to Ptolemy's list of Sanskrit names in Indo-China, the mention of the Chams or Annamese in history in the second century A.D., and also the Chinese reference to the foundation of the kingdom of Champa in 192 A.D. by Lien of the family of Kiu.[1]

Mainly on the basis of inscriptions and Chinese records, Majumdar has drawn up the lists of kings of the Hindu dynasties that ruled in Champa, beginning with Śrī-Māra, from the second century A.D. to A.D. 1180.[2]

So far as the architectural remains of Champa are concerned, they can hardly put up any claim to a comparison with those of Cambodia or Java in respect of purely technical design or artistic decorations. But the temples of Champa appear to have been erected earlier than those of Angkor Vāt and Boro-Budur.

The Cham temples have been found in groups at Myson, Dong Duong, Po-Nagar, and Pho Hai areas, and individually at Binh Lam, Khuong My, and Bang An.

M. Parmentier has made a technical classification of all these monuments under five headings.[3] What he calls the 'primitive art' is represented by the Myson and the Po Nagar temples of the seventh and the first quarter of the ninth centuries respectively. The 'cubic art,' deriving its name from the cube-shaped roof of the temples, is represented by the Myson temples of the eighth century, Po Nagar temple of the late ninth century, and the Dong Duong temple of the same period. The 'mixed art,' deriving its title from a combination of 'primitive' proportions and 'cubic' roof, is represented by the Dong Duong temple of the late ninth century.

[1] Majumdar : 'Champa,' Introduction, pp. xx–xxiv.

[2] *Dynasty of Sri Mara of Sixteen Kings from 250–529.*
Dynasty of Gangaraja of Fourteen Kings from 500–757.
Dynasty of Panduranga of Five Kings from 758–860.
Dynasty of Bhrigu of Seven Kings from 861–972.
Dynasty of Some Varman of Nine Kings from 972–1044.
Dynasty of Some Varman of Three Kings from 1050–1069.
Dynasty of Some Varman of Four Kings from 1070–1126.
Dynasty of Some Varman of Five Kings from 1139–1180.
—'Champa', Chap. III–X, pp. 19–105.

[3] M. H. Parmentier, *Inventaire Descriptif des Monuments Chams de L'Annam*, Vol. II, pp. 19 *et. seq.* quoted by Majumdar, 'Champa,' Chap. X, p. 258.

CHAM PILLAR, ELABORATELY CARVED

PLATE LIi

The 'classic art' is so called because of the architectural formula followed in the representation of the Myson temple of mid-eleventh century. The 'pyramidal art' dervies its title from its pyramidal form, as represented by the Bang An temple of the earliest tenth century, Po Nagar temple of the late twelfth century, and the Yan Pron temple of the fourteenth century. Lastly, what is called the 'derived art,' has departed from the recognized canons of the classical art and is represented by the Myson temples of the twelfth century, the Po Khaun Garai of the fourteenth century, and Po Rome of the mid-seventeenth century.

The Myson temples are situated in a valley, measuring about a mile in extent, south-east of Touranne. They are built in the valley proper, as also upon the low peaks of the neighbouring hills. They may be divided into some ten groups. The first group consists of the main shrine and three subsidiary temples on each side, of the same form but smaller in size, all built on one terrace in a quadrangular courtyard, surrounded by brick walls. They are cruciform (*svastika*) in plan and consist of several stages or storeys. 'In the first stage of the pyramidal roof, each side contains three pilasters. The second and third stages are repetitions of the first, though on a smaller scale.' The second group, within a square wall, contains the principal temple in the centre of the enclosure. 'A hall with double doors gives access to the court from the east. Two subsidiary temples occupy respectively the south-eastern and north-eastern angle. There are two other temples within the enclosure, in the south-west angle and in front of it. There are besides, seven miniature temples attached to the enclosing wall.' One of these temples 'has only two storeys and the roof of the upper one is ridge-shaped, with ogival ends.' There is a colonnade in front of the main shrine. The octagonal shaft of each column 'is fluted and ornamented at both ends. The base and capital are both executed with rare perfection. The abacus is decorated with the busts of four figures brandishing swords of a peculiar kind. The topmost member is a beautiful lotus.'

The third group is also enclosed with a wall. It consists of the main shrine, five other edifices, three temples, two subsidiary temples, all of the same orientation, and one gate tower. The main shrine is separated by an open space into the sanctuary and the vestibule. 'Internally the arched vault is not of a regular pyramidal character, but rises straight to a certain distance.'

The fourth group is 'enclosed by a continuous wall which forms a circuit round the northern, southern, and western walls.' There are two principal temples separated by a common court, two other subsidiary temples, two minor buildings, and another temple within the same enclosure. The fifth group is also enclosed by a wall, with a gateway in the middle of the southern wall. The main shrine had a tiled roof. Its 'inner chamber is square in plan, and has four wooden columns at the four angles. It opens by a doorway to the west, and has in the centre a richly sculptured pedestal carrying an enormous *liṅga*' (phallus of Śiva). There are three subsidiary temples, two edifices, and remains of several other buildings. In this group only one temple faces the east, the others having their façade towards the west.

The sixth group is also similar in plan, being enclosed by a wall with a single gateway. Here there is only one subsidiary temple, to the south of the main shrine in the centre of the enclosure.

The seventh group is similarly enclosed with a single gateway. In front of the main shrine, facing west, there is the usual hall (*mukha-maṇḍapa*). There is no subsidiary temple within the enclosure, but there appears to have been a residential chamber. Outside the enclosure, to the north-east, there is a temple with four entrances on the four sides.

The eighth group has no other building besides the main shrine, facing east, which is furnished with the usual front hall within the enclosing wall. There is also no gate-tower, which is substituted by a simple doorway.

The ninth group is also enclosed and has a gateway, but the main shrine and other temples have all disappeared.

The tenth group, at the middle height of a small peak overlooking the second, third, and fourth groups, 'consists merely of a long chamber.' It has two doorways at the two ends.[1]

The deities installed in the Myson temples include, besides the phallus of Śiva, Gaṇeśa, Skanda, Brahmā, Sūrya, Indra, and other gods and goddesses.

Dong Duong Group

The general plan of the Dong Duong temples appears to illustrate the design described in the *Mānasāra* and other *Śilpa-śāstras*. The

[1] For further details, *vide* Majumdar, *loc. cit.*, Vol. I, pp. 240–248; Parmentier, *loc. cit.* Plates LXVII—XCVII.

CHAM TEMPLE OF DUY HUYEM

Page 332

PLATE LIV

ANKCR VAT

whole compound is divided into four main courts. The outermost court, like all the rest, had an entrance porch on the east, preceded by two columns. Buildings in all the courts are mostly in ruins. In the third court there is a single hall with two side entrances. The second court contains a long chamber. In the first, or innermost court, is situated the main shrine of cross shape (i.e. *svastika* in plan) surrounded by four sanctuaries. There is, in front, an imposing building (*mukha-maṇḍapa*) with four bays. There are also two other temples and two residential blocks. The whole court is enclosed by a wall, with a porch on the east.

From the inscriptions it appears that 'the ruins at Dong Duong are those of a Buddhist temple and monastery, built by king Jayavarman in A.D. 875,' and that 'the temple was situated within the town of Indrapura, which was at that time the capital of Champa, and that the widowed queen of Indravarman, named Haradevī Rājakula, installed many gods and goddesses within the temple area. The actual discovery of Buddhist images among the ruins of the temple also demonstrate the Buddhist character of the building.'[1]

Po Nagar Group

The Po Nagar temple, otherwise known as 'the goddess of the city,' is situated, facing east, on a small hillock at the entrance of a valley. 'It commands a good view of the lagune at the foot of the hillock and of the sea close by.'

The temples were built within an enclosing wall in two rows from north to south, each containing three. The principal temple is in the front row. 'A steep staircase leads to a lower terrace containing an imposing hall with a colonnade.' There appears to have been a gateway also.

The superstructure of the main temple, wherein is installed a beautiful image of Umā, 'consists of a small member of ogival-shape, superimposed upon a bigger one of the same shape. Each of these stands upon two pilasters, between which, at the bottom, is a human figure decorated with a *mukuṭa* (crown) and with hands joined near the breast.' 'The roof consists of four stages. The interior of the roof is a pyramidal vault, ending in a long chimney to which are

[1] Majumdar, *loc. cit.*, Vol. I, p. 250 ; *vide* Parmentier, Plates XCVIII, *et seq.*

attached, at the height of the third stage of the roof, two cross-pipes which extend over the entire summit of the building. The vestibule is a copy of the main building in all its essential features.'[1]

This appears to be the best preserved and most beautiful of all temples in Champa.

One other temple of this group has a peculiar roof, consisting of a single curvilinear pyramidal dome of elegant shape, with two bulb-shaped stones as finials looking like the phallus of Śiva.

From inscriptions it is clear that there were several other buildings at Po Nagar. One of these has been identified as an apsidal Buddhist *chaitya*, with a central nave and two aisles.[2] In another inscription it is stated that 'King Satyavarma built a new temple and installed therein a new *mukha-liṅga*, together with images of other gods and goddesses.' In a third inscription of A.D. 817, Senapati Par is stated to have 'erected three temples with *maṇḍapas* (pavilions) and gates and installed gods and goddesses.'[3]

The Po Hai temples[4] on the top of a hillock consist of three shrines, facing east, in two different levels. The principal one is enclosed by a wall. 'The absence of corner towers brings out very prominently the resemblance of this type of temples with the storeyed *stūpas* of India, from which it seems to have been ultimately derived.'[5]

The Po Dam group consists of six temples,[6] also situated on a hill, but face the south, and the upper storeys of one with curved roof resemble some small temple in Boro-Budur.

The Po Rome temples consist of the principal shrine and another building.[7]

The Po Klong Garai temple comprises six buildings, built on a peak, commanding a fine view.[8]

The Ho Lai temples consist of three shrines built on a plain, and the Hung Thank group of five temples at the foot of a hill.[9]

[1] Majumdar, *loc. cit.*, Vol. I, pp. 252, 251 ; Parmentier, *loc. cit.*, Plate XXLI.
[2] Parmentier, Plate XXI, Vol. I, p. 127, quoted by Majumdar.
[3] For further details, *vide* Majumdar, *loc. cit.*, Vol. I, p. 258 : for inscriptions, Book III, pp. 41–218.
[4] Parmentier, *loc. cit.*, Parts I to III, pp. 29 *et seq.*
[5] Majumdar, *loc. cit.*, Vol. I, p. 254.
[6] Parmentier, Plates VI and VII; Majumdar, p. 255.
[7] Parmentier, Plates VIII to X; Majumdar, p. 255.
[8] Parmentier, Plates XI to XIV; Majumdar, p. 255.
[9] Parmentier, Plates XV to XIX; Majumdar, p. 256 ; and Parmentier, Plates XX and XXI : Majumdar, p. 256.

PLATE LV

PO-KLANG-GARAI

Page 334

PLATE LVI

P0-KLANG-GARAI (ANOTHER VIEW)

The remains of a few cave temples also have been found at several places in Champa. The Phu Duoc cave is oval in shape. 'The inner chamber has a vaulted roof, and two cells radiate from it.' 'The marble mountains near Hos Que contain several caves round a central hall, which is, however, open to the sky.' 'The caves of Phong Nha are of massive proportions.' This cave contains an image of Buddha and some other sculptures. There are some hundred inscriptions, one of which appears to contain the word 'Sāriputra,' thus indicating a Buddhistic sanctuary. The Chua Hang cave also contains a small image of Buddha. The caves near the Lac-Son village appear to have been 'transformed into Buddhist sanctuaries by the Chams.' In these caves there are some thirty-six inscriptions.[1]

The sculptures in connexion with the temples and caves comprise the images of both gods and goddesses, kings and queens, men and women, and animals. The actual iconographic proportions in *Tāla* or any other system are not available. But Dr. Majumdar declares that 'the features, at least of the upper part of the body, are well proportioned and the expression of face is pleasing.' But he comments that, 'like the Indian art, the images of gods in later periods became more and more deformed, till they assumed sometimes a monstrous appearance.' The figures of *dvārapālas* (doorkeepers) in temples are cited as examples.[2] Some of the human figures, comprising praying ones, mounted on elephants, lions, *apsaras* (nymphs), demons, etc., as also of musicians, are stated to be 'really charming.' The bas-reliefs on pedestals are stated to be so good as to be compared with those of Java.[2]

City Plan

The description of the city of Champa is available from a Chinese text.[3] It is stated to have been situated at a distance of about 6½ miles from the sea coast. 'At the north-west angle of the ramparts of the city were high mountains and a long chain of hills. To the north of these hills flowed a river, to the south also there was another river which joined the former to the east of the city.'

[1] Majumdar, *loc. cit.*, Vol. I, pp. 259–260; Parmentier, *loc. cit.*, Vol. I, pp. 218, Fig. 41, p. 317, Fig. 69, pp. 542–548, quoted by Majumdar.

[2] For further details, *vide* Majumdar 'Champa,' pp. 263–271; and Parmentier, *loc. cit.*, Figs. 78 to 107.

[3] *Chouei King Tchou* (A.D. 527) referred to by Dr. Majumdar, *loc. cit.*, p. 19.

'The city was surrounded by a wall about a mile and a half in circumference. On a brick wall, about 200 feet high, was raised a second brick wall of half that height, pierced by square loop-holes. On the walls were placed wooden boards supporting many-storeyed pavilions, on the roof of which again arose towers varying in height from 40 to 70 feet. There were four gates in the walls. The main gate was on the east. It opened near two islands in the river Houai. The western gate opened on a double ditch which turned to the north and reached a hill. The southern gate, likewise, opened on a double ditch. The northern gate opened on the river Houai.'

'Within the walls were a small enclosure, the assembly rooms, and brick palaces. There was a palace, opening to the east, of which the loose pieces supporting the rafter looked like the tail of an owl.' The towers are also stated to have been of an owl shape, 'with its tail turned towards the wind and touching the mountains and the clouds, looking as if towards the water and ascending to the highest peak of the mountains.'[1] In design, the city itself, it should be noticed, may correspond to the Kheṭa plan of the *Mānasāra*, while *pechaka* (owl) has been distinctly referred to in the *Mānasāra* as a site-plan, which appears to have been carried to the towers and palaces built within the city, probably of the same plan.[2]

There are also scanty remains of some fortified cities. The citadel of Srī Banoy, an irregular quadrangle in shape, is situated on the right bank of the river Song Luy. This 'shows greater knowledge in the art of fortification than any other.' Thank Ho, about ten miles from the mouth of the river Song Da Rang, is 'enclosed between a mountain and the left side of the river, and the open face is protected by a wall. It was also protected by reduits and towers and had several gates.' Of the citadel of Chausa and Coy Luy very little remains to enable a description.

Remains of 'a first class military fortification' have been discovered at Caban, the ancient capital town of Vijaya. 'They cover a rectangular area of over 1,500 yards from north to south and of 1,200 yards from east to west. It was protected by an arm of the Binh Dinh river on the north, and a strong wall, without any flanking, on either sides. The wall was built of earth with revetment of

[1] M. Auroussean, *B. E. F.*, Vol. XIV, no. 9, pp. 23–34. Dr. Majumdar, *loc. cit.*, Vol. I, pp. 19–20.

[2] *Vide Mānasāra*, Chap. VII; and *see* pp. 101–102, 104 of this volume.

limonite, and was pierced through by tunnels for the ingress and egress of a small brook. There are a number of high mounds on all sides which probably conceal some towers or gates.'[1]

This brief account of Champa architecture does not lack in the variety of structures. Except private dwelling-houses of simple character, all other types of buildings, namely, cities, forts, palaces, and temples have been referred to. In most cases their Indian origin is more than indicated. But there has been difference of opinion on this point, on account of the inaccessability of the *Śilpa-śāstra*, like the *Mānasāra*, wherein alone one can find the basic principles of Hindu architecture. Thus M. Parmentier, who has discussed the question of the Champa art at great length and who possesses a thorough knowledge of the art and architecture of Champa, was faced with a real difficulty. In order to come to the conclusion that Champa might have borrowed from India through the Indian colonizers, it was naturally necessary for Parmentier to see such structures in India of some earlier dates than those of Champa. On this ground he is perfectly justified in denying a connexion of the Champa art with that of Cambodia and Java. So far as India is concerned, even in the absence of archaeological remains, there are convincing literary evidences which clearly show that Champa art might have easily migrated from India.

Even on purely archaeological grounds, Dr. Majumdar and others have joined issue with M. Parmentier when the latter says that, 'with the exception of the curved roof, no typical element of Indian architecture appears in Cham style, nor is any typical motif of the Cham art traceable in the old Indian style.'

By way of refuting M. Parmentier, Dr. Majumdar rightly says that, 'to us, the characteristic feature of a Cham temple seems to be its storied roof of several stages, in gradually diminishing proportions, each of which is again a miniature of the whole. Now this is the characteristic feature of what is known as the Dravidian style, The *rathas* of Mamallapuram and temples of Cenjeeveram and Badami of the seventh century A.D. are cited as examples. The essential resemblance between the *śikharas* of normal Cham temples and of the Dharmarāja Ratha and Arjuna Ratha is also referred to. The elongated curved roof with ogival ends has its counterpart in

[1] Majumdar, *loc. cit.*, Vol. I, p. 261–262. Parmentier, *loc. cit.*, Plates IV, XXVII, XLIX, LV.

Gaṇeśa Ratha and Sahadeva Ratha. The third type of curved roof of Champa temples 'resembles Draupadi's Ratha, and is probably derived from those of North-Indian style, as Parmentier himself admits.' It is, however, clear and natural that the Chams did not blindly imitate the Indian prototypes, but added new elements of their own. 'But the fact,' concludes Dr. Majumdar, 'that their style was throughout based upon the essential and characteristic features of Indian style seems to be beyond question.' Dr. Majumdar is equally convinced that Cham sculptures bear striking 'agreement with the Indian style in both essential and non-essential elements.'[1]

Cambodia

Cambodia is situated to the south of Siam. It is included in a group of countries, without natural boundaries, comprising Burma, Siam, Annam, and Cochin-China. The ruined cities, palaces, and temples of Cambodia are astonishing from an architectural point of view. The famous temple of Angkor Vat and others are in a way more imposing than even the Boro-Budur of Java. The Hindu city-plan, which is missing in other parts of Insulindia, is fortunately available in Cambodia. The civil architecture, also, is a novelty of the archaeological remains without which the Hindu influence in arts and architecture in Insulindia cannot be complete.

There is a well-established tradition, which has been recognized by European authorities[2] also, that in 443 B.C., Preaṭhong, a Hindu prince, son of the king of Indraprastha (the modern Delhi), emigrated with a large number of his followers and settled at Choukan, north of Angar. 'In 125 B.C. the Chinese are said to have conquered the Cambodians. There is also a record that, in the first centuries of the Christian era, emigrants from Madras made their way into Cambodia, introducing the Brahman faith, the Sanskrit alphabet, and Indian rites and customs.'[3]

The Khmer and Sanskrit epigraphic texts give details of a dynasty of seven kings who reigned from A.D. 435 to 680. From the death of the last king Jayavarman to the commencement of the ninth century there are no records. In A.D. 802, Jayavarman II, who

[1] Majumdar, *loc. cit.*, Vol. I, pp. 272–274.
[2] Dr. Bastian (Vol. I, p. 393), *Tissandier* (p. 17), quoted by Fergusson, *History of Indian and Eastern Architecture*, Vol. II, p. 373.
[3] Fergusson, *loc. cit.*, Vol. II, p. 373.

may have been connected with the earlier dynasty, formed a new dynasty of eighteen sovereigns who ruled till A.D. 1201. To this monarch is attributed the foundation of the Cambodian kingdom, with its capital Angkor Thom. He is credited to have laid the foundations of the great city of Angkor Thom, the royal palace in its centre, the pyramid temples of Phimêanakas, the great temple of Bayon, and other structures.[1] Aymonier has correctly traced the origin to this great king of the colossal constructions which were raised during the four centuries following.[2] He is also of opinion that this king may have come from Java, with an acquaintance with the great temple of Boro-Budur. But there are some small earlier temples of comparatively small importance, built towards the end of the sixth or commencement of the seventh century, in which the origin of the Cambodian style may be traced. There are, however, striking similarities between the great temples of Java and Cambodia. The other kings of this long dynasty were also great builders. Thus 'the third king, Indravarman, besides building the temples of Baku and Bakong, completed and consecrated the temple of Bayon in Angkor Thom. To the fourth king, Yaśovarman, is attributed the completion of the great capital city, also the temple of Lolei and the pyramid temple of Phimêanakas in the centre of the palace enclosures. The ninth king, Rājendravarman, built two great temples, Ta-Prom being Brahmanical, and Bānteai Kedei, Buddhist. The tenth king also built several temples, of which the most important is the pyramid temple of Bapoun, immediately south of the royal palace in Angkor Thom. The eleventh king, Sūryavarman, who reigned for nearly a half century, was a great builder, the temples of Phnom Chisor, Vāt Ek, Phnom Bāset, Prah Vihear, and Prah Khan being attributed to him. His successor continued his work and built the temples of Banteai Ta Kean, Phimai, Pre Rup, and, probably, the temple on Mount Bakheng, south of Angkor Thom. Vāt Phu may have been built in 1090–1100 by one of the three following kings.

The sixteenth king, Sūryavarman II, who ruled from 1112 to 1152, completed the great temple of Angkor Vāt, which is said to have been laid by his predecessor. No further temples were built during the reign of the last two sovereigns.[3] Thus the actual building period in Cambodia may be placed between A.D. 802 and 1152.

[1] Fergusson, Vol., II, pp. 373–374. [2] E. Aymonier, *Cambodge*, III, p. 468.
[3] Fergusson, *loc. cit.*, Vol. I, pp. 374–375.

From an architectural point of view the great temples of Cambodia have been divided into four groups.[1] Those of Ta Prohm, Kedei, and Pre Rup, possessing generally three enclosures, are built more or less on the same level. Secondly, the pyramid temples, as Phimeanakas and Bapuon, consist of a series of narrow terraces rising one above the other. Those of Angkor Vāt and Bayon combine both the enclosed and raised terrace types, where the enclosures are within the other, each raised from 15 to 20 feet above the level of that outside, making the whole look like a pyramid. The fourth group comprises all smaller temples, consisting of three to five sanctuaries placed side by side, the centre one being the most important, and the whole surrounded by a wall or moat.

'The enclosures consist of a moat or stone wall. In some temples one or more of the enclosures take the form of a gallery or corridor, which is roofed over with horizontal courses of stone corbelled over till they meet at the top. In parts of the enclosures, as also in front of temples, are tanks of water with stone borders and steps round. Each enclosure is furnished with four *gopuras* or gateways ended with a tower raised from the centre of the top. The gateways on the north and south are invariably closed with imitation doors in stone. The principal entrance to the temples is, as a rule, from the east, except in cases like Angkor Vāt, which has a western entrance, the capital, Angkor Thom, being on the west.'

The remarkable feature of the pyramidal and raised-terrace group is their imposing approach by causeways of considerable length and their staircases, comprising 392 steps in front of the *gopura* of Phnom Chisor temple.

'The sanctuary is always situated on the axis of the principal entrance, generally on the east. In general design it takes the form of *śikhara* or tower, the lower portion rarely higher than the width, but crowned with a series of receding stages. On the three sides are false doorways, like on the north and south of the *gopura*, which are elaborately carved. The walls are of great thickness, sometimes 5 to 6 feet, deemed necessary to carry the superstructure, built with horizontal courses of stone or brick, corbelled out internally so as to meet in the centre.'

It is hardly necessary to say that all these are the common usual features of Hindu architecture applied with little alteration to Cambodian temples.

[1] Fergusson, *loc. cit.* Vol. II, pp. 376–380.

The largest temples in Cambodia are those of Angkor Vāt, Bayon, and Beng Mealeā. Angkor Vāt is the best preserved, but of later date. Bayon and Mealeā were built at a period 'when the architectural style of Cambodia had reached perhaps its highest development.'[1]

'Angkor Vāt' means 'the temple of the city.' It is situated about a mile to the south of the capital city of Angkor Thom, and between it and the lake Tonlé Sap.[2] 'It is almost an exact square and measures nearly an English mile each way. The walled enclosure of the temple measures 1,080 by 1,100 yards, and is surrounded by a moat 216 yards wide. The moat is crossed on the west by a splendid causeway, carried on piers on either side. This leads to the great gateway, five storeys in height, not unlike the *gopura* of a Dravidian temple, but extended by lateral galleries and towers to a façade more than 600 feet in extent. Within this a second raised causeway, 370 yards long, leads to a cruciform platform in front of the temple. On either side of this, about half way down, is a detached temple. . . . The general plan of the temple . . . consists of three enclosures, one within the other, each raised from 15 to 20 feet above the level of that outside it, so as to give the whole a pyramidal form. The outer enclosure measures 590 feet by 700 feet, and it covers, therefore, about 413,000 square feet. . . . There are three portals, adorned with towers on each face, and on either side of these are open galleries or verandahs, which, with their bas-reliefs, are probably the most remarkable features of this temple.'[3]

It looks like a pyramid 'more than 600 feet in breadth across its shortest width north and south, and rising to 180 feet at the summit of the central tower. It is consequently larger and higher than Boro-Budur, and surpasses the latter in its ornamentation as well as in the delicacy of its carvings.'[4]

The temple[5] proper is situated in the centre of the middle court. 'It measures 200 feet by 213 feet, and is crowned by five towers

[1] Fergusson, *loc. cit.*, Vol. II, p. 380.

[2] By a treaty, France obtained from Siam, in 1907, the provinces wherein Angkor Vāt and numerous other temples are situated.

[3] Fergusson, *loc. cit.*, Vol. II, pp. 380, 382.

[4] Except in the matter of colonnades of the Rameswara temple, both Boro-Budur and Angkor Vāt are stated by Fergusson to be superior for architectural design and sculptural decoration.

[5] The building which resembles the innermost temple is that at Ranpur in Godwar District of the Jodhpur territory. Its dimensions are nearly the same, 200 feet by 225 feet; like this, it has five spires similarly disposed and four open courts; and at Ranpur, as here, there are a certain number of snake figures.

or spires (*śikhara*), one on each angle, and one taller than the other in the centre, rising to a height of 180 feet. The central tower has four cells, one facing the central hall from each side.'[1]

The most wonderful features of the colonnades of Angkor Vāt are the sculptures that adorn their walls. 'These are distributed in eight compartments, one on each side of the four central groups of entrances, measuring each from 250 to 300 feet in length, with a height of about 6½ feet. Their aggregate length is thus at least 2,000 feet. The number of men and animals represented extends from 18,000 to 20,000. Generally speaking, the reliefs represent battle scenes of the most animated description, taken from the *Rāmāyaṇa* or the *Mahābhārata*.' There are other bas-reliefs, also, dealing with different subjects, 'one representing heaven, earth, and hell; one representing the second Avatāra of Vishṇu, the world-supporting tortoise, another dealing with the churning of the ocean with the great snake Nāga.'[2]

'The only other temples where sculpture is used in anything like the same profusion,' declares Fergusson 'are those at Boro-Budur in Java and that at Halebid'[3] in Mysore State.

'No trace of an arch of any description has ever been found in Cambodian architecture,' and there is no dome at Angkor Vāt. There are, however, 1,532 pillars in this single building. All these piers strikingly resemble the Roman Doric order.[4]

So far as the identity of the Angkor Vāt is concerned, Fergusson and others have no doubt that it was originally a Hindu temple, probably of Nāga-Vāsuki, and that it could not be a Buddhist temple. The reasons given are convincing. 'Though the god is gone, and the Buddhists have taken possession of the temple,[5] every angle of every roof is adorned with an image of the seven-headed snake, and there are hundreds of them; every cornice is composed of snake's heads; every convolution of the roofs, and there are thousands, terminates

[1] Fergusson, *loc. cit.*, II, pp. 388.

[2] *Ibid.*, II, pp. 385, 386.

[3] *Ibid.*, p. 386.

[4] Similar resemblance of Kashmir pillars with the Grecian Doric order has been recognized (Fergusson, *loc. cit.*, II, p. 389). It has been shown that the five Indian orders described in the *Śilpa-śāstras*, *Purāṇas*, and *Āgamas* are similar to the five Greek-Roman orders in respect of proportion and mouldings (*vide* the writer's *Encyclopaedia of Hindu Architecture*, under Stambha).

[5] It is in French hands and in possession of the Siamese bowzes, who have dedicated it to the worship of Buddha.

in a five- or seven-headed snake. The balustrades are snakes, and the ridge of every roof was apparently adorned with gilt dragons.'

'There is one thing more certain than another,' emphatically declares Fergusson, 'that Angkor Vāt was not originally erected by Buddhists or for Buddhist purposes.' This fact is abundantly proved. 'In the first place, there is no sign of *dagoba*, or of a *vihāra*, or of a *chaitya* hall in the whole building, nor anything that can be called a reminiscence of any feature of Buddhist architecture. More than this, there is no trace of Buddha, of any scene from his life, or from the Jātakas to be found among the sculptures.' Referring to the Buddhist temples at Bharaut, Sanchi, Amaravati, Gandhara, and Boro-Budur, Fergusson concludes, most unhesitatingly asserting, that 'there is not a trace of Buddhism in any of the bas-reliefs yet brought to light from Angkor Vāt, nor an integral statue of Buddha or of any Buddhist saint about the place.'[1]

The Siamese, who are now in possession of the temple, have introduced images of Buddha into the sanctuaries and other places, and, 'with the usual incuriousness of people of their class, assert (in Siamese records) that it was always so.'[2] The unfounded traditions of Asoka having sent missionaries to Cambodia and of Aśvaghosha's having visited the place, as also the account of a Chinese traveller,[3] who saw the country with Buddhist spectacles, in 1295–1297, have lent colour to the Siamese records.

The temple of Bayon is situated within the city walls of Angkor Thom. It was founded by Jayavarman II (A.D. 802–869), the first king of the dynasty, and was consecrated by Yaśovarman (889–910), the fourth king, about A.D. 900. That this long period of a hundred years was required for the construction of this great temple may be indicated by the fact that it had a double course of sculptural corridors, 'the aggregate length of which has been calculated to be over 36,000 feet, or nearly twice that of Angkor Vāt,' and that, while Angkor Vāt has nine towers, the temple of Bayon had fifty. Unfortunately it suffers from terrible ruin and a forest of trees has badly invaded it. Thus no general view is available. But the architects have recovered its wonderful plan. It is of a pyramidal form and belongs to the third group of Cambodian temple. 'The

[1] Fergusson, *loc. cit.*, Vol. II, p. 390–391. [2] *Ibid.*, p. 390.

[3] Translation by Abel Remusat, *Nouveaux Melanges Asiatiques*, Vol. I, pp. 78, *et. seq.*

principal difference between it and the Angkor Vāt is found in the second platform, and the great importance given to the sanctuary, as well as the richer and more elaborate ornamentation.' It had great entrance porches on the north, south, and west sides, and the entrance porch vestibule and two other halls preceding the sanctuary on the east side.

It appears to have been a Brahmā temple from the fact that the towers are decorated with the four great masks of Brahmā on each face. Their 'fine modelling and expression,' declares Fergusson, 'are only approached by the great Egyptian Sphinx.'[1]

Beng Méaleā

The temple of Beng Méaleā, probably of the ninth century, is situated about twenty miles east of Angkor Thom. It belongs to the first group of Cambodian temples, all the enclosures being more or less on the same level. Its exceptional features lie in the fact that, in the first enclosure on the south or left side, are two groups of buildings 'which are assumed to have been the palaces of the king and the queen respectively.' The palaces are identified by the smaller corridors and great halls, with side aisles, as throne or state reception rooms. 'The walls of the corridors are as those of Angkor Vāt and Bayon, the decoration being confined to the entrance portals and the towers.'[2] All the outer courts are filled with water, forming huge tanks.

This is also in a ruined condition. Its general view is thus not available. The plan has been, however, reconstructed.[3] The chief deity of the temple is missing. But it is clear from the general history of the dynasty that it was originally a Hindu temple.

Bapoun

The temple of Bapoun is an example of the pyramid type of Cambodian temple. It is situated immediately south of the palace in Angkor Thom. 'It bears considerable resemblance to the temple of Bayon, but the height of its second and third platform is much greater. Moreover, the Brahmā masks were not carved on the twenty-eight towers of Bapoun, nor are the walls of the corridor enriched with the bas-relief sculpture of Bayon and Angkor Vāt.

[1] Fergusson, *loc. cit.*, II, p. 392. [2] *Ibid.*, II, p. 396.
[3] *Vide* Fergusson, Plate no. 470; and M. L. Delaporte, *Le Cambodge*, Tome I. *Le Royaume Actuel*, par Etienne Aymonier.

But the richness in beauty of the carving is quite as fine as that of Bayon.'[1]

This is also in a ruined condition. Its other details are thus missing.[2]

City of Angkor Thom

The foundation of the city of Angkor Thom was laid by the first king, Jayavarman II (802–869), but not completed or occupied till the reign of Yaśovarman (889–910), the fourth king. This long period of a hundred years required for its construction is indicated by the greatness of the city, its palaces, temples, roads, and bridges. 'The city measured close upon 10,000 feet east to west, and 9,600 feet from north to south, giving a perimeter of 7½ miles to the enclosure walls. Those walls, about 22 feet high, were surrounded by a moat, 300 feet wide, and entered through five gates, one on the north, south, and west sides, and two on the east, the most important, called the Gate of Victory, leading to the palace.'[3] It was of what is called the *svastika* (cruciform) plan in the *Mānasāra* and other *Śilpa-śāstras*. It consisted of a central gateway, 52 feet square, with recessed angles and side wings. Three towers, with Brahmā masks on the four sides of each, rose above the central gateway and the side wings. The walls of the city were also of very great extent and of dimensions commensurate with its importance. Unfortunately no other details of the city proper are available.

'The palace enclosure, situated in the centre of the city, measured about 2,000 feet by 800 feet and was surrounded by a double wall, with moat between. In front of the palace enclosure was a great terrace over 800 feet long by 45 feet wide, and 15 feet high, the walls of which were sculptured with elephants. No traces of walls of any description have been found in front of this terrace, suggesting that it formed an open space where reviews took place before the king and his courtiers on the terrace. At the north end of this square is a cruciform (*svastika*) structure, about 30 feet wide and 60 feet long, richly decorated, with six bands of sculptured figures, and it

[1] Fergusson, *loc. cit.*, II, p. 398.

[2] The other examples of the pyramidal type are Phimêanakas, Bakheng, and Tā Kio, of which also the details are missing.

[3] Fergusson, *loc. cit.*, II, p. 401.

was on the top of this that the French explorers found the supposed statue of the leprous king[1] to whom the monument was ascribed.'[2]

The great temples of Angkor Vāt, Bayon, and Bapoun[3] and many smaller temples were built in this capital city. Some of the numerous temples appear to have been 'built as palaces for the king and occupied by him, his family, and courtiers.' 'In the outer court of Beng Méaleā are two groups of structures which have been described as the palaces of the king and the queen respectively. On the west side of Phimêanakas, and within the palace enclosure of Angkor Thom, are the foundations of buildings which are supposed to have been the residences of the king and his family, the women's quarters occupying the whole width of the enclosure against the west wall, in which there is no entrance gate. At Vāt Phu, near Basak, on either side of the causeway leading to the temple, is a structure of about 150 feet frontage, with a rectangular court at the back and surrounded with a corridor vaulted like those in the temples, and those are considered to be palaces. Again at Phnom Chisar, on the north side of the court, the sills of the windows are 6 feet from the ground, so that the corridor they lighted may have been occupied by women.' Concerning the accommodation necessary for a king and his retinue of thousands, Fergusson declares that only temples like Angkor Vāt, Beng Méaleā, Ta Prohm, and Prah Khan could possibly hold them. Though Bayon might have been occupied by the priests only, the series of magnificent halls in the enclosures of Angkor Vāt and Beng Méaleā 'would seem to have been provided for the needs of a great court.'[4]

Some of these great structures might have been used also as collegiate *maṭhas* of the Brahmans, with provision for accommodation for the numerous students and teachers.[5] Fergusson speaks highly on the perfection of the ancient roads and bridges. 'One great trunk road seems to have stretched for 300 miles across the country from Korat, in a south-easterly direction, to the Me-kong river. It was a raised causeway, paved throughout like a Roman Road, and

[1] King Yaśovarman II, the fourth monarch of the dynasty, who is credited with the completion of the capital Angkor Thom, of which the foundation was laid by the first monarch a hundred years earlier.

[2] Fergusson, *loc. cit.*, II, pp. 401–402.

[3] For details, *vide ibid.*, Fergusson.

[4] Fergusson, *loc. cit.*, II, pp. 399–400.

[5] Cf. Lājonquiere *Inventaire Descriptif*, Tome II, Introduction, p. 29.

every stream that it crossed was spanned by a bridge, many of which remain perfect to the present day.'[1]

One of these bridges was 400 feet in length and 50 feet in breadth, richly ornamented by balustrades and cornices, and representations of snakes and the snake-king. 'The extraordinary thing is,' states Fergusson, 'that it is constructed without radiating arches, but, like every structure in the place, by a system of bracketing or horizontal arches, and without cement. Yet it has withstood, for five centuries at least, the violence of the tropical torrent which it spans.'[1]

There can be no doubt about the sceintific skill of the architects who built the great Cambodian structures, cities, roads, and bridges. By way of an illustration, Fergusson refers to their mechanical skill employed in constructing the roofs of great structures wholly of hewn stone, without the aid either of wood or concrete or cement of any kind, and in dovetailing and joining them so beautifully that they remain watertight and perfect after at least five centuries of neglect in a tropical climate. 'When we put all these things together,' concludes Fergusson, 'it is difficult to decide whether we ought most to admire the mechanical skill which the Cambodian architects displayed in construction or the largeness of conception and artistic merit which pervades every part of their design.'[2]

About the Indian origin of the Cambodian art there is no doubt. 'Indian temples were constructed with pillars almost purely classical in design, and ornamented with bas-reliefs so strangely Egyptian in character.'[3] In Cambodia before the Hindu colonization there might have been a civilization and even some religion, but no art, declares Fergusson. 'Indians seem slowly, and only to a limited extent, to have been able to modify their religion towards Hinduism, probably because it was identical, or at least sympathetic, but they certainly endowed the Cambodians with an art which we have no reason to suppose they before possessed.'[4]

[1] Fergusson, *loc. cit.*, I, pp. 402.

[2] *Ibid*, II, pp. 403.

[3] It has already been pointed that what Fergusson considered to be the Greco-Roman orders are really Indian, fully described in the *Śilpa-śāstras*, *Purāṇas*, and *Āgamas*. Fergusson, like many early European scholars and historians, was obsessed by a prejudice. Whatever scientifically developed things were found in India were sought to be explained by the theory of importation instead of the natural process of indigenous origin.

[4] Fergusson, *loc. cit.*, II, p. 391.

SUMATRA

The great island of Sumatra is nearly four times as large as Java and the fifth island of the whole world in area, Greenland, New Guinea, Borneo, and Madagascar alone surpassing it. 'It lies almost equally in the northern and southern hemispheres, north-west of Java, and west and south of the Malay Peninsula, its western and northern shores being washed by the Indian ocean. It has a length of 1,000 miles and a maximum breadth of 230 miles. Of the vast area of this enormous island a large part is still unexplored and unknown. The interior plateaus, forests, and mountains are still the home of cannibal tribes and the haunt of elephants and tigers.'[1]

The origin of the name is ascribed by some to an abbreviation of the Malay words 'burut suma utara,' used by the people of Java to describe the situation of Sumatra to their 'north-west.' According to others, the name owes its origin to the Sanskrit form *samudra* or sea, given by the Hindu settlers to imply the ocean island. Yet a third derivation is found in Suvarṇa-dvīpa (island of gold), which is found mentioned in the *Rāmāyaṇa* in connexion with the search for Sītā, stolen by Rāvaṇa.

Sumatra as an island of gold is mentioned, besides in the *Rāmāyaṇa*, in Buddhist literature also.[2] 'From Chinese sources we learn that a Hinduized kingdom of Palembang (formerly known as Śrīvijaya) existed in Sumatra in the fifth century A.D. In the tenth century this kingdom . . . ruled over fifteen subject states. In the tenth century this Sumatran kingdom was conquered by Java, but soon recovered its independence. Early in the thirteenth century we find again a list of the subject countries of Śrīvijaya. In the fourteenth century it came under the sway of Majapapit kingdom of Java.'[3] Thus 'the history of the great island before its rediscovery by the Portuguese is wrapped in mystery.'[4]

'The archaeological monuments of the Hindu period in Sumatra are of small importance compared with those of Java.'

A king of the Sailendra dynasty of the kingdom of Śrīvijaya in Sumatra is stated to have built, in Central Java, the temple of Kalasan,

[1] A. S. Walcott, *Java and Her Neighbours*, pp. 275–276.

[2] B. R. Chatterjee, *India and Java*, I, pp. 22–28.

[3] *Ibid.*, p. 14.

[4] Walcott, p. 278.

of the Mahāyāna divinity Tārā. 'These Sumatran monarchs built on a grand scale in Java rather than in Sumatra.'[1] Thus, in Sumatra itself, no trace of Hindu monuments of religious character were found and recorded by the early visitors. Perhaps whatever monuments may have been there were of perishable materials and were easily destroyed by the Moslem invaders. But the existing civil architecture of the vast island must have been based upon the old tradition. So far as the peculiar horned houses of Sumatra are concerned, it will be noticed that their foundations on bamboo-pole or harder wood have their counterpart in the thatched houses in many parts of India. The horn itself may be seen in varying degrees in thatched houses in Bengal in particular. Their angularity increases in houses of those places where strong and stormy wind blows periodically. The interior arrangement and accommodation differ in accordance with the local conditions and the varying requirements of the occupants.

The horned houses are mostly dwellings. They are oblong in shape, with the front on one of the long sides. 'They are one storey high and stand several feet above the ground, on posts or piles. The walls are of wood or plaited bamboo, the front steps of wood, stucco-covered brick, or stone, the windows mere openings closed by means of shutters or screens, and the doors plain and usual.' The larger and better types of these houses are furnished with elaborate porches at the entrance, and the ends of the main structure rise in curves and are highly carved. The roof, of which the peculiarity lies in its simplest form, 'consists of a flexible ridge-pole running lengthwise off the house, supported only at the ends.' The top line is curved with raised ends and represents a crescent.[2]

'A development of the primitive form is found in the houses with wings at the ends, each wing necessitating an additional horn or peak in the roof. The horns are covered with metal in best houses.'[3] Facing each dwelling-house there are, as a rule, two small structures on high posts, which are used as rice barns or family granaries. 'Their entrances, for better security from men, rats, and snakes, are high up

[1] Chatterjee (p. 15), on the authority of Prof. Krom, *De Sutrantraansche Periode der Javansche Geschiedenis*, 1922.

[2] In India, in East Bengal in particular, the top line curves in a reverse manner, with a raised middle and the ends sloping downwards.

[3] Walcott, *Java and Her Neighbours*, pp. 314–315.

under the gables of their horned roofs, and reached only by the aid of ladders.'

'In every (horned) house of the richer and more prosperous, the front door opens on an oblong hall or living room, of equal length with the middle section of the roof or that between the central pair of horns. To the rear are the sleeping rooms and kitchen, and when the houses have wings, there are a few steps at each end of the main apartment leading to raised sleeping rooms or platforms, shut off by curtains. The houses are all raised high above the ground on posts, and this lower space is often fenced in with lattice and used as a cellar and carriage-house, probably sometimes even as a stable, piggery, or chicken house.'[1]

' There are two other distinctive buildings in every self-respecting highland village—the *balei* or meeting place, and the *misigit* or mosque.'

' The village graveyards are quite apart from the houses of worship and seem to receive little care, their plain, upright tombstones being often broken or fallen down.'[2]

Celebes

The term might have been derived from the Malay words ' Si Labih ' (land up there), or ' Seli-besi,' signifying iron kris. ' Celebes itself is fourth in size of the various islands, surpassed in this respect by New Guinea, Borneo, and Sumatra itself. Its length is roughly about five hundred miles, and its width is so varying that, while at the middle it is a scant twenty miles, at the north end it is over a hundred.' The inhabitants of the interior and the central Celebes, known as the head-hunting Toradjas, are still in a savage condition ; only those of the Minahasa District in the north, a small area in the neighbourhood of Macassar, and a few scattered settlements in near proximity to the coasts, are partly modernized. The people of the southern end of Celebes are nearly all Macassarese or Bugis, the latter being the seamen of the Archipelago, the greatest navigators and the most enterpising traders'.[3]

' The houses of the Kampongs vary in many details from those in Java. They are generally raised several feet above the ground on poles, and have gabled roofs, shuttered windows, and considerable

[1] Walcott, *ibid.*, pp. 324–325.
[2] *Ibid.*, pp. 315, 316.
[3] *Ibid.*, pp. 111, 112.

ornamentation in the way of carved woodwork. The walls are of matting or of neatly plaited bamboo, the roofs are of *nipa* or palm-leaf thatch.'[1]

The house of this type is very usual in villages in Bengal, with only this much difference that the space between the ground and the floor is filled with earth, forming a plinth.

There are several groups of islands where traces of ancient structures may be seen. The Ambonia, or Ambon, group includes Boeroc (Bourou), Cerum, the Bandas, the Arus, and many smaller islands of the Banda sea coast of Timor.[2] The Bandas include Banda Lontar, 'a crescent-shaped island, six miles long by a half broad; Banda Neira, two miles by one in dimension, and Gunong Api (the island of Volcano).'[3] On a steep hill, at the water's edge, there is a series of mediaeval fortifications, very little of which remains to enable an architectural description.[4]

There are the remains of an imposing old fort at Nassau also. 'A moat, now nearly dry, surrounds the walls. . . . This fortification must, in the old days, have been an almost impregnable stronghold, for its walls are, at least on the sides towards the sea, 500 feet long, 20 feet high, and over 15 feet in thickness.' Like the forts at Agra, Delhi, and other places, it is today occupied, laments Mr. Walcott, 'by peaceful dwellings, gardens, tennis courts, while trees and undergrowth have taken the place of cannon on its ramparts.'[5]

The Fort Belgica is an ancient structure. It is of pentagonal form with high exterior walls. 'Like Fort Nassau, Belgica is no longer in use for purposes of defence.'[6]

Bali

Bali is separated from Java by a narrow strait. Of all the peoples of Insulindia, the Balinese have retained to this day the religion of the early Hindu settlers. They call themselves 'men of Madjapahit,' and indeed many of them are descendants of subjects of the great Hindu kingdom of Eastern Java of that name, who fled across the

[1] Walcott, *Java and Her Neighbours*, pp. 115–116. [2] *Ibid.*, p. 166.
[3] *Ibid.*, pp. 174–175. [4] *Ibid.*, p. 174. [5] *Ibid.*, p. 178.
[6] *Ibid.*, p. 178.

straits before the incursion of the Muhammadans several centuries ago.'

'There are a number of fine Hindu temple ruins. The native Kampongs are enclosed by walls'.[1]

Borneo

The enormous island of Borneo[2] is situated towards the north-west of the Celebes and nearly due east of Sumatra. In size it is seven times that of Java and larger than France. The bulk of the inhabitants are Dyaks, closely affiliated with the Malays. 'The Dyaks are generally of sturdy build and splendid physique, but ugly of face and thorough savages in mental and moral character.'[3] It is notorious as the 'land of the wild Dyak, the orang-utan, and the great constrictor snakes, the land of vast impenetrable jungle and mosquito-infested swamps.'[4]

In the native State of Kotei, East Borneo, several inscribed stones have been discovered. These are undated documents. On the palaeographical ground they have been placed between A.D. 400 and 450.[5] All the four inscriptions[6] are written in Sanskrit and record the gifts made by king Mulavarman. To commemorate the gifts sacrificial pillars were erected. These pillars, like those of Asoka, are of considerable architectural interest. They are thoroughly original, Brahmanical in religion and Indian in design, and the most elegant productions of Indian art.[7]

This would clearly indicate not only the existence of some Hindu kingdom in Borneo, but also the Sanskrit language, and the art and architecture of the Hindu type. There are, however, no more architectural remains available.

[1] Walcott, *Java and Her Neighbours*, pp. 108, 109.

[2] 'Borneo was for many years a cause of dispute between England and Holland, and it was only in 1892 that the island was divided amicably between them, England's suzerainty over the north-western third being recognized by her rival claimant.' (Walcott, p. 107.)

[3] Walcott, *Java and Her Neighbours*, p. 107.

[4] *Ibid.*, p. 120.

[5] Dr. B. R. Chatterjee and Dr. N. P. Chakravarti have quoted (*India and Java*, II, p. 17) the views of M. Finot, Prof. Kern, and Prof. J. Ph. Vogel (*Bijdragen tot-de Taal-Land en Volken-kunde van Nederlandsche Indie*, 1918).

[6] A, B, C, and D, *see* Vogel and Chatterjee and Chakravarti, pp. 17–19.

[7] *See* under Stambha, writer's *Encyclopaedia of Hindu Architecture*.

JAVA

The Indo-Javanese connexion has been further established by Javanese tradition,[1] the Kavi chronicles like the *Nagarakṛitāgama* and the *Pararaton*, the inscriptions of the Malay Archipelago, the remnants of buildings, sculptures, paintings, and other archaeological remains, and the Chinese records. The Dutch, French, English and Indian scholars, historians, travellers and archaeologists have contributed largely to reconstruct the Hindu-Buddhist period of Javanese history.[2]

In point of time, the earliest reference appears to have been the passage in the *Rāmāyaṇa*, according to which the King Sugrīva, the friend and ally of Rāmachandra, is stated to have sent out search parties in quest of Sītā, among other places to the island of Java (Yavadvīpa) also. The exact dating of this passage is not possible, although the *Rāmāyaṇa* itself is an earlier composition than the other epic, *Mahābhārata*, the kernal portion of which must have been composed before 500 to 600 B.C. The Greek astronomer Ptolemy, who wrote his geography in the second century A.D., refers to this island as Jabadieu.

So far as the Indian colonization of Java is concerned, it is believed by many historians that a prince from Gujarat, with some 5,000 followers, settled in Central Java in A.D. 525, 599, or 603. (It is also a fact that the Hindus of Java had been conquered by the Muslim invaders before the first arrival of the Portuguese settlers in the beginning of the sixteenth century.) A reinforcement of 2,000 people was sent from Gujarat. 'From this period Java was known and celebrated as a kingdom; an extensive commerce was carried with Gujarat and other countries, and the Bay of Matārem was filled with adventurers from all parts.'

During the sovereignty of this unnamed prince and his two immediate successors, 'the country advanced in fame and prosperity. The city of Mendang Kamulan, since called Prambānan, increased in size and splendour; artists, particularly in stone and metals

[1] Sir Stamford Raffles, *History of Ancient Java.*

[2] Kern, Brandes, *Krom, Hindoe—Javaansche Greschiedenis.* A. S. Wallcott, *Java and Her Neighbours.* Messrs. R. C. Majumdar, B. R. Chatterji. N. P. Chakravarti, P. N. Bose.

arrived from distant countries, and temples, the ruins of which are still extant, were constructed both at this place and at Boro-Budur, in Kedu, during this period by artists invited from India.'[1]

'This is supported by an inscription found at Menankabu, in Sumatra, wherein a king who styles himself Mahārājādhirāja Āditya-dharma, the first king of Java, boasts of his conquests and prowess, and he proclaims himself a Buddhist, a worshipper of the five Dhyāni Buddhas, and records his having erected a great seven-storeyed *vihāra* in honour of Buddha.'[2]

Fah-hien's visit to the island in A.D. 414, on his way from Ceylon to China by sea, for five months, has further supported the Indian colonization of Java. 'In this country,' he says, 'heretics and Brahmans flourish, but the Law of Buddha is not much known.'[3] Commenting on this, Fergusson says, 'that there were Brahmans in these islands before the advent of the Buddhist emigrants in the seventh century seems more than probable from the traditions about the Brahman Tritresta on Tritāstri collected by Sir S. Raffles and others'[4]; but they seem to belong to a non-building class, as no early remains of Brahmanical buildings are available.

Boro Budur

The famous monument is locally known as the Tjandi Boro Budur. The phrase has been variously spelt and interpreted. The most acceptable interpretation would be the 'Shrine of the Many Buddhas.' It is undoubtedly a Buddhist monument and appears to have been built to shelter some portion of Buddha's ashes, which were taken by king Asoka from their original resting places and distributed in 84,000 parts throughout the Buddhist world, 'to be reburied under such sacred mounds and venerated by rapidly increasing bodies of converts in countries far remote.' From a critical examination of its carvings and sculptures it has been established that 'it was erected under the auspices of members of the northern sect or Mahayanists, the more progressive sect, which, in its growth, took over *en masse*

[1] Sir S. Raffles, *History of Java*, Vol. II, pp. 87 *et seq*. Lassen, *Indische Alterthumskunde*, Vol. II, ss. 1059, quoted by Fergusson, *History of Indian and Eastern Architecture*, II, p. 418.

[2] Fergusson, *History of Indian and Eastern Architecture* (1910), Vol. II, p. 419.

[3] Beal's Translation, p. 169, *Buddhist Records*, Vol. I, p. LXXXI.

[4] Fergusson, *loc. cit.*, Vol. II, p. 419. Refers to Lassen, *ref. sup.*, pp. 1063 *et seq.*

BORO-BUDUR

Page 354

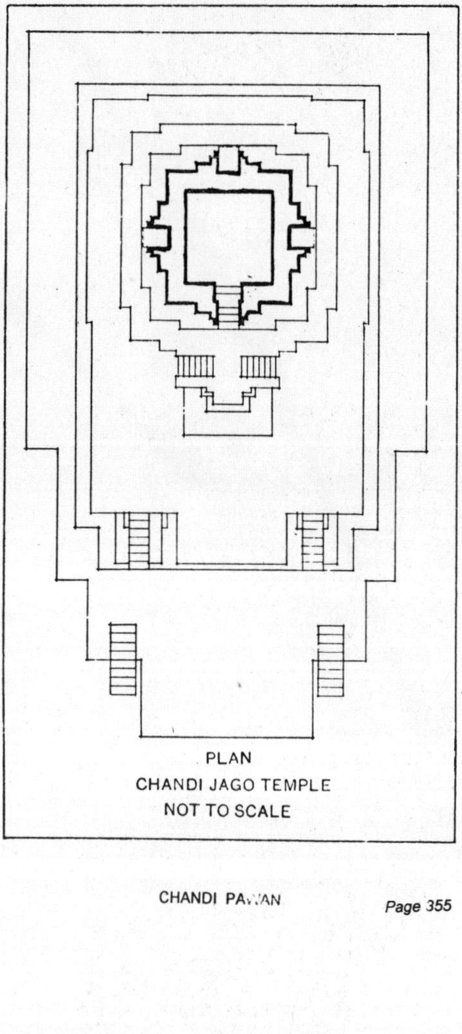

PLAN
CHANDI JAGO TEMPLE
NOT TO SCALE

most of the popular Hindu gods and their followers and eventually spread through Nepal and Tibet to China and Japan.' The shrine of Boro Budur appears to have been erected between the seventh and ninth century A.D., although Rhys Davids holds that it must have been erected in the thirteenth century. An inscription of A.D. 656 discovered in Sumatra mentions that a seven-storey temple was erected to the five Dhyāni Buddhas by the Mahārājadhirāja Aditya-dharma of Prathanna (or Great Java). It is, nevertheless, not quite settled if this temple refers to the shrine of Boro Budur, which, however, was built by a prince of the sect that worshipped the Dhyāni Buddhas and that it is usually spoken of as having seven storeys. This fact has been further corroborated by the inscriptions in old Javanese on the base walls of the shrine itself, which are dated to the ninth century by Professor Kern. Groneman, also, believes the shrine to have been in existence in the ninth century.[1]

'The fundamental formative idea of Boro Budur monument is that of a *dagoba* with five procession paths. These, however, have become square in plan instead of circular ; and, instead of one great domical building in the centre, we have here seventy-two smaller ones, each containing the statue of a Buddha ; and one large one in the centre, which was quite solid externally but had a cell in its centre, which might have contained a relic or some precious object.'

'With the idea of a *dagoba*, however, Boro Budur also combines that of a *vihāra*. There the cells, though only copied solid in the rock, still simulated the residences of the monks, and had not yet advanced to the stage we find in the Gandhara monasteries, where the cells of monks had become niches for statues.' 'The cells of the Māmallapuram are here repeated in every face. So great, indeed, is the similarity between the two, that, whatever date we assign to the one, drags with it that of the other. On the other hand, having so similar a Buddhist development in Java in the seventh century, it seems difficult to separate the monuments of the north-east of India from it by any very long interval of time.'

'The monument may be described either as a seven- or a nine-storeyed *vihāra*, according as we reckon the platform on which the seventy-two small *dagobas* stand as one or three storeys. It is, however, either for its dimensions or the beauty of its architectural design that Boro Budur is so remarkable, as for the sculptures that

[1] Walcott, *Java and Her Neighbours*, pp. 205–206.

line its galleries. These extend to nearly 5,000 feet, almost a mile, and as there are sculptures on both faces, we have nearly 10,000 lineal feet of bas-reliefs; or, if we like to add those which are in two storeys, we have a series of sculptures, which, if arranged consecutively in a row, would extend over nearly three miles of ground.'[1]

'The primary construction of the Boro Budur was effected by truncating a hill more or less pyramidal in form, filling out and slicing off its sides and sheathing them with stone, digging out central chambers below the level top, and covering this last with a domed or spired *dagoba*. The Boro Budur is not, as it appears, a solid mass of masonry, but a mass of earth over which has been built a thin shell of stone.'

The present condition of the site tends 'to decry rather than to enhance the proportions and architectural value of the monument. The hill on the top of which it has been built is low and irregular, overlooking a plain of waving palm trees. There is a dreary view of distant volcanoes and the indented peaks of a line of high mountains, from some hundred feet above the plain, which is the highest point of the shrine.'

'The form of the structure is that of a truncated step pyramid with base dimensions of about 400 feet, resting on a platform practically square and facing the cardinal points. Strictly speaking, the walls have thirty-six sides, not four, for each main wall juts out several times as it approaches the middle point from either end. There is not a single pillar or column in the whole structure, and no doors or windows are to be found—merely tier after tier of galleries joined by stairways to a top platform. The original base is now hidden by some 7,000 cubic yards of reinforcing stone blocks which form the present visible base.'

'Above the present base, the side walls are terraced in such a way as to form galleries about 7 feet wide, though one may walk between an outer wall, 5 feet thick, which is actually the parapet of the inner wall of the gallery next below, and an inner one, whose parapet similarly forms an outer wall for the gallery above. These galleries run continuously around the Tjandi, broken only by a stone stairway at the middle of each side. Their walls are adorned with over a thousand sculptured bas-reliefs depicting scenes from the life of Gautama Buddha in his various incarnations, groups of

[1] Fergusson, *loc. cit.*, Vol. II, pp. 424–425.

Buddhas, angels, and saints. Above these sculptures, on the parapets of the walls, are small recessed shrines, in all over 400, each containing a Buddha image a couple of feet high.'

'Above the four sculptured galleries rise three tiers of circular terraces, bearing, altogether, 72 bell-shaped, latticed *dagobas*, each about 5 feet in height and containing a lotus-enthroned Buddha, which may be seen through the lozenge-shaped openings in the sides. From the centre of the upper of these circular terraces rises what is left of the former apex of the shrine, a ruined *dagoba* about 30 feet high, containing in an interior chamber a large and apparently unfinished image thought to represent the Buddha yet to come. The cone- or parasol-shaped spire, which doubtless once covered this highest *dagoba*, has wholly disappeared.'

'The stairways of Boro Budur formerly had gate-houses at each landing and their arches are ornamented with great heads with bulging eyes. At the sides are the heads of *nāgas* with upper lips prolonged into short trunks.'[1]

The shrine, however, owes its fame more to its artistic detail than its purely architectural features. Its wall sculptures are remarkable. 'The subjects are almost beyond enumeration and include practically every phase of life and action. The scenes portrayed may still be seen in the Java of today. Kings and nobles, dancing girls and palace women, peasants and fishermen, bearded strangers from foreign lands, elephants and monkeys, deer and horses, birds and fish, fruit-trees and shade-trees, native houses, ships, war chariots, ploughs, musical instruments, state umbrellas, and hundreds of other things typical of the country are depicted here in a way that is wonderfully life-like and truthful. The representations of the scenes from the *Jātakas* (tales of Buddha's life in his earlier incarnations) are particularly interesting, for each one has its own story, and some of these are very very entertaining.' For instance, Walcott quotes the following from Dr. J. Groneman :

'The Lord (Buddha or incarnation of Vishṇu), being a turtle in the sea, perceives a ship sinking and surrounded by sharks and other fishes. Taking the crew and the passengers on his back, he carries them to the shore, where he offers them his own body as food.'[2]

[1] Walcott, *Java and Her Neighbours*, p. 212.

[2] *Ibid.*, pp. 211, 208–210.

There are two other smaller shrines in the Boro Budur group. The one known as the Tjandi (Chandi) Pawan (kitchen shrine) is situated in a grove at a short distance from the principal shrine. The structure has been restored, but the images housed therein are now quite gone. The other is situated at a distance of a mile and a half. This is known as the Mendoet Tjandi. ' This temple is pyramidal in form and about 60 feet high, with exterior walls elaborately sculptured. In an interior chamber, some 10 feet square, are three figures, one of which is definitely identified as Buddha, the others being variously denominated as Buddhas, Bodhisattvas, princely benefactors or worshippers, or even as adoring women.' This temple was built at a period slightly later than the Boro Budur.

There is in Java a Hindu group of temples also, comprising Prambavan, the Tjandi Loro Djonggrang. Unlike the Boro Budur and Mendoet shrines, these temples are monuments of the Hindu or Brahman faith. They have been built for the worship of Brahmā, Vishṇu, Śiva, Kālī, Durgā, Pārvatī or Laro Djonggrang (virgin), and Gaṇeśa. ' Unfortunately all but two or three of the original group of over a hundred had already fallen into the last stages of decay and ruin, and today, in spite of the conscientious work of the restorers, it is difficult to frame more than an imaginative conception of the appearance of the original whole.' ' In the plan of construction three circular walls enclosed three circular rows of small shrines, and in the centre stood a group of eight more important shrines arranged in an oblong, three on each side and one at each end to the north and south.' The central western temple is the most important and may serve as an example of the rest. ' It is pyramidal and rests on a base which is practically square. Its outer walls are covered with bas-reliefs and other sculptures of great artistic merit and careful workmanship, representing scenes from the *Rāmāyaṇa* and other tales of Hindu mythology. An entrance on each side is reached by a corresponding stairway, and an external gallery surrounds the structure at some distance from the ground level.'[1]

There are four chambers and a sort of entrance hall, the *mukha-maṇḍapa* of the *Śilpa-śāstra*. In the largest central chamber, which is about 20 feet square, is installed an image of Śiva, four-armed, bearded, and with a snake for a belt. In the western chamber is the image of Gaṇeśa. In the room to the south is again the image of

[1] Walcott, *Java and Her Neighbours*, pp. 216–217.

Siva, the recluse with trident and water bottle. In the north chamber is the image of Kālī, Loro Djonggrang, with eight arms and prominent breasts and hips, a feature so common in Hindu art. The goddess is represented in the life-size, 'standing on her sacred cow and grasping by the hair a small demon or evil spirit. This statue is responsible for the name of this entire group.'[1] In other buildings are Brahmā, Nandi (bull), and a few fragments.

'The exterior of these temples, built, like the Boro Budur, of small blocks of lava stone, are covered with elaborate carvings.' 'Grotesque representations of the monkey-king and his followers recur again and again, as do rather graceful groups of dancing girls (the three graces of the foreigners). The incidental ornamentations, borders, friezes, and the like, are particularly artistic, and might well be adapted to modern use.'

'The precise date of their erection is unknown, but, as in the case of the majority of the ruins of the Prambanan plain, it may roughly be given as the ninth century.' But their Indian origin and Hindu style is obvious.

The Tjandi Sewoe or Chandi Sewu, implying a thousand temples, is situated at a short distance from the Laro Djonggrang. 'Chandi Sewu is neither more nor less than Boro Budur taken to pieces, and spread out, with such modifications as were necessary to adapt it to the position.'[2] This group has suffered more seriously at the hands of vandals and from earthquakes, and no idea of the original can be gathered from the remains without a reference to the reconstructed diagrams. 'In this case there was a central cruciform (*svastika*) shrine of the usual truncated pyramid type, surrounded by four successively larger squares of small shrines, two and forty in all, and each about 11 feet square and 18 high. The entire enclosure, some 500 feet square, was protected by a wall, with a gateway on each side, through which passed a broad, straight avenue leading to the central edifice. These gates were guarded by pairs of grotesque, pot-bellied, kneeling stone figures, perhaps 10 feet high, with fierce moustaches, tusk-like teeth, and pop eyes, and with snakes as head, arm, and body ornaments.'

'The Tjandi Sewoe was built in 1094, according to old court documents still in existence in the Solo archives.'

[1] Walcott, *Java and Her Neighbours*, p. 218.
[2] Fergusson, *loc. cit.*, II, p. 435.

'There are many more ruined temples on this Prambanan plain and on one elevated piece of ground lie the scant remains of a former palace of the Mataram days.'[1]

There is a group of temples on the tableland at the foot of Mount Prahu, known as Dieng Plateau, about 35 miles north of Boro Budur 'They consist only of simple sanctuaries and are not remarkable for the beauty of their details. But they are Indian temples pure and simple and dedicated to Indian gods. What these temples tell us further is, that if Java got her Buddhism from Gujarat and the mouths of the Indus, she got her Hinduism from Telingana and the mouths of the Krishnā. These Dieng temples do not show a trace of the curve-lined *śikharas* of Orissa (*Vesara*) or of Indo-Aryan (*Nāgara*) style.' 'Nor are these temples Dravidian in any proper sense of the term. They are in storeys, but not with cells, nor any reminiscences of such; but they are Chalukyan, in a clear and direct meaning of the term.'[2]

There are numerous epigraphic references to a number of Hindu buildings erected in Java. The Janggal inscription of Central Java, in Grantha (Pallava) script and Sanskrit language, of the Saka year 654 (A.D. 732), 'refers to the reconstruction of a Śaiva temple on the model of a celebrated shrine in the holy land of Kunjara Kunja, to be identified with the Āśrama of Agastya of that name in south India.' Another inscription found at Dinaya in Eastern Java, dated Śaka 682 (A.D. 760), 'describes the construction of a black stone image of Agastya Ṛishi.' In another inscription of Śaka 785 (A.D. 863), in Sanskrit and Kavi (mixture of Sanskrit and Polynesian dialect), mention is made of a temple of Bhadraloka having been built by Agastya himself. In another inscription, found at the temple of Kalasan in Central Java, of Saka 700 (A.D. 778), this temple of Tārā is stated to have been built at the command of the Śailendra, king of Śrīvijaya, in his own kingdom. 'The great building activity continued in Central Java under the Mataram princes; for to this period of Hindu revival belongs the famous Prambanam group of temples with its magnificent reliefs depicting scenes of the *Rāmāyaṇa*.'[3]

Dr. Krom refers to several inscriptions relating to engineering operations for the drainage of a river. In a Kavi (old Javanese)

[1] Walcott, *Java and Her Neighbours*, p. 220.
[2] Fergusson, *loc. cit.*, Vol. II, p. 430.
[3] B. R. Chatterjee, *India and Java*, Part I, pp. 3, 4, 5.

inscription, of 932 Śaka, from Soerabaya, mention is made of a water-course. In another inscription of the same place, of 856 Śaka, the construction of dikes for regulating the course of the river is described.[1] The Tugu rock-inscription refers to 'a canal known as Chandrabhāgā, dug by the father of Pūrṇavarman, and then again to another canal Gomatī, dug by Pūrṇavarman himself.'[2]

The Dinaya inscription of 682 Śaka refers to king Devasiṁha who, having seen an image made of wood by his ancestors, ordered the sculptor and 'had a wonderful image of black marble prepared.'[3]

The inscription of Vieng Sa refers to 'excellent houses for the wielder of thunderbolt, the conqueror of Māra, and the producer of Jaya,' and also to the *chaitya* houses and *stūpas*.[4]

The only reference to town-planning has been supplied by the *Nagara Kṛitāgama* (science dealing with the city-plan). Therein is given a detailed account of the capital, Majapahita (Bilvatikta), 'with its deep tanks, avenues of *kesara* and *champaka* trees, public squares, market places, palaces, the royal pavilion (*bitāna*) where the prime minister, the *Āryas* (nobles), and the trusted five (the cabinet) approached the king. In the eastern part of the capital dwelt the Śaiva Brahmanas, in the southern part the Buddhists, and in the western part were the houses of the Kshatriyas, ministers and others.'[5]

Although no further details are available, it will be seen that similar distribution has been prescribed by the *Mānasāra* and other architectural texts. In view of the fact that temples, deities, reliefs, etc., were predominantly of Hindu style, it may safely be held that the town-planning and village schemes were also of Hindu origin.

[1] *India and Java*, II, pp. 22, 23. [2] *Ibid.*, pp. 26, 27. [3] *Ibid.*, pp. 37, 39.
[4] *Ibid.*, pp. 41, 42, 43, 44. [5] *Ibid.*, p. 11.

CHAPTER XI

HINDU ARCHITECTURE IN OUTER INDIA

CHINA

THE FOLLOWERS OF Buddhism in the whole world may be roughly estimated at 200 millions[1] or about one-eighth of the human race. Of these, as many as 150 millions may be allotted to China, and 50 millions to Tibet, Manchuria, Burma, Siam, Cambodia, and Ceylon. The rest of the 400 millions of Chinese population in China profess the doctrines of Confucius, the contemporary and rival of Gautama Buddha, and belong to the new sect known as Lao-tse or the Doctors of Reason, who are more progressive than others. To this want of dominent priesthood in China is ascribed the absence of monumental buildings, 'because in all countries where architecture has been carried to anything like perfection, it is to sacred art that it has owed its highest inspiration.' Again, 'religious and sectarian zeal is often a strong stimulus to sacred architecture, and this is entirely wanting in this remarkable people.' The want of a hereditary nobility and any strong family pride will similarly account for the absence of the domestic architecture of a durable description. 'At a man's death his property is generally divided equally among his children, consequently the wealthiest men do not build residences calculated to last longer than their own lives. The royal palaces are merely somewhat larger and more splendid than those of the mandarins, but the same in character, and erected with the same ends.' Thus the oldest civilized people of the world are 'almost wholly without monuments to record the past.' The Chinese are, however, the only people in the world 'who now employ polychromy as an essential part of their architecture : indeed, with them, colour is far more essential than form,' but 'colour, though most valuable as an accessory, is incapable of that lofty power of expression which form conveys to human mind.'[2]

This essential feature of Chinese art has defaced all individuality to the temples of the Buddhist, Taoist, and Confucianist. Thus, 'externally the temples are nearly all of the same type, and it is only

[1] The census of 1931 disclosed 12,786,806 Buddhists in India.

[2] Fergusson, *History of Indian and Eastern Architecture*, Vol. II, pp. 449-450.

from their interior decoration and by the statues placed in them that any distinction can be made.' Even the Muhammadan mosques are 'all in general form identical with the Buddhist and other temples, and can only be distinguished by their external decoration with texts from the *Quran*, and are not even to be recognized by the minaret, which in other countries has been their chief characteristic feature.' There is also no essential distinction between sacred and seculiar work. Thus 'the temple, the tomb, and the dwelling are symbolically repetitions of each other.'

The usual type of Chinese architecture is known as the Ting. It 'consists of a roof of concave section carried on short columns. If the roof is of great dimensions and elaborately decorated, it covers either a temple, an imperial hall of audience, or the official residence of a mandarin, if of small size and light construction, it is that of a house. In order to give more importance to the imperial structures, whether temples or reception halls, they are raised on platforms with triple terraces and balustrades round, and three flights of steps on the south front. The flight in the middle is subdivided into three, the central portion forming an inclined slope which is covered with dragons and clouds in relief, in some cases the treads of the steps on each side are also carved with dragons in relief, the terraces, balustrades and steps being all in white marble.'

The building materials are of various kinds. The city walls are built in brick, and the bridges in stone, with marble casing and balustrades. The raised platforms for altars, as well as some temples, and generally the imperial halls, are also built in marble. All other Chinese constructions are in timber. The roofs are covered with glazed tiles, yellow in imperial structures, and green, blue, or purple for others. The ridge and hip rolls, with the dragons and fishes which surmount their roofs, are all in glazed terra-cotta.'[1]

The Temple of Heaven, or the Great Dragon, a most magnificent temple built about the year A.D. 1420, is situated close to the southern wall of the capital city of Pekin, in a square enclosure measuring about a mile each way. From the outer gate a raised causeway leads to the temple, on either side of which, for the accommodation of the priests, are numerous buildings approached by frequent flights of steps leading down to a park beautifully planted. In the centre

[1] Fergusson, *History of Indian and Eastern Architecture*, Vol. II, p. 456.

part of the enclosure are two altars, distinguished as the north and south. The south altar consists of a circular platform of three concentric terraces, the upper one 90 feet in diameter, the middle terrace 150 feet, and the lower one 210 feet, all enclosed with balustrades and raised about 6 feet, one above the other. These terraces are ascended by four flights of steps on the north, east, south, and west sides respectively. In the centre of the platform are the five sacred vessels found in all Buddhist temples, over which a canopy is erected on the occasion of a celebration. There are eight flights of steps to the north altar, three of which are placed side by side on the north end, the central portion of the middle flight forming a gradual slope and covered with dragons and clouds in relief. In the centre of the upper terrace is the circular structure known as the Heaven's Palace. It has the appearance of a three-storeyed structure, but in reality consists of a central hall 90 feet in height with double aisles round. The roof, with its widely projecting eaves, and the drum below, are carried by four immense columns, 4 feet in diameter ; the second roof and drum are carried by twelve columns, as also the lower storey. The construction is of a very extraordinary kind. At the level of the upper part of the second roof, carved beams are tenoned into the four columns, over which, between each, are provided two other columns, forming a sort of attic storey, to support the roof and the internal dome.[1]

Although all temples in China, whether Confucian, Taoist, or Buddhist, are based on the same Ting type, 'generally speaking, the temple of a Buddhist monastery is enclosed by a wall, with a monumental gateway at the entrance and a series of three detached buildings beyond, placed one behind the other, on a central axis, with courts between, and communicating one with the other by means of covered corridors. The first building is the ex-voto hall, with statues; the second is the principal temple in which are the three images of the Buddhist triad, and the altar with the sacred vessels in front. The building in the rear contains sometimes a miniature *dagoba* in marble, in which are enclosed supposed relics of Buddha. To the right and left of the enclosure, and placed symmetrically, are other isolated structures, such as the bell-tower, the library, the pagoda, and the monks' dwellings.'[2]

[1] Fergusson, *History of Indian and Eastern Architecture*, Vol. II, pp. 459–460.
[2] *Ibid.*, p. 461.

The Buddhist temple of Honan is 'a parallelogram enclosed by a high wall, measuring 306 feet by 174 feet. In the shorter front, facing the river, is a gateway. This leads to a series of halls opening into each other, and occupying the whole of the longer axis of the internal court. The first and second of these are porches or ante-chapels. The central one is the largest, and practically the choir of the building. It contains the altar, adorned by gilt images of the three precious Buddhas, with stalls for the monks and all arrangements necessary for the daily service. Behind this, in the next compartment, is a *dagoba*, and in its rear another apartment devoted to the goddess Kuan-Yin, principally worshipped by women, in fact, the Lady Chapel of the church. Around the court are arranged the cells of the monks, their kitchen, refectory, and all the necessary offices of the monastery. These are generally placed against the outer wall, and open into the court. At Pekin there are several lamasaries or Buddhist monasteries of much more monumental character than that of Honan.'

'The usual form of temple,' says Fergusson, 'as seen in towns and villages, is very simple, rectangular on plan, with five bays in the front, which always faces the south, and three at the side, with a verandah and flight of steps in the centre of the south front leading to the central doorway.'[1]

Another type of later temples, dating from the fifteenth century, 'consists of a lofty square pedestal, which recalls the lower portion of the celebrated temple at Bodh-Gaya. The pedestal is subdivided into five storeys by string courses, each storey enriched with arcaded niches containing statues of Buddha, the whole crowned with five square *dagobas*, the centre one with thirteen projecting eaves.'[2]

The Chinese tombs are different from the Buddhist *stūpas* in their origin and in form. That is mostly due to the fact that while the *stūpas* contained the sacred relic of Buddha, the Chinese tombs are monuments built in memory of the ordinary dead, because the Chinese are well known, like all Turanian peoples, as the worshippers of ancestors. These tombs are 'often merely conical mounds of earth, with a circle of stones round their base.'

The Chinese pagodas 'owe their origin to the religion of Fo or Buddha, being nothing more than exaggerated *dagobas*.'[3] These pagodas are generally nine-storeyed in the south, but in the north

[1] Fergusson, *History of Indian and Eastern Architecture*, Vol. II, pp. 463–464.
[2] *Ibid.*, II, p. 464. [3] *Ibid.*, II, p. 468.

the storeys range from three to thirteen. The porcelain tower at Nankin and the pagoda in the Summer Palace, Pekin, are the best examples.[1] The former is known as the Temple of Gratitude, as it was erected (1412–1431) as a monument of gratitude to an empress of the Ming family.

It was octagonal in form, 236 feet in height. Its extraordinary feature lies in the fact that its brick walls, as well as the upper and under sides of the projecting roofs, were coated with porcelain. 'From the summit of the spire eight chains were suspended, to each of which were attached nine bells, and a bell was also attached to each angle of the lower roof, making 144 bells in all.' These when tinkling in harmony to the evening breeze 'must have produced an effect as singular as pleasing.'

The pagoda in the Summer Palace is 'divided into three storeys, with additional projecting eaves under the balconies. Four of the sides of the octagon are longer than the other four.' 'Altogether there is a play of light and shade,' declares Fergusson, 'and a variety about the ornaments in this tower, which is extremely pleasing. It is much more like an Indian design than any other in China, and with the circle of pillars round its base, and the *stambha*, which usually accompany these objects further west, it recalled the original forms as completely as any other object in this country.'[2]

The entrance gateways to temples and tombs, known as *pailus* or *paibangs*, are a class of monument almost universally employed as honorific monuments of deceased persons. 'The posts or piers always carry a rail or frieze bearing an inscription, which is in fact the object for which the monument was erected. The most singular features about them are the tile roofs at various levels, with which they are surmounted.'[3]

'Their origin is as distinctly Indian as the other,' declares Fergusson. Another curious thing noted by him is 'that at Sānchi, before the Christian era, we find them used as gateways to a simulated tomb. In India both the tumulus and the *pailu* had at that time passed away from their original sepulchral meaning, the one had become a relic shrine, the other an iconostasis. Two thousand years

[1] Photo. 499, 500, Fergusson, *History of Indian and Eastern Architecture*, Vol. II, pp. 470, 471.

[2] Fergusson, *ibid.*, II, pp. 471–472.

[3] For example, *see* the sketches made by Fergusson (*ibid.*, Vol. II, pp. 473, 475) of the Gateway near Canton and at Amoy.

afterwards in China we find them both still used for the purposes for which they were originally designed.'[1]

As has already been stated, 'there is virtually no difference in the architectural design of the temples and palaces.' In both cases the halls and palaces consist of a number of pavilions rather than of numerous suites of apartments and halls. 'The resemblance of temple and palace is further accentuated by the fact that in front of the great hall of the palace in the Forbidden City are similar platforms, with the triple terrace, balustrade, and flights of steps, which have been described in the Temple of Heaven and the Tomb of Yunglo.' In this Forbidden City the buildings are all of one storey, surmounted with the same type of roof as that employed in temples, and facing the south. But according to their importance, their height differs. 'The three principal halls are the Hall of Highest Peace (built in 1602–1722) where levees are held on special occasions, the Hall of Central Peace, and the Hall of Secure Peace. The first is the most important and it is preceded by a gateway and has nine bays instead of eleven on the main front. It is raised on a platform with a triple terrace, balustrade, and flights of steps.'[2]

'The principal difference between the palaces and Chinese dwellings of the better class lies in a much lighter system of construction. There is the same general disposition of the plan, viz., a series of detached blocks, separated by open courts or gardens, and placed in communication with one another by covered corridors.' The official rules are stated to prescribe the dimensions in width and height for all Chinese habitations, and the number of columns which may be used. 'The principal hall, for instance, is not allowed to be wider than three bays, if for a man of letters only, five, if for a mandarin, seven for a prince, and only the palace of the emperor may have nine or more bays.'

These rules were distinctly taken from the architectural texts of India. In the *Mānasāra Śilpa-śāstra* the rules regarding the length, breadth, height, and number of storeys of buildings for people of different ranks are discussed in great detail in a whole chapter (XI) on Dimensions. In the concluding portion of the chapter it is stated that 'there should be one to two storeys in the palaces of the kings of the

[1] Fergusson, *History of Indian and Eastern Architecture*, II, pp. 475–476.

[2] For plan and section, *see* Fergusson, *ibid.*, pp. 477, 478, and Winter Palace, Pekin, p. 482.

ninth order, one to three of the eighth order, one to four to the kings of the seventh order, three to eight storeys in palaces of the kings of the third order, three to nine storeys for those of the second order, and five to twelve storeys for the kings of the first order. One to three storeys are given to the crown prince and nobles. The buildings of the architects of first rank, engineers, military officers, chiefs, and twice-born in general, may possess one, two, or three storeys. The temples of gods may have one to twelve storeys. The stables, etc., are built in a single storey.'

The Chinese municipalities must have access to these guide books. We in India, however, have forgotten all these rules and have adopted instead those prevalent in the countries of our conquerors.

JAPAN

Although the accession of the first Mikado is dated 660 B.C., ' it was not till the second half of the sixth century A.D. that Japan reached the first step of civilization, along with the introduction of Buddhism, from Korea, in A.D. 552.' The revelations of Buddhism ' stirred the Japanese people to a loftier conception than those which the older Shinto religion had inspired,' and ' its earliest architectural structures date from the commencement of the seventh century.'[1]

Thus ' the architecture of Japan owes its origin to Chinese sources, the earliest examples remaining being those which were built by carpenters sent over from Korea. The Japanese temples, whether Buddhist or Shinto, are all of the Chinese Ting type. In Japan, as in China, the later developments have as a rule resulted only in further enrichments, the elaborate carving in the Japanese Buddhist temples being carried to excess. In the Shinto temple, on the other hand, the greatest simplicity prevails, more importance being attached to the quality of the wood employed, and to its structural execution, than to any display of diagram work or carving. The pagoda in Japan still retains the ancient design and timber construction of the earliest example remaining, at Hariuji, which was built by Korean carpenters in A.D. 607, and may be looked upon as the original type of, at all events, the Korean pagoda.'[2] This pagoda and temple, near Nara in Japan, are square on plan and built in timber. But the earliest remains of the pagoda in China are almost universally octagonal on plan, and were built in stone or brick. This difference is accounted for by the fact that all the early architecture of China was annihilated, and that the Japanese examples, ' in their design and execution, present a completeness of style which must have taken several centuries to develop ' through Korea. But the Chinese style of the Hariuji examples are not doubted by experts. There is, in fact, ' one example with square plan at Korea, but this, following the Chinese examples, was built in brick.' In the first century of the Christian era, however, the wooden construction developed in Korea owing to the presence of great forests therein, the perfected type of which is seen in the pagoda at Hariuji.'[3]

[1] Fergusson, *History of Indian and Eastern Architecture*, Vol. II, p. 487.
[2] *Ibid.*, Vol. II, pp. 486–487. [3] Plate LXII, Fergusson, *ibid.*, p. 496.

In Japan, also, no distinction was made ' between the temples and mortuary chapels, and the mausoleum of Ieyasu, at Nikku, built on rising ground, has the triple enclosure with three entrance gateways, and besides the main temple or mortuary chapel, has all the independent accessories, such as the torii, pagoda, sacred stable, store-houses, library, drum-tower, belfry, priest's residence, etc., which form the complement of an important Buddhist temple, and in addition a winding pathway up numerous flights of steps leading to the upper mortuary chapel and monumental tomb.'[1]

Thus the Buddhist monuments of India supplied the inspiration, but in Japan, as in China, although the composition was of the Indian type, the style was entirely different. So far as the civil architecture is concerned, the Japanese palaces were originally simple and unostentatious buildings. Since the sixteenth century, when the country came under military domination, palaces have been built within fortified enclosures surrounded by moats. ' The walls, 20 to 25 feet high, are built with a concave batter, the masonry of the quoins dipping down in order apparently to run less risk of being overthrown by earthquakes (as, in the event of an upheaval, the stones would fall back by their own weight into their original position).'[2] Like temples, palaces are all of one storey only. The floor is raised from 4 to 8 feet above the ground. In their design they belong to the Ting type of China, with Irimoya gables like those in the temples. ' In plan they consist of a number of blocks put in communication, one with the other, by covered corridors, not arranged symmetrically like those in the Forbidden City of Pekin, but disposed so as to overlook gardens and small lakes. The principal difference externally, when compared with the temples, lies in the less height and much flatter pitch given to the roof, so much so that they are not concave in section, the roofs having generally one uniform slope. Although externally the blocks have the appearance of constituting a single hall, they are usually subdivided by sliding screens into several rooms. Thus the residential block of the Imperial Palace at Kioto, measuring about 100 feet by 60 feet, is divided by partitions into fourteen rooms, the centre one of which, lighted only through the outer rooms, constituted the Mikado's sleeping apartment. The three rooms on one

[1] Fergusson, *History of Indian and Eastern Architecture*, Vol. II, p. 497.

[2] *Ibid.*, p. 499, *see* Plate LXV (Castle of Yedo, Tokio).

PLATE LIX (a)

TEMPLE HALL WITH SVASTIKA SCREEN WORK

A JAPANESE PAGODA

Peninsula is in the Mexican territory of Quintana ninhabited peninsula lying between the Chetumal ribbean Sea. It is equally desolate between the Bay Bacalar Lagoon. Before the Spanish conquest of the home of the Maya clans. The ancient Maya k of Chilan Balam of Chumayel records the migra- clans and describes also the migration of the Itzas za to Coba, which is about 50 miles to the east of he British Museum Guide to the Maudsley Collec- Sculptors has further reference to the period of the

ast coast of Yucatan live the Santa Cruz Indians, endants of the ancient Mayas. They have never been 'for five centuries they have successfully resisted all of the Spaniards and later of the Mexicans, to conquer These Indians, so far as is known, live the lives of thousand years ago. They worship the same gods he ancient religious ceremonies.'

was the first to discover the ruins of the great city of n information found in a recent translation of the Maya ook. He has also discovered a monolith and a once in the forests of Yucatan. 'It is a block of greyish et long, 18 inches wide, and 12 inches thick. It had stood upright, but now lay flat and embedded in the on one edge faint traces of sculpture were visible, ter part of the exposed surfaces had been worn quite he tropical downpours of an unknown number of rainy s has been the fate of many Maya inscriptions.'

nolith had been erected just in front of a great terraced ich stood between two others. All these pyramids were e usual Maya style, with blocks of cut limestone. The had three terraces and was 32 feet high. Its flat top, n there no doubt stood a wooden temple, long since as one 135 feet long and 64 feet across. Further inves- owed that these pyramids were at one end of a great which was surrounded by a massive stone wall. This wall to 15 feet thick at the base, and in the places where it has

side of this block form a s
one above the other, the fu
raised dâis indicating the
to all the rooms in a subd
verandah which constitutes
houses.' The palaces of the s
on the same lines as those c
round them are, however, in
at Kunamoto, now destroyed
towards the end of the sixtee
castles of the middle ages with
within the inner enclosure.'[1]

The simplest architectural e
non-existent in the ordinary
is the only feature which dist
otherwise the street in the grea
with monotonous houses. The h
and 'the design consists of a sq
with a tiled roof, the interior bein
screens about 6 feet high. In the
be internal courts with buildings c
a plan commonly followed in India
very early period and minutely elab
Śilpa-śāstras.

'The chief feature of the Japanes
faces the gardens and serves as a
floor of the house is raised about 10
being no basement of any kind, an
depends on the number of mats whic
measure 6 feet by 3 feet each. In a
reception room may have fifteen or si
four to eight or ten, by pushing aside
can be thrown into one room, and,
south is thrown open during the day
decoration of the interior is confined to
above the screens.'[2]

[1] Fergusson, *History of Indian and Eastern Archit*
[2] *Ibid.*, II, p. 501.

The Yucatan
Roo. It is an u
Bay and the Ca
and the Great
Yucatan it was
manuscript boo
tions of Maya
from Chichenit
Chichenitza. T
tion of Maya
Mayas.

Along the e
the direct desc
subdued, and
the efforts, firs
their country.
ancestors of a
and perform t

Dr. Gann
Coba, throug
manuscript b
populous site
schist, 12 fe
at one time
ground. Up
but the grea
smooth by
seasons. Th

'The mo
pyramid wh
faced, in th
central one
upon whic
perished, w
tigation sh
enclosure,
is from 12

Central America

The Yucatan Peninsula is in the Mexican territory of Quintana Roo. It is an uninhabited peninsula lying between the Chetumal Bay and the Caribbean Sea. It is equally desolate between the Bay and the Great Bacalar Lagoon. Before the Spanish conquest of Yucatan it was the home of the Maya clans. The ancient Maya manuscript book of Chilan Balam of Chumayel records the migrations of Maya clans and describes also the migration of the Itzas from Chichenitza to Coba, which is about 50 miles to the east of Chichenitza. The British Museum Guide to the Maudsley Collection of Maya Sculptors has further reference to the period of the Mayas.

Along the east coast of Yucatan live the Santa Cruz Indians, the direct descendants of the ancient Mayas. They have never been subdued, and 'for five centuries they have successfully resisted all the efforts, first of the Spaniards and later of the Mexicans, to conquer their country. These Indians, so far as is known, live the lives of ancestors of a thousand years ago. They worship the same gods and perform the ancient religious ceremonies.'

Dr. Gann was the first to discover the ruins of the great city of Coba, through information found in a recent translation of the Maya manuscript book. He has also discovered a monolith and a once populous site in the forests of Yucatan. 'It is a block of greyish schist, 12 feet long, 18 inches wide, and 12 inches thick. It had at one time stood upright, but now lay flat and embedded in the ground. Upon one edge faint traces of sculpture were visible, but the greater part of the exposed surfaces had been worn quite smooth by the tropical downpours of an unknown number of rainy seasons. This has been the fate of many Maya inscriptions.'

'The monolith had been erected just in front of a great terraced pyramid which stood between two others. All these pyramids were faced, in the usual Maya style, with blocks of cut limestone. The central one had three terraces and was 32 feet high. Its flat top, upon which there no doubt stood a wooden temple, long since perished, was one 135 feet long and 64 feet across. Further investigation showed that these pyramids were at one end of a great enclosure, which was surrounded by a massive stone wall. This wall is from 12 to 15 feet thick at the base, and in the places where it has

side of this block form a suite in which the floors are raised slightly one above the other, the further and highest room furnished with a raised dâis indicating the position of the imperial throne. Access to all the rooms in a subdivided block is obtained by the external verandah which constitutes the principal feature in all Japanese houses.' The palaces of the *shoguns*, or military regents, 'follow much on the same lines as those of the Mikado. The fortified enclosures round them are, however, increased in number, those of the castle at Kunamoto, now destroyed, which was built by Kato Kyomasa towards the end of the sixteenth century, resembling somewhat the castles of the middle ages with two or three outer courts and a keep within the inner enclosure.'[1]

The simplest architectural expression of the Japanese palaces is non-existent in the ordinary dwelling-house. The entrance door is the only feature which distinguishes one house from another, otherwise the street in the great cities presents a dull appearance with monotonous houses. The houses have rarely an upper storey and 'the design consists of a square or rectangular block covered with a tiled roof, the interior being subdivided into rooms by sliding screens about 6 feet high. In the better houses there may sometimes be internal courts with buildings on all sides or all round.' This is a plan commonly followed in India, and has been in vogue since the very early period and minutely elaborated in the *Mānasāra* and other *Śilpa-śāstras*.

'The chief feature of the Japanese house is the verandah, which faces the gardens and serves as a passage to all the rooms. The floor of the house is raised about 10 inches above the ground, there being no basement of any kind, and the importance of the room depends on the number of mats which cover the floor. Those mats measure 6 feet by 3 feet each. In a middle-class dwelling the chief reception room may have fifteen or sixteen mats, the smaller rooms four to eight or ten, by pushing aside the screens the whole house can be thrown into one room, and, as a rule, the side facing the south is thrown open during the day to ventilate the house. The decoration of the interior is confined to the upper part of the walls above the screens.'[2]

[1] Fergusson, *History of Indian and Eastern Architecture*, II, pp. 499–501.
[2] *Ibid.*, II, p. 501.

MAYA TEMPLE OF PATRON DEITY KULKULCAN UPON HIGH-TERRACED PLATFORM OF THE HINDU SIKHARA TYPE COVERING AN AREA OF ONE ACRE, CHICHEN ITZA, CENTRAL AMERICA

THE USUAL HINDU TYPE OF MASSIVE STONE COLUMNS AT THE DOORWAY OF THE KUKULCAN MAYA TEMPLE

remained intact, it is 12 feet high ; but for the most part the growth of the luxurious vegetation has thrown the stones down and the ruins are only 3 or 4 feet above ground. The wall is a mile and a half long and forms a semicircle with the two ends running down to the shore.'

This is obviously a defensive wall. It is significant that the only two walls of this kind which have hitherto been discovered are also in Yucatan, one being at Tuluum, on the east coast, and the other at Chicken Itza, in the northern interior.

'The space enclosed by this wall had evidently been densely populated in bygone times. For in the places where the Indians have cleared the undergrowth away, one could see that the ground was literally covered with potsherds, flint and obsodian chips, clay beads, spindle whorls, small human and animal heads, and other surviving evidences of human habitation. A great concourse of people must have lived there for many generations.'

The vast cave of Loltum is entered by 'great well-like holes in the north, through which one descends by ladders from ledge to ledge, arriving in immense rocky chambers whose floors are covered with stalagmites and cave earth, and from whose lofty roofs depend vast stalactites. Two of these holes are a mile apart. From the great chambers unexplored passages branch out in every direction.'

It is believed that 'subterranean passages from this cavern reach to the ruined city of Chicken Itza, 20 miles away. There is a tradition that during one of the innumerable internecine wars amongst the Mayas, which followed the breaking up of the central authority after the conquest of Mayapan, the inhabitants of a neighbouring village were driven to take refuge in this cave by a band of their enemies.'

The Mayas also 'erected magnificent temples and palaces, most of which now lie buried in the tropical forests. Some have been discovered, but there is no doubt that a great number of them yet remain to be discovered.'

These discoveries of Dr. Gann and Professor Morley of the Carnegie Institute are of great historical interest. The dates on the monoliths have been deciphered. Dr. Gann himself places the beginning of the Maya chronology in 3381 B.C. But it is considered to be mythological. According to Spinder's correlation the date on Dr. Gann's monolith corresponds to October 26, A.D. 333. Maya

Asura of the *Mahābhārata*, who built a wonderful hall for the king Yudhishṭhira, has been elaborately referred to above.[1] There are a number of manuscripts of the *Silpa-śāstra* ascribed to Maya.[2] As an architect, Maya is mentioned in the *Purāṇas* and other Sanskrit works also.[3]

The scanty remains of the Mayas of Central America, however, do not supply details for a satisfactory comparison with the temples, palaces, dwellings, etc., elaborately described in the *Mānasāra* and other *Silpa-śāstras*. But the walls referred to by Dr. Gann look like the city walls described in the *Mānasāra.* If the city within these walls could be identified together with its buildings, roads, plan, etc., it is not unlikely that we might have found there one of the numerous town-plannings minutely described in the *Silpa-śāstras*. It is, however, fortunate that Professor Grafton Elliot Smith, of University College, London, has been able to establish the Indian connexion with the Central American Maya ruins through the Indian Archipelago or Insulindia, of whose monuments a full account has been given in the preceding chapter.

Professor Elliot Smith disagrees with Dr. Gann and emphatically declares that the causeway that has been found was not built for the purposes of human sacrifices. There are similar causeways in Cambodia, ' which were designed purely for ceremonial purposes.' They may represent the circumambulatory path (*pradakshiṇa*) which is a common feature of Hindu architecture frequently referred to in the *Mānasāra* and other *Silpa-śāstras.*

' The whole Maya remains as discovered show,' declares Professor Elliot Smith, ' the closest possible relation with the civilization as it existed in Java and South-East Asia to what has been found in Yucatan. There is nothing in my mind that suggests that the form of civilization is indigenous, and I should be inclined to hold that the temples at Java were the prototypes of what has been found in Yucatan.'

' Unquestionably in the early days perishable wood structures were built,' continues the Professor, ' but when stone supplanted wood, you find pyramids being built precisely on the same lines that

[1] *See* above, pp. 247, 400 and note.

[2] *See* pp. 159–161, 205, 253, and the writer's *Encyclopaedia of Hindu Architecture*, Appendix I, *sub voce*.

[3] E.g. *Matsya-Purāṇa, see* above, pp. 245, 246, 247; 79, 97, 168, 169, 170, 171.

THE SARNATH TYPE OF MAYA GATE UNDERNEATH THE HALL OF THOUSAND PILLARS AT CHICHEN ITZA

TYPE OF PILLAR (UNDER CONSTRUCTION) SVASTIKA MANSION (FAST VERANDAH)

they were built in South-East Asia. . . . It is necessary to remember that, as Indian civilization spread eastwards, the type of pyramid, established by them become fashionable and was built in stone 'Further there was no question but that Maya carvings represented Indian elephants and Indians with typical head-dresses.'

Professor Elliot Smith explains how the Indian civilization penetrated into Central America: 'Indian navigator, it was known, had combed out the islands in the Pacific, such as Easter Island and many others, and it was unthinkable that they should not have discovered a continent that stretched from pole to pole.'

Thus under Asiatic, or rather Indian, influence the Central American civilization 'rose to great heights, but had already collapsed before the advent of the Spaniards, who may have given it the *coup de grace.*' 'The Maya civilization rose and fell. It fell so soon as the energy of the driving force that inspired it declined. That is,' declares the Professor, 'our view, and we do not believe in an indigenous culture that rose through its own impetus, and that fell as a result of foreign invasion.' 'At University College,' concludes Professor Elliot Smith, 'we are absolutely convinced that the Maya civilization (of Central America) was directly derived from India.'[1]

[1] 'Central News,' quoted from the *Morning Post,* by the *Statesman,* March 21, April 9, 17, 25, 1926, *vide* for fuller details and references, the writer's *Encyclopaedia of Hindu Architecture,* Appendix I, under Maya.

APPENDIX I

INDO-PERSIAN ARCHITECTURE[1]

'FREQUENT ALLUSIONS TO the inhabitants of the western zone of the Iran Plateau are found in Assyrian documents from about the eighth century B.C. They belonged to the Aryan family and were closely related to the Indo-Aryan. The kinship existing between the two branches was unsuspected by antiquity, and is clear beyond doubt to modern science, which bases its conclusions on the striking resemblance observable in the languages, the religious ideas, and even the original rites and physical characteristics of the Indo-Aryans and Persians.'

These linguistic, religious, and physical resemblances seem to have induced several scholars and historians, including archaeologists, to seek further resemblance between the Persian and the Indian architecture. The procedure of investigation appears to have been based on a larger assumption that in all matters of refinement and culture the West must have been the creditors and the East the borrowers. The possibility of indigenous growth was never taken into consideration except in case of the *Veda*.

The admission made in this connexion by Kennedy is free and frank. 'The pre-historic age in India is distinguished, not by periods of stone and copper and bronze, but by the spread of the Aryans, the consolidation of societies, and the elaboration of a cult. With the sixth and fifth centuries B.C. we reach the commencement of personal and dated history, and a great creative era—the age of Mahāvīra and of Buddha. But the material preceded the spiritual. The first stir of that new life arose from the contact with Western civilization, the breath of inspiration came from Babylon, and then from Persia. When the Greeks arrived, they found great and civilized peoples whose learning and whose capitals aroused their admiration. The records of that civilization were written on palm-leaves and on

[1] Originally published in (i) *The Calcutta Review*, February, 1930; (ii) *Oriental Studies*, Commemoration Volume of C. E. Pavry, 1933, pp. 3–14.

bark, or exhibited in brick and wood—things perishable, which have perished, and we are perforce reduced to search painfully among the flotsam and jetsam of time for any vestiges of the grandeur of antiquity.'

Then follows an interesting note: 'The progress of the Indians was necessarily of the slowest, for Persia could supply them with scarcely any models, and they had to discover everything themselves.'[1]

'Of the decoration of the earlier Buddhist monasteries we know practically nothing, but the decoration of the later *vihāra* caves of Nalanda, and of the *saṅghārāmas* of Gandhara, was Persian, and that not so much after the fashion of the Sassanians as of the Achaemenids. There is the same lavish employment of colour, the use of enamelled or metallic tiles upon the roof, the gilded rafters and elaborately painted ceilings, the rich capitals of the pillars, the application of inlaying. The two schemes of decoration are substantially the same.'[2]

'To the general question, then, concerning the direct influence of Babylon on Indian art, we must answer no.' But Kennedy thinks that 'a direct influence may be traced in one particular class of buildings and one particular locality—the Buddhist *vihāra* caves of Western India. . . . The four or five-storeyed *vihāras* . . . undoubtedly recall the impression of a Babylonian *zigurat* or temple, but are hollow throughout and built of wood.' In a note Kennedy adds, 'Fergusson has attempted[3] to connect certain Burmese and Sinhalese *dagobas* with the Babylonian type, and has suggested that connecting links once existed in brick and plaster in the valley of the Ganges. But there are two objections: (1) Had massive buildings of solid brick, either temples or *vihāras*, ever existed in the valley of the Ganges, they could not fail to have left their traces, as the *stūpas* have done. (2) The Indian buildings, so far as we know (apart from the *stūpas*, which are not buildings at all) were not solid, but hollow.'[4]

'The Babylonian *zigurats* represented exactly on a large scale the same idea of a mountain . . . the storied *vihāras* of India, with their retreating stages, are also imitation mountains. The artificial mountain of the Indians was necessarily a hollow shell, because all

[1] *J.R.A.S.*, 1898, p. 287. [2] *Ibid.*, pp. 284–285.
[3] *History of Indian Architecture*, pp. 202, 618, and *Cave Temples of India*, p. 34.
[4] *J.R.A.S.*, *ibid.*, p. 285.

their constructions was of brick and wood. . . . But the towering *vihāra* became a very different structure from the solid stories of the Zigurat, for India has rarely borrowed anything which she has not altered in adapting it.' This is a very convenient assumption. Kennedy himself admits that when he says, ' but we may conjecture that *zigurat* and *vihāra* had a common origin,' but he is generous to confess that ' these speculations may be fanciful,' and he ' will not deny it.'[1]

Thus Grünwedel and Burgess hold that ' the Persian style, which the Achaemenids employed in their buildings at Susa and Persepolis, has inherited West Asian forms in its constructive as well as in its decorative features. This Persian style, which shows many peculiarities, is unfortunately represented only by a few monuments upon which it is almost impossible to pronounce judgment. But undoubtedly its elements may again be recognized in the buildings of Asoka's day and of the older Indian style, dependent on that of Asoka, as grafted upon the native wooden style.'

' As chief elements, the following forms may be indicated. The Persian pillar with bell-shaped capital was adopted directly; it was set up by itself as an inscription-pillar ; the famous iron pillar of Delhi is a later example. In sculptures it is seen not only in representation of palace-halls, but also decoratively—often to divide spaces, and with many interesting variants. The bell-capital frequently serves as a basis for one or more lions or elephants, or for a religious symbol, (e.g. the wheel) when the pillar is considered as standing alone. If the pillar is used as a support in a building. the bell-capital serves as a base for an abacus on which, turned towards the sides, winged figures of animals (winged horses, gazelles, goats, lions, or sitting elephants) are placed. This last form resembles the Persian ' unicorn-pillar.' The appearance of the whole pillar in India, however, is rough and clumsy compared with Persian forms.'[2]

Fergusson detects Persian influence on pillars in front of the Bedsa cave south of Karle. ' The two pillars in front, however, are so much too large in proportion to the rest, that they are evidently

[1] *J.R.A.S.*, pp. 285, 286, 287.

[2] *Buddhist Art in India*, pp. 17–18. For illustrations, *see* Cunningham *Arch. Sur. Ind. Report*, Vol. V, Plates XLV, XLVI, pp. 187, 188 ; Burgess, *Archaeological Survey, W. Ind.*, Vol. IV, pp. 5, 12 ; and *Cave Temples*, Plates XVI, XXIII, XCVI.

stambhas, and ought to stand free instead of supporting a verandah. Their capitals are more like the Persepolitan type than almost any other in India, and are each surmounted by horses and elephants bearing men and women of bold and free execution.' In a note, he further adds that, ' in the Pitalkhora *vihāra*, we find the Persepolitan capital repeated with a variety of animals over it, for the Hindu artists, from their natural aptitude for modifying and adapting forms, very soon repeated the bicephalous bull and ram of the Persian columns by a great variety of animals, sphinxes, and even human figures in the most grotesque attitudes.'[1]

Of the more recent advocates of the Persian theory, Sir John Marshall is stated by Dr. Spooner to have inferred from the Sarnath capital that ' the Mauryan stonework had been wrought by foreign masons.'[2] Dr. Spooner himself has gone much further, and the idea which was almost within the grasp of Fergusson but ' missed,' altogether possessed him (Spooner), and he could not think of anything but Persian in the Mauryan period of Indian history.[3] He imagined to have explored everything as the result of his excavation at Kumrahar, Patna, which, however, did not proceed further than its initial stage, and could not unearth anything but a portion of a badly damaged pillar and the footmark of what he imagined to be a hall. Starting with a preconceived idea that ' the style of Asoka's sculptured capitals originated in Persepolis,' he began to see, at the very outset, ' the peculiar Persian polish in the columns,' some twenty-three hundred years after their erection, and (from this polish) it seemed to him ' not impossible that even in its design the building (i.e. the hall of which only the footmarks remain) might have been under Persian influence.' The Hall of a Hundred Columns at Persepolis, which is discussed later on, was a square hall with ten rows of ten columns evenly spaced in square bays. ' At Pataliputra,' Spooner himself emphatically declares, ' to be sure, we had only eight rows,' but he consoles himself with an equally emphatic assumption that ' there was every reason to suppose that others would be found, and possibly evidence for a porch as well, to correspond with the porch in Persepolis.' He further admits that ' the intercolumnation at Kumrahar was found to be five diameters, an intercolumnation

[1] *History of Indian and Eastern Architecture*, Vol. I, p. 138.
[2] *J.R.A.S.*, 1915, p. 66.
[3] *See later*, pp. 406–407.

not identical, perhaps, with that of the Persian throne-room, but still,' holds Dr. Spooner, 'one which is essentially Persepolitan. and never found in any other country of antiquity.' So far as the capitals are concerned, of which there appears to be striking similarity, as has been pointed out by all authorities, Spooner admits that 'no capitals had been recovered in Patna to help us in comparing the two buildings, nor had any pedestals been met with.' Spooner acknowledges the importance of the existence of capitals when he says, 'It may be true that, so far as Indian architecture is concerned, the only substantial point showing Persian influence is the capital.' He further admits that 'it may be true that no architectural plan in India, nor any type of building, as a whole, has hitherto been known which one could say was based directly on a Persian model'; yet, undeterred even by this consideration, Dr. Spooner goes on to build his castle of assumption and declares that a 'careful study of the stratification suggested that pedestals had, *in all probability*, existed, and the *indicated* dimensions and proportions justified the thought that these pedestals must have been themselves of Persepolitan type, round in plan, some 3 feet high, and inferentially, bell-shaped; though as regards this latter point,' he is forced to admit that 'no evidence exists.'[1]

Here it is necessary to observe that not a single monument of recognizable condition is available in Persia. Everything has been in ruins when seen by historians, and many objects have been cleverly restored by several archaeologists from scanty material but fertile imagination. But the restorers do not agree amongst themselves. The actual condition of the ruins and the manner of their restoration are pointed out later on.

As more tangible similarity between the Persian and the Indian architecture is apparent in the capitals of columns, it will be perhaps better to take into consideration this object to begin with. Columns in all countries can be classified into two broad classes in regard to their utility, namely, the free pillars, and those which are employed in buildings as support to the whole structure and, in ancient architecture in any case, as the regulator of the whole composition. As regards this regulating column, the question of proportion and intercolumnation alone can arise. So far as this column is concerned

[1] *J.R.A.S.*, 1915, *ibid.*, pp. 66, 67.

A FREE PILLAR IN THE KAILASA TEMPLE OF ELLORA

the capital is of minor importance, because in many places of its employment it becomes mixed up with the entablature and loses its prominency, if not its identity, also. Of the free pillar, on the other hand, the captial is the most prominent part. No other part draws the attention of the visitor so much, the free pillar having no other purpose to serve except being showy. Therefore, apart from the consideration of stability, the proportion between its length and width and between its component parts, namely, the pedestal, base, shaft, and capital, has no significance. But these are the factors which count much in case of the regulating pillar, because, apart from aesthetic consideration, any error in the proportion and in the composition of several parts, will often prove injurious, not only to the pillar itself, but also destructive to the whole building. Consequently the regulating pillar can hardly be considered without taking into consideration the building which it regulates.

These common characteristic features of columns in all countries may help us in distinguishing the really essential elements from the unessential ones. Before proceeding further it is necessary to take stock of what we find in India and what in Persia, and when.

The archaeological remains in India could not be dated much earlier than the fifth century B.C., the Piprahwa Stupa building of 450 B.C. being about the earliest. The discoveries made at Mahenjodaro and Harappa may take back by centuries the Indian architecture and other matters of the cultural progress of the country to a time which would make it impossible to further speculate on the Persian influence in India in any case. But before the artistic treasures unearthed in Sindh and the Punjab have been properly estimated and the scripts have been deciphered they can be hardly utilized in an article like this. We are, therefore, to limit our observation to the old materials, which are, fortunately, plentiful for the present purpose.

The extant Asokan pillars, with which alone a Persian connexion has been sought to be established, and which probably at one time could be counted by hundreds, do not number more than a dozen. The best known Asokan pillar is that removed from Topra to Delhi by Firoz Shah Tughlak in 1356. A fragment of a second was re-erected, also in Delhi, in 1867. Three others exist in Champaran district : the first of these is known as the Lauriya-Araraj, the second as the Lauriya Navandgarh pillar, and the fragment of the other was 'recognized—utilized as a roller for the station roads by a utilitarian member of the Civil Service.' The most complete shaft, bereft, however, of its capital, is the Allahabad pillar, to which a pedestal was added by Captain Smith, but which was again thrown down and re-erected by Jahangir (in 1605) to commemorate his accession. Four other Asokan pillars are in much damaged condition at Rampurwa, Nigliva, Rummindei, and Sarnath. 'It is more than probable that each of these Asokan pillars stood in front of, or in connexion with, some *stūpa* or building of some sort. At least we know that six or seven can be traced at Sanchi, and nearly an equal number at Amarabati, and, in the representation of topes at the latter place, these *lats* are frequently represented both outside and inside the rails. At Karle one still stands in front of the great cave.' The pillar at Eran, and the iron pillar at Mehrauli, near Delhi, belong to the Gupta period; the pillar at Pathari in Bhopal is ascribed to Rastrakuta King Parabala (A.D. 861).

The crowning ornaments of these pillars have been lost, but the capitals of some pillars still exist. The capital of the pillar at Lauriya Navandgarh is surmounted by a lion of bold and good design. The pillar at Sankisa, situated between Mathura and Kanouj, of which the greater part of the shaft has been lost, is surmounted 'by an elephant, but so mutilated that even in the seventh century the Chinese traveller Hiuen Tsiang mistook it for a lion.' The pillar at Karle is surmounted by four lions, 'which, judging from analogy, once bore a *chakra* or wheel, probably in metal.' The pillars at Bedsa, a dozen miles south of Karle, partly stand free and partly supporting a verandah: these pillars are surmounted by horses and elephants bearing men and women of bold and free execution. These capitals are stated to be 'more like the Persepolitan type than almost any others.' In a note, on the authority of Dr. Le Bon, Fergusson further asserts that, in the Pitalkhora *vihāra*, 'the Persepolitan capital is repeated with a variety of animals over it, for the Hindu artists, from their natural aptitude for modifying and adapting forms, very soon replaced the bicephalous bull and ram of the Persian columns by a great variety of animals, sphinxes, and even human figures in the most grotesque attitudes.'[1]

[1] *Indian and Eastern Architecture*, Vol. I, p. 138.

It is needless to point out that this 'great variety of animals' on the capitals of Indian columns has caused great inconvenience and discomfort to the advocates of the Persian theory, because, on Persepolitan capitals, the animals comprise only the bull, the unicorn, and possibly the lion too.

Another important factor, which Fergusson himself admits, is that the Persepolitan 'features are only found on the *lats* of Asoka, and are never seen afterwards in India, though common in Gandhara and on the Indus long afterwards . . . Persian form of capital long retained its position in Indian art.'[1] It is not stated how and why the Persian form did not influence the other Indian types, but the fundamental differences in the Indian types are explained: 'whatever the Hindus *copied*, however, was changed in course of time, by decorative additions and modifications, in accordance with their own taste.' With such an assumption any slight similarity in the most ordinary things of any two countries or peoples may establish relation of indebtedness of any one of the two to the other.

The great variety, and the undeniable differences from the Persian model, of the Indian columns can be verified by a reference to the capitals of pillars at cave no. 26 at Ajanta (Fergusson, *ibid.*, Vol. I, p. 154), at the Chaitya Cave of Kenheri (p. 164), at Bhaja (p. 178), at caves of Nahapana and of Gautamputra in Nasik (p. 185), at Sri Yajna Cave (p. 188), at Vihara no. 16 (p. 190), no. 17 (p. 192), no. 24 (p. 194), no. 1 (p. 195), at Ajanta, at Patna (p. 207), at Jamalgarh (p. 214), at Srinagar and at Shadipur (p. 257), in Bhima Rath at Mamallapuram (p. 332), *Dhvaja-stambha* at Elura (p. 346), *Dipa-stambha* in Dharwar (p. 347), in Tirumalai Nayyaka's *cheultri* at Madura (p. 387), at Vellor and at Pelur (p. 399), of the hall in the Palace at Madura (p. 414), of court in the palace in Tanjore (p. 415), at Ananta Gumpha in Orissa (Vol. II, p. 16), of an Indra Sabha cave at Elura (pp. 20, 21), of Bimala temple at Mount Abu (pp. 39, 42), at Chandravali, Mount Abu (p. 43), at Ranpur (pp. 46, 47), at Khajuraho (p. 53), at Gyaraspur (p. 54), at Amwa (p. 56), at Sravana Belgola (p. 75), at Mudabidri (pp. 76, 77, 78), at Guruvayankeri (p. 81), at Jajpur (p. 111), at Kailasa of Elura (p. 126), at Elephanta (p. 129), *Kīrtistambha* at Vadnagar (p. 136), at Udayapur in Gwalior (p. 146), and at Brindaban (pp. 157, 158).

[1] *Indian and Eastern Architecture*, Vol. I, p. 59.

This long list of existing pillars, when compared with the shorter one, comprising less than a dozen examples where certain similarity with the Persian type is possible, makes it all the more difficult to believe in the Persian theory so far as the Indian pillars are concerned. Moreover, there is another consideration, and that is, in a matter like the present one, perhaps more significant. Only the general principles and practicable rules and regulations for the guidance of artists are codified in standard treatises dealing with a subject like architecture. If any similarity can be clearly detected in the standard treatises of different countries, deficiency, due to the lack of sufficient archaeological remains, can be rectified. But so far as Persia is concerned there appears to have been no such treatise ever written. All that has been recorded in Persia are from the reports of foreign visitors, entirely based on their observation of the scanty remains. In India, fortunately, we possess in manuscripts many hundred *Śilpa-śāstras* dealing with architecture and the cognate arts in great detail. But the standard work, *Mānasāra*, was not accessible to scholars in text or translation until the publication of the writer's seven volumes including a dictionary, an illustrated encyclopaedia, and a number of measured drawings. It is needless to repeat what has been stated in these books. It is possible that, from the details gathered together in these books, readers may expect with greater reason a similarity between the Indian and the Greco-Roman orders rather than the Persian columns. Merely the conclusion may be reiterated here : 'The striking similarities in the names of the mouldings, like *padma* or cyma, *hāra* or bead, or in the names of orders like the *Miśrita* or Composite, may sometimes be attributed to inexplicable coincidence. But in view of other striking similarities between Vitruvius and the *Mānasāra*, such as the classification of orders into exactly five, and the divisions of subservient parts called mouldings, common to all the orders, into eight, and also the proportionate measurement varying equally from six to ten diameters, and tapering almost in the same way, there seem to have been something more substantial than mere coincidence. An influence, direct or indirect, of the one upon the other, seems highly probable.'[1]

In the absence of a direct influence, an indirect one through the Persian source should have been quite feasible, if there were really anything common save and except a few capitals.

[1] *Vide* p. 231, para. 2 of this volume.

So far as the antiquity and the variety are concerned, the Indian columns are so very remote and different from even the doubtfully restored columns of Persia, that no connexion seems to be probable. Synonyms of pillars are met with in the *Ṛig-veda*[1] and the *Atharva-veda*[2] ; the former of which, in any case, must be dated before the *Zend-Avesta* of the Parsis. As regards the variety, they are far too many to be referred to : they are given in detail in the writer's *Dictionary of Hindu Architecture.*[3]

The proportion and the intercolumnations of the Persian type are also essentially different from the Indian ones. The proportionate measures of the pedestal, base, shaft, capital and entablature, as well as the plan and intercolumnation, have been discussed in great

[1] *Ṛig-veda*, I, 59, 1 ; IV, 5, 1.

[2] *Atharava-veda* IX, 3, 1 ; Bloomfield, *Hymns of the A.-V.*, 343 *et seq.*

[3] *Aṅghri* (pp. 13-14), *Āyaka* (p. 67), *Āyikapāda* (p. 69), *Uchchhraya* (p. 78), *Kīrti-stambha* (p. 132), *Gaṇda-verenda*, bearing sun-eagle (pp. 161, 674), *Garuḍa-stambha* (pp. 163, 652, 655, 666, 667, 674, 675, 677), *Gṛiha-stambha* (p. 172), *Charaṇa* (p. 196), *Chitra-skambha* (p. 196), *Chitra-karṇa* (p. 196), *Jaṅghā* (p. 206), *Jayanti* (p. 208), *Jaya-stambha*, pillar of victory (p. 208), *Daṇḍaka* with 16 sides (p. 256), *Dvi-vajraka* (p. 281), *Dhāraṇa* (p. 282), *Dhvaja-stambha*, bearing a flag or banner (p. 282), *Dharma-stambha* (p. 282), *Dhānya-stambha* (p. 282), *Padmakānta* (p. 339), *Pāda* (p. 346), *Pālika-stambha* (p. 348), *Kulikāṅghrika* (p. 143), *Brahma-kānta* (p. 443), *Māna-stambha*, (pp. 654–656, 671), *Mūla-daṇḍa* (p. 511), *Yūpa-stambha* (517), *Ruchaka* (p. 526), *Rudra-kānta* (527), *Lakshmī-stambha* (p. 527), *Vajra-pāda* (p. 533), *Vajra* (p. 532), *Viskambha* (p. 557), *Vishṇu-kānta* (p. 557), *Vṛitta* (p. 563), *Sīlā-stambha* (p. 593), *Śiva-kānta* (p. 594), *Śubhaṅkari* (p. 595), *Sukhāṅghri*, (p. 595), *Śrīkara* (p. 597), *Saumukhya* (p. 642), *Skanda-kānta* (p. 643), *Sthūṇa* (p. 731), *Sthāṇu* (p. 731), of the Jains, Buddhists, Vaishṇavas, Śaivas (p. 677–8), Basava pillar (p. 673), Benefaction pillar (p. 667), Beauty pillar (p. 597), Boundary pillar (p. 661), Brahmadeva pillar (p. 676), Crocodile pillar (p. 677), Devotion pillar (p. 670), Diamond pillar (p. 533), Dwarf pillar (pp. 13–14, 86), Elephant pillar (p. 675), Fan-palm pillar (p. 677), Fortune pillar (pp. 652-653, 668), Foundation pillar (pp. 511, 655, 664, 667), Four-faced pillar (pp. 653, 654, 658), Gate pillar (p. 672), Gold pillar (p. 648), Granite pillar (pp. 654, 655, 656), Honour pillar (pp. 664–665, 666, 670–671), Lamp pillar (pp. 258, 661, 672, 673, 677), Lion pillar (pp. 655, 675, 676), Main pillar (p. 143), Memorial pillar (pp. 538, 674), Monkey pillar (p. 677), Monumental pillar (pp. 132, 282, 675), Octagonal pillar (p. 656), Phallus pillar (p. 667), Piety pillar (p. 659), Projecting pillar (p. 657), Quadrangular pillar (p. 653, 656, 657), Religious pillar (p. 282), Sacrificial pillar (pp. 663, 666, 669–670, 677), Satī pillar (pp. 660, 677), Sixteen-sided pillar (669), Stone pillar (pp. 593, 645, 652, 653, 657, 658, 659, 671, 673), Thieves pillar (p. 677), Thirty-two-sided pillar (p. 648), Town pillar (p. 665), Trident pillar (p. 652), Umbrella pillar (p. 676), Unshaken pillar (p. 673), Upper pillar (p. 143), Victory pillar (pp. 659, 664, 666, 670, 671, 677), Wall pillar (p. 139), War pillar (pp. 661-662), and Welfare pillar (p. 669). For further details and illustrations, *see* the writer's *Encyclopaedia* of *Hindu Architecture* under these terms.

Like the *Romaka siddhānta*, the name of an astronomical treatise based on Roman sources, one might expect, in case of borrowing, to find in this huge list pillars named after the Greeks, Romans, or the Parsis, but no such names are available.

detail in the writer's *Encyclopaedia of Hindu Architecture* and need not be repeated here. Only the conclusions, again, may be briefly referred to. The measures of the mouldings of twelve pedestals[1] classified under three heads, and of some sixty-four bases[2] under nineteen heads, have been given. Shafts are primarily divided into five orders, but there is a great variety described under the technical names, of which a long list has been given above. The capitals, too, which have drawn the attention of the archaeologists rather disproportionately, have been described under several types, none of which appears to have much resemblance with the Persian ones. Lastly, the entablature have been described under eight classes.[3]

The height of the pedestal is generally from a quarter to six times the height of the base. Pedestals are actually given nine heights, which are worked out by nine proportions. In the case where a pedestal is joined to the base, the height of the pedestal may be either equal to that of the base, or twice, or three times as much. Again the bases are given twelve heights varying from 30 *aṅgulas* (of $\frac{3}{4}$ inch each) to 4 cubits. The height of the shaft being divided into four parts, one is given to the base, which may or may not be accompanied by a pedestal. The height of the entablature, as compared with that of the base, may be equal to the latter, or less by a quarter, or greater by a quarter, half, three-quarters or twice. In cubit measure, these six heights may vary from $4\frac{1}{2}$ to 7 cubits. The height of the entablature, when compared with that of the shaft, may be half or three-quarters, or equal to, or greater by a quarter, half, or three-quarters of the latter.

Similarly the capitals are varied at pleasure, though not without regard to the diameter and length of the shaft, and the forms of the plainest of them are found, at a distant view, to bear some resemblance to the Doric and Ionic capitals, but those of a more elaborate kind are sometimes so overloaded with a sort of filigree ornaments as to destroy the effect of the beautiful proportions of the whole.[4]

The capital given to the first design is from a model found at Tiruvottiyur, near Madras, and is called *taraṅga* (wave)-*bodhikā*. It is one diameter high, and projects equal to its height.[5] The other form is from a temple at Mayalapura. It is called *suru-bodhikā* or roll capital.[5] The height of the third capital, called *Phalaka*, is

[1] *See* the writer's *Encyclopaedia*, under *Upapīṭha*. [2] *Ibid.*, under *Adhishṭhāna*.
[3] *Ibid.*, under *Prastara*. [4] The writer's *Dictionary*, *ibid.*, p. 704.
[5] *Ibid.*, p. 680.

three-quarters of the lower diameter of the column and is divided into thirteen parts. Its projection is one diameter.[1] The capital in the fourth variety takes three-quarters of the diameter.[2] The fifth capital, called *Pushpabandha* or band of flower, is equal to the upper diameter of the column. Its projection is equal to its height, but its altitude may be equal to the higher, lower, or the middle diameter of the column; and its breadth may be equal to its height, or four or five diameters.[3] There are many other varieties which are hardly necessary for the present purpose.[4] We may conclude with a more general direction: 'a capital, the height of which is from one to two diameters, and the breadth twice its height. is of the superior sort; that which in height is half the diameter, and in breadth from one to three diameters, is of the inferior sort.'[3]

The plan of the Hindu columns admits of every shape, and is frequently found in the round, quadrangular, and octangular forms, although sixteen-sided and thirty-two-sided cnes are also met with. They are richly adorned with sculptured ornaments.[5]

The intercolumnation may be two, three, four, or five diameters: it is measured in three ways—first, from the inner extremity of the base of one pillar to that of another; secondly, from the centres of the two pillars; and, thirdly, from the outer extremities of the pillars, including the two bases. There seems to be no fixed intercolumnation. This has been left to the discretion of architects, who are, however, required to be particularly careful with regard to beauty and utility.[6]

Similar details of columns may be briefly quoted from Perrot and Chipez's *History of Art in Persia*.

'A glance at the proportions of the Persian column, its thin and airy aspect would, almost by itself, make it clear that it would have been a poor support for a stone entablature.'[7] We have seen above that the Indian column is generally bulky. 'The shaft of the Persian column is always tall and slender. In the Palace of the thirty-six columns at Persepolis, the total height of the order, with base and crown, is in the proportion of twelve to one diameter of the shaft; whilst in the Pasargadae specimen, whose capital has disappeared,

[1] *Dictionary of Hindu Architecture*, by the writer, p. 683.
[2] *Ibid.*, pp. 687–698.
[3] *Ibid.*, p. 691.
[4] *Ibid.*, pp. 669–702.
[5] *Ibid.*, p. 703.
[6] *Indian Architecture*, by the writer, p. 45.
[7] Perrot and Chipiez, *History of Art in Persia*, p. 48.

the proportions are more airy and light.'[1] 'The Susian column, whose head is now in the Louvre, best characterizes the architecture of the Achaemenide sovereigns.'[2]

'The shaft in all the orders of the edifices is slender and slightly tapering towards the top. It is fluted in all instances save in the façades of the necropolis at Persepolis, and the single column that still remains of the Palace of Cyrus in the upland valley of the Polvar.'[3]

'In the oldest stone column standing among the ruins of the Palace of Cyrus at Pasargadae, we have a faithful representation of the primitive post, save that its material is stone and not wood. There is no fluting, the shaft being quite smooth. But what was its capital like? Nobody knows. As to the base, it is a simple round form interposed between the shaft and the ground, even more rudimentary than the cube which does duty now as a plinth in the rustic house.'[4]

'The complex column, with double capital and volutes, rose between the four enormous pillars of the monumental Propylæa on the Persepolitan platform; it upheld the ceiling of the central hall of the great Palace of Xerxes, and formed the supports, both internally and externally, in the main porch of the hall of a hundred columns, as well as those of the hypostyle hall of Artaxerxes at Susa.' In a note it is further stated that 'until recently only slight fragments of the capitals . . . had been recovered; nevertheless the number seen by Coste was sufficiently large to enable him to write as follows: "The flutes of the shaft are cut to a fine edge, and the capitals . . . consist of four distinct sections." Scores of shafts and chips of capitals were disengaged some ten years ago. In Plates (LXVII—LXIX) of the atlas published by the German Mission, entitled *Details of Columns*, will be found fragments of the bull-group, along with pillars adorned by volutes and the cylindrical form which intervenes between these and the pillar. Altogether they furnish all the elements requisite for a restoration of the column,'[5] but not for a comparison with the Indian column.

'All the columns have a base, which differs from one building to another.'[6] 'The type that prevailed all over the country in the golden age of Persian art is represented' in the great palace at Susa. It constitutes the true Persian base. 'The base is not

[1] *History of Art in Persia*, p. 53. [2] *Ibid.*, 86, 87. [3] *Ibid.*, p. 87.
[4] *Ibid.*, pp. 98, 99. [5] *Ibid.*, pp. 95. [6] *Ibid.*, p. 88.

infrequently carved into the lower drum of the shaft, and is singled with it, hence with it must stand or inevitably fall. Elsewhere, in the hypostyle hall of Xerxes, for instance, the base is cut into two, in it the torus belongs to the first drum of the shaft, whilst the principal member is a separate block—resting directly on the ground. Despite the elegance of its contour and the care displayed in its make, the base lacks independence, and does not sufficiently contrast with the column so as to allow of those charming effects which greet us '[1] in the Grecian and Indian support.

As regards the shape of the base, it is limited to a few types only. 'In the Palace of Cyrus it is a disc, or a reversed quarter round. A more complicated shape, composed of a rectangular plinth and a torus seamed by horizontal channellings is seen in one of the porticoes of the Gabre, in the central colonnade of the great Palace of Xerxes, at Susa, as also in the hall of a hundred columns.'[2]

The plinth is hardly seen or can be distinguished. The proportion between the component parts of the column is also lacking.

The Persian capitals, of which much has been made out by the early Indologists, may be referred to in all available details.

In every case the lower portion of the capital detaches itself very abruptly from the column, forms a horizontal line on each side, parallel to the architrave and at right angles with the axis of the shaft. There is no junction or intermediary moulding between the tapering column and the rectangular member at the beginning of the capital[3] akin to the achinus of the Doric and Indian capital.

'If, neglecting minor details, we only regard the shape as a whole, it does not seem unlikely that the first notion of it was suggested by the crowning tuft of a palm. The lower members of the capital would represent the dead twigs as they droop and fall about the stem of the tree, the upper members, whose forms look upwards, would stand for the young shoots, which dart forward past the sere foliage with a slight outward curve, the vertical stripes that scar the surface throughout would be reminiscent of the intervals of fillets which, in nature, separate the leaves of the terminal bunch.'[3]

In India, on the other hand, it should be noted, the analogy lies with the human body, the capital stands for the head, the shafts for the body, the base for the leg, and pedestal for the foot.

[1] *History of Art in Persia*, pp. 89, 90. [2] *Ibid.*, p. 88. [3] *Ibid.*, p. 92.

'Stolze (*Persepolis, Bemerkungen*) seems to think that in the capitals of the columns[1] the animals figured resemble the horse rather than the bull . . . the ornamentist hit upon a kind of compromise between the two quadrupeds, so as to add another conventional type to his repertory, which is not a whit more strange than that of the unicorn, found as support to many of the architraves.'

The animals that figured on Indian capitals, we have seen, are neither bull, nor even the compromised unicorn, but mostly lion, elephant, and man.

Nothing like the Indian cave temples have been disclosed from the Persian ruins. No discussion on the subject is, therefore, possible.

As regards the funerary architecture, 'although Susa would seem to have been the favourite city of the kings of Persia, nothing has been found in the immediate neighbourhood that resembles royal tombs.' 'Persia counted thirteen sovereigns from Cyrus to Darius Codomanus, including the Magi Smerdis. It would appear that four sovereigns had no special monument set up to them in the necropolis.'

'The internal evidence points to Xerxes, Artaxerxes Codomanus, and Darius Nothus as the princes that were entombed at Naksh-i-Rustem, whilst the younger cemetery at Persepolis was inaugurated by Artaxerxes Mnemon. There are then twelve princes and eight tombs, reckoning the Gabre.'

'All these tombs, with but slight differences of detail, are as like one another as it is possible to conceive; to describe one is to describe them all.'

'The total height of each is 22 m. 50 c. divided into three portions of almost equal size. (According to Coste the length of transverse limb of the façade at Naksh-i-Rustem is 18 m. 63 c., length of upper and lower limb 11 m. The height of tomb no. 10 at Persepolis is given at 24·50 c., middle portion, 17 m., length of upper division, 10.50 c.) The middle and longer compartment, in conjunction with the other two, forms what is called a Greek cross. The monument, properly so called, begins with the middle section, carved architecturally into four engaged columns and a lofty double recessed doorway, surmounted by an Egyptian gorge, and a row of dentels, so as to reproduce a palace façade. The upper portion of this doorway is solid rock, but the lower section is cut away, so as to provide

[1] Hypostyle hall of Xerxes at Persepolis, Perrot and Chipiez, no. 31 (p. 91), no. 32 (p. 93), no. 38 (p. 97), no. 43 (p. 112), no. 44 (p. 115).

an entrance to the vault excavated in the mass behind. The field contains a bas-relief of an essentially religious character: upon a stage the king is seen on a pedestal raised by four steps, in the act of worshipping. . . . Above, between the king and the altar, floats the image of Ahura-Mazda, borne on huge wings, behind which a solar disc is roughly suggested.'

So far as the 'Tower of Silence' is concerned it can claim no architectural skill or beauty, because it was never meant to be visited by anybody except the vultures.

There is nothing like the Persian tombs in India. The *stūpas*[1] and the *chaityas*[2] are entirely different monuments; their appearance, measurements, and architectural details are fundamentally different from those of Persian tombs. The *stūpas* were erected as towers to commemorate some events or sacred spots; as *dagobas* they contained relics of Buddha or of some Buddhist saints. For comparison in details, the topes at Sanchi, Sarnath, Amaravati, Gandhara, Jelalabad, Manikyala, the *dagoba* at Ajanta, and the temple at Bodh Gaya may be referred to.

According to Hodgson, the Indian *stūpas* in Nepal are known a *chaityas*. According to Fergusson,[3] the Buddhist *chaityas* at Bhaja, Nasik, Ellora, Karle, etc., correspond in every respect with the churches of the Christian religion rather than to the Persian tombs. 'Their plans, the position of the altar or relic casket, the aisles, and other peculiarities are the same in both, and their uses are identical, in so far as the ritual forms of the one religion resemble those of the other.' But the *chaityas* were much earlier buildings than even the Christian churches, because the ceremony of entombing sacred ashes and other relics is mentioned in the *Vedas*. In the *Rāmāyaṇa*, also, the Brahmanical *chaityas* are alluded to. Later on *chaitya* became a synonym for temple.

The *Avesta* condemns in no measured terms the worshippers of the Daevas or Demons, and, in a general way, whoever does not strictly observe the rules established by Zoroaster, in that he exposes himself to pollute the sacred elements: fire, earth, and water.

In the words of Herodotus (I, 121), the Persians 'have neither images nor temples nor altars, these they consider unlawful, and impute folly to those that make them. This is because they do not

[1] For details, *see* the writer's *Encyclopaedia, sub voce.*
[2] *Ibid., sub voce.*
[3] *Ibid.*, pp. 50–51.

believe, like the Greeks [and the Hindus] in the personality of the gods. Their practice is to sacrifice to Zeus on the summit of the highest mountains, and under the name of Zeus they understand the whole circumference of the heavens.' Cicero (*De Republica*, III, IX, 14, *De Legibus*, II, X, 26), by way of explaining the cause of Xerxes' burning of the temples of Athens, says that it was to punish the Greeks ' for their sacrilege in their foolish attempt " to shut up within walls the gods, before whom everything ought to be open and free, the gods, whose temple and habitation were the whole universe ".' The *Avesta*, however, ' contains no sign or token of the feeling imputed to the Persians by the Greek historian, and more explicitly the Roman orator.' The Persians burnt the Grecian temples probably ' to avenge the sacking of Sardes ' (Herodotus, VI, 96, 100).

King Darius claims, however, to have restored to the people, among other things, ' the temples that Gaumata the Magi had destroyed.'[1] The original term, of which ' temples ' is the translation, is *ayadana*, from the root *yas* signifying ' to adore.' The proper rendering of the word should be ' sacred place,' ' place of worship,' and need not mean temple at all.

On the façade of the rock-tombs referred to above, ' we have seen the king in the act of prayer, standing before an *altar* upon which the celestial fire is burning.' Up to the present nothing of this kind has been, however, found in Persia, though in many places monuments have been noticed to which the name of *atesh-gah* (fire-places) is applied by the natives. But for their dimensions, that are on a larger scale than those of the altars figured in the upper division of the royal tombs, crowned with sacrificial fire, they might be taken as replicas of these.

Even assuming the existence of altars in Persia, they could never look like the Indian altars, out of which the Hindu temple seems to have developed. The *Śūlva-sūtras*, which are but the supplementary portions of the *Kalpa-sūtras*, furnish us, as stated above, with interesting structural details of the large altars built of bricks, which, for ready reference may be reiterated here. These altars were constructed in different shapes, first enumerated in the *Taittirīya-saṁhitā* (V. 4, 11). Following this enumeration, *Baudhāyana* and

[1] Darmesteter, *Etudes Iraniennes*, tom. II, pp. 129, 130. The passage belongs to the first column of the inscription.

Āpastamba furnish us with full particulars. These altars, as stated above, were divided into ten classes according to their shape and other details: (1) *Chaturasra-Śyenachit*, so called because it resembles the form of a falcon and the bricks out of which it is composed are all square-shaped; (2) *Kaṅkachit*, in the form of a heron, is the same as the preceding one except the two additional feet; (3) *Alajachit*, is the same except the additional wings; (4) *Praugachit*, is an equilateral triangle; (5) *Ubhayataḥ-Praugachit*, is made up of two such triangles joined at their bases; (6) *Ratha-chakrachit*, is in the form of a massive wheel without spokes, as well as with sixteen spokes; (7) *Droṇachit*, is like a vessel or tube, square or circular; (8) *Parichayyachit*, has a circular outline and is equal to the *Ratha-chakrachit*, differing in the arrangement of bricks, which are to be placed in six concentric circles; (9) *Samuhyachit*, is circular in shape, and made of loose earth and bricks; and (10) *Kūrmachit* resembles a tortoise and is of a triangular or circular shape.

'Every one of these altars was constructed of five layers of bricks, which, together, came up to the height of the knee; in some cases ten or fifteen layers, and proportionate increase in the height of the altar were prescribed. Every layer in its turn was to consist of two hundred bricks, the first, third, and fifth layers were divided into two hundred parts in exactly the same manner, a different division was adopted for the second and the fourth, so that one brick was never laid upon another of the same size and form.'

'The first altar covered an area of 7½ *purushas*, i.e. 7½ squares, each side of which was equal to the height of a man (*purusha*) with uplifted arms. On each subsequent occasion the area was increased by one square *purusha*. Thus, at the second layer of the altar, one square *purusha* was added to the 7½ constituting the first *chiti*, and at the third layer two square *purushas* were added, and so on. But the shape of the whole and the relative proportion of each constituent part had to remain unchanged. The area of every *chiti*, whatever its shape might be—falcon, wheel, tortoise, etc.—had to be equal to 7½ square *purushas*.[1]

As regards the temple, the worshippers of fire (as an element), could hardly think of any, because the god of fire was never idolized by them, and only idol-worship needs a temple proper.[2] Dieulafoy's

[1] For further details, *see* the writer's *Indian Architecture*, pp. 7, 8.

[2] *See* above, pp. 21, 22, 23; and 'Fine Arts' (pp. 212–215), by the writer, *I.H.Q.*, June, 1929.

description of a building in ruins situated in the Susian Plan, which Perrot and Chipiez quote but criticize,[1] would hardly apply to a Hindu, Buddhist, or Jain temple. All we are really sure about is the *atesh-gah*, 'the sole monumental type and representative of the religious architecture in Persia.' This figured on the bas-reliefs of Persepolis and is encountered all over the country. On a coin, posterior to Alexander's, is figured a monument, by the side of which a king stands in the attitude of a prayer. 'A glance suffices to show that we are in face of an *atesh-gah*. Three altars with very salient horns rise upon a block of masonry, whose base and entablature the engraver has indicated, between the pillars at the angle, two parallel flights approach laterally the landing place that let to the platform.'

'If during the Parthian domination the Mazdian temple thus preserved its traditional form, it was not likely to lose it with the Sassanidae, when Mazdiasm became the state religion.' Then Perrot and Chipiez conclude with the remark, 'that the notion of a temple built by a Sassanian prince must be abandoned as illusory. All we know is that the sacred fire continued to ascend to heaven throughout the duration of the second empire, precisely as it had done during the first.'[2]

'Religious beliefs which discountenanced inhumation had not favoured the development of funerary architecture, and the monotheistic tendencies of a cult whose sanctuaries at the outset were the bare summits of lofty mountains, had retained throughout, even when it could command the resources of a mighty empire, the elementary and primitive form of the temple, an altar set upon a plinth more or less elevated, rising on an esplanade open to sky. Such simplicity and uniformity as these were in perfect harmony with the spirit of Magianism and in accord with the character of its rites.'

The principal effort of the Indian builder, on the other hand, was brought to bear upon the temples, which have been distinguished as male, female, and neuter; as round, oval, rectangular, quadrangular, octagonal, and of other shapes; as running to seventeen storeys; as having ninety-eight, forty-five, and ten types.[3] 'They display an exuberance of fancy, a lavishness of labour, and an elaboration of detail to be found nowhere else.' Even the most ardent

[1] *History of Art in Persia*, pp. 249–259. [2] *Ibid.*, pp. 250, 252.
[3] *See* the writer's *Encyclopaedia of Hindu Architecture*, under *Prāsāda* (temple).

advocate of Persian theory could not think of Persian influence upon Indian temples.

Sculpture is intimately associated with temples; in the absence of the latter the former cannot naturally develop. 'As to the statues of gods and goddesses, it is well-known that they could not obtain in Persia until the fourth century B.C., when Ochus, affirms Berosus, set up statues to Anahita in the principal towns of the empire. But the traces of those simulacra have not been preserved.' 'A descriptive passage in the *Vendidad-sada* may possibly apply to the images of Anahita.'[1]

'No statuary has been found which might have served to decorate their (Persian) palaces.'[2] But according to Plutarch[3] statues were actually made in Persia. He recounts that when the soldiers of Alexander entered the capital of Persia they cast down a statue of Xerxes from its pedestal. But Perrot and Chipiez think that 'the so-called statue may have been no more than an image carved upon a stela, like those of the bas-reliefs at Persepolis, representing the kings for whom the palaces were built.' 'As in Assyria, here also, bas-relief was the sculptor's favourite mode of expression.' Excepting small figures disinterred in the ruins of Susa, all sculptures were in low relief. The only monument left to represent the primitive period of Persian sculpture is the Cyrus at Pasargadae, but its head, hands, and feet are 'terribly defaced,' so that 'it is more especially,' admit Perrot and Chipiez,[4] 'from the costume that we surmise where the artist took his models.'

'Simultaneously with the king, the soldiers, and the tribute-bearers, animals too have become mere abstractions, and only interest the sculptor so far that they play a part in the festival given in honour of the monarch. To the lion is allotted the largest place in the bas-reliefs at Persepolis.'

'The fault of these representations resides in this, that neither king nor monster appear to fight in good earnest and for dear life. The attitudes of the conqueror and the vanquished are tame, conventional, and uniform.'[5]

[1] *Zend-Avesta*, translated by James Darmesteter, *Vendidad*, Chap. XXX, tome ii, p. 82. *See* also Perrot and Chipiez, p. 385.

[2] Perrot, 376.

[3] *Alexander*, by Plutarch, XXXVII.

[4] Perrot, 426.

[5] *Ibid.*, p. 436, *see* the details, pp. 436–439.

In India, on the other hand, we possess innumerable examples of sculpture and reliefs, both high and low. There is also most elaborate literary evidence furnishing all details. As in the buildings, so also in sculpture and painting, ' an exuberance of fancy, a lavishness of labour, and an elaboration of detail have been evinced in India.' In the early Vedic age, God is personified in natural phenomena, then He is given a human body, till at last He is conceived as having a thousand heads, a thousand eyes, and a thousand hands, etc. We see in the Pauranic age Brahmā is furnished with four heads, Śiva and other deities with three eyes, the goddess Śakti with ten hands holding various attributes, and the goddess of learning with a musical instrument and other objects, indicative of her profession. There are given, in the treatises known as *Silpa-śāstras*, the minutest measures of the several limbs of the images of not only the gods and goddesses, but also of sages, ordinary men and women, of animals and birds of well-known species, even of fish and insects.[1]

' The Hindu image-maker or sculptor,' Hadaway observes, ' does not work from life, as is the usual practice among the (modern) Europeans, but he has, in place of the living model, a most elaborate and beautiful system of proportions, which he uses constantly, combining these with those of observation and study of natural detail. It is, in fact, a series of anatomical rules and formulae, of infinitely more practical use than any European system, for the Indian one treats of the actual proportion and of the surface form, rather than the more scientific attachment of muscles and the articulation of bones.'[2]

Although there has been undeniable Grecian influence on the Gandhara (and Amarabati) sculpture, there can, thus, be no possibility of any Persian influence on the Hindu, Buddhist, or Jain sculpture or painting.[3]

The military and the civil architecture of a people are regulated by the local conditions. When by instinctive skill the bird builds its nest and the lion its cave to protect itself from the inclemency of weather, etc., it is but natural that a people should invent their own defence. It is, therefore, not expected in most cases that one people should influence another in ancient times in the building of

[1] *See* the writer's *Encyclopaedia of Hindu Architecture*, under *Tālamāna*.
[2] The writer's *Dictionary*, p. 244.
[3] The description of Vahuman can never correspond to that of Brahmā.

their villages, towns, and forts. Nor is this expectation falsified in the case of Persia and India.

Like buildings referred to above, the remains of the old Persian military architecture are but scanty for study and comparison. 'When Alexander invaded the country there were no walled cities.' 'No wall surrounded Ecbatana or Susa when Alexander entered them, but then, as now in those regions, every town kept its fortress in good order. Behind its thick friendly walls the king could take refuge and place his treasures in safety.' Of all the fortresses, the best known and the most ancient was that of Susa. The notion gained by Dieulafoy respecting the Susian defences is summed up in the following words :

'The fortification works consisted first of a deep broad ditch full of water, communicating with the Shāür, and a double rampart. The external or first wall was massive and built of crude bricks, in width 23 metres by 22 metres in height. Against the inner lining of the wall—separated from the masonry by a trail of small pebbles or gravel—leant a mass of earth beaten into a compact mass, 27 metres thick and 18 metres high. On this platform stood two groups of buildings which served at once as barracks and walk rounds. . . . The second rampart, 14 m. 70 c. broad, was constituted by two walls of unbaked brick, in thickness 3 m. 50 c. to 4 m. 60 c., between which damp earth was beaten down. Behind the second rampart ran a path. . . . Broadly stated, the enceinte was not furnished with bastions. . . . Towers had been distributed at the crenelated summits of the fortress, and its tracing had been so continued that the towers of the second rampart struck the middle of the curtains of the exterior wall.'[1] This would look like the scheme adopted at Babylonia and Assyria.

Recent historians, excavators, and archaeologists have equally found out inaccuracy in Herodotus's statement[2] about the seven walls encompassing Ecbatana, along the flanks of the hill at the summit of which stood the palace of Dejoces. Rawlinson's attempt[3] to seek the fortress with the sevenfold wall, not in the vicinity of Hamadan, but in Media Atropatene, at a place called Takht-i-Suliman, has also not been successful.

[1] Perrot and Chipiez, *History of Art in Persia*, p. 370.
[2] Herodotus, I, 98.
[3] *The Five Great Monarchies*, II, 268.

In India, along with frequent mention of villages, towns, and forts,[1] cities with a hundred enclosures are, however, referred to in the earliest extant literature of the world, the *Ṛig-veda.*[2] On this, Muir remarks,[3] as pointed out before that, although they are only alluded to as figurative expressions of the means of protection afforded by the gods, they no doubt suggest the idea of forts, consisting apparently of a series of concentric walls, as actually existing in the country at that time.[4]

In Buddha's time, in Northern India, 'we nowhere hear of isolated houses : they were all together, in a group, separated only by narrow lanes. Immediately adjoining was the sacred grove of trees of primeval forest . . . villagers united of their own accord to build mote-hills and rest-houses, reservoirs, to mend the roads between their own and adjacent villages, and even to lay out parks. . . . We are told of lofty walls, ramparts with buttresses, and watch-towers, and great gates ; the whole surrounded by a moat or even a double moat, one of water and one of mud.'[5]

Full details are available in the *Silpa-śāstras*, which are avowedly architectural texts. In the *Mānasāra*, villages are divided, as pointed out before, into eight classes according to their plans—*Daṇḍaka*, *Sarvato-bhadra*, *Nandyāvarta*, *Padmaka*, *Svastika*, *Prastara*, *Kārmuka*, and *Chaturmukha*. Every one of these villages is surrounded by a wall made of brick or stone; beyond this wall there is a deep and broad ditch. There are generally four main gates at the middle of the four sides, and as many at the four corners. Inside the wall there is a large street running around the village. There are two other large streets, each of which connects two opposite main gates. They intersect at the centre of the village, where a temple or public hall is generally built. The village is thus divided into four main blocks, each of which is again subdivided into many blocks by streets which are always straight and run from one end to the other of a main block.[6]

[1] *Ṛig-veda*, I, 58 ; 8, 144, 1 ; II, 20, 8 ; IV, 27, 1 ; 30, 20 ; VIII, 3, 7 ; 15, 14 89, 8 ; 95, 1.

[2] *Ibid.*, I, 166, 8 ; VII, 15, 14.

[3] *Sanskrit Texts*, V, 451.

[4] For further details, *see* the writer's *Indian Architecture*, p. 8.

[5] *Buddhist India*, Rhys Davids, pp. 42, 45, 49, 64–65, *Jataka*, I, 199.

[6] For further details, *see* the writer's *Dictionary*, pp. 180–186, and *Indian Architecture*, pp. 39–40.

Towns are also divided, as we have seen before, into eight classes—*Rājadhānīya-nagara*, *Kevalanagara*, *Pura*, *Nagarī*, *Kheṭa*, *Kharvaṭa*, *Kubjaka* and *Pattana*. The smaller towns are but an enlargement of the village, differing mostly in the matter of dimensions. According to the *Mānasāra*, the dimensions of the smallest town-unit are 100 by 200 *daṇḍas* (of 4 cubits each), and the largest 7,200 by 14,000 *daṇḍas*. There are generally twelve large streets in a small town.[1]

Forts are first divided into eight classes known as *Sibira*, *Vāhinīmukha*, *Sthānīya*, *Droṇaka Saṁviddha* or *Vardhaka*, *Kolaka*, *Nigama*, and *Skandhāvāra*. There is a further division according to the strategic position—mountain fort, forest fort, water fort, chariot fort, divine fort, marsh fort, and mixed fort. The mountain fort is again subdivided as it is built on the top, valley, or slope of a mountain. Everyone of the forts is surrounded with strong and high walls, and deep and broad ditches. The wall is made of brick, stone, and similar materials. It must be at least twelve cubits high and six cubits thick. It is provided with watch-towers.

In Persia there appears to have been nothing like these, so far as the Persian towns and forts can be judged from the scanty remains. Of the civil architecture in Persia fragmentary information regarding certain palaces only are available. Even such information is entirely lacking in regard to the less imposing, but decidedly more common, buildings where the bulk of the people used to live, and wherefrom alone the national life and habit could have been estimated for comparison with corresponding buildings in India. The historian divides these Persian buildings into three types, namely the open throne-room, the walled throne-room, and the inhabited palace.

'Capitals, as Ecbatana, Susa, and Persepolis, were not alone in possession of royal palaces, there were houses also in lesser centres where kings stopped a few days, so as to escape from the extreme cold and heat. Polycletus,[2] who has been cited by Strabo,[3] and who was a contemporary of Alexander and well versed in all things pertaining to Persia, writes, 'on the summit of the mound at Susa every king builds a separate palace for himself, with treasuries

[1] For further details, *see* the writer's *Encyclopaedia*, under *Grāma* and *Nagara*, and *Dictionary*, pp. 283–294, 259–262.

[2] Fragments collected by C. Müller, *Scritores rerum Alexandri Magni*, pp. 130–132.

[3] Strabo, XV, iii, 21.

and stores, a pile of building set apart receiving tributes levied in the course of his reign, and which must he kept as a monument of his administration.' 'But this statement lacks confirmation. Susa certainly had palaces as fine, as vast, and as grand as Persepolis, but nothing now appears above ground; what subsists is buried under an enormous accumulation of earth and rubbish, whence the English and French excavations have only disengaged the fragments.'[1]

According to Strabo[2] and Arrian,[3] Cyrus, after defeating Astyages, built in Pasargadae palaces and treasuries which existed at the time of the Macedonian invasion. The ruins at the village of Mished-i-Murghab are supposed to be the remains of these edifices. After clever restoration the general plan appears to be this: 'a four-pillared porch, with two lateral chambers, then comes a great hypostyle hall, divided into four aisles by two ranges of pillars which supported the ceiling . . . the number of pillars is not large; their dimensions, together with those of the building considered as a whole do not come near those displayed later at Persepolis and Susa, nor are the walls as thick as on the platform of the Takht-i-Jamshid.'[4] Of the 'small palace' and the Takht-i-Suliman (the stage of Solomon) little remains to give an idea of its plan.

At present the district where Persepolitan kings built royal palaces contains naught but villages. 'As to Persepolis, besides anonymous buildings in a poor state, four kings have left structures signed by them. Amongst all these edifices not two are alike. Again, neither the plan nor the dimensions of the colossal fabric, those we should call state apartments, throne-rooms, were uniform.'[5]

Several important structures of Persepolis have been restored. One of these is known as the platform: very little of it really remains, but contains four inscriptions and the signature of Darius. Its general plan is shown by a carriage-road winding round the southern face leading from the plain to the platform; it (the road) then went behind the edifice along the first slope of the hill, to approach again the esplanade towards the east angle, whence it mounted as far as the pair of tombs situated in the rock behind the level.[6] This level is reached by a 'superb staircase,' consisting of not more

[1] Perrot and Chipiez, *History of Art in Persia*, pp. 257, 266.
[2] Strabo, XV, iii, 3, 7, 8. [3] Arrian, III, xv, iii, 10.
[4] Perrot and Chipiez, pp. 268–269, 270. [5] *Ibid.*, p. 257. [6] *Ibid.*, pp. 282–283.

than a hundred and eleven steps, which is very common in India.[1]

'Four distinct horizontal plans may be counted on the platform. The lower stage is narrow and insignificant : it does not seem to have supported any edifices. The second level is approached by the great staircase, and takes up about three-quarters of the superficies of the platform, upon it were distributed the principal buildings —the propylaca and the hall of a hundred columns. Proceeding from north to south there is another esplanade, some three metres above this, which contains the relics of the most important and attractive of all the royal edifices, the hypostyle hall of Xerxes. Again, to the rear of this, is reached the terrace which carried two buildings, the palaces of Darius and Xerxes. Lastly, a building at the south-east angle appears to have had its floor on the third stage.'[2]

Dr. Spooner could not find such a platform at Kumrahar, Patna. Nor does the high plinth at Sanchi, or the Buddhist railings in many places, seem to resemble this Persian platform.

The propylaca was signed by Xerxes. Its principal remains are two great piers some eleven metres high, beyond projects, in round-boss, the foreparts of two quadrupeds, right and left of paved corridor, 3 m. 82 c. broad. Even after restoration, based on such scanty materials, it can never look like any Indian building, such as the great gateways of temples (Gopuram).

The hypostyle hall of Xerxes also contains his signature. But very little of it really remains. Its general character has been indicated by Perrot and Chipiez. 'Beyond the substructures is found the most important group of columns, of which three shafts alone remain.' Originally there were seventy-two pillars, which supported the ceilings.

'The stone base that supported the pillars tell us plainly,' say Perrot and Chipiez, rather too emphatically, 'what was the arrangement of the apartment. It was a hall 43 m. 50 c. square, and on its floor are found the marks of thirty-six columns, spaced equidistant from one another, as in the west and east porches.' 'All that is visible of another isolated structure are the foundation stones distributed in two ranges, which doubtless supported pillars. Their inter-columnation is 2 m. 50 c. In the absence of any fragment,

[1] Compare, for instance, the grand staircase at Sītākunda Hill, Chittagong, Bengal, which consists of more than a thousand steps.

[2] Perrot and Chipiez, pp. 284, 287.

sculptural or architectural, to throw any light on the subject, it is impossible to hazard a guess as to the probable use of this minor building.'

The claim of this hall as a queen among other Persepolitan monuments is stated to have been established by ' the imposing adjustment and the wealth of ornament displayed about the stairs by which it was approached, the extent of the ground it covered, the exceptional height and magnificence of its quadruple colonnade.' The area covered by this hall is stated to far exceed that of the Pharaohs of the nineteenth dynasty. The site occupied by the central pavilion is not more than 2,500 m. square, whilst that of the Egyptian colonnade is more than 5,000 m., but counting the annexes the total area would be not less than 7,500 square metres. This was clearly a reception room of Xerxes.

The hall of a hundred columns, also a reception, audience, or throne room, is but an enlargement of the hypostyle hall, around which chambers are distributed. It is called an anonymous building, as no inscription has been preserved of it, from which it might have been dated. It was walled on all its faces, with porchlike colonnade in front. In shape the built surface is a parallelogram 75 m. 82 c. from east to west, and 91 m. 16 c. from north to south. ' The principal façade was on the north side. . . . Counting the intervals between the bases, we get the number of pillars, which was sixteen, arranged in two rows of eight. Two great portals open upon the porch.'

' By setting up, in *imagination*, the original brick wall, 3 m. 25 c. thick which connected these minor buildings with one another, we get the whole area which it embraced, . . . no bearing wall stood here. Of ancient structures nothing remains save fragments of bases, and when these fail, their foundations, the intercolumnations are about those of the portico, 6 m. 20 c., measured from one axis to another, whilst all the bases are uniform in shape.' The number of the columns had to be ' made out ' merely from the marks of bases left on the floor. They were distributed in rows of ten each, and upheld the roof of a square hall. Their disposition is identical with that of the central pavilion of the great palace of Xerxes.

' In front of the palace we have *imagined* the soil furrowed by countless rills, masked by plants and shrubs which they feed into greenness, a contrivance still resorted to in modern Persia to obtain the equivalent of our lawns.'

'With data of this nature,' declare the archaeologists, 'to go by, it is easy to restore the edifice.'[1]

But with data of this nature no comparison with any Indian building will be convincing to the average reader conversant with the long past of India, despite Dr. Spooner's advocacy to connect this hall with the footmark of what he also imagined to be Asoka's palace.[2]

One other general important characteristic of Persian civil architecture is that 'no trace has been detected of a second storey about this (Palace of Darius) or any other Persepolitan edifice. To the present hour, Persian dwellings and palaces have but a ground floor, divided into apartments, the number of which depends upon the fortune of the owner. As to the great throne rooms (i.e. the hypostyle hall and the hall of hundred columns), their character excludes the notion of more than one storey, each shell, being a perfect unit in itself, was in no need of dependencies, so that we cannot suppose any having existed here. Aught more whimsical than the restoration of Fergusson, who places a second order of pillars above the ceilings of the hypostyle halls with a fire-altar for the king to worship at, cannot well be imagined, and will not bear the test of close inspection.'[3]

In India, even in the earliest Vedic period, which must precede the period of the Persian halls by several hundred years, mention is made of a sovereign 'who, exercising no oppression, sits down in this substantial and elegant hall built with a thousand pillars,'[4] and of residential houses with such pillars as are said to be 'vast, comprehensive, and thousand-doored.'[5] Mitra and Varuṇa are represented as occupying a great palace with 'a thousand pillars and a thousand gates.'[6]

There were such other buildings also : Atri is stated to have been 'thrown into a machine room with a hundred doors, where he was roasted.'[7] Vasishṭha desired to have 'a three-storeyed dwelling.'[8]

[1] Perrot and Chipiez : pp. 326, 341.

[2] *See* pp. 404–405.

[3] Perrot and Chipiez, pp. 337–338.

[4] *Ṛig-veda* (Wilson), II, 313.

[5] *Ibid.*, IV, 179.

[6] *Ibid.*, II, 41, 5 ; V, 62, 6 ; VII, 885, *Atharva-veda*, III, 12 ; IX, 3. Muir comments (Sanskrit Texts, V, 455) : 'this is but an exaggerated description of a royal residence such as the poet had seen.'

[7] *Ibid.*, I, 112, 7 ; Wilson's IV, 148.

[8] *Ibid.*, Wilson's IV, 200.

In the *Matsya-purāṇa*,[1] halls are divided into twenty-seven kinds according to the number of columns they are furnished with, the largest one having 64 pillars, the next 62, one following 60, and so on. They bear significant and artistic names: (1) *Pushpaka*, (2) *Pushpa-bhadra*, (3) *Suvrata*, (4) *Amrita-nandana*, (5) *Kauśalya*, (6) *Buddhi-saṁkīrṇa*, (7) *Gaja-bhadra*, (8) *Jayābaha*, (9) *Śrīvatsa*, (10) *Vijaya*, (11) *Vāstu-kīrti*, (12) *Śrutiñ-jaya*, (13) *Yajña-bhadra*, (14) *Viśāla*, (15) *Suślishṭa*, (16) *Śatru-mardana*, (17) *Bhāga-pañcha*, (18) *Nandana*, (19) *Mānava*, (20) *Māna-bhadraka*, (21) *Sugrīva*, (22) *Harita*, (23) *Karṇikāra*, (24) *Śatardhika*, (25) *Siṁha*, (26) *Śyāma-bhadra*, and (27) *Subhadra*. In shape they may be triangular, crescent, circular, quadrangular or square, octagonal, and sixteen-sided.

In the *Mānasāra* and other texts, where a very large number of halls and pavilions are elaborately described, various storeys of the halls are referred to: the storeys may vary from one to twelve.[2]

In the *Mānasāra* the royal palaces proper are divided, with regard to their size, storey, and other characteristic features, into nine classes and assigned to the nine classes of kings—(1) *Chakravartin*, (2) *Mahārāja* or *Adhirāja*, (3) *Mahendra* or *Narendra*, (4) *Pārshṇika*, (5) *Paṭṭadhara*, (6) *Maṇḍaleśa*, (7) *Paṭṭabhāj*, (8) *Prāhāraka*, and (9) *Astra-grāhin*. Each of the nine types of the palaces admits of nine sizes. Every one consists of a certain number of halls, audience-chambers, or throne-rooms. Thus the palace of the *Chakravartin*, or universal monarch, possesses up to seven halls, that of the *Adhirāja* or *Narendra* up to six halls, and so forth.[3] The chapter (XI) dealing with the dimensions of storeys, varying from one to twelve in residential buildings and temples, concludes with the rule directing the number of storeys in edifices according to the social status of their occupants.[4]

In the *Sabhā-parvan* of the *Mahābhārata* are referred to several halls belonging to the Pāṇḍavas (Chap. I), to Indra (Chap. VII), to Yama (Chap. VIII), to Varuṇa (Chap. IX), to Kubera (Chap. X), and to Brahmā (Chap. XI). The description of every one of these lacks in the architectural details which are necessary for any

[1] Chap. 270, verses 7–15, 16.

[2] For details, *see* the writer's *Encyclopaedia*, under Śālā.

[3] For more details, *see* the writer's *Indian Architecture*, pp. 57, 58, 59; *Encyclopaedia of Hindu Architecture*, under Prāsāda.

[4] *See* above, p. 106, and *Indian Architecture*, p. 42.

fruitful comparison. None of the ancient Indian halls or palaces appears to have any substantial resemblance with the Persian open, walled, pillared, or unstoreyed halls.

The only point of similarity between the Pāṇḍava hall and Spooner's Kumrahar hall, which is ascribed to king Asoka, is no more substantial than that Maya-Asura is stated to have built the former, while some unspecified genii are stated by Fa-hien to have built the latter.[1]

Thus Spooner seems to have hit upon a further discovery between the supernatural origin of Asokan buildings hinted by Fa-hien, and the equally mythological description, in the *Mahābhārata*, of the hall stated to have been built by Maya-Asura, of which, however, no architectural details are available for a comparison, either with the throne-room of Darius Hystaspes at Persepolis or with the foot-marks of the supposed Asokan hall at Kumrahar.[2] What Maya-Asura claims to have built for the Dānavas (genii) may be given in Spooner's own translation : 'the palaces, pavilions full of pleasures and abounding in delights a thousandfold, delightful gardens, too, and ponds of various kinds, and wondrous vestments, chariots that moved at will, and cities far extended, with high rampart walls, also thousands of wondrous vehicles most excellent, and pleasing caves to every comfort joined.'[3]

[1] Fa-hien's description of Asokan buildings at Patna is but mythical. 'The royal palace and halls in the midst of the city (of Pataliputra), which exist now as of old, were all made by spirits which he (Asoka) employed, and which piled up the stones, reared the walls and gates, and executed the elegant carving and inlaid sculpture work'—in a way which no human hands of this world could accomplish,—(James Legge, *A Record of Buddhistic Kingdoms*, p. 77).

[2] *J.R.A.S.*, 1915, p. 77.

For further discussion of Maya's hall, *see* the writer's article 'Ahura-Mazda and Maya-Asura' (Proceedings of the Fourth Oriental Conference, Vol. II, pp. 736–751), and his *Indian Architecture*, p. 166.

दानवानां पुरा पार्थ प्रसादा हि मया कृताः ॥
रम्याणि सुखगर्भाणि भोगाढ्यानि सहस्रशः ।
उद्यानानि रम्याणि सरांसि विविधानि च ॥
विचित्राणि च वस्त्राणि कामगानि रथानि च ।
नगराणि विशालानि साट्टप्राकारवन्ति च ॥
वाहनानि च मुख्यानि विचित्राणि सहस्रशः ।
बिलानि रमणीयानि सुखयुक्तानि वै भृशम् ॥
—(*Mahābhārata*, II, i, 14–17.)

[3] *J.R.A.S.*, 1915, p. 82.

At Kṛishna's suggestion, Maya is stated to have built a Sabhā for the king Yudhishṭhira—'a durbar hall, or throne room,' in the words of Spooner. But no details of this hall are given. It is simply stated that 'there could not be any parallel in the world of the mortals, and whereon all heavenly ideas were depicted in bṛicks, stones' (or wood). He declares himself as a great *poet of architecture* (a Ruskin), among the rivals of gods, and he is the Viśvakarman who was the heavenly architect among the gods.[1]

To Dr. Spooner, Yudhishṭhira's so-called 'throne-room' has sounded a note of similarity to the Asokan hall and thence to the Persepolitan 'throne-room' of a hundred columns.

And the supposed supernatural origin of practically all the architectural objects in India has a prototype in the Fa-hien's ascription of Asokan buildings to the genii.

Further, by way of establishing to a certainty the Persian origin of Indian architecture, Spooner imagined to have arrived at a number of wonderful discoveries,[2] namely :

(1) That the architectural structures described in the *Mahābhārata* are of Persian model.

(2) That the palaces to which the *Mahābhārata* refers are those of Pataliputra.[3]

(3) That the Kumrahar remains, dug out at the cost of a Parsi millionaire are identical with the Persepolitan structures (p. 71).

(4) That the temple at Bodh-Gaya was founded by the ancient Persians and that Gaya was an early seat of Magian worship (p. 411).

(5) That the ancestors of Buddha, the Sākyas of Kapilavastu, were of Zoroastrian origin (pp. 440, 441).

[1] अहं हि विश्वकर्मा वैं दानवानां महाकविः।
यदि त्वं कर्तुकामोऽसि प्रियं शिल्पवतां वर।
धर्मराजस्य दैतेय यादृशीमिह मन्यसे ॥
यां कृतां नानुकुर्वन्ति मानवाः प्रेक्ष्याधिष्ठिताः।
मनुष्यलोके सकले तादृशीं कुरु वै सभाम् ॥
यत्र दिव्यानभिप्रायान् पश्येम हि कृतांस्त्वया
असुरान्मानुषांश्चैव सभां तां कुरु वै मय ॥

—(*Mahābhārata, Sabhā-parvan*, I, 5, 9–12.)

See further details in the writer's *Indian Architecture*, p. 166, and his article on 'Ahura-Mazda and Maya-Asura' (Proceedings of the Fourth Oriental Conference), Vol. II, pp. 736–751.

[2] *J.R.A.S.*, 1915. [3] *J.R.A.S.*, pp. 405–6.

(6) That the Mauryas were Zoroastrians, the name having been derived from Persian Morva, and that they came originally from Meru, which is stated to have been situated in Persia (pp. 406, 408, 409).

(7) That Chandragupta Maurya was a Persian. Persepolis was his ancestral home (p. 409); he probably came with Alexander and was left behind to occupy the throne at Magadha, and made Persian architects build palaces after the Persian model, remains of which, even with Persian's mason's marks, are fancied to have been explored at Patna (pp. 422, 427).

(8) That the name Magadha is Persian in origin, derived from Persian Mugh or Magi (pp. 422, 427).

(9) That a portion of the *Atharva-veda*[1] containing the term, 'Magadha' must be of Persian origin (pp. 420, 421, 422).

(10) That Brahmā is not an Indian god, but an echo (or imitation) of the Zoroastrian arch-angel Vahuman (p. 449).

The obvious object of these speculations was to establish an all-round Persian influence over the Indian culture, which was no doubt older by several centuries. Spooner started with a prejudiced mind and over-enthusiasm has misled him from the field of archaeology proper to the subtle speculation of philosophy. It is needless to add that none of these theories has been worked out, and that none has found acceptance to any serious student of history.[2]

Thus there appears to be no similarity between Persia and India in civil, military, or religious architecture. In the light of all the aforesaid facts, the theory of Persian influence upon Indian architecture does no longer seem tenable. There is certainly a sort of similarity between a certain type of capital in India and Persia, that is all. But the Indian pillar as a whole, we have shown elsewhere elaborately,[3] shows affinity with the Greco-Roman order, and certain school of Indian sculpture bears the stamp of Grecian type.

In the light of all the facts briefly discussed above, merely to deal with the questions as they concern architecture, it seems impossible to think of any connexion between India and Persia.

[1] (i) That the *Garuḍa-purāṇa* also is of the Indo-Zoroastrian origin (p. 428).

(ii) That the Yoga system of Indian philosophy was derived from the Persian mummeries.

(iii) That the Tantric system and the Śakti cult of the Brahmans of Śāka-dvipa, which was the home of the Zoroastrian Magi (p. 447), were originated from the magic rites of the Persian goddess Ishtar (p. 435).

[2] For instance, compare V. A. Smith, *J.R.A.S.*, 1915, pp. 800–802.

[3] *See* the writer's *Encyclopaedia*, under Stambha (pillar); *Indian Architecture*, pp. 149–153.

APPENDIX II

THE FUTURE OF INDIAN ARCHITECTURE[1]

IN THE WAKE of political evolution the march of economic and social matters is natural and irresistible. Thus a movement to improve the present state of our housing and town-planning, if not our clothing and food also, should be welcome both to thinkers and practical men alike. Political freedom, just for its own sake, could have no meaning. But no real improvement can be based upon either national hatred or racial antagonism. It must proceed from an impartial study of history and a true perspective. The dictum, 'the best international is he who is profoundly national' (appearing in a circular letter from the chief organizer of a new school of Indian architecture), should be altered into 'the best national is he who is profoundly international.' For, otherwise, no real improvement can ever be effected. If our aim is nothing more than to try to revive what we had in the hoary past, irrespective of the changes the world has undergone in the meantime, we must be prepared for self-deception, both in practice and in principle. In order to be 'profoundly national' it would be impracticable, if not ungenerous and ungrateful, to start with an idea of disregarding everything foreign. It will also be a wrong policy to start with an exaggerated notion and prejudiced interpretation of historical facts. The above circular letter contains the following survey, which needs a dispassionate analysis and examination in order to realize the importance of India's past architecture and the possibilities of a future one :

'Architecture, the mother of all Arts, has been most assiduously cultivated in India through the centuries. The beginnings are found in the excavations of sites going back to a period contemporaneous with ancient Chaldea and Egypt : the ruins at Mohenjo-daro and Harappa take back the Indian Architectural tradition to 3000 B.C.'

'An artistic tradition in Hindu India carried from generation to generation as a caste craft and going back to over 2000 years, and responsible for many wonderfully magnificent structures, presents a record of which any civilization can be proud. The Turks and

[1] Originally published in the *Modern Review*, August, 1935.

Persians conquered Northern India from after A.D. 1000, and they brought some new ideas with the Muhammadan religion they professed. But they themselves became Indianized, and the great Islamic culture and art they brought merged into the Indian one, only to cause it to seek out a new path of development which culminated into the great Taj Mahal at Agra—a gem of Mogul architecture.'

'Indian domestic and religious architecture continued in a most flourishing condition up till the advent of the English and the invasion of Indian life by modern notions from Europe. In British India the native arts and crafts dwindled, owing to the craze for the new things of the West, and architecture also similarly suffered. India, it looked, was going to become a province of Europe in matters of architecture and art.'

In what sense can architecture be 'the mother of all arts'? What sort of architecture was 'most assiduously cultivated in India through the centuries' from 3000 B.C.? Which 'wonderfully magnificent structures' were carried from generation to generation as a caste-craft and going back to over 2000 years? How were the Turkish, the Persian, and the Mogul architectures 'merged into the Indian one'? Where has the 'advent of the English' destroyed the 'Indian domestic and religious architecture,' instead of the English architecture also being merged into the Indian one? And, lastly, why the 'craze for the new things of the West' 'was going' to convert 'British India' into 'a province of Europe in matters of architecture and art'? These are some of the most important questions which, raised though in an advertisement, should be clearly understood by all interested in the subject before an intelligent interest can be taken in the revival or introduction of an exclusively Indian architecture.

The denotation and connotation of the term 'architecture' must be brought home in order to adjudge the relative position of architecture with fine or refined arts—numbering some 518 according to Yaśodhara, a commentator of Vātsyāyana's *Kāmaśāstra.* Before that, the essential and exact difference between architecture on the one hand and civil engineering or mere art of building on the other hand should be made clear. The same structure, say, a railway station or a newspaper office may be built both architecturally as well as an object of mere engineering. If the main object of the railway building and the newspaper office were to supply necessary accommodation in the most convenient manner, and if no extra expenditure of money and thought were made for the sake of an artistic look or a symbolic expression, these buildings could not be designated as objects of real architecture, Indian or foreign. The artistic design and symbolic significance are not confined, it should be noted, to the external look alone.

The essence of architecture proper, however, lies in the 'fine art of designing and constructing ornamental buildings,' both externally and internally. The mere engineering buildings are not necessarily devoid of all ornaments and do not always look like godowns. However plain a builder may be, he is instinctively artistic in nature, and whatever is built by him must have some sort of art in it. But the real difference lies in the fact that, in architectural buildings like the Christian churches and the Hindu temples, the primary object is to exhibit an artistic design and a symbolic idea throughout; while in office buildings, railway station structures, and godowns, the engineering skill lies in providing required accommodation and facilities at the minimum cost. The question of utility is neither entirely ignored in temples, churches and mosques; nor are the beautifying measure, proportion, roof, ceiling, door, window, balcony, verandah, arch, porch, pillars and their mouldings deliberately turned out of the prison houses and barracks.

Architecture, thus comprehended, denotes all objects that are constructed according to a design and with an artistic finish. The guide book, like that of the Roman architect Vitruvius, upon which all western architecture is based, and the standard *Śilpa-śāstra*, like the *Mānasāra*, which has regulated all the known structures of India, have included sculptures also for discussion. Both these authorities deal almost equally with all details of the village-scheme, town-planning, fortified cities, and all the cognate subjects, such as the layout of roads, gardens, market-places, commercial ports and harbours, bridges, gateways, triumphal arches, enclosures, embankments, dams, railings, landing places, and flights of steps for hills and rivers, wells, tanks, trenches, drains, sewers, moats and similar objects. Buildings proper include religious, residential, military and commercial structures, and comprise temples, dwelling-houses, palaces, edifices and mansions, various halls and pavilions, secretariats, prison houses, hospitals for men, stables of animals, and nests for birds. Courts, compounds, blocks of larger edifices, as well as the auxiliary members and their component mouldings, are necessarily discussed. Doors, windows, verandahs and balconies, floors, roofs, domes, ceilings, pillars, arches and porches, which mostly constitute the distinguishing features of various styles in architecture, are elaborated in great detail. Articles of furniture are similarly treated, and include bedsteads, couches, tables, chairs, wardrobes, baskets, cages, nests, mills, lamps and lamp-posts. Thrones and crowns for deities and kings form a distinct branch. Personal ornaments and garments include various chains, ear-rings, armlets, anklets, foot-rings, waist-bands, jackets, headgear and footwear.

Thus architecture is, no doubt, at the root of some allied fine arts. But it can hardly be called the mother of mimicry, or jugglery, for instance. In fact, out of the five hundred and eighteen fine arts referred to above, hardly a dozen or score can at all be connected with architecture even as a sister, not to speak of as the mother.[1]

Before the next point is taken into consideration, the term 'Indian architecture' needs elucidation. Geographically, structures of whatever origin and style built anywhere and at any time in India, may bear the designation. Like modern scientific inventions, such as telegraphy, radio, gramophone, etc., architectural ornaments and styles of pillars, arches, domes, etc., migrate all over the civilized world. Thus structures with some distinguishing features of various European, Byzantine, Persian, and Mogul styles may be visible in India. They are not, however, usually designated as works of Indian architecture, which is generally understood in the restricted sense of Hindu architecture only.

If taken in this sense, the buildings and plans of towns opened out at Mohenjo-daro in Sindh and Harappa in the Punjab, which may go back to 3000 B.C. or even earlier, cannot yet be classified properly under Hindu architecture of later centuries until at least the scripts, the language, and the contents of the inscriptions have been deciphered, although, as stated above, the general plans and designs may bear a comparison with those described in the *Mānasāra*.[2]

The next source of information for the antiquity of Indian or Hindu architecture is entirely literary and is confined to the casual and scanty references found in the Vedic literature regarding the villages, towns, forts, and cities, hundred enclosures or fortifications figuratively expressed as the means for protection afforded

[1] *See* above, pp. 5–19. [2] *See* above, pp. 36–37.

by the gods, as well as stone-houses, carved stones, and brick edifices, and several articles of furniture.[1] In the *Ṛig-veda*, as quoted in Chapter II, mention is made of a sovereign 'who sits down in his substantial and elegant hall built with a thousand pillars,' and of residential houses with such pillars and said to be 'vast, comprehensive and thousand-doored.' Mitra and Varuṇa are represented[2] as occupying a 'great palace with a thousand pillars and 'a thousand gates.' Again Atri is stated[3] to have been 'thrown into a machine room with a hundred doors, where he was roasted,' and Vasishṭha desired[4] to have a three-storeyed building.

Although Muir criticizes[5] these references 'as exaggerated description of a royal residence such as the poet had seen,' they may be taken to support the contention of 'wonderfully magnificent structures going back to over 2000 years B.C.' It can also be admitted that architecture, like carpentry, weaving, and such other practical arts, was 'carried from generation to generation as a caste-craft,' when so many other professions used to be associated with one's birth. But such a condition of an art as disclosed by mere casual literary reference without any architectural details does not necessarily imply its merging capacity, which is really ensured by a settled, strong and 'profoundly' international government. The stale controversy, first between Fergusson and Rajendralal Mitra, and, subsequently, between Spooner and many modern scholars, has already been set at rest by the later archaeological finds and the discovery of architectural texts. No useful purpose will be served by re-examining the arguments so convincingly interpreted to explode the theory that whatever truly scientific and artistic architectural objects have been found in India must have been borrowed from abroad, though that source was unknown and unknowable. Hindu architecture does not seem to possess that capacity to merge in its fold whatever was introduced into India by the Persians in 500 B.C., and by the Turks, Moguls, and Pathans from A.D. 1000.

So far as the Persian architecture in Persia is concerned it is necessary to observe, as pointed out before, that not a single monument of recognizable condition was ever seen by even the earliest historians,

[1] *See* above, pp. 54–64.
[2] *Ṛig-veda*, II, 41, 5; V, 62, 6; *Atharva-veda*, III, 12; IX, 3.
[3] *Ibid.*, I, 112, 7. [4] Wilson's IV, 200. [5] *Sanskrit Text*, V, 455.

although some objects have been cleverly restored from scanty materials and fertile imagination. It has been shewn in detail in Appendix I, quoting from Herodotus (I, 121), that the Persian had 'neither images, nor temples, nor altars.' There is in India nothing like the Persian tombs divided into three portions of almost equal size. The middle and longer compartment, in conjunction with the other two forms what is called the Greek cross. It is carved architecturally into four engaged columns and a lofty double-recessed doorway, surmounted by an Egyptian gorge and a row of dentels, so as to reproduce a palace façade. The upper portion of this doorway is solid rock, but the lower section is cut away to provide an entrance to the vault excavated in the mass behind. Upon a stage the king is seen on a pedestal. Between the king and the altar floats the image of Ahura-Mazda, borne on huge wings, behind which a solar disc is roughly suggested. The Indian *stūpas*, *chaityas* and *dagobas* are entirely different monuments in appearance, measurement, and architectural details. The *atesh-gah*, having no affinity to a Hindu Buddhist, or Jain temple, is 'the sole monumental type and representative of religious architecture in Persia.' This consists of 'three altars, with very salient horns, which rise upon a block of masonry; between the pillars at the angle, two parallel flights approach laterally the landing place that led to the platform.' The remains of the plans of villages, cities, and forts are also scanty. 'When Alexander invaded the country of Persia there were no walled cities.' 'The fortification works consisted of a deep broad ditch, full of water, communicating with the Shaur and a double rampart. Behind the second rampart ran a path. . . . The enceinte was not furnished with bastions. . . . Towers had been distributed at the crenelated summits of the fortress.' This would look like the scheme adopted at Babylonia and Assyria, rather than in India. Of the civil architecture in Persia fragmentary information of certain unstoreyed halls and palaces only are available. They are divided, as stated before, into three types, the open-roofed, the walled throne-room, and inhabited palace. They were in capital cities, Ecbatana, Susa, Persepolis, and in lesser centres where the kings stopped a few days to escape from the extreme cold and heat. The restored Persian palaces and the halls, open, walled, pillared, or unstoreyed, have no substantial resemblance with the Indian buildings of the same types which have been referred to in the Vedic literature long before the Persian period. The contemporary

Indian buildings of the Persian period comprise the cities described in the *Rāmāyaṇa*, the numerous halls referred to in the *Mahābhārata*, and the *vihāra* (monastery), *ardhayoga* (bungalow type of old Bengal buildings), *prāsāda* (storeyed palaces), *harmya* (storeyed mansions comprising several rows or blocks), and *guhā* (cave-houses) which have been described in the Buddhist Vinaya text.[1] These buildings do not look like the Persian structures referred to above. The later Indian works of architecture, comprising villages, towns, forts, civil, military, and religious buildings, various articles of furniture and personal ornaments, including royal and divine crowns, etc., described in detail in our architectural texts, like the standard work *Mānasāra*, and referred to above, do not bear any resemblance to the scanty materials and the reconstructed monuments of Persia. Thus there appears to be no similarity between Persia and India in works of architecture proper. There is, however, a sort of similarity between a certain type of capitals of columns, bearing only the unicorn and bull in Persia, but with a larger variety of animals in India, including the lion and elephant, as well as man.

If Indian architecture had much merging capacity, the Muhammadan mosque would have borne the Hindu *śikhara*, and the Taj Mahal would have looked like a *dagoba*. 'The culture and art they brought could have been merged into Indian one only to cause it to seek out a new path of development,' if there were any noticeable modification of the Turkish and Mogul architecture in India for the better than it was in the lands of its origin.

The layout of existing villages and towns, and the orientation and the arrangement of dwelling-houses therein, would supply ample proof to hold the view that there was a deliberate policy of the Muslim invaders and conquerors of India to impose their own methods and principles of architecture in India. Thus, in the layout of villages and towns and in the orientation of still existing houses, the scientific principles of Hindu architecture, though more suitable for the soil and climate, are missing. 'A casual inspection of houses in cities of Bengal, Madras, Bombay, the Punjab, the United Provinces, and Bihar and Orissa may supply many convincing illustrations. Not only certain quarters of Lahore, Delhi, Meerut, Lucknow, Benares, Patna,

[1] *Mahavagga*, I, 30 4; *Chullavagga*, VI, 1, 2.

and Calcutta are named after the Pathans and the Moguls, but there are actually houses with the characteristic features of Arabian deserts and colder regions wherefrom the Moguls emerged.' These works of foreign architecture, unsuitable for the Indian climate and soil, have been rendered possible largely for political reasons. This is mostly due to the natural desire of the conquerors firmly to establish their domination and culture by removing the customs, habits, and traditions of the conquered as far as possible; and, partly, on account of the ignorance of the scientific methods of Indian architecture or a dislike to apply them in preference to their own. Thus, in muslimized structures in India are seen in abundance the Saracenic domes and arches introduced by the Muhammadans of Syria and Palestine, known as the Arab-Berber races of Northern Africa, who conquered Spain and Sicily and invaded France. In fact this style has materially affected the Hindu style in the layout of villages, towns, forts, as well as in civil buildings, instead of its being merged into the Hindu one. Byzantine architecture, introduced by the Turks of Byzantium, or Constantinople, and prevalent in the Eastern empire down to 1453, appears almost to have migrated to India, materially dispossessing the Hindu style. It is 'marked by the round arch springing from columns or piers, the dome supported upon pendentines, capitals elaborately sculptured, mosaic or other incrustations, etc.,' which are largely visible in Hindu buildings of the Muslim period in India. These features are visible not only in domestic structures of the Hindus, but they have also penetrated into some of the Hindu, Buddhist, and Jain temples of the period, belonging to western, northern, and eastern India, where the architectural traditions of the Hindus were entirely forgotten.

Thus the advent of the English in the eighteenth century could not destroy 'the Indian domestic and religious architecture,' even if they wanted to, because the domestic Hindu architecture of that time had already become largely muslimized. So far as Indian religious architecture, or the Hindu, Buddhist, and Jain temples, and monuments of Muslim origin are concerned, no traces thereof would have been found by this time if the British conquerors, instead of neglecting, not to speak of destroying, had not made an active effort to preserve them. The Preservation of Ancient Monuments Act of 1904, initiated by an Englishman, Lord Curzon, may be cited as an undisputed evidence. This fact will contrast well with the similarly undisputed marks of deliberate destruction of Hindu monuments in several places in western, northern, eastern, and central India. Many readers may have seen the condition of Somanath temple in Gujarat, the back portion of the original temple of Viśvanaṭh at Benares (the front portion whereof has been merged into a mosque), the chisel marks of destruction to remove the nose, nipple, and other pointed portions of sculptures at Ajanta, Ellora, and a hundred other places. Readers of history and Hindu culture, and of the Sanskrit, Pali, and Prakrit texts, are well aware that there would have been no traces of the manuscripts of the *Vedas*, the Buddhist and the Jain scriptures and canonical works, if, at the instance of the Indo-British Government, the early English, French, and German savants had not toiled, not only to preserve and publish them, but also to encourage and induce us to appreciate them. It was left for Sir Aurel Stein to discover and join together the full manuscripts of the Kashmir history, *Rāja-taraṅgiṇī*, from the three co-sharers of a Pandit in Kashmir, who had cut, breadthwise, the book of those manuscripts, written lengthwise on palm leaves, into three equal portions, along with other ancestral property. It was Böhtlingk and Roth who compiled the St. Petersburg Dictionary, of which Sir Monier William's and Apte's Sanskrit-English Dictionaries are but summaries, that have made the study of Sanskrit popular among most of the Indians themselves. The compiler of the Pali Dictionary was Childers, an Englishman. The writers of the histories of Indian literature are all Europeans. A retired British army officer, General Sir A. Cunningham, organized the archaeological researches in India, which alone rendered it possible to make excavations at many places like Harappa and Mohenjo-daro, the treasures whereof have supplied materials to the ungenerous critic to refer to the antiquity of Hindu architecture. It was again the English who established research centres like the Asiatic Society in India and abroad, the modern schools, colleges, and universities, and introduced the system of sending abroad Indian students for special training in cultural, scientific, and technical subjects, including engineering and architecture.

The object here is not to recount the blessings following from the 'advent of the English,' nor to make a contrast between different conquerors of India in their destructive and constructive efforts or in matters of modification, preservation, and reconstruction. The critic will be justified in accusing the English people, or the British Government in India, that they have not done all that they could do for us. But it will be untrue and incorrect to say that the 'advent of the English' has destroyed 'the Indian domestic and religious architecture.'

Who is responsible for the 'craze for new things from the West' which 'was going to convert British India into a province of Europe in matters of architecture and art,' if the statement is at all correct in some modified form? 'Craze' is certainly a subjective quality, and the desire to imitate the conquerors, whether Muslim, English or, French, is a historical fact and a usual weakness of all the conquered and subjugated peoples of the world. The British Government in India have no more compelled us than the earlier conquerors to take to their mode of living. If certain quarters of some big cities in British India have been turned into a 'province of Europe in matter of architecture,' and if certain so-called highly placed Indian families have developed a preference for European art, our own 'craze' for blind imitation is solely responsible for that.

The following complaint contained in the same document is substantially true, though incomplete:

'There is no institution in modern India where Indian youths can get proper training, either theoretical or practical, in the complex subject of Indian architecture. The very descendants of traditional architects and craftsmen, not to speak of the civil engineers trained in modern engineering institutions, owing to their deplorable ignorance of the history and spirit of Indian architecture due to lack of proper education, have failed to develop their indigenous architecture and have introduced ugly and hybrid styles, unfaithful to Indian traditions.'

The aesthetic sense of individuals differs, though in architecture there is a general standard of beauty. According to the standard treatises of Europe and of India the architectural beauty is largely dependent upon proportionate measurement of dimensions, disposition of component members and types of verandahs, balconies, doors, windows, arches, porches, parapets and domes. The aspect of the site and orientation of the buildings, together with the layout of surrounding courtyards, lawns and gardens, add to the beauty and utility alike.

The incompleteness of the complaint lies in the omission of the authority and authenticity of the source of information on these essential features of Indian architecture. It is again due to the British Government in India and the highly placed English officials, ungenerously and falsely accused of having destroyed Indian architecture, who have made available the archaeological materials and the original texts on architecture, the most authenticated sources of information on all architectural and allied subjects for critical study and reconstruction of our forgotten architecture and cognate arts. The establishment of the Archaeological Department itself is an innovation in India. The Bill introduced in the Assembly by an English Home Member, Sir Basil Blackett, to establish a permanen fund to carry on the work of the Archaeological Department could not be passed owing to the opposition of our own representatives. Under such adverse circumstances the distinguished Director General of Archaeology, Sir John Marshall, again an Englishman, a real scholar and lover of Indian culture, was the first and foremost to realize that no reconstruction of real Indian architecture is possible from the scanty archaeological remains, and that it could be done only with the assistance to be derived from the literary sources and numerous architectural texts if they could be scientifically edited, translated and illustrated. The architectural tradition, as truly said, has been lost. The professional craftsmen have all but disappeared. The terms of the *Śilpa-śāstras*, frequently referred to in the scriptures, *Purāṇas*, *Āgamas*, and all other branches of literature, had become unintelligible, obscure, and obsolete. Thus some Indian student possessing sufficient knowledge of our classics and several modern vernaculars, conversant with the principles of philology, and thoroughly educated in Indian history, culture, and archaeology had to be found, after much searching, for special training and experience abroad to tackle these valuable treasures, left so far unrecognized, neglected, and unutilized. The result has been the publication by the Government of the United Provinces, with the substantial assistance rendered by the Secretary of State for India and the Government of India, through the Oxford University Press, of seven volumes, covering some 5,000 quarto pages, dealing with the whole subject thoroughly and in a scientific manner. They comprise not only the standard text—the *Mānasāra*—its translation into English, and illustrations of architectural and sculptural objects described therein, but also an

Encyclopaedia of Hindu Architecture which will enable students, builders, engineers, and architects to study the original texts and the archaeological records that are gathered together therein, according to their own light, and, an introductory volume dealing with a historical survey of all architectural evidences of the past and finally the present volume, which will enable all unprejudiced readers to form a true perspective and which may remove ignorance and false notions from the mind of the professional misleaders.

A careful study of these volumes is indispensable in order to understand fully the methods and principles, rules and regulations, as well as the essential features of real Indian architecture. For without full and accurate knowledge the adaptability of Hindu architecture to modern conditions and requirements will either be lost sight of, or an ugly hybrid mixture will be inevitable.

A rigorous purity of style need not be strictly adhered to for practical or asthetic reasons. Such a conservative spirit may only gratify a profoundly national bigot. It cannot enhance the real importance of a great national art. Even to preserve artistic design and symbolic significance it will not be a practical proposition to lose sight of the adaptability of Hindu architecture for modern requirements. For neither the aspect of the existing towns and villages which have been haphazardly laid out, owing to political reasons, nor the external orientation and internal disposition of dwelling-houses erected unscientifically, owing to social and economic conditions, can be materially altered unless a catastrophe like an earthquake occurs frequently. Both commonsense and the ancient authorities, however, emphasize the aspect of sites and the orientation of buildings as the most essential factors in architecture. Provided the scientific calculation of strength and harmony and proportion of the component and auxiliary members, on which both stability and beauty depend, be maintained, there can be no harm if there be a modification by addition, omission, or alteration of the pillars and pilasters, doors and windows, arches and porches, balconies and verandahs, steps and staircases, parapets and crowning domes in order to suit different tastes and purses. Mouldings and ornamental sculptures are objects of individual taste and can be altered if the modification does not lead to incongruity.

It is this incongruity that has disfigured the residential buildings in the Lake area in Calcutta, decorated with ornaments and sculptures borrowed from Ajanta and Ellora caves. It is objectionable on this ground, more than anything else, to build residential houses with the figure of Gaṇeśa on the gateway or an elephant on the landing, a hospital building with a hawk on the front parapet or a school building with a monkey on the top, intending them to pass as productions of Hindu architecture in order to gratify the heart's craving of the enthusiastic builders for an Indian style. Self-deception is preferable to deliberate cheating, even if the latter is practised owing to ignorance. Some builders are natural architects, and they prefer their own design based entirely on the inspiration of an uneducated mind. Engineers and architects are not to blame for such architecture, which is very common in India. There can be no objection if a layman builder, though untrained, having studied or seen the objects of architecture in different countries, makes a choice or combination of styles in his own building in a place where there is no municipal board to sanction the plan. But it will be unfortunate if some innocent business magnate of Calcutta or Bombay finds, on completion of his house, that he was misled to believe by his advisers that his proposed residence will prove to be a fine piece of original architecture, though it may not follow any one method or principle and though it may consist of a porch from one country, a dome from another, office room and library from a third one, kitchen and dining-room from another country, and gardens and outhouses from a fifth place. Still more objectionable, even on moral grounds, would it be to cheat an enthusiastic builder that the Hindu style is nothing more or less than the monkey brand; or to give a misdirection to a profoundly nationalistic municipal corporation that the cause of the national architecture could be advanced only by discarding all that may look like English in the city plan, in laying out roads, and in sanctioning permission to independent private builders within their jurisdiction.

Insufficient and inaccurate knowledge, and an unjustifiable prejudice against everything English, appear to be at the root of the following quotation from the 'Prospectus of the first All-India Exhibition of Indian Architecture,' held in the Senate House of the University of Calcutta. 'By modern Indian architecture is meant the development of old Indian styles of architecture,' which is elucidated by expressly excluding all structures built after the British pattern by saying, 'that existed in India before the termination of the Mogul rule, but adopted to suit modern Indian requirements, viz., sanitation, economy, utility, etc.'

It is needless to repeat what has been shown above, that nothing much of real Hindu village, town, or dwelling-house remained intact before the termination of the Mogul rule. All that survived comprise a few temples of later dates in the South, where the Muslim domination did not spread far and wide. Even in the South the civil architecture has been modified to suit the needs of villagers, who became largely converted to Christianity more through non-British agencies of other European conquerors. Thus, before the termination of the Mogul rule, what remained of civil architecture was exclusively of Muhammadan origin. If, therefore, in order to modernize Indian architecture, the British patterns are to be excluded, it will be necessary to demolish and rebuild not only the Viceregal palace at New Delhi and all the Council halls, secretariat buildings and offices in central and provincial towns, but also the bridges, railways, schools, colleges, universities, art galleries, museums, hospitals, maternity homes, down to the prison houses and lunatic asylums. Will the reform, if at all possible from the scanty materials of such structures that can be reconstructed from the Persian, Turkish, Pathan and Mogul patterns alone, the knowledge of the Hindu source being absent, satisfy our sanitary, economic, and utilitarian requirements?

All interested in the revival of an Indian architecture must learn to distinguish its essential features from the unessential ones. And they must know what can be absorbed for our own advantage from not only the Muslim and the British styles but also from all the known and scientific methods that the civilized peoples of the world have evolved after long experience and repeated experiments. For, otherwise, India cannot expect to be modernized in architecture.

APPENDIX III

WHAT OTHERS THINK

OBSERVATIONS ON MĀNASĀRA ARCHITECTURE

DR. RABINDRANATH TAGORE[1]

ORDINARILY RESEARCH SCHOLARS seem to ignore the fact that the past is of interest to us only in so far as it was living, and that, unless they discover it for us in such a way as to make us feel its life, we may admire them for their patience and industry, but will not be the wiser for their labours. I have often felt sad that so much human talent and industry should disappear in the publication of matter where bones keep on rattling without forming for us an outline of the figure that once moved. I, therefore, cannot help congratulating Dr. P. K. Acharya of the Allahabad University for his great work *Mānasāra.* I am not qualified to pronounce judgment on ancient Indian architecture, but I can say this much that the learned author has succeeded in re-fashioning for us, out of the debris of the past, a picture of the forms of ancient architecture which, while it speaks much for his scholarly equipment, has the additional merit of interesting us in a real human way. The indirect glimpses it gives into the life of the people whose architecture he discusses are something for which his readers will have reasons to be grateful to him.

DR. C. Y. CHINTAMANI, D.LITT., D.L., EDITOR OF THE LEADER[2]

Dr. P. K. Acharya, Professor of Sanskrit, University of Allahabad, deserves high praise and warm congratulations on producing, as the result of seventeen years of devoted and self-denying effort, a truly monumental work on Hindu architecture, comprising no fewer than five volumes. The first volume is *A Dictionary of Hindu Architecture* ; the

[1] The *Visva Bharati Quarterly*, May—July, 1935, p. 115.
[2] The *Leader*, 6th August, 1933.

second, *Indian Architecture according to Mānasāra Śilpa-śāstra*; the third, *Mānasāra*—Sanskrit Text with Critical Notes; the fourth, *Architecture of Mānasāra*—translation in English, and the fifth, *Architecture of Mānasāra*—Plates I to CXXXV (Architectural) and CXXXVII to CLVII (Sculptural).

Dr. Acharya is richly qualified for the laborious task which he undertook in a spirit of dedication. He is an M. A. of Calcutta, a Ph. D. of Leyden, and Doctor in Literature of London. He is a member of the Indiân Educational Service whose services were lent to the University of Allahabad for engagement as Professor of Sanskrit. He has so won the regard and confidence of his colleagues of the University that he has for years been the Head of the Oriental Departments and also Dean of the Faculty of Arts. To his students he has been remarkably considerate and helpful, and, without sacrificing the demands of discipline and efficiency, has made himself deservedly popular among them.

For the production of the big work under notice, Dr. Acharya spared no pains whatsoever. He has discovered unknown ways and learnt new things 'after bitter experience and elaborate experiments.'

'The vast store of literature on the subject, and the inscriptions and other archaeological records have had to be ransacked. Extensive tours in company with trained architects and engineers have had to be undertaken, involving great expenditure of time, money, and convenience, from Landikotal on the borders of Afghanistan to Ramesvaram in the south, from Mohenjodaro in Sindh to Shillong in Assam, in order to examine ancient monuments throughout the country, including the cave-temples of Western and Central India, the monuments of the Indian States in Rajputana and Hyderabad, the hill temples of Kedarnath, Badrinath, Tunganath, etc. An encyclopaedic dictionary has had to be compiled wherein, for the first time, an attempt has been made to settle the meaning of, and explain in English, some three thousand technical terms by illustrative quotations from cognate literature. In addition, some two hundred measured drawings, diagrams, and sketches in line and in colours have had to be prepared at great trouble and expense.'

'Thus,' says Dr. Acharya, 'the peculiar pain of giving "rebirth" to a once fully-grown "barbarous" child of unknown origin has been brought home to the writer. The youthful enthusiasm has been put to a great trial through the continuous struggle for seventeen years. With great diffidence, therefore, this curious child is presented to the learned world. If received with sympathy and kindness even such a child may thrive and bring some solace to everybody responsible for and interested in it.' Dr. Acharya's diffidence does credit to his modesty. His work is the product of such uncommon scholastic zeal and enthusiasm, and of such rare merit that, we are quite sure, the learned author's sacrifice will be rewarded not merely by the appreciation of competent judges, but by 'lasting benefit' to the country. Dr. Acharya is right to hold that 'our architectural policy of the past few hundred years, based as it has been on foreign imitation, and in an entirely different climate and soil, has not proved quite successful in regard to temples and humble dwelling-houses, if not in regard to public edifices also.' We earnestly share Dr. Acharya's hope. To the layman, quite a new world, as it were, of India's greatness in a sphere of national life which has been comparatively neglected, is opened by our author's *magnum opus*. As we read Dr. Acharya's pages we are filled with wonder, admiration, and pride that the twin subjects of architecture and sculpture were treated with such scientific thoroughness and precision by our remote ancestors. And yet, we are the people who are condemned, by the arrogance of a ruling race, as unworthy of constructing the ugly barracks which our Public Works Department glories in putting up at extravagant cost to the tax-payer.

In undertaking and executing the present work, Dr. Acharya has had to combine in himself the triple office of editor, translator, and commentator; and he has wisely followed the sound rule: 'let an editor give what there is, and let the commentator say what might be and what ought to be.' Dr. Acharya placed before himself the following dictum for his guidance: 'What the learned world demand of us in India is to be quite certain of our data, to place the monumental record before them exactly as it now exists, and to interpret it faithfully and literally.' This he has successfully followed.

The seventy chapters (of the *Mānasāra*) deal with such varied subjects as the qualifications of architects, the selection of sites, the examination of soil, site-plans, the village, town-planning, forts, the dimensions of buildings, the bases and pedestals of columns, the features of buildings (one-storeyed to twelve-storeyed), courts, temples, pavilions, mansions, dwelling-houses, royal palaces, bedsteads and swings, thrones, arches, theatres, ornamental trees, crowns, altars, personal ornaments, furniture, various kinds of images and penalties for defective construction. No wonder that the author thinks that, like the medical works, this is ' the most practical of Sanskrit treatises ' He re-affirms ' the hope that a trial may be given to its method and principles, its rules and regulations, because the foreign imitation in architecture for a millennium has proved more or less unsuccessful and uneconomical.'

It is encouraging and pleasing to find that Dr. Acharya's great effort has won commendation from such men as Dr. Keith, Mr. Havell, Dr. Abanindra Nath Tagore, Dr. A. K. Coormaraswamy, Dr. Ganganatha Jha, Prof. Thomas, Sir Claude de la Fosse, Dr. Sten Knonow, Mr. K. N. Dikshit, Dr. Kali Das Nag, and several antiquarian journals. We may be permitted to quote, as typical of opinion generally, the following passage from Dr. Coomaraswamy's learned review in the *Journal of the American Oriental Society* :

' These two volumes, the latter (*Dictionary*) especially, are monumental works, and will be indispensable to every student of Indian architecture and realia. Only those who work along these lines will realize the great labour involved in the preparation of such books, especially when they are almost the first of their kind. The serious study of the Indian *Śilpa-śāstra* has been too long delayed, and a warm welcome may be extended to the Professor's undertaking.'

One last word. It is a pleasure for us to be able to acknowledge the uniform and ungrudging encouragement and assistance which the Government of the United Provinces, the Government of India, and other governments and a number of high-placed officials gave to Dr. Acharya to enable him to continue and complete his most admirable work. We once more congratulate the learned author.

PROFESSOR A. BERRIEDALE KEITH, D.C.L., D.LITT.[1]

Professor Prasanna Kumar Acharya has now completed his study of Hindu Achitecture by adding to his *Dictionary of Hindu Architecture* and *Indian Architecture according to Mānasāra Śilpa-śāstra*, the Sanskrit text of the *Mānasāra*, edited with critical notes, a translation in English

[1] The *Modern Review*, Calcutta, January, 1936.

of the Architecture of *Mānasāra*, and a collection of 157 illustrated plates in line and colour.

Full recognition has already been accorded by all students of Indian Art and Science to the fundamental value of Professor Acharya's earlier contributions to the elucidation of the Sanskrit texts on architecture, and the invaluable character of his *Dictionary* is admitted on all hands. The three new volumes which are now available form an indispensable part of his undertaking. They present the material on which the results stated in his earlier works were based, and they afford the means for further investigation into the many obscure issues which still remain to be solved. It is almost impossible to exaggerate the difficulties of producing a satisfactory text of such a work as the *Mānasāra*. It has been necessary to prepare the edition from eleven manuscripts, not one of which presents a readable or trustworthy text. It is clear, however, that, even if we had much older manuscripts than those which have been preserved, we would still find a text written in very defective Sanskrit. It is plain that the writers on technical science, whether medicine, or mathematics, or architecture, were far from being proficient in Sanskrit, and, after making all those conjectures which the state of the manuscripts renders legitimate, we are left with a text which, in many places, not merely violates the rules of Sanskrit grammar, but offers the most serious difficulty of translation. The editor has most wisely shown the utmost caution in his reconstruction of the text. He has made such amendments only as are indispensable for the constitution of an intelligible text; he has marked these clearly in the text itself and he has given in full all real various readings in his authorities. It is most improbable that any manuscripts will ever come to light which will enable us substantially to improve the style of the *Mānasāra*.

The translation of a work of this type presents endless difficulties, and the utmost credit is due to the author for the energy with which he has reckoned with the problems presented by the text. Even the most cursory examination shows how impossible it is without the aid of the translation and the explanations given in the *Dictionary* to understand with any precision the directions of the text. An indispensable adjunct to the translation and the *Dictionary* alike is afforded by the volume of illustrations of architectural and structural objects. It is impossible to exaggerate the importance of this feature of the work. The author describes the difficulties which he experienced in obtaining the means of producing these illustrations, and our most grateful thanks are due to Mr. H. Hargreaves, who placed at the disposal of Professor Acharya the services of Mr. S. C. Mukherji, a graduate in Sanskrit, who had received training in the methods and principles of Græco-Roman and modern architecture. The material is now available for an investigation of the question whether the extant monuments of Hindu architecture are based on the methods and principle which are set forth in the *Mānasāra.* It is interesting to note that the greatest difficulties were experienced in securing the services of a Śilpin to supply the sculptural drawings in line and in colours. It is hoped that the same artist may be available to execute the remaining sculptural drawings, some three hundred in number.

The labour involved in this great work has been lightened by the encouragement of many scholars, and it will be of particular interest to see whether his work in making available the true doctrines of the ancient Hindu authorities can be turned to practical benefit for India and for its people. The Ruler of Oundh, whose interest in Indian culture and art is well known from his contributions to the great edition of the *Mahābhārata*, intends to build a house according to the directions of the *Mānasāra*, and it may well be that modern India has something to learn in this as in other matters from the achievements of its past.

H. Hargreaves, Esq., lately the Director General of Archaeological Survey, Government of India[1]

These publications are the third, fourth, and fifth volumes of an *Encyclopaedia of Hindu Architecture* of which the first two volumes—*A Dictionary of Hindu Architecture* and *Indian Architecture according to the Mānasāra Śilpa-śāstra*—were published in 1927 and reviewed at length in the *Journal* for October, 1928.

In the third volume, Dr. Acharya now gives the complete Sanskrit text (based on eleven manuscripts written in five different scripts), as well as 315 pages of notes in English, from which an idea may be obtained of the imperfect condition of the available manuscripts. The fourth volume is the English translation, and, considering the

[1] *Journal of the Royal Asiatic Society*, London, October, 1935, pp. 777-9.

material on which it is based, the author has, on the whole, been successful in giving an understandable and readable text, though naturally obscurities are not entirely absent. The suggestion that the usefulness of the *Mānasāra* would be enhanced by illustrating it has been met by Dr. Acharya, who has issued the fifth volume as a collection of 157 plates. For the preparation of these drawings he has enlisted the assistance of K. S. Siddhalinga Swamy, a Silpin, working according to the tradition of the *Śilpa-śāstras* and whose illustrations of images and other objects are very successful, particularly his eleven coloured plates. For the illustrations of the architectural drawings Dr. Acharya is indebted in the main to Mr. S. C. Mukherji, whose knowledge of Sanskrit and training in architecture has enabled him to contribute 121 line-drawings of a suggestive and helpful nature. None of the drawings appears to have been based on either ancient remains or existing structures.

The importance of this *Encyclopaedia of Hindu Architecture* will be generally admitted, and Dr. Acharya is to be congratulated on the successful termination of his prolonged labours, in which he has displayed not only scholarship, but industry and indomitable perseverance. His work is, indeed, 'not the end but the beginning of a new line of Indology' and it will now be for Indian architects, archaeologists, and students of Indian arts and crafts to examine to what extent the principles laid down in the *Mānasāra* represent those of medieval Hindu architecture and art, and to consider if they are suitable for modern practice, for philologists to suggest solutions of the problems revealed by the textual imperfections, and for Sanskrit lexicographers to avail themselves of the technical terms now, for the first time, made available by the complete text.

MAHAMAHOPADHYAYA PT. GANGANATHA JHA, M.A., D.LITT., D.L.[1]

These are the three concluding volumes of the monumental work on *Mānasāra*, by the Allahabad Professor. The first two volumes—(1) *A Dictionary of Indian Architecture*, and (2) *Indian Architecture according to Mānasāra Śilpa-śāstra*—appeared a few years ago and have been appreciated by the world of scholars, as evinced by the fact that the gifted author is already preparing a second edition.

[1] *Modern Review*, April, 1934.

The third volume of the series, which is no. (1) of the three volumes under review contains the original text of the *Mānasāra* with (*a*) full alphabetical index and (*b*) critical notes. The original text of the treatise is so notoriously and hopelessly corrupt that credit is due to Dr. Acharya for having provided a readable text. Anachronisms and grammatical anomalies in which the text abounds are the common feature of many Sanskrit treatises on technical subjects,—such as Medicine and Astronomy-Astrology. But the text of *Mānasāra* is full of other defects as well. It must have cost the editor immense labour and not a little ingenuity to prepare a neat and readable text. The critical notes bear ample testimony to this.

The *Mānasāra*, it seems, was not meant by the author, whoever he was, to be a scholarly and scientific treatise; it appears to have been meant as a handbook for the guidance of practical builders and architects. This is the only explanation that we can find for the more-than-ordinary 'barbarous Sanskrit' in which the work has been described as having been written. This is also indicated by the fact that the author's name is nowhere mentioned; and it is difficult to find out who the author was. Like many encyclopaedic works, it has been attributed by pandits to the great Scholar-King Bhojadeva of Dhara.

This leads us on to the second of the three volumes under notice—which forms Volume IV of the series. Here, in the Preface, we are told in regard to the authorship of the original that, 'up till now, no tangible argument or proof has been found as to the possibility of the treatise being the compilation of a number of authors, instead of a single individual.' There is thus a lot of uncertainty on this point, and the only reasonable view to take at present appears to be the one hinted at in this sentence. It is a practical handbook, added to from time to time as experience dictated. This also will account for the diversity of language and style.

This volume contains a complete English translation of the original, with full alphabetical indices of Sanskrit and English terms. The translation is accurate and at the same time readable by itself, which cannot be said of most of our translations, which lose much of their readability through an attempt at literalness. Dr. Acharya has sailed clear of this difficulty and has succeeded in giving us a translation which can be read and understood by itself.

Some idea of the magnitude of the task to which Dr. Acharya set himself twenty years ago may be formed from the contents of the work. The whole work consists of seventy chapters, dealing with all the minute details relating to house-building, such as qualifications of architects, selection of site, erection of the gnomons for the orientation of buildings (a matter which is very badly understood by present-day builders), site-plans, village- and town- and fort-planning, dimensions, foundation, pedestal, columns, roofs, joinery and general features. All these are dealt with in relation to buildings of one to twelve storeys—(it seems we had sky-scrapers in ancient times). Next follow chapters dealing with royal palaces, royal entourage, cars, chariots, furniture, thrones, arches, central theatre and crowns. Lastly, there come temples and images, separate chapters being assigned to Jaina images, Buddhist images, images of sages, the comparative measures of images. Special chapters are also devoted to the casting of idols in wax and the chiselling of the eye. There are penalties also for defective construction.

The last volume of the series supplies elaborate plates providing full illustrations (drawn to scale) of architectural and sculptural objects. These are likely to be extremely useful to the extensive town- and village-planning that is going to be undertaken in Bihar. It represents the practical outcome of the experience of centuries, and is likely to be more adapted to the climatic conditions of the country than the ideas derived from experience in other climes and other countries.

While congratulating Dr. Acharya on the completion of his monumental work, one cannot resist the temptation of requesting him to bring out, in course of the present year, if possible (in view of the likelihood of its being useful in the rebuilding of Bihar), a smaller volume containing, in brief, the main conclusions, specially those relating to the planning of villages and towns and the building of houses. This volume should not contain more than 200 or 250 pages. The utility of the work would be immensely enhanced if a Hindi translation also appeared simultaneously with the English version.

Ramananda Chatterjee, Esq., Editor, Modern Review[1]

As many towns and villages in Bihar will have to be reconstructed, all those who are directly and indirectly connected with the work of reconstruction should have their attention drawn to the ancient

[1] *Modern Review*, April and May, 1934.

Indian ideas of village-planning, town-planning, and architecture in general. They are to be found in Professor Dr. P. K. Acharya's masterly edition of the ancient standard Sanskrit work *Mānasāra* in five sumptuous volumes. Those who do not know Sanskrit need not think that the work will not be of any use to them. For Dr. Acharya has given a full English translation of the work with critical notes. There are also numerous plates, which will help architects, engineers, and builders in their work.

European architecture has not been a complete success in India either from the artistic or from the economic point of view. We should give a trial to our own architectural rules and plans, which were not crude but scientific.

As the Government and non-official relief societies and the Maharajadhiraj of Darbhanga are going to spend lakhs of rupees, they would do well to spend a very much smaller sum to purchase copies of this work, for the preparation and publication of which the author has received encouragement and assistance from the Government of India, the Government of the United Provinces, and other Governments, and some high officials. The work has been published by the Oxford University Press.

It has been reported in the papers that in Nepal old temples, constructed according to ancient Indian methods, have not suffered so much from the earthquake as more modern buildings. There is reason to believe that buildings on the *Mānasāra* plans and methods would be durable and beautiful, as well as comparatively inexpensive.

The patriotism of Mahatma Gandhi, Pandit Madan Mohan Malaviya, Babu Rajendra Prasad, and other leaders need not be referred to. But it is not to their or anybody else's patriotism that it is necessary to appeal. The appeal is to common sense. And the common-sense view is that an elaborate and practical handbook of architecture, which has come down from antiquity and which embodies the age-long experience of many experts, native to the soil and the climate, should at least be given a trial. To dismiss it without such trial, is to insult ourselves as well as our ancestors. Of course, there should be adaptations to modern conditions, wherever necessary. The first two volumes of this monumental work were published in 1927 and were highly appreciated by savants and artists in India and abroad. They were reviewed in our Bengali magazine *Prabasi* and in the *Modern Review*.

Mānasāra is universally recognized as the standard Hindu treatise on Hindu architecture. But it has not hitherto been completely published after critical editing, nor comprehensively treated otherwise. A complete translation into English was also wanting. Its technical terms and 'barbarous' Sanskrit presented difficulties even to professional Indologists. Dr. Acharya has, after years of devoted labour, succeeded in overcoming these difficulties to a sufficient extent to be able to finish his work and thus to open up a new line of research. Scholars and the general public will be thankful to him for this service. There has been for some time a disposition on the part of a section at least of the Indian public to favour Indian architecture. But there has not been much definite and scientific knowledge of what that architecture stood for. Dr. Acharya's work will enlighten architects, engineers and craftsmen.

FREDERICK GRUBB, ESQ.[1]

Dr. Prasanna Kumar Acharya, I.E.S., Professor of Sanskrit in the University of Allahabad, has placed all scholars and researchers who are interested in Indian archaeology under a great obligation by the completion and publication of his monumental work on the *Mānasāra* architecture. Under instructions from the Government of the United Provinces the same author compiled some years ago *A Dictionary of Hindu Architecture*, together with a second volume on the same subject according to *Mānasāra Śilpa-śāstra*. Dictionaries available previous to that date, whether in Sanskrit, English or any other language, did not adequately explain the architectural terms of a remote past. For hundreds of years the texts of the *Vāstu-śāstras* had remained unexplored, waiting for someone possessed of the necessary erudition and industry to provide students with a dictionary which should enable them to make effective use of these unique manuscripts.

Since then Dr. Acharya has devoted a great deal of his time to the preparation of the three supplementary volumes recently published by the Oxford University Press.

The work as a whole comprises a comprehensive encyclopaedia of what to most people must be a rather abstruse subject. It includes

[1] (1) *Hindu* (Educational and Literary Supplement), 17th July, 1934. (2) *Tribune*, 20th July, 1934. (3) *Leader*, 23rd August. (4) *Hindustan Times*, 3rd September, 1934.

a scholarly introduction, the original text, English translation and 157 plates in line and in colour.

It is not too much to say that in the production of this great work in its present form Dr. Acharya has had to surmount myriads of difficulties, and he has apparently done so with remarkable success. No one would undertake a task of this magnitude except as a labour of love, for it is obvious that there could be no material return at all commensurate with the amount of work involved, covering as it has done in this case a period of seventeen years. When we remember other exacting duties which must fall to the lot of the Head of the Sanskrit Department (who is also the Dean of the Faculty of Arts) in a modern university, it is astonishing that Professor Acharya should have been able to accomplish his task so successfully. To decipher worn out manuscripts and to translate the technical terms into their English equivalent are alone worthy of great praise. But to illustrate the text with so many carefully-selected and well-executed sketches, diagrams and measured drawings is indeed a colossal achievement.

The canons and scientific precision of Hindu art and architecture are brought out so admirably in these volumes that the theme need no longer be looked upon as unintelligible, either by scholars or by the general inquirer. To the Western reader they ought to bring a new understanding of architecture in ancient India, for they open a means of approach hitherto unknown in this branch of study.

The final volume of sketches and drawings helps to make clear the main contents of the *Mānasāra.* It speaks in a language that will be universally understood, and the work as a whole should facilitate the classification of Indian architecture in general. Both the northern style and its southern counterpart are very well brought out in Dr. Acharya's work, though special reference to one or the other is limited. The unity of the whole is thereby emphasized, and even without technical knowledge of the subject the ordinary reader should be enabled to grasp something of the significance of Hindu art. Laws which have remained too long unwritten are now brought to light for the instruction of this generation in an ancient culture.

Professor Acharya acknowledges the co-operation in the production of this work of such outstanding international scholars as Dr. F. W. Thomas, Dr. L. D. Barnett, and Dr. J. Ph. Vogel, whose interest in the undertaking is a further testimony to its scientific importance. What the learned world demands from India in these matters is certainty of data, and this has undoubtedly been supplied as a result of the author's prolonged research. The *Mānasāra* manuscripts are in a class by themselves and they have now been given to the world in a form which must be of permanent value. All students of the arts of ancient India should feel greatly indebted to Dr. Acharya for the illumination which he has thrown upon a comparatively unknown branch of Sanskrit study. The five volumes together are certainly a notable contribution to the available literature on the subject, and their compiler deserves every congratulation on the completion of his task.

I ought perhaps to add that some acknowledgment is due to the Government of the United Provinces for the practical support which has been given to Dr. Acharya's research and the publication of its results. There ought to be no doubt as to the proper recognition of this work by the local educational authorities and universities in India. There is no other country in the world so rich in ancient lore of this character, and every encouragement should be given to the production and utilization of works which cannot but enhance the status of India in the realms of art and literature.

Professor J. Ph. Vogel, Leyden University, Holland[1]

It is now more than a century ago that the well-known *Essay on the Architecture of the Hindus*, by Ram Raz, Native Judge and Magistrate at Bangalore, was published. This book, which appeared after the author's death, was mainly a summary of a Sanskrit work on architecture, called *Mānasāra.* Ram Raz's Essay is a treatise of sixty-four pages, illustrated by means of forty-eight plates.

In the year 1914 a young Sanskrit scholar from Bengal, Mr. Prasanna Kumar Acharya, 'induced by youthful enthusiasm,' undertook the gigantic task of editing and translating the standard work on Indian architecture of which Ram Raz had only published a résumé. The Essay is, moreover, based on a single manuscript containing only fifty-eight chapters, whereas the whole *Vāstu-śastra* now published consists of seventy chapters.

It has taken Dr. Acharya more than twenty years to complete this enormous task, and he deserves no less credit for the perseverance with which he has carried it through than for the enthusiasm which

[1] Ex. *Actorum Orientalium*, Volumine XIV, Excerptum, pp. 224–25.

first induced him to undertake it. In 1918 he published a *Summary of the Mānasāra* as his Doctor's Thesis at the University of Leyden. In 1927 he brought out his *Dictionary of Hindu Architecture* and his *Indian Architecture according to Mānasāra Śilpa-śāstra*, both preliminary to the three final volumes, published in 1934, which consist of the Sanskrit text with appendices, index and critical notes (altogether more than 800 pages), the English translation with a copious index (another volume of some 800 pages), and a fifth volume of 157 partly coloured plates. These plates, it should be understood, do not form part of the original work; they have been prepared by three modern draughtsmen who have performed their task with considerable skill.

Dr. Acharya's edition of the *Mānasāra* is based on no less than eleven manuscripts, a full account of which will be found in his Preface. It is only the extent of the text which rendered the editor's task a laborious one. Owing to the nature of the subject, the work teems with technical terms known neither from ordinary literature nor from the *kosas*, and, consequently, sometimes very difficult to explain. But what is worse, it is couched in a language which has been rightly described as 'barbarous.' The text presented by the manuscripts (none of which is ancient) cannot be considered as correct. The editor is no doubt correct in assuming 'that the *Mānasāra* was never written in a chaste language and that its imperfections are original.' The same is true of other *Śilpa-śāstras*, as was pointed out by Bühler many years ago. It seems that works of this kind were composed by craftsmen who were moved by the ambition of writing Sanskrit without possessing the necessary knowledge of that difficult language. In these circumstances it is not surprising that the meaning of several passages is obscure and the translation uncertain. Moreover, none of the manuscripts contains any commentary, drawings, diagrams, or sketches.

Dr. Acharya presents his work with a laudable modesty. He regards the appearance of it only as a beginning of the study of the subject and there can be little doubt that it is bound to render great services to anyone engaged in the investigation of ancient Indian architecture. . . .

We have, therefore, every reason to be grateful to Dr. Acharya for the valuable work which he has accomplished at the expense of so much time and exertion.

RAJASEVASAKTA RAO BAHADUR S. KRISHNASWAMI AIYANGAR, M.A., PH.D.[1]

We welcome the publication of this monumental work on the architecture of the Hindus by Professor Prasanna Kumar Acharya of the Allahabad University. Professor Acharya has been engaged in the study of this subject ever since he obtained the Government of India scholarship to proceed to Europe, and has produced, as a result of his twenty years' study, five voluminous works on Hindu architecture.

It seems to be quite an accidental coincidence that this magnificent work on the *Mānasāra* should have been brought out almost at the centenary of its first notice in the *Journal of the Asiatic Society* of Great Britain and Ireland by Rama Raz, the talented pioneer in this field of work. Rama Raz was a typical product of the nineteenth century, and his work, practically the last one, as he died before the work was actually out, had to be brought out, such as it was, under disadvantages and difficulties that he had to overcome, quite comparable to those that Professor Acharya had actually to surmount. Rama Raz's notice was based upon the few scattered chapters, and from a few manuscripts collected from here and there, and put together not by any successful effort at translation, but by what could more or less be guessed at by references to living workmen and extant buildings, with such assistance as could be got from *pandits* whose knowledge of the science was by no means profound. Having regard to the disadvantage under which this first work was published, it must be regarded as a very creditable performance, even from the vantage point of our possession of the whole text and the far superior equipment that we have for understanding and appreciating the work as a whole.

The work *Mānasāra* is regarded, even among architectural works, as one of high authority. Among architectural works so far available, this is undoubtedly the most comprehensive and consists of seventy chapters, of which the first eight are devoted to preliminaries. The next forty-two deal with buildings as such, the remaining chapters being devoted to sculpture and iconography. The introductory matter consists really of the invocation to the gods and *rishis* who seem to be called

[1] *Journal of Indian History*, Vol. XIII, Part I, April, 1934.

by the name Mānasāra, which again would mean only *rishis* expert in architecture. The next one has to deal with measurements, qualifications of the architects and so on. The third has reference to the divisions of the subject. The next two chapters deal with characteristics of the soil and the selection of suitable sites for various classes of buildings. In these chapters, the soil test and the quality required for particular buildings are treated with sufficient elaboration for various kinds of buildings. Chapter VI deals with the orientation of buildings, in the course of which the principles of mechanics and gnomon, that is dial, etc., are described. The following chapter (VII) deals with site-plans. Thirty-two schemes of these are given, divided into squares for various purposes of structure. The section concludes in the VIII chapter with the ceremonies necessary to propitiate the deities of the sites, etc. . . .

This brief summary is enough to indicate that the *Mānasāra* is a complete work of architecture and sculpture as applied to the construction of temples and images, and all work of building connected therewith. Though we know of something like 300 works on these subjects, most of which exist only in manuscripts, none of them attains to the voluminous and the detailed treatment of the *Mānasāra*. A certain number have been published since, such as the *Mayamata*, *Śilparatna*, and *Manushyālaya-chandrikā* in the Trivandrum Sanskrit Series, and a few other elsewhere; but none of them comes up to the comprehensiveness or complete details of the *Mānasāra*. The Agamaic works, both *Śaiva* and *Vaishṇava*, have to deal with these very topics, as one of the main sections of these works, both *Vaishnava* and *Śaiva*, have reference to temple-worship. Some of them do give detailed description of these, the best among them being the *Kāmika Āgama*. This is a vast work of 160 chapters of which a fairly large number are devoted to these subjects. There again architecture is generally regarded as subsidiary to town-planning. The building of temples, of course, forms a part of town-planning. When we get to a description of temples, naturally it takes us on to the description of the making of images, being connected intimately with each other. Dr. Acharya draws attention incidentally to the fact that even Vedic Indians were not ignorant of stone forts or walled cities, stone houses, carved stones and even brick edifices, although they are generally regarded as being ignorant of these. A certain amount of information on these subjects could be collected from

Buddhist literature as Dr. Acharya points out, not to speak of the description of palaces and towns, such as we find in the *Rāmāyaṇa* and the *Mahābhārata* and work of that kind. The *Purāṇas*, like the *Āgamas*, contain elaborate chapters upon these subjects, as again they have to deal with the connected subject of temple-worship. A co-ordinated study of these gives a detailed idea of architectural notions of the Hindus, and these theoretical principles could be verified from even existing buildings where they do exist in some number.

We may conclude by congratulating Professor Acharya upon the monumental work that he has produced and brought to a term the labours of twenty years of devoted study. Though, accidental, so far as Professor Acharya is concerned, the publication of this work, the preface to which is dated 6th February, 1933, seems to be almost exactly the centenary of the completion of the first work on this subject by Rama Raz, as we have already noted. There could be no more appropriate celebration of the centenary of the publication for such an important work as the *Mānasāra* than this careful, complete, and an admirably adequate edition of the great work. Let us hope that this publication will lead to a scientific study of Hindu architecture with a view to the practical applications which Professor Acharya wants. We commend the work to those concerned with all our heart, and say amen to the wish of the learned editor and translator.

G. A. Natesan, Esq., Editor, Indian Review[1]

When about seven years ago Professor Prasanna Kumar Acharya published the two volumes, *A Dictionary of Hindu Architecture* and *Indian Architecture according to Mānasāra Śilpa-śāstra*, he challenged the attention of the world and gave an impetus to the study of a long-neglected subject. He has now completed his stupendous work with the publication of three volumes containing the Sanskrit text of *Mānasāra* with critical notes, a translation of it in English, and illustrations in line and in colours which run to 157 plates. The effort has cost him about twenty years of devoted research and the result is an achievement which has been deservedly acclaimed as monumental. His marvellous tenacity of purpose has enabled him to succeed where others have given up the colossal task in despair.

[1] The *Indian Review*, May, 1934, p. 313.

He has evolved cogency out of chaos and left students of Indology under a deep debt of gratitude.

Some idea of the magnitude of his labour can be gleaned from the fact that since 1834, when Ram Raz referred in his *Essay on the Architecture of Hindus* to the contents of a few chapters of *Mānasāra* from a fragmentary manuscript on which he had lighted, the field remained unexplored until in the year 1914 Professor Acharya stepped in with his great purpose and the scholar's enthusiasm. The unravelling of the obscure text of *Mānasāra* was in itself a formidable endeavour. Men like Dr. G. Bühler and Sir Ramkrishna Bhandarkar had stigmatized it as written in the 'most barbarous Sanskrit,' while the last of those who have laid testimony to the distracting business of translating *Mānasāra* is that eminent scholar Mahamahopadhyaya Dr. Ganganatha Jha. The first work confronting Professor Acharya was, therefore, to compile an encyclopaedia of technical terms and the collation of illustrative quotations from cognate literature. He had then to travel from one end of the country to the other collecting and arranging a text written in five different scripts, possessing eleven badly-preserved manuscripts, subject to five recensions and comprising more than 10,000 lines of a disheartening language. In spite of the forbidding nature of the undertaking, however, Professor Acharya has triumphed as editor, commentator and translator.

The great value of the work to students of Indian art lies in that *Mānasāra* is the 'most complete, scientific and probably the oldest extant record' of Hindu architecture dealing with everything for which the essence of measurement is required.

Professor Otto Stein, University of Prague, Czechoslovakia[1]

The publication of the *Mānasāra*, text and translation each forming a bulky volume, accompanied by a third one containing the plates, was preceded by two other contributions from the pen of Dr. Acharya, his *Dictionary of Hindu Architecture* and *Indian Architecture according to Mānasāra Śilpa-śāstra* (both *s.a.*, probably 1927 and 1928 respectively). The former work brought an alphabetically arranged

[1]*Archiv Orientalni*, Vol. 7 (1935), no. 1-2, pp. 248-58.

terminology of Indian technics, art, settlements, etc., with ample quotations from texts and inscriptions, and in two appendices a valuable list of Sanskrit works on architecture and of 'historical architects, with short notes on their works.' The second book was a preparatory one in regard to the present three volumes, giving a survey of *Śilpa-śāstra*, summaries and synopses of some texts, especially of the *Mānasāra*, of its position in the literature, drawing a comparison with Vitruvius, and finally summing up all the indications of the age of *Mānasāra* ; an appendix notes down a florilegium of grammatical peculiarities, to use an euphemistic expression, what Dr. Acharya himself calls a 'barbarous' Sanskrit. All that extensive work goes back to the year 1914, when Dr. Acharya took up what Professor Rapson predicted to him would become a life's undertaking. Now the scholar may be proud of having published the volumes, though they, according to his modesty, 'do not claim to be other than provisional.' No doubt, much more will have to be done in that field, but the credit of 'beginning of a new line of Indology, which, it may be perhaps hoped, is likely to prove not merely of cultural and historical interest, but possibly of some practical benefit to the country and to the nation' is due to Dr. Acharya.

From that edition of the *Mānasāra* the study of more than one field of Indology will get a new stimulus, as the interrelation of *Śilpa-śāstra* with many other disciplines is evident. In the first place, of course, the history of technical science, the history of Indian architecture and sculpture will draw the main profit ; the comparison between theory and practice is not only interesting, but might yield also chronological clues for the history of religious sects. The editor has done all he could to bring out a readable text in which every line has been settled after careful consideration, as is to be seen from the Critical Notes. But Dr. Acharya has done much more ; he has not satisfied himself with the edition, but he has rather for the first time brought out a translation of a *Śilpa-śāstra*. Everyone who will have to work in that field must either adopt his interpretation of the complicated materia or improve it by arguments ; but nobody, who is aware of the intricate terminology of technical *Śāstras* can deny the pioneer work done by Professor Acharya. He has, however, facilitated the understanding of, in some way, dead words by a special volume of plates, not less than 157 in number, illustrating the features of all the buildings, sculptures, idols, etc. As great as the merit of Dr. Acharya may be in bringing out such a volume, the assistance he got by Mr. S. C. Mukherji of the Archaeological Department, partly by Mr. R. L. Bansal and Sri Siddalingaswamy, by transforming the complicated indications of the text into drawings, appealing much more to a vivid comprehension than words, deserves the highest appreciation. And great is the obligation under which students of Indology may feel themselves laid to all the factors by the help of which such an undertaking has been effected in these days.

Silpa-Siddhanti K. S. Siddalingaswami Sri Jagadguru Nagalingaswamy Math

The world is much grateful to you for the great help you have done in publishing the *Mānasāra grantha* which is a valuable and precious guide to the artists. As far as we know there is scarcely a *grantha* of this type available to guide the artists. After I went through this *grantha* my desire was to give a series of pictures for all the *Mānasāra*. I am also trying for this. It was so long impossible to get a correct *grantha* in complete form. This difficulty has been solved by you.

Raja Sri Pratap Singh (of Mallapur, United Provinces)

I have been fortunate enough to see all your five volumes on the Hindu architecture. You have really taken great pains to revive the old art belonging to us which was dying out. You have done a great service . . . by completing such an important work. How much I wish to pay my respects to you in token of my appreciation for such a noble work.

Times Literary Supplement[1]

Architecture, like most phases of intellectual activity, finds a place in Sanskrit literature, incidentally in the *Purāṇa*, *Āgamas*, and similar works, and in detail in that extensive technical literature known as the *Śilpa-śāstras*, of which the best known example is the *Mānasāra*. Etymologically the word ' Mānasāra ' means ' the essence of measurement,' but in certain connexions seems to be applied to the author

[1] 7th February, 1935.

of the work, while in one passage in the treatise it has been used in both senses. There is nothing in the work itself to indicate the date of a compilation with certainty, but Dr. Acharya would place it provisionally between A.D. 500 and 700.

Dr. Acharya's three volumes appear most appositely, marking a centenary in the study of Hindu architecture, for it was in 1834 that Ram Raz published in English his *Essay on the Architecture of the Hindus*, based on a fragmentary manuscript of the *Mānasāra*. It may seem strange that the publication of a complete text of such importance should have been so long delayed, but Sanskritists were little attracted to a purely technical work having no claims to literary excellence and abounding in words used in a technical sense differing entirely from their derivative literal rendering and, moreover, not to be found in dictionaries. A belief that the *Mānasāra* is the standard Hindu work on architecture and sculpture prompted Dr. Acharya to undertake the difficult and laborious task of editing this text and has sustained him in his unremitting labours for some twenty years.

The three volumes now issued are the third, fourth, and fifth of an *Encyclopaedia of Hindu Architecture*, the author having in 1927 published, as the first volume, *A Dictionary of Hindu Architecture* treating of Sanskrit architectural terms, and, as the second, *Indian Architecture according to the Mānasāra Śilpa-śāstra*. In the third volume Dr. Acharya now makes available for the first time the complete Sanskrit text of the *Mānasāra*, based on eleven badly-preserved manuscripts written in five different scripts and has added three appendices, a Sanskrit index, and over 300 pages of critical notes in English. That the elucidation of the text calls for such extensive annotation witnesses to the difficulties presented by the defective manuscripts and the industry and scholarship of the author. In his preface to the English translation Dr. Acharya has indicated the method followed in its preparation and the limits imposed by the imperfect texts. Within those limits he has produced a clear and readable translation, and it is but rarely that we are left with such cryptic passages as 'He (Garuda) is known to have the posture of bent mixedness in the walking pose and collectiveness in the sitting pose.'

From the complete text it is now plain that architecture in the *Mānasāra* is taken in its widest sense and includes systems of measurement, selection of sites, town-planning, foundations, bricks, plinths, bases, pillars, entablatures, chariots, couches, thrones, crowns and personal ornaments, doors, windows, staircases, wells and drains and even balances and baskets and cages for birds and beasts. The carving and casting of images of deities, sages and donors and the making of cult objects occupy no fewer than twenty of the seventy chapters. That the *Mānasāra* is a practical work based on experience and actual measurement of the then existing architectural and sculptural objects can hardly be doubted, but mingled with the technical detail are many ritual rules and other extraneous matter, not however without considerable interest. Hindu fondness for classification is evidenced in the multiplicity of types, and we have thirty-two varieties of site-plans, fifty kinds of mouldings and sixty-four types of column bases and so on, until it becomes difficult to determine where reality ends. The importance of exact proportion and strict adherence to the rules annunciated is emphasized throughout the work, and this is based not only on aesthetic considerations, for a whole chapter is devoted to penalties arising from any deviation. For instance it is laid down that, 'If the staircase be less or greater the master would certainly be crippled,' and such might indeed happen from such a faulty construction; but it seems somewhat severe that 'if the height of a pillar be lower or higher the family and race of the master will be exterminated.' Light is thrown on the religious toleration of the age, for two chapters are devoted to rules for the making of Buddhist and Jain images.

Of storeyed buildings three styles are mentioned, namely, Nāgara, Vesara and Drāvida, and Dr. Acharya considers these terms as geographical and would render them as the architectural styles of North, East and South India respectively. These three terms, however, occur several times in the text in connexion with such different objects as the *linga*, *yoni* and cars, and there merely in the sense of square, circular or hexagonal. But whatever the meaning of Nāgara, Vesara and Drāvida, it is impossible to escape from the feeling that the architecture of the *Mānasāra* is, in general, that of South India, for the many-storeyed *gopura*, the clustered columns, heavy entablatures, numerous court-yards, halls of a thousand columns, etc., have still their living examples at Tanjore, Tiruvalur, and Srirangam, but are not only absent nowadays in Northern India but were equally so in the period assigned to the *Mānasāra*, as excavation at numerous sites in that region have revealed no traces of such monuments, and the buildings of Northern India described by the Chinese pilgrims, who were in India between A.D. 500 and 700, are not those of the *Mānasāra*. That eight of the eleven manuscripts consulted by Dr. Acharya were in South Indian scripts is not without significance.

Although it is impossible to be perfectly certain of the interpretation of all the terms used in the *Mānasāra*, Dr. Acharya has felt that an endeavour should be made to illustrate as far as possible the architectural and sculptural forms detailed therein, and the fifth volume consists of 157 plates. For these he has naturally had to rely upon others, but has been fortunate in obtaining for the preparation of those illustrating sculpture and ornament the assistance of K. S. Siddhalingaswamy, 'A Silpin by heredity,' and a master working to the living Sastraic tradition, whose drawings, eleven of them in colour, seem thoroughly in keeping with the spirit of the text. For most of the architectural illustrations he is indebted to Mr. S. C. Mukerji, a trained architect and a graduate in Sanskrit, whose 121 line drawings are a praiseworthy attempt to interpret the very difficult text. In general he has done this with success, but the staircase in Plate XCIX appears too European in style, the Bengali roof of the canopied throne of Plate CXXX, and the foiled arch of the late Mughal type of the *Pushpa-torana* on Plate CXXXII are more than doubtful for so early a period as that assigned to the *Mānasāra*, while the representation of the *Kalpa-vriksha* on Plate CXXXV deviates from the text description of this wonder-working tree, of which an early sculptural example exists in the Indian Museum, Calcutta, and inspiration for which might have been sought in the garlanded trees of the Bharhut and Sanchi gateways and railings.

League of Nations, Information Meusuelles[1]

Editorial : Le *Mānasāra*, cette œuvre classique sur l'architecture hindoue, a fait, ces dernières années, l'objet de la publication de cinq fort volumes, comptant ensemble près de 3.000 pages. Les deux premiers volumes, parus en 1927, sont épuisés. Nous ne pouvons donc faire état ici que des trois derniers, et, plus particulièrement du quatrième *Architecture of Mānasāra* qui est la traduction en anglais du texte sanscrit original contenu dans le troisième volume. Le cinquième réunit les illustrations auxquelles le texte se réfère.

[1] June, 1934.

Le texte publié est basé sur les onze manuscrits existants, réunis par Sir Austen Chamberlain, alors secrétaire d'Etat pour les Indes, en vue de la rédaction de cet ouvrage. A l'exception d'un seul, ces manuscrits sont tous fragmentaires et aucun ne comprend des commentaires, dessins ou diagrammes. Si des spécialistes avaient déjà cité des extraits de l'un ou de l'autre de ces manuscrits, nul n'en avait encore tenté la traduction. Quelques textes sanscrits sur l'architecture ont bien été imprimés au cours des dernières années, mais aucun n'avait été jusqu'à présent traduit en anglais ou commenté en aucune langue, hindoue ou européenne. C'est à Sir John Marshall, directeur général de l'Archéologie, que l'on doit l'idée de la publication d'une édition établie sur des bases scientifiques de cet ouvrage essentiel sur l'architecture hindoue. La traduction du texte original devait être accompagnée des commentaires nécessaires, de dessins et diagrammes Dans la préface de l'ourvage actuel, P. K. Acharya retrace les différentes étapes de la préparation de l'ouvrage qui parait maintenant, aprés dix-sept ans d'un labeur continu. D'un grand intérêt, aussi bien culturel qu'historique, il semble appelé à rendre également des services pratiques. La politique de l'architecture aux Indes, basée depuis quelques siècles déjà sur l'imitation étrangère, en dépit des conditions climatériques toutes différentes, n'a pas toujours eu des résultats heureux. On perçoit de ce fait la portée pratique que peut presenter la *Mānasāra.* Il reste à vérifier si les monuments parvenus jusqu'à nous, ont été édifiés selon les règles et principes exposés dans le *Mānasāra*. Si, tout en tenant compte des conditions actuelles, il est avéré que ces méthodes sont scientifiquement applicables, il serait intéressant de les expérimenter sur des constructions modernes

Les deux premiers ouvrages publiés à ce sujet, par M. Acharya et actuellement épuisés (*A Dictionary of Hindu Architecture, Indian Architecture according to Mānasāra*) ont suscité un tel intérêt qu'ils l'ont amené à mettre le problème à l'étude de la façon la plus systématique dans l'état actuel de nos connaissances. Le texte original est souvent très défectueux et l'interprétation n'en est pas toujours certaine. C'est grâce à la collaboration de Mr. S. C. Mukherji, B.A., G.D. ARC., A.I.I.A., attaché au département archéologique qu'ont été ètablies les illustrations, interprétation graphique aussi fidèle que possible du texte. Aprés plusieurs tentatives qu'il fallut abandonner, 32 dessins de sculptures, au trait et en couleurs, ont été exécutés par Silpa

Siddhanti Sivayogi Sri Siddalingaswamy, chef du monastére Jagadguru Nagalinsgaswamy. Nul n'était mieux placé, à tous égards, pour entreprendre cette tâche qui lui coûta six mois de travail, aprés des essais et expériences qui ne durérent pas moins d'un an. Conscient des difficultés que présentait la tâche de traduire un texte aussi mutilé, traitant de sujets aussi techniques l'auteur s'est attaché à serrer le texte d'aussi près que possible, et a éviter toute interprétation hasardeuse Dans une préface très documentée, il indique brièvement le contenu de chacun des 70 chapitres qui composent l'ouvrage et dont les huit premiers servent d'introduction, les 42 suivants traitant de questions d'architecture, les vingt derniers consacrés à la sculpture. Une liste de manuscrits traitant des sujets analogues est donnée à la suite du dictionnaire d'architecture hindoue. Ces mêmes manuscrits sont briévement analysés dans la préface du tome IV.

La date du *Mānasāra*, longuement discutée dans le premier volume, ne pourra être vraiment fixée que le jour oû l'on aura réussi à identifier l'auteur du traité—à moins qu'il ne s'agisse d'une compilation. Le sens même du titre reste incertain. Dans le texte même, *Mānasāra* est employé dans plusieurs acceptions différentes. Ceux qui estiment que l'ouvrage a ete inspiré plus ou moins directement par le roi de ce nom, font remonter le document au VIIe siècle, d'autres reculent cette date jusqu'à 450 environ ; d'autres encore, s'appuyant, sur des similitudes avec le traité de Vitruve (25 av. J.-C.) estiment qu'il peut avoir été composé aussi bien quelques siècles avant qu'aprés ce dernier ouvrage.

La préface du troisième volume (*Mānasāra*—Sanskrit Text with critical notes) donne la description détaillée des onze munscrits sur lesquels est basée la publication de ce texte.

Pravāsi, the leading Bengali Magazine[1]

Editorial : Allahabad Viśwa-vidhyālayer Saṁskrita vibhāger adhyaksha adhyāpak doctor Prasanna Kumar Acharyer pāṇḍitya dīrgha-kāl-vyāpī pariśram o adhyavasāyer guṇe prāchīn Bhāratavarsher sthāpatya o mūrti-śilpa sambandhīya Mānasār nāmak prasiddha granther ekṭi utkrishṭa Saṁskaraṇ prakāśita haiyāchhe. Taj-janya tini pṛithivīr samuday prāchya-vidyānurāgīr kritajñatā-bhājan. Ihāte

[1] Chaitra and Vaishak, B. S. 1341.

Mānasārer mūl saṁskṛita, saṁskṛita pariśishṭa, pratyek śabda kon kon prishṭhāy āchhe tāhār anukramaṇikā, pratyek adhyāyer nānā pāṭha-bhed o ṭīkā, samagra grantha-khānir Iṅgreji anuvād, Iṅgrājite vistārita vishay-sūchī o śabda-sūchī, grantha-kārer rachita saṁskṛita o dīrgha Iṅgreji bhūmikā, evaṁ 157 sumudrita plate anek-sata gṛihādir naksā o mūrtir chitra āchhe. Bahu-saṁkhyak mūrti-chitra bahu-varṇe mudrita. Āj-kāl prāchin Bhāratīya sthāpatyer prati śikshita-śreṇīr lokder kichhu dṛishṭi paḍiyāchhe. Kintu sthāpatya o mūrti-śilpa sambandhe prāchīn Bhāratīyader gaveshaṇā, anuśīlan o jñān ki-rūp vistārita o suspashṭa chhila, tāhā kam loke-i jāniten evaṁ sakaler jānibār upāy-o chhila nā. Doctor Ācharyer grantha dekhile tāhā jānā yā-i-be. Grantha-khānir mūlya lekhā nā-i. Sakale kinite pāribenā baṭe, kintu sakal viśwa-vidyālayer library-te, sakal baḍa kalejer, viśeshataḥ engineering college-r library-te, Art school sakaler library-te, baḍa baḍa engineer-der o gṛiha-nirmātā company-der pustak- saṁgrahe ihā rakshita ha-o-yā ekānta āvaśyak. Ihā Bhārata-varsher ye sav viśwa-vidyālaye engineering vibhāg āchhe tāhār aṅgībhūta engineering college-gulite evaṁ viśwa-vidyālayer sahit samparka-śūnya engineering college o vidyālay-samūhe agrasar chhātrader adhītavva pustak-baliyā nirddhārita ha-o-yā kartavya. Āmāder viśvās e-i ye, yadi Sir Āsutosh Mukhopādhyāya ekhan jīvita thākiten, tāhā ha-i-le tini niśchay-i e-i pustak-khāni Kalikātā (Calcutta) viśwa-vidyālayer engineering upādhi-prārthi-der avaśya-pāṭhya grantha-samūher anyatama baliyā nirddhāraṇ kariten. Ekhan i-hā antatah Kāshir Hindu Viswa-vidyālayer engineering college-e adhīta ha-o-yā uchit. Grantha-khānike viśwa-vidyālayer adhītavya karile paroksha suphal e-i ha-i-be ye, prāchīn Bhāratīya-der sthāpatya o mūrti-śilper jñāner parimāṇ sambandhe satya dhāraṇā janmi-be. Tā-chhāḍā, e-i ubhav śilpe prāchīn-erā yadi kona bhram kariyā thāken, nūtan jñān o gaveshaṇār prabhāve tāhār śaṁsodhan ha-i-be. Kāraṇ prāchīn vā ādhunik kona lekhak-der-i kona vishayer jñān sampūrṇa vā chūḍānta na-he.

Viśal-Bhārat, the leading Hindi Magazine[1]

'Mānasār' sthāpatya kalā-kā ek atyant prāchīn saṁskṛit granth hai. Is grantha-kā astitva sau-savā-sau varsha pahale se jñāt thā;

[1] Braj Mohan Verma : Jeth, V.S. 1991.

lekin uskā prakāśan ab-tak na ho sakā thā. Granth iṁjīniyaro-n, śilpiyo-n, mūrtikāro-n aur kārīgaro-n ke liye vyāvahārik ḍhaṅg par likhā gayā thā, aur jān paḍtā hai ki unhī-n logo-n-ke hāth-me rahā. Prāchīn kāl me-n chhāpe-khāne to the nahī-n, sabhī granth hāth-se hī nakal kiye jāte the. 'Mānasār'-kā kām jinhe-n paḍtā thā, ve prāyaḥ be-paḍhe-likhe śilpī aur kārigar hote the. Unke dvārā nakal kiye jāne-me-n aśuddhi-yā-n rah jānā sambhava hī nahī-n, varan avaśyambhāvī thā. Phal yah huā ki samay-ke pher-se 'Mānasār'-kī jo pratiyā-n vartmān kāl tak pahu-n-chī-n, ve aśuddhiyo-n-kā bhaṇḍār ban ga-ī-n. Unkī bhāshā itnī aśuddha ho gaī hai ki Sir Bhaṇḍārkar aur Dr. Bühler ne uskī bhāshā ko atyant, 'barbar' saṁskṛit likhā hai.

Srī Prasanna Kumār Ācharya-ne bīs varsha-ke sudīrgh pariśram ke bād 'Mānasār'-ko tīn jildo-n me-n prakāśit kiyā hai.

'Mānasār' apne ḍhaṁg-kā anokhā granth hai. Is-se Bhāratkī Prāchīn sabhyatā aur kalā-par jo prakāś paḍegā, uskā mūlya ānkā nahī-n jā saktā. Pustak sattar adhyāyo-n-me-n vibhakta hai . . . Samāj-kī vibhinna śreṇiyo-n-kī haisiyat-ke anusār un-ke makān bhī ek-se le-kar bārah talle tak-ke batāye gaye hai-n, aur unkī har tarah-ki lambāī-chauḍāī-kā anupāt-ādi viśad-rūp-se sam-jhāyā gayā hai. Yah suṇ-kar āścharya hotā hai ki abse lag-bhag do hazār varsha pahale Bhārat-me-n bārah talle ūn-che aur tālābo-n-ki buniyāde-n, khambhe, unke bhed aur ākār, chhate-n, gumbad, śikhar, imāratī sāmān (patthar, īn-ṭen, lakḍī aur dhātu-kī chīze-n), toraṇ, nāliyā-n, sīḍhiyā-n aur zīne, ahātā, āngan, darvāze, khiḍkiyā-n, mahārābe-n ityādi sthāpatya-se sambandha rakhne vālī pratyek vastuke vivaraṇ 'Mānasār'-me-n maujūd hai-n. Iske atirikta, savāriyā-n, rath simhāsan, furniture-kī chize-n aur Hindu, Bauddha, Jain mūrtiyā-n ityādi banāne-ke sambandh-men bhī vyavahārik śikshā 'Mānasār'-men maujūd hai.

Sriyut Āchārya-ne jin kaṭhinā-iyo-n-kā sāmnā karte huye is kārya-ko kiyā hai, unhe-n dekhte huye, unkī jitni prāśaṁsā kī jāy thoḍī hai. Bhārat-sarkār aur Yukta-Prāntīya sarkār ne is mahān granth-ke prakāśan-me-n jo sahāyatā dī hai, uske liye ve bhī badhāī-ke pātra hai-n.

Zarurat is bāt-kī hai ki Bihār-ke punar nirmāṇ-ke kāryame-n jo iṁginiyar tathā anya log bhāg le rahe hai-n, ve is granth-ko achchhī tarah paḍhe-n aur navīn vaijñānik āvishkāro-n aur jānkariyo-n kā āvaśyak samāveś karke 'Mānasār' me-n varṇit sthapatya aur nagar-rachanā ādiko kām-men lāyen. . . .

Is pustak-kā Hindī-me-n nikalnā atyanta āvaśyak hai.

HINDUSTANI, THE LEADING HINDI QUARTERLY[1]

Prayāg-viśva-vidyālaya ke saṁskṛit-vibhāg ke adhyaksha Doctor Prasanna Kumār Āchārya, I.E.S., M.A., PH.D., D.LITT., mahodaya ne jis yogyatā aur pariśram se pāñch jildo-n men prāchīn-Bhārtīya-vāstuvidvā saṁbandhī vishayo-n par prakāś ḍālā hai, uske liye ve hamāre dhanyavād ke pātra hāi-n. Prastut pāñch jildo-n ka prakāśan kar hamāre prānt kī sarkār ne prāchīn Bhāratīya saṁskriti ke adhyayan me Bhāratīya itihās ke jijñāsuo-n ke liye ek atyant upayogī sāmagrī upasthit kar apnī udārtā aur jñānāśraya kā parichaya diyā hai. . . . yah āśā karnā anuchit nahī-n ki in grantho-n ke adhyayan se bhavishya me Bhārtīya itihās par bahut kuchh prakāś paḍ sakega aur hamārā ajñāt vigat bahut kuchh prakāś-maya ho kar hamāre sāmne upasthit hogā aur hame-n apnī prachīn saṁskṛiti aur vigat unnat avasthā kā parichaya karā sakegā.

[1] 1935, Mr. Satyajeevan Verma, M.A.

INDEX

A

B

D

E

F

G

K

L

M

O

P

S

W

X

Y